1/46
Rec'd Readings

1. Abraham Lincoln & the Union
Stephenson - Due Oct. 22nd

2. The Agrarian Crusade -
Buck - Due

3. The Age of Big Business
Hendricks

4. Woodrow Wilson & the World War
Seymour.

POLITICAL AND SOCIAL HISTORY

OF THE

UNITED STATES

1829–1925

BY

ARTHUR MEIER SCHLESINGER

PROFESSOR OF HISTORY

HARVARD UNIVERSITY

New York

THE MACMILLAN COMPANY

1929

PRINTED IN THE UNITED STATES OF AMERICA

Set up and electrotyped. Published June, 1925. Reprinted November, 1925; April, 1926; January, 1927; March, December, 1928; May, 1929.

TO

GEORGE WELLS KNIGHT

IN GRATITUDE

PREFACE

MORE than four thousand Americans living today have, in their lifetime, spanned the century of history covered by this volume. This fact suggests not only the extreme youth of the United States as a nation but also the bewildering speed with which America has changed from a primitive frontier country to one of the greatest powers, politically and industrially, in the world today. It is the purpose of this volume to recount this marvelous story with a special view to the needs of college students. While the major emphasis is placed on political development, political forces are regarded as being constantly responsive to the changing conditions of social life. The life of the people, therefore, forms a significant though not the principal thread of the story. Even within these limits the problem of selecting material has proved a difficult one. Accordingly, it seems desirable to explain why some of the familiar landmarks of history textbooks are ignored, and new ones somewhat venturesomely set up.

In the first place, in the choice of material an effort has been made to keep in mind the two basic respects in which the American population has differed from the people of any modern European country — the fact that the United States has been, in the main, a nation of people living on farms and in crossroads villages in a condition of economic independence, and the fact that European colonization, far from ceasing in the mid-eighteenth century, has been sending to American shores a continuous stream of foreign-born settlers. The former circumstance has led the people to develop those traits of character, mental predispositions and economic wants peculiar to such a mode of living. In all the great political decisions which they have made, the agricultural environment has been a potent, and usually the controlling, factor. The recurrent tides of immigration have likewise powerfully influenced the national destinies in countless ways, have given us some of our greatest men, and have helped to produce a people that is neither English nor German nor Irish nor Italian, but "American."

In the second place, constant stress has been placed on the great dynamic currents which have shaped the nation's life. In the author's judgment, these were, and still are, (1) the growth of nationality; (2) the struggle for greater democracy; (3) changes in the methods of production and distribution (as evidenced, for instance, by the introduction of machinery and the social adjustments necessitated thereby); (4) the constant striving for social amelioration, including the contest for free public schools, improvement in the lot of women and children, and the successive movements for humanitarian reform; and (5) the expansion of the national boundaries.

All these are envisaged as continuous and continuing processes. For example, the contest over nationality is treated not merely as a conflict between the antagonistic interests of different sections, terminating in the Civil War. It is also depicted in its significant later phases as it has been affected by the growing strife between capital and labor and by the heterogeneous racial makeup of the population. In a similar fashion, the policy of expansion is traced from the time when it was chiefly actuated by a desire to secure adjacent territory to afford elbow room for the American people, to the more recent period, when, after the manner of imperialism, it has become concerned with the extension of political or fiscal control over remote alien peoples.

From these five guiding principles emerges what is tantamount to a sixth, namely, a recognition that American history is, and always has been, an inseparable part of the world stream of development. As Professor Haskins observed in the course of his presidential address to the American Historical Association in 1922, "Ireland has a potato famine in 1848, and Boston has an Irish mayor in 1922. Karl Marx and Engels publish their *Communist Manifesto* in this same 1848, and two generations later Bolshevism appears in the lumber camps of the Pacific Northwest." Indeed, the more one studies the history of the United States, the more one becomes convinced of the unity of all history. In reality, the five main currents of American development are, in no sense, peculiar to the United States, but were equally operative in the history of Western Europe during the same period. So far as space has permitted, an effort has been made to show the essentially international character of such significant movements, for example, as abolition, the extension of the suffrage, the consolidation of nationality, the efforts for universal peace, and the development of imperialism.

In the preparation of this volume I have drawn heavily on the standard historians, and even more so on the countless authors of special articles and monographs. In the words of the Reverend Thomas Prince of Boston, a historian of the eighteenth century, "I have laboured after accuracy; and yet I dare not say that I am without mistake; nor do I desire the reader to conceal any he may possibly find." The bibliographical notes at the ends of chapters, while making no pretensions to completeness, may prove helpful in directing teachers to the main secondary authorities on the topics treated. Of the many friends who have generously aided in the completion of the manuscript, only a few can be mentioned. Professor Louis Pelzer and Dr. Bessie L. Pierce of the University of Iowa, Mr. George Carver of the University of Pittsburgh and Dr. H. E. Miller of Brown University read the manuscript, in whole or in part, and made valuable suggestions. Mr. John F. O'Brien and Mr. Kenneth L. Bowersox, formerly members of the Graduate College of the University of Iowa, combed much of the manuscript for errors. To Professor H. C. Hockett of the Ohio State University I am indebted for a painstaking and helpful examination of the entire production. At all stages I have had the counsel and assistance of my wife, Elizabeth Bancroft.

A. M. S.

CAMBRIDGE, MASS.
May, 1925.

CONTENTS

PART ONE. THE AGE OF THE COMMON MAN

PART TWO. THE CONTEST OVER NATIONALITY

PART FOUR. GREATER AMERICA

MAPS AND CHARTS

POLITICAL AND SOCIAL HISTORY OF THE UNITED STATES 1829–1925

CHAPTER I

THE RISE OF THE COMMON MAN

The Opening of a New Era

When Andrew Jackson entered the presidency in 1829, a current of unrest and revolt was coursing through the entire western world. The passion for democracy and the longing for nationality, which had been flouted by the Congress of Vienna (1815) in settling Continental affairs after the Napoleonic storm, were beginning to shake the thrones of Europe again. Within a few months the flood burst its barriers. In France the Revolution of 1830, led by Lafayette, drove out Charles X who reigned by "divine right," and set up a middle-class monarchy resting upon a popular but highly restricted suffrage. In the same year Belgium, which had been forced upon the King of Holland by the diplomats of Vienna, raised the flag of independence, and established a monarchy based upon the most liberal constitution on the European Continent. In Germany, Italy, and Poland, revolutionary ardor flamed up and subsided, leaving behind no gains for democracy except liberal constitutions in four petty German states.

The changes that took place in Great Britain were perhaps the most significant of all. Additional civil and political rights were conferred upon the Roman Catholics in 1829. Three years later, with England on the verge of a violent upheaval, Parliament enacted the Reform Law — one of the landmarks of English constitutional history. The scheme of representation in Parliament was made more equitable, and the great landowners were required to share the franchise with men of the manufacturing and merchant classes. The electorate was nearly doubled thereby, and the first great step thus taken toward confiding the control of the government to all the people.

The growth of popular power abroad gave thoughtful Europeans a desire to study the great democratic experiment in the United States. In the decade or so after 1829, scores of Englishmen and Frenchmen visited our shores, and in due time, reported their observations in book form. Some saw in American democracy a proof of their preconceived notion that the mass of men were unfit for self-government. For example, Michel Chevalier, the French economist, likened popular rule in the United States to "the despotic humor of a full-grown democracy, passing more and more into radicalism," whereas the parallel movement in his own country impressed him as "the rising of a democracy . . . yet in embryo, and which, if it please God, will never come to maturity."

Others, like Harriet Martineau, the English historian, concluded that democratic government, with all its faults, was amply justified by its good works. This opinion was fully shared by Alexis de Tocqueville, a Frenchman who toured the United States in 1831, and whose remarkable volume *Democracy in America* formed the most luminous commentary on American institutions prior to the appearance of James Bryce's *American Commonwealth* a half century later.

Frontier Influences

The views and opinions of these visitors are of particular interest, for they were formed at a time when the mighty forces of democracy and nationality, which had thrown Europe into turmoil, were engaged in transforming the fabric of accustomed political thought and practice in America. A number of conditions conspired to bring the United States to a new era about 1829. Fundamental among these were the westward expansion of the population, the birth of a labor movement in the East, and the broadening of the suffrage.

Since the dawn of the century the United States had become a new nation in territorial extent and population. From a country bounded by the Spanish Floridas and the Mississippi River on the south and west, the national borders in 1829 stood flush with the Atlantic and the Gulf on the south, and stretched far westward to the Rockies, with certain claims to a portion of the Pacific Seaboard in dispute with Great Britain. A Union composed of sixteen states clinging to the Atlantic coastal plain had blossomed into twenty-four mighty commonwealths, two of which (Louisiana and Missouri) lay west of the Mississippi. The country intervening between the Mississippi and the Appalachians was all carved into states, with the exception of the areas now known as Michigan, Wisconsin, and Florida, which, however, possessed territorial governments.[1] Since 1800 the population of the United States had more than doubled, increasing from five and one third millions to thirteen millions; and while in 1800 only one twentieth of the people lived west of the mountains, in 1830 nearly one third of them were to be found in that region.

The West in 1829 possessed a unity of outlook and interest and a political solidarity that were to be conspicuously absent twenty years later. Up and down the Mississippi Valley, from north to south along the line of settlement, the frontiersman struggled with the same tasks of subduing the wilderness, conquering the savage Indians, killing wild animals, and creating social conditions suitable for rearing a family. The difficulties of the pioneer of the Old Northwest in hewing a clearing out of the hard woods of that region were matched by the trials of the Mississippi frontiersman in coping with the pine forests of the South. The sharp cleavage between "North" and "South," which was already apparent in the seaboard states, was, for the most part, lacking in the Mississippi Valley. Indeed, at this period, the Mississippi Valley may be regarded as a section by itself with interests and needs just as homogeneous and important as those of the two sections east of the Appalachians.

The people in the Mississippi Valley were different, in many respects, from those who continued to dwell along the Atlantic Seaboard. As James Bryce observed at a later time in *The American Commonwealth*, "What Europe is to Asia, what England is to the rest of Europe, what America is to England, that

[1] Kentucky and Tennessee had, of course, become states before 1800. Michigan Territory in 1829 embraced within its borders the present state of Wisconsin.

the Western States are to the Atlantic States, the heat and pressure of life always growing as we follow the path of the sun." The same influences which had caused European peasants to settle in the thirteen colonies later served to attract many of the farmers and city dwellers of the East into the virgin wilds west of the mountains. The superior economic opportunities offered by the interior, the freedom from the hampering restraints of settled communities, the lure of the adventurous life, all played their part in transplanting to the Mississippi Valley men and women of energy, initiative, and ambition.

The hardships and rewards of pioneer life served to accentuate these traits. The settlers in the frontier states became self-reliant to the point of lawlessness. Their excessive pride was hardly to be distinguished from plain boasting; their unconventionality too often took the form of crudeness and coarseness. As some one has aptly said, they were "men with the bark on." Foreign visitors with their fastidious European background, like Charles Dickens and Mrs. Frances M. Trollope, saw only the unpleasant aspects of frontier existence — the rowdyism, debauchery, and lack of culture — and failed to perceive that these qualities were merely externals masking the essential soundness and strength of Western character.

The three outstanding traits of the West of 1829 were the individualism of the people, their belief in the capacity of the common man, and their strong nationalism. The abundance of land and natural resources made it possible for any energetic individual to gain a livelihood, and made him scorn the thought of government aid or interference in his ordinary economic pursuits. The absence of distinctions among men as property owners tended to make the people disregard wealth as a criterion of fitness and to look upon all men as essentially equal. Whenever occasion demanded and obvious advantages were to be gained, the frontiersmen resorted to mass action, and showed that instinctive capacity for practical coöperation and self-government that we like to think of as distinctively American.

Their nationalism was, in part, the result of their diverse origins. Coming from many states and even from lands across the sea, they could find common ground only in their allegiance to the government of all the states — that government which had permitted them to acquire their lands upon easy terms and had granted them full rights of self-government through admission into the Union. Ordinarily they were little concerned about the details of political organization or about fine distinctions turning on questions of constitutional construction. Theirs was a democracy as yet without organization, one that depended upon personal leadership.

Since 1812, when the "War Hawks" had rushed the country into the second war with Great Britain, the influence of the West had been steadily growing. In 1828 it elected 47 of the 213 members of the House of Representatives and 18 of the 48 members of the Senate — a greater proportion than any other section. Politically and otherwise, the West had become a dominant force in American national life.

The Awakening of Labor

Another factor in the democratic upheaval of Jackson's time was the organization of a labor movement in the urban centers of New England and the Middle Atlantic states. Mechanics and factory workers occupied only a small place in American life in 1829, for the United States was predominantly a nation of independent farmers, with less than seven per cent of the people living in cities of 8000 or over. Conditions of employment had, however, become unendurable to the urban working class, and they launched a movement of protest that was more influential than their mere numbers justified.

In the earlier days of the republic, the skilled work of the community had been carried on under simple conditions. A youth learned the trade of shoemaker or carpenter or printer during an apprenticeship of several years, and was then prepared to take his part in the bustling life of the town as an independent workman or "journeyman." Owning the simple tools of his trade, he sometimes associated himself with other journeymen under the direction of a "master workman," and the men worked together on terms of personal intimacy and substantial economic equality. If the trade was of an indoor nature, the work was usually performed in the house of one of the workmen.

The westward movement of population and the linking up of

various parts of the country by highways and canals in the first decades of the nineteenth century upset this primitive mode of industry. Whereas mechanics working at a trade had hitherto sought merely to supply the needs of the community in which they lived, the way was now open to sell their wares in distant parts. These broader operations, however, required more capital than the average workman possessed, for large quantities of raw materials had to be kept on hand and attractive terms of credit extended to possible purchasers. As a result, men of capital and enterprise, who had never themselves been workmen, came to take a lead in the development of the skilled trades. Eager for large profits, they bought only from workmen who produced goods at the cheapest rates; and since women and children worked at lower wages than men, the former were drawn into the trades in unprecedented numbers.

In consequence, the skilled workers in the towns found their status fundamentally changed. Instead of being independent producers, they were rapidly becoming dependent for employment upon the favor of the "merchant-capitalist," and the new conditions of competition were causing their hours to grow longer and their wages smaller. The hours of labor ordinarily extended from "dark to dark," a regulation meaning an average workday of from twelve to thirteen hours, six days a week, the year round. Such conditions prevailed throughout the towns of the northern seaboard, and were to be found, in a lesser degree, in a few Western towns like Cincinnati, Louisville, and Pittsburgh.

In those parts of New England and the Middle Atlantic states where the factory production of cotton and woolen goods had taken root, the distress of the wage-earners was even greater. Whereas the simple processes of spinning and weaving had hitherto been largely carried on in the home by the housewife and her children to supply local needs, the introduction of the power-loom in 1814 made all such methods cumbersome and uneconomical, and necessitated the adoption of different arrangements.

The great impetus given to American manufacturing by the embargo and the protective tariffs following the War of 1812 was mainly responsible for the rapid development of the textile industry. Under the new conditions men of capital purchased costly machines and placed them in special structures called "mills" or "factories," and the women and children who could be spared from the home made up the mass of the factory workers. Unable to purchase machines for themselves, the wage-earners were dependent upon the factory owner, who was in a position to dictate the wages, hours, and conditions of labor under which his employees must work.

The conditions in the factories were, with a few bright exceptions, more degrading for the employees than those existing in the skilled trades. The factories were large, gloomy buildings without proper ventilation, light, or sanitation. The wages were low; the work-day lasted, as in the skilled trades, from "dark to dark." About sixty per cent of all the workers in the cotton mills of the Atlantic Seaboard from Virginia northward were women in 1831. Seven per cent were children under twelve years of age. Speaking of the latter, an address issued by the workingmen of Massachusetts in 1834 declared: "To look at the pale and dirty, and spiritless beings, as they pour out of the factory to their hurried meals at the sound of a bell; and . . . to see the lazy motion of their jaded limbs, and the motionless expression of their woebegone countenances, must give a pang to the feeling heart which can never be forgotten."

Since the mills depended for their motive power upon nearby waterfalls or easily available deposits of "stone coal" (as anthracite was called), the introduction of the factory system assisted the rapid growth of cities at strategic points. Thus, the city of Lowell, Massachusetts, which in 1820 had only 250 people, possessed in 1840 a population of over 20,000, collected there largely to work in the mills. Into these cities the wage-earners were crowded, living in congested quarters amidst unwholesome moral influences.

Other conditions not directly connected with the problem of making a living added to the hardness of the lot of the common man. Many laws on the statute books were survivals from colonial times when the idea of discrimination between social classes was universally accepted, but these laws were no longer in harmony with the democratic trend of the times. Thus, educational advantages were virtually denied to the masses of the people, either through lack of provision for free, public schools, or because the long working hours of child wage-earners made attendance impossible. In 1833 probably one million children of the ages from six to fifteen in the entire country were not in any school, and eighty thousand of these were in the state of New York.

The militia laws were another source of discontent. The well-to-do could escape service through payment of a fine, while the man less fortunately situated must serve or go to prison. Furthermore, state laws continued to provide imprisonment as the penalty for indebtedness, and debtors' prisons swallowed thousands of worthy but unfortunate men. Legal fees were regarded as unreasonably high, with the consequence that poor people were discouraged from seeking protection for their rights before the courts.

The banking system of the time also aroused bitter criticism from the working class. Chartered by the states, these banks were permitted to conduct business without adequate safeguards for the depositors or the public, so that laborers were often forced to accept their wages in bank-notes of doubtful or fluctuating value.

In the latter part of the twenties the wage-earners began an active campaign to secure greater rights for their class. Before that time a sullen discontent had occasionally shown itself in strikes and in the temporary formation of local trade unions. Individuals might escape the hardships of their class by moving to the frontier; but most of the wage-earners were discouraged from taking this step by large families, poverty, or lack of ambition. They were accordingly forced to work out their salvation at home.

In the year of Jackson's election to the presidency (1828), a "Working Men's" party was organized in Philadelphia. New York followed in the next year, and within a short time Working Men's parties of varying strength were to be found in all the seaboard states north of Maryland. Candidates were nominated for local and state offices and for Congress, campaigns were conducted, and more than fifty newspapers were founded to acquaint the public with the grievances of the wage-earning class.

These local parties never combined into a national organization, for they were primarily interested in reforms that could be secured through action of the states. They sought legislation that would make life less burdensome for the poor people and which would create broader opportunities for the common man. The main items in their program were summarized by the *Mechanics' Free Press* of Philadelphia on April 16, 1831: "Universal education, abolition of chartered monopolies, equal taxation, revision or abolition of the militia system, a less expensive law system, all officers to be elected directly by the people, a lien law for laborers, no legislation on religion." The abolition of imprisonment for debt might properly have been included in this list.

In 1832 most of the Working Men's parties disappeared, but the "Workies" had succeeded in arousing the public to the need for changes in the existing laws. Their voting strength was very largely taken over by the Democratic party, which under Jackson's vigorous leadership combated all class distinctions. As will appear in Chapter V, most of the reforms that the Working Men's parties espoused were soon carried into effect either by action of the state governments or by the federal government.

The dissolution of the Working Men's parties was merely preliminary to a more intensive organization of the working class along economic lines. Energetic attention was everywhere given to the formation of trade unions or "trade societies." At first the various trade societies in a city were unconnected with one another, but in 1833 New York succeeded in linking all the trade societies of the city into a stable central body called a "General Trades' Union." Other large cities did likewise, and in 1834 the General Trades' Unions of the various cities joined together in a central federation or "National Trades' Union," not unlike the American Federation of Labor of our own day.

About the same time, some of the stronger crafts, like the handloom weavers and the printers, began to organize on a national basis as separate trades. By 1836 the union membership in the cities of the northern seaboard had climbed to something like three hundred thousand. Through the use of the strike and other methods of pressure, they succeeded in securing more humane conditions of employment. By winning a decisive strike in Philadelphia in 1835, involving seventeen different trades and occupations, the organized labor forces succeeded in establishing their most cherished reform, the adoption of a ten-hour work-day in place of the old "dark to dark" day. The activity of the working class and their zeal for humanitarian reform proved to be an indispensable part of the democratic movement of the time.

The Extension of the Suffrage

The heightened importance of the common man in state and national politics had been made possible only by drastic changes in the suffrage regulations that had existed when Washington was President. According to the older conception, only such white men might vote as owned real estate, or possessed some other substantial property interest in the orderly progress of society. A larger amount of property was required of officeholders than of mere voters. In some states, in addition, certain religious qualifications for officeholding were imposed. The result was that in the early years of national independence the electorate constituted much less than half of the adult male population.

But as new states were formed on the democratic frontier, a different notion of the relation of the people to their government arose. As a man of those times asserted, "our community is an association of persons — of human beings — not a partnership founded on property." By 1829 eleven new states had been added to the original thirteen, nine from the western country and two from the northern frontier. In all these communities the conditions of economic and social equality were conducive to the belief that political equality was a natural right of all white men. Accordingly, all the new states entered the Union with white manhood suffrage, absolute or virtual, and officeholding was put on the same basis as voting.[1]

The example of the frontier commonwealths reacted upon the older states. With the suffrage confined in the Eastern states to landholders and taxpayers, the growing class of wage-earners were denied the ballot; and since the seaboard states desired to stay the westward exodus of their working population, concessions were necessary. Moreover, new generations of men,

[1] It is to be noted that New Hampshire, a state possessing many frontier characteristics, had provided in its new constitution of 1792 for white manhood suffrage.

born since the achievement of national independence, had grown up, and for them the aristocratic colonial ideals had lost meaning. Just as these later Americans discarded the courtly colonial costume for the less lovely but more practical long trousers and short-cropped hair — the *sans culottes* of the French Revolution — so they abandoned many political ideas that were sacred to the Fathers of the republic.

The result of these influences appeared in sweeping modifications of the voting regulations of the seaboard states. Between 1810 and 1826, Maryland, South Carolina, and New York adopted white manhood suffrage, Connecticut removed all restrictions except the requirement of tax payment or military service, and Massachusetts reduced her former qualifications to tax payment. The Virginia constitutional convention of 1830 removed the chief restrictions on the franchise, although universal suffrage for white men was not granted until twenty years later.

These changes were stubbornly opposed by the upholders of the old order. Daniel Webster and Justice Joseph Story united with the venerable John Adams in resisting the reform in Massachusetts. In New York the famous jurist, Chancellor James Kent, insisted that manhood suffrage would put it "into the power of the poor and the profligate to control the affluent," and that "every department of the government" would be "at the disposal of those who are ignorant of the importance and nature of the right they are authorized to assume."

In Virginia the opponents of manhood suffrage were led by such distinguished personages as James Madison, James Monroe, Chief Justice Marshall, and John Randolph, men who had differed with one another on many political questions in the past. When Randolph made caustic allusion to the evils of government by "King Numbers," the champions of the new order replied that "there is no other monarch save King Cypher, King Blood, King Sword, or King Purse." By 1829 the principle of white male suffrage was firmly established throughout the Union, although several states held off for a few years more.

The last real contest against the reform, and the most dramatic of all, occurred in Rhode Island. Upon winning independence, Rhode Island had retained as her state constitution the colonial charter which she had received from Charles II in 1663.

This instrument required voters to be owners of real estate to the amount of at least $134. With the growth of an industrial population in the cities, this restriction became exceedingly irksome. Under the leadership of Thomas Dorr, a man of education and good family, a suffrage party was organized in 1834, and a campaign of agitation begun which resulted in the calling of a constitutional convention by the legislature later in the year. The governing class was arrogant and disinclined to make concessions, and nothing was accomplished by the convention.

A few years later the movement got under way again. In April, 1841, a huge mass meeting was held in Providence, the spirit of which was well expressed by a slogan of the gathering: "Virtue, Patriotism, and Intelligence *vs.* $134 Worth of Dirt." Without any legal warrant for the action, this assemblage summoned a constitutional convention to frame a "People's Constitution." Hoping to allay popular clamor, the Rhode Island legislature hastened to call a constitutional convention also. The rival conventions assembled about the same time in the fall of 1841, and each drew up a constitution. The unauthorized "People's Constitution" granted white manhood suffrage; the constitution drafted by the legitimate convention provided for a suffrage somewhat less liberal. When submitted to the people at separate elections, the former constitution was approved by an overwhelming majority, and the latter defeated.

The Dorr party now set up a state government under the "People's Constitution" with their leader as "Governor." The action was illegal, and Dorr's government led a precarious existence for several months. There was some half-hearted fighting with the legal government, and finally Dorr was captured and sentenced to life imprisonment. But the governing class had learned its lesson. In 1843 a new constitution was promulgated which granted substantially all that the rebels had demanded. Native-born Americans were permitted to vote if they had paid a tax of one dollar or served in the militia; naturalized citizens continued to be subject to a slight property qualification. Incidentally, Dorr himself was set at liberty.

The broadening of the suffrage throughout the Union brought into existence a type of democracy which made that of Revolutionary days seem like a limited aristocracy. Several hundred thousands of men had become enfranchised who had been regarded as sheer outsiders in the management of the government by the founders of the nation. Many of the new voters were uneducated, untrained as yet in political thinking, and apt to follow a magnetic leader irrespective of the policies he advocated. The adoption of white manhood suffrage meant the introduction of a new and uncalculated spirit into the conduct of public affairs.

Out of these new influences and conditions there rose a new America, for the full sweep of the new tendencies was to be felt in almost every avenue of human endeavor and achievement, political, social, and intellectual. They led to the creation of new economic and political interests and attachments. They gave a great impetus to the establishment of a tax-supported public school system. They set in motion the first organized movement for women's rights. They produced a notable crop of humanitarian legislation, and inspired socialistic projects for the betterment of society. To the same source is also to be ascribed the growth of a truly American literature.

Jackson's Accession to Office

If Andrew Jackson had not been elected President in 1828, it is almost certain that the choice would have fallen on someone like him. There were, nevertheless, special reasons to account for his selection. Jackson was the very personification of the contentious, self-confident democracy of the West. Born of humble parentage in the backwoods of South Carolina in 1767, he had migrated to the newer frontier of Tennessee at the age of twenty-one. There his public career began almost at once, for he was a natural leader, and by virtue of a compelling personality, he quickly commanded the respect and devotion of the people. Indeed, as a result of the Battle of New Orleans in 1815 and his later campaigns against the Indians in the Southwest, his name became a household word throughout the West and even throughout the nation.

In the course of time, he outgrew the uncouthness of his earlier years, and acquired an impressive dignity of manner. His sincerity and integrity were undoubted, and his private morals without blemish. A somewhat reluctant candidate for the presidency in 1824, he polled a larger popular vote than any of his rivals. The circumstances of his defeat in the House of Representatives caused countless thousands to regard the "Old Hero" as a martyr, sacrificed by a "corrupt bargain" on the altar of the political ambitions of John Quincy Adams and Henry Clay.

In addition to his strong hold on the public, he was also the most available man about whom the diverse antiadministration forces could rally, since little was known of his political opinions. Prominent political organizers, like Senators Martin Van Buren of New York and Thomas H. Benton of Missouri, though they had backed other candidates in the previous election, now came to his support.

There were reasons of a different kind to account for his popularity in the South Atlantic states. With the growth of factory industry in the Northeast, the planters of the Southeast had found their own interests drifting apart from those of the Northern manufacturers. The South, as an agricultural section dependent upon slave labor for the production of staple crops, like cotton and tobacco, had no share in the manufacturing development fostered in the North by the protective tariffs of 1816, 1824, and 1828.

From early colonial times the planters had been accustomed to purchase their manufactures in Great Britain, the cheapest market in the world, where also they sold most of their cotton. They found that, under the protective system, they were paying a considerably higher price for the same goods in the North without any corresponding benefits to themselves. Under spur of their need, they studied the tariff question afresh, and came to the conclusion that the protective system was not only inequitable but also unauthorized by any rational construction of the Constitution. In reality, a part of their economic distress was due to a steady decline in the price of cotton, resulting from the spread of cotton culture into the fresher lands to the west, but the Southern leaders laid the whole blame to the more obvious cause.

Their sense of grievance flamed forth in 1828 in the "South Carolina Exposition," secretly drafted by John C. Calhoun and issued by the South Carolina legislature. This document proclaimed the right of a state to suspend or nullify the tariff as unconstitutional until the states should declare a contrary opinion through an amendment to the Constitution. Though more restrained in their pronouncements, the legislatures of Georgia, Mississippi, and Virginia also resolved that the protective policy was impolitic and unconstitutional.

In Jackson these Southerners saw a man who was without pronounced tariff views, and who, being a slaveholder himself, would probably espouse their side of the question. As Vice-President, Calhoun did all in his power to aid the Tennesseean's cause, and at his behest, his kinsman and political henchman, Duff Green of Missouri, went to Washington in 1826 and founded the *United States Telegraph* as the national organ of the Jackson forces.

The election of 1828 proved to be a victory for the "Old Hero" and for the new social and political order which he symbolized. In his own right he commanded the vote of the pioneer farmers of the West. Assisted by the powerful influence of Calhoun, his vice-presidential candidate, he received an equally ardent backing from the planters of the South Atlantic states. In the northeastern states the odds favored Adams, and he received virtually the solid support of New England. But with the aid of Martin Van Buren and his co-workers, Jackson won a majority of the electoral votes of New York and the entire vote of Pennsylvania. The new administration went into office with an electoral majority of 178 as against 83 for Adams and the National Republicans.

SELECT BIBLIOGRAPHY

General. The earlier years of the present volume are treated, with a wealth of detail, by the standard comprehensive histories, notably Edward Channing, *A History of the United States* (6 v., New York, 1905–1925, in progress), covering the period 1000–1865; H. von Holst, *The Constitutional and Political History of the United States* (8 v., Chicago, 1876–1892), treating the period 1750–1861; J. B. McMaster, *A History of the People of the United States* (8 v., New York, 1883–1913), dealing with the period 1784–1861; James Schouler, *History of the United States* (7 v., New York, 1895–1913), treating the period 1783–1877; and Woodrow Wilson, *A History of the American People* (5 v., New York, 1902), covering the years from 1492 to 1900. McMaster was the first general historian to stress American economic and social conditions. Judged by present-day standards, his material is not always well digested, and his treatment is lacking in interpretation. Channing presents a pleasing contrast in these respects. Schouler is a well-balanced general account of the older type. Von Holst's trenchant narrative needs to be read with a knowledge of his strong antislavery predispositions. Wilson's work is notable for its brilliant style and interpretation rather than for independent research.

In a class with these standard histories are the great coöperative works. The first of these was Justin Winsor, ed., *Narrative and Critical History of America* (8 v., Boston, 1884–1889), covering the years from 1000 to 1850. It contains many penetrating essays and invaluable bibliographical information. A. B. Hart, ed., *The American Nation: a History* (28 v., New York, 1904–1918), treating the period 1300–1917, gives attention to social and economic conditions as well as to political development, and is perhaps the best comprehensive history of the United States yet written. Allen Johnson, ed., *The Chronicles of America* (50 v., New Haven, 1918–1921), represents a successful attempt to popularize American history without sacrifice of scholarly accuracy. The volumes, which cover the period from pre-Columbian days to 1919, are not always well coördinated.

Much of value is also to be derived from the smaller coöperative histories, notably the *American History Series* (7 v., New York, 1892–1902), to which J. W. Burgess was the chief contributor and which carries the story to 1877; the five related volumes in the *Home University Library* (New York, 1911–1914), written by C. M. Andrews, T. C. Smith, William MacDonald, F. L. Paxson, and P. L. Haworth; and W. E. Dodd, ed., *The Riverside History of the United States* (4 v., Boston, 1915). Individual volumes of these coöperative works will be cited in succeeding chapters in appropriate connections.

The Opening of a New Era. Excellent brief accounts of the revolutionary era of 1830 in Europe may be found in such standard manuals as C. J. H. Hayes, *A Political and Social History of Modern Europe* (2 v., New York, 1916–1924), C. D. Hazen, *Europe since 1815* (2 v., New York, 1923), and E. R. Turner, *Europe, 1789–1920* (Garden City, 1920). H. T. Tuckerman, *America and Her Commentators* (New York, 1864), discusses the views of foreign visitors to our shores down to the date of publication. The most useful survey is the collection of source extracts entitled *American Social History as Recorded by British Travellers* (New York, 1923), edited, with excellent introductory essays, by Allan Nevins.

Frontier Influences. The various essays of F. J. Turner, collected in his *The Frontier in American History* (New York, 1920), remain unexcelled as an interpretation of the westward movement. His interpretation should be contrasted with that of Edward Channing, *History of the United States*, V (New York, 1921). The best systematic account is F. L. Paxson, *History of the American Frontier, 1763–1893* (Boston, 1924). For other authorities, see bibliographical note at the close of chapter xvi in H. C. Hockett, *Political and Social History of the United States to 1828* (New York, 1925).

The Awakening of Labor. This subject is thoroughly discussed by Helen L. Sumner and E. B. Mittelman in J. R. Commons, *History of Labour in the*

United States (New York, 1918), I. Good summary accounts appear in Mary R. Beard, *A Short History of the American Labor Movement* (New York, 1920), and S. Perlman, *A History of Trade Unionism in the United States* (New York, 1922). See also Norman Ware, *The Industrial Worker, 1840–1860* (Boston, 1924).

The Extension of the Suffrage. The best work is K. H. Porter, *A History of Suffrage in the United States* (Chicago, 1918). See also C. E. Merriam, *A History of American Political Theories* (New York, 1903), chapter v.

CHAPTER II

JACKSONIAN DEMOCRACY

Democracy Triumphant

The scenes at Jackson's inauguration gave boisterous evidence of the conviction of the common people that they had at last come into possession of the government. Ten thousand visitors from all parts of the country thronged Washington to witness the event. The President-elect walked to the Capitol with a small company of friends, his erect figure and uncovered white head in plain sight of the cheering hosts. The oath of office was administered by the venerable Chief Justice, John Marshall, whose whole life had been a protest against the political tenets of the Jackson party. After the ceremonies an official reception was held at the White House. The impatient multitude broke into the interior, stood in muddy boots on the damask-covered chairs, and mobbed the waiters carrying refreshments. In the scornful phrase of Jackson's adversaries, "the millennium of minnows" had arrived.

Jackson himself was in no sense responsible for the unruly behavior of his admirers at the inauguration, but in making his appointments to office, he acted frankly upon the principle that the government belonged to the people. Though a man of strong personal convictions, he perceived the wisdom of selecting the heads of the executive departments from the principal factions of the Democratic party. The Van Buren element was recognized by the appointment of Van Buren himself as Secretary of State. Three other department heads were political friends of Calhoun.[1] John H. Eaton of Tennessee, Secretary of War, was the personal choice of the President, and William T. Barry of Kentucky, the new Postmaster-General, was also a Jackson supporter.

[1] S. D. Ingham of Pennsylvania, Secretary of the Treasury; John Branch of North Carolina, Secretary of the Navy; and John M. Berrien of Georgia, Attorney-General.

With the exception of the Secretary of State, the group as a whole was not a strong one. In the course of a long public career Martin Van Buren had, by sheer force of ability and political skill, risen from humble beginnings to the political leadership of the important state of New York. Tactful and urbane in his personal relationships and adroit in political manipulation, he was regarded by many of his contemporaries as a mere crafty politician. That he was more than that, however, his service as Secretary of State and his later political career were to show.

Jackson did not regard his official associates as men upon whom he cared to lean heavily for advice. For this purpose he gathered about him a number of intimates who enjoyed his complete confidence and who were derisively dubbed the "Kitchen Cabinet" by the National Republicans. The dominant personality of the Kitchen Cabinet was Amos Kendall, an astute politician and former editor of Kentucky, and with him were associated a group of somewhat variable composition, chief among whom were Isaac Hill, editor of the *New Hampshire Patriot*, William B. Lewis of Tennessee, who for many years had been Jackson's political mentor, and Duff Green, editor of the *United States Telegraph*. All these men had been active in state politics, and the majority of them belonged to what Webster called "the typographical crowd." Indeed, Jackson was the first President to realize the importance of being on cordial terms with the newspaper men of the country. The fact that he bestowed many offices upon newspaper editors throughout the land was no doubt a powerful assistance to him in interpreting public opinion and in securing wide publicity and popular support for his policies. The members of the Kitchen Cabinet were, with the exception of Duff Green, favorable to Van Buren's political aspirations, and indeed Van Buren and Eaton of the President's official circle may be regarded also as members of the Kitchen Cabinet.

Jackson's accession to the presidency was marked by the adoption of a new principle in the selection of federal officeholders. Under the earlier Presidents, public officials had enjoyed a feeling of security, and ordinarily continued their tenure during good behavior. To be sure, the spirit of partisanship had never been wholly absent in making appointments. Thus, when Jefferson in 1801 found the government positions monopolized by the Federalists, he made some dismissals and filled all vacancies with members of his own party. With the rapid falling off of the Federalist party in the subsequent years, the entire public service became filled with Republicans. As Republican Presidents, Madison and Monroe had little temptation to make widespread changes, and the civil service attained a new stability. Men grew old in the service; Richard Rush once spoke of the War Department as the "octogenarian department."

Meantime the practice had grown up in most of the Northern and Western states of basing appointments and removals from office upon party service. In New York and Pennsylvania this system attained its greatest development, and party organization in those states was not unlike the modern "political machine." With the reappearance of factional strife under John Quincy Adams, it was natural that attempts should be made to extend the system to the federal government; but the high-minded Adams sternly set his face against the practice.

The triumph of the democratic forces under Jackson opened the way for the nationalization of the "spoils system." The idea of an official aristocracy was repugnant to the common man, and most people were ready to indorse the doctrine that "to the victor belong the spoils." Furthermore, many people felt that "rotation in office" would give the newly enfranchised masses a chance to receive training in the actual conduct of public affairs. Jackson announced the new creed in his first annual message to Congress. Averring that public office had come to be regarded as "a species of property," he insisted that long continuance in office was likely to breed indifference to the public welfare. This danger, he believed, outweighed any advantages that might be derived from the experience or training of the officeholder, especially since any man of intelligence could quickly qualify himself to perform the duties of any government position.

Jackson's frank avowal created more alarm and excitement among the official class, and in the country at large, than his performance actually warranted. While he removed more officeholders than any previous President, the changes were not nearly as extensive as the outcries of the opposition represented. The best available evidence shows that, in the first year and a half of his administration, 919 removals and changes had been made for all purposes, or approximately one eleventh of the entire federal civil service. Although most of these changes were made for partisan reasons, some of them were caused by misconduct in office and others by resignation or death. Jackson's appointments were made exclusively from the ranks of the Democratic party; and among the men who received postmasterships, customs offices, and other positions were fifty-six editors of influential newspapers. The public excitement over the administration's patronage policy subsided after these first sweeping changes. By the close of Jackson's eight years in office, it is estimated that about one fifth of all federal officeholders had been changed.

The spoils system was one of the cruder manifestations of triumphant democracy.[1] Jackson adopted the new practice in the spirit of reform and without any appreciation of its dangers and abuses. The new system, thus established, received the unwavering support of all later Presidents and parties until the administration of President Grant, forty years later.

The Question of Internal Improvements

When Jackson entered office, his views upon many national questions were unknown even to his close friends, and were perhaps not clearly formulated in his own mind. But in the course of his first administration a series of important problems arose for settlement, and his action with regard to them was so clear-cut and decisive that no one could remain in doubt as to Jackson's sentiments when he came up for reëlection in 1832. Since his party was made up of heterogeneous elements, it was inevitable that his spirited course should result in alienating from him a portion of his original supporters.

The first of these great questions concerned the attitude of the federal government toward expending money for the promotion of roads, canals, and other public works. The facilities for transportation and communication in 1829 were still primitive.

[1] With the introduction of the spoils system another vicious practice grew up in national politics, namely, campaign assessments on official salaries for party purposes. Previous to an election, officeholders were asked to contribute a percentage of their salaries for party expenses in the campaign. At first voluntary and occasional, the custom in the course of a few decades hardened into a form of official taxation, unjust and burdensome to the helpless victims.

In the older seaboard states the construction of turnpikes had somewhat increased the ease of travel; but in the country at large the roads were poor, and travelers in the interior had still to rely upon the stagecoach, postchaise, or private conveyance unless they were so fortunate as to be able to travel by water. It was particularly important, for the sake of national unity, that the difficult barrier formed by the Appalachian System should be pierced at as many points as possible, and communication between the interior and the seaboard be facilitated. This need, which seemed very real to a generation that remembered the transportation difficulties of the War of 1812, received additional support from men like Henry Clay and John Quincy Adams, who perceived the commercial, as well as political, advantages of promoting an interchange of trade between the Eastern manufacturers and the Western farmers.

No one denied the desirability of the more rapid development of the country by means of internal improvements; but since the early days of the republic, the question had been warmly discussed whether the general government was warranted by the Constitution to assist in such enterprises, or whether the matter did not belong more properly to the action of the states. Nevertheless, Congress since 1806 had from time to time made gifts of money or grants of land for internal improvements, and under the nationalistic impulse of the War of 1812, Calhoun, Clay, and other leaders of the younger generation had sought energetically to commit the government to a comprehensive program of public works.

Their efforts were of no avail during the terms of Madison and Monroe. Neither President was willing to support the plan unless all constitutional doubts should be swept away by an amendment to the Constitution. Monroe's veto of a bill in 1822 for collecting tolls on the Cumberland Road drew forth a letter of commendation from Jackson, then in private life. Van Buren, who sympathized with Monroe's constitutional scruples, introduced a resolution in the Senate in 1825 for a constitutional amendment, but that body left it unnoticed.

Thrown back on their own resources, some of the more enterprising states acted for themselves, either through legislative subsidies or private companies or through combinations of the two. The Erie Canal, completed by the state of New York in 1825, was only the greatest of such projects. With the ascendancy of John Quincy Adams and his Secretary of State, Henry Clay, the federal government reversed its attitude toward internal improvements. Despite bitter factional opposition, considerably more than twice as much was spent for roads, canals, and harbor improvements under Adams as under all the preceding Presidents.

When Jackson became President, the situation with reference to internal improvements was badly complicated politically. The National Republicans were, of course, ardent supporters of a federal system of public works; but Jackson's own followers were divided on the issue. Vice-President Calhoun, though he had sloughed off most of his earlier broad-construction convictions, continued to uphold the policy of internal improvements. Van Buren, on the other hand, disapproved of the policy. Jackson himself had indicated his earlier attitude in his letter to President Monroe; but as a member of the Senate (1823–1825), he had not always voted consistently with the view he had then expressed. Van Buren took an early occasion to discuss the matter with his chief, and ascertained that the Monroe letter represented Jackson's real convictions.

Jackson was soon given an opportunity to make a public announcement of his position. On May 20, 1830, Congress passed a bill authorizing the government to buy stock in a company which was planning to build a road from Maysville to Lexington, two towns in Kentucky. The bill represented a popular demand, and the proposed improvement lay in a section of Kentucky that was friendly to the President. Van Buren stated afterward that not one in twenty believed that Jackson would dare to reject it. Against the advice of many of his Western friends, he prepared a ringing veto message which Van Buren helped to compose. This message, dated May 27, asserted that the Maysville Road, as a work of merely local utility, was not entitled to federal aid under any reasonable construction of the Constitution. He furthermore called attention to the selfish "scramble for appropriations," which was an inevitable feature of the policy of federal help, and declared that the paramount object of the government should be retrenchment and economy in order to pay off the national debt. He concluded by repeating the familiar injunction that, if the people really desired federal aid, the Constitution should be amended to that end.

Jackson's opposition proved a strong deterrent to further expenditures by Congress during his presidency for roads within the boundaries of the states. The chief, though not only, exceptions were the continued aid given to the Cumberland Road and an appropriation for a highway in Alabama in 1833. In Jackson's mind, subsidies for roads in the territories and for the improvement of navigable rivers and harbors possessed greater constitutional justification, and expenditures for such purposes during his presidency actually exceeded the total appropriations under John Quincy Adams for internal improvements. The question of federal aid to railroads did not become important in Jackson's time; and it was not until 1850 and later that the system of land grants to railroads was fairly inaugurated.

Jackson's stand against public improvements at federal cost did not cause the great popular outcry that Clay and the National Republicans had so confidently expected. The President's instinct proved a better guide to an understanding of the common man than the judgment of the experienced politicians. Within his own group of followers the Maysville veto had the effect of drawing the President closer to his Secretary of State and of revealing possibilities of discord between himself and Calhoun. The Southerners generally applauded Jackson's veto, and felt more strongly than ever that he could be relied upon to back up strict-construction principles.

The Georgia-Indian Controversy

The popular belief that Jackson was a strict constructionist was strengthened by his action in the Georgia-Indian controversy. The westward flow of white settlement across the Appalachians had early raised the question of extinguishing the Indian title to the land in that region. Since the War of 1812 the United States government had been rapidly pushing its purchases of Indian land. By 1829 all of Ohio and most of Indiana, Illinois, the lower peninsula of Michigan, Louisiana, and Arkansas had been cleared for white settlement. The Indians, however, still retained possession of extensive tracts in the Gulf region and Tennessee. The relations between the two races in these states became one of the thorny problems of Jackson's presidency.

In 1802, when Georgia ceded its western lands to the United States, the federal government had agreed to extinguish the Indian title to lands within the state "as soon as the same can be peaceably obtained upon reasonable terms." By a series of treaties the United States had, in the spirit of this agreement, bought out the Indian title to a considerable portion of the lands "peaceably" and "upon reasonable terms." Yet in 1825 the Creeks and Cherokees still held nearly ten million acres in Georgia, and, together with the Choctaws and Chickasaws, owned a total of more than nine million acres in the nearby states of Alabama, Tennessee, and Mississippi. These tribes exercised complete rights of self-government within their domains, and were not subject to the laws of the states wherein they dwelt. Their privileged position excited the utmost impatience of the white planters who saw some of the best cotton lands occupied by a backward race, and who believed furthermore that no constitutional warrant existed for the presence of an independent alien community within the borders of a state.

Although the neighboring states had almost as great an interest in the matter, the leadership in the movement against the Indians fell to Georgia. Early in John Quincy Adams's administration Georgia began a bitter controversy over the matter with the federal government. The treaty of Indian Springs in 1825, which ceded a large portion of the Creek lands in Georgia and Alabama, was disregarded by President Adams as having been illegally negotiated. In Georgia this was looked upon as a bit of misdirected Puritan conscientiousness, and before a satisfactory adjustment was reached, threats of warlike action were exchanged between the state and federal governments. However, in 1827, the Creeks consented to a treaty ceding the last of their lands in Georgia to the United States.

The Cherokees, who had developed farming as an important industry and who were the most highly civilized of all the Southern tribes, realized that their turn would come next. Although their rights were protected by a series of treaties with the United

States, they sought to render security more secure by adopting a constitution in 1827, which asserted their position as one of the sovereign and independent nations of the earth. This bold defiance led the Georgia legislature to pass a law in December, 1828, providing that after June 1, 1830, all Indians should become subject to the laws of the state. Mississippi and Alabama followed the example of Georgia a little later with similar legislation.

As a frontiersman and Indian fighter, President Jackson knew the red man of old; and he believed further that the Indian character would be debased rather than uplifted by constant association with the more advanced race. His instinctive sympathy, therefore, lay with Georgia in the controversy. He outlined his policy in his first annual message to Congress on December 8, 1829. Denying that the Indians had any constitutional right to an independent government within the limits of a state,[1] he asserted that they must either agree to migrate beyond the Mississippi, with the help of the United States, or else submit themselves to the laws of the state like the whites and give up all their lands not under cultivation. In accordance with Jackson's recommendation Congress passed a law on March 10, 1830, which authorized him to locate, on lands west of the Mississippi, all Indians who surrendered their holdings. The sum of $500,000 was appropriated for the expense of their removal.

The resolution of the Cherokees remained unshaken by these developments. When the Georgia authorities took the necessary steps to extend their jurisdiction over their lands, the Indians, acting upon the advice of white friends, turned to the Supreme Court for relief.[2] In the case of Worcester *v.* Georgia, Chief Justice Marshall roundly declared that the Cherokees possessed the status of "a nation" under protection of the federal government and that the action taken by Georgia against the Indians was unconstitutional and void. When Jackson learned of this decision, he is reported to have said, "John Marshall has made

[1] The Constitution (Art. IV, Sec. 3) says that "no new State shall be formed . . . within the Jurisdiction of any other State . . . without the consent of the Legislatures of the States concerned as well as of the Congress."

[2] There were three cases in all: Cherokee Nation *v.* Georgia (1831), Worcester *v.* Georgia (1832), and Graves *v.* Georgia (1834).

his decision; now let him enforce it!" Jackson was not willing to concede on this or any other occasion that the executive, as a coördinate department of the government, did not have as good a right as the judiciary to decide questions of constitutionality.

Since the Supreme Court was helpless to act effectively without executive support, the Indians had to bow to the inevitable. The Cherokees eventually made a treaty with the United States in 1835, surrendering their lands for five million dollars and receiving a tract beyond the Mississippi with their expenses of transportation. The Choctaws and Chickasaws accepted the liberal terms offered by the United States in 1830 and 1832, and began their removal westward. In the case of the Sac and Fox Indians in Illinois, and the Seminoles in Florida, the United States had to resort to forcible measures of ejection. The former incident, known in history as the "Black Hawk War," occurred in 1832. The unwillingness of the Seminoles to migrate from Florida was inspired, in part, by fear of discovery and apprehension on the part of a large number of fugitive slaves who had joined the tribe. The Seminole leader was the brave Osceola, and the struggle dragged on from 1834 to 1842 before the savages were willing to submit to the will of the United States. Distressing as were many features of the removals, the country as a whole approved of the government's course.

On its constructive side, Jackson's aggressive Indian policy led to the creation of an extensive territory in the fertile valley of the Arkansas as a final home for the dispossessed Southern tribes. Under a law of 1834 and certain supplementary acts, Congress made permanent provision for these Indians, who in the past had constantly been subject to white encroachment. The land was granted to them in perpetuity with virtually full rights of tribal government. No white man could go into the Indian country without a license, and no spirituous liquors were to be permitted there. The office of the Commissioner of Indian Affairs was created, with special oversight of the Indians, and provision was made for supplying the tribes with domestic animals and agricultural implements. This Indian country formed the nucleus of the state of Oklahoma, which was admitted into the Union many years later.

The Great Debate on the Nature of the Union

The internal-improvements question and the Georgia-Indian dispute were hardly more than opening skirmishes in the great struggle over the question of the nature of the Union and the respective rights of the states and the federal government under the Constitution. On December 29, 1829, Senator Samuel A. Foot of Connecticut offered a resolution in Congress, suggesting the desirability of stopping the further survey of the public domain, and of restricting the sale of public lands, for a certain period, to those already on the market. The proposal was at once assailed by Thomas H. Benton of Missouri as an attack on the West. In an elaborate speech he declared that the material prosperity and political security of the West depended upon the rapid settlement of the country. He charged that Foot's resolution was provoked by the jealousy of the seaboard North, and by the self-interest of the manufacturers who wished to check the flow of their underpaid employees to the frontier.

The Southerners, who had long been smarting under the protective-tariff policy of the Northern industrialists, saw an opportunity of welding the interests of the trans-Appalachian states and the seaboard South by showing that the two sections were equally sufferers at the hands of a common enemy. With the introduction of this new element into the situation, the question of the public lands receded into the background. Thenceforward it was the divergent needs and interests of sections that were debated.

The logical spokesman for the South Atlantic section, John C. Calhoun, could not as Vice-President assume his proper rôle, but his place was ably taken by Senator Robert Y. Hayne, a fluent and persuasive orator from Calhoun's state. Hayne's severe indictment of New England and the seaboard North at once brought into the arena Senator Daniel Webster of Massachusetts, the ablest constitutional lawyer in the country and the greatest public speaker that the nation had yet produced. From January 19 to 27, 1830, these two giants engaged in a forensic contest that crowded the galleries of the Senate with excited auditors.

Senator Hayne condemned the steady trend toward national consolidation, and particularly the employment of this enlarged national power for selfish sectional advantage. Restriction of land sales, he said, would not only curb the growth of the agricultural states, but would contribute to the upbuilding of manufacturing and thus perpetuate the unconstitutional protective system. Obviously the states must look to themselves for protection against encroachments by the federal authority. The means for so doing had already been pointed out by the Virginia and Kentucky Resolutions of 1798–1799 and the South Carolina Exposition of 1828.

Hayne then reiterated the doctrine that the states as independent sovereignties had joined together to form the Union, and had conferred upon the general government only certain powers specified in the Constitution. The Union, therefore, was a compact among sovereign states, and each state as a party to the compact could judge when the federal government exceeded its constitutional limits. If a state declared a federal law to be unconstitutional, it was the duty of the general government "to acquiesce in the solemn decision," and to appeal to the country for an amendment to the Constitution expressly granting the disputed power. The claim that the federal government was the exclusive judge of its own authority, he held, was not warranted by the Constitution, and would result in making the general government "a government without limit of powers."

Webster, while protesting that New England had always been friendly to the West, directed his chief attack against Hayne's constitutional arguments. He denied that the Union was merely a compact among the states, and asserted that the national Constitution had been formed by the people of the entire country just as the people within each state had instituted their state constitutions. The federal government could not be regarded, therefore, as occupying a subordinate relationship to the states, since "the general government and the state governments derive their authority from the same source." Furthermore, the people had provided in the federal Constitution for a judiciary vested with the authority of settling all questions of constitutional law.[1]

In his view, the doctrine of nullification was not only uncon-

[1] Webster referred to the provisions that the Constitution and the federal laws made pursuant thereto shall be the supreme law of the land, and that the jurisdiction of the federal courts shall extend to every case arising under the supreme law. See the Constitution, Art. VI, Par. 2, and Art. III, Sec. 2, Par. 1.

stitutional but impracticable, for under its operation the tariff would be void in South Carolina, but in Pennsylvania and Kentucky, where protection was in favor, it would be in force. There would thus be "four and twenty interpreters of constitutional law, each with a power to decide for itself, and none with authority to bind anybody else," and the Constitution would be reduced to a "collection of topics for everlasting controversy." The states were not without redress, he pointed out, if the acts of the general government seemed oppressive to them, for they might lawfully amend the Constitution at their pleasure or choose new officers for the government at the elections. They might even appeal to the right of revolution, the inherent right of every people. But the South Carolina doctrine of defying the Union while remaining within it meant inevitably armed defiance of the federal government, or treason.

The Webster-Hayne debate was the formal opening of the historic controversy concerning the nature of the Constitution, which thirty years later was to plunge the nation into civil war. The debate of 1830 was, of course, inconclusive in settling the vital issues at stake, but the adherents of each side claimed a victory for their champion. That both of the great debaters loved their country and were stating the only principles upon which they believed the Union could survive, we can well believe. That both men spoke with full knowledge of the selfish sectional advantages to be derived from their constitutional contentions is also true.

Hayne pleaded for the states, Webster for the nation. Hayne's arguments breathed the spirit of the past, and probably reflected the attitude of the country when the Constitution was first adopted. Whatever may have been the true legal character of the Constitution in 1787, the new frame of government would almost certainly have failed of acceptance if the ratifying conventions had believed the federal government to be beyond state control except by the amending process, or that the Supreme Court would be the final interpreter of the Constitution in all cases whatsoever.

Webster, on the other hand, held that the Federal Convention had devised a truly national system — a position with which modern students are inclined to agree. Though ingenious arguments could be, and were, urged against his view, the tide of American development had strongly set in its favor. The American people had been undergoing a process of nationalization since 1787. The heritage of a common history, the great increase of population, the habit of working together for common purposes, the patriotic pride born of wars against a common enemy, the strong nationalism of the new Western states, and Marshall's series of great constitutional decisions had united to bring into being a Union that was quite unlike the one the people of 1787 had thought they were creating.

The Split in the Democratic Party

The appearance of this portentous issue boded ill for continued harmony within the Democratic party. Other influences, however, were already at work to drive a wedge between the Jackson-Van Buren following, on the one hand, and the Calhoun faction, on the other. The friends of Calhoun looked upon the South Carolinian as the logical successor of Jackson to the presidency in 1836, but this plan did not accord with the desires of the Kitchen Cabinet, who were grooming Van Buren for the position. Events now occurred in rapid succession, which firmly established Van Buren in Jackson's regard and led to the latter's complete alienation from Calhoun.

The first of these incidents was known as the "Eaton Affair." Shortly before his appointment as Secretary of War, John H. Eaton had married a lively young widow who, under her maiden name of Peggy O'Neil, had been the life of her father's tavern in Washington and whose free manners had set tongues wagging. The leaders of Washington society determined to ostracize Mrs. Eaton, and at cabinet functions and official receptions they studiously ignored her. The whole affair might have been merely a tempest in a teapot except for the fact that Jackson, who believed the wife of his intimate friend to be unjustly accused, resolved to make himself her champion. On every occasion he showed her marked courtesy; he even lectured his cabinet members on the attitude that their wives should take toward her. Very conspicuous in the campaign against Mrs. Eaton were Mrs. Calhoun and the wives of the Calhoun members of the cabinet, and Jackson soon began to think of the Calhouns as abetters in an intrigue to discredit his administration. Van Buren, who as a widower was free from family restraints, won new favor with his chief because of his chivalrous attentions to Mrs. Eaton.

The breach between Jackson and Calhoun was further widened by an event that occurred at the anniversary celebration of Jefferson's birthday on the evening of April 15, 1830. The Southern Democrats planned to make the affair a nullification demonstration; and as Jackson had not yet committed himself on the issues raised in the Webster-Hayne debate, they hoped to surprise him into an utterance favorable to the Southern position. Jackson and Van Buren took counsel in advance, and agreed that the occasion would give the President an effective opportunity to disclose his real convictions. Therefore, when Jackson was called upon for a toast, he declared in ringing tones: "Our federal Union: it must be preserved!" Calhoun sought in vain to retrieve the situation by offering as his sentiment: "The Union: next to our liberty most dear! May we all remember that it can only be preserved by respecting the rights of the states . . . ."

The final break between the two men was precipitated by the revival of an incident, dating back to the year 1818, when Jackson's course in invading Spanish Florida had been sharply criticized in President Monroe's cabinet. Since Jackson in this affair believed that he had been merely carrying out the wishes of the government, he had felt angered and humiliated by the strictures on his conduct. For many years he thought that he had escaped official censure only through the stout friendship of John C. Calhoun, then Secretary of War. The time now being propitious, the Kitchen Cabinet managed to get the real facts before him. Sometime in May, 1830, he learned that Calhoun, instead of being his defender, had been his most aggressive critic. To a man of Jackson's temperament, only one course of action was now possible. After giving Calhoun a chance to explain, he sent him a letter, terminating their relations and venting his bitter disillusionment in Cæsar's reputed words to his false friend, "*Et tu, Brute!*"

The President now proceeded to reorganize his administration frankly upon a Jackson-Van Buren basis. Always alive to the importance of an active newspaper support, he abandoned the *United States Telegraph* as the administrative organ because of its pro-Calhoun leanings, and induced Francis P. Blair, a Kentucky friend of Amos Kendall, to come to Washington to found a new organ in December, 1830. Blair proved to be a prince of partisan editors, and throughout the administrations of Jackson and Van Buren, his newspaper, the *Washington Globe*, thundered forth Jacksonian policies, giving the cue to the Democratic press the country over.

Jackson's next step was to purge his cabinet of the Calhoun element. Van Buren and Eaton readily saw the wisdom of the move, and prepared the way by tendering their resignations early in April, 1831. In view of all the circumstances the three Calhoun members could but follow their example. The President then chose a cabinet composed of men who enjoyed his confidence, headed by the distinguished jurist, Edward Livingston of Louisiana, as Secretary of State, and Louis McLane of Delaware, as Secretary of the Treasury.[1] Thereafter the Kitchen Cabinet, as such, played a less important rôle, though Kendall and Blair came closer to the President than ever before, and Kendall was eventually taken into his official family as Postmaster-General in 1835. The latter an English visitor in America at this time called a "twilight personage" who was supposed by Jackson's critics to be "the moving spring of the whole administration; the thinker, planner, and doer."

Jackson sought to look after Van Buren's interests by submitting his nomination as Minister to Great Britain; but the Senate was torn by factionalism, and on January 25, 1832, the nomination was defeated by the casting vote of Vice-President Calhoun. When the result was announced, Senator Benton shrewdly remarked to a Senator who had voted against the nomination, "You have broken a minister and elected a vice-president." This occurrence undoubtedly stiffened the President's already strong determination to secure a public vindication of Van Buren from the assaults of his enemies.

[1] The other members were: Lewis Cass of Michigan, Secretary of War; Levi Woodbury of New Hampshire, Secretary of the Navy; Roger B. Taney of Maryland, Attorney-General; and W. T. Barry of Kentucky, Postmaster-General. Barry was the only holdover from the previous cabinet.

SELECT BIBLIOGRAPHY

Democracy Triumphant. The general events of Jackson's presidency receive detailed treatment in the comprehensive works already cited: Edward Channing, *A History of the United States*, V (New York, 1921); H. von Holst, *The Constitutional and Political History of the United States*, III (Chicago, 1881); J. B. McMaster, *A History of the People of the United States*, V–VI (New York, 1900–1906); James Schouler, *History of the United States*, III–IV (New York, 1894); and Woodrow Wilson, *A History of the American People*, IV (New York, 1902). Reliable single-volume surveys are William MacDonald, *Jacksonian Democracy* (in *The American Nation*, XV, New York, 1906), and F. A. Ogg, *The Reign of Andrew Jackson* (in *The Chronicles of America*, XX, New Haven, 1920). W. E. Dodd's discussion of the period in his *Expansion and Conflict* (*The Riverside History of the United States*, III, Boston, 1915) is valuable for an insight into the interplay of social forces and political conduct. The most recent study, C. G. Bowers, *The Party Battles of the Jackson Period* (Boston, 1922), places chief emphasis upon the picturesque aspects of the epoch.

The biographies of the statesmen of the period usually include a full discussion of pertinent political events. Of particular value are J. S. Bassett, *The Life of Andrew Jackson* (2 v., Garden City, 1911), Gaillard Hunt, *John C. Calhoun* (Philadelphia, 1908), T. D. Jervey, *Robert Y. Hayne and his Times* (New York, 1909), H. C. Lodge, *Daniel Webster* (Boston, 1899), W. M. Meigs, *Life of Thomas Hart Benton* (Philadelphia, 1904), W. M. Meigs, *The Life of John Caldwell Calhoun* (2 v., New York, 1917), Carl Schurz, *Henry Clay* (2 v., Boston, 1899), and E. M. Shepard, *Martin Van Buren* (Boston, 1900).

The origin of the spoils system is best set forth in C. R. Fish, *The Civil Service and the Patronage* (in *Harvard Historical Studies*, XI, New York, 1905). See also M. Ostrogorski, *Democracy and the Organization of Political Parties* (2 v., New York, 1902).

The Question of Internal Improvements. The political phases of this problem are portrayed and analyzed in R. G. Wellington, *The Political and Sectional Influence of the Public Lands, 1828–1842* (Cambridge, 1914). A. B. Hulbert, *The Paths of Inland Commerce* (*The Chronicles of America*, XXI, New Haven, 1920), gives a good account of the development of roads, canals, and early railways, summarized from the same author's *Historic Highways of America* (16 v., Cleveland, 1902–1905). F. L. Paxson, *History of the American Frontier, 1763–1893* (Boston, 1924), is also of importance.

The Georgia-Indian Controversy. The standard treatment of this subject is U. B. Phillips, "Georgia and State Rights" in American Historical Association, *Annual Report for 1901*, II, 3–224. It should be supplemented by Annie H. Abel, "The History of Events Resulting in Indian Consolidation West of the Mississippi" in American Historical Association, *Annual Report for 1906*, I, 233–450.

The Great Debate on the Nature of the Union. The biographies of Webster and Hayne (already cited) are useful in supplying a personal setting. J. W. Burgess, *The Middle Period* (*The American History Series*, New York, 1897), while unduly brief on the Webster-Hayne debate, gives an incisive analysis of the constitutional problems of the years from 1817 to 1858. C. E. Merriam, *A History of American Political Theories* (New York, 1903), chapter vii, is the best objective study of the growth of political theory concerning the nature of the Union.

CHAPTER III

JACKSON'S FIGHT FOR NATIONALITY AND POPULAR RIGHTS

South Carolina Nullification

The divided condition of the Democratic party helped to prepare the way for South Carolina's dramatic defiance of the federal government in 1832–1833. The South Carolinians had expected, or at least had hoped, that Jackson would use his power as President for a removal of the tariff injustices against which they had protested in the Exposition of 1828. But Jackson's messages to Congress had, from the outset, shown that, while he favored a modification of the Tariff of 1828, he did not share the Southern view of the unconstitutionality of protection. Indeed, his position was that of moderate protectionist.

When Congress enacted a new tariff law in July, 1832, he signed it without hesitation. The new rates, which were to go into effect on March 3, 1833, were in many respects an improvement over the "Tariff of Abominations" of 1828, but they were frankly based upon the protective principle. The average level of duties was reduced from 41 to about 33 per cent. In the House of Representatives, the bill received overwhelming support from the Middle Atlantic states and the states west of the Appalachians. New England was evenly divided. South Carolina and Georgia voted strongly in the negative, but Virginia and North Carolina voted as strongly in the affirmative.

The people of South Carolina had been closely following the course of events. During the summer of 1830 the nullifiers in South Carolina, calling themselves the "State Rights party," had agitated for a state convention to consider the propriety of nullification, but their efforts had been defeated by the Union party under the leadership of Joel R. Poinsett. In the subsequent months, Calhoun issued a series of addresses and papers in aid of the State Rights party, restating and clarifying the nullification theory for the people at large.

The new tariff measure of 1832 brought matters to a crisis. Immediately after its passage, the South Carolina members of Congress issued an address to their fellow-citizens, asserting that "all hope of relief from Congress is irrevocably gone," and that the people could now look only to themselves. The new South Carolina legislature, elected on the express issue, summoned a special state convention to meet on November 19, 1832.

Five days after this body assembled, they adopted by an overwhelming vote an "Ordinance of Nullification," declaring the tariff laws of 1828 and 1832 unconstitutional and void within the state from and after February 1, 1833. All state officials (excepting the members of the legislature) were required to take an oath to obey the Ordinance, appeals were prohibited to the United States Supreme Court in cases involving the Ordinance, and the state legislature was instructed to adopt the necessary measures to make the Ordinance effective. The document closed with a threat of secession from the Union in case Congress should pass any law for the employment of force against the state.

Three days after the adjournment of the state convention, the legislature met on November 27 and passed a series of acts providing the necessary machinery for the enforcement of the Ordinance within the state, and making warlike preparations against the possibility of armed intervention by the federal government. Shortly thereafter, Calhoun resigned the vice-presidency, and was chosen by the South Carolina legislature to Hayne's seat in the Senate, where he could act as the champion of the state in the national arena.

Jackson had been kept fully informed of these proceedings. His own instinct was to deal vigorously and decisively with the recalcitrants, but since he believed that behind the nullification program lay a genuine grievance, he was not disinclined to listen to Van Buren and other counselors, who advised that South Carolina be afforded some relief from her economic distress. The policy of the administration became thus a mixture of principle and expediency, of the sword and the olive branch.

In November, 1832, Jackson strengthened the garrison at Fort

Moultrie in Charleston Harbor. Seven revenue cutters and a ship-of-war were sent to Charleston with orders to be ready for instant action. Arms and munitions were placed at convenient and safe places, some of them across the North Carolina border, and Jackson intimated his intention of personally leading the forces against the South Carolina rebels if the crisis came. On December 10, he issued his resounding proclamation against the nullifiers.

This nationalistic pronouncement was the joint production of Jackson and Livingston, two Westerners. South Carolina, the President declared, stood on "the brink of insurrection and treason," and he appealed to the people of the state to reassert their allegiance to that Union for which their ancestors had fought and bled. Instead of being "a compact between sovereign States," he affirmed, like Webster, that the United States was "a Government in which the people of all the States, collectively, are represented." As for his own course of action, the laws of the United States must be executed. "I have no discretionary power on the subject; my duty is emphatically pronounced in the Constitution." Acting in the spirit of this proclamation, he asked Congress on January 16, 1833, for additional legislation to enable him to enforce the tariff law.

Jackson's bold stand for national supremacy came as a surprise to many who had observed his earlier course in championing a strict construction of the Constitution. But it is only fair to note that he was fully as consistent in his constitutional convictions as Webster or Calhoun. He held with the former that the Union was indestructible, and with the latter that the powers of the federal government should be construed narrowly; but he failed to find in a literal reading of the Constitution any justification either for Calhoun's nullifying doctrine or for Webster's belief in national consolidation. He occupied, as Calhoun admitted, a position "between the parties." That his treatment of South Carolina contrasted sharply with his attitude toward Georgia during the Indian controversy arose naturally from his conviction that the executive department was as competent as the Supreme Court to decide questions of constitutionality. In the Georgia affair he regarded the pronouncements of the federal judiciary unconstitutional, whereas in the nullification controversy he held that a protective tariff was warranted by the Constitution.

In accordance with Jackson's desire, a "force bill" was promptly introduced in the Senate. By its terms the President was empowered to change the location of custom-houses for their greater security, the jurisdiction of the United States Circuit Courts was extended to all cases arising under the revenue laws, and the President was authorized to employ the armed forces of the United States to enforce federal laws and the processes of the federal judiciary.[1] Denounced as the "Bloody Bill," the proposed law met with the bitterest opposition of John Tyler of Virginia, Calhoun, and other Southern leaders, but found an equally ardent advocate in Daniel Webster.

Meantime, Jackson's friends in Congress were pressing a bill for scaling down the tariff duties. Their efforts, embodied in the Verplanck bill, made little progress, however. It soon became clear that, in the critical juncture, there was only one man who could still the raging elements and pilot a compromise measure through Congress. This was Senator Henry Clay, the great advocate of protection and father of the "American System." On February 12, 1833, he introduced his compromise tariff, and with Calhoun's assistance, the bill was hurried through Congress, ready for Jackson's signature on March 1. The law provided for an enlargement of the free list, and for a gradual reduction of all other duties until they should reach a general level of twenty per cent in 1842. On the same day the "Force Bill" was adopted by Congress.

The nullification leaders had been anxiously watching the progress of events at the capital. They had felt certain of receiving support from other Southern states, but to their surprise these without exception denounced the course of South Carolina as unwise and unconstitutional. The Ordinance of Nullification was to go into effect on February 1, 1833; but on January 21 a public meeting of State Rights leaders in Charleston voted, on their own responsibility, to suspend the Ordinance until the action of Congress should be learned. After the adjournment of Congress, the South Carolina convention reassembled on March 11,

[1] The provisions authorizing the employment of force were limited in duration to the end of the next session of Congress.

and formally rescinded the Ordinance of Nullification. As a last gesture of defiance, the convention adopted an ordinance nullifying the "Force Bill."

Each side derived encouragement from the outcome of the dispute, and it is not an easy matter to decide where the real victory rested. The Jackson administration had committed the federal government unqualifiedly to the principle of the supremacy of the Union, but, on the other hand, South Carolina by a show of resistance had secured a large measure of the practical relief she had demanded. There can be no doubt that the controversy deepened and strengthened the conviction that the interests of the slave states and free states were diametrically opposed.

The nullification episode had a profound effect on the later development of the state-rights theory. The Southern leaders saw that nullification was certain to be ineffective in practice, for in a test of force the general government would always be able to execute federal law in a nullifying state. Accordingly, talk of nullification gradually dropped into the background, and Calhoun and his followers during the next thirty years placed chief stress upon the right of an aggrieved state to secede from the Union. The episode also had the effect of estranging many Southern Democrats from Jackson's leadership. Unwilling to support the President, they had either to form an antiadministration *bloc* within the party or to cast their political fortunes frankly with the party of Clay and Webster. Those who chose the latter course played an important part in the formation of the Whig party in 1834.

The United States Bank Controversy

While the controversy over nullification was still unsettled, there occurred the mighty struggle of the United States Bank for recharter, an event which strained Jackson's leadership to the uttermost. From its foundation in 1816, the United States Bank had been unpopular in the newer parts of the country and with the working classes in the Eastern cities. This was due, in part, to a feeling of suspicion and distrust toward banks in general, an attitude very largely justified by the circumstances of the times.

Banks in those early years were everywhere incorporated by special acts of the legislatures. In place of the modern system, whereby any persons who wish to establish a bank must meet certain conditions plainly set forth in a law of general application, charters were frequently granted as rewards for party service or for similar reasons. Banks founded under such circumstances were apt to lack proper provision for their financial security. Add to this the dire need of the Western settlers for money to buy implements, build roads, and improve their properties, and one can understand why banks were inclined to loan freely, make excessive issues of paper notes, and employ other "wild-cat" methods of finance. Bank suspensions and failures were frequent. Such conditions inflicted great suffering upon the whole community, especially upon the farmers, wage-earners, and other poor people into whose pockets the worthless bank notes found their way.

The great bank at Philadelphia with its various branches fell a natural heir to this popular antagonism notwithstanding the strict conditions of its charter. It incurred further hostility on its own account during the Panic of 1819 when the Bank officials found it necessary to foreclose mortgages on large quantities of real estate, especially in the West, which were later sold at an advance. It also became a target of opposition of the state banks. Among other things, these institutions strenuously objected to the activities of the great federal Bank in attempting to keep their paper issues within more conservative limits by promptly returning their notes to them for redemption. Several states passed laws intended to hamper or destroy the branches of the United States Bank within their boundaries, but the federal Supreme Court intervened with decisions that upheld the constitutionality of the Bank and declared its immunity from state interference.[1]

Meantime the United States Bank had been handling the funds of the government, assisting the collection of taxes and the negotiation of public loans, and performing other valuable fiscal services. Under direction of its capable president, Nicholas Biddle, it became a prosperous and powerful institution. It intrenched itself firmly in the affections of the older sections of

[1] McCulloch *v.* Maryland (1819), Osborn *et al.* *v.* The Bank of the United States (1824).

the country, particularly among the business classes and men of capital. But the violent democratic surge which swept Jackson into office served to give new life to all the old objections to the Bank, and supplied a fresh argument against it. Democracy, being based upon the principle of equality, is always opposed to all forms of privilege, and to none more than a financial monopoly. Although the United States Bank bore the name of a government bank, it was, in reality, a private corporation in which the government was a minority stockholder and appointed but one fifth of the Board of Directors. As the one overshadowing monopoly in the country, against it was directed all the passionate hatred that a half-century later fell upon trusts and railways.

Indeed, this fear was not altogether without foundation. Whether or not the Bank had ever abused its power, it was in a position to do so by reason of the exclusive privileges it enjoyed from the government and its vast economic power. At the outset, the stock of the Bank had been distributed among more than thirty-one thousand holders; but by 1831 the number of stockholders had dwindled to a little more than four thousand, and the majority control had gravitated into the hands of Biddle and two members of the Board of Directors. More than four hundred of these stockholders lived in Europe, and of the remainder, the vast majority lived in the financial centers of the seaboard. In the eyes of the new democracy the existence of this great moneyed monopoly, with its closely centralized control, constituted a menace to free government.

Jackson entered office with the frontiersman's prejudice against banking corporations; and his antipathy was sharpened by the suspicion, probably unfounded, that the Bank had worked against his party in several states during the campaign of 1828. Without loss of time he announced in his first annual message that it was none too soon for Congress to consider the advisability of renewing the Bank charter at its expiration in 1836. For himself he questioned both its constitutionality and the desirability of its continued existence. In his next two annual messages he returned to the subject.

His attitude was not wholly destructive, for he proposed as a substitute for the existing institution a bank of limited powers that would be a branch of the United States government, and that would, among other duties, handle the public funds. His ideas were somewhat vague, but his proposal, as we shall see, was eventually worked into definite form by the Van Buren administration as the Independent Treasury System. In these official pronouncements Jackson expressed himself as yet with a degree of caution, for the leaders of his party, including Secretary McLane of the Treasury Department, were far from united in support of his views. Indeed, two committees of Congress, controlled by the Democrats, reported in 1830 in favor of both the constitutionality and expediency of the Bank.

The approach of the presidential election of 1832 brought matters to a crisis. Clay and Webster urged Biddle to apply for a recharter without further delay, for they believed that Jackson would be unwilling to hazard his chances of reëlection by a veto. If he were so foolhardy, they were convinced that his action would spell certain victory for the National Republicans in the campaign. Biddle readily fell in with the plan. Being a man with an eye for the main chance, he had long been prepared for the occasion. Through heavy loans to prominent newspaper editors, hitherto unfriendly to the Bank, he had secured their powerful help in creating a favorable public opinion.[1] He had placed many Congressmen under personal obligations to the Bank through the extension of loans, accommodating in this manner thirty-four members in 1829, fifty-two in 1830, and fifty-nine in 1831.[2] Furthermore, the United States Bank had a political tower of strength in Daniel Webster, who was one of its directors and salaried attorneys.

The application for recharter was made early in 1832, and on July 3, Congress passed the bill. On July 10 came the President's flaming message of veto. If Jackson showed in this message little knowledge of the principles of banking and finance, he at least made it unmistakably clear to the "farmers, mechanics, and laborers" that he was unalterably opposed to legislation that would "make the rich richer and the potent more powerful."

[1] Thus, the *New York Courier and Enquirer*, originally an opponent of the Bank, changed its attitude after it had borrowed $53,000 from Biddle. Other newspaper editors who were heavy borrowers were Duff Green of the *United States Telegraph*, Gales and Seaton of the *National Intelligencer*, and certain prominent editors of New York and Philadelphia.

[2] The total amount of loans to Congressmen was $192,161 in 1830, $322,199 in 1831, $478,069 in 1832.

Reasserting his earlier belief that the Bank was unconstitutional, he emphasized the great danger to free government from "such a concentration of power in the hands of a few men irresponsible to the people"; and he further pointed out that the profits of the Bank, derived from loans to Western farmers, went into the pockets of capitalists in the East and Great Britain.

The veto created a profound sensation. The *Washington Globe* heralded it as a "second Declaration of Independence," freeing the country from the grasp of a moneyed monopoly and frustrating the plot of "the aristocracy of England to raise a revenue in America." But to Biddle and his associates, the message was "a manifesto of anarchy." Whether Congress or the President had correctly gauged the will of the people remained to be decided in the impending presidential election.

The Presidential Campaign of 1832

The campaign of 1832 was opened by the Anti-Masons, a party new to the national political scene. This party had originated under strange circumstances. In 1826, William Morgan of Batavia, New York, a former member of the Masonic order, had written a pamphlet purporting to reveal its secrets. Shortly thereafter he was abducted by certain overzealous members, and after being carried as far as Niagara Falls, his later fate became shrouded in mystery. The belief spread like wild fire through the rural districts of New York, Pennsylvania, and New England that he had been murdered, and all the latent democratic prejudice against exclusive secret societies was galvanized into active hostility. Churches took up the matter, deprived Masonic clergymen of their pastorates, and expelled Masonic laymen from membership. Other secret organizations were involved only in less degree; thus the honorary scholarship society, Phi Beta Kappa, founded in 1776, felt obliged to abandon its secret character at this time.

The movement quickly found its way into local and state politics, and Anti-Masonic parties were formed in many states. So popular did the new issue seem that certain astute young political leaders believed they might use it as a rallying point for the forces opposed to Jackson. Under the direction of such men as William H. Seward and Thurlow Weed of New York and Thaddeus Stevens of Pennsylvania, the party was organized on a national basis. At a national convention held on September 26, 1831, candidates were nominated and a platform adopted. William Wirt, former Attorney-General, was named for the presidency notwithstanding his statement to the convention that he had joined the Masons early in life and would not favor any "blind and unjust proscription" of the order.

This effort to fuse the anti-Jackson elements proved a failure, largely because of the personal popularity of Henry Clay, whom the National Republicans proceeded to nominate by unanimous vote in a national convention at Baltimore on December 12, 1831. John Sergeant of Pennsylvania was named for the vice-presidency. The platform condemned Jackson's attitude on the great questions of the day. Jackson's renomination by the Democrats was, of course, a foregone conclusion, but in order to give a semblance of wide popular sanction to the vice-presidential choice, a national convention was held in Baltimore on May 21, 1832. Van Buren was triumphantly named for the second place, and Jackson's reëlection was recommended to the country.

In the campaign that followed, the Anti-Masons did not play an important part; the real contest occurred between Jackson and Clay. The issue that occupied the foreground was the Bank question. Charges and countercharges were made, and the Democrats accused the Bank of attempting to influence the voters by calling in loans and contracting the currency. Jackson's stand was eagerly indorsed by the Working Men's parties in different states.

But beneath the consideration of specific questions lay a fundamental division of opinion between the merchant, manufacturing, and financial classes of the country, on the one hand, and the laboring and agrarian elements on the other — between those who feared the new democratic upheaval and those who desired to give Jackson their *carte blanche* approval. The outcome was an enthusiastic indorsement of "Jacksonism." The President received 219 electoral votes, Clay 49, Wirt 7. To Jackson fell most of the electoral votes of the West, the Middle Atlantic states, and the South Atlantic states. The Calhoun party in South Carolina, unwilling either to vote for Jackson or to join the opposition, cast the eleven votes of the state for John Floyd of Virginia.

The campaign signalized the adoption of certain new democratic practices by political parties, which have survived to the present time. For the first time, party conventions, representative of the rank and file of the voters, were called into being.[1] This was a welcome advance over the old congressional caucus scheme of nominating, which had broken down in 1824, or the haphazard system of nominations by state legislatures and popular conventions, which had prevailed in 1828.

The adoption of platforms was likewise an innovation, essentially democratic in its purpose of giving the voters advance notice of the policies and plans of the party if elected. Nor is it to be overlooked that this election marked the first widespread use of cartoons for campaign purposes. By means of this shrewd and sometimes grotesque symbolism, political parties found it possible to instruct countless voters whose interest could have been excited in no other way.

The Transfer of Deposits

Jackson interpreted his reëlection as a mandate from the people to crush the Bank beyond hope of recovery. He moved as quickly as the circumstances permitted, for he feared that delay would give Nicholas Biddle a chance surreptitiously to create a condition of commercial depression through a sudden contraction of loans and thus reëstablish the Bank in popular favor. Jackson's weapon lay at hand in that provision of the Bank charter which authorized the removal of the public funds from the Bank at the discretion of the Secretary of the Treasury. Finding that Secretary McLane was unwilling to take this step, he appointed William J. Duane of Pennsylvania to the office, and when the latter refused to issue the order, he replaced him with a bitter anti-Bank Democrat, Roger B. Taney of Maryland.

Late in September, 1833, the order went forth that no more government funds should be deposited in the United States Bank, and that the ten million dollars already in its custody should be

[1] The Democratic convention chose to make its nominations contingent upon a two-thirds majority vote, a custom that is still followed.

gradually withdrawn in the ordinary course of meeting the expenses of the government. As a substitute depository a careful selection was made of the stronger state banks, and stringent restrictions were imposed upon them in order to preclude the possibility of financial irregularities. In general, the favored banks were required to perform any or all of the services hitherto rendered by the United States Bank in their vicinity. The administration hoped, by these measures, to insure a gradual contraction of loans on the part of the United States Bank, and to provide relief to borrowers through the gradual expansion of the facilities of the sound state banks. Twenty-nine deposit banks were designated by January 1, 1835, and the number rose to eighty-nine by November 1, 1836.

The National Republicans, aided by the Calhounites, did what they could to condemn and oppose the transfer of the government funds, and the deposit banks were contemptuously dubbed "pet banks." In spite of Jackson's precautionary measures, the winter, spring, and summer following the cessation of deposits brought severe business depression to the country, a condition which Jackson's friends attributed to the malice of "Nicholas I." When Taney in accordance with the law reported the removal of deposits to Congress, the Senate pronounced his reasons insufficient, denounced Jackson's part in the proceedings, and refused to confirm Taney as Secretary of the Treasury. The House, however, approved of the transaction; and as a result of Benton's dogged loyalty, the resolutions censuring Jackson were eventually expunged from the Senate journals on January 16, 1837.

Foreign Affairs under Jackson

Jackson's conduct of foreign affairs lacked much of the ceremonial and formalism of earlier administrations, but it was marked by vigor and crowned with success. One difficult problem was presented by the unsatisfactory trade relations existing with the British islands in the West Indies. Ever since the close of the Revolutionary War the United States had coveted the direct trade with the British West Indies, which had contributed so largely to the prosperity of the thirteen colonies. Repeated attempts had been made, from Washington's time down, to secure the prize, but these had ended in failure or else in partial and temporary concessions.

When Jackson entered office, the two countries were again at a deadlock; neither British nor American vessels could trade directly between the British West Indies and the United States. Jackson acted without hesitation. At his request, Congress in May, 1830, authorized the President to open the ports of the United States to British vessels as soon as England accorded us similar privileges in her colonial ports in America. Had this move failed, Jackson planned to recommend a nonintercourse law between the United States and Canada. Great Britain, however, willingly met the terms offered. Jackson's success was no doubt facilitated by growing doubts in British official circles as to the wisdom of the old monopolistic commercial attitude of Britain toward her colonies.

The settlement of long-standing claims of American citizens against France proved more difficult. These claims had risen from the injuries and losses inflicted upon American commerce under the Berlin and Milan decrees and other arbitrary orders of France during the Napoleonic wars, and ever since 1815 had been the subject of negotiation between the two countries. The accession of Louis Philippe to the throne by the July revolution of 1830 invited a reopening of the question, and in 1831 a treaty was concluded, whereby France agreed to pay the United States $5,000,000 in six annual installments in full satisfaction of the spoliation claims.

The treaty proved to be unpopular in France, however, and the French Chamber of Deputies persistently refused to vote the necessary funds. Finally, in great exasperation, Jackson in December, 1834, urged Congress to authorize reprisals on French property in the United States should payment be further deferred. Although Clay persuaded Congress to withhold the desired legislation, France was greatly irritated by the President's action. The French minister at Washington was recalled, and the American minister at Paris was given his passports.

In April, 1835, France, with a characteristic Gallic touch, authorized payment of the spoliation claims provided that a suitable apology should be offered for the President's words. Jackson responded by recommending the employment of commercial coercion against France, but in the course of his message to Congress, he expressly disclaimed any intention "to menace or insult the Government of France." On the basis of this avowal good relations were restored.

A foreign problem of a quite different kind was presented by the Texan war for independence in 1836. Beginning in the early twenties, American settlers had flocked over the border into Texas, allured by the generous land policy of Mexico. Soon they formed a majority of the sparse population of the region. Separated by a wide stretch of uncultivated area from central Mexico, these new-fledged Texans were at first little conscious of their political subordination to the Mexican government. Moreover, the intermittent revolutions which had afflicted central Mexico since its separation from Spain in 1821 left the people of Texas, for the most part, undisturbed. Efforts were made by President Adams in 1825 and 1827, and by President Jackson in 1829 and 1835, to purchase the province from Mexico; but the proposition was not entertained by that government.

Meantime, conditions in Texas had become increasingly irksome, and the minds of the frontiersmen, impatient of restraint or regulation, began to turn to thoughts of revolution. In 1824 Mexico forbade the further importation of slaves within her borders. Three years later Texas and Coahuila were united into a single province, so that the Mexican population of Coahuila outnumbered and therefore governed the Texans. In 1829 Mexico, imitating the example of other Spanish-American republics, abolished slavery throughout her dominion, but the storm of protest caused a withdrawal of the decree in the case of Texas. In 1830 further immigration from the United States was forbidden, additional military posts were established in Texas, and troops were dispatched to enforce Mexican law there.

Affairs reached a crisis shortly after the Centralist revolution of 1834 in Mexico. Under the leadership of Santa Anna the federal system of government, copied after that of the United States, was overthrown, and a centralized autocratic government substituted, in which Texas and the other provinces became mere administrative subdivisions. Underneath these specific causes of irritation lay, of course, profound differences in race, religion, customs, and political methods between American Texas and the Spanish-Indian people of Mexico.

The Texan uprising began in 1835 as a protest against Santa Anna's *coup d'état*. But when Santa Anna undertook the subjugation of Texas, rebellion turned into revolution. A Texan convention declared independence in March, 1836, and adopted a constitution on the American model. The new republic legalized the institution of slavery, and asserted that its territory extended on the south and west to the Rio Grande River, that is, beyond the limits of Texas as a Mexican province. Some light is thrown on the nature of the revolt by the fact that the Declaration of Independence was signed by three Mexicans and fifty-three Americans, and of the latter forty-eight hailed from the slave states.

Fierce hostilities ensued, marked by Mexican successes in the early weeks; but on April 21, 1836, Sam Houston, the Texan commander, inflicted a disastrous defeat on the Mexicans on the banks of the San Jacinto River, taking Santa Anna himself as prisoner. The Mexican leader bought his release by agreeing to the independence of Texas (an act not binding upon Mexico) and ordering his troops to retire beyond the Rio Grande. The actual independence of Texas was thus won. Although Mexico refused to recognize the new republic, she was unable to send another army against the Texans.

The official attitude of the United States toward the uprising had been one of neutrality, but ardent popular sympathy with Texas prevented a strict enforcement. Volunteers were openly recruited and ships-of-war fitted out within American jurisdiction. Without their help it is doubtful if Texas could have defeated Mexico. In July, 1836, the Texan government made overtures to the United States for annexation, and in September the people of Texas approved annexation by an almost unanimous vote. The proposal found quick response in the United States, and in view of the earlier attitude of the American government, might have been expected to carry the day in Congress.

But conditions had changed in both the United States and Texas. The growth of antislavery feeling in the North gave the proposal the appearance of a plot to increase the slave area of the United States. Furthermore, under the existing circumstances, annexation promised a war with Mexico. Former President John Quincy Adams, rounding out a distinguished career in the House of Representatives, declared against the acquisition of additional slave territory. Daniel Webster counseled delay until it was known whether Texas had a *de facto* government. Calhoun, on the contrary, advocated immediate recognition of independence and admission into the Union.

Torn by a multitude of counsels, Congress contented itself with authorizing the President to appoint a diplomatic agent whenever he believed that Texas independence should be recognized. This step Jackson took on March 3, 1837, the day before he left the presidency. In this whole affair the President had acted with unusual circumspection. His enemies ascribed it to his desire to preserve party harmony and facilitate the election of Van Buren in 1836.

SELECT BIBLIOGRAPHY

South Carolina Nullification. The best detailed accounts are D. F. Houston, *A Critical Study of Nullification in South Carolina* (in *Harvard Historical Studies*, III, Cambridge, 1896), and the more recent one by C. S. Boucher, entitled *The Nullification Controversy in South Carolina* (Chicago, 1916). For a different approach to the subject, see Edward Stanwood, *American Tariff Controversies in the Nineteenth Century* (2 v., Boston, 1903), I. The general relationship of state-rights doctrines to regional self-interest is discussed in A. M. Schlesinger, *New Viewpoints in American History* (New York, 1922), chapter x.

The United States Bank Controversy. The most thorough treatment, R. C. H. Catterall, *The Second Bank of the United States* (Chicago, 1903), emphasizes the fiscal elements of the controversy. The account in W. G. Sumner, *Andrew Jackson* (Boston, 1899), is suggestive and informing, but prejudiced. Horace White, *Money and Banking* (Boston, 1914), sheds much light on the general banking methods of the times.

The Presidential Campaign of 1832. S. R. Gammon, Jr., *The Presidential Campaign of 1832* (in *Johns Hopkins University Studies*, XL, no. I, Baltimore, 1922), discusses the election in detail, including the rise of the convention system. The relation of the Anti-Masonic party to the complex political situation is authoritatively set forth in Charles McCarthy, *The Anti-Masonic Party* (in American Historical Association, *Annual Report for 1902*, I, 365–574). See also Edward Stanwood, *A History of the Presidency* (2 v., Boston, 1898–1916), I.

Foreign Affairs under Jackson. This subject in its general bearings is lucidly discussed in J. S. Bassett, *The Life of Andrew Jackson* (2 v., Garden City, 1911), II; J. W. Foster, *A Century of American Diplomacy* (Boston,

1900); and C. R. Fish, *American Diplomacy* (New York, 1924). An authoritative work on the subject treated is F. L. Benns, *The American Struggle for the British West India Carrying Trade, 1815–1830* (in *Indiana University Studies*, X, Bloomington, 1923). Of the many works on Texas, the most useful for an understanding of American interest in the Texan Revolution are Justin H. Smith, *The Annexation of Texas* (New York, 1911), and G. L. Rives, *The United States and Mexico, 1821–1848* (2 v., New York, 1913), I.

CHAPTER IV

THE DEMOCRATS AND THE WHIGS, 1833–1842

The Rise of the Whigs, 1833–1837

The political factions opposed to Jackson had no hope of success so long as they remained divided and working at cross purposes. In consequence, the experiment was again tried early in his second administration of bringing all the dissatisfied elements together under a common party name. These groups were the National Republicans and the Anti-Masons, and they found ready allies in those Democrats, particularly in the South, who had been antagonized by the President's "nationalist heresies" or his imperious ways.

Since they agreed only in an implacable antagonism to "King Andrew I," in 1833 or 1834 they adopted the name of "Whigs," a term which at once said much and told little. Reminiscent of the Whig party in England, the new Whigs stood for Congressional supremacy and against "executive usurpation." But as to their constructive principles and policies they prudently kept silence, for their views were too diverse to command a united support of their own membership. Indeed, as will presently appear, they refrained from drawing up a platform until the eve of the election of 1844.

In Clay and Webster the Whigs possessed two of the ablest and most brilliant statesmen of the time. John Tyler of Virginia was the chief spokesman of the Southern wing of the party. Calhoun counted himself a Whig so long as Jackson remained in power, but he was never entirely reconciled to his new affiliations. In point of organization and discipline the Whigs were inferior to the Democrats. Loosely banded together, they relied chiefly on the magnetic personalities of their great leaders to solidify their membership. The dominant influence in the party, numerically and intellectually, was the National Republican strain; but this element, despite its distinguished leadership, could never hope for electoral success without the support of its Southern allies. In general, the people of substance and position were to be found within Whig ranks, for they were the classes whose vested interests were imperiled by the radical doctrines of Jacksonian Democracy.

In the public-land question the leaders of the new party found ammunition at hand with which to attack and embarrass the Jackson administration. Since 1820 the minimum price of land had been $1.25 per acre in tracts of eighty acres or more. The Act of 1820 accorded with the feeling of that early time that the price should not be so high as to discourage thrifty settlers but that, nevertheless, the public domain should be a source of profit for the federal government. Under the operation of this law, the revenue from land sales did not exceed two million dollars in any year prior to 1830, but thereafter there occurred a startling increase, due largely to the activity of speculators. In 1836, with land sales totaling nearly twenty-five millions, the government actually received more money from this source than from tariff duties.

The newer states chafed under this system. They wished to accelerate settlement and thereby promote the development of their material resources. If any revenue was to arise from the sale of the public domain, they believed it belonged of right to the states within whose bounds the lands lay. They had a doughty champion in Senator Benton, who as early as 1824 began the introduction of "graduation bills," designed to reduce the price of slow-selling lands, by progressive stages, to a merely nominal sum.[1] The business classes of the North Atlantic seaboard, however, had no intention of assisting a scheme which would help to depopulate their cities and further diminish their labor supply. This attitude was clearly revealed by Foot's resolution in 1829 (see page 28). On the other hand, the Westerners had allies in the Southern planters, who favored any plan that would cripple the growth of Northern manufacturing, and in the working

[1] The main features of Benton's plan were: a reduction of the price of unsold lands each year until within four years the price stood at twenty-five cents an acre; the donation to actual settlers of lands which were not sold after being offered at fifty cents an acre; and the cession of all lands, which were not bought after being offered for one year at twenty-five cents an acre, to the states in which they lay. The details of the plan subsequently underwent considerable modification.

class of the Northern cities, who saw in cheaper lands a chance of escape from wage-labor.

The question did not assume an acute form in Congress until 1832. Then Henry Clay, with a shrewd eye on the approaching presidential election, proposed a measure which he believed would harmonize the discordant interests of the Northeast and West and win the political support of both sections. His bill provided for the distribution of the land revenues among all the states (in proportion to their membership in the electoral college) for a period of five years, each state's share to be expended substantially as the state might decide. Clay's plan was acceptable to the Eastern manufacturers because the price of land remained unchanged, and to the West it offered a substantial inducement in the form of gifts to the state treasuries.

The bill, after passing the Senate in July, died in the House of Representatives; and Jackson, in his first message to Congress after the election (December, 1832), put himself squarely on record against the distribution scheme. Instead, he urged that "as soon as practicable" the public lands should cease to be a source of revenue and should be sold at nominal cost to settlers. Tracts remaining unsold should "in convenient time" be ceded to the states within whose borders they lay.

The various elements of the Whig party, including the Southern contingent, rallied to the support of Clay's distribution plan. Although the Calhounites had earlier favored a reduction in the price of western lands, they now experienced a change of heart, partly because they believed that the Compromise Tariff would check the growth of Northern manufactures, and partly because of their dawning conviction that cheap lands meant the settlement of the West by free settlers. On March 1, 1833, Clay's proposal, somewhat modified in detail, passed Congress, only to receive a pocket veto from Jackson, who declared distribution to be both unwise and unconstitutional.

At this juncture a new factor was introduced into the situation by the extinction of the national debt. The proceeds from tariff duties and land sales had been large in recent years, and the excess revenue was applied toward a reduction of the debt. In January, 1835, the last of the debt was discharged. At once a surplus of public funds began to pile up in the "pet banks," and

Congress had to consider the problem of disposing of the government's excess income. Stoppage at the source through a reduction of taxes was not feasible, since the tariff duties were fixed by the Compromise of 1833, and a strong sentiment in the seaboard states opposed lowering the price of public lands. Clay renewed his proposal of distributing the land revenues, and although his bill again passed the Senate by a party vote in May, 1836, it failed in the Democratic House.

Calhoun now assumed leadership in the fight, and advocated a plan of disposing of all surplus funds of the government irrespective of source. As adopted in June, 1836, the act provided that all money in the treasury on January 1, 1837, in excess of five million dollars, should be deposited with the states (in proportion to their representation in the electoral college) in four equal quarterly payments. Although Jackson's constitutional scruples were quieted by the fiction that the money was a loan rather than an outright gift, he signed the bill with palpable reluctance. The impelling reason for his approval was probably his desire to do nothing to embarrass Van Buren's chances in the approaching presidential election. The distribution of the surplus, amounting to $37,469,000 on January 1, 1837, was never completed, for, as will appear, the execution of the law was interrupted by the Panic of 1837, whose coming it hastened.

The plans of the Democratic organization for the election of 1836 had long been laid. Jackson's dominant will had consolidated his miscellaneous following of 1828 into a compact organization though at the cost of defections from the ranks. Jackson's mind was fixed upon Van Buren as his successor, and at a Democratic national convention held at Baltimore on May 20, 1835, he had his way. The Western membership was recognized by the choice of Colonel Richard M. Johnson of Kentucky, a well-known frontier fighter, for the vice-presidency. By authorization of the convention, a committee later issued a statement of Democratic principles pledging the candidates to a continuation of Jackson's policies.

The Whigs were too heterogeneous to unite upon a single man or upon a common platform; therefore all thought of a national convention was abandoned. Instead the plan was adopted of nominating several men for President, each of whom might be expected to win the votes of his own geographic section. In this way it was hoped that Van Buren would be prevented from receiving a majority in the electoral college, and, as in 1824, the election be thrown into the House of Representatives. Webster was put forward by the Massachusetts legislature; Senator Hugh L. White, a former Democrat of Tennessee, by the legislatures of Tennessee and Alabama; and William Henry Harrison, a popular military hero of the old Northwest, was nominated by a state convention of Pennsylvania.

The central figure throughout the canvass was not Van Buren but Jackson, and the old political battles were fought out anew before the people. The working-class element rallied to the Democratic ticket, attracted by Jackson's overthrow of the "Money Monster" and his action in establishing a ten-hour day in the Philadelphia navy yard in 1836. The outcome of the election was a surprise to the Whigs. Van Buren received 170 electoral votes, forty-six more than the total vote polled by all his opponents. Johnson, however, had only 147 votes against a combined opposition vote of the same number. For the first and only time in our history, the choice of a Vice-President devolved upon the Senate, which proceeded to elect Johnson by a vote of 33 to 16. As in 1832, South Carolina chose to bestow her eleven electoral votes on candidates of her own selection.

Van Buren and the Money Question

Martin Van Buren has not received his just dues at the hands of posterity, partly because his merits were obscured by the picturesque personality of his predecessor and, in part, because his administration coincided with a period of economic depression. By his contemporaries he was known as the "Little Magician," and his enemies asserted that his political code consisted chiefly of "noncommittalism" or the ability to straddle public issues. Yet his record as Chief Executive, though lacking in the attributes of creative statesmanship, was that of a man of strong convictions and stubborn purpose. The fact that he preferred to persuade rather than antagonize an opponent argued no absence of moral courage.

The Panic of 1837, which crashed upon the country shortly

after Van Buren entered office, was due, at bottom, to the orgy of speculation and overexpansion through which the nation had been passing. Astonished at the evidences of feverish enterprise in all parts of the country, a European visitor in this period was provoked to remark that whereas his own countrymen boasted of their past, the Americans bragged of their future. The phenomenal development of the Western country has already been alluded to. The increased purchase of public lands after 1830, however, was only in part the result of actual settlement; it was caused more largely by speculators who borrowed wildly and invested deeply in lands for the purpose of reselling at a profit. In the planting states much the same sort of thing was going on. A rise in the price of cotton in 1835 caused thousands of Southwestern planters to buy slaves and lands on credit, in the expectation of paying for them out of their profits. The fever of speculation also infected the older sections of the country, and sent real-estate values soaring in the cities.

In a similar fashion, public improvements were everywhere being carried out on an extensive scale. Between 1830 and 1834 the number of steamboats grew from 130 to 230. Canals were projected and begun in many parts of the country, especially in the old Northwest. State governments were involved in these enterprises as well as private persons and companies. The newly invented steam railway came in for special attention. Since 1826 "rail" roads or tramways, operated by horse power or stationary engines, had been in use for local commercial purposes in certain parts of the country, but in 1829 the importation of a steam locomotive from England revealed the vast possibilities of the railroad for general public use. Peter Cooper and other American inventors improved upon the English model, and state legislatures granted charters and appropriations to assist in developing the new mode of transportation. The railway mileage increased from 23 in 1830 to almost 1500 at the close of Jackson's administration.

In general, the construction of public works far outran the needs of the country, and tied up millions of borrowed capital in enterprises that would for many years be unproductive. Moreover, the carnival of speculation was based largely on bank credits and paper money of doubtful value. The number of state banks had increased from 329 in 1829 to 788 in 1837, and under the loose laws of the time, the specie basis of many of the banks was entirely inadequate. The destruction of the United States Bank removed a conservative influence, and the deposit banks loaned out public funds to borrowers with a liberal hand.

The artificial prosperity would have collapsed sooner or later, but the crisis was hastened by two measures adopted in the last months of Jackson's presidency. One of these was the Specie Circular. Since 1834 President Jackson had become increasingly alarmed at the amount of doubtful paper money which the government was receiving for lands and taxes. Benton had sought to get Congress to provide that "hard money" only would be accepted in payment for public lands, but besides winning for himself the sobriquet of "Old Bullion," he had been able to accomplish nothing. In April, 1835, Jackson, on his own authority, began to issue orders forbidding public officers to accept bank notes of the smaller denominations, hoping thereby to increase the circulation of specie and check the unbridled speculation. These measures proving insufficient, the administration on July 11, 1836, issued the famous Specie Circular, which directed all government agencies to receive only gold and silver in payment for public lands. Since "hard money" was scarce, especially in the West, an acute check at once was given to land speculation, discredit was cast upon all paper notes, and private creditors began to demand payment in coin.

The effects of the Specie Circular were sharpened by the withdrawal of federal funds from the "pet banks" for apportionment among the state governments, beginning on January 1, 1837. In order to accumulate sufficient money for this purpose, the deposit banks called in many of their loans, and money began to grow tight. They succeeded in paying two of the quarterly installments and half of the third, but then the payments ceased.[1] The situation was further complicated by the untimely failure of certain great business houses in Great Britain, which had invested heavily in American securities, and by poor crops in the West in 1835 and 1837.

The cotton merchants in the South were the first to break, followed closely after by Northern factories and warehouses.

[1] Eventually the federal government recovered all but $50,000 from the deposit banks.

On May 10, 1837, the banks of New York City suspended, and in all, 618 banks failed during this fatal year. Bankruptcies multiplied in every direction. The discredited bank notes depreciated in value, and prices shrank to a hard-money level. Twenty thousand wage-earners were thrown out of work, wages were cut, and the cities were crowded with the unemployed. For the organized labor movement, which had attained such considerable proportions, this was a death-blow. The local societies, city assemblies, national federation, and national trade unions were crushed out of existence, not to be revived for many years, when new conditions necessitated their reëstablishment. So overwhelming was the disaster to the country that industrial depression was felt throughout the remainder of Van Buren's administration, and indeed business conditions did not return to normal until 1842.

President Van Buren summoned a special session of Congress on September 4, 1837, to deal with the situation. His recommendations revealed his complete accord with the financial ideas of Jackson and Benton, and his full adherence to the doctrines so popular with the urban wage-earners.[1] To tide over the immediate stringency, Congress, at the President's suggestion, authorized the borrowing of money through the issuance of ten million dollars' worth of treasury notes. As a measure to safeguard the public finances for the future, he offered a plan known as the "Independent Treasury" or "Subtreasury." He proposed that the government should take charge of its own funds instead of depositing them in state banks or in a centralized national bank, and that the principle of the Specie Circular should be extended to all taxes and payments due to the government. An Independent Treasury, he argued, would not only keep the public funds safe from harm but would also prevent their use for the encouragement of private speculation.

[1] Since 1835 a struggle had been raging in New York within the Democratic party over fiscal policies. By this message Van Buren placed himself on the side of the Loco-Focos (so-called) and the workingmen. Aided by the President's favor, the Loco-Focos gained control of the New York Democracy; and in 1838 a law was passed, providing for ample specie reserves for state-bank notes, and permitting any group of qualified men to establish a bank under a general law. During the next decade Massachusetts, Maryland, South Carolina and other older states followed New York by instituting safe and conservative banking systems. The new system spread to the old Northwest, beginning with Illinois in 1851. These laws furnished a model for the National Bank legislation of 1863–1864.

The Whigs, led by Clay and Webster, hotly opposed this scheme. They accused the President of being impervious to popular suffering. They insisted that, if the United States Bank had been rechartered, the panic would never have occurred. With an eloquence born of renewed hope, they directed their efforts toward the establishment of a third United States Bank. Calhoun, however, now abandoned his erstwhile allies, and gave his unreserved support to the Independent Treasury and the Van Buren administration.

The Independent Treasury bill passed the Senate in 1837 and again in 1838, failing both times in the House of Representatives. Van Buren's persistence was finally rewarded, and on July 4, 1840, his plan was adopted by Congress. By its provisions the United States was directed to provide vaults and safes as depositories for government funds in certain specified cities, and the requirement was added that after June 30, 1843, all payments to or by the United States should be made in gold or silver. The Whigs, though overborne, were not convinced, and six years more of political controversy were necessary before the plan became firmly engrafted into the federal fiscal system.

The Overthrow of the Democrats

In dealing with the public issues of the day, Van Buren faithfully kept the pledge, made in his inaugural address, to tread in the path of his "illustrious predecessor." Indeed, some historians have gone so far as to speak of his administration as "a third term of Andrew Jackson." In the matter of internal improvements Jackson's policy was continued for another four-year period. Van Buren showed his interest in labor welfare by issuing an order in 1840 for the establishment of the ten-hour day on all government works.

As respects the public lands, Van Buren, like his predecessor, recommended a reduction of the price, with the eventual transfer of unsold lands to the states in which they lay. He also advocated the right of preëmption on the part of settlers (or "squatters," as they were called) who occupied public lands in advance of sale. As earlier, Benton championed the rights of the Western pioneers; but he had to meet the vigilant opposition of Clay, who continued to agitate for the distribution of the land revenue among the states. Three times the Democrats passed Benton's "graduation bill" for a progressive lowering of the price of government lands, but the bill was each time defeated in the House of Representatives. Although a general preëmption law could not be passed, two acts, each authorizing preëmption for a period of two years, were adopted in 1838 and 1840. The final victory of the preëmption principle was destined to come in 1841 at the hands of the Whigs who now opposed its adoption.

Van Buren's public acts awakened no enthusiasm among the masses. Lacking Jackson's compelling qualities of leadership, he was unable to invest his struggle for the Independent Treasury, or his efforts for a liberal land policy, with those elements of the dramatic which had attended the "Old Hero's" every move. But it may well be doubted whether even Jackson's popularity would have been proof against the opprobrium which fell to his successor because of the severe industrial depression from which the country was suffering.

The tactics of the Whigs in the campaign of 1840 were shrewdly designed to take advantage of the weaknesses of the President's position. Their national convention met at Harrisburg on December 4, 1839, the first in the history of the party. Henry Clay confidently expected the nomination, but this did not accord with the plans of the practical politicians, who feared that his long public record would antagonize some of the diverse elements necessary for victory. Democratic appreciation of the Whig dilemma was shown by the scornful suggestion of the *Hartford Times* that the nominee, when chosen, be called "the federal-whig-abolition-amalgamation-conservative-anti-masonic-striped pig-foreign missionary candidate." When the voting began, Clay was in the lead, but after repeated balloting, the prize went to William Henry Harrison of Ohio. General Harrison met the requirements of the situation perfectly. During the quarter of a century which had elapsed since the War of 1812, he had done nothing to excite active antipathy, and his fame as the hero of Tippecanoe and the Thames had become a popular tradition. As a concession to the Southern Whigs John Tyler was nominated as his running-mate. The convention adjourned without adopting a platform.

The Democrats at their Baltimore convention on May 4, 1840, unanimously renominated Martin Van Buren, though they were unable to unite upon a candidate for the vice-presidency. The platform indorsed the Independent Treasury, and declared against the exercise of "doubtful constitutional powers" by the federal government. Specific condemnation was visited upon the proposed United States Bank, the protective principle, and federal appropriations for internal improvements. A third party, organized by anti-slavery enthusiasts, took part in the campaign, but its proceedings were unimportant save as a harbinger of the future.

The Democrats were on the defensive throughout the campaign. With the country afflicted with hard times and low wages, the party in power was hard pressed to justify the policies of the Van Buren administration and of Jackson before him. The Whigs, at odds among themselves, either avoided a discussion of policies or suited their public utterances to the section in which they spoke. By the Democrats these tactics were viewed with contempt. In a heedless moment a prominent Eastern newspaper spoke of Harrison as a man content to remain on his backwoods farm if he might have a pension, a log cabin, and a barrel of hard cider. No remark could have been more imprudent at a time when the mass of the Western people lived in log cabins, and the Whigs used their opportunity to the utmost.

"The battle is now between the log cabins and the palaces, between hard cider and champagne," declared Henry Clay in campaign speeches. Daniel Webster apologized publicly because he had not been born in a log cabin, but eagerly claimed that honor for his elder brother and sisters. "If ever I am ashamed of it," he thundered, "may my name and the name of my posterity be blotted forever from the memory of mankind!" Horace Greeley, a young New York journalist whose newspaper career had been interrupted by the Panic of 1837, established a campaign sheet called *The Log Cabin*, which quickly attained a weekly circulation of eighty thousand copies.

The log cabin became the election symbol of the Whigs, and the campaign was turned by them into a joyous romp. Giant mass meetings and barbecues were held everywhere, torchlight processions paraded the streets, "Tippecanoe and Tyler too" became the popular slogan. The women were almost as active as the men. The enthusiasm easily lent itself to song, and such ditties as "Old Tippecanoe" and "Little Van is a used-up man" were on everyone's lips. In contrast with the "Honest Farmer of North Bend," Van Buren was pictured as a man who used gold spoons and dressed himself before costly French mirrors. "The campaign was an apotheosis of tomfoolery," declared Andrew D. White in after years.

The outcome was a sweeping victory for the Whigs, Van Buren receiving only 60 votes out of the 294 in the electoral college. The Whigs had made politics so entertaining that the popular vote was nearly twice as great as in the previous election. In reality, the victors had little cause for jubilation. Harrison had received only about six per cent more of the popular vote than Van Buren, and the Whigs faced the responsibility of office, divided among themselves as to a program of public policy.

The Quarrel between Tyler and the Whigs

Of Harrison's capacities for the presidency the country was never to learn, for he died within one month of his inauguration. Sixty-eight years of age when he took the oath of office, his strength was taxed beyond endurance by the demands of the hungry Whig office-seekers who forgot their former distaste for "spoils." Clay, preferring his regnant position in the Senate, declined Harrison's offer of the post of Secretary of State, and the honor went to Daniel Webster. Four of Clay's intimate friends, however, were appointed to cabinet positions.[1]

Harrison's death brought into the presidency John Tyler, a strict-constructionist, antiprotectionist, anti-Bank Democrat, who had left his party because of Jackson's dictatorial course, and whose views were at variance with the dominant Whig leadership. Apprehending disagreement between Tyler and himself, Clay determined to seize the command and impose his views upon the new President. On June 7, 1841, he offered in the Senate a series of resolutions which outlined the Whig program of legislation. These resolutions may be regarded as a belated

[1] Thomas Ewing of Ohio, Secretary of the Treasury; G. E. Badger of North Carolina, Secretary of the Navy; John Bell of Tennessee, Secretary of War; and J. J. Crittenden of Kentucky, Attorney-General.

announcement of the platform which the national convention had feared to adopt in advance of the election. Clay's main proposals were: the repeal of the Independent Treasury Law, the distribution of the proceeds of public-land sales, revision of the tariff, and the incorporation of a bank. Since Tyler had not been pledged to these policies as a candidate, he cannot fairly be criticized for acting upon his own judgment concerning them.

The Independent Treasury Act was quickly repealed with the President's assent on August 13, 1841. Clay's pet measure for distributing the land revenues encountered greater difficulty. To many persons it seemed unwise to give away a portion of the national income when the government was borrowing money for its current expenses. Furthermore, the pioneer West, now as earlier, preferred to have the price of lands reduced; and Tyler was known to oppose distribution for fear that the resulting loss of revenue would be used as an excuse for raising the tariff.

To win enough votes for passage, the distribution bill, as adopted on September 4, 1841, contained important concessions to the opposition. The right of preëmption, so dear to the hearts of Westerners, was made permanent.[1] It was further enacted that the public-land funds should be distributed among the states provided that the tariff should not be increased beyond the twenty-per-cent level fixed by the Compromise of 1833. Clay agreed to the proviso because he believed that, if once the principle of distribution was accepted by Congress, he might later induce that body to repeal the restricting clause.

Clay's optimism failed to make due allowance for Tyler's deep-seated convictions. In 1842 Congress twice passed measures for raising the tariff and retaining the distribution feature, but both bills were vetoed. Forced to decide between a high tariff and distribution, the Whigs chose the former. On August 30, 1842, Congress enacted a tariff law which, by its increased rates, rendered inoperative the distribution provided for in the Act of 1841. The tariff duties were restored to the general level of those of 1832. The new law was generally satisfactory to the protectionists, and could be justified in the eyes of others because of deficiencies in the existing revenues.

[1] Squatters were granted the priority right to purchase 160 acres at the minimum rate of $1.25 per acre when the lands were offered for sale by the government.

The open break between Tyler and the Clay Whigs was precipitated by the struggle to create a new centralized bank. No measure was more important in the eyes of Clay's followers, but it was scarcely to be expected that they could fashion a bank that would meet the approval of a man of Tyler's constitutional views. When he vetoed a bill in August, 1841, for creating a "Fiscal Bank," they tried again in September with a bill providing for a "Fiscal Corporation." This measure, though framed in an effort to meet the President's supposed objections, proved no more acceptable to him. His second veto brought down upon his head a tempest of wrath and charges of party treachery. In a formal manifesto the Whig members of Congress disavowed all further political connection with him. The members of the cabinet resigned, except Webster, who lingered on until May 8, 1843, chiefly because he wished to complete certain delicate negotiations with Great Britain (see page 68).

The President, repudiated by the party which had elected him, reorganized his cabinet by the appointment of five former Democrats, who had left their party for the same reasons as himself. The stormy contests of Tyler's administration killed the bank project beyond possibility of resurrection, and robbed the distribution question of its vitality as a Whig issue. In the absence of the Independent Treasury, state banks were once more employed as depositories of the public funds.

The United States and Canada, 1837–1842

In international affairs the anomalous position of the Texan Republic, refused annexation by the United States and denied recognition by Mexico, continued to excite attention in the United States, but the most critical relations in these years were with our neighbor to the north, Canada. One set of difficulties was a by-product of the Canadian rebellion of 1837. In 1791 the greater part of Canada had been divided into two provinces, each with its own government: Lower Canada, controlled by descendants of the original French settlers along the St. Lawrence, and Upper Canada, north of the Great Lakes, populated largely by Loyalists who had fled the United States during the Revolutionary War. In the former province racial antipathy and religious jealousy were productive of much ill feeling; in the latter the pioneer farmers became increasingly resentful at the exactions and selfish sway of the large landed interest and the Anglican clergy.

In 1837 the smoldering discontent flared forth into an armed attempt for independence. The uprising had slight popular support and was easily crushed by Great Britain, but while it lasted, it aroused much sympathy in the United States. Furthermore, it proved to be a turning point in the evolution of British colonial policy, for, on the basis of an investigation made by Lord Durham, Upper and Lower Canada were joined under one government in 1840 with large powers of self-government. Modern Canada thus owes its beginning to an unsuccessful revolt.

The Van Buren administration did its best to prevent the use of American soil as a base of insurrectionary operations. Nevertheless, the United States became involved in December, 1837, when the *Caroline*, an American steamer in the rebel service, was seized by Canadian militia while on the American side of the Niagara River. One United States citizen was killed, and the vessel was sent drifting and afire over the Falls. The excitement caused among our border population was presently intensified by the arrest of Alexander McLeod, a Canadian, who boasted in a New York saloon of having killed the American. The British government demanded his release on the plea that, if guilty, he had acted under orders, but the United States replied that the federal government lacked authority to interfere with the proceedings of a state court. The situation promised to lead to dire consequences, but fortunately the New York court acquitted McLeod in October, 1841.[1] Webster subsequently acknowledged to the British authorities that such a violation of our sovereignty might be permissible if necessary for self-defense.

In April, 1842, Lord Ashburton arrived in the United States as special minister to clear up all matters at issue between the two countries. The chief of these was the long-vexed question of the northeastern boundary of the United States, which had been inadequately defined in the Treaty of 1783. After earlier attempts to reach an agreement had failed, the matter had been

[1] Webster, in order to prevent the same difficulty from rising in the future, secured an Act of Congress providing that a subject of a foreign power on trial in a state court might be brought into a United States court on a writ of *habeas corpus*.

referred in 1827 to the King of the Netherlands for adjudication. The United States, however, had been unwilling to accept the settlement proposed. In 1838–1839, armed collisions, dignified as "the Aroostook War," occurred on the Maine border in a portion of the disputed region, and for the time being, the northern frontier bristled with warlike preparations.

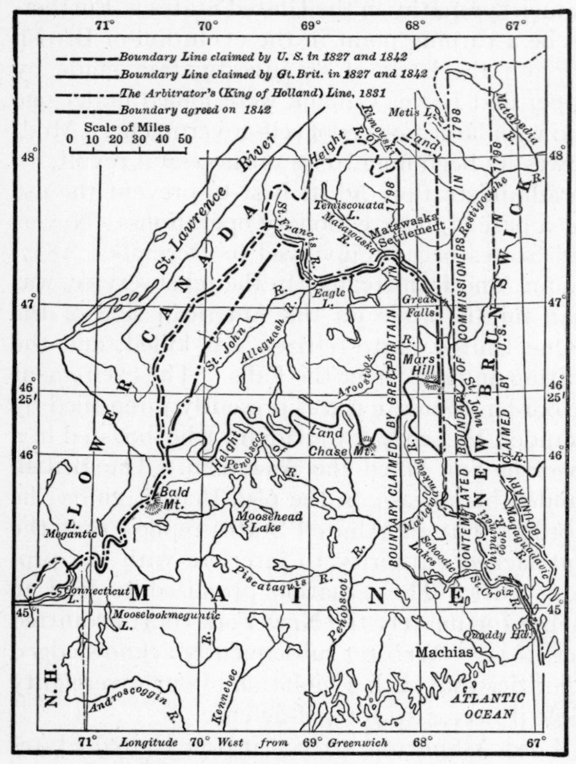

THE MAINE BOUNDARY CONTROVERSY

The adjustment of the boundary question proved to be a complicated matter since Maine and Massachusetts insisted on being represented along with the federal government in the negotiations.[1] But all difficulties were eventually surmounted. The treaty, signed on August 9, 1842, established a compromise line somewhat less favorable than the one proposed by the King of the Netherlands. To offset this disadvantage, the people of Maine received special trading privileges in the adjoining province of New Brunswick, and the United States agreed to make special payments to Maine and Massachusetts. Thus, for the first time, the northeastern boundary was defined in intelligible terms, and

[1] When Maine separated from Massachusetts, the latter retained part ownership of Maine's public lands, a considerable portion of which lay in the disputed region.

no disputes of importance have since arisen concerning it. Two other provisions of the treaty arranged for joint action of the two countries in suppressing the slave trade in African waters, and for the extradition of criminals.

BIBLIOGRAPHY

The Rise of the Whigs. A helpful discussion of the subject in its general bearings appears in John Fiske, *Essays Historical and Literary* (2 v., New York, 1902), I. The tangled relations of the Southern Whigs with the national organization are straightened out in A. C. Cole, *The Whig Party in the South* (Washington, 1913). The operations of the party in two Northern states receive special study in D. R. Fox, *The Decline of Aristocracy in the Politics of New York* (in *Columbia University Studies*, LXXXVI, New York, 1919), and H. R. Mueller, *The Whig Party in Pennsylvania* (in *Columbia University Studies*, CI, no. 2, New York, 1922).

For a connected account of the development of public-land policy, see Shosuke Sato, *History of the Land Question in the United States* (in *Johns Hopkins University Studies*, IV, Baltimore, 1886). The intricate politics of the land question is given penetrating analysis in R. G. Wellington, *The Political and Sectional Influence of the Public Lands, 1828–1842* (Cambridge, 1914). F. L. Paxson, *History of the American Frontier, 1763–1893* (Boston, 1924), should also be consulted.

Van Buren and the Money Question. Van Buren's presidential policies are sympathetically expounded in E. M. Shepard, *Martin Van Buren* (Boston, 1900). E. R. Johnson and T. W. Van Metre, *Principles of Railroad Transportation* (New York, 1921), and Eliot Jones, *Principles of Railway Transportation* (New York, 1924), contain useful information on early railway development.

For an understanding of fiscal problems, D. R. Dewey, *Financial History of the United States* (New York, 1922), D. R. Dewey, *State Banking before the Civil War* (Washington, 1910), W. A. Scott, *The Repudiation of State Debts* (New York, 1893), E. G. Bourne, *The History of the Surplus Revenue of 1837* (New York, 1885), and David Kinley, *The Independent Treasury of the United States and its Relations to the Banks of the Country* (Washington, 1910), are of special value.

The Overthrow of the Democrats. The picturesque features of the campaign of 1840 have made it a favorite subject for the standard historians and the biographers of the period. As in the case of all other campaigns to 1916, a convenient summary appears in Edward Stanwood, *A History of the Presidency* (2 v., Boston, 1898–1916), I. A special work written from the Whig point of view, with source extracts, is A. B. Norton, *The Great Revolution of 1840* (Mt. Vernon, Ohio, 1888).

The Quarrel between Tyler and the Whigs. John Fiske discusses the Whig schism in his *Essays Historical and Literary* (already cited), I. L. G.

Tyler, *The Letters and Times of the Tylers* (3 v., Richmond, 1884–1896), gives a strong presentation of the Tyler case.

The United States and Canada, 1837–1842. The evolution of Canadian self-government forms the theme of A. W. Tilby, *British North America, 1763–1867* (London, 1911), and J. L. Morison, *British Supremacy and Canadian Self-government, 1839–1854* (Glasgow, 1919). O. E. Tiffany, *Relations of the United States to the Canadian Rebellion of 1837–1838* (Ann Arbor, 1905), is the most satisfactory treatment of this subject. For a detailed study of the boundary dispute, J. F. Sprague, *The Northeastern Boundary Controversy and the Aroostook War* (Dover, Maine, 1910), and H. S. Burrage, *Maine in the Northeastern Boundary Controversy* (Portland, 1919), should be consulted.

CHAPTER V

DEMOCRACY AND SOCIAL REFORM

The Struggle for Free Public Schools

The democratic upheaval in the realm of politics, exemplified by Andrew Jackson, was merely one phase of the demand of the common people for larger rights and opportunities. The epoch of the thirties and forties was characterized by an invigorating faith in the perfectibility of mankind, and there resulted a real emancipation of the intellectual and spiritual life of the masses. While the reform spirit in America had its own sources of support, it was thoroughly in harmony with a world current of development. Great Britain was undergoing a similar ferment of social improvement and uplift. The champions of British reform, such as John Bright, John Howard, Lord Ashley, Sir Robert Peel, Robert Owen, and Lord Brougham, received constant inspiration from the parallel movements in the United States, and in turn afforded great encouragement to American reformers.

The American struggle for democracy in education merits special consideration, for it far outstripped similar efforts abroad. Furthermore, with the exception of the antislavery contest and the labor struggle, no question in American history has aroused such bitter controversy, and none has been more important to the welfare of the American people. In the earlier years of the nineteenth century, the prevailing idea was that only a minority of the population needed to be educated, and that this was a function of the church or of private enterprise rather than of the government. It is true that the principle of free public education had been recognized since colonial times in most parts of New England, but the practice fell sadly short of the theory. Where free schools were maintained elsewhere, as in New York and Pennsylvania, they were regarded as charitable institutions for pauper children, and the instruction offered was extremely rudimentary. A person who had mastered the "three R's" was an educated man at that time, while the absence of this knowledge was by no means a matter of reproach.

But the spread of manhood suffrage and the growing importance of the common man in American life led to a new conception of education. Clear-sighted statesmen perceived the danger of universal suffrage based on universal ignorance. De Witt Clinton in New York, Thaddeus Stevens in Pennsylvania, and Abraham Lincoln in Illinois were among those to raise their voices for an educated electorate as a safeguard of democratic government. Educational leaders like Horace Mann in Massachusetts and Henry Barnard in Connecticut and Rhode Island gave a wise direction and practical application to the new trend in education. As we have seen, the efforts of these reformers were supported by a vigorous and incessant agitation carried on by organized labor in the cities of the northern seaboard. The labor leaders demanded free, tax-supported schools open to the children of all classes without taint of charity. "Our government is republican; our education should be equally so," declared the Workingmen's Committee of Philadelphia in 1830 after five months spent in investigating educational conditions in Pennsylvania.

The great battle for free public education was fought out in the second quarter of the nineteenth century. The friends of the new system were at first regarded as visionaries or dangerous fanatics, and the opponents of free schools were considered by the former as unconscionable conservatives and the foes of progress. A Rhode Island farmer threatened to shoot Barnard if he ever caught him on his land advocating "such heresy as the partial confiscation of one man's property to educate another man's child." In state after state the agitation was conducted. Hard legislative fights were waged, and bitter contests took place with religious and private-school interests which held that their vested rights were being disturbed. Fortunately, the gradual development of national wealth in the shape of taxable property made possible a governmental support hitherto not practicable.

At first, various substitutes for government ownership and operation were tried. For example, denominational and pauper schools were subsidized out of public funds, private schools were exempted from taxation, grants of land were made for their endowment. But these makeshifts failed to meet the imperious needs of the times. Gradually, in one state after another, free tax-supported education was provided by legislative enactment. The public school system was common throughout the North and the Northwest by the forties, and by 1850 the battle may be said to have been won so far as these sections were concerned. Not only did America lead the world in this respect, but it should be added that today few countries have facilities of free education comparable to those of the United States.

The demand for tax-supported schools embraced not only elementary instruction but the high school as well. At the same time the school curriculum was greatly enriched. A new emphasis was placed on the study of civics, and the states passed laws prescribing the subject of history for the first time. The South, with its plantation economy, caste system, and negro slavery, was slower to respond to these new influences. While some progress was made, the real educational awakening did not occur there until after the Civil War.

Higher education also received a tremendous impulse in this period. The great pioneers in this field were the religious denominations, though they were often aided by land grants and subsidies from the states. Between 1820 and 1850, eighty-seven private colleges were founded in all parts of the country, and in the next decade the number was swollen by ninety-one more. It is clear that the public school system had to be firmly established before the people could envisage higher education as a proper function of the government. Nevertheless, beginning with the University of Virginia in 1819, fifteen state universities were founded by 1850, mostly in the West and the new South. They were as yet inadequately supported by the states, and the great epoch of state-university expansion did not come until after the Civil War.

The Beginning of the Woman's Rights Movement

The democratic idealism of the second quarter of the nineteenth century overleaped sex barriers. While it freed white men from most of their ancient fetters, it also awakened women to a realization of their onerous position in society. As in early colonial times, the rights of women before the law were circumscribed by the principles of the English common law. The unmarried woman, in most respects, enjoyed the same legal rights as a man; but custom required her to marry early, and with marriage she virtually lost her separate identity in the eyes of the law. She forfeited title to all her personal property, even if it had been acquired before matrimony, and she was deprived of all personal control over her real property for the duration of the marriage. A husband had the right to control his wife's conduct and punish her in the same degree as he did his children, and to appropriate to his own uses any wages that she earned outside the home.

The father was the sole guardian of the children during his lifetime, and could dispose of them by will at his death. Conversely, the husband was held responsible for many of the crimes and torts committed by his wife, and was entitled to collect damages for injuries inflicted upon her. Feminine education was disregarded, or else, in the well-to-do classes, confined to needlework, dancing, and the cultivation of manners and morals. Susan B. Anthony's teachers refused to instruct her in long division, and were at a loss to understand why a girl should want to learn it. Of course, women were not permitted to vote.

The awakening of women began with the visit of Frances Wright, a Scotchwoman of advanced views, to this country in 1827. Her appearance before audiences to deliver lectures on slavery, theology, and woman's rights shocked the public, unaccustomed to seeing a woman in such a rôle; but her example soon aroused to action such great figures in the American feminist movement as Sarah and Angelina Grimké from South Carolina, Lucretia Mott, a Quakeress of Philadelphia, and Mrs. Elizabeth Cady Stanton of New York. Keenly alive to the humanitarian trend of the times, these women devoted their energies not only to feminism but also to antislavery, labor welfare, and temperance reform. They had to brave the fierce contempt of most of their own sex as well as that of the men, and they stood in constant peril of physical violence at the hands of mobs because of their bold and "unwomanly" conduct.

In 1840 several feminine delegates from the United States were denied admission to a World's Antislavery Convention in London because of their sex. This indignity prompted the American women to resolve to launch a militant and organized crusade for equal rights. After a few years' delay, a woman's rights convention was held at Seneca Falls, New York, on July 19, 1848, the first in the history of the world. The delegates drew up an impressive declaration of sentiments patterned closely upon the Declaration of Independence. They asserted "that all men and women are created equal," and demanded equality with the male sex before the law, in educational and economic opportunities, and in voting. Though greeted by the ridicule and condemnation of press and pulpit, woman's rights conventions came to be almost yearly occurrences until the outbreak of the Civil War.

The feminist leaders were not altogether without friends among the men. Prominent at their meetings were the great antislavery agitators, William Lloyd Garrison and Wendell Phillips. Ralph Waldo Emerson, John Greenleaf Whittier, and Horace Greeley wrote and lectured in their behalf. Young Abraham Lincoln, beginning a legislative career in Illinois, announced his approval of the principle of sharing the government with those who bore its burdens, "by no means excluding the women."

Although the period was one of agitation rather than of accomplishment, nevertheless definite improvement in the position of women was achieved. In 1839 Mississippi granted to married women the control of their own property, and similar laws were enacted in the next decade by Texas, Indiana, Pennsylvania, New York, California, and Wisconsin. In 1821 Emma Willard opened a seminary for girls at Troy, New York, and in 1837 the first women's seminary of college rank, Mt. Holyoke, was opened by Mary Lyon in Massachusetts. These marked the beginnings of higher education for women. By 1860 the number of such institutions increased to sixty-one

Coeducation was an even more venturesome undertaking, but Oberlin College in 1833 and Antioch College in 1853, both in Ohio, led the way. Not till the University of Iowa acted in 1858 were women admitted to any state university. Notwithstanding these promising beginnings, women were still far from the goal of sex equality. A long and discouraging struggle loomed ahead before success was to crown their efforts.

Humanitarian Crusades

The democratic humanitarianism of the times also evoked a new sense of public responsibility for the weak and unfortunate members of society. In 1826 began the first organized movement against strong drink. In the absence of organized sports and the many facilities for amusement and recreation common today, the use of intoxicants in the United States was well-nigh universal. Liquor was even served at funerals, and was sold openly from booths at the chief colleges on public days. The movement started in Boston with the formation of societies pledged to total abstinence. Within five years more than one thousand of these bands were formed in all parts of the country. After 1840 the agitation fell under the direction of the "Washington Societies," which soon recruited a membership of half a million.

The policy of self-imposed abstinence, however, proved disappointing in its results, and under the leadership of Neal Dow of Maine, the reformers began to demand the passage of state prohibitory legislation. As a consequence Maine in 1846 passed the first prohibition law in American history. By the end of 1856, thirteen states in the North and West had taken definite action for the abolition of the sale of alcoholic stimulants. But in most of these states the laws were later repealed or modified,[1] and the prohibition movement did not again become a vital issue until a generation later (see pages 318–321).

This period saw substantial progress toward the abolition of imprisonment for debt, a practice inherited from colonial times. It was estimated in 1829 that about seventy-five thousand persons were annually imprisoned for debt in the United States, more than half of them for sums less than twenty dollars. The burden of such laws fell chiefly upon the wage-earners and the unemployed, and the Working Men's parties joined with the philanthropists in agitating for an abandonment of the practice. As new states were admitted from the West, the constitutions usually provided that no citizen should be imprisoned for debt unless he refused to give up his estate. In the older states the laws were gradually modified so as to make it increasingly difficult for a

[1] New Hampshire and Vermont, however, remained "dry" until 1904; and Maine, save from 1856 to 1858, retained prohibition until the Eighteenth Amendment (1919).

creditor to incarcerate a debtor, and impossible where only small amounts were involved.

Much attention was given to prison reform. For the first time prisons began to be regarded as instruments of reformation as well as of punishment. The New York State Prison at Auburn and the Eastern Pennsylvania Penitentiary at Philadelphia were pioneers in this movement. However defective their discipline may appear today, their systems attracted the admiration and study of de Tocqueville, Charles Dickens, and many other European humanitarians.

Great improvement also occurred in the care of the insane. Instead of treating these unfortunates as criminals or leaving their custody to private persons, state legislatures began to recognize the obligation of the community to provide proper care and surroundings for them. Dorothea L. Dix of Massachusetts, who was also active in prison reform, was one of the foremost leaders in this field. By 1847 she had visited eighteen state penitentiaries and hundreds of jails and almshouses. Her labors resulted in the establishment of insane asylums in twenty states and in the founding of many additional jails and almshouses conducted on a reformed plan.

The question of the statutory limitation of the factory workday to ten hours was much discussed. Organized labor had forced the shorter day upon employers in the leading mechanical branches in the thirties, and President Van Buren's order of 1840 establishing the ten-hour day on all government works gave further sanction to the reform. The agitation for legislative action by the states produced little result until 1847 when New Hampshire enacted the first ten-hour law for factory labor. In the next five years similar measures were adopted in Pennsylvania, Maine, Rhode Island, Ohio, and California.

The idealism underlying these humanitarian efforts was most clearly mirrored in the numerous communistic experiments that were carried out in various parts of the country between 1825 and 1850. These enterprises received their main inspiration from the writings and teachings of the leaders of the rising Socialist movement in Europe, and the abundance of cheap land invited a degree of social experimentation impossible in the crowded districts of the Old World. In 1825 Robert Owen, a Scotch manufacturer and reformer, set the example by establishing at New Harmony, Indiana, a community where labor and property were to be in common. The plan was adopted in other states.

After 1840 the number of such communities rapidly multiplied under the influence of Albert Brisbane's book, *The Social Destiny of Man* (1840), and Horace Greeley's editorials in the influential *New York Tribune*, both men being followers of the French Socialist, Charles Fourier. Over forty communistic projects were attempted from 1840 to 1850, all based upon an illimitable faith in humanity, and, like the Owenite communities, all unsuccessful in their effort to transform society overnight. Of these, the best known was Brook Farm, near Boston, which counted among its members and friends Emerson, Thoreau, Hawthorne, and Margaret Fuller. It continued from 1841 to 1846; subsequently Hawthorne gently satirized it in *The Blithedale Romance*.

Another significant outcropping of the high aspirations of the period showed itself in the launching of the first organized nonsectarian movement for the prevention of war. In 1815 peace societies had been formed in New York, Ohio, and Massachusetts, the first of the kind in the world. The Anglo-American Convention of 1818 for establishing an unfortified boundary between Canada and the United States gave a great impetus to the movement, which spread to other states. In 1828 the American Peace Society was founded in New York by William Ladd through a merger of nearly fifty local organizations. Its constructive program called for the codification of international law by a congress of nations, meeting periodically, and for the establishment of a permanent world court with power to make decisions, though not to enforce them, in disputes arising between nations.

Meantime the peace movement had taken root abroad, particularly in England. In 1843 a universal-peace congress was held in London, attended by thirty-seven American delegates. Elihu Burritt, one of the foremost leaders of the American movement, went to Europe four years later, and as a result of his labors, the international congress, held at Brussels in 1848, passed resolutions indorsing the American peace plan. Thereafter congresses were held almost yearly, and the hopes of the peace advocates beat high. But the movement was badly disrupted by the outbreak of the Crimean War (1854–1856) and of the American Civil War, and organized agitation for world conciliation did not become important again until the first decade of the twentieth century.

The Improving Standard of Life

The welfare of the masses and their comfort of living were greatly improved by a number of important inventions between 1825 and 1850. Kerosene lamps were devised, the friction match superseded the use of flint, improved cookstoves were put on the market. The shortage of wage-labor in the farming districts proved an incentive to the invention of labor-saving implements. After 1825 the threshing machine began to supplant the flail and roller, and shortly thereafter the Fairbanks platform scale, the mower, and the reaper were invented.

In 1825 the first successful attempt was made to generate steam with anthracite coal, and in 1837 the first furnace for smelting iron with anthracite was built. The English *Great Western*, a wooden-hulled side-wheeler with coal to heat its boilers, inaugurated regular steam navigation across the Atlantic in 1838, although the bulk of ocean freight continued to be carried in American sailing vessels.

Outside of the plantation states, the material conditions of American life were singularly even, and generous in promise. "Go-ahead-ativeness" characterized the typical American, causing Dickens to remark, "whenever an Englishman would cry 'All right!' an American cries 'Go ahead!' which is somewhat expressive of the national character of the two countries." An easy livelihood might be gained by all who were industrious, and few great private fortunes existed. Business and industry continued to operate on a small scale. For financial support the economic development of the country relied chiefly upon foreign investors, especially British capitalists.

The difficulty of maintaining a united nationality in the face of rapid geographical expansion was somewhat eased by the mechanical ingenuity of the people. Railway mileage steadily progressed from the first steam railroad of 1829. By 1850 one could travel over the iron highways from Maine to North Carolina, from the Atlantic Seaboard to Buffalo on Lake Erie, and from the western end of Lake Erie to Chicago or Cincinnati. The electric telegraph, invented in 1835 by S. F. B. Morse, was first practically applied in 1844, and from the outset possessed vast social and political significance. In 1847 the rotary printing press, devised by Richard M. Hoe, was first used, and by revolutionizing the processes of newspaper publishing, made possible the important position of the newspaper in American life.

Religious Readjustments

The new spirit in American life was reflected in the spiritual strivings and ecclesiastical revolts of the age. The stern Calvinistic theology, which had so long held sway in New England, felt the first impact of the democratic tide. Under the leadership of W. E. Channing, Unitarianism was organized about 1825 by dissenting members of the Congregational Church, on a creed opposing the somber doctrines of total depravity and predestination and affirming the infinite possibilities of man's development. The new system exerted an influence altogether out of proportion to its number of adherents, and attained its loftiest expression in the philosophic movement known as "Transcendentalism," of which Emerson was the foremost exponent. The spread of Unitarianism throughout New England was halted only by the work of men like Horace Bushnell, who sought to reconcile the Calvinistic theology of the old Congregational system with the new precepts of democracy.

Other sects were experiencing similar difficulties. The Quakers were rent in twain by the teaching of Elias Hicks. The Campbells, father and son, led a departure from the established Presbyterian order. Universalism began a rapid expansion at this time, and in the West there occurred a swift growth of the Methodists, Baptists, and Presbyterians and other denominations which were able to satisfy the spiritual cravings of a people impatient of theological hair-splitting. The itinerant preachers penetrated into the wilderness, bringing messages of hope and faith to the isolated inhabitants. The greatest of them, Bishop Francis Asbury of the Methodist Church, who died in 1816, traveled nearly three hundred thousand miles in the course of his labors, preached more than sixteen thousand sermons, and ordained some four thousand ministers. In the more settled western communities, the pent-up religious enthusiasm of the frontiersmen found expression in tumultuous revivals and campmeetings.

Of the many new sects that rose in this period the most extraordinary, in the light of its subsequent history, was the Mormon Church. It was organized at Fayette, New York, in 1830 by Joseph Smith, who asserted he had found, inscribed on golden plates, a marvelous tale of a Biblical tribe which had migrated to the New World from the Tower of Babel, had been the ancestors of the American Indians, and had possessed as their great hero the prophet Mormon. The new sect, though Christian in its tenets, possessed too many novelties to be acceptable even to a people accustomed to innovation in religion. Although steadily increasing in wealth and numbers, the Mormons were driven from state to state until finally, in 1847, they were led by Brigham Young on a courageous overland journey to the "promised land" in the valley of Salt Lake, Utah. There they proceeded to build up a great and thriving commonwealth.

The First Flowering of American Literature

It was not strange that the spirit of national self-confidence and democratic aspiration should find utterance in a great outpouring of literature. The new literary ideals were summed up in 1837 by Emerson in his Phi Beta Kappa address at Harvard, "The American Scholar," which has been termed "America's intellectual Declaration of Independence." He made an eloquent appeal for individuality, sincerity, and realism in the intellectual life of America.

In reality, the new movement had gotten under way during the first quarter of the century, when Washington Irving and James Fenimore Cooper had boldly cast off the customary dependence of American writers upon England in literary manners. Irving's *Sketch Book* (1820) revealed America as a land of legend and romance, equal in interest to the Old World. The abundant literary output of his riper years, instinct with grace and charm, caused Thackeray to call him "the first ambassador whom the New World of letters sent to the Old." In the *Leatherstocking Tales*, published from 1823 to 1841, Cooper made the American pioneer, Natty Bumppo, and the silent-footed Indian chief, Uncas, permanent figures in world literature.[1]

The decade of the thirties saw the full flowering of American letters. As might be expected, the chief center of literary activity was the old settled portion of the country; Massachusetts was particularly prominent. Henry Wadsworth Longfellow, John Greenleaf Whittier, Oliver Wendell Holmes, and James Russell Lowell commenced at this time their creative work of glorifying the commonplace things of life in poems of simple and genuine feeling. Emerson began to preach the doctrine of individualism and the nobility of man in imperishable prose and verse. Nathaniel Hawthorne and Edgar Allan Poe exemplified the versatility of American genius by giving literary expression to the somber and supernatural in man's experience, the former finding his inspiration in the annals of New England Puritanism, and the latter in the self-absorption of a morbid mentality. America owes its early ascendancy in the art of the short story very largely to the work of Irving, Hawthorne, and Poe.

The trend of the times awakened a new interest in the history of the republic, and marked the beginnings of modern American historical scholarship. In the thirties Jared Sparks took up his vast labors of editing historical documents, eliminating and softening such phrases and allusions in the writings of the Fathers as seemed to him unsuited to their dignity. In 1834 George Bancroft published the first volume of his monumental history of the United States, a work based upon a laborious examination of source materials but colored by the author's enthusiastic championship of democratic institutions. Before the close of the decade Irving and William H. Prescott had amply shown the ability of American scholars to portray with literary distinction the history of Spain and of Spanish America.

Although the writers of the time derived their enduring fame from their literary achievements, most of them took an active interest in the humanitarian and political struggles of the age.

[1] *The Deerslayer* (1841), *The Last of the Mohicans* (1826), *The Pathfinder* (1840), *The Pioneers* (1823), and *The Prairie* (1827).

Whittier was preëminently the poet laureate of the antislavery crusade, throwing himself into the contest with all the militant fervor that smoldered under his calm Quaker exterior. Longfellow published his *Poems on Slavery* in 1842. Lowell acted for a time as editor of the *Pennsylvania Freeman*, and later mercilessly lampooned the proslavery politicians in the *Biglow Papers* (1848). Henry D. Thoreau, our first great nature writer, went to jail rather than pay a tax which would help the government then engaged in what he regarded a war of conquest with Mexico.

Cooper showed his interest in the agitation for political democracy by writing a series of propagandist novels, now forgotten, in behalf of the cause in the early forties. Bancroft was an ardent anti-Bank man; and his prominence as a public figure soon drew him into the maelstrom of Democratic politics, where he was rewarded by Polk with a cabinet position, and subsequently received various diplomatic appointments. In the case of William Cullen Bryant, a brilliant poetic career was seriously hampered by his distinguished editorship of the *New York Evening Post* from 1826 to 1878.

As protagonists of the democratic movement, Bryant, Bancroft, and other literary men explained and interpreted Jacksonian Democracy to the educated classes of the East, and helped to make democracy respectable in their eyes. Even the unworldly Hawthorne held various political offices in the customs service, and when he wrote a campaign biography of his college friend Franklin Pierce in 1852, he was repaid by the lucrative post of consul at Liverpool.

SELECT BIBLIOGRAPHY

Democracy and Social Reform. Excellent chapters on the social, intellectual, and humanitarian aspects of the democratic upheaval may be found in Edward Channing, *A History of the United States*, V (New York, 1921), and J. B. McMaster, *A History of the People of the United States*, V (New York, 1900). These matters are discussed in smaller compass in A. M. Schlesinger, *New Viewpoints in American History* (New York, 1922), chapter ix, and in H. U. Faulkner, *American Economic History* (New York, 1924), chapter xv.

The Struggle for Free Public Schools. The educational awakening is set forth with reference to its social and political background in E. P. Cubberley, *Public Education in the United States* (Boston, 1919). Other works of value in this connection are E. G. Dexter, *A History of Education in the United States* (New York, 1904), E. E. Brown, *The Making of Our Middle Schools* (New York, 1907), and E. E. Slosson, *The American Spirit in Education* (in *The Chronicles of America*, XXXIII, New Haven, 1921). The great fathers of the public school system are treated in B. A. Hinsdale, *Horace Mann and the Common School Revival in the United States* (New York, 1898), and W. S. Monroe, *The Educational Labors of Henry Barnard* (Syracuse, 1893). On the development of colleges and universities, the most important treatise is C. F. Thwing, *A History of Higher Education in America* (New York, 1906).

The Beginning of the Woman's Rights Movement. The legal aspects receive attention in E. A. Hecker, *A Short History of Women's Rights* (New York, 1914). Belle Squire, *The Woman Movement in America* (Chicago, 1911), and H. A. Bruce, *Woman in the Making of America* (Boston, 1912), though popular accounts, throw light on the early phases of the feminist movement. The following biographies should be consulted: Katharine Anthony, *Margaret Fuller* (New York, 1920), Catherine H. Birney, *The Grimkê Sisters* (New York, 1885), and Anna D. Hallowell, *James and Lucretia Mott* (Boston, 1884). See also Gamaliel Bradford's readable *Portraits of American Women* (Boston, 1919). J. M. Taylor, *Before Vassar Opened* (Boston, 1914), is a valuable work on the early history of higher education for women.

Humanitarian Crusades. Much information concerning the temperance movement appears in J. G. Woolley and W. E. Johnson, *Temperance Progress of the Century* (Philadelphia, 1903), A. F. Fehlandt, *A Century of Drink Reform in the United States* (Cincinnati, 1904), and G. F. Clark, *History of the Temperance Reform in Massachusetts 1813–1883* (Boston, 1888). Prison reform is historically considered in F. H. Wines, *Punishment and Reformation* (rev. by W. D. Lane, New York, 1919). H. E. Barnes, *A History of the Penal, Reformatory and Correctional Institutions of the State of New Jersey* (Trenton, 1918), is a study of more than local importance. On the treatment of the insane, consult H. M. Hurd and others, *The Institutional Care of the Insane* (4 v., Baltimore, 1916), and Francis Tiffany, *Life of Dorothea Lynde Dix* (Boston, 1890).

Detailed descriptions of the Utopian communities appear in J. H. Noyes, *History of American Socialisms* (Philadelphia, 1870), Charles Nordhoff, *The Communistic Societies of the United States* (New York, 1875), and W. A. Hinds, *American Communities and Coöperative Colonies* (Chicago, 1908). A succinct account may be found in Morris Hillquit, *History of Socialism in the United States* (New York, 1910), part i. The much-neglected early peace movement is given a sketchy chapter in Julius Moritzen, *The Peace Movement of America* (New York, 1912).

The Improving Standard of Life. For the inventions of the period, E. W. Byrn, *The Progress of Invention in the Nineteenth Century* (New York, 1900), is very satisfactory. George Iles, *Leading American Inventors* (New York, 1912), and Holland Thompson, *The Age of Invention* (in *The Chronicles of America*, XXXVII, New Haven, 1921) tell the story of several important inventors and their work. E. L. Bogart, *An Economic History of the United States* (New York, 1922), gives an excellent compact account of economic conditions. The lighter phases of life are treated, in a somewhat flippant manner, in Meade Minnigerode, *The Fabulous Forties* (New York, 1924).

Religious Readjustments. Information regarding religious life and doctrinal controversy may be gleaned from Daniel Dorchester, *Christianity in the United States* (New York, 1895), L. W. Bacon, *A History of American Christianity* (in *American Church History Series*, XIII, New York, 1897), and H. K. Rowe, *The History of Religion in the United States* (New York, 1924). The *American Church History Series* (13 v., New York, 1893–1897) contains denominational histories and also an historical account of the Roman Catholic Church in the United States.

The First Flowering of American Literature. The literary awakening is a favorite theme of the historians of American letters, and is most fully treated in *The Cambridge History of American Literature* (W. P. Trent and others, eds., 4 v., New York, 1917–1921), I–II. W. J. Long, *American Literature* (Boston, 1913), is valuable for showing the relationship of political and social conditions to literature.

CHAPTER VI

SLAVERY AND SECTIONALISM

The Growth of the Slavery System

From the time that Tyler found himself a President without a party to the crushing of the South on the battlefield in 1865, slavery was the overshadowing question in American politics. Many of the developments of these years were due solely to the normal and expanding energies of the American people, but such matters inevitably became entangled in the skein of sectional politics, and were usually dealt with from the standpoint of proslavery or antislavery advantage.

Slavery was not new in the United States in 1841. Indeed, it was one of the oldest of American institutions, and was thoroughly hedged about with constitutional and statutory sanctions. Once universal throughout the thirteen colonies, it had, by the force of circumstances, come gradually to assume the aspect of a sectional system. After the Missouri Compromise of 1820, the slaveholding area was confined to the region south of a line formed by the southern border of Pennsylvania, the Ohio River, the northern limits of Missouri, and, in the remainder of old Louisiana Territory, the parallel 36°30′.

In the closing years of the eighteenth century, slavery was not regarded as filling any indispensable economic need. This opinion was shared by leading men in the South, who believed that, if let alone, the institution would die out of its own accord in due course of time. But certain new influences presently upset their calculations, and intrenched the system more strongly in the South than it had ever been before. On the one hand, the demand for raw cotton increased tremendously with the growth of textile manufacturing in England and the building up of the industry in New England. On the other hand, Whitney's invention of the cotton gin (1793), with its improvements, made available for manufacturing purposes short-staple cotton, the only kind that could be grown away from the seaboard region.

This significant discovery occurred at a time when population was beginning to flow across the mountains into the territory south of the Ohio River. Consequently, as quickly as the initial difficulties of pioneer life in Alabama, Mississippi, and Tennessee were overcome and the Indians removed, cotton culture was rapidly extended throughout the Southwest. Thus the forces which had made for the unity of the trans-Appalachian country — common frontier problems and a common dependence upon the Mississippi River — grew continually less important, and the forces of divergence — differences in climate, soil, economic interest, and social characteristics — became constantly more significant.

Instead of the small frontier farm, the great plantation became the unit of economic and social life in the Southwest. In 1824 the annual cotton production of the seaboard states was almost double that of the interior South, but by 1841 this ratio was reversed. From this time on, it is safe to regard the South, from the Atlantic to the Mississippi River and beyond, as a compact political unit agreeing on all fundamental policies affecting cotton culture and slavery, though still superficially divided in allegiance between the two great national parties. The Northern states did not undergo a similar welding process, remaining divided between the frontier farming regions of the Northwest and the manufacturing and financial districts of the older states.

Under the altered circumstances, the Southern planters came to regard their material prosperity as inseparably connected with the system of forced labor. Cotton culture was singularly adapted to the employment of slaves. The work was simple, requiring only primitive implements. It gave employment for nine months in the year, and permitted the use of women and children as well as "prime field hands." It enabled the white overseers to superintend large gangs of laborers working at the same time. Unable to conceive of a free black population living harmoniously with the white race, the Southerners of that day could not foresee that many of these advantages would also accrue from wage labor, and indeed that the cost to the planter under such circumstances would be considerably less.

Political leaders of the South, the professional classes, and the clergy now no longer apologized for slavery, but became ardent champions of the "peculiar institution." Slavery was said to have the sanction of the Bible as well as of the American Constitution. It was held to shower benefits upon the negro, and was proclaimed as the only secure basis for white civilization. These men in their private lives were of gentle breeding and fine character; their sincerity and good intentions are not to be judged by the more advanced conception of human rights that prevails in our own day. Indeed, Southern publicists insisted the relations of capital and labor were more humane under the slavery system than under the wage system of the North, where the factory-hands earned a bare subsistence, toiled amidst unsanitary conditions, and suffered in old age from unemployment and poverty.

The question of the well-being of the negroes under the system of enforced servitude cannot rightly be disposed of with a few generalizations. Nevertheless, it seems safe to say that the material conditions of slave life were considerably easier in the three decades prior to 1830 than in the three decades thereafter, and that at all times the house servants were better treated than the field hands. The old patriarchal system of plantation government, with easy-going methods of management and personal oversight of the slaves by a beloved master, was still characteristic of Southern life in the earlier period.

After 1830, however, a decided change began to be apparent, not so much in the border slave states, where the negroes were still regarded as a convenience rather than as an economic necessity, as in the states farther south where the "Cotton Kingdom" was strongly intrenched. With the introduction of large-scale methods of cotton production in the Lower South, the master ceased to have close personal supervision over his slaves, and employed professional overseers whose reputation depended on their ability to exact from them a maximum amount of work. Under such a régime the system tended to become thoroughly commercialized, and to lose its semifeudal character.

Moreover, the outbreak of the Nat Turner rebellion in Virginia in 1831, in which sixty whites were murdered by the slaves, stimulated Southern lawmakers to restrict the freedom of action of negroes by drastic legislation.[1] The severity of these "Slave Codes" was increased by the determination of the planters to protect their labor system from the rising tide of antislavery propaganda in the North.

While many planters continued to treat their negroes with great indulgence and every provident master was mindful of the necessity of keeping them in efficient working condition, too many instances of heartless cruelty are a matter of record, and the system inevitably involved the constant breaking of family ties. The most trenchant criticism of slavery, however, was not the actual inhumanity of the masters, but the potentialities for brutality and repression, which are inherent in any system of human bondage. Furthermore, since the slave was merely a piece of property, an "animated tool," no provision was made to promote his sense of self-reliance or to foster his intellectual development. Slavery, remarked F. L. Olmsted, a keen Northern student of Southern conditions, "withholds all encouragement from the labourer to improve his faculties and his skill, destroys his self-respect, misdirects and debases his ambition, and withholds all the natural motives which lead men to endeavor to increase their capacity of usefulness to their country and the world."

Society in the South was distinguished by its high degree of stratification. Of the five or six million white people in 1841, the number of persons in slaveholding families formed about one third. In South Carolina, Alabama, Mississippi, and Louisiana, exclusive of the largest cities, the number reached one half of the whole population. But the proportion of families that possessed great plantations and owned fifty or more slaves was much smaller, constituting a little more than two per cent of the entire number of slaveholding families. Consequently the especially privileged class, as in any other kind of social organization, formed a mere fraction of the population; their primacy was maintained by sheer force of intellect, social prestige, and politi-

[1] Some typical provisions forbade negroes to carry guns, to be absent from the plantation without written permission, to be taught to read and write, or to assemble without the presence of a white man. The Slave Codes were most severe in the states having the largest number of blacks.

cal acumen. Men of this class lived a prodigal life, and with their womenfolk, created that atmosphere of gentility, chivalry, and profuse hospitality which still gilds the prewar South in the minds of the romantic.

Next in the social scale came those well-to-do farmers who owned only a few slaves, and also the professional classes of the South — the lawyers, physicians, clergymen, and teachers — who were dependent upon the aristocracy for their incomes and were in close alliance with them. Most of the small slaveholding farmers, however, were unprosperous and unprogressive, and these made up a somewhat lower layer in the social order. Olmsted gives an unpleasant picture of their poor houses, unwholesome food, and lack of comfort, thrift, and refinement.

The most degraded class among the master race were the so-called "poor whites," a poverty-stricken, slaveless, uneducated, outcast element of the population, which lived in remote valleys of the mountains or else sought half-heartedly to wrest a livelihood from the lands which the planters had abandoned or refused to occupy. In a society differently composed, such folk might have found opportunities for employment and eventually for rising in the social and economic scale; but in a social organization which deemed manual toil a badge of inferiority, their lot was well-nigh hopeless. Only once in a generation could a man of indomitable spirit, like Andrew Johnson of eastern Tennessee, break through the fetters of poverty and ignorance that bound him to his station, and reach high political preferment in his state. Generally speaking, the life of the "poor whites" was happy-go-lucky and not given to introspection, and in matters of political import they were usually willing to follow the lead of their economic and social superiors.

With the passage of years, cotton culture and its labor system came to represent a vast investment of capital. From a crop of negligible importance, its production leaped in 1800 to about thirty-five million pounds, rose to one hundred and sixty million pounds in 1820, and reached a total of more than eight hundred and thirty-four million pounds twenty years later. The monetary value of the cotton crop in 1850 was $105,600,000, and at that date seven eighths of the world's supply was grown in the South. The slaves increased correspondingly in number and value.

About the time of the invention of the cotton gin the price of a good field hand was $300, in 1828 it had become $800, and in 1853, $1200. In 1850 the value of slave property in the entire South amounted to more than one and one-quarter billion dollars.

Thus was built up the superstructure of cotton capitalism in the South, as significant in its influence upon national destinies in the years before the Civil War as industrial capitalism has been in the period since. Inevitably the major purpose of Southerners in national politics came to be the protection and enlargement of the vested interests represented by the cotton-slavery system. As will presently be seen, one of their main objects was to extend the cotton-growing area beyond its existing confines, for, because of the wasteful system of cropping a piece of land until it was exhausted, cotton culture was ever on the move, and unlimited quantities of fresh and fertile lands were required. Furthermore, the South needed new territory out of which additional slave states might be created to offset the admission of new free states. Antislavery Northerners became quickly aware of this growing influence in national affairs; they called it the "Slave Power" or the "Slavocracy," and pictured it as a never-sleeping, malevolent conspiracy for proslavery aggrandizement.

The Rise of Antislavery Agitation

Antislavery agitation in the North did not become militant until the fourth decade of the century. Prior to this time there existed abolitionist newspapers and societies, which devoted their efforts to conducting a quiet, persistent campaign of education on the subject, trusting thereby to bring a gradual end to slavery. Much of this work was carried on by people who lived in or adjoining the slave states, and who hoped to persuade the slave-owners to voluntary emancipation. An organization had been formed in 1816 by leading men of both sections for the purpose of returning liberated negroes to Africa, but though the American Colonization Society continued in existence, the impracticability of the scheme quickly became apparent.[1] Indeed, antislavery men soon began to charge that the slaveholders favored the plan

[1] In the best days of the Society, the number of negroes transported did not equal one twenty-fifth of the natural increase of the race by births.

as a means of getting rid of ambitious and troublesome individuals.

The new phase of antislavery agitation, which began about 1830, owed much to the dynamic democratic idealism of the times and to the fierce new interest in social justice for all classes. It was, in a sense, the American counterpart of a worldwide movement which had achieved the abolition of human bondage in Mexico and the other Spanish-American republics in the preceding decade, and which inspired Parliament in 1833 to provide for gradual emancipation in the British West Indies. The new antislavery movement in America was combative and uncompromising, defying all the constitutional and legal guarantees protecting the slavery system, and insisting upon immediate abolition without compensation. It took no account of the difficulties and dangers involved in wholesale liberation, and valued emancipation above the preservation of the Union.

These extremists found an unexcelled leader in William Lloyd Garrison, a young man twenty-five years of age, of Massachusetts nativity, who possessed the fanatical heroism of a martyr with the crusading ability of a successful demagogue. He was ably seconded by Wendell Phillips, who was ostracized by his Boston friends when he lent his eloquent tongue to the unpopular cause. In 1831, Garrison founded his newspaper, the *Liberator*, and this at once became a rostrum from which he poured vitriolic editorials upon the slaveowners and all their practices. In 1832, he established the New England Anti-Slavery Society, and within a year this grew into a national body called the "American Anti-Slavery Society," pledged to a program of immediate, uncompensated emancipation.

Garrison's sensational methods awakened many Northerners to the evil character of an institution which they had long since come to regard as established and unchangeable. Not all of them, however, were willing to subscribe to his law-defying tactics, for they held that reform should be accomplished by legal and peaceful means. The chief spokesman of this more moderate element was William Ellery Channing, the Unitarian minister of Boston and an able pamphleteer.

Still another antislavery element consisted of quiet church-going citizens, who, under cover of night, helped to spirit escaping slaves away to safe refuges in the North or over the border into Canada. Known as the "Underground Railroad," an elaborate network of secret routes for the fugitives was firmly established in the thirties in all parts of the North. A formal organization of the Underground Railroad workers, with Robert Purvis as President, was effected in Philadelphia in 1838. Their most successful operations were in the old Northwest. In Ohio alone, it is estimated that not less than 40,000 fugitive slaves were assisted to freedom during the years from 1830 to 1860.

The number of local antislavery societies increased until in 1840 there were about two thousand of them with a membership of perhaps 200,000. Women took an active part in the agitation by circulating antislavery petitions, holding prayer-meetings and conventions, and raising large sums of money by fairs. In 1835 Oberlin College threw open its doors to negro students, thereby becoming the first coracial college in America, and making itself a center for abolitionist propaganda in the West.

In 1840 certain antislavery leaders, acting against the wishes of Garrison, gave a new turn to the movement by organizing the Liberty party and nominating J. G. Birney of New York and Thomas Earle of Pennsylvania as candidates for the approaching election. Typical of antislavery parties in subsequent campaigns, the platform took a less doctrinaire position than that of the Garrisonians. It called on Congress to abolish slavery in all the territories and in the District of Columbia, and branded the Fugitive Slave Act of 1793 as unconstitutional. The Liberty ticket polled only 7000 votes in 1840, but in the next few years new men joined the party, like Salmon P. Chase of Ohio and Charles Sumner of Massachusetts, who added to the idealism of the founders a knowledge of the arts of political manipulation. Many men, like Abraham Lincoln and Horace Greeley, sympathized with the purposes of the party, but refused to join it because they believed that its objects could be more speedily accomplished through the agency of the old parties.

The Northern public as a whole held aloof from active participation in the antislavery movement. Busy with their own concerns, they thought of slavery as a problem for the Southern people to solve through state action, and as a moral question rather than a political issue. The unbridled agitation of the antislavery zealots seemed to them to threaten the integrity of the Union, and the latter was dearer to their hearts, even in 1860, than the destruction of slavery. In the early stages of the militant movement, agitators in Northern cities were harshly dealt with by mobs. In one tragic affair at Alton, Illinois, Elijah P. Lovejoy, an abolitionist editor, was murdered by a proslavery mob in November, 1837. Even Abraham Lincoln, then a Whig member of the Illinois legislature, felt called upon to declare in a formal protest in 1837 that, while he believed slavery to be "founded on both injustice and bad policy, . . . the promulgation of abolition doctrines tends rather to increase than abate its evils."

In this growing warfare between the enemies and friends of slavery, the federal government sought at first to occupy a neutral position, for the issue crossed party lines and might easily disrupt the old established parties. But the energy of the antislavery propaganda soon snared the government at Washington in the toils of controversy. In 1835 a mob in Charleston, South Carolina, burned a sack of abolitionist literature which they found in the postoffice. The matter came to the attention of the Postmaster-General, and he made a ruling to the effect that, though all such papers must be accepted at the postoffices, the postmasters might withhold them from delivery if they believed them to be incendiary in character. This extraordinary ruling was hotly debated in Congress, and notwithstanding Calhoun's efforts to the contrary, the right to use the mails was restored by a law of 1836. Drastic penalties were provided for postmasters who interfered with the delivery of mail matter.

The proslavery forces were also resolved to check the flood of antislavery petitions which poured into the House of Representatives. These memorials generally asked for the abolition of slavery in the District of Columbia. In 1836 the House passed a "gag resolution" for the purpose of preventing consideration of such petitions. At each subsequent session, the readoption of the "gag resolution" was fought by Joshua R. Giddings of Ohio and ex-President Adams, the two pillars of antislavery strength in Congress. Finally, in 1844, they had the satisfaction of seeing the rule abandoned by a vote of 108 to 80.

These efforts at repression by the proslavery elements defeated their own purpose. They involved apparent denials of the constitutional guarantees of freedom of the press and the right of petition, and thereby caused many Northerners, who had remained indifferent to the injustices of the negro, to be deeply stirred by the assaults of the "Slave Power" on the rights of white men.

As the foremost moral issue of the age, the antislavery question inevitably challenged the attention of the great religious bodies. In 1844 the Methodist Church split upon the issue of whether a bishop could hold slaves, and the Southern members organized the "Methodist Episcopal Church South." In the same year the Baptists came to grief over the question whether slave owners might be sent out as missionaries, and a Southern Baptist Church resulted. A significant effect of these divisions was the increased membership of the sectionalized branches, thus attesting the conviction of churchgoers in each section as to the relation of Christianity to slavery. In 1853 the New-School Presbyterians divided into two branches over the question, but the other great national churches ignored it, condoned the practice of slaveholding, and remained united until the outbreak of the Civil War.

SELECT BIBLIOGRAPHY

The Growth of the Slavery System. Two of the best discussions of slavery and its significance in American history may be found in A. B. Hart, *Slavery and Abolition* (in *The American Nation*, XVI, New York, 1906), and W. E. Dodd, *The Cotton Kingdom* (in *The Chronicles of America*, XXVII, New Haven, 1919). The first volume of J. F. Rhodes, *History of the United States* (8 v., New York, 1892–1919), which begins nominally at 1850, contains two well-balanced chapters on slavery and the slavery controversy. The colored man's point of view is set forth in Benjamin Brawley, *A Social History of the American Negro* (New York, 1921).

On the political aspects of the controversy, C. S. Boucher, "*In Re* That Aggressive Slavocracy" (in *Mississippi Valley Historical Review*, VIII, 13–79), represents a reaction from the overdrawn statements of the older historians of antislavery leanings. The economic phases of the cotton-slavery system are authoritatively examined in U. B. Phillips, *American Negro Slavery* (New York, 1918). M. B. Hammond, *The Cotton Industry* (in American Economic Association, *Publications*, new series, no. 1, New York, 1897), is the standard work on that subject. For Southern economic and social conditions, there is much of value in the coöperative work edited by

J. A. C. Chandler and others, *The South in the Building of the Nation* (13 v., Richmond, 1909–1913), V and VII. See also Edward Ingle, *Southern Side-lights: a Picture of Social and Economic Life in the South a Generation before the War* (New York, 1896). A shrewd analysis of the sources of strength of the "Slave Power" may be found in A. N. Holcombe, *The Political Parties of To-day* (New York, 1924), chap. v.

The Rise of Antislavery Agitation. A. B. Hart, *Slavery and Abolition* (previously cited), is excellent on the general bearings of the antislavery movement, as is also Jesse Macy, *The Antislavery Crusade* (in *The Chronicles of America*, XXVIII, New Haven, 1919). On the colonization efforts, see E. L. Fox, "The American Colonization Society, 1817–1840" (in *Johns Hopkins University Studies*, XXXVII, no. 3, Baltimore, 1919). W. H. Siebert, *The Underground Railroad from Slavery to Freedom* (New York, 1898), is the most detailed treatment of this subject, and contains valuable maps. For a discussion of the religious ramifications of the controversy, consult J. N. Norwood, *The Schism in the Methodist Episcopal Church, 1844* (Alfred, New York, 1923).

Additional information on the antislavery movement may be gleaned from the biographies of the leaders, notably W. P. and F. J. Garrison, *William Lloyd Garrison* (4 v., New York, 1885–1889), Lorenzo Sears, *Wendell Phillips, Orator and Agitator* (New York, 1909), W. S. Kennedy, *John G. Whittier, the Poet of Freedom* (New York, 1892), W. H. Channing, *The Life of William Ellery Channing, D.D.* (Boston, 1899), and J. F. Morse, Jr., *John Quincy Adams* (Boston, 1898).

CHAPTER VII

SLAVERY AND EXPANSION, 1843–1848

The Annexation of Texas

Though the old parties strove to keep the slavery question out of national politics, their efforts were defeated by the revival, under Tyler, of the movement for the acquisition of Texas. Texas had again offered herself to the United States in 1837, shortly after the American recognition of her independence; but her overtures had been rebuffed, and in 1838 she formally withdrew her offer. Unlike Van Buren, President Tyler strongly favored annexation, and when Webster retired from the State Department in May, 1843, he felt free to prosecute his designs.

The case for annexation was greatly strengthened by the interest which Great Britain had been showing in Texas, and by the consequent fear that Texas might become a British protectorate organized on a basis of free trade and free labor. This apprehension was not entirely unfounded, but for political purposes in the United States, it was magnified by the administration much beyond what the facts actually warranted. On the other hand, the desire to acquire Texas was warmly assailed by the anti-slavery men as a scheme of the cotton capitalists to gain more slave territory. Furthermore, Mexico notified the United States that annexation would be regarded as a declaration of war.

Tyler appointed Abel P. Upshur of Virginia, an ardent annexationist, as Webster's successor. Negotiations were pushed with Texas, though Upshur's sudden death in February, 1844, left the completion of the arrangements to the deft hands of Calhoun, his successor in office. As signed on April 12, 1844, the treaty provided for the annexation of Texas as a "territory." The Senate debated the treaty behind closed doors, and on June 8 finally rejected it by a vote of 35 to 16. The reasons for this action were complex. Some Senators who favored annexation were unwilling to take the step at the cost of war with Mexico; others wished the matter to go over until the voters had expressed their will in the approaching presidential election.

The major parties had already held their national conventions when the vote on the treaty was taken in the Senate. Since early in the year, Henry Clay and Martin Van Buren had been regarded the logical candidates of their respective parties. Both deplored the entry of the Texas question as a campaign issue, and acting probably by prior agreement, each published his views in April as opposed to immediate annexation. In the case of Van Buren this was, of course, merely a reaffirmation of the policy he had pursued when President.

So great was the popular demand for Clay's candidacy that, when the Whigs met on May 1, they nominated him unanimously. In the interest of political expediency the platform omitted all reference to the Texas question. Theodore Frelinghuysen of New Jersey was named for Vice-President. The Democratic convention meeting on May 27 proved to be a theater of intrigue. Although a majority of the delegates were pledged to Van Buren, his Texas pronouncement had made him unacceptable to the Southern contingent. Calhoun's supporters wished to secure the prize for their chief, but while not strong enough to do this, they were able to keep Van Buren from getting the necessary two-thirds vote. The outcome was the nomination of a "dark horse," James K. Polk, ex-Governor of Tennessee, a strong annexationist, who had not been deemed a presidential aspirant prior to the convention. The second place on the ticket went to George M. Dallas of Pennsylvania.

The platform was the acme of political adroitness. Instead of avoiding the pivotal issue, the party boldly announced its support of "the re-occupation of Oregon and the re-annexation of Texas." But by using the words "*re*-occupation" and "*re*-annexation," the Democrats sought to clear these demands of the stigma of aggression, and by coupling Oregon with Texas, hoped to establish the nonsectional character of the demand for expansion.

Tyler allowed himself to be nominated by a convention of officeholders on a platform of "Tyler and Texas," but withdrew when he saw that his candidacy would only draw votes away from Polk. The Liberty party again offered a ticket, headed by James G. Birney, and the platform declared unequivocally against the extension of slavery.

In the campaign that followed, the Democrats made their appeal to the country upon the basis of national expansion rather than slavery extension. Clay, on the other hand, began to fear the loss of Southern votes because of his preconvention declaration against immediate annexation; and in later letters, designed for Southern reading, he explained and equivocated until no one knew definitely where he stood. Polk was victorious by a popular plurality of less than 40,000 and an electoral vote of 170 to 105. Though polling no electoral votes, the Liberty party won 62,000 popular votes. The popular strength of Polk and Clay was so closely divided that the balance of power lay with the Liberty party in New York, Ohio, and Indiana. Had the antislavery party chosen to vote for Clay in New York, he would have won the thirty-six electoral votes of that state and a majority of the electoral votes of the country.

Van Buren's repudiation by the Democratic national convention, followed by Polk's election, marked a turning point in the history of the Democratic party. Henceforth every Democratic candidate for President down to the Civil War was either a Southerner or a "doughface," that is, a pro-Southern Northerner. The radical democracy of the Jackson-Van Buren régime succumbed to the resolute purposes of Southern leaders intent on advancing cotton culture and its peculiar labor system. The death of Jackson in 1845 removed a potent counter-influence, and his great lieutenants, Van Buren and Benton, soon found themselves at cross purposes with the new leadership of the party.

Tyler, who still had four months in office after the election, hastened to capture for himself the honor of acquiring Texas. Declaring to Congress in December, 1844, that the American people had spoken in the election, he recommended that, since a two-thirds Senate majority for a treaty was out of the question, Congress should annex Texas by means of a joint resolution, which only required a majority vote in each house. Notwithstanding a flood of petitions and memorials from the free states against the measure, Congress followed the President's advice on February 28, 1845. Their action authorized the admission of Texas as a state of the Union. It further provided that Congress must approve of the Texan constitution, that all boundary disputes in which Texas was involved should be adjusted by the United States, and that the public debt of the new state should not become a charge on the federal government.

Although the acquisition of Texas, with its results, was destined to intensify sectional antagonism in American politics, it should be noted that the action of the United States was fully justified in international law. Texas had maintained a separate existence for nine years without any serious attempt on the part of Mexico to reconquer her. Moreover, her independence had been recognized by the leading European powers as well as the United States. On July 4, 1845, a Texan convention summoned for that purpose accepted annexation with only one dissenting vote, a decision later confirmed by popular referendum. At the next session of the American Congress, annexation was completed by the passage of a formal resolution admitting the state (December 29). The national territory was thereby enlarged by an area more than three times the size of present-day Italy.

The Partition of the Oregon Country

James K. Polk, the new President, was not the nonentity that history often pictures him. Lacking in personal magnetism and dramatic flourishes, he was a serious, methodical man of inflexible purpose and great executive capacity. His term was crowded with important events, and judged by his record, he was the greatest expansionist who ever occupied his high office. His cabinet appointments, headed by James Buchanan of Pennsylvania in the State Department and Robert J. Walker of Mississippi as Secretary of the Treasury, evidenced the dominance of Southern influence in his administration.[1] Unwilling to trust Blair who had been editor of the official Democratic organ in Washington since Jackson's first administration, Polk forced him to sell his paper, the *Washington Globe*, by taking away the

[1] The other members of his cabinet were: William L. Marcy of New York, Secretary of War; George Bancroft of Massachusetts, Secretary of the Navy; John Y. Mason of Virginia, Attorney-General; Cave Johnson of Tennessee, Postmaster-General.

government printing. In its place was established the *Washington Union* with a trusted friend, Thomas Ritchie, in charge.

Since the campaign pledge respecting Texas had been virtually carried out by the time Polk took the oath of office, he was free to give his attention to the settlement of the Oregon question. That vast domain, lying west of the mountains and extending from the forty-second parallel on the south to 54° 40′ on the north, had been held by Great Britain and the United States since 1818 under an agreement of joint occupation. Since the region was remote both from Great Britain and the settled parts of the United States, neither country made any serious effort to colonize it for a number of years. British interests were largely confined to the Columbia River basin where the Hudson's Bay Company, which in 1821 had absorbed the North West Company, carried on fur-trading. American energies were mainly engaged in handling the commerce between Oregon and China.

Missionary enterprise paved the way for the colonization of Oregon with permanent American settlers. In 1834 the first organized band of farmers went overland under the lead of Methodist missionaries, and two years later another band, led by Presbyterian or Congregational missionaries, made the trip. Other migrations followed, although up to the end of 1841 the total number of immigrants probably did not exceed four hundred. Their presence necessitated some provision for self-government, and upon their own initiative steps were taken by the settlers in 1841, which culminated two years later in the adoption of a temporary constitution, to remain in effect until the United States government should make other arrangements. The American settlements were located almost exclusively south of the Columbia.

Beginning as early as 1826, the two governments had exchanged views with respect to a division of the Oregon country. The United States insisted on a westward extension of the forty-ninth parallel, which already formed the international boundary east of the Rockies. But since this arrangement would deprive the British of trading and fishing advantages in the Columbia River and of the control of the ocean outlet of the waters east of Vancouver Island, the latter demanded the Columbia River as the dividing line.

By 1843 it became apparent that a final adjustment of the rival claims could not be much longer delayed. In that year no less than one thousand American settlers crossed the plains and mountains to the fertile valleys of the northwestern coast. Petitions for American occupation of the entire domain began to inundate Congress. As has been seen, the Democrats shrewdly capitalized the growing popular interest by inserting a plank in their platform of 1844 for the "re-occupation of Oregon," and "Fifty-Four Forty or Fight" was a telling slogan with the Western voters.

The campaign demand for the entire Oregon country was not, however, taken very seriously by the Democratic President, for in July, 1845, Polk renewed the earlier American offer to divide the country at the forty-ninth parallel. When Great Britain again declined, he chose to remember the platform pledge, and in his message of December 2, 1845, he asserted the American claim to all Oregon, appealed to the Monroe Doctrine, and asked Congress to authorize the termination of the joint occupancy. Congress acquiescing, the President in May, 1846, served upon Great Britain the one year's notice required by the treaty.

Fortunately, Great Britain did not regard the issue as sufficiently important to meet defiance with defiance, especially in view of the declining importance of the fur trade in the disputed region. She reopened negotiations, and on June 15, 1846, a treaty was signed for the partition of the Oregon country at the forty-ninth parallel on the mainland, and then along the middle of the channel between Vancouver Island and the mainland to the Pacific Ocean.[1] The Hudson's Bay Company was granted freedom of navigation of the Columbia. Polk's game of bluff had proved successful, and the United States received a stretch of territory equal in size to the combined areas of France, Portugal, and Greece.

The War with Mexico

The United States escaped war with Great Britain only to plunge into war with Mexico. Although the annexation of Texas

[1] The water boundary later gave rise to disputes over the ownership of certain islands, and the matter was finally adjusted by arbitration under the Treaty of Washington (1871).

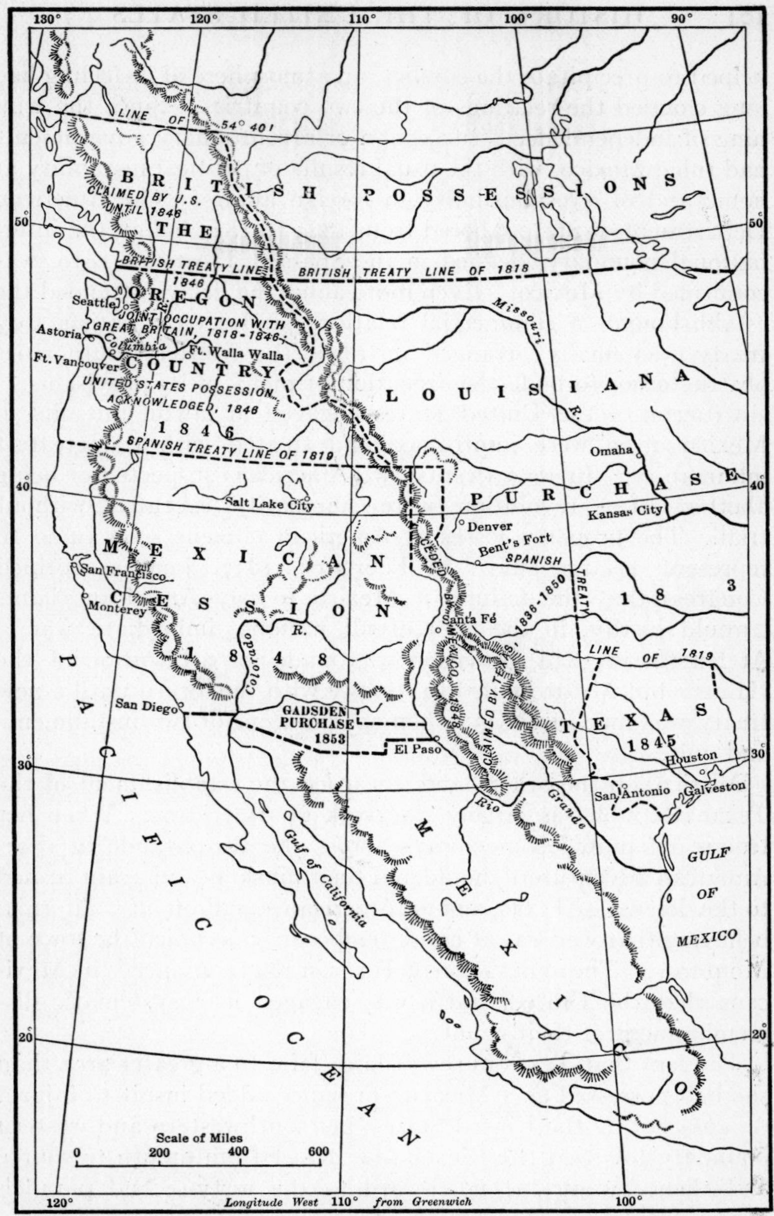

THE OREGON COMPROMISE AND THE MEXICAN CESSIONS, 1846–1848

helped to precipitate the conflict, an atmosphere of ill-feeling had long clouded the relations of the two countries. Since the winning of independence a succession of revolutionary governments had ruled Mexico, with the usual results of political instability at home and of irresponsibility in foreign affairs. The American Department of State labored from 1825 to 1835 before the international boundary, defined in the Spanish Treaty of 1819, was confirmed by Mexico. Even more annoying delays attended the establishment of commercial relations, and after a satisfactory treaty was finally arranged in 1831, the Mexican authorities obstructed or forbade the execution of many of its provisions.

Citizens of the United States engaged in lawful pursuits in Mexico often were imprisoned and treated with the greatest inhumanity. In 1835 twenty-two Americans suspected of being abetters of a revolution were summarily executed without trial. The property losses of American citizens soon came to represent a large sum. In February, 1837, Jackson notified Congress that the failure of Mexico to pay American claims "would justify, in the eyes of all nations, immediate war."[1] At length, in 1839, provision was made for arbitration of the claims; but Mexico failed to comply with the award until a new treaty was made in 1843, when she paid one or two installments and quit.

Mexico, on the other hand, regarded the establishment of the Texan Republic as largely the work of Americans. When her troops attempted some forays across the Rio Grande in 1842, American adventurers shouldered their muskets and again rushed to the defense of Texas, and an American squadron off California, believing that war was at hand, temporarily occupied the town of Monterey. The annexation of Texas in 1845 convinced the Mexicans that the United States was engaged in a systematic dismemberment of their country.

The fact that Texas in revolt laid claim to a greater area than she had possessed as a Mexican province added insult to injury. As annexed by the United States, her southwestern and western boundary followed the Rio Grande River from mouth to source and thence went due northward to the forty-second parallel,

[1] Other nations were similarly involved with Mexico. In 1838 France lost patience and collected her claims at the cannon's mouth.

whereas Mexican Texas had not extended beyond the Nueces River.[1] The added area, while comprising sparsely populated country in general, included the Mexican settlements at the mouth of the Rio Grande and the ancient Spanish city of Santa Fe in New Mexico.

It is probable, as recent students have maintained, that the prospect of war with the United States in 1845 was welcomed by Mexico rather than otherwise, for the Mexican generals, experienced in countless revolutions, had an inflated idea of their own prowess. Moreover, they counted heavily on the advantage of fighting on their own soil, and misled by the patient diplomacy of the United States for the last twenty years, believed that the American people would never support a war.

That Polk had no wanton desire to wage war with Mexico is clear, but he was obsessed with the notion of acquiring her northwest provinces, and this ambition was hardly consonant with the continuance of peaceful relations. However, he intended to accomplish his purpose by pacific methods, if possible. The Mexican treasury, chronically empty, was in need of replenishment. Furthermore, northwestern Mexico was remote from the seat of central authority, thinly peopled, and only loosely attached to the Mexican political system. Accordingly, in November, 1845, he sent John Slidell of Louisiana as Minister to Mexico to induce that government to accept the Rio Grande boundary of Texas in return for the American cancellation of claims against Mexico. Slidell was further instructed to offer $5,000,000 for New Mexico, as the country westward to California was called, and as for California, he was told that "money would be no object when compared with the value of its acquisition." But the Mexican government, having severed diplomatic relations after the annexation of Texas, refused to receive Slidell, who returned to the United States in March, 1846, with his mission unaccomplished.

In Polk's mind the situation now justified war. In the summer of 1845 troops under General Zachary Taylor had been sent into the disputed area beyond the Nueces, and on January 13, 1846,

[1] "The boundary was probably asserted partly in the hope of making it good, and partly with the idea of having a liberal basis for compromise in the final settlement with Mexico." Justin Smith, *The Annexation of Texas*, p. 19.

THE WAR WITH MEXICO ON ALL FRONTS

Year	Northeastern Mexico	Northwestern Mexico	Central Mexico
1846	May 8 Taylor's victory at Palo Alto		
1846	May 9 Taylor's victory at Resaca de la Palma		
1846	May 13 U. S. declaration of war		
1846		June 14 Uprising of American settlers at Sonoma, California	
1846		June 26 Kearny leaves Leavenworth for Santa Fe	
1846		July 7 Commodore Sloat takes Monterey, California	
1846		July 9 Naval seizure of San Francisco	
1846	July 14 Taylor occupies Camargo		
1846		Aug. 13 Commodore Stockton takes Los Angeles	
1846		Aug. 18 Kearny takes Santa Fe	
1846	Sept. 20–24 Taylor captures Monterey, Mexico		
1846		Sept. 25 Kearny leaves Santa Fe for California	
1846	Nov. 15 Commodore Conner takes Tampico		
1846	Nov. 16 Taylor occupies Saltillo		
1846			Nov. 18 Scott is appointed to command Vera Cruz expedition
1846		Dec. 6 Kearny's victory at San Pascual, California	
1846	Dec. 29 Taylor occupies Victoria		
1847			Jan. 3 Scott orders troops from Taylor
1847	Jan. 28 Santa Anna begins march against Taylor		
1847			Feb. 19 Scott reaches Tampico
1847	Feb. 22–23 Taylor's victory at Buena Vista		
1847	Mch. 1 Doniphan occupies Chihuahua		
1847			Mch. 9–29 Scott's operations against Vera Cruz
1847			Apr. 8 Advance on Mexico City begins
1847			Apr. 17–18 Scott's victory at Cerro Gordo
1847			Apr. 19 Scott occupies Jalapa
1847			May 15 Scott occupies Puebla
1847			Aug. 19 Scott's victory at Contreras
1847			Aug. 20 Scott's victory at Churubusco
1847			Aug. 24–Sept. 7 Armistice
1847			Sept. 8 Scott's victory at Molino del Rey
1847			Sept. 13 Scott's victory at Chapultepec
1847			Sept. 14 Scott enters Mexico City

they had been ordered to the banks of the Rio Grande. On Saturday, May 9, 1846, the President notified his cabinet of his intention to recommend war to Congress within the next few days. That night news came which enabled him to put the cause of war before the country in its most appealing light: Mexican forces had crossed the Rio Grande, and fought a skirmish with some American troops on April 24.

Polk's message of May 11 therefore adverted only briefly to the longstanding grievances of American citizens, the violation of treaty rights, and the wrongful interferences with American trade. Mexico, he declared, has "shed American blood upon the American soil. . . . War exists, and, notwithstanding all our efforts to avoid it, exists by the act of Mexico herself." Congress responded with an authorization of men and money. The next day (May 13) Polk told his cabinet that "In making peace with our adversary, we shall acquire California, New Mexico, and other further territory, as an indemnity for this war, if we can."

The military operations lasted for about a year and a half. The Mexicans outnumbered the invaders, and, for the most part, offered a stiff resistance; but they were overcome by the superior morale and stamina of the American forces, most of whom were volunteers. The fighting occurred in three distinct geographic areas. In order to assure the territorial objectives of the war, an American squadron in the Pacific seized the ports of California, and an overland expedition under Colonel S. W. Kearny, setting out from Fort Leavenworth on the Missouri, obtained control of New Mexico through the occupation of Sante Fe on August 18. Simultaneously with these operations, General Taylor began an invasion of northern Mexico from his point of vantage on the Rio Grande, gained brilliant victories at Palo Alto and Resaca de la Palma on May 8 and 9, took Monterey on May 24, and defeated a Mexican relief expedition under General Santa Anna at Buena Vista on February 22 and 23, 1847.

Polk, who was responsible for the plan of campaign, had hoped that these blows might bring the enemy to terms, but now he saw it was necessary to strike at the heart of the country. In March, 1847, an army under General Winfield Scott was transported to Vera Cruz, and a direct overland march begun on the capital city. Every step of the way was contested. The scaling of the mountain wall beyond Vera Cruz involved a severe struggle at Cerro Gordo on April 17 and 18; and finally, when the central plateau of Mexico was reached, there was hard fighting at Contreras, Churubusco, and Chapultepec in August and September. On September 14, 1847, Mexico City was taken, and the country lay at the mercy of the invaders.

MILITARY OPERATIONS OF THE MEXICAN WAR

Not desiring to prolong the war unnecessarily, Polk had sent Nicholas P. Trist of Virginia along with General Scott with instructions to negotiate a peace the moment the Mexicans were willing to make the required territorial concessions. But the sweeping victory of the American forces caused an outburst of imperialistic sentiment in the United States, which found expression in a demand for the annexation of all Mexico. Even Polk's cabinet was divided over what should be done, and Secretary of State Buchanan, with a hopeful eye on his chances in the approaching presidential election, declared in a public letter, "Destiny beckons us to hold and civilize Mexico." Polk, however, was not to be moved from his original purpose, and he accepted the treaty which had meantime been signed by Trist at Guadalupe Hidalgo on February 2, 1848.

By its provisions Mexico acknowledged the Rio Grande boundary of Texas, and ceded to the United States the territories then known as "New Mexico" and "Upper California." The international boundary thus established is the same as today, except for the small addition of territory made by the Gadsden Purchase (1853) south of the Gila River. In return, the United States agreed to pay fifteen million dollars and to assume the payment of all American claims against Mexico.[1]

Thus, at a war cost of twelve thousand lives and nearly one hundred million dollars, the United States gained a domain nearly two and one half times as great as France, and deprived the Republic of Mexico of two fifths of her territory. In this connection, it may be noted that, although the Latin-American republics had been assured by the United States of protection against European imperialism only twenty-five years before, those countries now learned that the United States did not regard the Monroe Doctrine as a self-denying ordinance.

Polk's craving for territory was not yet appeased. In a message to Congress in April, 1848, he hinted at the desirability of annexing the strife-afflicted Mexican province of Yucatan, in order to forestall similar action by Great Britain or Spain. A month and a half later he tried to buy Cuba from Spain, alleging that the covetous eyes of European powers were fastened on her declining power there. Polk's offer was met by the reply that Spain would sooner see Cuba "sunk in the ocean."

The great enlargement of the national area under Polk was, in its immediate results, productive only of strife and discord in American politics, for the question of slavery extension was inextricably bound up in that of national expansion. Its indirect effects were equally disastrous to national harmony. The energy and success of Polk's plans inoculated the popular mind with an

[1] These claims were later adjudged to amount to $3,208,315.

exultant faith in the manifest destiny of the United States to absorb all North America in her boundaries.

"Manifest Destiny" became the slogan of the Democratic party from this time to the outbreak of the Civil War, though it was corrupted by the party leaders into a purely sectional doctrine for the acquisition of semitropical lands suitable for slavery. This zeal for expansion could not well be reconciled with a strict construction of the Constitution, for, as Jefferson admitted when Louisiana was annexed in 1803, the Constitution nowhere explicitly authorizes additions of territory. It appeared, therefore, that even Southern Democrats were willing to forget their constitutional scruples if the interests of the "Cotton Kingdom" could be served thereby.

Politics and Public Opinion under Polk

Although foreign affairs occupied the dominant place in Polk's administration, he did not fail to give due attention to those well-established articles of Democratic faith: the Independent Treasury, and a tariff for revenue only. In his first annual message he called for the restoration of the Independent Treasury, discarded by the Whigs in 1841. Congress accordingly passed an act on August 6, 1846, which, in the main, was the same law that Van Buren had labored so long to secure. The system, thus again set in motion, proved its worth, and remained continuously in existence until abandoned under the provisions of the Federal Reserve Act of 1913.

In pursuance of recommendations made by Secretary of the Treasury Walker, Congress enacted a new tariff law on July 30, 1846, which had as its ideal the raising of revenue rather than the protection of industry. While the bill was before Congress, reduction of duties was opposed by members from New England and the Middle states, but favored by the farmers and planters of the West and South. The Walker Tariff enlarged the free list, and made the average rate on dutiable imports 26.5 per cent. Financially the new act proved a marked success. The average annual yield was forty-six million dollars as compared with twenty-six million dollars under the Whig tariff of 1842.

In 1854–1856, the revenue from tariff duties actually exceeded the normal expenditures of the government, and accordingly the Democrats scaled down the rates once more in 1857 by about five per cent, at the same time increasing the free list. This era of low tariff duties was also a period of great industrial prosperity in the United States; but one cannot safely draw conclusions from this fact, for, as we shall see, many other conditions were working toward the same end, such as the gold discoveries in California, the increase in immigration, and the rapid development of the West.

After the conflict with Mexico began, much of the time of Congress was taken up with discussions of wartime legislation. In the first flush of enthusiasm the war was extremely popular with the country; but the Whigs in Congress, while voting the necessary military appropriations, quickly adopted the policy of criticizing the causes and purposes of the struggle. The most resolute opposition came from antislavery sources, for men of this stripe regarded the conflict as an arrogant proslavery war of conquest. In this spirit, for example, the Massachusetts legislature resolved in April, 1847, that the war, "unconstitutionally commenced by the order of the President," was being waged "for the dismemberment of Mexico" with "the triple object of extending slavery, of strengthening the Slave Power, and of obtaining the control of the Free States."

Irrespective of party, the antislavery forces in Congress resolved to exclude slavery from any territory that might be acquired from Mexico. On August 8, 1846, Polk asked Congress to vote him two million dollars in order that he might be ready at any time to treat with Mexico for territorial cessions. David Wilmot, a Pennsylvania Democrat of the antislavery wing of the party, moved in the House of Representatives an amendment to the appropriation bill, providing that in all ceded provinces slavery should be forever prohibited. The issue was now joined. In August, 1846, and again in February, 1847, the "Wilmot Proviso" was adopted by the House after a severe struggle, but notwithstanding the support of Webster and other Northern Whigs in the Senate, the measure failed of passage there on both occasions.

At length the House was persuaded to vote the appropriations without restriction in March, 1847. By this time, however, the

Wilmot Proviso had served its purpose of arousing the country to the importance of the question of slavery in the Mexican cessions. Northern legislatures indorsed the exclusion of slavery; Southern legislatures just as roundly condemned the proposal. In general, the Democrats in Congress met the issue with a united front, but the Whigs were badly shaken by the contest. On every significant vote the Southern Whigs voted solidly with the Democrats against the Wilmot Proviso, and the Northern Whigs took the antislavery side.

The principle underlying the Wilmot Proviso was also evoked in the discussions in Congress over the territorial organization of Oregon. In messages of 1846 and 1847, Polk urged Congress to establish a regular territorial government in Oregon in place of the provisional government set up by the settlers (see page 101). Although everyone recognized that Oregon was certain to be free soil, the Southern members did not wish to yield the point without obtaining some corresponding sectional advantage. Bills passed by the House to organize Oregon as a free territory failed in the Senate in 1846 and 1847; but a third bill, of 1848, was approved by the Senate with an adroitly conceived amendment to the effect that the Missouri-Compromise line should be extended to the Pacific. The Senate hoped in this way to commit Congress in advance to the policy of permitting slavery in the Mexican acquisitions south of 36° 30′. The House was adamant, the need for action great, and on August 13, 1848, an act was adopted authorizing a free-soil government in Oregon with no mention of the Missouri-Compromise provision.

As the presidential election of 1848 drew near, the leaders of the great parties found themselves confronted with the same dilemma that had dismayed them in 1844: forces beyond their control had thrust forward the question of slavery extension as the paramount issue of the campaign. Since this question cut across party lines, the old-party managers determined, if possible, to evade it. The Democrats, holding their national convention at Baltimore on May 22, adopted a platform which defended the Mexican War as "just and necessary" but said nothing about slavery in the new accessions. For President the party nominated Lewis Cass of Michigan, a zealous expansionist and anti-Wilmot man who had recently proposed "squatter sovereignty" as a solution for the question of slavery in federal territories. With his name was coupled that of General W. O. Butler of Kentucky, a Mexican-War veteran.

The Whigs, meeting at Philadelphia on June 7, resorted again to the plan of staking their chances on a military hero. Notwithstanding the lukewarm support of the Whigs, the Mexican War had yielded greater popular credit to them than to the party in power. The guilt of starting the war belonged to the latter, but the glory of victory belonged to the former, for both Taylor and Scott were nominally of the Whig persuasion. Although Clay was as usual an aspirant for the honor, the presidential nomination went with great enthusiasm to Zachary Taylor of Louisiana. Besides his war fame, the fact that Taylor was the owner of three hundred slaves would, it was thought, make an especial appeal to Southern voters.

The true character of the nomination was amply evidenced by the General's bald announcement prior to the convention that he would run, even if the Whigs failed to nominate him, and that he would be their candidate only if "allowed to maintain a position of independence to all political parties." Millard Fillmore of New York, a suave man of moderate ability, was nominated for second place. The Ohio delegation made a determined but fruitless effort to put the convention on record in favor of the Wilmot Proviso, and the convention adjourned without framing a platform.

The opportunity for a third party based on an antislavery program was the best that had yet presented itself. Deeply stirred by the debates in Congress on the Mexican War and the Wilmot Proviso, the antislavery members of the old parties were becoming increasingly restless with their traditional affiliations. In the pivotal state of New York, the Democratic party split wide open, one wing under Van Buren's leadership espousing the Wilmot principle of dealing with the Mexican cessions, and the other, led by William L. Marcy of Polk's cabinet, taking the opposite position. Van Buren's followers were called the "Barnburners," because, like the old Dutch farmer, it was said they were willing to burn the barn in order to get rid of the rats; whereas the administration Democrats, for some obscure reason, were known as the "Hunkers." Angered by the treatment they received at the hands of the Democratic national convention, the Barnburners repudiated the nomination of Cass.

Another new source of support appeared in the organized activities of Eastern wage-earners, who were just beginning to recover from the shattering effects of the Panic of 1837. Under the leadership of the New York land reformer, George Henry Evans, the National Reform Association had been founded in 1844, and the National Industrial Congress the next year. These bodies undertook an aggressive agitation for free homesteads for actual settlers.[1] Their purpose was to extend a helping hand to the struggling white workingmen in the East, but their cause was eagerly championed by the antislavery men who favored any measure calculated to keep the territories free.

In order to present a united front, the various free-soil elements came together in a national convention at Buffalo on August 9. Senator John P. Hale of New Hampshire and ex-President Van Buren, who had already been nominated respectively by the old Liberty party and the Barnburners, agreed to defer to the will of the convention, and the choice of the new Free Soil party fell on the latter. Charles Francis Adams, son of John Quincy Adams, was named for the vice-presidency. An eloquent platform, written mainly by Salmon P. Chase, was adopted. It denounced the "Slave Power," declared that Congress must convert all federal territories into free soil, and indorsed the policy of free homesteads for landless settlers.

The campaign of 1848 was marked by no such enthusiasm as that of 1840 or 1844. The old-party managers effectually hushed up any discussion of dangerous issues. Though many citizens were dissatisfied with this temporizing policy, they continued nevertheless to vote the "regular ticket," or else stayed away from the polls, in preference to voting the third-party ticket. Under partisan pressure, Taylor issued a public letter in which he described himself as a Whig, "decided but not ultra." Taylor was victor by an electoral majority of thirty-six votes over Cass, just the vote of New York. The new party evinced remarkable strength. Though failing to gain any electoral votes, Van

[1] Petitions for this purpose poured into Congress from 1846 to 1852. In the latter year Senator Walker of Wisconsin presented a petition which was so numerously signed as to be fifty-two feet in length.

Buren polled nearly 300,000 popular votes, and the Free Soilers held the balance of power between the two old parties in eleven Northern states, including all those of the old Northwest. If Van Buren had not split the Democratic vote in New York, Cass would have carried the state and won the presidency.

SELECT BIBLIOGRAPHY

Slavery and Expansion. G. P. Garrison, *Westward Extension* (in *The American Nation*, XVII, New York, 1906), and N. W. Stephenson, *Texas and the Mexican War* (in *The Chronicles of America*, XXIV, New Haven, 1921), are excellent general surveys of the expansion movement which closed with the Peace of Guadalupe Hidalgo. See also Katharine Coman, *Economic Beginnings of the Far West* (2 v., New York, 1912), and Cardinal Goodwin, *Transmississippi West (1803–1853)* (New York, 1922).

The Annexation of Texas. A detailed treatment is J. H. Smith, *The Annexation of Texas* (New York, 1911). The chapters on Texas in G. L. Rives, *The United States and Mexico, 1821–1848* (2 v., New York, 1913), are valuable. E. D. Adams studies a special phase of the subject in his *British Interests and Activities in Texas, 1838–1846* (Baltimore, 1910).

The Partition of Oregon. E. I. McCormac, *James K. Polk* (Berkeley, 1922), sheds much light on all the problems of Polk's presidency, domestic and foreign. Excellent accounts of the Oregon episode may be found in Joseph Schafer, *A History of the Pacific Northwest* (New York, 1918), and F. L. Paxson, *History of the American Frontier, 1763–1793* (Boston, 1924). Very helpful is the discussion in J. S. Reeves, *American Diplomacy under Tyler and Polk* (Baltimore, 1907).

The War with Mexico. This subject is carefully treated in J. B. McMaster, *History of the People of the United States* (8 v., New York, 1883–1913), and in the second volume of Rives, *The United States and Mexico* (already cited). Though an exhaustive treatment, J. H. Smith, *The War with Mexico* (2 v., New York, 1919), is somewhat marred by the author's controversial tone.

Politics and Public Opinion under Polk. In addition to the general histories and biographies, such works should be consulted for fiscal and tariff measures as David Kinley, *The Independent Treasury of the United States and Its Relations to the Banks of the Country* (Washington, 1910), Edward Stanwood, *American Tariff Controversies in the Nineteenth Century* (2 v., Boston, 1903), and F. W. Taussig, *The Tariff History of the United States* (New York, 1923).

On elections and platforms, Edward Stanwood, *A History of the Presidency* (2 v., 1898–1916), I, is good, as usual. Of special interest is T. C. Smith, *The Liberty and Free-Soil Parties in the Northwest* (in *Harvard Historical Studies*, VI, New York, 1897). Information on George Henry Evans and his land-reform movement may be gleaned from J. R. Commons and others, *History of Labour in the United States* (2 v., New York, 1918), I.

CHAPTER VIII

A NATIONAL CRISIS, 1849–1852

The Union in Danger

Zachary Taylor, the new President, was a man of high character, sturdy honesty, and strong personality, with extensive experience in war but none in statecraft. He consulted leading Southern Whigs before naming his official advisers, and finally selected a cabinet composed of three Northerners and four men from the slave states.[1] Since the presidential election had settled nothing, Taylor was left free to act as he would on matters of public policy. To the disappointment of his Southern supporters, he honestly sought to weigh public questions without regard to partisan or sectional bias. Indeed, he formed a warm personal liking for William H. Seward, the antislavery Whig Senator from New York, and in August, 1849, he declared in a public speech, "The people of the North need have no apprehension of the further extension of slavery."

With the exception of Lincoln, never was a newly-elected President confronted with such grave and significant problems. Most of them had been created and left unsettled by the Polk administration, and all of them were intimately connected with the slavery system. The question of major importance concerned the policy which Congress should adopt toward slavery in the new Southwest, and on this issue the members of Congress were sadly divided. Indeed, during the heated debates over the Oregon situation, four distinct and mutually antagonistic views had been enunciated.

One group proposed to divide the territories once more between

[1] John M. Clayton of Delaware, Secretary of State; William M. Meredith of Pennsylvania, Secretary of the Treasury; George W. Crawford of Georgia, Secretary of War; William B. Preston of Virginia, Secretary of the Navy; Reverdy Johnson of Maryland, Attorney-General; Jacob Collamer of Vermont, Postmaster-General; Thomas Ewing of Ohio, Secretary of the Interior (a newly created department).

slavery and freedom, as had been done in 1820 at the time of the Missouri Compromise. This was preëminently a practical man's solution of the difficulty. Moreover, it had the sanction of historic precedent, for while the original line 36° 30′ applied only to old Louisiana Territory, the Joint Resolution of 1845 had extended it through Texas in case additional states should be created out of the area. Polk and many others believed that it should now be carried through the Mexican cessions to the coast.

A second group insisted upon the total exclusion of slavery from the territories. This plan also had historic sanction, for it had been embodied in the Ordinance of 1787, and had formed the gist of the Wilmot Proviso. But it was essentially an extremist position. Indeed, this element not merely maintained that Congress should, as a matter of humanity, forbid slavery in the territories, but also contended, according to the Liberty platform of 1844, that "the fundamental truth of the Declaration of Independence, that all men are endowed by their Creator with . . . life, liberty, and the pursuit of happiness, was made the fundamental law of our national government by that amendment of the Constitution which declares that no person shall be deprived of life, liberty, or property without due process of law." As respects the new accessions, the advocates of Congressional prohibition enjoyed a strategic advantage, for slavery had had no existence there while a part of Mexico, and they argued that under international law this condition of freedom persisted until changed by an express act of Congress.

According to a third group, the fate of slavery should be left to the decision of the respective territorial legislatures. Since this method involved settlement by local action before the territory became a state, it was termed, somewhat derisively, "squatter sovereignty." Yet no proposal seemed so happily inspired, or so likely to meet the requirements of the situation. It appealed to the democratic instincts of a people accustomed to making vital social decisions by a majority vote of those persons most closely concerned, and at the same time promised to relieve the federal legislature of all responsibility in the matter. In 1847 Lewis Cass of Michigan announced his espousal of this solution, and as might be expected, it found warm support among the self-reliant farmers of the Northwest. Within a few years

Stephen A. Douglas of Illinois, who happily renamed the doctrine "popular sovereignty," was to become its foremost champion.

The fourth group denied absolutely that slavery could legally be prohibited in the federal territories under any contingencies or circumstances. Among the chief upholders of this view were Calhoun and his disciple, Jefferson Davis of Mississippi, and the doctrine became indelibly associated with their names. Briefly expressed, these men maintained that, since the states were joint owners of the territories, each state was entitled to its full and equal rights in any territory, including the right of its citizens to carry their property there, slave or otherwise. In other words, the right of property in slaves subsisted in the federal territories irrespective of Congressional or local enactments to the contrary. The doctrine of constitutional protection represented at this time merely the views of certain Southern extremists in the Democratic party, for most of the leaders favored the squatter-sovereignty plan as a compromise acceptable to both the Northern and the Southern wings.

Before Polk left office, he sent a special message to Congress urging the immediate formation of territorial governments in California and New Mexico,[1] but his recommendation failed. The House of Representatives would not accept the President's suggestion of extending the Missouri-Compromise line to the Pacific, nor could the two branches agree on any other disposition of the question.

An unforeseen event now supplied a new and urgent reason for the speedy organization of the new Southwest. In January, 1848, gold was discovered in the Lower Sacramento Valley in California. Like a contagion, the news spread throughout the country, precipitating a headlong rush of gold-seekers from all parts of the world. In the single year 1849, more than eighty thousand immigrants arrived in the new El Dorado. Settlers already on the Coast abandoned their work to take part in the hunt, and in the mad excitement, soldiers and sailors deserted from the service of the United States. Many desperate and

[1] The New Mexico of that time included most of the present state of that name, all of Arizona except the part later included in the Gadsden Purchase (1853), all of Utah and Nevada, and parts of Colorado and Wyoming.

lawless men joined the "Forty-Niners," and human passions were under only a light restraint where sudden wealth tempted and the reins of government were weak. There were no land laws, mining titles were disputed, organized bands of ruffians terrorized the community. As Taylor said, it was imperative "to substitute the rule of law and order there for the bowie-knife and revolvers." The need in the remainder of the ceded territory, known as New Mexico, was less urgent, but it was plainly desirable that its political organization be effected without unnecessary delay.

Without waiting for Congress to assemble, President Taylor with soldierly directness endeavored to simplify the situation by counseling the people of California and New Mexico to frame state constitutions and seek immediate admission to the Union. His purpose was to save Congress the vexatious problem of the status of slavery prior to statehood, since all parties recognized the right of the people to make their own decision when they adopted a state constitution. California needed no urging, and in October, 1849, a state constitution prohibiting slavery was adopted and later ratified, subject, of course, to the consent of Congress. The action of New Mexico was more tardy, but in May, 1850, a free-soil constitution was framed and ratified for the consideration of Congress. When Congress met in December, 1849, Taylor recommended statehood for both districts as soon as their constitutions should be submitted to that body.

The situation was not susceptible of such simple solution, however. The fiercest sectional antagonism had been kindled by the exciting discussions of the last few years in Congress, and the original problem of territorial adjustments had become entangled and complicated with certain collateral questions affecting slavery. One of these concerned the boundary between Texas and New Mexico. Although the federal government had maintained the Rio Grande boundary from mouth to source in its dealings with Mexico in 1845, this line had been ignored when the United States established a military government in New Mexico at Santa Fe during the war. The antislavery members in Congress were in full agreement with the latter policy, for, since Texas was slave soil, they were anxious to confine its area to the narrowest limits. But the Texans were bitterly resentful, and harbored an additional grievance because of the refusal of the United States to assume their war debt at the time of annexation, when Texas surrendered her chief source of revenue, the customs duties, to the federal government.

Another question involved the existence of slavery in the District of Columbia. To the Southerners slaveholding seemed right and proper in this area, since the land had originally belonged to Maryland, and the capital city was inclosed on all sides by slave territory. But to their opponents it seemed an ugly blot on the national escutcheon, and for many years the antislavery petitions to Congress had had as their purpose the elimination of this evil.

A final source of contention arose from the growing difficulty encountered by slaveowners in the recovery of runaway slaves. In the case of Prigg *v.* Pennsylvania, the Supreme Court had held in 1842 that the master of a slave had a right to regain him under the Act of 1793 without obstruction from any conflicting state laws, but it had also decided that the federal statute did not require state authorities to assist in the rendition of fugitives. Some Northern legislatures thereupon withdrew the use of state magistrates, prosecutors, and jails in fugitive-slave cases. This, along with the heightened efficiency of the Underground Railroad, necessitated the adoption of a new and stronger fugitive-slave law, if that provision of the Constitution was to mean anything.

Nor was the excitement over these questions confined to the halls of Congress. Throughout the South, resolutions denouncing antislavery aggression were adopted by mass meetings and state legislatures, and the cry of disunion was raised with increasing frequency and violence. A state convention of Mississippi called a Southern "popular convention" to meet at Nashville, Tennessee, in June, 1850, to consider what action should be taken to meet the crisis. In the North public sentiment was equally tense. The legislatures of all the free states excepting Iowa passed resolutions favoring Congressional prohibition of slavery in the territories, and a number of them demanded action looking toward the abolition of slavery in the District of Columbia.

The Compromise of 1850

The responsibility of harmonizing these jangling interests fell upon a Congress whose passions were deeply stirred by the reiterated appeals to sectional prejudice. Perhaps no Senate of the United States has contained more distinguished men than the one which began its sessions in December, 1849. In it were Webster, Clay, Calhoun, and Benton, giants of an era fast departing, and Jefferson Davis and Stephen A. Douglas, who within a decade were to head the wings of a hopelessly divided Democracy. There, too, were Chase and Seward, destined to become the chiefs of a party yet unformed. The Free Soilers, led by Joshua R. Giddings, held the balance of power in the House, and a contest of three weeks was necessary before Howell Cobb, a Georgia Democrat of moderate views, was chosen Speaker.

The hopes of the nation rested on the aged Henry Clay, who had just been reëlected to the Senate after an absence of seven years. Viewing the troubled scene with eyes illumined with the calm wisdom of his years, he arose in his seat on January 29, 1850, and offered his famous resolutions for compromise. Though his plan comprised eight parts in all, his main proposals may be summarized as follows: (1) California should be admitted with her free-soil constitution; (2) territorial governments should be established in the remainder of the Mexican cessions, and "as slavery does not exist by law and is not likely to be introduced" there, Congress should take no action either for the introduction or the exclusion of slavery; (3) Texas should yield in her boundary dispute with New Mexico, in return for which the United States would assume the Texan debt contracted prior to annexation; (4) the slave trade, but not slavery, should be abolished in the District of Columbia; and (5) Congress should enact a more effective fugitive-slave law.

A significant and memorable debate followed, lasting through many weeks. In a speech of February 5 and 6, Clay, beginning with faltering voice but gaining strength with his theme, pointed to the ominous spectacle of the state legislatures, "twenty-odd furnaces in full blast generating heat and passion and intemperance," and called upon the two sections to make mutual concessions for the sake of the Union. He denied vigorously the right or possibility of peaceful secession. Analyzing the compromise resolutions in detail, he maintained that the proposals formed a middle ground honorable to both groups. When he concluded, a great throng of men and women, many of whom had come long distances to hear him, rushed forward to shake his hand and embrace him.

On March 4, Calhoun with the shadow of death already upon him appeared, too ill to read his own address but still full of that grim energy which had made him the foremost champion of cotton capitalism in his generation. He charged that the present crisis had been brought about by Northern aggression, which had succeeded in banishing slavery from nearly three fourths of the territory added to the original states. In the recent schisms in the Methodist and Baptist churches, he saw the first snapping of the cords of union. As for the proposed compromise, he branded it as a betrayal of his section. The Southerners could be satisfied with nothing less than a stoppage of antislavery propaganda, a faithful execution of the Fugitive Slave Act, the enjoyment of equal rights with Northerners in the acquired territories, and an amendment to the Constitution restoring the former equality of the sections. In making this last proposal, he had in mind a provision for the election of dual presidents, one from the slaveholding and one from the free states, each with a veto on the acts of Congress.

On March 7, Webster, the third of the great triumvirate, entered the lists. Clay had consulted him before offering his resolutions to the Senate, and Webster now marshaled his vast oratorical powers in behalf of conciliation. He met Calhoun's charge of Northern aggrandizement by pointing out that "the general lead in the politics of the country, for three-fourths of the period . . . since the adoption of the Constitution, has been a Southern lead." In words reminiscent of his reply to Hayne, he denied that peaceful secession was possible. But he addressed himself particularly to the task of making the compromise acceptable to the free states. He deplored the violence of abolition agitation, admitted that the Northern people had failed in their duty of returning fugitive slaves, and declared that "an ordinance of nature" had settled, "beyond all terms of human enactment, that slavery cannot exist in California or New Mexico."

The "Seventh-of-March Speech" came as a thunderclap to the antislavery men of New England, who had hoped that Webster would assume the leadership of the opponents of slavery extension. He was denounced by public meetings on every hand, and Whittier expressed the thought of thousands when he wrote in his poem, "Ichabod":

> All else is gone; from those great eyes
> The soul has fled:
> When faith is lost, when honor dies,
> The man is dead!

But such people strangely misapprehended the real significance of Webster's career. Though he had shown his personal convictions by disapproving of the Mexican War and supporting the Wilmot Proviso, the religion of his life was his devotion to an indivisible American nationality. To him, politics was a matter of the patient adjustment of interests, and when the Union was in jeopardy, he sank all lesser issues in the greater one. Indeed, his speech struck a responsive chord in the hearts of people of moderate views throughout the land.

The debate over the compromise now became general. Douglas, the Illinois Democrat, gave his support to its passage, whereas the Mississippi Democrat, Jefferson Davis, joined Calhoun in the opposition. Benton, however, denounced the pro-Southern features of the compromise. The antislavery extremists found spokesmen in two Senators serving their first terms — Seward, the New York Whig, and Chase of Ohio, who owed his election to a combination of Free Soilers and Democrats. Denying that the Constitution recognized human bondage, these men demanded that the territories remain free soil, and Seward created a sensation with his defiant assertion that for antislavery men "there is a higher law than the Constitution." These words, in the succeeding decade, were to become a rallying cry of the opponents of slavery.

On April 18, 1850, the compromise resolutions were referred to a Senate committee of thirteen with Clay as Chairman. On May 8 the committee made its report in the form of three bills. The first of these — at once dubbed the "Omnibus Bill" — dealt with all the questions affecting the newly acquired Southwest. California should be admitted with its free-soil constitution;

the remainder of the region should be divided at the thirty-seventh parallel into the two territories of New Mexico and Utah, and organized without mention of slavery; and the claims of Texas to a portion of New Mexico should be satisfied by a payment of ten million dollars. The second bill provided for a stringent fugitive-slave act, and the third, for the prohibition of the slave traffic in the District of Columbia.

These definite proposals seemed for the time to have little effect on the Senate. The tempests of sectional passion continued to rage unabated, and although there were majorities for the separate measures of the "Omnibus Bill," it proved impossible to secure a majority vote for all of them taken together. Fortunately, other conditions and events now began to make their influence felt. The convention of nine slaveholding states, which met at Nashville on June 3, was dominated by moderates, and called merely for the westward extension of the line 36° 30′. On July 9 the President died unexpectedly, and was succeeded by Fillmore, who, unlike Taylor, favored the compromise, and whose approval plainly appeared in his appointment of Webster as Secretary of State. Under these auspicious circumstances the various proposals comprising the compromise plan were embodied in separate measures, and, one after another, passed Congress, in most cases by decisive majorities. Between the ninth and twentieth of September all the bills became laws with the President's signature.

It may well be asked which side gained the major advantage from the sectional bargain of 1850, and the answer is not easy to give. The outlawing of the slave traffic in the District of Columbia might be balanced against the drastic Fugitive Slave Act. The boundary concession of Texas was offset by the federal gift of ten million dollars. But the crux of the settlement was the provision made for the newly acquired Southwest. Here the North won a clear advantage in the admission of California, for thereby the nation-old balance of free and slave states in the Senate was destroyed.

In the case of New Mexico and Utah, however, the essence of the compromise lay in a postponement of the issue. Territorial governments were authorized, with the proviso that the territories should eventually be admitted as states "with or without slavery,

THE STATUS OF SLAVERY AFTER THE COMPROMISE OF 1850

as their constitution may prescribe at the time of their admission." But Congress did not specify whether slavery might or might not exist in these regions prior to statehood, and instead, merely provided that all cases arising which involved title to slave property should be referred to the Supreme Court. To that tribunal, then, was left the question of the legality of slavery in the new territories. In this disposition of the matter, the various antagonistic factions found crumbs of comfort, for each was convinced that its own peculiar interpretation of the Constitution would be sustained by judicial sanction.

From the standpoint of posterity, however, the fact of supreme importance was that a peace had once more been patched up between the sections, and the fateful crisis postponed ten years. Had the South seceded in 1850, it may well be doubted whether the Northern people were as yet sufficiently united in opinion to wage a war to preserve the Union.

The Appeal to the Country

The Compromise had the sanction of Congress; it remained to be seen whether the general public acquiesced in the decision. Fortunately, the material conditions of the country were conducive to a cessation of sectional bickering, for the country was entering on an era of great prosperity. The gold discoveries in California, by swelling the country's specie supply, had stimulated industry, advanced wages, and raised the general level of prices. The repeal of the English "Corn Laws" in 1846 — coincident with the Walker Tariff — was another factor in the business advance, for thereby an unimpeded market was opened for our surplus grain. For this the farmers were prepared as a result of an ever wider application of machinery to the work of harvesting. Manufacturing shared in the general prosperity; indeed, in 1850, the annual value of American factory products temporarily passed that of agriculture. To the commercial and financial interests of the country the slavery controversy was a seriously disturbing factor — it was "bad for business." Lulled by a sense of material well-being, the American people turned, with profound relief, to the pleasant task of wooing the profits of industry.

Nevertheless, the political leaders left no stone unturned to make the Compromise acceptable to the country. In January, 1851, a pledge was signed by forty-four Congressmen of both parties, declaring their opposition to any candidate for public office, who did not regard the Compromise as a final disposition of the slavery question. Thirty-four of the signers were from the slave states. In the North the principal objection to the Compromise was the drastic Fugitive Slave Act, and upon this law was poured out the wrath of all unreconciled antislavery people. But under the leadership of Webster, Douglas, and Cass, conservative opinion rallied to the cause of harmony. Giant "union meetings," held in New York, Boston, and other cities, approved the Compromise measures, and pledged a rigid execution of the Fugitive Slave Act.

The irreconcilable element was stronger in the South, where, of course, the objections were based upon quite different grounds. In 1850–1852, special state conventions met in Georgia, Mississippi, Alabama, and South Carolina to consider the advisability of secession. The admission of California was an especially bitter pill for the Southerners. The stormiest contests occurred in South Carolina, Georgia, and Mississippi, but gradually the sober second thought of the people everywhere asserted itself in favor of conciliation. The temper of the section was best expressed by the resolutions drawn up by the Georgia convention in 1850, widely known as the "Georgia Platform." These resolutions yielded grudging adherence to the Compromise measures, but served notice on the North that a lax enforcement of the Fugitive Slave Act or any further restrictions by Congress on slavery would be resisted, "even to the disruption of the Union."

The presidential election of 1852 gave the people another chance to express themselves. The Democrats entered the campaign with a united front, for the Van Buren faction, which had bolted the party in 1848, was now back in the fold. At their Baltimore convention on June 1, they adopted a platform which affirmed the Compromise measures, including the Fugitive Slave Act, to be a final settlement of the slavery question. Cass, Buchanan, and Douglas were the chief contenders for the nomination.

With scant respect for the gray hairs of the veteran statesmen, Douglas's candidacy was represented by his supporters as a contest between "Young America" and "Old Fogyism." So evenly was the convention divided that none of the three could be chosen, and after forty-nine ballots the nomination went, almost by default, to Franklin Pierce, a "dark horse." Pierce was a handsome and prepossessing man of average attainments, a supporter of Polk's imperialistic policy, who, after serving in the New Hampshire legislature and in Congress, had taken some part in the Mexican War. William R. King of Alabama was named for Vice-President.

The Whigs came together two weeks later in the same city, but the shadow of dissolution was already upon them. Through superior strategy, the Southern delegates managed to foist a platform on the convention, which committed the party of Webster and Clay to the doctrine of state rights. Like their opponents, the Whigs also declared for the maintenance of the Compromise measures, including the Fugitive Slave Act. The Northern faction, however, succeeded after fifty-three ballots in nominating its candidate, Winfield Scott, over the heads of Fillmore and Webster, either of whom would have represented in a special sense the inviolability of the Compromise. William A. Graham of North Carolina was chosen for the second place.

One dissonant note alone was heard in this chorus of sectional concord. The remnants of the Free Soil party, calling themselves "Free Democrats," nominated John P. Hale of New Hampshire, on a platform which repudiated the Compromise and demanded free labor and free homesteads in the federal territories.

From the first, Democratic victory was assured. The Southern Whigs were openly suspicious of Scott's antislavery support in the North, and Northern Whig opinion of the situation was best expressed in the popular saying, "We accept the candidate but spit upon the platform." Scott exerted himself to curry favor with the new German and Irish voters, but his fulsome compliments only exposed him to the ridicule of the Democrats. Equally futile were the efforts of his party managers to create enthusiasm for him as the hero of two wars. Pierce received 254 votes to 42 for his opponent, the largest majority in the electoral college since Monroe's almost unanimous election in 1820. The popular support of the Free Democrats showed a loss of nearly one half from the last election. The people had declared unqualifiedly for the finality of the Compromise, and apparently a new era of good feeling was at hand.

SELECT BIBLIOGRAPHY

A National Crisis, 1849–1852. The best account of the Compromise of 1850 and its background is perhaps that found in J. F. Rhodes, *History of the United States*, I (New York, 1892). A better understanding of the slavery adjustments in Utah and New Mexico may, however, be gained from Hermann von Holst, *The Constitutional and Political History of the United States*, III (Chicago, 1881), or Carl Schurz, *Henry Clay* (Boston, 1899), II. Edward Channing, *A History of the United States*, VI (New York, 1925), treats the period 1848–1865 in the light of the latest researches.

S. E. White's readable volume, *The Forty-Niners* (in *The Chronicles of America*, XXV, New Haven, 1918), is a dependable treatment of the California gold-rush.

On party politics the standard histories and biographies are helpful. A special study is R. F. Nichols, *The Democratic Machine, 1850–1854* (in *Columbia University Studies*, CXI, no. 1, New York, 1923). M. J. White, *The Secession Movement in the United States, 1847–1852* (New Orleans, 1916), contains much of value on that subject.

CHAPTER IX

THE UNDOING OF THE SECTIONAL TRUCE, 1852–1856

EUROPE IN FERMENT

Many influences were at work to destroy the sectional adjustment of 1850 almost as soon as it was consummated. From a world point of view, the middle of the nineteenth century was a time of reform and innovation rather than of conservatism and compromise. The twin forces of democracy and nationalism, which had shaken Europe with popular upheavals in 1830, had paused temporarily, only to generate a new and more formidable series of uprisings in 1848, the so-called "Year of Revolutions." Fifteen separate revolts took place in the latter year, with varying degrees of success.

A revolution of the French people founded the Second Republic on a basis of manhood suffrage, though this victory was followed four years later by the establishment of a new monarchy under Louis Napoleon. The oppressed nationalities under the rule of Austria seethed with revolt. As the result of popular tumults in Vienna, the Hapsburg Emperor in great fright granted a constitution, which, however, he later rescinded. Hungary declared a republic, and under the leadership of the heroic Louis Kossuth, waged a gallant but unsuccessful war for independence. All Italy was swept with a storm of resolve to throw off the Austrian yoke, but a succession of rebellions ended in failure.

A similar fate met a promising revolutionary movement in the disjoined German States to create a united, liberalized Fatherland. Outbreaks were forestalled in Holland and Denmark only by the foresight of the monarchs in appeasing the popular demands. In Switzerland an attempt at secession was put down by armed force, but a new constitution was adopted, making of the Swiss communities a strong, compact, federal union.

Even Great Britain was shaken by the current unrest. The Reform Act of 1832 had conferred no benefits on the working classes, and encouraged by the commotions on the Continent, the "Chartists" (as they called themselves) demanded a further democratization of the British government, including manhood suffrage. Reform, however, was not to come until 1867.

Although the "Year of Revolutions" yielded few immediate tangible gains for popular rights, the foundations of the Old Order were irretrievably shaken, and the next twenty years — so momentous in the history of our own country — were to witness the triumph of the nationalist ideal and important advances toward the goal of democracy in all the great states of Europe. The people of the United States watched with approval these stirring events across the Atlantic, for the same forces of democracy and nationality that were struggling to remake Europe were also the moving principles of American development. The national Democratic convention of 1848 sent "fraternal congratulations" to the new French Republic, and rejoiced that the spirit of popular rule was "prostrating thrones and erecting republics on the ruins of despotism in the Old World."

Two years later Daniel Webster, as Secretary of State, sent a note to Austria, justifying the right of the American people "to cherish always a lively interest in the fortunes of nations struggling for institutions like their own," and declaring grandiloquently that, compared with free America, "the possessions of the House of Hapsburg are but as a patch on the earth's surface." To friends, Webster defended the boastful tone of this letter by his desire to "touch the national pride" and shame Americans "who should speak of disunion."

President Fillmore, by authorization of Congress, sent a warship to Turkey to convey the exiled Hungarian patriot, Kossuth, to the United States. Arriving in December, 1851, Kossuth was tendered great public ovations in the Eastern cities, was dined by the President in Washington, and was formally received by each house of Congress. Nevertheless, it was made clear to him that the American people still considered the Atlantic Ocean a barrier to armed intervention in the internal affairs of Europe, and that his cause must derive what benefit it could from their moral support and pecuniary contributions.

The Coming of the Foreigners

The revolutionary disturbances of 1830, and particularly of 1848, sent thousands of refugees flying to America. The greatly increased immigration of this period, however, was due principally to bad economic conditions abroad. The number of annual arrivals rose from 23,000 in 1830 to 84,000 in 1840 and to 297,000 in 1849, reaching floodtide in 1854 with 428,000. In the decade from 1845 to 1855, the newcomers totaled approximately three millions, as compared with hardly more than one third of that number in the entire preceding period of national independence. A sympathetic observer, writing in the *Democratic Review* in 1850, declared that "from every degree of latitude and of longitude, and from every isle and continent under the whole heaven, the flood of emigration has poured in upon the United States. . . . There has been nothing like it in appearance since the encampment of the Roman empire, or the tents of the Crusaders."

Most of the immigrants were desperately poor, and the voyage across the Atlantic exposed them to hardships and sufferings which severely tested their mettle. Although Scandinavians and other European nationalities were to be found among the newcomers, and on the Pacific Coast Chinese coolie laborers were being eagerly welcomed to perform the menial labor of the gold-mad whites, the great mass of the immigrants consisted of German peasants and workingmen dissatisfied with economic or political conditions in the Fatherland, and of peasants from central and southern Ireland, embittered by British rule or forced to leave because of the potato famines of 1847 and later.

In the decade following the German Revolution of 1848, nearly one million Germans arrived in the United States, among them Carl Schurz, Franz Sigel, and other leaders of education and ability. Most of them settled in the newer parts of the country north of the Ohio River, or beyond the Mississippi. St. Louis, Milwaukee, Cincinnati, and Cleveland attracted strong colonies, and in nearly one half the cities of Ohio the Germans and the "Pennsylvania Dutch" (descendants of German immigrants of colonial days) held nearly or quite the balance of political power. However, the bulk of the Germans sought the soil, usually in company with their countrymen, and proved to be hardy and successful pioneers. Wherever they went, they carried with them their zeal for schools and education, their love of music, and the liberal social customs of the homeland. Some of them took an active part in the agitation for free homesteads.

The Irish immigrants, on the other hand, chose to remain in the crowded cities of the North Atlantic Seaboard, or else became workers on turnpikes, canals, and railroads. Indeed, the hard manual labor upon the great public improvements of the time was performed mainly by the Irish. They lived, for the most part, in conditions of wretched poverty in the Eastern cities; and everywhere they settled, they added to the traditional anti-British feeling of Americans their own bitter hatred of that country — a fact that was quickly observed and capitalized by vote-seeking politicans.

This sudden growth of immigration inevitably begot a strong nativist or antiforeign sentiment on the part of Americans of older stock. In the seaboard manufacturing districts the workingmen were dismayed by the influx of cheap Irish laborers with their lower standard of living. Moreover, most of the Irish were Catholics, and the rapid increase of Catholic churches, convents, and parochial schools caused widespread apprehension in New England and the Middle Atlantic states. The ease with which unscrupulous native politicians managed to corrupt newly naturalized voters gave further cause for alarm, and seemed to threaten the integrity of American republican institutions.

In the West, the chief source of friction grew out of the unfamiliar social customs of the Germans, especially their laxity with respect to the Sabbath — practices which ran counter to the inherited Puritan austerity of the older inhabitants. Though the existence of slave labor caused most of the immigrants to avoid the Southern states, there, too, nativist feeling flourished. The slaveholders ascribed the alarming growth of Northern population to the large foreign infusions, and viewed immigration as an inexhaustible stream which would fill up the federal territories with the enemies of slavery.[1]

[1] A Southern editor claimed in 1855 that immigration was increasing the population of the free states to an extent that would entitle that section to five additional members of Congress and of the electoral college every year.

As early as the thirties, the feeling against the Irish had broken out in the form of mob violence. In 1834 a convent in Charlestown, Massachusetts, was burned. Three years later the Irish quarter of Boston was sacked, and similar outrages occurred in other Eastern centers. The movement got into local politics, and on one or two occasions "Native American" parties were formed in New York and Philadelphia to prevent the election of naturalized citizens to municipal office. In 1845 a national organization of Native Americans was effected, which claimed a membership of more than one hundred thousand;[1] and in 1850 the movement assumed the guise of a secret society under the name, known only to its members, of the "Supreme Order of the Star-Spangled Banner." For a few years, the society showed little sign of thriving, although presently, under unexpected circumstances, it was to form the backbone of the spectacular Know-Nothing movement.

The deeper significance of this peaceful foreign invasion was not, however, to be found in the short-lived manifestations of nativist feeling, but in the influence of the alien elements on the growing sectional controversy. From 1850 to 1860 the foreign-born population of the United States increased eighty-four per cent, and most of these newcomers massed themselves in the states and territories of the North. There they naturally gravitated to the party that opposed slavery and strove for an indivisible Union, for they were unaccustomed to slavery in Europe and many of them were veterans of wars for national unification. Moreover, they brought with them the traditions of a defiant and bitter republicanism. Temporarily many of them joined the Democratic ranks because of the appeal of the party name; but as the issue between the sections became increasingly clear, they gave their support to the antislavery cause, and after the organization of the Republican party, thronged into it.

The Rise of a New Generation

Of greater immediate danger to the maintenance of sectional harmony was the advent of a new generation to the control of

[1] Taylor was indorsed by the Native Americans in 1848, and in 1852 they nominated Daniel Webster, though without asking his permission. Upon his death before the election, they substituted the name of one Jacob Broom of Philadelphia. Less than three thousand votes were polled.

public affairs. By the close of 1852, the master figures of the older generation had passed from the political scene. Calhoun died in the Compromise year, Clay and Webster followed before Pierce's election. Van Buren was definitely out of politics after his party treason in 1848, and Benton was retired by Missouri from the Senate in 1851 after thirty years of service. Calhoun excepted, the distinguishing trait of these men had been their single-minded devotion to the Union, for their public life had been shaped by the dominant nationalism which had marked the years from the second war with Great Britain to the close of Van Buren's presidency.

The new leaders, however, had been reared in an era of sectional controversy. Young in years and experience, they lacked the poise and caution of the older statesmen, and they faced the problems of the age with all the arrogant assurance which fresh generations bring to a consideration of weighty public issues. On the central question of the time they held intense convictions, and felt lightly the obligation of maintaining a sectional peace that had been dictated by the leaders of a departed era.

The new generation, moreover, represented two radically different points of view. From the free states came Seward of New York, Chase of Ohio, Sumner of Massachusetts, and Thaddeus Stevens of Pennsylvania, all of whom entered Congress in the years from 1849–1851 as uncompromising foes of slavery extension and relentless antagonists of the "Slave Power." Though ever professing to uphold the Union, they were ready to risk harmony and peace within the Union for the sake of righting what they considered a terrible wrong.

Southern interests were no less ardently upheld by Davis of Mississippi, on whom fell the mantle of Calhoun, and by W. L. Yancey of Alabama, and Alexander H. Stephens, Robert Toombs, and Howell Cobb of Georgia. These men frankly measured the value of the Union in terms of the welfare of their section, and on every occasion proclaimed the right of secession as a measure of redress for the South. The Compromise ideals of the preceding era were perhaps best represented by John J. Crittenden of Kentucky, Clay's successor in the Senate, and by John Bell, Senator from Tennessee, men of lesser stature than the sectional champions.

Stephen Arnold Douglas, the Illinois Senator, is a man harder to classify, but he was one of the regnant political figures of the epoch. Idolized by Western Democrats as the "Little Giant," he embodied in his person the two ideals so dear to the frontier: enthusiastic attachment to nationality, and an unfaltering faith in local self-rule as a solvent of human ills. As the foremost Democrat in the free states, his position gave him an unusual opportunity to act as a conciliator and arbiter between Northern radicals and Southern "fire-eaters."

The fifties, however, were not a time when a man who sought a middle ground between extremes could attain success — certainly not a man who, like Douglas, failed utterly to comprehend the intensity of the moral opposition to slavery. His solution for the slavery question in the territories, that of "popular sovereignty," showed that in his social thinking he had not advanced beyond the democratic philosophy of Jackson's day. Yet Douglas's patriotism cannot be doubted by posterity, and his formula deserved a better reception than it received from his contemporaries. A believer in the destiny of the West and an examplar of its aspirations, he retained his hold on his section unshaken until Abraham Lincoln emerged from private life in 1858.

Despite the twenty years of abolitionist propaganda, the new antislavery leaders had a vast amount of inertia and indifference to overcome in the North if their cause was to be successful. To this end, certain literary forces were of incalculable value. The first of these was the advent of a new type of journalism. By 1850 the official party organs, located at Washington and subsidized by government printing, were rapidly on the decline, to be entirely discarded at the close of the decade. Such journals made dull reading for any but bigoted partisans, and their high subscription price further narrowed the circle of their influence. The gradual assumption by the government itself, after 1846, of the task of executing the public printing contributed to the eclipse of the old-fashioned party papers,[1] but more important in bringing this about were the improved news facilities resulting from the telegraph and the railroad, the rise of New York as a financial

[1] The office of Superintendent of Public Printing was created in 1852, and the Government Printing Office was established in 1860.

and news center, and the creation of a great reading public through the free public schools.

The new journalism flowered most luxuriantly in New York, and unlike today, most of the newspapers were owned by their editors. Selling at a price within the reach of all, the newspapers sought to make a broad popular appeal with headlines, attractive news "stories," and trenchant editorials.[1] The period produced the greatest editorial writers in our history — men like Greeley of the *New York Tribune*, Henry J. Raymond of the *New York Times*, James Gordon Bennett of the *New York Herald*, Samuel Bowles of the *Springfield* (Massachusetts) *Republican*, J. W. Forney of the *Philadelphia Press*, and Joseph Medill of the *Chicago Tribune*. William Cullen Bryant, who as editor of the *New York Evening Post* had been an exemplar of vigorous independent journalism since 1826, continued to make a special appeal to the educated classes in the East.

In national circulation and influence no other newspaper approached the *Tribune*, edited by the brilliant and eccentric Greeley. He was by temperament a reformer, and none of the agitations of the time, from spiritualism to scientific farming and Irish freedom, failed to challenge his interest. But his soul-consuming passion was his detestation of slavery, and to this cause he gave increasingly of his attention during the fifties. The circulation of his newspaper increased five-fold from 1850 to 1860; its sectional character is shown by the fact that practically all of its subscribers lived in the free states. The weekly edition was preëminently the journal of the rural districts of the North, which regarded it as a sort of political Bible. The antislavery forces could not have found a more effective vehicle of agitation and education.

No less important in accounting for the change of Northern sentiment was the appearance of that great propagandist novel, *Uncle Tom's Cabin*, written by Harriet Beecher Stowe of Cincinnati, Ohio. Composed with great intensity of feeling, the book did not picture the average condition of the slave, but showed, by melodramatic contrast, the best and worst possibilities of his

[1] The *New York Sun* was the pioneer among the "penny papers," beginning its career as early as 1833. Of the newspapers mentioned later in the paragraph, all were founded prior to 1850 except the *New York Times* (1851) and the *Philadelphia Press* (1857). Medill formed his connection with the *Chicago Tribune* in 1855.

life. The story, first appearing as a serial in the *National Era*, an antislavery newspaper at the capital, was published in book form in March, 1852. At once it began its record-breaking career with a sale of three hundred thousand copies in the first year. The stage possibilities of the story appealed first to the theatrical managers, and then to the political managers, and presently thousands of men and boys who never read a book were thrilled and swayed by the dramatized version. Mrs. Stowe's interpretation of the slavery system was of immeasurable influence in shaping the thinking of Northern youths who came of voting age in the years from 1852 to 1860; in the South it was anathema.

The Revival of Sectional Discord

The first active steps toward a disturbance of the sectional accord were taken by moral enthusiasts of the North in defiance of the new Fugitive Slave Act. Inasmuch as the Supreme Court had decided in Prigg *v.* Pennsylvania (see page 120) that state authorities need not assist in the capture of runaways, the Act of 1850 clothed the federal government with far-reaching powers for the purpose, and the negro whose freedom was at stake was denied trial by jury or other ordinary opportunities of establishing his innocence. The law was energetically put into operation by the slaveowners. In some instances, fugitives who had been living in the North for a number of years and had married there were seized under the statute, and carried away into slavery again.

Northern communities, which thus saw some of the worst features of the slavery system enacted before their very eyes, were easily incited to riotous opposition. One of the cases that occasioned nationwide attention occurred in Boston in February, 1851, when a runaway named Shadrach was rescued from the United States marshal by a mob, and spirited away into Canada. In October of the same year, Jerry McHenry, a negro who had been several years a resident of Syracuse, New York, was arrested as an escaped slave, but a mob led by Gerrit Smith effected his rescue, and saw him safely on his way to the Canadian border.

When President Pierce was sworn into office on March 4, 1853, he expressed the fervent hope in his inaugural address that "no sectional or ambitious or fanatical excitement may again threaten the durability of our institutions or obscure the light of our prosperity." Yet some of his first acts aroused serious misgivings as to his good faith. In making up his cabinet he first offered the post of Secretary of State to a New York Democrat tinctured with Free-Soil-ism; but under pressure of Southern leaders, he reversed his decision, and gave the place to William L. Marcy, a New York proslavery Democrat. To the important position of Secretary of War he appointed Jefferson Davis, who had been an implacable opponent of the Compromise.[1]

Furthermore, in his inaugural address, Pierce hinted broadly at the desirability of tropical expansion as a bulwark to "obvious national interest and security." He thereby made known that he was an apostle of the doctrine of "Manifest Destiny," aspiring to carry out the imperialistic plans that Polk and his Secretary of State, Buchanan, had inaugurated. This utterance struck a popular chord with the Southern planters. Although plans for tropical expansion had received little encouragement from the Whigs when in power, certain irrepressible spirits among the Southern people had fitted out filibustering expeditions during the years 1851–1853 in a fruitless effort to help the Cubans cast off the yoke of Spain.

With the assistance of his Secretary of State, Pierce prepared to translate his words into action. In August, 1854, Buchanan, Pierre Soulé, and John Y. Mason, the American ministers to Great Britain, Spain, and France, were instructed to confer on the best means of acquiring Cuba. Meeting together in Belgium in October, they drew up a remarkable document, known in history as the "Ostend Manifesto." Their recommendation was, in brief, that if Spain refused to sell Cuba to the United States, "by every law, human and divine, we shall be justified in wresting it from Spain, if we possess the power." The administration was not prepared to go to such lengths. The recommendation was coldly pigeonholed, but it produced wild excitement in the free states when its contents became public.

The net result of the efforts at expansion southward was an

[1] The other members of his cabinet were: James Guthrie of Kentucky, Secretary of the Treasury; James C. Dobbin of North Carolina, Secretary of the Navy; Robert McClelland of Michigan, Secretary of the Interior; James Campbell of Pennsylvania, Postmaster-General; Caleb Cushing of Massachusetts, Attorney-General.

acquisition of minor importance. In 1853 James Gadsden, representing the United States, purchased from Mexico at a cost of ten million dollars a strip of land lying to the south of the Gila River. By this act a boundary dispute was settled with Mexico, and the United States acquired a tract of land which, according to surveys of the War Department, was needful for the building of a transcontinental railroad along a southern route.

The Repeal of the Missouri Compromise

While the conditions and influences that have been set forth show that a revival of sectional strife was unavoidable, the dramatic incident that brought affairs to a sharp crisis occurred several months before the movement for Cuban annexation had reached the stage of the Ostend Manifesto. This was the passage of the Kansas-Nebraska Act.

The region lying between the Iowa-Missouri boundary and the Rocky Mountains had never been provided with territorial organization, and remained, for the most part, a vast reserve for wild Indians and roving buffaloes. Situated north of the line 36° 30′, the entire domain was potentially free soil by the Compromise of 1820. The need for extinguishing the Indian title and opening the country to white settlement was becoming urgent at mid-century. As population increased in the Mississippi Valley, ambitious spirits began to look to the virgin lands farther west. Furthermore, national security rendered desirable a continuous zone of settlement from the heart of the nation to the far-flung communities on the Pacific Coast. Already a transcontinental wagon route (the "California and Oregon Trail") traversed the region, and men of vision were agitating for the construction of a transcontinental railroad, with government aid.

On January 4, 1854, Douglas as Chairman of the Senate Committee on Territories introduced a bill for the organization of this entire region as the "Territory of Nebraska," and an accompanying report explained that it was intended that slavery in the proposed territory should be dealt with according to the basic principles of the Compromise of 1850. According to Douglas, these were: (1) the right of the territorial legislature to admit or exclude slavery (popular sovereignty), and (2) that all cases involving the ownership of slaves should be settled ultimately by the Supreme Court.

The measure excited a storm of criticism and protest, and in order to win the majority vote necessary for its passage, Douglas proceeded to make certain alterations in his bill. In its final form, the measure proposed the creation, not of a single territory, but of two territories, Kansas and Nebraska, with the fortieth parallel as the dividing line. The Missouri Compromise was explicitly repealed, and the people of the territories were authorized to regulate their domestic institutions as they chose, "subject only to the Constitution of the United States." All questions involving title to slaves might be appealed to the Supreme Court.

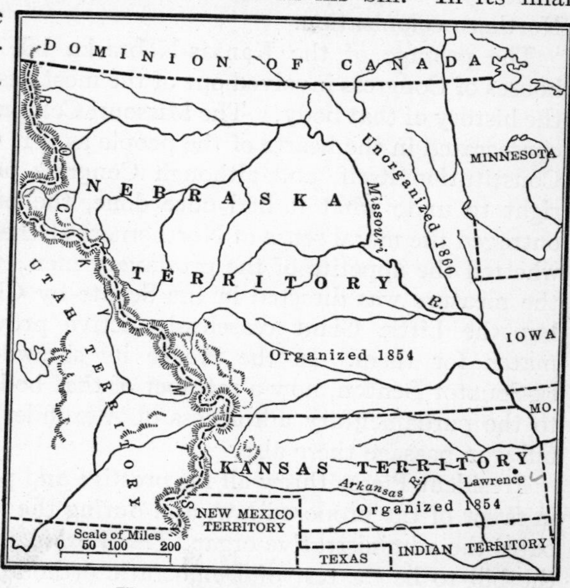

KANSAS AND NEBRASKA, 1854

From the standpoint of practical politics, Douglas undoubtedly won favor for his cause by claiming that the slavery regulations of 1850 for New Mexico and Utah had been intended as a rule of universal application; but the historian finds no warrant for this assumption. Furthermore, he was on extremely doubtful ground in reading his own doctrine of popular sovereignty into the territorial settlement of 1850 (see pages 125–126). Indeed, not all who supported the Kansas-Nebraska Act believed that popular sovereignty would be the outcome. For example, Senator A. G. Brown of Mississippi said, "If I thought that in voting for the bill as it now stands, I was conceding the right of the people in a territory to exclude slavery I would withhold my vote. . . . It leaves the question where I am willing it should be left — to the ultimate decision of the courts." The provision for two territories in place of one helped to facilitate passage, for it was believed that Kansas, lying next to Missouri, would become slave soil, and Nebraska be left to the slower processes of Northern colonization.

The passage of the Kansas-Nebraska bill through the two houses of Congress involved one of the most desperate contests in the history of that body. The Missouri Compromise had become consecrated in the hearts of the people as if it were a part of the Constitution itself, and although Congress possessed the legal right to undo what it had once done, the proposal for repeal outraged the moral sense of Northerners at the same time that it whetted the appetite of the proslavery men. The fight against the measure was directed in the Senate by Chase and Sumner, but the Little Giant ceaselessly active proved more than a match for them. In the House its shrewdest assailant was ex-Senator Benton, now a member of that body, but due largely to the parliamentary adroitness of Alexander H. Stephens, the bill won passage there also.

President Pierce threw all his prestige and power of patronage in favor of the proposed law, and during the progress of the debates the administrative organ, *The Washington Union*, declared the bill to be "a test of Democratic orthodoxy." An analysis of the voting shows that it was passed with the support of a practically solid South, assisted by many of the Democrats of the old Northwest. The bill, which became a law on May 30, 1854, was clearly a Democratic measure; but throughout the struggle, party considerations had been secondary to sectional advantage.

So far-reaching were the effects of the Kansas-Nebraska Act that the motives which led to its introduction are a matter of continuing interest. At the time, Douglas was accused by his antislavery opponents of making a conscienceless bid for Southern support for the presidency, but it is hardly probable that a man of his political acumen would have risked certain antagonism in the free states for the sake of gaining additional favor in the South. Douglas himself found ample justification for the measure in the democratic character of his plan and in his belief that popular sovereignty would permanently "withdraw the question of slavery from the halls of Congress and the political arena." It is only fair to say that nothing in his career, before or after 1854, warrants us in doubting his unselfish devotion to the principle of local home rule.

Other factors were, however, involved in the situation. The growing agitation for a transcontinental railroad had created rivalry between the commercial interests of the Northwest and the Southwest, which saw in such an artery of trade a means of nourishing sectional prosperity. An engineering survey, conducted by the War Department, reported the superior practicability of a southern route; but the enterprising leaders of the Northwest were not willing to yield the point, and they believed that the rapid settlement of the Nebraska country would be a potent argument for a centrally located route. The situation bore an especial appeal for Douglas who, as a loyal citizen of Chicago, had done all he could, while in state politics, to make that city a great railway center. Consequently, the economic interest of the Northwest, as well as its democratic idealism, favored the Kansas-Nebraska bill. The South was willing to forego its claims because of the chances for slavery extension made possible by the provision for popular sovereignty.

Additional support for the bill resulted from a factional fight in the Democratic party in Missouri. Senator David R. Atchison of that state was meeting hot competition in his campaign for reëlection, and in order to win popular favor, he publicly promised his slaveholding constituents in the summer of 1853 that the rich prairie lands west of the state would be opened to settlement without the Missouri-Compromise restriction. Like the Illinois Senator, he also desired to connect his state with the Pacific by railroads. When he resumed his duties in Congress in December, 1853, he prepared to make good his promise. If Douglas had not fathered the Kansas-Nebraska bill, it seems certain that Atchison would have been its author.

The Kansas-Nebraska Act before the Country

No law ever passed by Congress produced such momentous consequences as the Kansas-Nebraska Act. While the bill was yet before Congress, Chase predicted, "It will light up a fire in the country which may, perhaps, consume those who kindle it." The reasons are not far to seek. The Act revived all the old animosities over slavery extension, after the nation had persuaded itself that that disturbing question was finally put to rest in 1850. It furthermore involved the repeal of the sacrosanct Missouri Compromise. Hardly less important was the fact that the self-interest of the Northern masses and European immigrants was directly threatened by the new law. They had long accustomed themselves to think of the new territories as a Promised Land to which, in the fullness of time, they would fall heir. These expectations seemed likely now to be defeated by the establishment of the slavery system there. Greeley declared that Douglas and Pierce had made more abolitionists in three months than Garrison and Wendell Phillips could make in half a century.

To the national Whig party the Act dealt a deathblow. Already weakened by sectional differences, the two wings of the party now found themselves occupying opposing camps. Not a Northern Whig had voted for the measure while most of the Southern Whigs had supported it. There followed, during the next few years, the dispersion of the Whigs into the ranks of other parties. The Democrats suffered in less degree. Though their numbers were somewhat reduced by the defection of "Anti-Nebraska" Democrats in the North, this loss was more than balanced by accessions from the Southern Whigs. Alexander H. Stephens and Robert Toombs, former Whig leaders, were among the new converts. Naturally the party became more firmly allied than ever with cotton capitalism.

The most significant outcome of the Kansas-Nebraska contest, however, was the creation of two new parties. One of these was the Republican party. Even before the Act was passed, the antislavery leaders in Congress had issued an appeal to the people, denouncing it as "a gross violation of a sacred pledge" and "an atrocious plot to exclude from a vast unoccupied region immigrants from the Old World and free laborers from our own States." Three political factions were ripe for union on a program opposed to slavery extension: the Northern Whigs, the old Free Soilers, and the Anti-Nebraska Democrats. Another source of strength lay in the immigrant farmer population of the West, whose probable political course was charted by the anti-

Nebraska editorials that characterized eighty out of eighty-eight German newspapers.

Horace Greeley took an active part in agitating for independent political action through the columns of the *Tribune*, but the party actually came into being as the result of a spontaneous uprising of the people in the Western states. On February 28, 1854, a local gathering at Ripon, Wisconsin, proclaimed the formation of a new party; other localities fell in with the movement; and on July 6, a giant mass-meeting, held in an oak grove on the outskirts of Jackson, Michigan, launched a statewide organization under the name, "Republican party." By the fall of 1854 the new organization was active in all the states of the Upper Mississippi Valley and in some Eastern states, though the name, "Republican," was not yet everywhere used.

In the East the party made slower progress, for there it encountered a powerful competitor in the newly formed American party. This party was an outgrowth of the strong prejudice of native citizens against the rising tide of foreign immigrants and especially of Catholics. It had as its nucleus the Supreme Order of the Star-Spangled Banner, and was organized as a secret society with grips, pass-words, oaths, and ritualistic ceremonies.[1] By the uninformed public the members were known as "Know Nothings," since, when asked concerning the mysteries of the order, the invariable response was, "I know nothing." As a matter of fact, each member took a solemn oath to oppose any but American-born Protestants for office.

The secrecy and charm of novelty attracted many persons into membership, and the party was strongest in the Eastern states where the alien stocks were found in the largest numbers. Moreover, with the political elements in turmoil, it gained accessions of strength from people in all parts of the North, who hoped, by magnifying the new issue, they might still manage to keep the slavery question out of national politics. Many Southern Whigs also joined the Know Nothings rather than to make common cause with their traditional enemies, the Democrats; indeed, to oppose immigration seemed to proslavery men a means of curbing the growth of abolitionism.

[1] See Rhodes, *History of the United States*, II, 53–55, for an interesting description of the organization and ritual of the American party.

The fall elections of 1854 evinced the remarkable growth of the two new parties. Without making any public campaign, the Know Nothings carried Massachusetts, Rhode Island, Connecticut, New Hampshire, Kentucky, and California, and lost six other states only by small margins. The Republicans swept Maine and Vermont, and all the states of the old Northwest excepting Illinois. The Democrats lost their majority in the House of Representatives and the control of nine states besides. Everywhere the Whigs revealed lamentable weakness, and their success in carrying New York was due to the fact that Seward thought it best to remain in the party until after his reëlection to the Senate.

The Know Nothings, vastly elated by their successes, looked forward to capturing the presidency in 1856. Fully aware that much of their strength had come from voters who opposed a revival of sectionalism, they now sought to retain this support by adding to their ritual a "Union oath," whereby all members were pledged to oppose the election of disunionists to office. It was impossible, however, for any party to steer a middle course. The Northern and Southern wings inevitably fell into contentions over the slavery question, and by 1856 the party was squarely committed to popular sovereignty! Since this doctrine was, in a special sense, the pride and possession of the Democrats, the fate of the American party was therewith sealed.

The Republican legislatures, elected in 1854, proceeded to pass acts for the purpose of impeding or defeating the execution of the new Fugitive Slave Act. Known as "Personal Liberty Laws," these statutes usually prohibited the use of local jails to confine fugitives, and punished severely the seizure of a free negro with intent to enslave him. They were hailed by the South as incontrovertible evidence of the aggressive and lawless character of the new party. On one occasion, at least, Republican zeal afforded interesting confirmation of the old adage that politics makes strange bedfellows. In 1854 a Milwaukee mob effected the rescue of a negro named Glover, arrested under the Fugitive Slave Act. The Wisconsin Supreme Court held that the federal statute was "unconstitutional and void"; and when the United States Supreme Court subsequently reversed the decision, the legislature, in a paraphrase of the Kentucky Resolutions of 1798, resolved that the several states which had formed the federal compact, being "sovereign and independent," had "the unquestionable right to judge of its infractions" and to resort to a "positive defiance" of all unauthorized acts of the general government.

In the North, the Republicans steadily gained in popular favor. Seward, a tower of political strength, assumed the leadership of the party in the East in 1855; the fiery discussions of Republican leaders in Congress helped to educate the masses of the North; and in 1856 occurred a brutal assault on Charles Sumner, which, in a different manner, aided the Republican cause. In actual operation, the fruits of popular sovereignty in Kansas had been violence, fraud, and bloodshed. Using this situation as his text, Sumner delivered an address in the Senate on May 19–20, 1856, in which he stigmatized popular sovereignty as "the crime of crimes," venomously attacked the aged Senator Butler of South Carolina, and declared that Douglas's part in the proceedings had been that of Sancho Panza to Don Quixote.

Two days later, while Sumner was working at his desk in the Senate chamber, Preston Brooks, a member of the House and Butler's nephew, appearing suddenly from behind, beat him over the head with a cane into insensibility. The ferocity of the assault enraged the North, and symbolized in the minds of thousands the ruthless aggression of the "Slave Power." Sumner's injuries made it impossible for him to perform his Senatorial duties regularly until December, 1859; meantime, the Republican party gained fresh converts by reason of his martyrdom. An attempt to expel Brooks from his seat failed; every Southern member save one voted to sustain him.

The Republicans held their national convention at Philadelphia on June 17, 1856, the anniversary of Bunker Hill. Chase and Seward, the two foremost men of the party, were passed over for the presidency because of the enemies they had made on bygone issues, and the nomination went to John C. Fremont of California, a young man, almost unknown in politics but renowned as an intrepid explorer of the Far West. He was thought also to have a strong hold upon the German vote. For Vice-President, W. L. Dayton of New Jersey was chosen over Abraham Lincoln, the Western candidate. The platform declared for the exclusion of slavery from all federal territories as an obligation imposed by the Constitution, denounced the attempt to force slavery on Kansas, and stigmatized the Ostend Manifesto as "the highwayman's plea that 'might makes right.'"

The Know Nothings met in national convention at Philadelphia on Washington's birthday, 1856. The sessions were marked by angry debates between the antislavery and proslavery delegates, ending with the withdrawal of most of the former from the convention. The platform opposed the election of immigrants and Catholics to office, advocated a twenty-one-years' residence for naturalization, proclaimed the indestructibility of the Union, and favored popular sovereignty in the territories. Millard Fillmore, who had signed the Compromise of 1850, was nominated for President, and A. J. Donelson of Tennessee for Vice-President. Later in the year these nominations were indorsed by a national convention composed of remnants of the old Whig party.

Meeting in Cincinnati on June 2, the Democrats feared to nominate either Pierce or Douglas because of their close connection with the Kansas-Nebraska Act, and instead, chose James Buchanan of Pennsylvania, who had been safely out of the country as Minister to Great Britain during most of the controversy. John C. Breckinridge of Kentucky was selected for second place. The platform vindicated popular sovereignty and the Kansas-Nebraska Act as founded on the Compromise of 1850, and condemned the "political crusade" of the Know Nothings as contrary to "the spirit of toleration and enlightened freedom which peculiarly distinguishes the American system of popular government."

The campaign was a thrilling one. In the North the Republicans conducted a canvass rivaling that of 1840 in enthusiasm, and having behind it what the earlier campaign lacked — a dynamic moral conviction. With the slogan of "Bleeding Kansas," they sought to arouse the latent fear of every Northerner against the aggressions of the proslavery "Buchaneers." They made an especial appeal to the wage-earners, circulating campaign literature which represented slaveholders as declaring, for example, that "Slavery is the natural and normal condition of the *laboring man*, whether WHITE or *black*."

The conservative elements of the country became visibly

alarmed by the success of these tactics, and the Republicans were, in turn, assailed as a radical sectional party. Both Buchanan and Fillmore took occasion to declare that the election of Fremont would cause a division of the Union. Southern pamphleteers charged that the antislavery men were "committed to Socialism and Communism — to no private property, no church, no laws, no government — to free love, free lands, free women and free churches." When the votes were counted in November, it was found that conservatism had triumphed. Buchanan received 174 electoral votes, including the support of every slave state except Maryland; Fremont won 114 votes, representing eleven Northern states; and Fillmore received the eight votes of Maryland. The Democratic party was returned to office, but the surprising vote polled by the Republicans marked them as a party with a future.

SELECT BIBLIOGRAPHY

The Undoing of the Sectional Truce. The conflict of policies and personalities in the period from 1850 to 1860 receives critical treatment in J. F. Rhodes, *History of the United States*, I–II (New York, 1892), J. B. McMaster, *A History of the People of the United States*, VIII (New York, 1913), James Schouler, *History of the United States*, V (New York, 1894), and T. C. Smith, *Parties and Slavery* (in *The American Nation*, XVIII, New York, 1906). The most recent review of the decade appears in Edward Channing, *A History of the United States*, VI (New York, 1925).

Europe in Ferment. Good brief accounts of the mid-century revolutions in Europe may be found in such manuals as C. J. H. Hayes, *A Political and Social History of Modern Europe* (2 v., New York, 1916–1924), II; J. S. Schapiro, *Modern and Contemporary European History* (Boston, 1923); and E. R. Turner, *Europe since 1789* (Garden City, 1924). The interest and influence of the American people in these developments is illustrated, in the case of France, in E. N. Curtis, *The French Assembly of 1848 and American Constitutional Doctrines* (in *Columbia University Studies*, LXXIX, no. 2, New York, 1918).

The Coming of the Foreigners. Excellent chapters on this subject appear in S. P. Orth, *Our Foreigners* (in *The Chronicles of America*, XXXV, New Haven, 1920), H. P. Fairchild, *Immigration* (New York, 1913), and F. J. Warne, *The Tide of Immigration* (New York, 1916). See also J. B. McMaster, *A History of the People of the United States*, VI–VIII (New York, 1906–1913). Of a more specialized character are R. B. Anderson, *The First Chapter of Norwegian Immigration (1821–1840)* (Madison, 1895), K. C. Babcock, *The Scandinavian Element in the United States* (in *University of*

Illinois Bulletin, XII, no. 7, Urbana, 1914), Ernest Bruncken, *German Political Refugees in the United States during the Period from 1815–1860* (Chicago, 1904), A. B. Faust, *The German Element in the United States* (2 v., Boston, 1909), I, and H. J. Ford, *The Scotch-Irish in America* (Princeton, 1915).

The Rise of a New Generation. Perhaps the best biographies of the Northern leaders are Frederic Bancroft, *The Life of William H. Seward* (2 v., New York, 1900), A. B. Hart, *Salmon Portland Chase* (New York, 1899), G. H. Haynes, *Charles Sumner* (Philadelphia, 1909), J. A. Woodburn, *The Life of Thaddeus Stevens* (Indianapolis, 1913), and Allen Johnson, *Stephen A. Douglas* (New York, 1908). For the Southern statesmen, see W. E. Dodd, *Jefferson Davis* (Philadelphia, 1907), Louis Pendleton, *Alexander H. Stephens* (Philadelphia, 1908), U. B. Phillips, *The Life of Robert Toombs* (New York, 1913), and J. W. Du Bose, *The Life and Times of William Lowndes Yancey* (Birmingham, 1892).

Much information on the new era in journalism may be obtained from J. M. Lee, *History of American Journalism* (Boston, 1923), Elmer Davis, *History of the New York Times* (New York, 1921), Richard Hooker, *The Story of an Independent Newspaper* (New York, 1924), and Allan Nevins, *The Evening Post* (New York, 1922). For a biographical approach, consult G. S. Merriam, *The Life and Times of Samuel Bowles* (2 v., New York, 1885), and W. A. Linn, *Horace Greeley* (New York, 1903).

The Revival of Sectional Discord. M. G. McDougall, *Fugitive Slaves* (in *Fay House Monographs*, no. 3, Boston, 1891), and W. H. Siebert, *The Underground Railroad from Slavery to Freedom* (New York, 1898), give information on the execution of the Fugitive Slave Act of 1850. P. N. Garber, *The Gadsden Treaty* (Philadelphia, 1924), is a detailed study of our diplomatic relations with Mexico from 1848 to 1857.

The Repeal of the Missouri Compromise. The legislative history of the Kansas-Nebraska Act may be followed in the standard histories. The question of the motives behind the measure has provoked considerable discussion among historians. Rhodes lays it all to Douglas's personal ambition for the presidency. According to P. O. Ray, *The Repeal of the Missouri Compromise* (Cleveland, 1909), the Act should be understood as a campaign pledge made by Senator Atchison of Missouri in his contest for reëlection. F. H. Hodder regards the Act as one phase of the rivalry between Northern and Southern commercial interests to secure the terminus of the proposed Pacific railway. See his "Genesis of the Kansas-Nebraska Act," in Wisconsin Historical Society, *Proceedings for 1912*, 69–86.

The Kansas-Nebraska Act before the Country. The changes in the party situation may be traced briefly in Jesse Macy, *Political Parties in the United States, 1846–1861* (New York, 1900), and at greater length in Francis Curtis, *The Republican Party* (2 v., New York, 1904), L. D. Scisco, *Political Nativism in New York State* (in *Columbia University Studies*, XIII, no. 2, New York, 1901) — of more than local interest, and A. C. Cole, *The Whig Party in the South* (Washington, 1913).

CHAPTER X

THE DRIFT TOWARD DISUNION, 1855–1860

Projects for Slavery Extension

The new Chief Executive was a man of average attainments, whose chief title to distinction consisted in his unwavering fidelity to his party. Though a Northerner, Buchanan had always been favorable to the political objects of cotton capitalism, and, entering the presidency at advanced years, he surrounded himself with advisers who shared the same point of view. At the head of the cabinet he placed Lewis Cass of Michigan, then in his seventy-fourth year and widely known, because of his Southern sympathies, as the "archdoughface." Four other members were from slave states, and two from free states.[1]

To the new administration fell the complex and delicate task of pouring oil on the troubled waters of sectional dissension. This was a task ill suited to its genius, since one of Buchanan's dominant purposes was to find new territory for the expansion of the Southern economic system. The admission of California as a part of the Compromise of 1850 had destroyed the ancient balance of free and slave states in the Senate, and the rapid increase of population in the North produced two more free-soil states during Buchanan's term — Minnesota in 1858 and Oregon in 1859. In the President's mind, the security of the Union depended upon a restoration of the old equality of the sections; his attitude toward the great problems of the time is to be understood in the light of this conviction.

Like the two Democratic Presidents who preceded him, he urged upon Congress a policy of tropical annexation. Since westward expansion had built up the power of the free states, it

[1] Howell Cobb of Georgia, Secretary of the Treasury; J. B. Floyd of Virginia, Secretary of War; Isaac Toucey of Connecticut, Secretary of the Navy; Jacob Thompson of Mississippi, Secretary of the Interior; A. V. Brown of Tennessee, Postmaster-General; Jeremiah S. Black of Pennsylvania, Attorney-General.

seemed logical to Buchanan that "Manifest Destiny" should now direct the march of the American population southward. He predicted in a message of 1858 that Central America would fall to the United States by the natural course of events "at no distant day." In 1858 and again in 1859, he urged that the United States assume a protectorate over northern Mexico, and in the latter year he asked for authority to invade that country to restore order. His efforts were ill-timed. With the public mind agitated over the question of the extension of slavery within our existing boundaries, Congress did nothing with the President's foreign program.

The attempt to apply popular sovereignty in Kansas, begun under Pierce, had reached a critical stage when Buchanan entered office. Popular sovereignty in practice proved to be a quite different thing from popular sovereignty in theory. If the new territory had contained a settled population when Pierce signed the law, the slavery question might perhaps have been quietly decided by a popular referendum. Since, however, the region was virtually without white inhabitants, the Kansas-Nebraska Act precipitated a mad scramble on the part of each section for political control.

The New England Emigrant Aid Society was formed in April, 1854, by some wealthy citizens of Massachusetts for the purpose of financing and equipping Northerners who wished to settle in Kansas, and through this and other channels, free settlers soon began to pour into the territory. The Southern planters, hampered by their smaller numbers and their possession of slaves, did not find it practicable to meet this Northern competition by similar methods; but the border Missourians, organized in secret lodges, held themselves ready at a moment's notice to cross into Kansas and seize control of the voting places. Each set of contestants regarded the other with horror and indignation. To antislavery men the Missourians were all "Border Ruffians," unkempt, blood-thirsty, and lawless, whereas the Southerners looked upon their Northern brethren as "military colonies of reckless and dangerous fanatics" and "Hessian mercenaries."

The intense rivalry resulted in the establishment of two groups of settlements and separate territorial governments. The

Northerners located their towns in the valley of the Kansas River, naming their principal settlement "Lawrence" in honor of the chief patron of the Emigrant Aid Society. Atchison and Leavenworth on the Missouri River and Lecompton on the Kansas River were the leading proslavery towns. When the election of the first territorial legislature took place on March 30, 1855, the free-soil settlers formed a majority of the population, but the proslavery forces carried the day through the illegal interference of the "Border Ruffians" at the polls. The legislature so chosen proceeded at once to adopt laws for the protection of slavery. Declining to accept the outcome of the election, the free settlers, upon their own initiative, held a constitutional convention at Topeka in October, at which they drew up, for submission to Congress, a state constitution prohibiting slavery. Meanwhile, they organized a *de facto* government of their own.

Popular sovereignty was rapidly becoming a travesty, but President Pierce might have saved the situation by declaring both governments irregular and illegal and instituting a new election under protection of the federal troops. On the contrary, he sided with the proslavery legislature, and declared he would exert his whole power "to support public order in the Territory." A bill to admit Kansas under the Topeka constitution passed the House of Representatives on July 3, 1856, but received scant consideration from the Senate.

Emboldened by Pierce's attitude, the pro-Southern leaders in Kansas undertook active measures to crush the Topeka government. The free-soil "Governor," Charles Robinson, and his chief associates were indicted for treason, and on May 21, 1856, a proslavery force, acting as a posse, invaded Lawrence and sacked the town. A few days passed, and then the country heard, for the first time, the name of John Brown. Born in Connecticut, he had grown to manhood amid frontier conditions in Ohio, and in October, 1855, had removed to Osawatomie, Kansas. He had imbibed an intense hatred of slavery in childhood, and the conviction gradually grew on him that he was, in some way, divinely appointed to accomplish its extermination. "A stern Calvinist and a Puritan, he would have found the religious wars of Europe or the early days of the Massachusetts colonies an atmosphere suited to his bent," remarks one historian.

Incensed by the attack on Lawrence, Brown resolved, in the spirit of Old-Testament justice, to slay five proslavery men in expiation for the death of an equal number of free soilers. On the night of May 24, 1856, he and his band fell upon a settlement on Pottawatomie Creek, and ruthlessly executed his purpose. The massacre acted as fuel to the spreading flames. It was the beginning of a reign of terror lasting several months, during which parties of men from each side roamed the country, plundering and killing. In all, two hundred lives were lost, and two million dollars' worth of property destroyed. Only by a vigorous employment of the United States troops was the civil strife finally brought to an end by Governor J. W. Geary in November, 1856.

The regular election of a new territorial legislature was to occur in October, 1857; and the pro-Southern leaders realized that, if the free soilers took part, the slavery interests would lose their majority in that body. Therefore, while their lease of power continued, they hastened to set machinery in motion for the adoption of a state constitution, which, when ratified by Congress, would fasten slavery on Kansas. This proved easy, for the free soilers refused to take part in the election of delegates to a constitutional convention (June, 1857). Only one eighth of all the possible voters participated, and the delegates chosen were proslavery without exception.

The convention assembled at Lecompton in September, and drew up a proslavery constitution. Fearing that their object might be defeated by popular vote, the convention refused to give the voters a clear choice between accepting or rejecting the proposed instrument — the people were, in effect, permitted merely to affirm whether they favored the Lecompton constitution with or without the further introduction of slaves. The free-soil party, outraged by this perversion of popular sovereignty, refrained from voting; and the Lecompton constitution, as framed by the convention, was adopted at an election in which less than seven thousand votes were cast. At the October election, 1857, the free-soil party won a majority of both houses of the regular territorial legislature, and they resubmitted the constitution to popular vote on the express issue of acceptance or rejection. The instrument was defeated by a majority of more than ten thousand. The proslavery men, denying the legality of the second submission, stayed away from the polls in turn.

Notwithstanding the irregular character of these votes, no reasonable man could doubt that a majority of the Kansans were opposed to the proslavery constitution. Nevertheless, when the instrument came before Congress for acceptance, President Buchanan under influence of his Southern advisers insisted that favorable action be taken (February, 1858). If popular sovereignty was merely a cloak to extend slavery into free territory, Douglas might have been expected now to support Buchanan's position. On the contrary, he declared that the Lecompton constitution was a fraud upon the rights of the Kansas people, and in bold and open defiance of the administration, he set about to prevent its ratification. Feeling ran high in Congress, Buchanan personally threatened Douglas with political oblivion, and the administration newspapers accused him of having turned "Black Republican."

In spite of Douglas's efforts, the Senate approved the Lecompton constitution, but in the House the "Anti-Lecompton" Democrats managed to prevent its passage. The deadlock was finally broken by a compromise measure, the "English Bill," enacted on May 4, 1858. This law authorized a resubmission of the Lecompton constitution to popular vote, with the provision, however, that, in case of acceptance, Kansas should receive a specified grant of government lands within the state, and in case of rejection, statehood should be postponed until the population reached the number (93,560) necessary for a Representative in Congress. The bill was manifestly unfair and Douglas voted against it, but at least it gave the voters a chance to reject the whole instrument. Under its terms, the Kansans repudiated the Lecompton constitution by a vote of 11,300 to 1,788 in August, 1858. As a result, Kansas remained a territory until January, 1861, when the secession of the Southern states made possible its admission into the Union as a free state.

The contest over Kansas added immeasurably to the ill-feeling between the sections, for the nation was deeply stirred by the dramatic and relentless struggle. Although the contest was conducted by extremists and fanatics on each side, the law-abiding citizens of each section came to regard these leaders as fairly representing the convictions and purposes of the mass of people of the other.

THE SUPREME COURT AND SLAVERY EXTENSION

Buchanan had given notice in his inaugural address of his expectation that all controversy over the status of slavery would soon be stilled by a forthcoming judgment of the Supreme Court. Two days later, on March 6, 1857, the famous decision of Dred Scott *v.* Sandford was announced. Dred Scott was a Missouri slave who some twenty years earlier had been taken by his then master, an army surgeon, to reside at various posts in the free state of Illinois, and subsequently to a fort in the northern part of the Louisiana Purchase, where slavery was forbidden by the Missouri Compromise. Returning to Missouri he became discontented with his lot, and aided by some antislavery lawyers, began suit for his liberation on the score of his residence on free soil.[1] Meantime he was sold to an absentee master residing in another state.

After a long period of litigation, the case finally reached the federal Supreme Court. Dred Scott's right to sue his master in the United States courts rested upon the constitutional provision which gave the federal judiciary jurisdiction in cases arising between citizens of different states. The Supreme Court, therefore, had to decide the preliminary question, was he really a citizen? before it could consider the question, was he a freeman? If the Court followed its customary practice and if it decided against his citizenship, it would not seek to pass upon the more important question of his freedom.

The majority of the Court held that Dred Scott was not a citizen, declaring that negroes had not been citizens of any state at the time of the formation of the Constitution, and that the Constitution was not, in their judgment, intended to apply to any but the white race. Here, according to precedent, the case should have ended, but Chief Justice Taney and his associates felt that an opinion on the merits of the case from the highest tribunal in the land would remove a dangerous question from the

[1] The fact that the Missouri Compromise was repealed in 1854 had, of course, no bearing upon Dred Scott's rights under that law while it was still in force.

political arena. The Court, therefore, declared that the Missouri Compromise had all along been unconstitutional and void, for Congress had no right to enact a law which arbitrarily deprived persons of their property, slave or otherwise, in the territories of the United States.[1] Accordingly, Dred Scott was not entitled to freedom, and masters had a constitutional right to hold slaves anywhere in the federal domains. The Court attached no importance to Dred Scott's sojourn in Illinois, declaring that, since his residence was only temporary, his status as slave or free depended on the laws of Missouri and not of Illinois.

The decision created fierce excitement. Two of the justices, John McLean of Ohio and B. R. Curtis of Massachusetts, dissented from the majority opinion. Judge Curtis, challenging the assertion that no negroes had ever been citizens in any of the states, insisted that Dred Scott was a citizen within the meaning of the Constitution. The Missouri Compromise he justified by the constitutional power of Congress to "make all needful rules and regulations" for federal territories, and denied Taney's contention that this grant of authority was limited to the original area of the United States. He further contended that the judgment of the Court on the Missouri Compromise was an *obiter dictum*, that is, an opinion concerning points not properly before the judges, and hence of no legal binding effect.

Republican indignation was unrestrained. Not even in Jefferson's time had the federal judiciary come in for such bitter condemnation. Republican writers made the most of the fact that seven of the nine judges were Democrats, and that five of these came from slave states. Greeley declared in the *Tribune* that Taney's decision was "entitled to just so much moral weight as would be the judgment of a majority of those congregated in any Washington bar-room." Thousands of copies of the dissenting opinions were printed and circulated as campaign documents. In reality, the party was in a bad predicament, for if the Dred Scott decision were accepted as binding, then the Republican platform was unconstitutional and the party must disband.

The outcome of the case was, of course, a great victory for the

[1] "Nor shall any person . . . be deprived of life, liberty, or property, without due process of law." Constitution, Amendment V. As has been seen, the antislavery side cited the same passage, but stressed the word "liberty" instead of "property."

Southern Democrats since it gave judicial sanction to the extreme theory of slavery in the territories. The Northern Democrats accepted it with mental reservations, for Douglas and his followers realized that the doctrine of the Dred Scott case ran counter to, if it did not outlaw, the theory of popular sovereignty.

The Widening of the Sectional Breach

The Republicans, elated by their excellent showing in the campaign of 1856, were eager to try their fortunes again in the fall elections of 1858. To Northern indignation over "Bleeding Kansas" was now added resentment over the Dred Scott decision, and both meant new converts to Republicanism. In 1857 occurred another event which, in the minds of the unthinking, increased the unpopularity of the party in power — a financial storm broke on the country that did not entirely clear away during Buchanan's term of office.

As in the case of the Panic of 1837, the presence of unbounded resources had stimulated the industrial and financial world to overoptimistic investments in anticipation of the future development of the country. Railroads had been rapidly pushed westward, so that the Atlantic Seaboard was now connected by iron bands with the great plains. Manufacturing likewise had begun a rapid development in the Ohio Valley, and cities like Cincinnati, Louisville, and St. Louis were noted as centers of the readymade clothing industry. The heavy indebtedness incurred by railways, manufacturers, and promoters of all kinds far exceeded any possibility of a profitable return within a reasonable period.

The crash came in the summer and autumn of 1857. Fourteen railway corporations, including the Erie, Reading, Illinois Central, and Michigan Central, failed to meet their obligations; banks and insurance companies closed their doors; factories suspended operations. In all, more than nine thousand firms failed in 1857–1858, with total liabilities approaching $400,000,000. With tens of thousands of wage-earners out of work, "hunger meetings" of a semirevolutionary character were held in the larger Eastern cities. The Western farmers were involved likewise in the general depression. Crops were scarcely moved in some localities, and grain exports diminished one half. Only the

South escaped the prevailing hard times, a circumstance which led Senator J. H. Hammond of South Carolina to affirm the superior soundness of the Southern economic system and to reiterate the exultant conviction that "Cotton is King."

The autumn of 1858 saw the Republicans conducting vigorous campaigns for state and Congressional offices throughout the North, and in every state, except Illinois and Indiana, the administration party lost ground. Even Pennsylvania, the President's own state, turned its back on him because of the effect of the Panic on the iron industry and the unpopularity of the Tariff of 1857 (see page 111). The election in Illinois possessed certain features of unusual interest. Against the advice of Greeley and other Eastern leaders, the Illinois Republicans nominated for United States Senator Abraham Lincoln, then a lawyer of local prominence with some experience in the state legislature and Congress. The Easterners desired Douglas's reëlection without opposition, for since his break with the Buchanan administration over the Lecompton constitution, they hoped to induce him to unite with the Republicans and lead the party to speedy triumph in the nation.

Since the actual selection of the Senator rested with a new state legislature not yet chosen, the rival candidates devoted themselves eagerly to the task of acquainting the people with the issues at stake. A series of seven debates was arranged, two in northern Illinois, where the New England elements in the population were dominant; two in southern Illinois, or "Egypt," where proslavery sympathy was rampant; and three in the intermediate region. Upon the lean and ungainly Lincoln rested the burden of the attack, for he was challenging Douglas's right to continue in the Senate, and was spokesman for a new party.

Launching his offensive in his speech accepting the nomination, he strove to convince the people of the aggressive proslavery purposes of the Democrats. Before it was too late, he asserted, the free-soil North must take a bold stand against the "Slave Power," for the Dred Scott decision was merely an entering wedge for a later decision which would legalize slavery throughout the Northern states. "'A house divided against itself cannot stand.' I believe this government cannot endure permanently half slave and half free. . . . It will become all one thing or all the other." By these words, Lincoln was expressing not a purpose but the perception of a great truth, but Douglas, seizing the opportunity, made an adroit countercharge that the Republicans were plotting to destroy slavery within the Southern states.

Lincoln next undertook to disabuse his own party brethren of the notion that Douglas deserved Republican support because of his stand against the Lecompton constitution. This he accomplished by showing that Douglas's opposition had not been actuated by free-soil sympathies but by his popular-sovereignty views. With fine rhetorical effect, he recalled that Douglas had declared in Congress, "If Kansas wants a slave-State constitution, she has a right to it; if she wants a free-State constitution, she has a right to it. It is none of my business which way the slavery clause is decided. I care not whether it is voted down or up."

Finally, Lincoln wished to place his rival indubitably on record with regard to the Dred Scott decision. Southern Democratic leaders had been anxiously watching Douglas since the decision, for Taney's judgment that slavery could exist in all federal territories contradicted Douglas's doctrine of 1854 that slavery might be excluded by the territorial legislature. By asking Douglas to reconcile the two pronouncements Lincoln placed him in a dilemma.[1] If he reaffirmed the right of popular sovereignty, he would retain the loyalty of the Illinois farmers, deeply imbued with frontier ideals of democracy, but such a declaration would rob the Dred Scott decision of its vitality and make the Southern Democrats unwilling to support him for President in 1860. On the other hand, a confession that popular sovereignty had been outlawed by the Dred Scott decision would insure his defeat in the impending Senatorial election.

Douglas's reply is known as the "Freeport Doctrine," or as the Southern Democrats called it, the "Freeport Heresy." He drew a distinction between theory and practice in the application of the Dred Scott decision. In theory, slavery might exist

[1] Lincoln's question was: "Can the people of a United States territory, in any lawful way, against the wish of any citizen of the United States, exclude slavery from its limits prior to the formation of a state constitution?"

throughout the public domain; in practice, no master would take his slave into any territory where his rights of ownership were not fully protected by territorial law. Therefore, Douglas concluded, the failure of a legislature to enact such a body of law, or "slave code," would have the practical effect of banishing slavery from the territory.[1] Douglas took his stand with his neighbors and friends, and his utterance at Freeport won him reëlection to the United States Senate. But it cast dismay into the ranks of the Southern Democrats who realized that he was the best vote-getting candidate the party could nominate in 1860.

The year 1859 found the sectional strife once more assuming the ominous form of anarchy and bloodshed. Since his gory exploit in 1856 at Pottawatomie Creek, John Brown's ill-balanced mind had continued to brood over the evils of slavery, and he now laid plans to accomplish a more desperate stroke against it — nothing less than its overthrow through a servile insurrection. His scheme was as wild and quixotic as could be imagined. He proposed to establish himself in the mountain fastnesses of Virginia, North Carolina, and Tennessee, and with the aid of runaway slaves, levy war against the South, and eventually, through a Constitutional amendment, abolish slavery. As a first step, he planned to pillage the United States arsenal and rifle works at Harper's Ferry.

Consulting betimes with extreme abolitionists like Gerrit Smith, and collecting a modest store of money and munitions, he made a surprise attack on the unguarded federal works on Sunday night, October 16, 1859. His band at this time consisted of twenty-one followers, three of them his own sons, and five of them negroes. Excepting Brown and his son Owen, the men ranged in age from eighteen to twenty-nine. Several neighboring slaveholders, including a member of the Washington family, were arrested and brought in as prisoners.

With the coming of daylight on Monday the countryside was aroused. Men with all sorts of weapons poured into the village, and, supported by some militia companies, began a counterattack

[1] This was Douglas's soundest contention, but, as a matter of fact, he also claimed that, since the Dred Scott decision merely forbade *Congress* to exclude slavery from the territories, the *territorial legislature* still retained that power, at least until the Supreme Court should declare to the contrary. In other words, a free-soil legislature might prevent the existence of slavery by "unfriendly legislation."

on the invaders. By this time the telegraph had spread far and wide the news of the raid, and late Monday evening Colonel Robert E. Lee arrived in charge of a company of United States marines. Early the next morning Brown and his surviving followers were overpowered and taken prisoners.

A thrill of horror ran through both North and South. To credulous Southerners John Brown's fanatical attempt came as a confirmation of the worst charges that had been made against the "Black Republicans." Conservative-minded Northerners repudiated the exploit, for they rightly saw in Brown's deed an assault not against the South but upon all organized society and upon democratic methods of securing progress. Even the Republican platform of 1860 denounced his "lawless invasion" as "among the gravest of crimes."

Brown was promptly tried on the charges of conspiracy, treason, and murder, and was publicly hanged on December 2, 1859. The nobility of his bearing in these last weeks impressed all who saw him; he gloried in his "martyrdom," and believed to the end that he was but an instrument in the hands of God. It was this indomitable and self-forgetting spirit, not his bloody deeds, which caused Northerners a few years later to venerate him as one of the saints.

The Presidential Campaign of 1860

Congress, assembling a few days after Brown's execution for a session which lasted into June, 1860, proved to be a scene of defiant debates, of charges and countercharges, between the leaders of the opposing sections and parties. Threats of secession were made with increasing arrogance by Southern "fire-eaters," and Senator Seward was openly accused of having instigated John Brown's criminal adventure. "The members on both sides are mostly armed with deadly weapons," Senator J. W. Grimes of Iowa wrote to his wife at the time, "and it is said that the friends of each are armed in the galleries." On several occasions, violent collisions between members were only narrowly averted.

The administration party controlled the Senate, but in the House a Democratic majority of twenty-five in the previous

Congress was changed to a Republican plurality of twenty-one. Since the Republicans did not command an absolute majority, the contest for the election of a Speaker threw things into a turmoil at the very outset of the session. The struggle lasted for nearly two months, during which forty-four ballots were taken, but finally the Republicans carried the day by substituting a moderate-minded member of their party for John Sherman, their original candidate.

The discussions were embittered by frequent Southern allusions to an abolitionist tract, entitled *The Impending Crisis of the South*, which sixty-four Republican Representatives, including Sherman, had formally indorsed in print. The animus of this new assault on slavery was entirely different from that of *Uncle Tom's Cabin*. The author asked the pregnant question, for whose good was slavery? The book was written by Hinton R. Helper, a "poor white" of North Carolina, and fortified by facts gleaned from the United States census reports, he maintained that the direct benefits of slavery accrued only to a fraction of the Southern whites. This minority alone possessed the splendor, luxury, and culture of which the South boasted, while the mass of their brethren lived in poverty and illiteracy, deprived of equal economic, social, and political rights. The slavery system had plunged the South "into a state of comparative imbecility and obscurity," whereas the North without this encumbrance had risen "to a degree of almost unexampled power and eminence." It was a bold and convincing argument on behalf of the Southern white proletariat against cotton capitalism. Aided by the gratuitous advertising given it by the Southern "fire-eaters," Helper's tract gained an enormous circulation in the North, and won friends for the Republican cause among people who had been untouched by the miseries of the negroes.

The fundamental antagonism between the slavery system and free white labor was brought directly home to the Northern workingmen and farmers in an even more striking way by Buchanan's veto of a homestead bill in June, 1860. For more than a decade energetic efforts had been made to secure the passage of a law giving actual settlers free farms from the public domain. In Congress, Andrew Johnson, a "poor white" Democrat of Tennessee, had agitated for such legislation, Northern workingman associations had been equally ardent in its support, and it will be remembered that the antislavery parties in 1848 and 1852 had included such a demand in their platforms.

In 1854 a free-homestead bill passed the House of Representatives by Northern votes, only to suffer defeat in the Senate. Again in February, 1859, a similar bill, adopted by the House, failed in the proslavery Senate. The House vote in 1859 disclosed that only seven Northerners opposed the measure and only five Southerners supported it. The antagonism of the proslavery men was actuated by self-interest, for they saw truly that, despite friendly court decisions, the federal territories would quickly fill with Northern farmers and workingmen if colonization should be accelerated by the inducement of free farms.

In March, 1860, the matter came before Congress once more. In view of the nearness of the presidential election, the Democrats hesitated to go too far in their opposition, since the measure was extremely popular in the old Northwest and with the Germans and other naturalized citizens of the North. Nevertheless, the House bill providing for free homesteads proved unacceptable to the Democratic Senate. After much wrangling and mutual defiances, the two houses finally agreed on a bill in June, which authorized heads of families to purchase tracts of 160 acres at the nominal charge of twenty-five cents per acre, one fifth of the then existing price. Buchanan, stalwart in defense of the slavery interests, vetoed the measure, alleging it would tend to depopulate the older states, deprive the frontiersmen of their "noble spirit of independence," and might even "introduce among us those pernicious social theories which have proved so disastrous in other countries."

Throughout these trying months the proceedings of Congress were marked by a consciousness of the approach of a presidential campaign. The opposing leaders did everything possible to discredit each other in the eyes of the people, and the Democrats made a last effort to patch up their internal differences. Upon Douglas's return to the Senate after his victory over Lincoln, the proslavery leaders warned him that the South would have none of him unless he agreed to support the enactment, by Congress, of a slave code applicable to all federal territories. This was the reply of the Southern Democrats to his assertion at Freeport that slavery might be excluded from a territory by the failure of the local legislature to enact protective laws.

He proved unshakable, and the matter was brought to a sharp issue in February, 1860, when Jefferson Davis offered a set of resolutions reaffirming the Dred Scott decision and declaring the obligation of Congress to provide a territorial slave code. These resolutions were eventually passed by the Democratic Senate, but Davis's motive in introducing them at this juncture was to notify Douglas of the price he must pay to secure Southern support in the impending Democratic convention.

The Democrats assembled on April 23, 1860, at Charleston, South Carolina, the very hotbed of disunionism. Contrary to precedent, it was decided to frame the platform before nominating candidates. Thereupon two platforms were submitted to the convention, one reiterating Davis's demand for a Congressional slave code, and the other reaffirming Douglas's position at Freeport. The Douglas Democrats were in the majority, and when the Northern platform was adopted by a vote of 165 to 138, the delegations of South Carolina, Georgia, Arkansas, and the five Gulf states angrily departed from the hall. Balloting now began for a candidate, but in fifty-seven votes, Douglas was unable to secure a majority equal to two thirds of the original membership of the convention.

His nomination was eventually accomplished at an adjourned session held at Baltimore on June 18, after the adoption of a rule authorizing nomination by a two-thirds affirmative vote of the delegates present. H. V. Johnson of Georgia became his running mate. Meantime, the Southern Democrats decided to place a ticket of their own in the field, and after several meetings of preparation, they held a national convention in Baltimore on June 21, at which they unanimously adopted the Southern platform rejected at Charleston, and chose as their candidates John C. Breckinridge of Kentucky and Joseph Lane of Oregon.

While the Democrats were quarreling among themselves, the Republicans had proceeded with high confidence to the selection of their ticket. The contest for the presidential nomination lay between candidates offered respectively by the East and the West, Seward of New York and Lincoln of Illinois. The former was the most prominent man in the party, and seemed, by reason of a long and distinguished public career, to have a prior claim to the honor. Lincoln's greatest asset, on the other hand, was his obscurity. Despite his debates with Douglas, he was scarcely known outside of his own state. Furthermore, unlike Seward, he had not offended influential factions in doubtful states in past political contests, nor had he antagonized prominent leaders within the party. In addition, his candidacy would make a special appeal to the laboring people of the North, for he was the son of "poor white" parents, and a self-educated man whose homely qualities of character were impressed upon the public by the sobriquet, "Honest Old Abe, the Rail-Splitter."

At the Chicago convention on May 16, Lincoln's convention manager, David Davis, left no stone unturned to secure support for his candidate, and by promises of cabinet positions to influential Republicans in those states, he won over the Indiana and Pennsylvania delegations. Lincoln knew nothing of these agreements, though he later felt constrained to carry them out. Seward's friends were likewise active, but when the balloting occurred, Lincoln was successful on the third trial. Hannibal Hamlin of Maine was chosen as the vice-presidential candidate.

The platform was framed with the special purpose of attracting Northern voters who had not yet identified themselves with the party. Declaring anew for the exclusion of slavery from the territories, the platform demanded the immediate admission of Kansas, and vigorously denounced "the new dogma that the Constitution, of its own force, carries slavery into any or all of the Territories." It advocated free homesteads, and with a squint at the Pennsylvania iron districts disgruntled with the Tariff of 1857, demanded a tariff to encourage "the industrial interests of the whole country." As for threats of disunion, the Republicans declared that "the union of the States must and shall be preserved."

A fourth convention was held on May 9 at Baltimore, composed, for the most part, of old men who were one in spirit with the venerable statesmen who had saved the country from disunion in 1850. Calling themselves the "Constitutional Union party," they adopted a brief platform recognizing "no political principle other than the Constitution of the country, the union of the States, and the enforcement of the laws," and nominated

John Bell of Tennessee and Edward Everett of Massachusetts as their candidates.

The campaign that ensued, though less exciting than that of 1856, may in its consequences be regarded as the most important in American history. For a second time, the Republicans asked the voters to support them in a great humanitarian crusade for the extinction of slavery in the territories. "Free Homes for the Homeless" proved to be an effective slogan for the party,

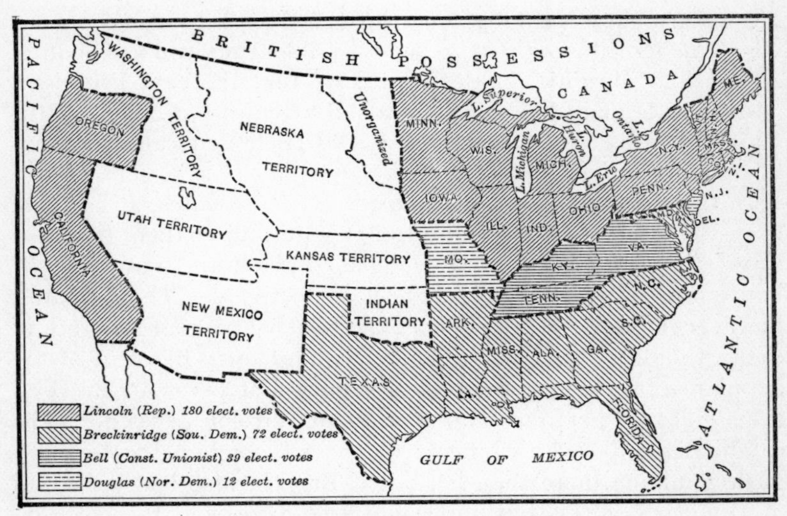

THE ELECTORAL VOTE IN 1860

especially in the old Northwest. They also inaugurated a systematic campaign to win the foreign vote, and in these efforts Carl Schurz, a political refugee of the German Revolution of 1848, was a tower of strength. Seward campaigned vigorously in behalf of his erstwhile rival, and in St. Louis and other German centers, took occasion to praise the "onward striving, freedom-loving German inhabitants."

In Pennsylvania and New Jersey, the tariff issue was urged by the Republicans to the virtual exclusion of all other questions. The great masters of literature, men like Longfellow, Bryant, Whittier, Emerson, and Lowell, all actively supported the Lincoln ticket, and Lowell wrote in the newly established *Atlantic*

Monthly, "We believe this election is a turning-point in our history." The large financial interests of the East, on the other hand, feared that Republican victory would mean secession and a general derangement of business. William B. Astor and other wealthy men are said to have contributed two million dollars to prevent Lincoln from carrying New York state.

In the last weeks of the campaign, Douglas became alarmed at the growing earnestness with which the Southern leaders threatened secession on the event of a "Black Republican" victory. He undertook a speaking tour through five slave states, everywhere pledging his support to an indivisible American nationality. At Norfolk, Virginia, he declared flatly that the next President, "whoever he may be, should treat all attempts to break up the Union by resistance to its laws, as Old Hickory treated the nullifiers of 1832."

In the electoral count, Lincoln received 180 votes, all of them from the free states, Breckinridge 72 votes, all of them from the slave states, and Bell and Douglas divided the votes of the border states, receiving 39 and 12 respectively. These figures, however, do not correctly reflect the relative popular strength of each candidate, for Lincoln received about forty per cent of the popular vote, Douglas more than twenty-nine per cent, Breckinridge eighteen per cent, and Bell about thirteen per cent. The candidates opposed to Lincoln received a combined vote of almost a million more than he, but if Breckinridge had polled all of Douglas's votes, Lincoln would still have won the election. The Republicans, however, failed to win a majority in either branch of Congress.

SELECT BIBLIOGRAPHY

Projects for Slavery Extension. In addition to the general histories, G. T. Curtis, *Life of James Buchanan* (2 v., New York, 1883), is useful for this period. Efforts to secure Cuba receive detailed discussion in J. M. Callahan, *Cuba and International Relations* (in *Johns Hopkins University Studies*, extra vol. XXI, Baltimore, 1899). The Kansas struggle has given rise to an extensive literature written by partisans of the various free-soil leaders. Perhaps the most objective account is L. W. Spring, *Kansas; the Prelude to the War for the Union* (Boston, 1907).

The Supreme Court and Slavery Extension. Two of the best discussions of the Dred Scott decision may be found in J. W. Burgess, *The Middle Period* (in *The American History Series*, New York, 1897), and Charles Warren, *The Supreme Court in United States History* (3 v., Boston, 1922), II.

The Widening of the Sectional Breach. The Panic of 1857 is given special study in C. F. Dunbar, *Economic Essays* (O. M. W. Sprague, ed., New York, 1904). On the Lincoln-Douglas debates, biographies of the participants are helpful. See also the introductory essay in E. E. Sparks's edition of the *Lincoln-Douglas Debates* (in Illinois State Historical Library, *Collections*, III, Springfield, 1908). Of the numerous lives of Brown, O. G. Villard, *John Brown, 1800–1859; a Biography Fifty Years After* (Boston, 1910), is the best balanced.

The Presidential Campaign of 1860. The efforts for a free-homestead law are painstakingly traced in G. M. Stephenson, *The Political History of the Public Lands from 1840 to 1862* (Boston, 1917). The fullest account of the campaign is E. D. Fite, *The Presidential Campaign of 1860* (New York, 1911). J. W. Burgess, *The Civil War and the Constitution* (2 v., in *The American History Series*, New York, 1901), opens with a description of the election and its preliminaries.

CHAPTER XI

THE GREAT DECISION, 1860–1861

THE MOVEMENT FOR SOUTHERN INDEPENDENCE

The election of Lincoln roused a tempest of emotions in the breasts of Southern leaders. Did the triumph of the "Black Republicans" justify the execution of the oft-threatened withdrawal from the Union? Notwithstanding the fulminations of the "fire-eaters," the tide of American nationality ran strong in the South, and a decision involving the dismemberment of a nation which Southern statesmen had played so vital a part in building was not lightly to be made. The right of secession was generally admitted, but did the existing circumstances justify the exercise of the right?

In an address before the Georgia legislature, Alexander H. Stephens on November 14 declared emphatically in the negative. He pointed out that "The president is no emperor, no dictator," that he could "do nothing unless backed by power in Congress," and there the Republicans lacked a majority. If the new Chief Executive should violate the Constitution, then would be the time to act. Certain other Southern leaders favored secession, not as an irrevocable step, but as a means of intimidating the federal government, believing, with T. R. R. Cobb of Georgia, that "We can make better terms out of the Union than in it."

But the psychology of the situation played inevitably into the hands of the extremists. Twenty-five years of increasing sectional bitterness had caused the two branches of the American people to lose faith in each other. Dr. Francis Lieber, a political economist who knew intimately the people of both sections, wrote in 1860, "It sometimes has occurred to me that what Thucydides said of the Greeks at the time of the Peloponnesian War applies to us at the present. 'The Greeks,' he said, 'did not understand each other any longer, though they spoke the same language;

words received a different meaning in different parts.'" Exaggerated fears of what *might* happen under a "Black Republican" administration became transformed into a conviction of impending calamities. Moreover, Lincoln's kindly and essentially conservative nature was unknown to most Southerners, who, however, were well apprised of his threatening sentiment that the Union must become all slave or all free. Was it not better for the South to secede, they reasoned, before the abolition party completely dominated the federal government?

The extremists had their firmest hold in the southernmost tier of the planting states, where cotton capitalism was strongest. Here, amidst a dense slave population, sensitiveness to antislavery criticism was exceedingly keen. Under the leadership of such men as J. H. Hammond and R. B. Rhett of South Carolina, Robert Toombs of Georgia, and W. L. Yancey of Alabama, the secession movement made swift headway. Jefferson Davis at first counseled delay and cautious action, but soon aligned himself with the separationists.

In every instance, the seceding states, thoroughly schooled in the constitutional views of Calhoun, sought to observe legal forms in severing the bonds of union. Special state conventions were summoned to enact ordinances of secession, since, by a similar procedure, the Constitution had originally been accepted. Appropriately enough, South Carolina took the lead. Upon receipt of the news of Lincoln's election, the legislature, which had remained in session for the express purpose, issued a call for a state convention. On December 20, 1860, that body amid intense excitement formally repealed the act of 1788 ratifying the Constitution, and "dissolved" the "union now subsisting between South Carolina and other States, under the name of the 'United States of America.'" By February 1, 1861, similar action had been taken successively by Mississippi, Florida, Alabama, Georgia, Louisiana, and Texas.

The ordinances of secession were usually accompanied by an official statement of the justifying causes. In general, three reasons were assigned. Much was made of the growing strength and aggressiveness of the antislavery forces, as exemplified in the Personal Liberty laws, John Brown's raid, defiance of the Supreme Court, and the inflammatory utterances of Republican leaders.

Such acts were held to violate the "constitutional compact" and thereby to release the Southern states from their obligations.

In the second place, slavery was vindicated from the assaults of those who opposed it on moral and economic grounds. In the words of the Mississippi convention, slave labor "supplies the product which constitutes by far the largest and most important portions of the commerce of the earth . . . and by an imperious law of nature none but the black race can bear exposure to the tropical sun. These products have become necessities of the world, and a blow at slavery is a blow at commerce and civilization."

But the most fundamental justification of all, in the minds of Southerners, may be summed up in the modern expression: the right of self-determination. The South demanded the right to live its own life in its own way, under such social institutions as were satisfactory to itself. In this sense, the official statements of causes may be regarded as declarations of independence. As Mississippi said, "We must either submit to degradation and to loss of property worth four billions of money or we must secede from the Union framed by our fathers, to secure this as well as every other species of property. For far less cause than this our fathers separated from the Crown of England."

Secession by the separate states was a preliminary to the formation of a Southern federal government. On February 4, 1861, a congress of delegates from the seceded states met at Montgomery, Alabama, organized a *de facto* government under the name of the "Confederate States of America," and adopted a provisional constitution (later made permanent). Jefferson Davis was chosen President, though much against his wishes, for he aspired to command one of the armies of the new nation. As a concession to the moderates, the vice-presidency was bestowed on Alexander H. Stephens, who had done more than any other Southerner to delay and defeat secession. The laws of the United States not inconsistent with the Confederate Constitution were continued in force.

The Constitution was closely modeled upon that of the United States, but there were certain significant departures. One body of provisions was designed to establish beyond cavil or dispute the Southern position on the various sectional questions that had arisen in the past. Congress was forbidden to subsidize internal improvements (except as an aid to navigation), or to lay protective tariffs, or to grant bounties. Negro slavery was to be protected by Congress in all territories, and no law should ever be passed to deny or impair the right of property in slaves. A second group of clauses provided for certain reforms in governmental procedure, suggested by experience under the old Constitution. For example, the President was limited to a single six-year term, he was given the right to veto items in appropriation bills, an executive budget system was introduced, and a simpler method of amending the Constitution provided for.

Only seven states were represented in the Montgomery Congress, but the architects of the new nation expected the early adhesion of the eight remaining slave states which still cleaved to the old Union. Indeed, in their high enthusiasm, they anticipated an extension beyond these natural limits. Stephens, now an ardent supporter of the Confederacy, predicted in a notable speech at Savannah on March 21, 1861, "Looking to the distant future, and perhaps not very far distant either, it is not beyond the range of possibility, and even probability, that all the great states of the north-west will gravitate this way." The sequel was to show that the Confederate leaders were too optimistic, even in regard to all those states whose domestic institutions were like those of the Lower South.

The North and Secession

The Northern people watched the progress of events in the Lower South with bewilderment and indecision. Few had anticipated such an outcome of a Republican victory, for the threats of the Southern "fire-eaters" had been looked upon as sheer braggadocio. Nor was the North a unit on the slavery question — a fact amply evident from Douglas's success in polling one and one third million Northern votes. In any contingency, many people preferred a permanent disruption of the Union to the alternative of a terrible fratricidal war.

Antislavery radicals declared publicly that the departure of the slave states was good riddance. "If the cotton States shall decide that they can do better out of the Union than in it," wrote Greeley in the *New York Tribune*, "we insist on letting them go in peace." In a similar spirit, a national convention of workingmen at Philadelphia resolved in February, 1861, that "our Government never can be sustained by bloodshed but must live in the affections of the people; we are, therefore, utterly opposed to any measures that will evoke civil war." On the other hand, there were those who could declare, like Senator Baker of Oregon, "We of the North are a majority of the Union, and we will govern our Union in our own way."

The responsibility for formulating a policy to cope with the crisis devolved upon the President and Congress, but their course was inevitably influenced by the uncertain state of public opinion. Buchanan was at this time nearly seventy years of age, by nature timid, and long accustomed to view public questions through Southern spectacles. Dreading the thought of taking any action likely to precipitate a civil war, he no doubt felt an obligation to keep things in an unchanged condition until the new administration took hold.

In his message of December 4, 1860, he outlined his policy to Congress. He denied absolutely the constitutionality of secession, but, on the other hand, he declared that the Constitution nowhere conferred on the federal government authority to compel a state to remain in the Union by force.[1] Charging that the North was the chief offender in the troubles that had arisen, he proposed an amendment to the Constitution, which would concede the extreme Southern contentions in regard to the Dred Scott decision, the Fugitive Slave Act, and the unconstitutionality of the Personal Liberty laws.

Unfortunately for Buchanan's peace of mind the situation called for more than well-intentioned words. What was to be done about the seacoast forts and other public property which the United States owned within the borders of the Confederacy? The cabinet, in which three Southern members still continued, gave him conflicting counsel, and Buchanan was torn alternately between the advice of proslavery disunionists and Northern

[1] In one portion of his message, he made allusion to the obligation of the President to enforce the laws throughout the land, but unlike either Jackson in 1832 or Lincoln when he entered office, he failed to find therein ample power for the suppression of an unlawful movement against federal authority. Still, if Buchanan had begun a second term in March, 1861, it is not impossible that his course might have been quite like Lincoln's.

nationalists. The most critical situation existed in Charleston Harbor where Major Robert Anderson and a small body of men occupied Fort Sumter. Old General Winfield Scott urged prompt and decisive action upon the President, and sought to stiffen his resolution by recounting the military measures which he had taken at Jackson's behest to meet a similar crisis in South Carolina.[1] Buchanan's indecision caused the resignation of Cass as Secretary of State in December.

Finally, in January, 1861, Buchanan was emboldened to dispatch an armed steamship, the *Star of the West*, to Fort Sumter, laden with military supplies and reënforcements of two hundred soldiers. Upon her arrival at daybreak on January 9, the Confederate batteries opened fire; and since Major Anderson, ignorant of the government's plans, was unprepared to give her prompt support, she turned about and forthwith returned to New York. The firing upon the *Star of the West* was really an act of war, but Buchanan was not disposed to make an issue of the affair. Meantime, the South Carolinians took peaceable possession of two unoccupied forts in Charleston Harbor and of the custom house and United States arsenal. Elsewhere in the Confederacy the federal forts and arsenals, being unprotected, were also quietly taken over, with the single exception of Fort Pickens at Pensacola, which remained in Union hands throughout the war.

Buchanan's inaction may be, in part, accounted for by the belief of statesmen in both sections that civil war might yet be averted, as in 1850, through the adoption of compromise measures. The most conspicuous champion of this solution was Crittenden of Kentucky, Clay's successor in the Senate and a Constitutional Unionist. He proposed a constitutional amendment reëstablishing the Missouri-Compromise line in the territories, with the protection of slavery south of the line. Though the plan had the half-hearted support of leading Southern Senators and was warmly advocated by Douglas, the Republicans would have none of it. They believed with their President-

[1] It is interesting to note that Jackson's Nullification Proclamation and Webster's speech advocating the Force Bill were reprinted in convenient form at this time, and enjoyed a wide circulation in the North. About this time, also, appeared the last volume of James Parton's *Life of Jackson*, and that author's account of "Old Hickory's" manner of opposing nullification had its effect in molding public sentiment.

elect that such an arrangement would merely redouble proslavery efforts for territorial expansion southward. "The tug has to come, and better now than later," advised Lincoln. Countless other proposals were brought before Congress, but the only action officially taken fell pathetically short of the necessities of the occasion — the submission to the states on March 2, 1861, of a proposed amendment pledging Congress never to interfere with slavery within the boundaries of a state.

Efforts for conciliation were also undertaken outside of Congress. In December, 1860, a caucus of the Governors of seven Republican states met in New York City, and agreed to recommend to their legislatures the repeal of the Personal Liberty laws. Such action was taken by Rhode Island in January, and Massachusetts and Vermont followed shortly with drastic modifications of their statutes. Had any real hope inhered in this course of action, other Northern states would have imitated their example.

A final attempt at adjustment was made by the border states under the leadership of Virginia. A "Peace Convention," attended by twenty-one states, assembled at Washington on February 4, 1861, with ex-President Tyler in the chair. Upon a close vote, a constitutional amendment was proposed, to the effect that no territory should be annexed without the consent of a concurrent majority of the Senators from the free and from the slave states. Despite the advocacy of Crittenden and Douglas, the plan received but seven favorable votes in the United States Senate.

As Lowell wrote in the *Atlantic Monthly*, the "panacea of palaver" had failed. Nevertheless, the months of discussion served a useful purpose in convincing the Northern people that, every peaceable means of settlement having been tried, no alternative remained but war.

Responsibility for the next move fell squarely upon the shoulders of the man whose election had precipitated the crisis. It seems an act of divine providence that Abraham Lincoln should have been called to the helm of state to undertake a task which, as he told his neighbors in Springfield upon departing for the capital, was "greater than that which rested upon Washington."

Born in 1809 in the border state of Kentucky, there coursed

through his veins the blood of a vigorous stock inherited on the one side from New England and on the other from Virginia. A frontier boy migrating with his parents to Indiana and then to Illinois, he imbibed from his pioneer surroundings a passionate belief in nationalism and an ardent faith in the common man. Notwithstanding his great stature and rude strength, he was by nature gentle, and his broad humanity arrayed him instinctively on the antislavery side. He had little patience, however, with the precipitate methods of the abolitionists, who, he believed, hurt rather than helped their cause, and even less with those zealots who valued the freedom of the negro above national preservation.

To the great majority of his countrymen, he was an unknown quantity when he entered the presidency. Indeed, his true greatness did not dawn on most men until after his death. Being of the common clay himself, his mind was attuned to the unspoken hopes and thoughts of the masses. "The Lord must love the plain people," he once said in his whimsical way, "that's why he made so many of them." But unlike the first great American commoner, Jackson, he regarded himself as an instrument, rather than the dictator, of events. Conscious of his political inexperience, he counseled with all sorts and conditions of men; but he formed his political principles with the utmost care, and when once convinced of their truth, never yielded them, though he was not above making temporary concessions.

He was unbelievably tender toward every antagonist. For all his hatred of false ideas, he never had a vindictive impulse directed toward the men who differed with him. As a recent biographer has said, "Destruction for the idea, infinite clemency for the person — such was his attitude." His literary style, the evolution of years, blended simplicity, directness, and candor, and was marked by a splendidly ordered progression of ideas. Lincoln would be the first to protest against the attempts that have been made to idealize him. He was human in every pore. Homely to the verge of ugliness, awkward in manner, he sometimes shocked dignified statesmen by receiving them in slippered feet. Addicted to story telling, his humor was not always in the best taste, and gave him a reputation for flippancy on grave occasions. His greatest mistakes were made as an administrator, for he was often unfortunate in his judgments of men. But these qualities made him resemble the average man, and endeared him to the plain people.

Lincoln arrived in Washington ten days before the close of Buchanan's term, escaping a plot to assassinate him as he passed through Baltimore. The day of the inauguration dawned, disagreeable and stormy. Most of the participants were agitated and apprehensive. General Scott kept an anxious eye upon the crowd, which was commanded by cannon. Chief Justice Taney, author of the Dred Scott decision, administered the oath of office in words scarcely intelligible from emotion. Then came Lincoln's inaugural address, delivered with deep feeling and a trace of nervousness, and containing his long-awaited announcement of policy.

Dwelling first upon the nature of the Union, he affirmed that it possessed the "vital spark of perpetuity," and was, in reality, "much older than the Constitution," for it was the product of a fundamental nationalism which had united the colonies in their efforts against Britain. The so-called ordinances of secession were "legally void," he said, and all violent efforts to uphold them "insurrectionary or revolutionary." As for his own duty in the crisis, the Constitution expressly enjoined the President to execute the federal laws in all the states. "The power confided to me will be used to hold, occupy, and possess the property and places belonging to the Government and to collect the duties and imposts." He closed with an eloquent and touching appeal for a restoration of the ancient bonds of affection.

The address possessed an undertone of vigorous nationality, but it was phrased cautiously, with the object of preventing the spread of the secession movement to the eight slave states as yet unaffected. In an unobtrusive way, Lincoln announced the principle upon which the federal government later waged war against the South. Ignoring Buchanan's assertion that the federal government had no authority to use force against seceding states, Lincoln dwelt on his constitutional duty to execute the laws in all parts of an indivisible country. In his mind, the whole situation reduced itself to a transaction between the national authority, on the one hand, and lawless persons or groups, on the other. This was in accord with the central principle of the

Constitution that the federal government operates directly upon individuals and not upon states.

Lincoln surrounded himself with a cabinet that at once commanded the confidence of the Northern people. All elements which had contributed to Republican success were represented, including Lincoln's chief rivals for the nomination. Seward was appointed Secretary of State, Chase, Secretary of the Treasury, Simon Cameron of Pennsylvania, Secretary of War, and Gideon Welles of Connecticut, Secretary of the Navy. The slave states still loyal were recognized by the offer of three places. J. A. Gilmer of North Carolina declined, but Edward Bates of Missouri accepted the post of Attorney-General, and Montgomery Blair of Maryland, that of Postmaster-General.[1]

The President had scarcely announced his policy toward secession before events forced him to put it into effect. On the day after the inauguration came word from Major Anderson that he could hold Fort Sumter only about a month longer unless reënforced and provisioned. The circumstances called for prompt action. All the members of the cabinet, except Blair and Chase, advised evacuation, and General Scott delivered his weighty opinion that to relieve the fort now would require a force of 20,000 troops — which did not exist. But Lincoln, almost without support, pitted his judgment against that of his more experienced counselors. It seemed to him that the abandonment of Sumter without resistance would not only impair the morale of the North, but would, in a sense, constitute a recognition of the Confederacy.

In accordance with a prior agreement, he therefore notified Governor F. W. Pickens of South Carolina of his intentions, and on April 6, ordered the dispatching of a relief expedition with provisions for the Sumter garrison. The Confederates at once sent a summons of surrender to Anderson, and when he refused, their batteries opened fire on April 12. By the next day the position had become untenable, and just as the relief ships — which could in no case have really helped him — were appearing in the offing, he surrendered with the honors of war. The period

[1] Caleb B. Smith of Indiana was appointed Secretary of the Interior. Cameron was succeeded by Edwin M. Stanton of Pennsylvania as Secretary of War in January, 1862. Other changes also took place.

of irresolution was at last ended. The nation — "a house divided" — faced the terrible certainty of civil war.

The Appeal to Arms

The bombardment of Fort Sumter had an electrifying effect upon the people of all sections. All hesitation was now swept from the minds of the Northern people. On April 15, 1861, President Lincoln issued a call for 75,000 volunteers for three months, followed early in May by a further call for 42,000 volunteers for a term of three years. Other proclamations increased the regular army by about 23,000 men, enlisted 18,000 men for the navy, and declared the coast of the Confederacy under blockade. Although the Northern people were of many minds concerning the downtrodden negro, patriotism clearly demanded of them the maintenance of an undivided nation. "For my own part," wrote Lincoln, "I consider the central idea pervading this struggle is the necessity of proving that popular government is not an absurdity. We must settle this question now, whether, in a free government, the minority have the right to break up the government whenever they choose. If we fail, it will go far to prove the incapability of the people to govern themselves."

The drums beat in every town and village, and the rush to arms of the young men was universal. Greeley and other editors, casting aside their earlier timidity, rallied strongly to the cause of the Union. Douglas, destined to live but a few months longer, pledged his full support to the President in an Associated Press interview, and in a great speech in Chicago declared, "There can be no neutrals in this war; only patriots — or traitors."

The news of Fort Sumter likewise enkindled the people of the seven Confederate states. President Davis issued a proclamation for 100,000 men, and his call was as eagerly obeyed as President Lincoln's in the North. Regiments sallied gayly forth from the Southern hamlets, as if on holiday parade, little dreaming how awful a struggle was about to begin.

Both sides now anxiously awaited the action of the eight slave states which had thus far continued loyal. Fringing the northern border of the Confederacy were Arkansas, Tennessee, North Carolina, and Virginia. These states were less identified with cotton production than the Lower South, having fewer slaves as well as a larger proportion of nonslaveholding whites. The majority of the people believed in the right of secession, but until now had denied that sufficient provocation existed. But their

THE PROGRESS OF SECESSION

doubts were dissipated by the attempt to relieve Sumter, followed by Lincoln's call for troops. Virginia took the fateful step on April 17, Arkansas on May 6, North Carolina two weeks later, and Tennessee on June 24.

No state left the Union with greater reluctance than Virginia. Her statesmen had been indispensable to the winning of independence and the framing of the Constitution, and she had furnished five Presidents of the United States. Her history was closely, almost inextricably, entwined with that of the nation. On April 5 her state convention had rejected secession, but after Lincoln's call for troops, the tide of disunion feeling swept all before it. With Virginia went Colonel Robert E. Lee, a man of noble character and superb military ability, who declined the command of the Union army out of loyalty to his state. The importance of Virginia's action gained immediate recognition by the removal of the Confederate capital from Montgomery to Richmond.

The mountaineers of northwestern Virginia, however, refused to accept the decision of the state. These folk, prevailingly Scotch-Irish and Pennsylvania-German in stock, owned few slaves, and had long been pitted against their tidewater brethren in state politics. Protected from Southern interference by federal military operations, they determined to separate from Virginia, and erect a state of their own. As a preliminary step, a convention was held at Wheeling in June, 1861, which set up a loyal government of Virginia, composed chiefly of representatives of the mountainous counties and those counties under federal military control adjoining Washington. Francis H. Pierpont was chosen Governor, and the new "state government" was prudently installed within Union lines at Alexandria.

A later convention representing only the people of forty-six northwestern counties was then held in November, and with the consent of the Pierpont government, application was made for admission into the Union as the state of "West Virginia." Congress acted tardily, and the new commonwealth finally entered the Union in June, 1863, with a constitution providing for gradual emancipation. West Virginia runs up like a wedge between Ohio and Pennsylvania, and from a military standpoint, the action of the inhabitants secured to the federal authorities the command of important rail and telegraph facilities between the Middle Atlantic states and the Ohio Valley.

Between the enlarged Confederacy and the free states lay the four remaining slave states — the "border states" of Maryland, Delaware, Kentucky, and Missouri. Financial investment in slaves steadily diminished from the Gulf northward, cotton capitalism was nonexistent in these states, and slaves were regarded as only one among many forms of property. Torn in their affections between South and North, and having substantial economic ties with both, these states knew not which way to turn.

Maryland was saved to the Union by the prompt and vigorous

action of the federal authorities. Inclosing the District of Columbia on three sides, it would have been a fatal military error to permit the state to pass under enemy control. When the Maryland disunionists severed telegraphic communications between Washington and the North and sought to prevent the passage of Union troops, Lincoln suspended the writ of *habeas corpus*, ordered numerous arrests of suspects, and stationed troops at strategic points throughout the state. In consequence, by the middle of May, 1861, all danger of secession was gone. With Maryland went Delaware as a matter of course; in any case, slaves formed an insignificant fraction of the latter's population.

Farther to the west, Lincoln's native state of Kentucky, standing athwart the military highway between North and South and rent by internal dissension, found a temporary solution for her problem in May, 1861, in a declaration of neutrality. Lincoln's policy here was in marked contrast with his treatment of Maryland. Feeling confident of her ultimate decision, he respected Kentucky's negative position, and quietly labored to promote the spread of nationalist sentiment. When the Confederacy violated her neutrality in September by sending troops to occupy Columbus, the newly chosen legislature raised the Stars and Stripes over the state capitol, and declared for the Union.

In Missouri the state government was disunionist, but the state convention, called to consider the question of secession, proved unexpectedly to be dominated by nationalist sentiment. A contest ensued between the two bodies, each claiming to represent the true will of the people, and each summoning military force to its support. Under the audacious leadership of Francis P. Blair, Jr., and Captain Nathaniel Lyon, supported by militia companies of St. Louis Germans, the forces of nationalism triumphed. The state convention in July, 1861, deposed the pro-Southern Governor, and established a loyal government. Thereafter there was never any real danger of secession, although the conflict between the two antagonistic elements continued in modified form throughout the war. In the case of all the border states save Delaware, thousands of citizens, unwilling to accept the decision of the majority, flocked into the Confederate armies.

The Embattled Hosts

The people of each section entered the war with high hopes for an early victory. Both sides prayed to the same God, and Southerners accepted almost implicitly the declaration of the Reverend B. M. Palmer, the great Presbyterian divine, that "In this great struggle, we defend the cause of God and religion." From a strictly mundane point of view, however, the North enjoyed a decided advantage. Twenty-three states with a population of twenty-two millions were arrayed against eleven states containing nine million people, and in the latter instance three and one half millions were slaves. Though the Southern white population was more homogeneous, the diversified makeup of the Northern people proved a source of strength rather than otherwise, for in proportion to their numbers, more English, German, and Irish immigrants served in the Union armies than native-born Northerners.[1] The Irish regiments often carried the green flag along with the American colors.

The industrial superiority of the North even exceeded its preponderance in man power. Whereas the South was purely an agricultural section, the free states had abundant facilities for the manufacture of arms and munitions, clothing and other necessary supplies. Indeed, three of the most powerful allies of the North in the war were mechanical agencies, devised by human ingenuity and developed to high efficiency in the decade or so before 1860.

One of these was the McCormick reaper, with its various competitors. Patented originally in 1834, the first model had undergone constant improvement until it had become possible for one person with a team of horses to cut as much grain as twenty men swinging cradles. Three thousand reaping machines were manufactured in 1850, twenty thousand in 1860, and seventy thousand in 1864. The farmers of the Upper Mississippi Valley were the chief purchasers, and with the westward movement of the center of wheat production, the harvester works had been

[1] Franz Sigel, Carl Schurz, and other Germans who had been prominent in the Revolution of 1848 gave the benefit of their military experience to the untrained federal armies, and rose high in the service. Count Zeppelin, who later perfected the dirigible airship in Germany, served as a cavalry officer and engineer, beginning in 1863. He made his first ascent in a military balloon in this country.

transferred from Virginia to Cincinnati, and in 1847 to Chicago. "The reaper is to the North what slavery is to the South," declared the Secretary of War in 1861. "By taking the places of regiments of young men in the Western harvest fields, it releases them to do battle for the Union at the front, and at the same time keeps up the supply of bread for the nation and the nation's armies."

Hardly less important was the sewing machine. In 1846 Elias Howe, a poor, struggling inventor of the traditional type, produced the first practicable sewing machine, and in the next few years important improvements were devised by A. B. Wilson, Isaac M. Singer, and others. After 1852 the contrivance began to be widely used in Northern homes, and between that year and 1860, 130,000 machines were made and sold. This invention quickly revolutionized the manufacture of men's clothing, hitherto a household industry, for power-driven sewing machines were introduced into the factories, and the era of cheap ready-made clothing dawned. Men's shirts which had required 14 hours and 20 minutes for making by hand could now be made in one hour and 16 minutes.

Between 1850 and 1860 the annual output of clothing factories grew from $48,000,000 to $80,000,000. With the invention of the McKay sewing machine in 1861, the large-scale production of cheap factory-made shoes became practicable. In the first year after its general adoption, 1,500,000 pairs of shoes were manufactured, double the quantity in any previous year. Since manufacturing was located exclusively in the North, the benefit of these inventions accrued only to that section, and though the wage-earners joined the armies in large numbers, the production of clothing, undergarments, and shoes, so necessary for the comfort of the soldiers, actually increased during the war period.

The spread of railway mileage in the North since 1850 had an even more direct relationship to federal military success. Besides the Baltimore and Ohio, saved to the Union by the loyalty of the West Virginians, the North in 1860 was traversed from coast to interior by three or four other fairly continuous roads, forerunners of later "trunk lines." The extension of railroads westward during the decade had drawn the Ohio Valley section and the

Eastern states closer together, and had created mutual economic ties. During the war the railway net helped to promote the rapid movement of troops and supplies. Among the early wartime laws was an act of January, 1862, giving the President authority to commandeer the railroads and telegraph lines, if necessary for military purposes. A Director of Railroads was appointed, and more than two thousand miles of track, chiefly in the border states, were taken over and operated by the government for the duration of the conflict.[1]

The principal advantage of the South in the struggle consisted in its geographic position and in the fact that the people were fighting on their own soil. Though proper railway facilities were lacking, the Confederacy, with a compact, well-watered territory, could protect its military frontier with a minimum of exertion and upon a smaller war budget than the North. The Union forces, on the other hand, operating on unfamiliar ground, were constantly drawing farther away from their base of supplies.

Moreover, the aristocratic social system of the South was conducive to the development of natural leaders and the cultivation of the martial spirit. Many of the Confederate generals had fought as youths in the Mexican War, and when secession occurred, an undue proportion of able officers resigned their commissions to join the Southern armies. It was a common boast south of Mason and Dixon's line that any Confederate could lick three Yankees, which provoked President Davis's sober retort, "Only fools doubted the courage of the Yankees or their willingness to fight when they saw fit."

The chief hope of the Confederacy lay in a speedy victory, or else in foreign intervention. For the latter, they relied upon their virtual monopoly of the world's cotton supply, a product so necessary for the operation of British textile mills. Time fought on the side of the North, for, with sufficient delay, raw armies

[1] Curiously enough, another invention was neglected, which would have greatly increased the destructive power of the army adopting it. This was the breechloading rifle. It had been used in the German Revolution of 1848, and in 1857 a board appointed by the Secretary of War had reported unanimously in favor of a single-shot breechloader. Since the old muzzle-loader required sixty seconds to load and fire as against four seconds for the new gun, the superiority of the latter would seem obvious. But the Ordnance Department was averse to innovation, and the purchase of breechloaders did not become a regular policy until 1864. Perhaps 100,000 breechloaders were in the hands of the Union soldiers by the close of the war.

might be whipped into shape, material resources efficiently utilized, and effective military leadership developed.

In reality, from a military point of view, neither side was prepared for a great war. As someone has remarked, the Americans are an intensely warlike but an unmilitary people. Munitions and equipment were lacking at the outset. Few officers on either side had ever commanded so much as a regiment, and as for commanding armies, there was no experience. Many of the opposing Generals were West Point men, graduates from the same course of study and often classmates. The regimental and company officers in the volunteer armies were commissioned by the Governors, and though this system was quickly altered in the South, politicians continued to be appointed to high military positions in the North. There were 2,537 Union Generals of all grades during the war. Moreover, the insistent clamor and officious meddling of Greeley and other editors embarrassed the success of Northern military plans, and frequently served as a source of information to the enemy.

Both sides faced the task of creating efficient fighting units out of the ranks of a people accustomed to peaceful pursuits. Of course, in the first flush of war enthusiasm, the calls for troops were met in both sections by an excess of volunteers. Numerous organization camps were established where the raw recruits, many of them mere youths, were hastily taught the manual of arms and the rudiments of warfare, and then hurried to the front. Enthusiasm began to wane, however, when the war promised to last much longer than originally expected, and when individuals saw a chance to reap unusual profits by staying in civilian occupations. Under these circumstances, both governments supplemented the system of voluntary enlistments with the offer of bounties, and when that failed to raise sufficient troops, with compulsory recruiting.

The purpose of the bounty system was to stimulate enlistments. Beginning in July, 1861, the federal government offered a special inducement of $100 to each volunteer, an amount increased during the year 1863 to $302 for raw recruits and $402 for veterans.[1] States, counties, and cities granted additional bounties, especially after conscription was adopted by Congress, for the draft was

[1] A private's pay was $13 a month until May 1, 1864, when it was raised to $16.

applied only to those districts which did not fill their quotas. In 1864 a volunteer in New York County might obtain a county bounty of $300, a state bounty of $75, and a federal bounty to new recruits of $302 or of $402 to veterans. At the same time an Illinois district paid an average bounty of $1,056. The system was bad, for it led to the crime of "bounty-jumping." Unprincipled men would enlist, claim the bounty, desert, reënlist elsewhere under a different name, and repeat the process. In all, the federal government paid out $300,000,000 in bounties, and the state and local government expended an additional amount of $286,000,000.

Conscription was first resorted to on August 4, 1862, when President Lincoln ordered a draft of 300,000 militia through the medium of the states. The results were unsatisfactory, and on March 3, 1863, Congress enacted the statute upon which all later drafts were based. This Act operated directly upon the people of the nation. All unmarried men between the ages of twenty and forty-five and all married men between twenty and thirty-five years of age, if fit for military service, were made subject to compulsory enlistment at the President's call. In each draft the names were to be selected by lot. Certain classes were exempt: high public officials, men who were the sole support of dependent families, and criminals. A drafted man might escape service by providing an acceptable substitute or by paying $300.

The Conscription Act provoked considerable antagonism in the North, for it was thought by many to be unconstitutional, and was undoubtedly contrary to the traditional military policy of the nation. But by others it was viewed as the only truly democratic system of recruiting an army. The laboring classes and poor people generally raised loud objections to the provision which enabled the well-to-do to purchase cheap exemption. Difficulties were encountered when the first draft under the law was undertaken. According to the official report of the Provost Marshal General, "Every imaginable artifice was adopted to deceive and defeat the enrolling officers. Open violence was sometimes met with. . . . In certain mining regions organized bodies of men openly opposed the enrollment, rendering it necessary that the U. S. authorities should send troops to overcome their opposition."

The most notorious resistance took place in New York City in July, 1863. When the officials in charge began to make public the lists of drafted men, it appeared that most of the names were of laboring men and mechanics. Rioting ensued, and for four days the city was at the mercy of a mob, composed principally of immigrants, and presently enlarged by the addition of thieves and ruffians. Houses and shops were pillaged and burned, and death dealt freely to negroes, who were blamed as the cause of the war and the draft. Only when the troops arrived and the streets were raked with cannon and howitzers was peace restored. The loss in killed and wounded was estimated at one thousand. The draft went on generally throughout the country, and while it did not actually furnish many soldiers to the army, it greatly increased enlistments.

In the South, also, bounties were offered to accelerate enlistments. Conscription was resorted to earlier than in the North. By acts of April and September, 1862, President Davis was empowered to impress into service all able-bodied male whites between the ages of eighteen and forty-five. The exempted classes were numerous, including state and Confederate officials, preachers and teachers, persons employed in railway transportation and important war industries, newspaper proprietors, and the overseers on the larger plantations. Toward the end of the war, an act of March, 1865, even provided for the enforced service of negro slaves.

The exercise of the conscription power by the Confederate government violated the strong state-rights tradition of that section, and led to energetic opposition on the part of R. B. Rhett and Vice-President Stephens and by some of the states. Governor J. E. Brown of Georgia pronounced the law unconstitutional, and refused to permit its enforcement within his state, though he was zealous in raising troops by state action. At Governor Z. B. Vance's instigation, the North Carolina legislature formally protested against conscription, and later passed a law, in direct contravention of the act of Congress, exempting additional classes from military service.

The total number of officers and men in the Southern armies during the war was approximately 1,200,000 as compared with 2,675,000 in the Union service. The latter figure includes

54,000 whites and more than 100,000 negroes recruited within the confines of the Confederacy.

SELECT BIBLIOGRAPHY

The Great Decision. On the events of these critical months of 1860–1861, J. F. Rhodes, *History of the United States*, III (New York, 1895), is detailed and judicious. Other well-balanced narratives appear in F. E. Chadwick, *Causes of the Civil War* (in *The American Nation*, XIX, New York, 1906); J. B. McMaster, *A History of the People of the United States*, VIII (New York, 1913); and James Schouler, *History of the United States*, V (New York, 1891). See also Edward Channing, *A History of the United States*, VI (New York, 1925).

The Movement for Southern Independence. N. W. Stephenson, *The Day of the Confederacy* (in *The Chronicles of America*, XXX, New Haven, 1919), gives a good general account. The subject may be approached from contrasting points of view in U. B. Phillips, " Georgia and State Rights " (in American Historical Association, *Annual Report for 1901*, II, 3–224), and C. H. Ambler, *Sectionalism in Virginia from 1776 to 1861* (Chicago, 1910). Consult also biographies of leading participants, such as W. E. Dodd, *Jefferson Davis* (Philadelphia, 1907), Louis Pendleton, *Alexander H. Stephens* (Philadelphia, 1908), and Gamaliel Bradford, *Lee the American* (Boston, 1912).

The North and Secession. A special study is Mary Scrugham, *The Peaceable Americans, 1860–1861* (in *Columbia University Studies*, XCVI, no. 3, New York, 1921). For the outgoing President's attitude, consult G. T. Curtis, *Life of James Buchanan* (2 v., New York, 1883), II. The earlier biographies of Lincoln were concerned mainly with the discovery of new material concerning him, the later chiefly with an understanding and interpretation of his personality and career. Of the former type perhaps the ablest are the monumental, though uncritical, *Abraham Lincoln; a History* (10 v., New York, 1890), by J. G. Nicolay and John Hay, and *The Life of Abraham Lincoln* (4 v., New York, 1906) by Ida M. Tarbell. Of the newer lives, two of the best are Lord Charnwood, *Abraham Lincoln* (New York, 1917), and N. W. Stephenson, *Lincoln* (Indianapolis, 1922).

The Appeal to Arms. J. C. McGregor, *The Disruption of Virginia* (New York, 1922), is an excellent treatment of the antisecessionist secession of the Virginia mountaineers. Thomas Speed, *The Union Cause in Kentucky* (New York, 1907), throws light on the situation in Lincoln's native state. For Missouri, see John McElroy, *The Struggle for Missouri* (Washington, 1909).

The Embattled Hosts. Some idea of the economic resources of the North may be gained from E. D. Fite, *Social and Industrial Conditions in the North during the Civil War* (New York, 1910). F. L. Paxson, " The Railroads of the ' Old Northwest ' before the Civil War " (in Wisconsin Academy, *Transactions*, XVII, pt. i, Madison, 1912), is also important in this connection.

For conditions in a particular state, Frederick Merk, *Economic History of Wisconsin during the Civil War Period* (in State Historical Society of Wisconsin, *Publications*, I, Madison, 1916), is valuable. The best account of Southern economic conditions appears in J. C. Schwab, *The Confederate States of America . . . A Financial and Industrial History* (New York, 1901).

For a comparison of sectional military strength, see J. C. Ropes and W. R. Livermore, *The Story of the Civil War* (3 v., New York, 1894–1911, in progress), I. Northern military legislation is summarized in F. L. Huidekoper, *The Military Unpreparedness of the United States* (New York, 1915). The military problems of the Confederacy behind the lines are dealt with in A. B. Moore, *Conscription and Conflict in the Confederacy* (New York, 1924).

CHAPTER XII

THE WAR OF AMERICAN NATIONALITY

Naval Operations of the Civil War

The Confederate armies, for the most part, fought on the defensive in the Civil War. To the North fell the task of invasion and conquest. From the outset, the federal authorities realized that, to suppress the rebellion, two objects must be attained: the Confederates must be prevented from receiving munitions and supplies from the outside world, and their armies must be crushed.

Without the accomplishment of the first purpose, it may be doubted whether success could have been attained in the second. Yet, when Lincoln inaugurated the blockade by proclamations of April 19 and 27, 1861, the United States navy was woefully inadequate for the task. It consisted of some ninety vessels, most of them small and antiquated and some of them absent on distant cruises, whereas the seacoast to be guarded was 3,500 miles in length. Nevertheless, by pressing all sorts of vessels into service, the blockade was already reasonably effective by summer.

Federal naval operations were, in general, lacking in spectacular exploits, though constant watchfulness was required to thwart the efforts of the blockade-runners. Evasion of the blockade was not only an adventurous but also a lucrative business, and occasional vessels, like the *Ad-Vance* which made eleven successful trips, showed the possibilities of the traffic. Some much-needed supplies gained access to the Confederacy in this way. Nevertheless, blockade-running never assumed formidable proportions.

As the prewar supplies became depleted, the Southern people began to suffer acute discomfort. Salt, coffee, tea, soap, paper, clothing, and matches were extremely hard to get at any price. Perhaps most serious of all was the scarcity of common medicines, like quinine and morphia, indispensable for the treatment of sick and wounded soldiers. The lack of salt also created difficulties, for salt meat formed a large part of the army ration.

The Confederates made one ingenious but unsuccessful effort to relieve the situation. On March 8, 1862, there suddenly appeared off Hampton Roads, Virginia, a Confederate vessel, the *Virginia*, made over from the former United States frigate *Merrimac* and covered with iron plates. The wooden ships of the blockading fleet were helpless before the iron monster, two warships being sunk and one driven aground. But the federal authorities had also been experimenting with the new type of vessel, and the ingenuity of John Ericsson, a Swedish immigrant, had contrived an armored vessel of a different model. On the next day the *Monitor*, a low-decked ironclad vessel with a revolving turret carrying heavy guns, took up the gage of battle for the North. Though neither vessel won a decisive victory, the *Virginia* was prevented from doing further mischief. This marine duel was epochmaking in the history of naval architecture, for it proved conclusively that the day of the wooden war vessel was past. A fleet of "monitors" was presently built by the United States, and performed important service during the remainder of the war.

The work of the navy was not confined to the maintenance of the blockade, for vessels of war coöperated with the land forces in opening up the Mississippi and other rivers. In Lincoln's expressive language, "Uncle Sam's web-feet" were present not only on "the broad bay, and the rapid river, but also up the narrow, muddy bayou, and wherever the ground was a little damp." The navy was also responsible for the eventual destruction of the Confederate raiders engaged in harassing Northern commerce on the high seas.

Military Activities in the East

The federal operations on land were determined, in part, by the objectives of the fighting, and partly, by the physical features of the country. From the early days of the war, one of the major purposes was the capture of the Confederate capital. Other important objectives were the military control of mountain

MILITARY OPERATIONS OF THE CIVIL WAR ON ALL FRONTS

Year	In the West	In the East	Year
1861	July 5 Engagement at Carthage, Mo. Aug. 10 Engagement at Wilson's Creek, Mo. Sept. 2 Capture of Fort Scott, Mo. Nov. 7 Battle of Belmont, Mo.	April 12–14 Attack on Fort Sumter. June 3 Engagement at Philippi, W. Va. June 10 Engagement at Big Bethel, W. Va. July 8 Engagement at Laurel Hill, W. Va. July 21 First battle of Bull Run, Va. Aug. 28–29 Capture of Fort Hatteras, N. C. Sept. 12–15 Fighting at Cheat Mt., W. Va. Oct. 21 Engagement at Ball's Bluff, Va. Nov. 7 Capture of Port Royal, S. C.	1861
1862	Jan. 19–20 Battle of Mill Springs, Mo. Feb. 6 Capture of Fort Henry, Tenn. Feb. 16 Capture of Fort Donelson, Tenn. Mch. 7–8 Battle of Pea Ridge, Ark. April 6–7 Battle of Shiloh, Tenn. April 7 Capture of Island No. 10. April 14 Capture of Fort Pillow, Tenn. April 28 Capture of New Orleans, La. May 30 Capture of Corinth, Miss. June 6 Occupation of Memphis, Tenn. Sept. 14–16 Battle of Munfordsville, Ky. Sept. 19 Battle of Iuka, Miss. Oct. 3–4 Battle of Corinth, Miss. Oct. 8 Battle of Perryville, Ky. Dec. 29 Sherman's repulse at Vicksburg, Miss.	May 4 Capture of Yorktown, Va. May 5 Battle of Williamsburg, Va. May 25 Battle of Winchester, Va. May 31–June 1 Battle of Seven Pines, Va. June 25–July 1 Seven Days' Battles, Va. Aug. 9 Battle of Cedar Mt., Va. Aug. 30 Second battle of Bull Run, Va. Sept. 14 Battle of South Mt., Md. Sept. 17 Battle of Antietam, Md. Dec. 13 Battle of Fredericksburg, Va.	1862

passes and navigable streams and the seizure of railway junction points — means whereby the economic life of the South and the transport of troops and munitions might be paralyzed. Since the Appalachian System, one hundred and fifty miles wide, divides the South into two unequal parts, each area became promptly a theater of war. During the first three years and more, a series of simultaneous campaigns took place on opposite sides of the mountain barrier, conducted with little or no relation to each other. West of the Mississippi River lay a third theater of warfare, involving military operations of distinctly minor importance.

To take a look ahead, the subjugation of the South proved to

MILITARY OPERATIONS OF THE CIVIL WAR ON ALL FRONTS

	In the West	In the East	
1863	Dec. 31–Jan. 2 Battle of Murfreesboro, Tenn. May 16 Fighting at Champion Hill, Miss. July 4 Capture of Vicksburg, Miss. July 9 Capture of Port Hudson, La. Sept. 9 Occupation of Chattanooga, Tenn. Sept. 19–20 Battle of Chickamauga, Ga. Nov. 23–25 Battle of Chattanooga, Tenn. Dec. 6 Occupation of Knoxville, Tenn.	May 2–5 Battle of Chancellorsville, Va. June 13–15 Engagement at Winchester, Va. July 1–3 Battle of Gettysburg, Pa. Sept. 7 Capture of Fort Wagner, S. C.	1863
1864	Feb. 14 Occupation of Meridian, Miss. April 8 Battle of Sabine Cross Roads, La. May 13–16 Fighting at Resaca, Ga. May 18 Fighting at Rome, Ga. June 27 Battle of Kenesaw Mt., Ga. July 22 First battle before Atlanta, Ga. Aug. 5 Capture of Mobile Bay, Ala. Sept. 2 Capture of Atlanta, Ga. Sept. 26–27 Fighting at Ironton, Mo. Nov. 30 Battle of Franklin, Tenn. Dec. 15–16 Battle of Nashville, Tenn. Dec. 20 Capture of Savannah, Ga.	May 5–6 First battle in Wilderness, Va. May 8–12 Battle of Spottsylvania, C. H., Va. June 1–3 Battle of Cold Harbor, Va. June 19 Siege of Petersburg, Va. begins. Sept. 19 Battle of Opequan, Va. Sept. 21 Battle of Fisher's Hill, Va. Oct. 19 Battle of Cedar Creek, Va.	1864
1865	May 26 Kirby Smith's surrender at Baton Rouge, La.	Jan. 15 Capture of Fort Fisher, N. C. Feb. 17 Capture of Columbia, S. C. Feb. 18 Capture of Charleston, S. C. Feb. 22 Capture of Wilmington, N. C. Mch. 19 Fighting at Goldsboro, N. C. April 1 Battle of Five Forks, Va. April 2 Occupation of Petersburg, Va. April 3 Occupation of Richmond, Va. April 9 Lee's surrender at Appomattox, Va. April 26 Johnston's surrender at Hillsboro, N. C.	1865

be a slow, difficult, and much interrupted process. Having been blockaded by sea, the Confederacy was gradually cut off from its western territory and deprived of its main internal lines of communication. Richmond, against which the North began to move within the first three months of the war, did not fall until nearly four years later, when the process just described had been completed and a Union army, operating from the West, had circled the southern end of the mountains and advanced northward along the coast, prepared to join forces with the troops assailing Richmond.

From the very first, both sides realized the importance of decisive operations in Virginia. The rival capitals stood only one hundred miles apart, located respectively on the Potomac and the James, rivers running in a roughly parallel direction. The intervening country, however, is traversed by numerous streams, subject to sudden freshets and flowing southeasterly into Chesapeake Bay. Lying athwart an invader's path, they afforded the Union troops maximum difficulty in their efforts to march overland on Richmond, while furnishing the Confederates natural moats of defense. Another feature of Virginia topography proved a constant menace to Northern security. Along the western border of old Virginia lie two mountain ranges, separated by the valley of the Shenandoah, a river flowing northerly into the Potomac at Harper's Ferry, above the federal capital. This valley formed an excellent passageway into the North, and under the protective screen of the mountains, Confederate commanders were constantly threatening Washington or harrying the rear of federal armies.

Lincoln's enterprise in preventing the secession of Maryland in the spring of 1861 had the strategic value of giving to the United States the control of the Potomac River. Spurred on by the popular clamor of "On to Richmond," General Irvin McDowell attacked the enemy at Manassas Junction on the little stream of Bull Run, twenty-five miles west of Washington, on July 21, 1861. Both armies were raw and undisciplined, but the superior leadership of the Confederate General, Joseph E. Johnston, threw the Union forces into confusion and caused a disgraceful rout. Lincoln now placed General George B. McClellan in command of the Army of the Potomac. Though he showed marvelous energy and success in whipping his armed mob into an efficient fighting unit, the remainder of the year passed without offensive operations.

The campaign of 1862 opened with McClellan's decision to launch a drive against Richmond from an unexpected quarter — the shore of Chesapeake Bay — thereby avoiding the difficult overland march. His plan was to ship his army to Fortress

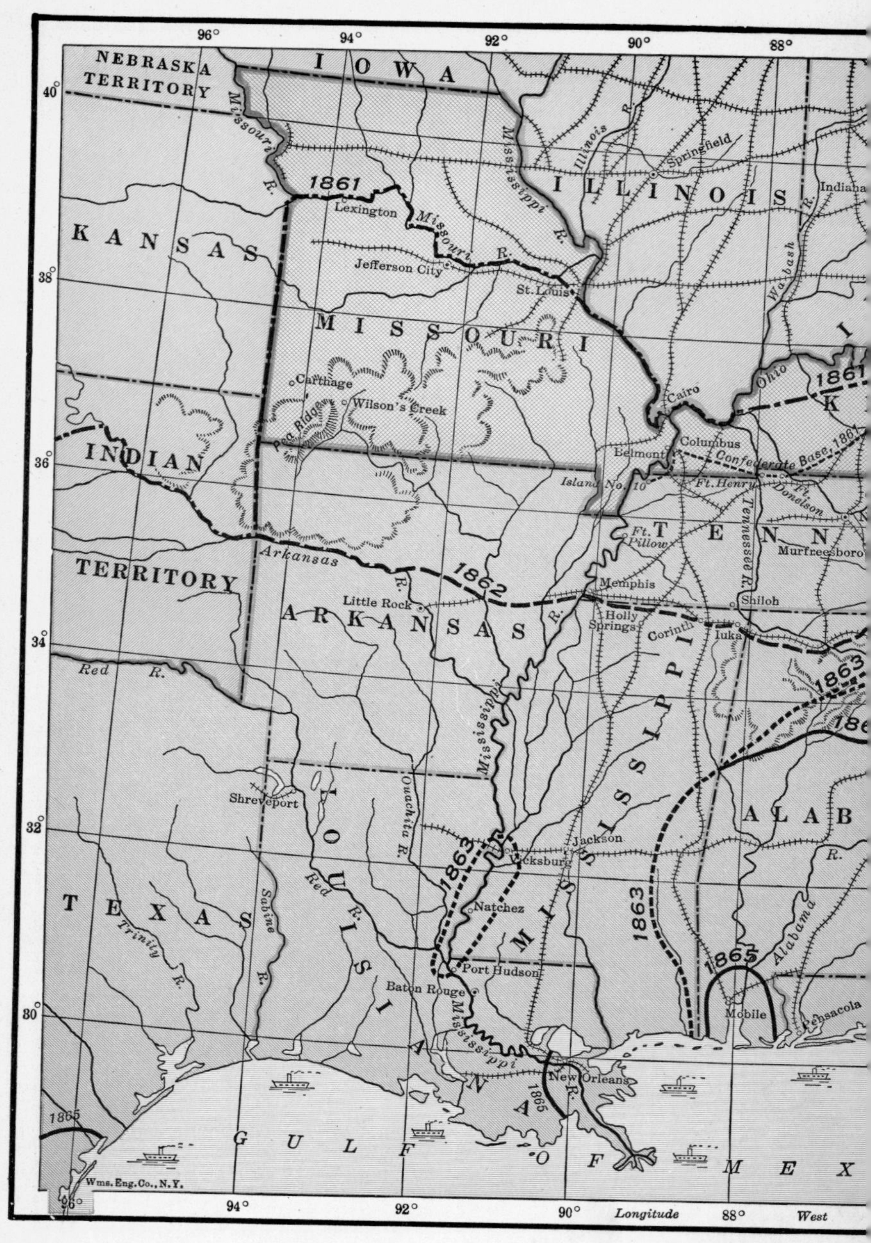

THE THEATER OF

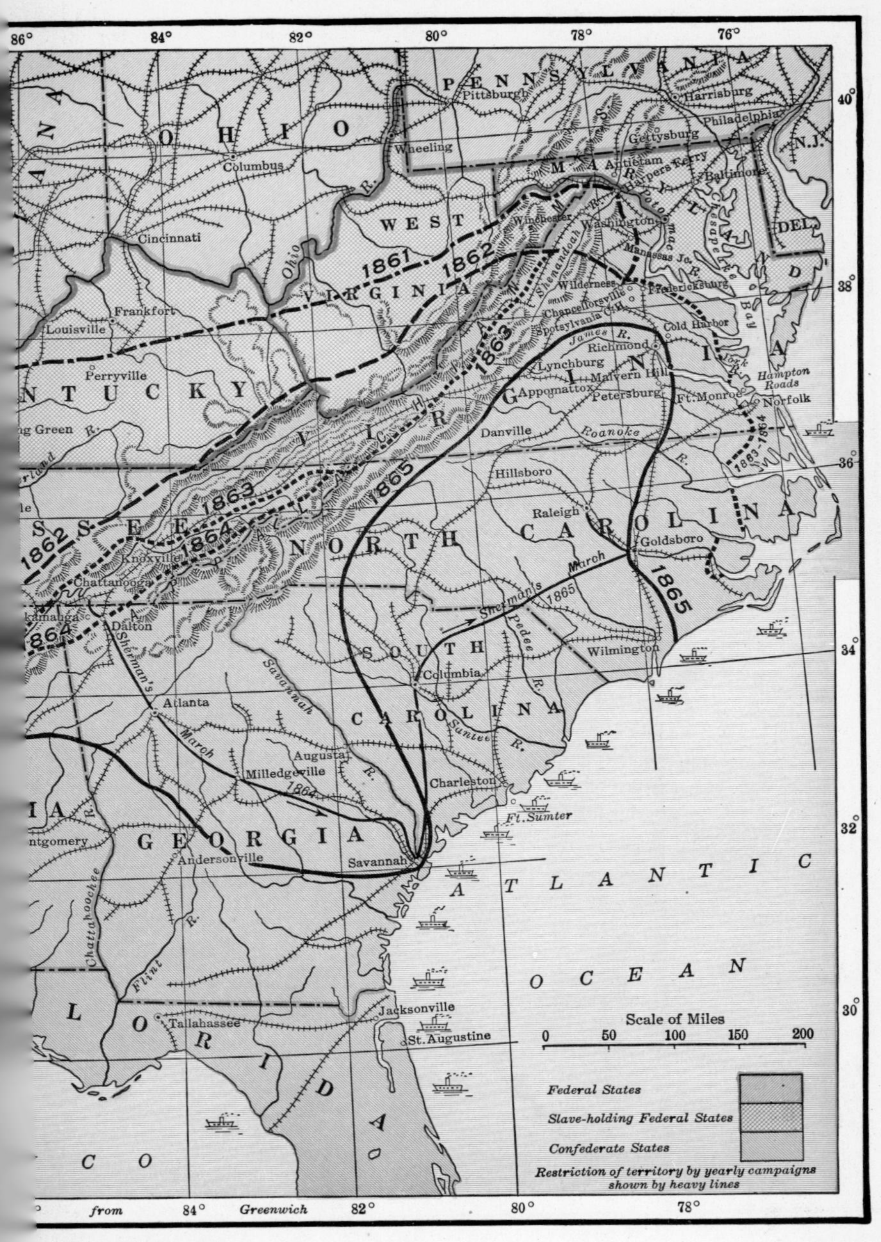

ARFARE, 1861–1865

Monroe, and then to advance up the peninsula between the York and James rivers and capture Richmond. The Peninsular Campaign was marked by McClellan's characteristic timidity and overcaution. Arriving at Fortress Monroe on April 2, he took Yorktown, his first objective, a month later after a prolonged siege. Advancing slowly in the face of stubborn resistance, he battled his way across the Chickahominy, and by the early days of June, came within sight of Richmond. Though his force outnumbered Lee's army of defense by thirty thousand, he allowed the latter to assume the offensive, and in the Seven Days' Battles (June 25–July 1), was driven steadily backward, both sides suffering terrible losses.

The opportunity for victory having passed, the army was recalled, and McClellan was replaced by General John Pope, a man of small ability, enjoying a temporary fame for some inconsiderable successes in the West. Boastful and overconfident, he began the overland march against Richmond only to meet needless disaster at the second Battle of Bull Run on August 30, 1862. Lee, seeing an opportunity to invade the North, quickly seized it. Offensive operations in the North might cause a pro-Southern uprising in Maryland, give him possession of Washington, and bring the war to a speedy close. In the first days of September he crossed into Maryland by way of the Shenandoah Valley. As Lee advanced northward, McClellan, again in command, paralleled his movements with an army vastly superior in numbers.

On September 17, the armies met on the banks of Antietam Creek, near Sharpsburg, Maryland. Desperate fighting ensued with heavy casualties. Lee was forced to give way, but due to McClellan's inactivity, he effected a retreat into Virginia without further losses. Lincoln urged McClellan to undertake a strong counteroffensive while the Confederate forces were still disorganized, but again he procrastinated. When late in October the federals once more undertook the overland march on Richmond, he was presently replaced by General A. E. Burnside. The latter had protested against his own appointment on the plea of incapacity, and the sequel justified his candor, for he was defeated with heavy slaughter at the Battle of Fredericksburg on December 13. The Eastern campaign of 1862 ended in a draw, with the advantage distinctly on the side of the South.

The campaign of 1863 began inauspiciously for the North. With "Fighting Joe" Hooker in command, the Union forces once more attempted the overland advance on Richmond. At Chancellorsville a bloody battle took place on May 2–5, resulting in a severe defeat for the federals. The Confederate victory was gained at a high price, for it cost the life of General T. J. ("Stonewall") Jackson, who, next to Lee, was the ablest Southern commander. Lee saw the way open for a second invasion of the North, and again using the Shenandoah Valley for this purpose, the Confederate forces crossed the Potomac late in June.

The Union army, with General G. G. Meade in command, moved on Gettysburg in southern Pennsylvania, the meeting place of several important highways, occupied the heights that dominated the region, and awaited attack. Here occurred three days of terrific fighting on July 1–3, 1863, involving casualties of nearly forty thousand men, shared almost equally by the two sides. In the end Meade won the advantage. Lee's invasion was checked, though he retired southward in such good order that the Union General feared to risk another battle. The remaining months passed with small skirmishes and combats but no general battle. Accordingly, the close of the year 1863 saw the Northern army as far away from Richmond as at the opening of the war.

The federal operations in the East had all along possessed an advantage over the enemy in larger armies and superior equipment, but had suffered from inferior leadership. With unexampled patience Lincoln had tried a succession of generals, but without satisfactory result. The campaign of 1864 opened with the appointment of yet another commander, Ulysses S. Grant. A former West Pointer, he had entered the war in 1861 as a Colonel of Illinois volunteers, and through his military successes in the West, had won rapid and deserved promotion. On March 9, 1864, he was appointed to the newly revived position of Lieutenant General with supreme command, under the President, of all the Union armies.

Grant differed from his predecessors mainly in his pertinacity and in his resolution to overwhelm the South by his superiority in men and resources. To fight hard with simple tactics was the new policy. Furthermore, his plans embraced concerted movements by the armies of the East and the West. For himself he reserved the Eastern command.

On the night of May 3 the Army of the Potomac began the oft-attempted march on Richmond by crossing the Rapidan, and encamped the next day in the Wilderness, a densely wooded tract of low ridges and treacherous swamps, ten miles across. Here Lee measured his strength with his new opponent in an inconclusive two days' battle (May 5–6). Grant now moved southeastward toward Spottsylvania Court House, and for the next month he was almost constantly engaged in desperate combat while he battered his way stubbornly toward Richmond. Lee was the greater strategist, and Grant's men were constantly being hurled against well-chosen intrenched positions, protected from attack by the new device of wire entanglements.

Two costly engagements — at Spottsylvania on May 8–12, and Cold Harbor on June 1–3, the latter near the scene of McClellan's misadventure — caused Grant to decide upon a change of base to the James River, south of Richmond. By this time he had lost fifty-five thousand men, or about half his original force, but fresh troops kept his ranks full. Repeated attacks failed to pierce the Confederate resistance. Grant then proceeded to lay siege to Petersburg, an important railroad junction connecting Richmond with the South. When Lee sought to draw him off in July by sending General J. A. Early down the Shenandoah Valley in a raid against Washington, Grant retaliated in August by dispatching General P. H. Sheridan with a force which defeated Early by weight of numbers at Winchester and elsewhere. Sheridan ravaged the valley so thoroughly that it could never be used again for a Confederate invasion. The year closed with Grant still before Petersburg, twenty-two miles from Richmond.

Grant's remorseless advance in 1864 foreshadowed the end. The South was rapidly approaching exhaustion. By the spring of 1865, the Confederate positions in Petersburg and Richmond were no longer tenable, and on April 2, Lee abandoned them, intending to effect a junction with General J. E. Johnston's army, then in North Carolina, or if that failed, to secure himself in the mountain fastnesses. But Northern cavalry got ahead of him, tearing up railway lines he had hoped to use, and blocking possible mountain passes. On April 9, Lee found himself at

Appomattox Court House, some seventy miles west of Petersburg, surrounded by the enemy and with no alternative but surrender.

A conference was held by the two Generals — Lee, erect, attired in a new full-dress uniform of Confederate gray with a jeweled sword; Grant in the shabby blue uniform of a private, wearing the straps of Lieutenant-General but without a sword. The terms of surrender were magnanimous. The officers were permitted to retain their sidearms, and both officers and men rode off on their own horses. On his return from the conference, Grant quieted the noisy demonstrations of his soldiers by reminding them, "The rebels are our countrymen again."

The Campaigns in the West

In the early years of the war the gloom of the Northern people was dispelled only by the steady progress made by the federal forces in the West. The decision of Missouri, Kentucky, and West Virginia in 1861 to remain with the Union placed the original battle front on a line somewhat north of the center of those states, and deprived the Confederacy of the Ohio River which would have formed a splendid boundary for defense and offense. When the campaign of 1862 began, the prime objective of the North was to open up the Mississippi, and thereby accomplish the double purpose of isolating the Confederate states west of the river and of providing the Upper Mississippi Valley with its accustomed channel of commerce.

The key to the situation was the military control of the Tennessee and Cumberland rivers, two tributaries of the Ohio, which penetrated southward toward the heart of the Confederacy. The first important movement, therefore, was an expedition up these streams by a combined gunboat fleet and army under the command of General U. S. Grant. In the early weeks of February, 1862, Fort Henry and Fort Donelson, situated on these rivers near the Kentucky-Tennessee border, surrendered with more than 14,000 prisoners. The expedition pushed on, capturing Nashville, the Tennessee capital, on the Cumberland, and continuing the southward advance along the Tennessee. Grant's objective now was the village of Corinth in northern Mississippi, one of the most important railway centers in the South, lying at the junction point of roads from Memphis, Vicksburg, Mobile, and Chattanooga. After desperate fighting on April 6–7 at Pittsburg Landing and Shiloh, where the federals departed from the river, the advance was continued under General H. W. Halleck. On May 30, 1862, Corinth was occupied.

Meantime, important progress had been made elsewhere in weakening the Confederate hold on the Mississippi. Union forces operating from the north captured Island No. 10 (April 7), an important river fort near the Kentucky-Tennessee border, and the occupation of Corinth forced the Confederates to abandon Fort Pillow and Memphis. A naval force under D. G. Farragut, operating from the Gulf of Mexico, secured the reduction of New Orleans on April 28 after ten days' fighting.

In September and October, 1862, the Confederates made a desperate attempt to compel the withdrawal of the Union forces by a raid into the North. Braxton Bragg and Kirby Smith moved rapidly into Kentucky, and actually approached within a few miles of Cincinnati, causing great consternation in that city. The Kentuckians failed to rally to the Confederate cause; and fearing defeat, the Southern forces retreated, fighting important battles at Perryville, Kentucky, and at Murfreesboro, Tennessee. In consequence, the year closed with the North in possession of the western half of Tennessee, and in control of the Mississippi River save for a stretch of 200 miles guarded at either end by the Confederate strongholds of Vicksburg and Port Hudson.

The first business of the campaign of 1863, on the part of the North, was to complete the task left unfinished in the preceding year — that of freeing Mississippi navigation. This involved one of the most difficult operations of the war, for Vicksburg was a natural stronghold, perched on a high bluff commanding the Mississippi, and almost unapproachable from the north or northeast on account of swamps. In April Grant began his active campaign against Vicksburg, assisted by a gunboat flotilla. Weeks passed with nothing to show but blocked attacks, heavy losses in battle, and the death of men from malaria and smallpox. Finally, on July 4, the Confederates, stricken with disease and on the verge of starvation, gave up the fight. Thirty thousand men surrendered. Five days later, when Port Hudson was taken, the "Father of Waters" again flowed "unvexed to the sea."

The Union forces in Tennessee were now ready to undertake the conquest of the remainder of that state, their special objective being Chattanooga in the extreme southeastern portion, which commanded the shortest railway route between Richmond and Atlanta. A skillful campaign, conducted by General W. S. Rosecrans, brought the desired culmination on September 9, 1863; but General Bragg's army, strengthened by reënforcements from Lee, turned on the federals at Chickamauga Creek on September 19–20, and drove them back into Chattanooga, to which it laid siege. Grant now took command in person, and in a hot battle lasting three days (November 23–25), he dislodged the Confederates and forced them to retreat into Georgia. The campaign of 1863 thus reopened the commercial outlet of the Upper Mississippi Valley, rent the enemy country in twain, crippled the Southern transportation system, completed the conquest of Tennessee, and placed the Union army in a strategic position for a new sundering of the Confederacy.

General W. T. Sherman, who had performed valiant service under Grant, was placed in command of the army at Chattanooga when the latter was promoted to the supreme command early in 1864. To him fell the task of penetrating the mountains of northwestern Georgia and capturing Atlanta, the principal railroad center left to the Confederacy and its most important manufacturing city. Marching from Chattanooga early in May with an army outnumbering his foe almost two to one, he gradually forced the enemy to give way, arriving before Atlanta in July. Several hard engagements were fought in the vicinity, and the Confederate General, J. B. Hood, saved his army from capture only by evacuating the city on September 2. Hood now endeavored to compel the retirement of Sherman's army by threatening his line of communications and his base of supplies at Nashville, but suffered an irreparable defeat at the Battle of Nashville on December 15–16, at the hands of General G. H. Thomas.

Meantime Sherman, undeterred by Hood's operations in his rear, determined upon a southeasterly march across Georgia to the ocean. This would enable him to establish a safe base, which could be supplied by sea from the North, and to strike a devastating blow at the granary which fed Lee's army. He believed that, if the war in all its frightfulness and ruin were brought home to the people of the Lower South, the desire to continue the conflict would disappear and the Confederate armies melt away.

Beginning the advance on November 12, 1864, his army of sixty thousand men, marching in four columns, foraged on the country, destroyed 265 miles of railway, and left in their wake a swath, sixty miles wide, in which nothing of military value remained. According to Sherman's own estimate, the damage inflicted amounted to one hundred million dollars; four fifths of it he classed as "simple waste and destruction." He met with no opposition worthy of the name, and on December 20, took possession of Savannah. Accordingly, the campaign of 1864 ended with the Confederacy severed in a new direction, and Sherman in a position to sweep northward along the coast toward Grant's army in Virginia.

On February 1, 1865, the northward advance began. The lay of the land made it necessary for Sherman's force to cross innumerable streams swollen by spring freshets. Everywhere a desperate enemy obstructed their progress. The Union soldiers lived off the country, and systematically destroyed railways and machinery. On February 17, the Confederates abandoned Columbia, the South Carolina capital, and in the confusion of federal occupation it was partly destroyed by fire, probably started by drunken stragglers of both armies. Charleston fell into the hands of the federal fleet without a battle when her railroad connections with the interior were cut.

The march through South Carolina was marked by pillaging and general lawlessness because of hatred of the soldiers for the "cradle of secession." On March 19, Sherman's advance ran into the Confederate forces under General J. E. Johnston at Goldsboro in central North Carolina, and was temporarily checked. Operations were soon resumed, and when news of Lee's capitulation reached Johnston, he asked Sherman for terms of surrender. The two men met in conference at Hillsboro, and on April 26, Johnston yielded on the same terms that had been accorded Lee a few weeks earlier. The two surrenders occurred within ninety miles of each other.

The operations west of the Mississippi River never assumed important proportions, and had little effect upon the campaigns farther east. Much of the fighting was desultory and guerilla in character. It was not until the spring of 1862 that the Confederates gave up hope of imposing their will upon Missouri. The Southern forces succeeded in regaining a good part of the state by September, 1861, but the issue was definitely settled against them at the bloody Battle of Pea Ridge, in northwestern Arkansas, on March 7–8, 1862. General S. R. Curtis, the victor in this fight, then proceeded to enlarge his area of authority until at the close of the year the northern half of Arkansas was in Union hands. General J. M. Schofield replaced him in 1863, but could not complete the task.

The center of Confederate power was at Shreveport in the Red River Valley in northwestern Louisiana. Various unsuccessful attempts were made by the Union forces to dislodge the enemy from this region in 1863 and 1864, but General Kirby Smith retained possession until the end of the war. He surrendered at Baton Rouge on May 26, 1865, with a force of 18,000 men.

War Activities of Noncombatants

The courageous exploits of the troops in the field need not obscure the heroism and self-sacrifice of the noncombatants connected with the army or of the civilian population behind the lines. In no previous conflict had such resolute efforts been made to ameliorate the horrors of war and to look after the welfare and comfort of the soldiers. This attitude was a testimonial to the new humanitarian regard for the well-being of the common man.

The casualties of the battlefield were so great that the Medical Department of the United States Army quickly found its resources overtaxed. Accordingly, its labors were supplemented by the services of volunteer nurses. Perhaps the most famous of these was Clara Barton, who resigned a government clerkship to take up the work of nursing and of organizing hospital supplies. Walt Whitman the poet gave of his strength so generously in a similar mission of mercy that he became permanently broken in health. At the beginning of the war, there was no organized ambulance or field hospital service, but when Jonathan Letterman became Medical Director of the Army of the Potomac in June, 1862, he brought about epochmaking reforms, which became patterns for the other armies.

The Civil War was one of the first wars in history in which anæsthetics were used to alleviate the pain of operations. This great boon to suffering humanity was a recent discovery. In 1844 Dr. Horace Wells, a dentist of Hartford, Connecticut, demonstrated that nitrous oxide gas might be used as an anæsthetic. Two years later Dr. W. T. Morton, a Boston dentist, applied ether as an anæsthetic, being guided in its selection and use by Dr. C. T. Jackson, a chemist of that city.[1] Chloroform, the third well-known anæsthetic, was first used for this purpose by Sir James Y. Simpson of Edinburgh in 1847. Prior to these discoveries, a patient in a severe surgical operation had to be restrained by force, and was bound by straps to the table. Since a slight inaccuracy of the surgeon's hand might cause fatal results, anæsthesia added greatly to the number of recoveries as well as to the relief of suffering. Chloroform was most widely used for this purpose during the Civil War.

Unfortunately, antiseptic surgery was, as yet, an undeveloped science,[2] and in order to prevent wound infections, the army surgeons freely resorted to amputations. There were 30,000 amputations in the Northern armies, the great majority of them successful, and for many years following the war, armless and legless veterans were a pathetic reminder of the great conflict. Sanitary science was also in a primitive state. Notwithstanding the heavy losses incurred in fighting, the deaths from dysentery, camp fevers, pneumonia, and other diseases proved to be almost twice as great.

In no war in history before the World War was organized relief work carried on by civilians on so vast a scale. With the opening of hostilities, women all over the North began to meet in Ladies' Aid Societies to make bandages, shirts, towels, and other supplies. In New York City they formed the Women's Central Relief Association under the leadership of Dr. Elizabeth

[1] Dr. Crawford W. Long of Georgia had made the same discovery in 1842, but did not publish his results.

[2] The discoveries of Louis Pasteur of France and Baron Lister of England ushered in the era of antiseptic surgery about 1867.

Blackwell. At the solicitation of this body, the United States government in June, 1861, approved the creation of a national organization, under the name of the "United States Sanitary Commission," charged with the duty of assisting in the welfare of sick and wounded soldiers and of their dependent families. Though this body was to coöperate with the United States government, it was independent of it, being supported entirely by private contributions. Most of the local Aid Societies throughout the North immediately affiliated as branches of the Sanitary Commission.

Under the presidency of the noted Unitarian divine, Dr. H. W. Bellows, the Sanitary Commission developed an elaborate organization, employing at times five hundred agents. Its work was comparable to that of the American Red Cross (established in 1881) during the World War. Storehouses were located in Boston, New York, Philadelphia, Cincinnati, Cleveland, Chicago, and Louisville, to which the local branches sent supplies of bandages, clothing, and food. Railroads and express companies gave their services free of charge. Supplies were gathered through private appeals, the work of the local branches, and the enterprise of church societies, but the leading means employed, especially in the later years, were the "Sanitary Fairs."

The first of these was held at Lowell, Massachusetts, followed soon by Lawrence and other towns of the state, and later by all the leading cities of the North. New York and Philadelphia netted one million dollars each by their fairs. At the latter city and at Baltimore, President Lincoln attended the opening day of the fair. The wonderful devotion of the women inspired his oft-quoted eulogy, "If all that has been said by orators and poets since the creation of the world in praise of women were applied to the women of America, it would not do them justice for their conduct during this war." A total of seven million dollars was raised by the Sanitary Commission in this and other ways during the war.

Through the labors of the Commission, the conditions of camp life were greatly improved, and assistance was given in caring for the wounded on the field of battle and in the hospitals. In the few days following the Battle of Gettysburg, clothing and food valued at $75,000 were distributed among the soldiers, including such delicacies as poultry, butter, eggs, milk, lemons, coffee, and ice. More than two hundred tons of supplies were distributed by the Commission in the Wilderness Campaign in 1864. In many parts of the North, convalescent camps were set up. Likewise, hospital cars were furnished, and surgeons employed to inspect the military hospitals and spy out unsanitary conditions. During the latter part of the war, Soldiers' Homes and Soldiers' Rests were established at all important railroad junctions, where the wants of traveling and wounded soldiers might be cared for.

To supplement the work of the Sanitary Commission, the United States Christian Commission was established in November, 1861, upon the initiative of the Young Men's Christian Association, a nonsectarian religious organization formed a few years earlier. The Christian Commission was primarily an enterprise for carrying on evangelical work among the soldiers although attention was also given to their physical comfort. Most of the Northern pastors at some time or other participated in the labors of this Commission. Free reading rooms were provided in the camps, where magazines, newspapers, and religious literature might be perused. Its unique service, other than its religious labors, was the establishment of a system of diet kitchens for injured soldiers, which extended to every corps of the army.

The dependent families of the fighters presented a serious problem. A number of the states provided monthly payments for them, and sometimes counties took similar action. The soldiers often turned over their bounty money to their families, thereby affording temporary relief. Millions of dollars of private contributions were disbursed for the same purpose. In one year the citizens of Philadelphia raised $600,000 for soldiers' dependents, and in another year slightly more. But even with such assistance many women were forced, or chose, to become breadwinners. They worked in munition plants or clothing factories, or else they took charge of the farming, thereby saving the homestead at the same time that they kept up agricultural production.

In the South the burdens borne by the women were even heavier, for a larger proportion of the white men were at the front. Relief work was not organized; but the proud Southern women brought into use old spinning-wheels and looms in order to make clothing for the soldiers, they denied themselves meat and drink that it might be sent to the army, they worked in munition factories and nursed wounded soldiers. Living in an invaded country, they experienced the horrors of war all about them — homes destroyed, fields devastated, hostile soldiers everywhere.

The disbanding of the troops and their dispersion into civilian life occurred without shock or incident. Nearly a million Northern soldiers were mustered out in 1865. Most of the discharged veterans took their final payment with them as a "nest egg," and with free farms awaiting them on the Western frontier and abundant openings in the new manufacturing industries, they were quietly absorbed into the ranks of civil life.[1] The Confederates wandered home, on foot and horseback, penniless. Their slaves were gone, their plantations laid waste or unworked. Peace meant to them the building of a New South.

SELECT BIBLIOGRAPHY

The War of American Nationality. Well-balanced, brief accounts of the military and naval operations may be found in J. F. Rhodes, *History of the Civil War* (New York, 1917, condensed and revised from his more elaborate work); J. K. Hosmer, *The Appeal to Arms* and his *Outcome of the Civil War* (in *The American Nation*, XX, XXI, New York, 1907); William Wood, *Captains of the Civil War* (in *The Chronicles of America*, XXXI, New Haven, 1921); F. L. Paxson, *The Civil War* (in *The Home University Library*, New York, 1911); G. C. Eggleston, *The History of the Confederate War* (2 v., New York, 1910); T. A. Dodge, *A Bird's Eye View of Our Civil War* (Boston, 1897); and W. B. Wood and J. E. Edmonds, *A History of the Civil War in the United States* (London, 1905). The most recent treatment is that of Edward Channing, *A History of the United States*, VI (New York, 1925). Two of the best war biographies are G. F. R. Henderson, *Stonewall Jackson and the American Civil War* (2 v., New York, 1898), and Sir Frederick Maurice, *Robert E. Lee, the Soldier* (Boston, 1925).

Naval operations receive special attention in A. T. Mahan, *Admiral Farragut* (New York, 1892), D. D. Porter, *The Naval History of the Civil War* (New York, 1886), and J. T. Scharf, *History of the Confederate States Navy* (Albany, 1894). In F. M. Bennett, *The Monitor and the Navy under Steam* (Boston, 1900), may be found a description of Ericsson's invention and of the revolution wrought in naval warfare.

War Activities of Noncombatants. Some light is thrown on the medical side of the war by C. B. Johnson, *Muskets and Medicine, or Army Life in the*

[1] Bryant, Longfellow, Greeley, and other public-spirited citizens petitioned Congress to establish a home for disabled Union volunteers, and thereby began a movement which resulted in eight fine national institutions in different parts of the country. Many of the states in the North and the South also established "homes" for disabled veterans and for soldiers' orphans.

Sixties (Philadelphia, 1917). A detailed discussion of the discovery of anæsthetics is appended to F. R. Packard, *The History of Medicine in the United States . . . to 1800* (Philadelphia, 1901). T. L. Livermore, *Numbers and Losses in the Civil War* (Boston, 1901), continues to be the best authority on that obscure subject.

For the services of women, consult L. P. Brockett and M. C. Vaughan, *Woman's Work in the Civil War* (Philadelphia, 1867), and J. L. Underwood, *The Women of the Confederacy* (New York, 1906). The most complete account of the principal relief organization is C. J. Stillé, *History of the United States Sanitary Commission* (Philadelphia, 1866), but an excellent summary appears in E. D. Fite, *Social and Industrial Conditions in the North* (New York, 1910).

CHAPTER XIII

WARTIME PROBLEMS NORTH AND SOUTH

Filling the War Purse

The financing of the war placed an enormous strain upon a people unaccustomed to heavy taxation. When Lincoln entered office, the treasury was practically empty, custom receipts almost at a standstill, and public credit on the ebb. In December, 1861, specie payments were suspended by the banks of the North, an action soon followed by the government. Thereafter the people could not secure gold and silver for use in trade, and the country went on a paper-money basis.

Responsibility for a fiscal policy rested on Salmon P. Chase, Secretary of the Treasury, and his two coadjutors in Congress: Senator W. P. Fessenden, Chairman of the Finance Committee, and Thaddeus Stevens, Chairman of the House Ways and Means Committee. Since all these men lacked experience in public finance, the resulting policy was one of trial and error, involving costly blunders at times though effective in the long run. There were three main sources of war revenue: taxation, the issuance of legal-tender notes, and the borrowing of money.

The imperative need for funds caused the government to revolutionize its policy of taxation. Hardly a session of Congress passed without some increase in the custom duties until the Act of 1864 advanced the average rate to forty-seven per cent, an unprecedented figure at that time though not excessive as compared with more recent tariffs. The chief purpose of this series of laws was to protect Northern industries from foreign competition, and thereby enable American manufacturers to pay heavy internal taxes. A total of $305,360,451 was raised from tariff duties during the war.

The first comprehensive internal-revenue law was passed in July, 1862. It levied a bewildering variety of duties, including taxes upon luxuries (such as liquors and tobacco), stamp duties, licenses upon occupations, and taxes upon manufactured products, advertisements, billiard tables, meat, railroads, insurance companies, inheritances, and incomes. These rates were increased in 1864. With internal-revenue duties the country had been unfamiliar for more than a generation, and the income-tax feature was a brand new departure. The first tax on incomes, in 1861, authorized a rate of three per cent on the excess of all incomes above $800. In 1862, and again in 1865, this was increased until incomes between $600 and $5000 were taxed at five per cent, and above $5000 at ten per cent. The total sum derived from the internal-revenue and income taxes during the war amounted to $356,846,136.

In legal-tender notes or "greenbacks," the government found another source of wealth. By the simple process of resorting to the printing press, the United States acquired abundant funds to expend for soldiers' wages and war supplies. This paper money was not unlike the Continental currency of Revolutionary days. It was fiat money, unsupported by a gold reserve; creditors were compelled to take the greenbacks at face value; and their ultimate redemption in gold depended on the good faith and future financial ability of the nation. In February, 1862, Congress authorized $150,000,000 worth of these notes. They were to be receivable for all debts due to or from the United States government, except import duties and interest on bonds, which were made payable in coin. Further inflation was provided in Acts of 1862 and 1863 until, at the close of the war, greenbacks to the amount of $431,000,000 were in circulation.

From a fiscal point of view, the legal-tender notes were a forced loan from the people to the nation. The greenbacks, after they left the government's hands, suffered a rapid depreciation both because of their superabundance and because the people's confidence in the government wavered during times of military misfortune. A decided impetus was thereby given to the ascending cost of living, though wages lagged behind the rise in prices. Workingmen, notwithstanding the fact that they were better paid than before the war, found that a day's wages would not go so far. In July, 1864, one hundred greenback dollars were worth thirty-nine dollars in gold; in April, 1865, sixty-seven dollars.

On account of the relatively high value of the precious metals, the small silver coins much needed in retail trade disappeared from circulation during 1862. The resulting embarrassment caused cities, and even business houses, to issue paper and metallic substitutes for use in local trade. In July, 1862, Congress sought to improve the situation by authorizing the use of postage stamps, but this inconvenient medium gave way in March, 1863, to small paper notes ("shinplasters"), issued by the government in denominations as low as three cents. Eventually $50,000,000 of such currency was authorized — a welcome addition to the resources of the treasury.

The main reliance of the government, however, was on borrowing money by means of the sale of bonds and treasury notes. In order to compete with commercial investments, high rates of interest were offered. The two issues of "five-twenties" (bonds redeemable at the government's option from five to twenty years after date), authorized in 1862 and 1864, bore interest at six per cent, and the "ten-forties," issued in 1864, paid five per cent interest. Short-term loans were effected through treasury notes, offered in smaller denominations, and sometimes carrying interest as high as 7.3 per cent (the "seven-thirties.") In all, the government obtained a revenue of $2,621,916,786 by such means — more than three times as much as from all the other sources combined.

The need for increasing the sale of bonds was an important factor in hastening the adoption of the National Banking Act of 1863. Other causes, however, were more fundamental. On January 1, 1862, there were in the United States fifteen hundred banks that issued bank notes. Chartered under the laws of twenty-nine states, they possessed different privileges, and operated under different restrictions; their bank notes were based on a great variety of securities, unlike either in quality or amount. In some states, there were boards of bank commissioners which made frequent and thorough examinations, while elsewhere no such boards existed or else existed only in name. All told, about seven thousand different kinds of bank notes were in circulation, to say nothing of successful counterfeits. The situation was much improved over that of Jackson's day, but depositors in many states were still uncertain as to the security of their funds, and bank notes in constant use might, or might not, be worth their face value. Some system of federal regulation and control seemed to be called for.

The National Banking Act of 1863, as amended by the law of 1864, did away with these irregularities, supplied a safe and uniform bank currency, and provided a new market for the sale of government bonds. Incidentally, it enlisted a strong and active financial interest in behalf of the security and welfare of the Union.

Banks chartered under the new system were required to purchase federal bonds to the extent of one third of their capital stock, and to deposit them with the Secretary of the Treasury. On the basis of this security they might issue bank notes up to ninety per cent of the market value of the bonds they owned. They must also keep on hand a cash fund for the current redemption of notes, and as a safeguard for their depositors. Depositors received additional protection from the provision for periodical examination by federal inspectors. The United States government assumed responsibility for the ultimate redemption of national-bank notes. Many of the state banks were at first reluctant to become national banks because of the restrictions imposed by the new system; but when Congress in March, 1865, levied a tax of ten per cent on all state-bank notes, their attitude changed. The legislation of 1863 and 1864 remains the foundation of our national banking system to this day.[1]

The expenditures of the United States for the army and navy from 1861 to 1865 amounted to more than three billion dollars. This figure, however, does not include the interest charges on the war debt. Furthermore, several years elapsed after the peace before the appropriations for military and naval purposes were brought down to a normal basis, and in the last year of the conflict, pensions began to swell the expenses of the government. In 1879, an estimate was made of the expenditures growing out of the war down to that date, showing a total of $6,190,000,000. But even this amount does not take into account the extraordinary expenses for war purposes borne by the states.

[1] The system was changed in some details by subsequent acts, particularly the Law of 1908, which permits a national bank to deposit certain other securities besides United States bonds as a basis for its note circulation. It was also affected, in certain respects, by the establishment of the Federal Reserve System in 1913 (see pages 470–471).

The financial difficulties of the Confederacy were incomparably greater. The North had the revenue machinery of the United States government through which to work; the South had to build from the ground up. At the outset, however, the Confederacy had over a million dollars in its treasury, practically all of it confiscated from federal mints and custom houses in the South. The Confederate Congress and several of the states took action, also, to prevent the payment of private debts owing to Northern merchants and bankers.

Like the United States, the Richmond government expected to obtain a substantial revenue from custom duties. The federal blockade, however, quickly put an end to this expectation. The Confederate Congress then requested each state to levy a property tax for the general treasury — the old requisition system of the Articles of Confederation — but the results were disappointing. Finally, in April, 1863, the Congress adopted an internal-revenue measure, comparable to the federal Act of 1862, and including comprehensive excise duties, taxes on incomes and profits, licenses upon occupations, and a ten-per-cent tax on farm produce payable in kind. The levy on farm products caused bitter resentment among the agricultural classes, particularly in North Carolina.

Borrowing was also resorted to, through long-term bonds and short-term treasury notes, at high rates of interest, but this method proved less successful than in the North where money for investment was plentiful. The first bond issue, made in 1861, brought into the treasury all the available specie in the South. Accordingly, the bond issue of 1862 was made payable in produce, whereby the government came into possession of large quantities of cotton, tobacco, sugar, and other commodities that were a drug on the market. In 1863, however, some success was met in selling a bond issue of $15,000,000 in Great Britain and on the Continent.

Like the North, the Confederacy also adopted the tempting expedient of irredeemable paper money. This currency was receivable in payment of taxes, though it was not made legal tender in private transactions. In its extremity, the Confederate government issued nearly one billion dollars of this currency during the war, with the inevitable result of rapid depreciation and inflated prices. The total volume of such money was swollen by unrecorded issues of state governments, banks, and private business firms. Of course, the enormous war debt of the South was outlawed by the failure of the rebellion, and the Fourteenth Amendment of the federal Constitution, adopted in 1868, declared expressly that neither the United States nor any state should ever pay any part of it.

The Restraint of Civil Liberty

In both North and South the power of the general government was stretched to the utmost under the strain of war. President Lincoln performed acts that would ordinarily have been unconstitutional and which could be justified only by his authority as Commander-in-Chief of the Army and Navy. Greater caution was exhibited by President Davis, but in both sections the exercise of "war powers" was bitterly denounced as tyrannical by minority elements. In general, however, the assumption of extraordinary powers was sustained by the public opinion of each section in view of the necessities of the situation.

Lincoln's suspension of the writ of *habeas corpus* and the frequent arbitrary arrests made by the administration came in for particular condemnation. While the Constitution is not entirely clear on the point,[1] early decisions of the Supreme Court had implied that this valued safeguard of the private citizen could be set aside only by Congress. Without consulting Congress, however, Lincoln suspended the writ of *habeas corpus* in Maryland in 1861, at a time when the fate of that state was hanging in the balance and the arbitrary imprisonment of all suspects seemed imperative to nip treason in the bud.

On September 24, 1862, he renewed the suspension in a proclamation directed against all persons, wherever found, seeking to discourage enlistments or guilty of any other "disloyal practice." Promptly hundreds of men in all parts of the North were arrested on suspicion, and imprisoned without hearing or trial, or else sentenced by military tribunals without jury. On March 3, 1863, Congress passed a law designed to regulate the suspension of the writ of *habeas corpus* and providing that suspects should

[1] Constitution, Art. I, Sec. 9, Par. 2.

not be kept in prison more than twenty days without indictment by a grand jury. The President, however, ignored this law, political arrests continued to be made, and the military authorities even went so far as to suppress temporarily the circulation of the *New York World* and certain other Democratic papers. On the other hand, Lincoln sought to mitigate the rigors of this policy by paroling many political prisoners.

The administration acted with an excess of zeal, and in many cases, violated the constitutional rights of individuals. This view was adopted by a decision of the Supreme Court in the case of *ex parte* Milligan, which was rendered, however, in 1866, too late to be of service. Milligan was an Indiana Democrat who had been sentenced by a military tribunal in 1864. According to the Supreme Court, the constitutional defenses of an individual under criminal prosecution could not be set aside by the government in those parts of the country where the regular courts were "in the proper and unobstructed exercise of their jurisdiction."

In the South, President Davis, acting under express authorization of his Congress, declared martial law and suspended the writ of *habeas corpus* in disaffected districts and at important military points in February, 1862. Strong opposition developed against this interference in the usual sphere of state action. In 1863–1864, the North Carolina courts contested the legality of the measure, and freely issued the writ to persons imprisoned by Confederate authority. A Georgia statute of 1864 declared that the refusal to grant *habeas corpus* would subject the judge to a penalty of $2,500. In this campaign of protest, Vice-President Stephens was a leader, and "military despotism" was roundly denounced in resolutions of public meetings and legislative memorials. The Confederate Congress gradually restricted the President's authority in this respect, and finally withdrew it altogether on August 1, 1864. The Southern newspaper press was left entirely without censorship or control.

The Abolition of Slavery

One of the most momentous results of the sectional conflict — emancipation — came from the exercise of war powers by the federal authorities. The abolition of slavery was, by no means, a necessary consequence of the collision of arms. The central purpose of the dominant political party was merely the restriction of slavery to the states wherein it already existed. Moreover, Congress, in defining the nature and object of the war, had explicitly declared in July, 1861, that the hostilities were not being waged for the "purpose of overthrowing or interfering with the rights or established institutions" of the South, but "to preserve the Union with all the dignity, equality, and rights of the several States unimpaired; and that as soon as these objects are accomplished the war ought to cease."

When the popular agitation for emancipation rose high in 1862, Lincoln took further occasion to define the position of the government in a letter of August 22, elicited by an editorial of bitter criticism in Greeley's *Tribune*. "My paramount object in this struggle," he declared, "is to save the Union, and is not either to save or destroy slavery. If I could save the Union without freeing any slave, I would do it; and if I could save it by freeing all the slaves, I would do it; and if I could save it by freeing some and leaving others alone, I would also do that."

Lincoln's personal convictions of the iniquity of slavery had not altered since his debate with Douglas in 1858; but as President of the entire American nation, he shrank from righting one wrong at the cost of another, and no principle of the federal Constitution was more deeply implanted than the right of each state to control its own domestic institutions. Furthermore, he realized the folly of committing the Northern people to a policy which many of them were not yet prepared to accept. He and Douglas had divided the vote of the North between them in the presidential election, and those who supported Lincoln had voted against the extension, not the existence, of slavery. When the war broke out, many thousands who sprang to the defense of the Union would have refrained from enlisting had they believed they were fighting a "nigger war."

Nor did the President ever lose sight of the fact that the four border states which had clung to the Union were slave states. Abolition would not only be an act of injustice to the loyal whites of those states, but might drive them into the arms of the enemy. Had Lincoln been permitted, undisturbed by men or events, to work out his own solution of the problem, he would have instituted everywhere a program of gradual emancipation, with compensation to the masters and the removal of the freedmen to Liberia or Latin America.

Under the pressure of circumstances, however, steps were taken, almost from the beginning of the war, looking to the further restriction or eventual abolition of slavery. On April 16, 1862, a law was enacted for the compensated liberation of the three thousand slaves in the District of Columbia. Two months later (June 19), the Republicans placed on the statute books the principle which had brought them into being eight years before — the exclusion of slavery from the federal territories.

Lincoln desired further to bring about emancipation in the border states, for he realized that their permanent loyalty could not otherwise be secured. At his suggestion, Congress on April 10, 1862, expressed its willingness to aid these states financially in a program of gradual abolition, and Lincoln held earnest conferences with the border-state Congressmen to bring this about. The latter, however, remained unmoved, asserting their constitutional right to hold slaves, and declaring that any scheme of compensation, even with federal assistance, would inflict ruinous taxation on their people.

The problem of dealing with the question in the seceded states proved much more complicated and difficult. To antislavery extremists the war presented a providential opportunity to deal a death-blow to slavery in the South, for, in their minds, the disloyal conduct of the planting class absolved the North from all obligations to respect Southern property rights. They entirely misunderstood Lincoln's legal scruples and political caution, and fiercely assailed him as a traitor to the holy cause of freedom. Such Republicans called themselves "Radicals," and as will be seen, their quarrel with the President over emancipation caused them to criticize him on other scores as well. In the cabinet they had a champion in Chase; in the House of Representatives, in Thaddeus Stevens. Outside of Washington their great spokesmen were Greeley of the *Tribune*, and General John C. Fremont, who was an ambitious politician as well as a mediocre soldier.

The problem was not merely one for abstract disputation. The movement of the army into the South brought the troops into direct contact with the slaves, and raised questions which called for an immediate decision by the government. In the first month of the war, an overwhelming number of slaves flocked into the camp of General B. F. Butler in Virginia. Should these be returned to their masters under the Fugitive Slave Act? On May 24, 1861, Butler propounded the ingenious doctrine that the fugitives were contraband of war, being a form of property used by the Confederates in hostile war service, and that accordingly they should be confiscated. His position was promptly approved by the War Department, and when Congress passed the First Confiscation Act on August 6, 1861, providing for the seizure of property used for insurrectionary purposes, it expressly stipulated that slave property used for such purposes should likewise be subject to confiscation.

No sooner was this problem decided than General Fremont, then in command in Missouri, raised the issue in a different form. By a proclamation of August 30, 1861, he decreed the forfeiture of all property belonging to disloyal citizens of Missouri, and the emancipation of their slaves. This was exceeding the provisions of the First Confiscation Act, for the cause he assigned for liberation was the hostile service of the master, not of the slave. Lincoln, believing the step premature, repudiated it by an order of his own. In May, 1862, General David Hunter, commanding the recovered territory around Beaufort, South Carolina, imitated Fremont's example by declaring free the slaves of Florida, Georgia, and South Carolina. Again Lincoln intervened and revoked the order.

On July 17, however, Congress passed the Second Confiscation Act, which applied, in a modified form, the principle for which Fremont and Hunter had stood. After inflicting drastic penalties on all persons convicted of treason, the law declared that, when the slaves of rebel masters were taken captive or sought refuge within federal lines, they should "be forever free of their servitude and not again held as slaves." Two months later Lincoln said, "I cannot learn that that law has caused a single slave to come over to us."

In revoking General Hunter's order, Lincoln had declared, "Whether it be competent for me, as Commander-in-Chief of the Army and Navy, to declare the slaves of any State or States, free, and whether at any time, or in any case, it shall have become a necessity indispensable to the maintenance of the Government . . . , are questions which, under my responsibility, I reserve to myself." This pivotal question was never entirely absent from his thoughts. He was constantly weighing the political considerations involved, at home and abroad, and particularly whether an act of liberation would prove an effective blow in weakening the enemy. At a secret cabinet meeting on July 22, 1862, he announced that he was prepared to take the fateful step, and read to his advisers the draft of the proclamation. Seward suggested further delay until the United States could speak with the authority of a successful combatant, for, in view of the recent military reverses, the proclamation might be regarded as our "last shriek on the retreat." The wisdom of this advice was at once recognized.

The public was kept in ignorance of the action soon to be taken, and the clamor of the Radicals in the subsequent weeks reached an unprecedented pitch. The Confederate reverse at Antietam provided an appropriate occasion, and on September 22, 1862, the President issued the preliminary Proclamation of Emancipation. Justifying the act as a "necessary war measure," he declared the freedom of the slaves in all parts of the Confederacy that should be engaged in rebellion on January 1, 1863. When the latter date arrived, he issued the definitive proclamation, designating the states and portions of states affected, and announcing that ex-slaves would be received into the armed forces of the United States. The proclamation did not apply to the four border states, nor did it affect the status of slavery in Tennessee and those districts of Virginia and Louisiana already conquered. Elsewhere the slaves became free by the executive edict, although actual liberation did not come to them until the federal power had sufficiently extended the area of its authority into enemy territory.

The propriety of emancipation as a war measure can be measured only by the results which flowed from it. Slaves continued to throng into federal lines, though perhaps not in greater numbers than before. However, 104,387 negroes enlisted in the Northern armies from Confederate territory, and rendered services in guarding and repairing railroads and in fighting, which, in Lincoln's judgment, hastened the final victory. Of even greater importance was the effect of the proclamation on public opinion abroad, for thereafter, as will be seen, there was no further danger of foreign intervention.

Lincoln's action gave a mighty impetus to the movement for emancipation, which did not spend itself until universal freedom was accomplished. The next steps were taken by the states. On June 24, 1863, the Missouri convention provided for gradual emancipation, but changed its plan to immediate liberation in

THE PROGRESS OF EMANCIPATION, 1863–1865

January, 1865. During 1864 immediate abolition was decreed by Maryland and by conventions of unionists in Virginia, Arkansas, and Louisiana. Similar action was taken early in 1865 by Tennessee.

Meantime, a strong sentiment had been developing to make abolition universal by a constitutional amendment. Thoughtful people doubted whether the President's war measure would remain operative when peace should be restored. In any case, the freeing of the individual slaves would not necessarily prevent the Southern states from reëstablishing the institution of slavery at some future time. Therefore, on February 10, 1864, the Judiciary Committee of the House reported the familiar Thirteenth Amendment, which forbids slavery and involuntary servitude except as a punishment for crime anywhere within the United States or places subject to its jurisdiction.

The House was unable to marshal the necessary two-thirds vote for its passage, but the Senate acted favorably. The amendment was an issue in the presidential election of 1864, and Lincoln's reëlection emboldened the House to reverse its former vote in January, 1865. The proposed amendment was ratified by the requisite number of states, and became a part of the organic law on December 18, 1865. Its direct practical effect was to free the slaves in Kentucky and Delaware, and to substitute immediate for gradual emancipation in West Virginia.

Political Divisions during the War

The Civil War saw the development of factionalism within the ranks of both political parties. In the Republican party the main divisions were known as the "Radicals" and the "Conservatives," and as has been seen, their chief source of difference was the abolition question, though the Radicals also criticized Lincoln's management of the war. The Conservatives held with the President that national preservation was paramount, and abolition a secondary consideration. In elections, the two factions maintained a united front, and since the practice was adopted early in the war of nominating proadministration candidates under the name of the "Union" party, they also succeeded in commanding the support of one section of the Democrats. These "War Democrats," as they were called, retained their belief in the historic economic doctrines of their party, but believed that, in the existing crisis, the question of the Union overshadowed all other issues.

Most of the Democrats, however, continued in the old party organization, and throughout the war conducted political contests against the Union party. A majority of them supported the war, but charged Lincoln with incompetence and denounced his assumption of autocratic war powers. Their slogan became, "The Constitution as it is and the Union as it was," and in Horatio Seymour of New York they possessed their most effective leader.

A militant minority, headed by Clement L. Vallandigham, an Ohio Congressman, disapproved of the war, and demanded immediate peace without terms. Their stronghold was the old

Northwest, particularly those parts in which the people, like Vallandigham himself, were descendants of settlers from the slave states. In order to carry on their propaganda more effectively, many of the Peace Democrats joined a secret, oath-bound order variously known as the Knights of the Golden Circle, the American Knights, and the Sons of Liberty. This pacifist element was execrated by the public at large, and quickly won the name of "Copperheads" — an epithet soon applied indiscriminately to all Democrats.

The first test of strength between the contending forces came in the fall elections of 1862. For this event the Democrats were in an advantageous position. The Northern people, discouraged by an almost unbroken series of military defeats, were suffering a reaction from the buoyant patriotism of 1861, and were outraged by the revelations of corruption in war contracts, uncovered by investigating committees of Congress. Many of them, furthermore, were disconcerted by the jibes of the Democrats that the Emancipation Proclamation had changed the contest into an "abolition war."[1] The increasing number of arbitrary arrests gave additional grounds for dissatisfaction. As a result, the administration party lost ground in many parts of the country. Horatio Seymour was elected Governor of New York, and the Democrats won the elections in New Jersey, Pennsylvania, Ohio, Indiana, Illinois, and Wisconsin. The Republicans managed to retain a majority in Congress, though the Democratic membership was greatly increased.

The next year proved an even more critical one for the administration forces. The Peace Democrats in the Indiana legislature blocked every measure for the support of the war, and the lower house of the Illinois legislature declared for an immediate armistice and a peace convention. The President informed Charles Sumner that he was more fearful of "the fire in the rear" than of the enemy's military prowess. In the fall of 1863 the efforts of the Peace Democrats reached a dramatic climax. The Demo-

[1] A favorite bit of Democratic verse ran as follows:

> Honest old Abe, when the war first began,
> Denied abolition was part of his plan;
> Honest old Abe has since made a decree,
> The war must go on till the slaves are all free.
> As both can't be honest, will some one tell how,
> If honest Abe then, he is honest Abe now?

crats of Ohio nominated for governor C. L. Vallandigham, who had recently been convicted by a military court for his violent public denunciations of "King Lincoln," and banished from Northern soil. He conducted his campaign from a safe refuge in Canada, and for a time, it seemed that he might be elected.[1] The candidate of the Union party was an able War Democrat, John Brough. Vallandigham received 187,000 votes in the election, but he was defeated by a majority of 101,000. The federal victories at Vicksburg and Gettysburg proved a decisive campaign argument against him.

Vallandigham's defeat marked the turning of the tide in favor of the administration, though Lincoln still had much political opposition to encounter both within and outside of his party. The Radical Republicans, bent on preventing his renomination, sought to forestall such action by nominating Fremont at a mass convention at Cleveland on May 31, 1864. Their platform demanded a more vigorous prosecution of the war and a constitutional amendment to end slavery. But the maneuver was not successful. When the Union party convened at Baltimore a week later, they renominated the President on the first ballot, thus deciding, in Lincoln's homely phrase, that it was "not best to swap horses while crossing the river." Andrew Johnson, a War Democrat of Tennessee and the then Military Governor of that state, was chosen as his running mate. The platform praised Lincoln's management of the war, and called for universal emancipation by constitutional amendment.

The Union nominations were received without enthusiasm by the people; the prospects for success were gloomy, especially in view of unsuccessful military operations during July and August. Advised by Thurlow Weed, Greeley, and others of his almost certain defeat, Lincoln recorded his own impressions on August 23 in a private memorandum. "This morning," he wrote, "as for some days past, it seems exceedingly probable that this Administration will not be reëlected."

The situation was alleviated somewhat by the action of the Democratic national convention at Chicago on August 29. The platform, written under Vallandigham's influence, declared the

[1] Edward Everett Hale's famous story, "The Man Without a Country," was written for the purpose of affecting public sentiment at the time of this campaign.

war a failure, and demanded an immediate armistice with a peace convention to restore the federal Union. But General George B. McClellan, the victor of Antietam, was selected as the Democratic candidate, and in his letter of acceptance he virtually repudiated the platform. The net effect produced on the country was perhaps well summarized by a travesty of the platform in the *New York Tribune:* "Resolved that the war is a very good war, and most unrighteous war, and while it should be stopped at once, it must be carried on with vigor."

Nevertheless, the success of the Union ticket seemed far from assured. Special efforts were again made to secure the support of the wage-earners. In a letter of March 21 to the Workingmen's Association of New York, Lincoln declared that "Labor is the superior of capital and deserves much the higher consideration," and called the rebellion, "in fact, a war upon the rights of all working people." A campaign broadside appealed, "Workingmen, stand by your order. Lincoln and Johnson were poor men and worked for their living." In September, Sherman, Farragut, and Sheridan won their great victories, and, as Seward said, this news "knocked the bottom out of the Chicago nominations." Fremont withdrew from the contest on September 17, and Lincoln was elected by an electoral majority of 212 to 21, though he secured only fifty-five per cent of the popular vote.

Europe and the Civil War

The stronger European governments, with a single exception, sympathized with the South in the Civil War. It was the purpose of the Confederates to convert this sympathy into a recognition of Southern independence, coupled, if possible, with armed intervention. The Lincoln administration, on the other hand, sought to defeat this expectation, and to keep the Confederates from building vessels and obtaining munitions in Europe. The efforts of both sides centered upon Great Britain, for it was well understood that the policy of Napoleon III of France would be governed by that of Britain.

British sentiment on the American conflict was far from unanimous. The governing class was friendly to the Confederacy, for the British nobility looked upon the Southern planters as fellow aristocrats, and rejoiced that the great American experiment in popular government seemed on the verge of collapse. Citing Congress's own declaration at the opening of the war, they denied that the North was fighting to abolish slavery, and held with the *London Times* that "The contest is really for empire on the side of the North and for independence on that of the South." The manufacturing and commercial classes were also favorable to the Confederacy, for cotton was an essential product to keep their factories going, and they viewed with approval the adherence of the South to the doctrine of free trade. Even Charles Dickens the novelist, who hated slavery and social injustice in all its forms, expressed only dislike for the North in his private letters during these years.

From the outset, however, the United States had influential friends in Parliament, who, though in the minority, were strong enough to prevent the government from taking extreme measures. Such great champions of humanitarian reform as John Bright, Richard Cobden, and William E. Forster declared insistently that the cause of the South was the cause of slavery and the "Slave Power." In this position they were joined by the wage-earners in spite of the fact that the latter were the chief sufferers from the cotton stringency and that their misery was only partly alleviated by the organized philanthropy carried on by friends of the North. As if to offset Dickens, Tennyson and Darwin were warm supporters of the Union. The influence of this pro-Northern sentiment was strengthened by the fact that English crop failures in 1860–1862 caused Northern grain to be in greater demand than Southern cotton.

Nevertheless, relations between the two countries were badly strained in the early years of the war, and extremists on both sides eagerly acclaimed the possibility of war. On May 13, 1861, the British government issued a Proclamation of Neutrality, an action quickly followed by other European countries. Such a proclamation was not equivalent to a recognition of Southern independence, but it granted the Confederates privileges and advantages in British ports all over the world equivalent to those accorded loyal Northerners. The act also contravened Lincoln's contention that a rebellion, and not an international war, was in progress — a position from which Lincoln himself had unwittingly departed when he established the Southern blockade. However justified the proclamation may have been, it bore the appearance of action taken precipitately since it was issued on the very day that the American minister, Charles Francis Adams, arrived in England.

Six months later occurred the *Trent* affair, which brought the two nations to the brink of war. An American man-of-war, commanded by Captain Charles Wilkes, stopped the British steamship *Trent* on the high seas on November 8, 1861, and forcibly removed the Confederate commissioners, J. M. Mason and John Slidell, with their secretaries, who had taken passage on the vessel from Havana for Southampton, two neutral ports. The news was received with extravagant joy in the North, but England blazed with resentment. The British government made peremptory demands for the liberation of the prisoners, and coupled the act with extensive naval preparations and the dispatching of eight thousand troops to Canada.[1] Since the seizure had not been authorized by the American government and, indeed, ran counter to all previous American policy as to the freedom of the seas, Lincoln allowed sufficient time to pass for public sentiment to cool, and then on December 26, ordered the surrender of the men with a suitable explanation.

No sooner was this matter settled than a new difficulty arose from Great Britain's lax interpretation of her neutral duties toward the surreptitious construction of Confederate cruisers. In March, 1862, the newly built *Florida* was permitted by the authorities to sail from Liverpool, and in July the *Alabama* departed in the same manner. In both instances Adams protested vigorously, and presented advance evidence to prove the Confederate ownership of the vessels.

That the British authorities were swayed by their friendship for the South cannot be gainsaid. Indeed, by the middle of September, 1862, Lord Palmerston, the Prime Minister, decided that the time was at hand to recognize Confederate independence. Arrangements were made for a cabinet meeting with a view to proposing to France and other powers joint action in the matter, but before the meeting was held, several things intervened to render such a step impossible. Adams let it be known that the United States would sever diplomatic relations, but perhaps a more important influence was the Union victory at Antietam on September 17, 1862, followed by the Emancipation Proclamation. With her own strong antislavery traditions, Great Britain could not adopt a policy which would serve to perpetuate slavery in America.

From this time to the close of the war, the British government stringently enforced her neutrality obligations. In 1863, the authorities seized three vessels destined for the Confederacy, two of them ironclad rams of great destructive power. Meantime the *Florida* and the *Alabama* were engaged in their mission of harassing Northern merchantmen, and before their capture, wrought damage to Northern commerce to the extent of more than fifteen million dollars.

Napoleon III was even more friendly to the South than the British leaders. To the Confederate commissioners he intimated a willingness to open French shipyards to the construction of commerce destroyers, and work on several vessels was actually begun. Though the cotton shortage had caused unemployment in certain sections of France, Napoleon's chief motive was his desire to cripple the military strength of the United States, and thereby create conditions favorable for the realization of the long-cherished dream of reëstablishing a French empire in the New World.

About six months after the war began, he induced Great Britain and Spain to join with him in an armed expedition against Mexico for the purpose of collecting the unpaid claims of their subjects. In January, 1862, the allied forces occupied a number of custom houses, and a few months later Great Britain and Spain, coming to terms with Mexico, withdrew. The French General, left to his own devices, proceeded, under Napoleon's instructions, to overthrow the existing Mexican government, declare a monarchy, and place Maximilian, an Austrian archduke, on a throne supported by French bayonets. All this was, of course, in direct violation of the Monroe Doctrine, but being engaged in a struggle for national existence, America could do nothing but protest and bide her time. With the close of the Civil War, the United States became master of the situation. Napoleon was warned once more, and the French troops finally withdrew in the spring of 1867. Without foreign support

Maximilian's government collapsed, and he himself was executed.

Spain's rôle during the Civil War was in feeble imitation of that of France. In 1861 she annexed the Dominican Republic on the island of Santo Domingo. In 1864 she declared war on Peru, and seized the Chincha Islands, valuable for guano. The United States protested vigorously in both instances, and announced again the principles of the Monroe Doctrine. With the termination of the Civil War Spain quietly yielded both claims.

Russia, Prussia, and the Scandinavian countries were favorable to the North, Russia conspicuously so. Czar Alexander II, who had emancipated the serfs in 1861, was strongly influenced by his antislavery sympathies, and no doubt also by the fact that the European powers friendly to the South were unfriendly to his own country. At a critical time in the war (September, 1863), one Russian fleet visited New York and another San Francisco, and their presence there gave much moral support to the cause of the Union both at home and abroad.

The Northern people felt a deep debt of gratitude to Russia, and consequently, shortly after the war, when Russia proposed the sale of Russian America (Alaska) to the United States, the American government was agreeably disposed, though the territory in question was looked upon as a barren expanse of ice with no possibilities of development. The purchase price was fixed at $7,200,000, and the Senate ratified the treaty on April 9, 1867, with but two dissenting votes. As the future was to disclose, the United States had unwittingly made a noble purchase. Incidentally another European monarchy was eliminated from the Western Hemisphere.

SELECT BIBLIOGRAPHY

Wartime Problems North and South. Domestic and international controversies in the North are treated in a judicial spirit in J. F. Rhodes, *History of the United States*, III–V (New York, 1895–1904). Well-balanced accounts, briefer in scope, may be found in J. K. Hosmer, *The Appeal to Arms* and his *Outcome of the Civil War* (in *The American Nation*, XX–XXI, New York, 1907); and N. W. Stephenson, *Abraham Lincoln and the Union* (in *The Chronicles of America*, XXIX, New Haven, 1918).

Filling the War Purse. An excellent concise analysis of federal finances and of the new national banking system is given in D. R. Dewey, *Financial*

History of the United States (New York, 1922). Very helpful, also, is J. J. Knox, *A History of Banking in the United States* (rev. by Bradford Rhodes and E. H. Youngman, New York, 1903). A biographical approach is afforded by A. B. Hart, *Salmon Portland Chase* (New York, 1899), E. P. Oberholtzer, *Jay Cooke, Financier of the Civil War* (2 v., Philadelphia, 1907), and T. E. Burton, *John Sherman* (Boston, 1906). For Southern finances, J. C. Schwab, *The Confederate States of America* (New York, 1901), is exceedingly important.

Political Divisions during the War. Much light on the general subject is cast by a series of monographs worked out for separate states, namely, G. H. Porter, *Ohio Politics during the Civil War Period* (in *Columbia University Studies*, XL, no. 2, New York, 1911); A. C. Cole, *The Era of the Civil War, 1848–1870* (in *The Centennial History of Illinois*, III, Springfield, 1919); Edith E. Ware, *Political Opinion in Massachusetts during Civil War and Reconstruction* (in *Columbia University Studies*, LXXIV, no. 2, New York, 1916); O. B. Clark, *The Politics of Iowa during the Civil War and Reconstruction* (Iowa City, 1911); S. D. Brummer, *Political History of New York State during the Period of the Civil War* (in *Columbia University Studies*, XXXIX, no. 2, New York, 1911); and C. M. Knapp, *New Jersey Politics during the Period of the Civil War and Reconstruction* (Geneva, New York, 1924).

Of importance in this connection, also, is W. B. Weeden, *War Government, Federal and State, in Massachusetts, New York, Pennsylvania, and Indiana, 1861–1865* (Boston, 1906). The Peace Democrats receive careful study in E. J. Benton, *The Movement for Peace without Victory during the Civil War* (in Western Reserve Historical Society, *Collections*, no. 99, Cleveland, 1918). All such narratives, however, take on new meaning after a perusal of the volume entitled *American Caricatures Pertaining to the Civil War* (New York, 1918). N. W. Stephenson, *The Day of the Confederacy* (in *The Chronicles of America*, XXX, New Haven, 1919) gives a good picture of Southern life and politics.

Europe and the Civil War. Excellent summaries appear in J. W. Foster, *A Century of American Diplomacy* (Boston, 1900), and C. R. Fish, *American Diplomacy* (New York, 1924). See also C. F. Adams, Jr., *Charles Francis Adams* (Boston, 1900), and his *Studies Military and Diplomatic, 1775–1865* (New York, 1911). T. L. Harris, *The Trent Affair* (Indianapolis, 1896), is a special study. A brief account, written by two Englishmen, is Brougham Villiers and W. H. Chesson, *Anglo-American Relations, 1861–1865* (London, 1919). For the Confederate side, consult J. M. Callahan, *The Diplomatic History of the Southern Confederacy* (Baltimore, 1901), John Bigelow, *France and the Confederate Navy* (New York, 1888), and M. L. Bonham, *The British Consuls in the Confederacy* (in *Columbia University Studies*, XLIII, no. 3, New York, 1911). P. F. Martin, *Maximilian in Mexico* (New York, 1914), is the best treatment of that subject.

CHAPTER XIV

THE POSTWAR SOUTH

Wartime Efforts at Reconstruction

The problem of postwar readjustment in the seceded states was a threefold one. It was primarily a humanitarian and sociological question, so far as it concerned the adaptation of the emancipated negro to the new conditions of freedom. In its political and constitutional aspects, it involved the reorganization of the Southern state governments and the resumption of their former relations with the general government. As an economic problem, it dealt with the revival of the war-deranged industry of the South under the changed conditions imposed by a free-labor system.

The questions thus raised were complex and unprecedented, and, unfortunately, their settlement devolved upon a people, divided for a generation by political and economic differences, freshly emerged from a fratricidal war, and sustaining the relation of victor and vanquished. Personal animosities, partisan prejudices, and misguided zeal inevitably played a large part on both sides in working out a program of reconstruction. The welfare of the negro, at first envisaged as a philanthropic and humanitarian enterprise, soon became a bone of political contention, and was given a place in the Congressional plans for political reconstruction. Only in the matter of economic readjustment were the Southern people permitted to work out their salvation without federal interference.

The need for extending aid to the negroes rose early in the war when fugitive slaves began pouring into the Union camps in Virginia and elsewhere. Acting in coöperation with the government, private organizations in the North sprang at once to the service of relieving the needy and of offering religious and educational instruction to the ignorant. The American Missionary

Association was the first in the field, but scores of other organizations quickly joined in the work, including the United States Sanitary Commission and even some philanthropic societies in Great Britain. Some of the military commanders also gave direct aid to the refugees.

In September, 1861, the first of a series of freedmen's schools was opened at Fortress Monroe. More than three thousand men and women eventually became engaged in social and educational service among the negroes, and the aggregate of the money contributions reached millions of dollars. While many mistakes were made by overzealous individuals, much suffering was relieved, many negroes were saved from a life of ignorance and vice, and some progress was made in guiding them along the uncertain way between slavery and freedom.

Nevertheless, as the Union armies conquered additional territory and the number of refugees multiplied, the scope of the work became too vast for private agencies to handle efficiently, and the chief responsibility inevitably fell upon the government itself. A few days after the final Proclamation of Emancipation, efforts were begun in Congress to secure the establishment of an official bureau of emancipation, but it was not until early in 1865 that a majority of Congress were convinced that the government might properly undertake the task. The Freedmen's Bureau Act of March 3, 1865, created a "Bureau of Refugees, Freedmen and Abandoned Lands" with local branches throughout the South. It was charged with the duty of providing food and clothing for the temporary relief of the former slaves, and of allotting them tracts of land from abandoned estates (not to exceed forty acres), at a low rental, with the privilege of eventual purchase. The law was limited in duration to one year after the close of the war.

Major General O. O. Howard was placed at the head of the work, and he performed competent service in a difficult situation. Besides centralizing and coördinating the activities of the private societies, the Bureau assumed a general guardianship of the emancipated people. It strove to impress them with the idea that freedom did not mean idleness, and to assist them in their dealings with the unfriendly white population. That it greatly facilitated the process of social reorganization cannot be doubted.

In some cases, however, the local agents of the Bureau were unfit, and such men wrought more harm than good by raising false hopes in the breasts of their wards and unduly antagonizing the whites. For example, in the autumn of 1865, the idea gained currency among the negroes that on New Year's Day the United States government would give each freedman "forty acres and a mule." Accordingly, many of them refused to contract for farm labor during the coming year.

While attempts were being made to solve the negro problem, the question also presented itself of how a "seceded" state might recover its former status in the Union. Such a situation was unforeseen by the framers of the Constitution, and that instrument offered little guidance in the circumstances. Lincoln believed that the task of political reorganization belonged to him, since he, as Commander-in-Chief of the Army and Navy, had imposed military law on the South, and might therefore declare the conditions of its withdrawal. Congress, on the other hand, maintained that reconstruction was properly a function of the law-making branch, inasmuch as the Constitution guaranteed to every state a republican form of government and made Congress the judge of the admission of its own members. In time this difference of opinion became intensified by the revelation that the executive department favored a policy of clemency and conciliation in contrast to the more drastic course deemed necessary by Congress.

In the nature of the case, the first moves fell to Lincoln, for as quickly as Confederate territory was conquered, provision had to be made for its government. Incapable of cherishing animosity toward beaten opponents, he desired to give the erring states every practical assistance in quickly recovering their old place in the Union. Since the early days of the war he had recognized the Pierpont government in Virginia as the lawful government of that state (see page 182), believing that when the Confederate power was crushed, the loyal legislature would quietly extend its authority over all the inhabitants. When Tennessee, Louisiana, and Arkansas passed under federal control in 1862 and 1863, he appointed military governors to take charge until acceptable civil governments could be established.

On December 8, 1863, he issued his Proclamation of Amnesty,

which outlined a general plan of procedure for the guidance of the Southern people. He offered to pardon all who should take a prescribed oath of loyalty to the United States, with the exception of certain classes, such as prominent Confederate officials and persons who had joined the rebellion after resigning high federal positions. Whenever as many as one tenth of the number of voters in 1860 should thus recover the franchise in any state, they might reëstablish a state government, which would thereupon be recognized as the true government by the President. Congress, he pointed out, must decide for itself whether members from the state should be admitted to seats. Measures adopted by the states for the assistance of the "laboring, landless, and homeless" negroes would "not be objected to by the National Executive." From other sources, we know that Lincoln did not favor negro suffrage, except possibly for educated men and veterans of the war.

Under this "ten-per-cent plan," constitutional conventions were held and state governments organized during 1864 in Tennessee, Louisiana, and Arkansas. Though these governments were but "as the egg is to the fowl," Lincoln believed "we shall sooner have the fowl by hatching the egg than by smashing it."

To many members of Congress, the President's plan seemed too lenient, not to say in excess of his authority. Accordingly, Congressmen chosen from the reorganized communities were not admitted to membership; and in July, 1864, Congress set forth its views in a measure, known from its authors, as the Wade-Davis Bill. This bill made Congress instead of the Executive the ultimate authority on reconstruction, and imposed on the Southern states more stringent conditions than had the President, particularly the requirement that a majority of the white men must take an oath of allegiance. To this bill Lincoln applied a "pocket veto," though he issued a new proclamation in which he offered it as a possible alternative to his own plan. He was not inclined to quibble over details if the end he was seeking could be as well attained in another way.

His attitude toward the Wade-Davis Bill is an augury of how he might have dealt with Congress when the return of peace made reconstruction the paramount public issue. But hardly had Lee and Johnston surrendered their armies before he fell victim to an assassin's bullet. In consequence, his place was taken on April 15, 1865, by a man ill-fitted, by temperament or training, to assume the reins of government at such a trying juncture.

The Quarrel over a Southern Policy

The rise of Andrew Johnson from humble origins was even more extraordinary than that of Lincoln himself. Indentured at the age of ten to a tailor in a mountain hamlet of eastern Tennessee, he had been taught to read by a fellow apprentice, but the art of writing he acquired in manhood from his wife. When scarcely of voting age, he became Mayor of his village, and this proved to be the first step in a political ascent which took him to the state legislature, to the Governor's chair, to the national House of Representatives, and in 1857 to the Senate. By dint of a combative nature and tenacious will, he became a political power in a state where public leadership was ordinarily monopolized by the planting aristocracy. A Democrat of the Jacksonian school, he vigorously opposed the secession of Tennessee, and his vice-presidential nomination in 1864 was a concession to the War Democrats in the Union party. Long experience in public life wore off some of his rough edges, and revealed his sterling qualities of intellectual courage and inflexible purpose. Unfortunately the situation before him called also for tact and patience, and these qualities were utterly foreign to his contentious makeup.

Lincoln's death at the hands of a drink-crazed Southern zealot put the North in an ugly humor. While the excitement was at fever heat, Johnson offered large rewards for the arrest of Jefferson Davis and other leaders as accomplices in the terrible deed. Misled by this impulsive action, the Radicals confidently expected the President to announce a vengeful policy toward the South. On cooler thought, however, Johnson announced his acceptance of the reorganized governments in Virginia, Tennessee, Louisiana, and Arkansas, retained his predecessor's cabinet without change, and on May 29, 1865, issued a proclamation which made clear his essential agreement with Lincoln's reconstruction policy.

Although his proclamation excluded certain additional classes from the franchise in the remaining states, he directed that constitutional conventions should be held as speedily as practicable on the basis of a loyal white suffrage. When these conventions met, he made known his expectation that they should declare invalid the ordinances of secession and repudiate their war debts, and further that their first legislatures should ratify the pending Thirteenth Amendment. The reorganization of the remaining seven states proceeded along these lines, and by December, 1865, when Congress assembled for the first time under the new President, all the states save one had substantially complied with his terms, Texas completing her handiwork in April, 1866.

Congress accordingly was confronted with the question of admitting the members-elect from the ex-Confederate states, and they decided in the negative. The conviction continued strong in that body that reconstruction was the proper business of the legislative branch. Moreover, the President's terms seemed far too mild to guarantee the future good behavior of the Southern people. Idealists like Charles Sumner maintained that the freedmen were entitled to the ballot as an inherent human right. A similar view was championed by Thaddeus Stevens and other strong party men, though for a different reason. They perceived that abolition, by rendering inoperative the constitutional provision for counting only three fifths of the slaves in apportioning representation, would actually enhance the strength of the Southern whites in Congress and the Electoral College. The seceded states would thereby gain nine additional Representatives on the basis of the census of 1860. In their judgment, it was a situation pregnant with dangerous consequences for the Republican party, unless it should be counteracted by bestowing the vote on the negroes.

Such fears and misgivings were greatly accentuated by the conduct of the newly-established governments. Men prominent in the Confederacy were beginning to take an active part in Southern politics again. The election of an ex-Confederate Senator as Governor of South Carolina and of Alexander H. Stephens as United States Senator from Georgia seemed to evince an impenitent spirit on the part of the people. Moreover, the attitude of the Southern law-makers toward the former slaves created alarm and indignation.

These legislatures were engaged in enacting statutes which, in many respects, curtailed the rights of freedmen as compared with those of the white race. Based upon a deep conviction of the incapacity of the negro to adjust himself readily to conditions of freedom, the "Black Codes" aimed chiefly to impose restraints which might discourage idleness, vagrancy, and race disturbances. For example, while permitted to enjoy ordinary civil rights like making contracts and owning property, the blacks were, in some states, subjected to special penalties for breaking labor contracts, forbidden to give testimony in cases involving whites, and prohibited from bearing arms without a license. A few legislatures even went so far as to provide that idle negroes should be subjected to a fine which, if unable to pay, they must work out at a fixed rate in the service of an employer. However justifiable such laws were in the eyes of the former master class, they seemed to the North a deliberate effort to nullify the result of the war, and to reëstablish, under color of legality, the former system of human bondage.

The Congress, which began sitting on December 4, 1865, contained conservative, moderate, and radical Republicans. If President Johnson had shown a disposition to conciliate the moderates, he might have commanded a majority of Congress in support of a slightly modified version of his own plan. On the contrary, his dogmatism and violence soon drove his natural allies into league with the Radical leaders, Stevens and Sumner, iron-willed, imperious men who for two years were virtual dictators of Congress.

The two Houses created a Joint Committee on Reconstruction for the purpose of formulating the conditions upon which the Southern members might be admitted to seats, and then, while waiting for the report of the committee, proceeded to pass a series of acts to safeguard the former slaves from the Black Codes and other Southern discriminations. The first of these measures, the Freedmen's Bureau bill of February 6, 1866, prolonged the life of the Bureau for an indefinite period, enlarged its powers, and gave it the right to appeal to the military whenever civil rights were denied to freedmen. The bill was promptly negatived by the President as inexpedient and unconstitutional, and in an intemperate speech on Washington's Birthday, he classed Sumner and Stevens with Jefferson Davis as traitors to the basic principles of our government.

This, however, was the last time that Johnson was able to thwart the will of Congress. In April, 1866, Congress adopted over his veto the Civil Rights Act, which accomplished the purpose of the earlier bill in a more thorough way. All persons born in the United States, excluding Indians not taxed, were declared to be citizens of the United States, and as such, entitled to absolute equality of treatment before the law, any "statute, ordinance, regulation, or custom to the contrary notwithstanding." Violators of the Act were punishable by fine or imprisonment or both, and the military power might be employed, if necessary, to enforce its provisions. The right of Congress to enact such a law was open to question; but its supporters, insisting that the negroes were virtually in a condition of "involuntary servitude," based its constitutionality upon the enforcement clause of the Thirteenth Amendment.

Since January, the Joint Committee on Reconstruction had been taking testimony with reference to conditions in the South, and on the last day of April, 1866, it reported to Congress its conclusions. Its chief proposal was that a comprehensive amendment dealing with Southern conditions should be added to the Constitution, and that, when this was accomplished, any Southern state which had ratified it might gain representation in Congress. Ratification of the proposed amendment would thus become the condition on which Congress would accept Presidential reconstruction.

After some modification at the hands of Congress, the amendment eventually became the Fourteenth Amendment. It dealt with every important aspect of the Southern situation. By the first section, the principles of the Civil Rights Act were securely imbedded in the Constitution, and thereby all question of the constitutionality of the statute was set at rest.[1] The second

[1] This portion of the amendment has figured in so many court decisions that the exact phraseology is a matter of importance: "All persons born or naturalized in the United States, and subject to the jurisdiction thereof, are citizens of the United States and of the State wherein they reside. No State shall make or enforce any law which shall abridge the privileges or immunities of citizens of the United States; nor shall any State deprive any person of life, liberty, or property without due process of law; nor deny to any person within its jurisdiction the equal protection of the laws." Though ostensibly evoked by the necessities of the freedmen, few negroes ever brought cases under it; and its chief effect has been to enable the federal courts to protect corporations from invasions of their vested rights by state laws and city ordinances. The prohibitions on state authority are very comprehensive.

section represented an attempt to meet the desires of both the theorists of racial equality and the practical politicians. By its provisions, the states were given the option of enfranchising all adult male citizens or suffering a reduction of representation in Congress. The third section was intended to check the rapid return of rebel leaders into politics, and therefore barred from officeholding ex-Confederates who had been federal or state officials before the war, until they should be pardoned by Congress. The next section declared that the war debt of the South should never be paid nor that of the Union repudiated, and further that the former masters should never be compensated for the loss of their slaves.

On June 13, 1866, the amendment was sent to the states for ratification. The Radicals evidently believed that the Southern governments were sufficiently reconstructed to ratify a constitutional amendment even if they might not send members to Congress. On July 19, Tennessee ratified, and five days later Congress declared her entitled to representation. The other Southern legislatures voted down the amendment by overwhelming majorities.

The contest over reconstruction policy had reached a temporary deadlock. With Congress and the President at odds over the Southern question, the fall elections of 1866 gave the people a chance to act as arbiter between them. The President's friends sought to attract the support of the moderates of both political parties, but their promising efforts were unwittingly defeated by Johnson himself when he undertook a "swing round the circle" and made a series of blustering speeches in the large cities of the Middle West. Though the charges of drunkenness made by the Radicals were untrue, his tactics were better suited to the rough-and-tumble politics of eastern Tennessee than to a dignified national campaign.

The President's cause was further discredited by a bloody race riot in New Orleans on July 30, an incident which convinced many that the South did not intend to deal fairly with the freedmen. Both factions endeavored to win the soldier vote by assembling special conventions of the veterans — these efforts may be said to mark the formal entry of the powerful "old-soldier" influence into postwar politics. The outcome of the campaign was a stinging defeat for the administration candidates and an overwhelming victory for the Radicals, who secured more than two thirds of each House of Congress. Thereby the popular will expressed approval of a policy of severity toward the South.

The Reign of the Radicals

When Congress assembled in December, 1866, the Radicals, elated by the recent election, decided to brush aside the governments set up by the President in the ten remaining states, and to exceed their own former demands. Stevens desired to place the South under military government pure and simple, and a bill embodying this idea passed the House. When it reached the Senate, its terms were somewhat softened, although Sumner succeeded in forcing into it the additional requirement of negro enfranchisement. Congress accepted Sumner's alteration, notwithstanding the fact that at the very time negro suffrage prevailed in only six states of the North — in New York and all the New England states except Connecticut.

The new plan of Congress was set forth in the basic Reconstruction Act of March 2, 1867, and the supplementary legislation of March 23 and July 19, 1867, and March 11, 1868. The ten Southern states were to be divided into five military districts under command of United States Generals, who were charged with preserving order and with continuing or supplanting civil officials as they saw fit. The people of a state might gain representation in Congress when a constitutional convention elected by the adult males of both races (excluding those disfranchised as former rebels) should frame a constitution establishing negro suffrage, when this constitution should be ratified at a popular election of white and black voters and accepted by Congress, when the new state legislature should ratify the Fourteenth Amendment, and when this amendment should have become a part of the federal Constitution.

The feeling between the President and Congress was constantly growing more vindictive. Johnson vetoed all the important Reconstruction Acts, and in turn, Congress set about to hamper and defeat his purposes in every conceivable way. One of their efforts was the Tenure of Office Act of March 2, 1867, which made the President guilty of a "high misdemeanor" if he removed an officeholder without the consent of the Senate. The statute specifically included cabinet officers, who, unless dismissed with the Senate's permission, were to hold office "during the term of the President by whom they may have been appointed and for one month thereafter." Johnson vetoed the bill on the ground that it reversed a time-honored practice of the government and was unconstitutional, but his opposition was overridden.

Not content with halfway measures, the Radicals sought diligently for a pretext to depose the President. In their inflamed state of mind, his stubborn resistance to the measures which they thought necessary was identical with treason to the Constitution itself. Throughout the year 1867 the Judiciary Committee of the House labored to find evidence which would justify his impeachment on one of the grounds named in the Constitution — "treason, bribery, or other high crimes and misdemeanors" — and in December, by a vote of five to four, reported to the House in favor of such action. But the House decided to await more specific evidence of his misconduct.

Their opportunity came on February 21, 1868, when Johnson dismissed from office Edwin M. Stanton, Secretary of War, whose collusion with the Radicals had made his continuance in the cabinet intolerable to the President. Three days later the House amid intense excitement voted to impeach the President for "high crimes and misdemeanors." The charges against him were set forth in eleven articles involving much duplication and confusion of thought. The principal accusations were that his removal of Stanton constituted a "high misdemeanor" under the Tenure of Office Act, and that he had attempted to bring Congress into contempt in his "swing round the circle" in 1866.

The trial in the Senate began on March 5, 1868, with Chief Justice Chase presiding. The prosecution was conducted by Stevens, Benjamin F. Butler, and five other members of the House, and the defense was represented by distinguished legal talent. It soon appeared that the charge against Johnson, based upon the Tenure of Office Act, lacked foundation, for the protection afforded by that statute extended to cabinet members for only one month after the term of the President who had appointed them, and Stanton, a Lincoln appointee, had continued in office for almost three years after Lincoln's death. Nothing daunted, the Radicals turned their chief efforts toward removing the President for reasons of general party expediency.

The excitement throughout the North was great, with public sentiment antagonistic to Johnson. When the final votes were taken in May, the decision of the Senate stood thirty-five to nineteen for conviction, one vote short of the necessary two-thirds majority. Seven courageous Republicans joined with the twelve Democrats in making this result possible. To posterity it is clear that Johnson had done nothing to merit removal. As Senator Lyman Trumbull said before casting his ballot for acquittal, "Once set the example of impeaching a President for what, when the excitement of the hour shall have subsided, will be regarded as insufficient causes, and no future President will be safe who happens to differ with a majority of the House and two thirds of the Senate on any measure deemed by them important."

Meantime, the new Congressional plan of military reconstruction was put into effect in the South. Mississippi applied to the Supreme Court for an injunction to restrain the President from carrying out the legislation on the ground of its unconstitutionality, but in vain. A similar application by Georgia met the same fate. The Supreme Court was unwilling to interfere in a controversy which it regarded as purely political in character.[1]

Notwithstanding Johnson's personal disapproval of the Radical scheme, he appointed the district commanders as required by the law, and these officials proceeded to establish the paramount authority of the federal government in the unreconstructed states. Wherever possible, the commanders sought to coöperate with the existing governments, but when this proved difficult, they did not hesitate to depose the Governors (as in Louisiana, Texas, Georgia, and Mississippi), or to substitute military tribunals for the ordinary civil courts. All elections under existing state laws were forbidden, and in due course, the commanders provided for the registration of voters preparatory to the holding of constitutional conventions in each state. Negro voters were in the majority in South Carolina, Florida, Alabama, Mississippi, and Louisiana, and the whites in Virginia, North Carolina,

[1] Mississippi *v.* Johnson; Georgia *v.* Stanton; *Ex parte* McCardle.

Arkansas, and Texas. In Georgia the numbers were about equal.

The result of the elections was a group of constituent assemblies unlike any others in the history of the American nation. The chief part in the conventions was taken by the "Carpetbaggers" — ambitious Northerners who had gone South chiefly for mercenary purposes. With them were allied a small number of Southern whites — the detested "Scalawags" — who had forsaken their white neighbors to become converts of the Radical

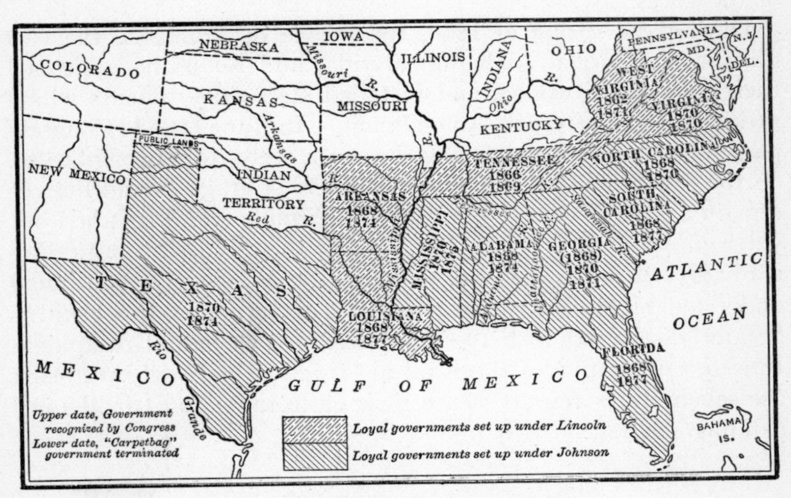

THE PROCESS OF RECONSTRUCTION

cause. All the conventions also contained negroes, bent on tasting the vague but inebriating joys of political privilege. In the case of South Carolina this element was in the majority. The bulk of the colored members were of little consequence, however, except as they were pawns in the hands of white or black leaders.

During the late winter and spring of 1868 the work of the conventions was performed in all the states but Texas. The constitutions framed under these unpromising conditions embraced many excellent features, none more laudable perhaps than the mandatory provisions for the inauguration of free public-school systems. All the constitutions guaranteed the civil and political equality of the negroes, and some of them carried the principle of disfranchising ex-Confederates beyond any previous enactments.

As the time approached for submitting the new frames of government to popular vote, a vigorous opposition appeared among the native white population. The antagonistic elements professed to be the defenders of "Caucasian civilization" against the inroads of "African barbarism," but the hand of the national military authority was too strong for them. Only in Mississippi, where the white-disfranchisement clause was unusually severe, was the ratification of the new constitution defeated by a majority of the votes cast.

During the spring of 1868, the people of Arkansas, the two Carolinas, Georgia, Alabama, Florida, and Louisiana approved their new constitutions, and installed state governments which ratified the Fourteenth Amendment. In June, 1868, Congress passed legislation for restoring the seven states to representation, on the fundamental condition that negro suffrage should forever remain a part of their organic laws. Virginia and Texas had not yet completed the process of adopting their constitutions. Accordingly, these two states, along with Mississippi, continued under federal military rule while the attention of the country became distracted with the approaching presidential campaign. Indeed, one motive of the Radical leaders in hurriedly restoring the seven states was to secure their electoral support in the impending election.

Grant and the Radicals

The Radicals were first in the field, and while the impeachment trial was still in progress, they held their national convention at Chicago on May 20, under the name of the "National Union Republican party." Ulysses S. Grant and Schuyler Colfax of Indiana, the latter Speaker of the House and an extreme Radical, were nominated on a platform affirming unqualified approval of Congressional reconstruction and pledging payment of the public debt in gold. Recommended by his fame as the "Hero of Appomattox," Grant's nomination took place on the theory which came in with Jackson, that any red-blooded American is capable of holding any office, and that special training for administrative work is unnecessary. As a matter of fact, Grant's political affiliations, so far as he had had any, had been Democratic, but in the months prior to the impeachment trial he had become friendly to the Radicals because of a bitter quarrel with Johnson.

The Democrats were in a difficult position. Discredited by Southern secession and Northern Copperheadism, the party faced the problem of rehabilitating its former strength. For this purpose they must develop new leaders and new issues, a task which could hardly be accomplished in one or even two presidential compaigns. There was an uncomfortable amount of truth in the remark of Kate Chase, politician-daughter of the Chief Justice, that "when the South seceded, the brains of the party went with it." When the Democrats convened in New York City on July 4, they determined to clear their skirts of past offenses and strike out along fresh lines — a course of policy which in time became known in party circles as the "New Departure."

As it happened, a new issue lay ready at hand. Certain wartime bonds were about to fall due, which had been issued under a statute requiring the interest to be paid in coin and the principal in "dollars." Hard times in the Middle West, especially in the year 1867, caused the farmers of that region to insist that the "bloated bondholders" be paid off in the depreciated greenback dollars which they themselves used. "The same currency for the bondholder and the ploughholder" became a popular cry, and George H. Pendleton, a Democratic leader in Ohio, made himself the foremost exponent of the "Ohio Idea," as it was called. The plan was also warmly supported by those Democrats who looked upon the war debt as having been incurred for an unrighteous purpose.

Accordingly, in the spirit of the "New Departure," the Democratic platform declared "the questions of slavery and secession" to be "settled for all time to come," demanded the adoption of the "Ohio Idea," and denounced Radical reconstruction as unconstitutional. Andrew Johnson had some support for the presidential nomination, but Pendleton was the favorite in the early balloting. August Belmont and a group of Eastern Democrats, appalled by the financial heresy of the platform, succeeded in preventing his nomination, and on the twenty-second ballot the choice fell on ex-Governor Horatio Seymour, who reluctantly assented. Francis P. Blair, Jr., of Missouri, an extreme opponent of Radical reconstruction, was named as his running mate.

Grant's election was assured from the outset. Republican orators easily diverted popular attention from the financial issue by "waving the bloody shirt," that is, denouncing the war record of the Democrats. Both platforms promised pensions to the ex-soldiers, but naturally the Republican pledge was looked upon as more certain of results. Toward the end of the canvass there was a strong movement by business men to defeat the Democrats. Grant received 214 electoral votes to 80 for Seymour, though he polled only fifty-three per cent of the popular vote as compared with forty-seven per cent for the opposition.

The new President was purely a product of the war. Although a graduate of West Point, he had left the army in 1854 rather than stand trial on a charge of drunkenness. He had next turned his hand successively to farming and real estate but without success, and when the war opened, he was clerk in his father's leather store in Galena, Illinois, at a salary of $800 a year. Inexperienced in civil administration and of an uncommunicative nature, he had no perception of the subtleties of political management, or of the constant need for conference and conciliation within the party — qualities essential for leadership in a democracy. Moreover, he was a very poor judge of men. His greatest asset was his personal popularity.

The new administration proceeded at once to dispose of the two questions raised by the campaign, namely, the financial issue and the completion of reconstruction. On March 18, 1869, Congress stopped further agitation of the "Ohio Idea" by formally pledging the payment of the public debt in coin. On the Southern question Grant was inclined to follow his own independent judgment, but gradually fell under the influence of the professional politicians in Congress, particularly Benjamin F. Butler, an unscrupulous spoilsman of demagogic gifts who had amassed a fortune while in the army service. These men believed that a stern policy was necessary for the preservation of the Republican party in the South, and influenced the President to that end.

When Grant recommended that the remaining unreconstructed states be permitted to vote separately on their constitutions and the harsh disfranchisement clauses, they argued that he was being too lenient. As an additional condition, they therefore proposed that, since the Fourteenth Amendment had become a part of the Constitution in July, 1868, the three states be required to ratify the pending Fifteenth Amendment. This amendment, which was purely a Radical creation, provided that "The right of citizens of the United States to vote shall not be denied or abridged by the United States or by any State on account of race, color, or previous condition of servitude." Its adoption was urged as the only sure way of establishing negro suffrage, left optional in the previous amendment, and of safeguarding the negro after the Southern states were once again full members of the Union.[1]

The Radicals carried their point, and in the first three months of 1870, Virginia, Mississippi, and Texas complied with the new conditions, and were declared entitled to representation in Congress. The process of reconstruction was not yet completed, however, for the reconstructed legislature of Georgia, under control of the Democrats, had aroused the ire of the Radicals by expelling all the negro members from their seats. On Butler's initiative, the state was once more placed under military rule by Congress in December, 1869, required to ratify the Fifteenth Amendment, and finally restored in July, 1870. In the case of the last four states, Congress, upon readmitting them, affixed a final "fundamental" condition, namely, that negroes should never be disqualified from holding office. The Fifteenth Amendment was proclaimed in effect on March 30, 1870.

The Struggle for White Dominion in the South

Although all the ex-Confederate states had now recovered their former relations with Congress, the Radical leaders were disinclined to allow them to manage their internal affairs without further interference. They feared that the Southern whites, left to their own devices, would reassert their accustomed superiority over the emancipated race, and undo the results attained by

[1] Furthermore, the action of Ohio, Michigan, Kansas, and Minnesota in 1867 of refusing to incorporate negro suffrage in their state constitutions made the Radicals fearful that the Fifteenth Amendment might fail of ratification.

the Fourteenth and Fifteenth amendments. Nor were their fears without foundation. The effect of military reconstruction in the South had been to stand the social pyramid on its apex, with the natural ruling class abased by the elevation of the freedmen and their white allies. The whole process seemed grotesque and intolerable to the former master class. Even as a consequence of the war, it seemed without justification since military rule and negro suffrage were imposed upon them two or more years after the return of peace.

Their resentment was increased by the behavior of the former slaves. While most of the freedmen remained quiet, ambitious individuals, encouraged by mulattoes and white leaders from the North, set about to rouse their people to a bristling sense of race consciousness. One outcome was the widespread formation of "Union Leagues," secret oath-bound societies composed predominantly of blacks, and pledged to the maintenance of the new political order. The organization of these Leagues was accompanied by a certain amount of violence toward the old master class, the waylaying of men, and the burning of houses and barns. The better elements among the whites were at first driven to anger, and later to real alarm.

Most exasperating of all, however, was the conduct of the new state governments installed upon the withdrawal of military reconstruction. These governments were dominated by Carpetbaggers in the higher offices, and by negroes and Scalawags in the subordinate positions. For example, in the case of the seven states restored in 1868, four of the Governors and ten of the United States Senators were men who had never seen their respective commonwealths prior to the war. The highest offices occupied by negroes at this time were Lieutenant-Governor in Louisiana and Secretary of State in South Carolina. Every state legislature contained a substantial negro contingent, and in South Carolina the black members outnumbered the whites eighty-eight to sixty-seven.

In a well-known account, from which the following excerpt is taken, James S. Pike, a Northern newspaper man, described the legislature of South Carolina: "The Speaker is black, the clerk is black, the door-keepers are black, the little pages are black, the chairman of the Ways and Means is black, and the chaplain is coal black. . . . No one is allowed to talk five minutes without interruption, and the one interruption is the signal for another and another. . . . Every one esteems himself as good as his neighbor, and puts in his oar, apparently as often for love of riot and confusion as for anything else. . . . But underneath all this shocking burlesque upon legislative proceedings . . . there is something very real to this uncouth and untutored multitude. . . . Seven years ago these men were raising corn and cotton under the whip of the overseer. Today they are raising points of order and questions of privilege. . . . It is the evidence of an accomplished result. . . . It means liberty. . . . It is their day of jubilee."

The new ruling class had, for the most part, no large property interests. In Alabama, for instance, the total taxes paid by the members of the legislature were estimated at less than one hundred dollars. Since the taxes would fall upon the detested aristocracy, the legislators were not deterred from extravagant expenditures. Indeed, there was a real need for unusual outlays of money, for roads, bridges, and public buildings had fallen into disrepair, and a public educational system had to be built from the ground up. The vast increase, however, in the cost of government was due chiefly to other causes — to the irresponsible character of the lawmakers, their ignorance of the rudiments of finance, and, most of all, to downright corruption and fraud. A conservative estimate in 1872 put the increase in indebtedness of the eleven states at about $132,000,000, much of which consisted of loans and guarantees to wildcat railroad enterprises.

The orgy of misgovernment rose highest in Louisiana and South Carolina. In the latter state, a free restaurant and bar was maintained for the convenience of the legislators, while included in the item, "legislative supplies," were such articles as hams, perfumes, suspenders, bonnets, baskets of champagne, and a coffin. The public printing bills during the eight years of Carpetbag rule exceeded by $717,589 the total amount expended for that purpose in the entire previous history of the state since 1789.

Southern whites, trained in a different social philosophy, stood aghast at the social and political chaos, which threatened to engulf everything in life most dear to them. How could the fine fruits of their civilization be saved from "Africanization"?

From Congress no relief could be expected, and the Supreme Court had turned a deaf ear to their pleas. Members of the old master class therefore resorted to that mode of collective resistance which oppressed peoples have often employed against tyrannical rulers. They organized themselves into secret ritualistic societies for the purpose of counteracting the new order with a reign of terrorism and coercion.

The best known of these organizations was the Ku Klux Klan, founded in 1866 at the little country town of Pulaski, Tennessee, as a source of diversion for youths accustomed to the excitements of army life.[1] The mysterious nocturnal ceremonies of this new order aroused the superstitious fears of the colored people in the neighborhood, and profiting by this fact, the members soon gave their chief energies to intimidating and disciplining aggressive blacks. The Pulaski idea spread like wildfire through the rural districts; similar groups or "Dens" sprang into existence throughout Tennessee and the nearby states. At a secret meeting at Nashville in April, 1867, the Dens were brought together into a unified system under the name of the "Invisible Empire of the South," with officers bearing awe-inspiring titles.

The chief work of the Klan fell to the Dens. Appareled in ghostly manner and riding white-sheeted horses with muffled hoofs, the members would visit the homes of unruly negroes and objectionable whites at dead of night, and warn them to cease their activities or to depart from the neighborhood. If the Grand Cyclops of the Den were a strong character, violence was kept at a minimum; but if he were rash or weak-willed, the midnight visitations might result in whippings, maimings, or even death.

Therein lay the fatal weakness of the order: the turbulent spirits were apt to predominate, or in any case, its methods might, without warrant, be imitated by the criminal elements of the community for purposes of loot or personal vengeance. A realization of this fact caused the men at the head of the organization to order its disbandment in the early spring of 1869. This, however, left the situation worse than before, for although the conservative members everywhere withdrew, the

[1] The name had no particular significance. "Ku Klux" came from "Kuklos," the Greek word for circle, and as William Garrott Brown has said, "Klan" followed "Ku Klux" as naturally as "Dumpty" follows "Humpty."

Dens did not dissolve, but remained more than ever in the hands of the irresponsible leaders.

Through a misapprehension of the true state of affairs, Northerners applied the term "Ku Klux" to all secret movements of terrorism in the South. In reality, the largest and perhaps most important of these underground organizations was the Knights of the White Camelia, established at New Orleans about the same time as the Ku Klux Klan, and drawing its members from the states from Texas to the Carolinas. Operating under the nominal control of a Supreme Council at New Orleans, the real power, as in the case of the Klan, was wielded by the local "Circles," and the methods and purposes of the two orders were virtually identical. Other bodies engaged in similar work were the Pale Faces, the White Brotherhood, and the Constitutional Union Guards.

The excesses and disorders instigated by these organizations led inevitably to repressive measures on the part of the federal government. The will of Congress was set forth in the Force Act of May 31, 1870, the Federal Elections Law of February 28, 1871, and the Ku Klux Act or "Bayonet Bill" of April 20, 1871. The object of these laws was to break up the secret societies, and secure a rigid enforcement of the Fourteenth and Fifteenth Amendments, particularly of those portions guaranteeing the civil and political equality of the negro. For this purpose, the President was empowered to use the troops, and even to suspend the writ of *habeas corpus*. When circumstances seemed to warrant, the appointment of federal supervisors of Congressional elections was authorized.

Under these laws hundreds of men were tried for "conspiracy" before the United States courts, and a number were convicted. Troops were freely employed, and in the fall of 1871 the writ of *habeas corpus* was suspended in nine counties of South Carolina. By the end of 1872 "Ku Kluxing" had virtually disappeared. It is a significant commentary on the zeal of Butler and the Radicals that the essential provisions of all these laws, except the Federal Elections Act, were declared unconstitutional by the Supreme Court in a series of decisions from 1875 to 1882.[1]

[1] United States *v.* Cruikshank (1875), United States *v.* Reese (1875), and United States *v.* Harris (1882). An act of 1875 granting equal privileges to both races in hotels, churches, railways, etc., was also held unconstitutional. Civil Rights Cases (1883).

In spite of all handicaps, the Southern states made steady progress toward the recovery of white supremacy. Already in 1869 the obnoxious "Parson" Brownlow government had lost its hold in Tennessee. After the passage of the repressive acts of 1870–1871, the native whites began to substitute craft for force in dealing with the black voters. The franchise had come to the negroes through no exertions of their own, and a denial of the right violated no long-cherished convictions of the race. The mere threat of violence, subtly conveyed, deterred thousands of freedmen from appearing at the polls, and afforded insufficient evidence for prosecution under the provisions of the new federal legislation.

In 1870 and 1871, the Carpetbag governments were dislodged from power in North Carolina, Virginia, and Georgia. In May, 1872, Congress passed the General Amnesty Act, which removed the political disabilities of most of the persons excluded from office by the Fourteenth Amendment, and thereby permitted nearly 150,000 of the ablest citizens of the South to return to active political life.[1] Moreover, the Scalawags were growing tired of their alliance with ex-slaves and Northern adventurers, and were beginning to make common cause with their white neighbors. As a result, Alabama, Arkansas, and Texas were "redeemed" in 1874, and Mississippi in the next year.

Only the presence of federal troops enabled the Carpetbaggers to retain their hold in the three remaining states. The two political elements came to a death-grapple in these states in the presidential election of 1876, with the result that the electoral returns were in doubt, and as will presently appear, the whole nation thrown into turmoil. The election of Tilden, the Democratic candidate, would have meant the withdrawal of the troops, but, as it happened, the seating of Hayes had the same result, for Hayes represented that wing of the Republican party which had grown desperately tired of federal interference in Southern politics. Early in 1877 the troops were removed, and South Carolina, Florida, and Louisiana lapsed quietly into the control of the whites.

[1] About 750 Southerners remained unpardoned. Not until June, 1898, when North and South joined in the war against Spain, were the last of the disabilities removed.

The Postwar Settlement with Great Britain

The close of the Civil War left a legacy of angry feeling between the United States and Great Britain. The pro-Southern course of the latter caused the Northern people, however inconsistently, to view with approval an active Irish movement to throw off the British yoke. Late in 1865 the "Fenians," embracing many Irish-Americans, met in Philadelphia and organized the "Republic of Ireland." By popular appeals the leaders succeeded in raising large sums of money for the cause of Irish freedom, much of which was spent in riotous living. One faction of the Fenians resolved to bring the British government to terms through the seizure of Canada, and in 1866 and subsequent years, made repeated efforts to invade that country from American soil. The United States authorities took resolute and, for the most part, successful steps to suppress these lawless enterprises.

Sovereign of many subject peoples, Great Britain began to see the importance of insisting on high standards of neutral conduct on the part of foreign powers when her own paramount authority might at any moment be challenged by secession movements. In 1868, the American Minister at London, Reverdy Johnson, succeeded in negotiating what is known as the Johnson-Clarendon Convention. All existing claims were to be submitted to a joint commission, and when agreement was impossible in any instance, to an umpire to be chosen by lot. The Americans felt that the agreement failed to safeguard their interests adequately, and early in 1869 the Senate refused it by a vote of 44 to 1.

In this rejection Senator Sumner played a leading part. He contended that America was entitled to $15,000,000 for direct damages inflicted by the *Alabama* and other cruisers, and that, in addition, Great Britain owed the United States a bill of more than $2,000,000,000 for indirect damages on account of the decline of our merchant marine, the assistance given Confederate raiders in British colonial ports, and the effect of the premature recognition of Confederate belligerency in prolonging the conflict. To satisfy this debt, he desired Great Britain to cede us Canada.

Sumner's extravagant demands temporarily dampened British ardor for a settlement, but early in 1871 the two governments appointed a joint commission to arrange for an adjustment of all outstanding differences. The outcome was the comprehensive Treaty of Washington, signed on May 8. This effected a new twelve-year arrangement with regard to the fisheries, granted free navigation of the St. Lawrence and other waterways in which Canada and the United States had a mutual interest, and submitted controverted questions to special arbitration tribunals. A dispute over the international boundary along the channel separating Vancouver Island from the state of Washington was referred to the Emperor of Germany, who later gave judgment in favor of the United States. The claims of British subjects for damages suffered from military operations during the Civil War were submitted to a tribunal, which eventually made an award of nearly $2,000,000.

The most important settlement of all concerned the question of unneutral conduct by the British government during the war. The treaty contained a frank expression of British "regret" for what had happened, and laid down certain principles which were to guide the arbitrators and were to govern the observance of neutrality in the future. The court of arbitration consisted of one representative from each country and of three other members chosen respectively by Switzerland, Italy, and Brazil. Meeting at Geneva, the arbitrators excluded Sumner's indirect claims from consideration, and in September, 1872, awarded direct damages of $15,500,000 for the *Alabama* and other depredations. The outcome was a signal triumph for the cause of international peace and good will. Two great nations had found a better method than the sword for the settlement of their differences.

The Significance of the Civil War and Reconstruction

The epoch of the Civil War and Reconstruction left an indelible impress upon American history. The great constitutional issue upon which the war was avowedly fought was resolved, once for all, in favor of the supremacy of the Union. Although the decision was reached under purely American conditions, it coincided with a mighty movement for the consolidation of nationality in other parts of the world. By 1861 the unification of Italy under constitutional forms was attained. In 1867 the dual monarchy of Austria-Hungary was founded. Four years later the present French Republic was organized, and in the same year the establishment of the German Empire completed the unification of the German States. In Canada the provinces from Ontario east (Newfoundland excepted) were united in 1867 into the Dominion of Canada, with full powers of local self-government and provisions for enlargement of the Dominion when the western territories should be ready for admission.

It is impossible to believe that questions of nullification and secession will ever again seriously disturb the domestic politics of the United States, notwithstanding the fact that since the Civil War the national power has expanded beyond the dreams of a Marshall or a Webster. The problem of American nationality remains, but in a new, though perhaps not less portentous, form. In this more recent phase, it has to do with the preservation of national unity in the face of the clashing interests of economic classes and of unassimilated immigrant groups in our population.

The war also resulted in the destruction of slavery and of the power of the cotton capitalists — the real, though unconfessed, cause of the struggle. The United States was the last of the great western nations to do away with human bondage, Russia having preceded her in 1861. The undoing of the "Slave Power" meant the removal from national politics of an aggressive political force, whose place in the nation was presently to be taken by the rise of a new capitalist class, domiciled in the North and based on manufacturing and railway holdings.

The effects of emancipation upon race relations in the South demonstrated that the war, though striking the shackles from the slave, had left a problem in its wake almost as serious — the negro problem. In spite of the frantic efforts of Reconstruction statesmen, the difficult question of race adjustments had to be worked out, in the long run, by the peoples most directly concerned. As will presently be seen, the negroes never received from the Southern whites the full measure of rights accorded them by the Fourteenth and Fifteenth amendments.

Another outcome of the war was the creation of a political entity known as the "Solid South." As the states one after another shook off Carpetbag control, their prewar preference for the Democratic party was unutterably deepened by angry memories of their humiliation at the hands of the Republicans. The ex-Confederate states became a solidly Democratic section irrespective of the candidates running or the issues at stake.[1] Ordinarily the border slave states followed their lead.

But in matters nonpolitical, the two sections began to grow together again, particularly as the generation which had lived through the sectional conflict began to pass from the scene. Many influences worked to this end. A beginning was made by certain Carpetbag legislatures when they required the study of national history in the Southern schools for the first time.[2] In the economic rehabilitation of the South, Northerners took an active part, and many of them took up their abode there. Publicists like Henry W. Grady of Georgia and Henry Watterson of Kentucky directed the thoughts of their people toward the future, and energetically preached the gospel of a "New South."

Furthermore, thoughtful Southerners came to realize that, however galling the process of reconstruction had been, the Radicals had stopped short of the crowning blunders: they had confiscated practically no enemy land, and put no one to death for a political offense. Old passions and prejudices, nourished on out-worn issues, gradually lost their vitality in the face of new economic and political problems of equal concern to both sections. The outbreak of the Spanish-American War in 1898 sealed the reunion in spirit of the antagonists of 1861.

The Economic Reconstruction of the South

Another consequence of the Civil War was the industrial reorganization of the South. Although these changes were a phase of the great Economic Revolution that was affecting the entire country, they were the immediate results of the derangement of Southern economic life wrought by the war. As the scene of the conflict, the South had suffered losses that were well-nigh irreparable — bridges wrecked, towns destroyed, railroads torn up. Cotton culture had been neglected and the plantations had gone to wrack and ruin, so that land had depreciated to half its prewar

[1] The first break in the Solid South came in 1920 when Harding carried Tennessee.

[2] In addition, Arkansas in 1868 and Missouri in 1869 required all public school teachers to take oaths of loyalty.

value. In addition, the wealthy had been impoverished by the collapse of Confederate bonds and currency and the confiscation of slave property. Equally serious was the shortage of labor. The casualties of the war had fallen chiefly on the young white manhood of the South between the ages of eighteen and thirty-five. As for the negroes, they had suffered severely from privation and disease, and moreover, in their new freedom, were in a wrong frame of mind to seek ready employment with the former master class.

In the face of heavy odds the great planters sought to re-establish agriculture on its former large-scale basis. Their efforts were unavailing, for they had to operate on borrowed capital, and were hampered by the excessive taxation of the Carpetbag governments as well as by the irresponsible character of their negro labor. Salvation seemed possible only through a breaking-up of the great estates. Accordingly, the plan was generally adopted of leasing or selling tracts of from forty to eighty acres to negroes and "poor whites."

The result was a more careful utilization of the land through the rotation of crops and the use of fertilizers. Already by 1870 the average yield of cotton per acre was greater than in 1860, although it was not until 1876 that the total crop equaled that of 1860. The reconstruction of agriculture was a slow and difficult process, but patience and enterprise eventually rendered the South more productive under free labor than under slavery. Increased attention was also paid to other farm products, and in time, the total value of these minor crops came to exceed that of cotton.

Simultaneously with the breakdown of the plantation system occurred the first advances in manufacturing. Conditions were favorable for this development. Water power abounded, raw cotton lay at the door of the factories, and the "poor whites" with their women and children formed an abundant supply of cheap labor. Moreover, Northern capital was ready and eager to finance the new enterprises. By 1880 the Southern states manufactured nearly one fourth as much cotton as New England. The development of the iron industry came a little later.

Thus, in a short span of years, the South changed from a semi-feudal order of society and industry based upon slavery to a modern system of society and industry based upon wage labor. The social consequences were far reaching. The new order involved the emancipation of the "poor whites" in as real a sense as the Thirteenth Amendment had that of the negroes. To them had at last come the opportunities of free employment, education, and self-improvement, for which Helper had pleaded in the *Impending Crisis;* to their hands was to fall the political leadership of the South.

SELECT BIBLIOGRAPHY

The Postwar South. A detailed account of the reconstruction period may be found scattered through J. F. Rhodes, *History of the United States*, IV–VII (New York, 1899–1906). For an understanding of the Southern point of view, W. L. Fleming, *The Sequel of Appomattox* (in *The Chronicles of America*, XXXII, New Haven, 1919), and P. J. Hamilton, *The Reconstruction Period* (in G. C. Lee and F. N. Thorpe, eds., *The History of North America*, 20 v., Philadelphia, 1903–1907), XVI (1905), are especially valuable. The constitutional phases are penetratingly discussed in W. A. Dunning, *Essays on the Civil War and Reconstruction* (New York, 1904), and his *Reconstruction Political and Economic* (in *The American Nation*, XXII, New York, 1907). See also J. W. Burgess, *Reconstruction and the Constitution* (in *The American History Series*, New York, 1902), in this connection. The colored man's side of the story is recounted in G. W. Williams, *History of the Negro Race in America* (2 v., New York, 1883), II.

A number of single-volume histories begin with 1865, and afford useful surveys of events down to their dates of publication: C. A. Beard, *Contemporary American History* (New York, 1914); P. L. Haworth, *Reconstruction and Union* (in the *Home University Library*, New York, 1912); F. L. Paxson, *The New Nation* (in *The Riverside History of the United States*, IV, Boston, 1915); P. L. Haworth, *The United States in Our Own Times* (New York, 1920); C. R. Lingley, *Since the Civil War* (in Max Farrand, ed., *The United States*, III, New York, 1920); D. S. Muzzey, *From the Civil War* (in his *The United States of America*, II, Boston, 1924); and L. B. Shippee, *Recent American History* (New York, 1924). E. P. Oberholtzer, *A History of the United States since the Civil War* (New York, 1917–), is a new comprehensive history, of which two volumes have thus far appeared.

Wartime Efforts at Reconstruction. The most careful discussion of relief work among the negroes is P. S. Peirce, *The Freedmen's Bureau* (in *University of Iowa Studies*, III, no. 1, Iowa City, 1904). A different phase of wartime reconstruction is examined in C. H. McCarthy, *Lincoln's Plan of Reconstruction* (New York, 1901).

The Quarrel over a Southern Policy. This theme is developed with a wealth of incident and illustration in D. M. Dewitt, *The Impeachment and Trial of Andrew Johnson* (New York, 1903). A useful résumé is C. E.

Chadsey, *The Struggle between President Johnson and Congress over Reconstruction* (in *Columbia University Studies*, VIII, no. 1, New York, 1896). Of particular interest are B. B. Kendrick, *The Journal of the Joint Committee of Fifteen on Reconstruction* (in *Columbia University Studies*, LXII, New York, 1914), and H. E. Flack, *The Adoption of the Fourteenth Amendment* (Baltimore, 1908).

The Reign of the Radicals. The actual operation of reconstruction in the South is studied in a series of monographs: W. L. Fleming, *Civil War and Reconstruction in Alabama* (New York, 1905); J. W. Garner, *Reconstruction in Mississippi* (New York, 1901); C. W. Ramsdell, *Reconstruction in Texas* (in *Columbia University Studies*, XXXVI, no. 1, New York, 1910); W. W. Davis, *The Civil War and Reconstruction in Florida* (in *Columbia University Studies*, LIII, New York, 1913); J. G. de R. Hamilton, *Reconstruction in North Carolina* (in *Columbia University Studies*, LVIII, New York, 1914); C. Mildred Thompson, *Reconstruction in Georgia* (in *Columbia University Studies*, LXIV, no. 1, New York, 1915); T. S. Staples, *Reconstruction in Arkansas* (in *Columbia University Studies*, CIX, New York, 1923); H. J. Eckenrode, *The Political History of Virginia during the Reconstruction* (in *Johns Hopkins University Studies*, XXII, nos. 6–8, Baltimore, 1904); J. R. Ficklen, *History of Reconstruction in Louisiana (through 1868)* (in *Johns Hopkins University Studies*, XXVIII, no. 1, Baltimore, 1910); Ella Lonn, *Reconstruction in Louisiana after 1868* (New York, 1918); J. S. Reynolds, *Reconstruction in South Carolina* (Columbia, South Carolina, 1905); and J. W. Fertig, *The Secession and Reconstruction of Tennessee* (Chicago, 1898). See also E. W. Knight, *The Influence of Reconstruction on Education in the South* (in *Teachers College Contributions to Education*, no. 60, New York, 1913).

Grant and the Radicals. For the election of 1868, Edward Stanwood, *A History of the Presidency*, I (Boston, 1898), is of service. L. A. Coolidge, *Ulysses S. Grant* (Boston, 1917), is a good brief biography.

The Struggle for White Dominion in the South. Carpetbag and negro rule is dealt with in the various Southern states in the series of monographs previously cited. Good short sketches of the Ku Klux Klan may be found in W. G. Brown, *The Lower South in American History* (New York, 1902), and E. P. Oberholtzer, *A History of the United States*, II (New York, 1922). A more thorough treatment is J. C. Lester and D. L. Wilson, *Ku Klux Klan, Its Origin, Growth, and Disbandment* (W. L. Fleming, ed., New York, 1905). "The Federal Enforcement Acts" are analyzed by W. W. Davis in J. W. Garner, ed., *Studies in Southern History and Politics* (New York, 1914).

The Postwar Settlement with Great Britain. Good discussions of the Treaty of Washington may be found in C. F. Adams, *Lee at Appomattox* (Boston, 1903), E. P. Oberholtzer, *A History of The United States*, II (New York, 1922), and C. E. Hill, *Leading American Treaties* (New York, 1922). On the Geneva arbitration, T. W. Balch, *The Alabama Arbitration* (Philadelphia, 1900), is of particular value.

The Economic Reconstruction of the South. The best general accounts appear in Holland Thompson, *The New South* (in *The Chronicles of America*, XLII, New Haven, 1919), W. L. Fleming and others, *The South in the Building of the Nation*, VI (Richmond, 1909); and P. A. Bruce, *The Rise of the New South* (in *The History of North America*, XVII, Philadelphia, 1905). Of a more specialized character are Broadus Mitchell, *The Rise of Cotton Mills in the South* (in *Johns Hopkins University Studies*, XXXIX, no. 2, Baltimore, 1921), and R. P. Brooks, *The Agrarian Revolution in Georgia, 1865–1912* (in *University of Wisconsin Bulletin*, no. 639, Madison, 1914).

CHAPTER XV

THE VANISHING FRONTIER AND THE AGRICULTURAL REVOLUTION, 1860–1890

The Economic Revolution

While the smoke still lingered over the battlefields of the Civil War and the Carpetbaggers were in the heyday of their power, a throng of events, mute, irresistible, and all-comprehensive, was laying the foundations of a new nation — the America of today. In its lasting effects, the "Economic Revolution," as it has been called, was, in truth, more significant than the war itself. In the period from 1860 to 1890, it wrought changes in American life so sudden and profound that even today we have scarcely learned to adjust ourselves to them.

The roots of this great transformation reached back into the prewar period, when, as we have seen, steam and machinery first began to invade American industries. Scattered factory districts had sprung up along the northern Atlantic Seaboard and, to a certain extent, in the region north of the Ohio River. The total amount of capital invested in such establishments was, however, not large. The people continued to rely upon foreign countries for the bulk of their manufactured goods, or else made the articles with primitive tools in their own homes. Likewise, railway development had not passed beyond the period of its infancy.

A new era of growth opened with the Civil War. The demand for munitions, iron and steel manufactures, textiles and food supplies had the stimulating effect of a hothouse. Every nerve of industry in the North was quickened, and improved agricultural implements were called upon to supply the loss of man power on the farm. Moreover, the high war tariffs, by granting manufacturers a virtual monopoly of the American market, accelerated the expansion of the factory system. Hardly less important was the amassing of great fortunes out of government contracts, land grants, and financial speculation, for thereby a vast surplus of private capital, eager for investment, was created.

Another potent factor in the economic progress resulted from the absence of Southern members from Congress for nearly a decade after 1861. Unhampered by sectional jealousy, Congress was able to adopt many measures of vital economic import to the North. For example, as will presently appear, the policy of free homesteads for settlers was inaugurated, lavish subsidies were granted to railway enterprises, and the protective tariff system of war times was quietly converted into a permanent peace policy.

But the Civil-War phase was merely the prologue to the play. In the quarter of a century following Appomattox, the Economic Revolution reached its full momentum, being accelerated by abundant capital, brilliant industrial leadership, American inventive genius, vast unexploited natural resources, and cheap labor. Of great importance, also, was the heavy demand levied upon American manufactures and railways by the new and growing communities of the West, and by the necessities of the postwar South.

Between 1860 and 1890, the United States was transformed from a nation mainly employing primitive methods of agriculture and importing most of her manufactures from abroad, into an industrialized country with an export trade in farm and factory products that reached the outer fringes of the globe. Had a person who died previous to the Economic Revolution returned miraculously to life in 1890, the changed aspect of American life would have seemed no less amazing than that depicted by Edward Bellamy and H. G. Wells in their fanciful accounts of human society in the future. The economist, Edward Atkinson, wrote in 1888, "greater progress than ever before has been made during the present generation, dating from 1865 . . . in providing for the means of subsistence, shelter, and clothing, and in organizing the machinery for distributing the necessaries of life." Three years later he declared, "there has never been in the history of civilization a period, or a place, or a section of the earth in which science and invention have worked such progress or have created such opportunity for material welfare as in these United States in the period which has elapsed since the end of the civil war."

Such tremendous changes could not occur without altering the habits and hopes and needs of the people and creating new political, economic, and social problems. Never before had American society suffered from such a severe attack of "growing pains." It was in these years that machine-industry rose to its present dominant position in American civilization, and that most of the conveniences and inventions which have softened and embellished everyday life came into common use.

The social, political, and intellectual consequences of the Economic Revolution form the main themes of American history in the period since the Civil War. Such problems as industrial monopoly, the money question, immigration, labor discontent, political corruption, the tariff, agrarian unrest, and the unequal distribution of wealth, all have their roots in this new substratum of American life. To it, also, is attributable much of the ardent nationalism which today characterizes the American spirit. Even the rise of the United States as a world power, presently to be considered, can be rightly understood only in its relation to the Economic Revolution. In the long run, the new nation had to face the grave question whether political agencies and instrumentalities, devised in the eighteenth century by a people predominantly agricultural and possessing easy means of subsistence, could be adapted to the pressing needs of a vastly expanded population rapidly becoming urbanized and industrialized.

The revolutionary character of the upheaval will become clearer from a closer examination of the great fields of economic activity in which the main changes occurred, namely, agriculture, manufacturing, transportation, mining, and communication.

The Opening of the Great West

The expansion of agriculture was closely related to the swift spread of American civilization over the vast unoccupied spaces west of the Mississippi in the generation following 1865, for the transplantation of a white population into this region was a major factor in the agricultural revolution. This imperial domain, already providing space for ten states on its borders, was an ocean of grassy prairie which, starting at the Mississippi, rolled far westward until it reached a zone of arid plains, which in turn extended to the foothills of the Rocky Mountains. Then, for nearly a thousand miles from east to west, the Rockies and the Sierra Nevadas, embosoming lofty plateaus, heaved up their enormous bulk, concealing huge treasures of silver, gold, and the baser metals.

Thousands of miles of this region were inhabited only by warlike tribes of roving Indians and by herds of wild buffalo. It required twenty-five days for a passenger to make the overland journey from St. Joseph on the Missouri to the Pacific Coast by the stagecoach system, established in 1858, and more than ten days for the swift pony express, organized in 1860, to carry a letter to San Francisco. The frontier line of settlement on the east ran north through the central part of Texas and, in a general way, followed the western limits of the states bordering on the Mississippi River, including, however, the eastern sections of Kansas and Nebraska. On the Pacific Coast, well-settled districts adjoined San Francisco and San Diego and were to be found in the Columbia and Willamette valleys.

The Americans of 1865 looked upon the intervening region as a well-nigh inexhaustible land reserve which would afford ample room for expansion and provide farms and natural resources for the people for generations to come. Yet, a quarter of a century later, virtually all of the country was carved into states and territories, and the last of the arable lands had passed from the possession of the government into private hands!

Three influences hastened the white colonization of the Great West. One of these was the passage in May, 1862, of the Homestead Act, whose adoption had been prevented by the slavery interests before the war. By its terms any adult citizen could acquire a farm of 160 acres, without cost to himself excepting for a small fee, upon condition of occupancy and improvement for a five-year period. Under this law, nearly 56,000,000 acres were transferred to private owners by 1880.

The other two influences were the penetration of the country by the railways, and the subjugation of the aborigines. In regard to the former, it should be noted that the project of joining the Pacific Coast with the Mississippi Valley by rail was not a new one, for the idea had been urged in one form or another since the steam locomotive had demonstrated its practicability. But the outbreak of the Civil War emphasized the need of cementing political and commercial relations between the two sections, and the Southern Congressmen were no longer in a position to object, as formerly, to a central route for the railway.

On July 1, 1862, Congress voted a charter to the Union Pacific Railway, the first federal charter to be granted to a corporation since the United States Bank. By this Act the track was to be simultaneously constructed — westward from Omaha, Nebraska, and eastward from Sacramento, California. The eastern portion was to be built by the Union Pacific Railroad Company, and the western division by the Central Pacific Railroad Company, a California corporation. Each division was granted a right of way, two hundred feet wide, from the federal public domain, with the privilege of securing construction materials from adjacent public lands. In order to make the enterprise more attractive to investors, the government agreed to aid the Company with land grants and outright loans. The law, as revised in 1864, provided for a gift of ten alternate sections on each side of the track, and for a loan of six-per-cent United States bonds at the rate of $16,000, $32,000, or $48,000 per mile according as the roadbed was laid in the plains, the plateau country, or the mountains. In addition, the Company was authorized to borrow money on its own bonds, which were to be secured by a first mortgage on the railroad property.

Owing to various delays, the work of construction was not begun in earnest until 1866. Building operations in the eastern division were in charge of the Credit Mobilier, a construction company organized by leading stockholders of the Union Pacific under the leadership of Oakes Ames of Massachusetts. At the western end, the work was energetically prosecuted by another construction company under the direction of ex-Governor Leland Stanford, President of the Central Pacific. The labor demand was met on the Coast by Chinese coolies, who, in their basket-hats, queues, blue blouses, and flapping pantaloons, performed the same grinding toil that was being performed in Nebraska and Wyoming by Irish "Paddies" and ex-soldiers.

Because of the hostility of the Indians the building operations assumed a semimilitary aspect. The construction trains were equipped to resist attack, and the laborers had to be equally adept with picks and shovels, and rifles and pistols. Every mile of grading was done under the protection of scouts. As they advanced toward each other, the two Companies erected stations and water-tanks, established supply depots, and virtually built towns. The engineering difficulties were often appalling. In traversing the Sierra Nevadas, frequent tunnels and deep rock-cuttings were necessary, while long, high trestles spanned the numerous ravines and gorges. The railway workers had no assistance from steam shovels, steam derricks, and other modern appliances for railroad building; it was virtually a "hand-made" road.

The imagination of the whole country was captured and held by the steady progress of the iron highway, and the managers exerted continued pressure for speed. Their motives were not wholly disinterested, for the company which laid the higher mileage of track would receive the greater share of the government's largess. One result was a tendency toward waste, slovenly construction, and dishonest practices, sufficiently scandalous to provoke a subsequent Congressional investigation. Circuitous lines were substituted in some places for straight lines, either to avoid obstructions or in order to increase the length of track. Often little time was spent in ballasting ties, in masonry work, or in making certain that the rail joints rested on the ties.

On May 10, 1869, the two tracks came together at Promontory Point, northwest of Ogden, Utah, and the "wedding of the rails" was celebrated with an impressive ceremony. Telegraph connections were made in such a way that the blows of the silver sledge, which drove gold spikes into the connecting rails, were recorded in the principal telegraph stations throughout the country. The great adventure was at an end. Of the completed road, the Union Pacific had built 1,086 miles, and the Central Pacific 689. The two oceans, separated hitherto by a month of travel, were now but seven or eight days apart.

The zeal for rail communication with the west coast did not spend itself with the Union Pacific. Before that line was completed, Congress had granted charters to the Northern Pacific (1864), for linking Lake Superior with Puget Sound; the Southern Pacific (1866), originally called the "Atlantic and Pacific" and extending eventually from New Orleans to San Francisco; and the Atchison, Topeka and Santa Fe (1866), which when completed started west from Kansas, crossed the desert regions south of the Rockies, and ended in San Francisco. All these roads were aided by land grants even more munificent than those given the Union Pacific, but no direct financial aid was extended by the government. By 1884, four great lines joined the central valley of the continent with the Pacific Seaboard, and a fifth one paralleled them beyond the Canadian border.

The continental railways were vitally interested in the settlement of the territory they traversed, for settlers meant increased traffic and, moreover, a rise in the value of the railroad lands. They therefore encouraged immigration and settlement; and their literature, scattered throughout the East and in Europe, helped to attract people to the new regions.

The Pacification of the Indians

With the completion of the Pacific railways the chief bar to the rapid and unobstructed occupation of the Great West was the presence of wild Indians. There were perhaps 300,000 savages west of the Mississippi in 1860. Besides the semicivilized tribes moved by the Jackson administration to Indian Territory in the Valley of the Arkansas, the main groups were the Sioux of the Mississippi, located in Minnesota; the Plains Sioux, in the Dakotas north of the Platte; the Cheyenne and Arapaho, in the region to the south of the Valley of the Yellowstone and North Platte; and the Apache, Comanche, and Kiowa, in the Southwest. These tribes held their lands under treaty guarantees of the United States government; and in return for annual gifts of food, munitions, and clothing, they bound themselves to maintain peace, keep within their preserves, and allow migration along their trails.

Before 1861 the trans-Mississippi Indians were generally on friendly terms with the United States, but thereafter for twenty-five years, almost incessant conflict disturbed the relations of the two races, with the periods of greatest intensity falling within the years 1862–1867 and 1875–1886. It was the most extensive Indian warfare in which the United States ever engaged. The hostilities really consisted of a multitude of petty wars, for, though the outbreaks were due to certain widespread causes, the savages did not, as in earlier times, seek to repel their foe through general tribal federations. More than one hundred pages were required to print a list of engagements of the troops with the Indians between 1868 and 1882 alone. Between 1865 and 1880, the cost of the border warfare to the United States government amounted to $22,000,000.

The mainspring of trouble was the increasing pressure of white population, and the resulting friction between two types of civilization, one progressive and predatory, and the other backward and unenterprising. Similar difficulties had been solved in the past by removing the offending tribes to some remote part of the country, off the beaten tracks. But now the two races stood face to face on the last frontier. The land-hungry whites viewed the redskin as an obstacle to social progress. Whenever it was to their interest to do so, they seized Indian country, thereby violating solemn treaty stipulations between the savages and the government. In the end, the federal authorities invariably acquiesced in the outrages, and, by new agreements, removed the bands to less desirable tracts.

Indeed, the "Great White Father" at Washington, perplexed by divergent counsels, knew not which way to turn. On the one hand, the army officers on the plains insisted on a policy of stern repression or even extermination. It was General "Phil" Sheridan who coined the saying, "There are no good Indians but dead Indians," a sentiment heartily echoed by other frontier fighters. But the officials of the Department of the Interior, who had peacetime charge of the Indians, were inclined to regard the tribesmen as sinned against rather than sinning — the victims of ruthless aggression. In this humanitarian position they had wide support among the cultivated classes of the East, whose agitation was to lead eventually to the adoption of a more enlightened policy.

Unfortunately, the idealistic professions of the Department of the Interior were not always apparent in practice. The agents employed to execute its policy were apt to be political appointees, and ill-fitted for their task. The result was unscrupulous and dishonest dealings with both the savages and the Department.

Another source of irritation rose from the practice of white traders in charging the natives exorbitantly for goods. Their traffic in liquor often resulted in fatal drunken brawls.

In the desire to be just to the Indian, it is not necessary to idealize him. He was at best an uncomfortable neighbor, patterning his ideals of conduct on barbarous models, and often lazy, licentious, and meddlesome. As Colonel Richard Dodge declared, in the savage mind men attained renown "just in proportion to their ferocity, to the scalps they have taken, or the thefts they have committed." Nevertheless, President Hayes may be believed when he asserted in a message to Congress in 1877 that the Indians "have been driven from place to place. . . . In many instances, when they had settled upon land assigned to them by compact and begun to support themselves by their own labor, they were rudely jostled off and thrust into the wilderness again. Many, if not most, of our Indian wars have had their origin in broken promises and acts of injustice on our part."

The first series of wars began in 1862 while the Civil War was in progress.[1] The chief area of conflict was Minnesota, where the Sioux, under the leadership of Little Crow, broke from the reservation and went on the warpath, leaving behind them burning dwellings, devastated fields, and slaughtered men, women, and children. In September, 1862, General H. H. Sibley broke the back of the revolt at Wood Lake. Congress confiscated the entire reservation in 1863, and removed the tribe to less desirable quarters near Fort Thompson on the Missouri.

A war with the Cheyenne in Colorado followed shortly thereafter in 1864, provoked by the increasing encroachments of miners on Indian country. Portions of the Arapaho, Apache, Comanche, and Kiowa tribes were involved in varying degrees, and in characteristic fashion, war parties harried the frontier, burning, scalping, and killing. The worst massacre, however, was not perpetrated by the savage enemy but by United States troops. Under command of Colonel J. M. Chivington, they surrounded an unsuspecting Cheyenne village on Sand Creek in Colorado on November 28, 1864, and killed and mutilated the men, women, and children. Peace was restored in October, 1865,

[1] It has been said that Confederate emissaries incited the Indians to hostilities, but historical students have been unable to authenticate this charge.

but in 1868 the Cheyenne were again on the warpath under their famous chief, Black Kettle. General G. A. Custer, his antagonist, adopted Chivington's policy of fighting the Indians with their own weapons, and, under cover of night, his troops captured Black Kettle's camp with heavy slaughter. The chieftain was killed, and the blow proved decisive in crippling the power of these tribes.

Meantime, in 1866, the Plains Sioux under Red Cloud began war upon the United States troops because of the effort of the latter to open up and fortify an emigrant road through their choicest hunting-grounds — from Fort Laramie along the Powder River to the mines of Montana and Idaho. The Indians claimed that a treaty of 1865 granting this right of way had been made by persons without authority to bind them. Aided by the Cheyenne, they offered a fierce resistance which continued until the government abandoned the forts early in 1868.

By the summer of 1867 the United States troops were generally getting the upper hand. Consequently, in July, 1867, Congress empowered a commission of three generals and four civilians to study conditions in the West and work out some means for promoting Indian welfare without impeding the advance of white civilization. When the commission ceased its labors fifteen months later, it had cleared away all legal obstacles to the building of the Pacific railways through Indian country, had persuaded most of the Apache, Comanche, and Kiowa bands to locate in Indian Territory, and had induced other tribes to lessen their reservations or accept new ones in remote districts. President Grant, coming into office at this time, was a warm advocate of the policy of peace on the plains, and in April, 1869, Congress created a Board of Indian Commissioners to supervise all government expenditures for the Indians. Although inefficiency and corruption were not eliminated, distinct improvement appeared in the management of the reservation tribes under the new plan.

Notwithstanding these well-meant efforts, events were preparing for a new eruption of hostilities. The opening up of the Great West by the railroads, with the consequent stimulus to white settlement, involved for the redskin not merely the loss of much of his choicest land but also the destruction of his chief

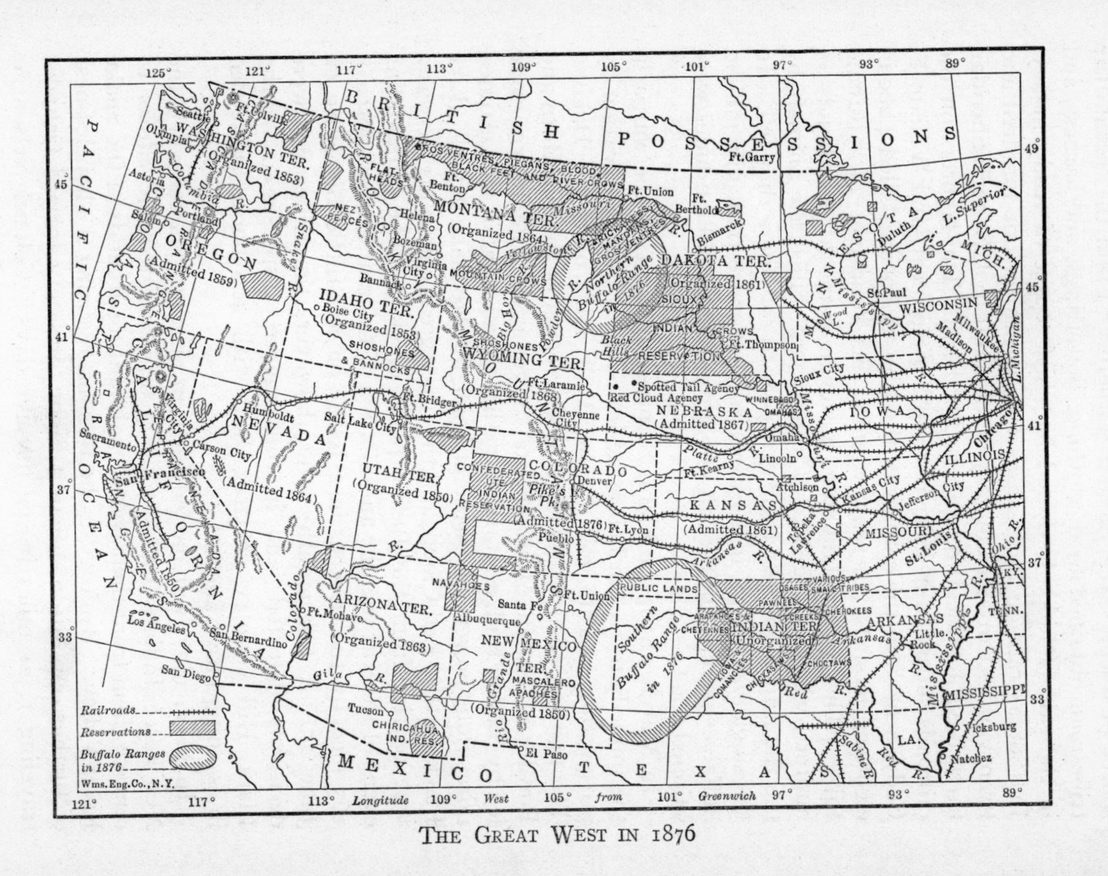

THE GREAT WEST IN 1876

source of livelihood — the buffalo herds. From the buffalo the tribesman obtained food, clothing, bowstrings, and harness, and in the sale of hides he found his chief source of ready money. In 1868 a train on the Kansas Pacific ran for one hundred and twenty miles through a mighty herd, and it took General Sheridan three days to ride through another herd. The laborers on the railroads subsisted in large part on buffalo meat, and William F. Cody, a scout in the employ of the Kansas Pacific, killed 4,280 in eighteen months, thereby winning his sobriquet of "Buffalo Bill." The worst slaughter, however, came at the hands of hunters, who, for the sake of amusement, killed the animals by the thousands and left their carcasses to rot where they fell. In the single year 1873, it is estimated that more than five million buffaloes were slain, though not three-quarter million hides were shipped East.

In March, 1876, the Plains Sioux again went on the warpath, the immediate reason being the invasion of their reservation by prospectors seeking gold in the Black Hills of South Dakota. The fighting occurred mainly in the region of the Big Horn and Powder Rivers in Montana and Wyoming. The braves were led by Sitting Bull, a strategist rather than a fighter, who claimed miraculous powers by virtue of being a "Medicine Man." Like Black Kettle, Red Cloud, and the other great chieftains, he was a true patriot from the Indian point of view. The outstanding event of the war was the annihilation of General Custer's force of 265 men by the savages in a battle on the Little Big Horn on June 25. A few months later, however, the tribesmen were decisively defeated, and in consequence, dispossessed of the Black Hill country. Sitting Bull with 400 bucks succeeded in escaping into Canada.[1]

In May, 1877, war flamed forth in another quarter when the Nez Percé Indians under Chief Joseph resisted the efforts to remove them from their traditional hunting grounds in the Snake River Valley. By August, the Indians, realizing the hopelessness of further opposition, began a flight for safety toward Canada, traveling 1,321 miles in seventy-five days. Colonel Nelson A.

[1] In 1881 he returned to the United States upon General N. A. Miles's promise of amnesty. In December, 1890, he was arrested as chief instigator of the Messiah craze among the Indians, and in the subsequent fighting, was killed.

Miles inflicted a crushing defeat on the band in October, 1877, and the savages were removed to unhealthy lands in Indian Territory where they dwindled in numbers.

The last notable uprising occurred in Arizona and New Mexico among the warlike Apache. Fighting under the leadership at first of Victorio and then of Geronimo, they succeeded from 1882 to 1886 in defying the efforts of the United States to concentrate the scattered bands on reservations.

Throughout the long period of border warfare, the United States troops performed valiant service under difficult conditions. Fighting operations required eternal watchfulness, instant preparedness, and dauntless personal daring. No one knew when, out of the vast expanse of treeless plain, small bands in war-paint would strike the border settlements, killing the men and carrying off the women and children. In the annals of plains fighting perhaps no names stand higher than those of General Sheridan, General W. T. Sherman, and General Miles.

Every mile of Western railway increased the military effectiveness of the United States in the later years. By the middle of the eighties, the Indian question was no longer troublesome as a problem of military police, but little or no progress had been made in solving the question in its broader aspects, that is, as a process of assimilating the tribesmen to modern American life. Nevertheless, a quarter-century of frontier fighting had made the Great West safe for white civilization, and placed the best lands at the disposal of the more advanced race.

Westward Migration and the Agricultural Revolution

With the exception of the large Mormon settlement in Utah, dating from 1848, the first notable influx of settlers into the Great West resulted from the discovery of mineral wealth — gold, silver, copper, and lead. In 1859 a fabulously rich vein of silver, known as the "Comstock Lode," was discovered in the present Nevada, precipitating a rush of fortune-hunters from all over the country. About this time, some prospectors struck gold in Colorado, and a headlong stampede began for "Pike's Peak or Bust." Valuable mineral deposits were also found in Montana, Idaho, Wyoming, and Arizona in the following years.

"Boom towns" sprang up throughout these regions, whose denizens led a turbulent and precarious existence. An inhabitant wrote in after years of Virginia City, Nevada: "This human hive, numbering at least ten thousand people, was the product of ninety days. Into it were crowded all the elements of a rough and active civilization. . . . Gold was abundant, and every possible device was employed by the gamblers, the traders, the vile men and women that had come in with the miners into the locality, to obtain it. Nearly every third cabin was a saloon. . . . Many of these places were filled with gambling tables and gamblers. . . . Hurdy-gurdy dance-houses were numerous. . . . Not a day or night passed which did not yield its full fruition of vice, quarrels, wounds, or murders."

These lawless conditions were, of course, only a passing phase, difficult to control because of the remoteness of the camps from the seats of law and authority. In many cases, the solider elements of the community took the law into their own hands, formed bands of "Vigilantes," and overthrew the reign of the "bad man" and the desperado.

Following close on the heels of the prospectors and miners came the cattlemen. Stock-raising had long been an important industry in Texas; and in 1866 it was discovered, largely by accident, that Texas longhorn cattle could be driven north across the unfenced public domain, feeding as they went, and arrive at the railway shipping points in Kansas larger and fatter than when they started. Soon the "Long Drive" became a regular event, and for hundreds of miles the trails were dotted with herds of from one to ten thousand cattle moving ceaselessly northward. Meantime, the cattle industry expanded rapidly in the trans-Missouri region, due to the demand of the railway laborers and mining camps for fresh beef and to the improved marketing facilities afforded by the completion of the railroads. Immense ranches appeared overnight, as it were, in Colorado, Wyoming, Kansas, Nebraska, Dakota, and elsewhere, and Western cities became important centers for the slaughter and dressing of cattle.

Ranch life introduced a stirring and colorful mode of existence, with the picturesque cowboy as its central figure. "Of all the babes of that primeval mother, the West," wrote the late Emerson Hough, "the cowboy was perhaps her dearest because he was her last." The immense profits of the "cattle kings" were made possible by the benevolent neglect of the government. After branding their cows, they permitted the animals to roam at will over the public domain, and then, at the spring or summer "round-up," the cowboys sought them out and brought them together for the drive to market. Cattle, costing only a few dollars, raised in vast numbers, fed on free pasturage, and requiring but few men to attend them, could be sold in several years for four or five times the original investment.

Peace did not always dwell on the ranges. The ranchmen often waged small civil wars with each other over cattle stealing, the changing of brands, and other such matters. Sometimes, to vary the routine, they made common cause against the sheep-herders, who soon appeared to appropriate their share of the free lands and free grass.

By the mid-eighties the halcyon days of the cattlemen were over. Not far behind the rancher creaked the prairie schooner of the farmer, bringing his womenfolk and children, his draft horses, cows, and pigs. Backed by the provisions of the Homestead Act, he staked off his claim, inclosed it with a barbed-wire fence, and with the aid of the government, ousted the ranchman from the lands of which the latter held illegal possession. Artificial barriers began to render difficult the "Long Drive," and destroyed the unity of the free grazing lands of the West. The romantic "cow country" gave way to settled communities and prosaic fields of wheat, corn, and oats. In order to survive at all, the cattle industry had thereafter to adapt itself to fenced, or fairly defined, pastures and herding, and to operation on a relatively small scale.

In the hands of the pioneer farmers agriculture advanced at an unparalleled pace. To them and their brethren on the older frontier was due the tremendous agricultural development which constituted one phase of the Economic Revolution. The farms of the nation were increased in a single decade, 1870–1880, by an area equal to that of the British Isles and Sweden combined, and between 1880 and the close of the century, a domain was added equal in extent to the British Isles, Sweden, Norway, Denmark, Holland, Belgium, and Switzerland.

In Minnesota and Dakota, wheat-growing was the main re-

A STATISTICAL VIEW OF CERTAIN ASPECTS OF THE ECONOMIC REVOLUTION

	1860	1880	1890
Population and Wealth			
No. of people	31,443,321	50,155,783	62,622,250
Population per sq. mile	10.4	16.6	20.7
% of population in towns of 8000 or over	16.1	22.6	29.2
National wealth	$16,159,616,000	$43,642,000,000	$65,037,091,000
Wealth per capita	$513.9	$850.2	$1,038.6
Agriculture			
No. of farms	2,044,077	4,008,907	4,564,641
Improved farm land in acres	163,110,720	284,771,042	357,616,755
Value of all farm property	$7,980,493,063	$12,180,501,538	$16,082,267,689
Value of farm implements	$246,118,141	$406,520,055	$494,247,467
Value of farm products	?	$2,212,540,927	$2,460,107,454
Wool production in pounds	60,264,913	232,500,000	276,000,000
Wheat production in bushels	173,104,924	498,549,868	399,262,000
Corn production in bushels	838,792,740	1,717,434,543	1,489,970,000
Cotton production in bales	4,861,292	5,761,252	7,311,322
Cane sugar production in tons	119,040	92,802	136,503
Manufacturing			
No. of mfg. plants	140,433	253,852	355,415
Value of domestic manufactures	$1,885,861,676	$5,369,579,191	$9,372,437,283
Capital invested in manufactures	$1,009,855,715	$2,790,272,606	$6,525,156,486
No. of wage-earners	1,311,246	2,732,595	4,251,613
Importation of foreign mfres.	$261,264,310	$423,699,010	$230,685,581
Exportation of Am. manufactures	$48,453,008	$121,818,298	$178,982,042
No. of patents issued in year named	4,778	13,947	26,292
Transportation			
Vessels built for foreign trade (tons)	2,546,237	1,352,810	946,695
Vessels built for domestic purposes (tons)	2,807,631	2,715,224	3,477,802
Railway mileage in operation	30,626	93,267	163,597
No. of passengers carried	?	?	520,439,082
Tons of freight carried 1 mile	?	?	79,192,985,125
Mining			
Production of gold	$46,000,000	$36,000,000	$32,845,000
Silver production (commercial value)	$156,800	$34,717,000	$57,242,100
Tons of coal mined	13,044,680	63,822,830	140,866,931
Gallons of petroleum mined	21,000,000	1,104,017,166	1,924,552,224
Production of pig iron (tons)	821,223	3,835,191	9,202,703
Production of steel (tons)	—	1,247,335	4,277,071
Production of tinplate (lbs.)	—	—	2,236,743
Production of copper (tons)	7,200	27,000	115,966
Communication			
No. of postoffices	28,498	42,989	62,401
Mileage of post routes	227,908	343,888	427,990
Postal receipts	$8,518,067	$33,315,479	$60,882,098
No. of telegrams sent	?	29,215,509	63,258,762
Banks and Savings			
No. of national banks	—	2,045	3,214
National bank capital	—	$454,606,073	$607,428,365
Deposits in national banks	—	$833,701,034	$1,521,745,665
No. of savings banks	278	629	921
Deposits in savings banks	$149,277,504	$819,106,973	$1,524,844,506
No. of depositors in savings banks	693,870	2,335,582	4,258,893

liance of the farmer. South of the wheat belt, corn predominated in Kansas, Nebraska, and Iowa, and went to market either as grain or in the converted form of hogs. The production of corn and wheat doubled between 1860 and 1880, and doubled again in the next twenty-year period. Cultivated lands completely surrounded the old Indian Territory. Many of the farmers were immigrants from Germany and the Scandinavian countries, who settled in the new lands in colonies. By 1880 the United States had become the greatest wheat-exporting nation in the world.

Much of this progress resulted from an increased use of improved farm implements. With every farmer a landowner, machinery was necessary to make up for the scarcity of wage labor in the planting, cultivation, and harvesting of crops. The decade 1870–1880 saw the most rapid introduction of agricultural implements. Improvements had continued to be made upon the early reaper until it became the "complete harvester." Of the new inventions, the grain binder (1875) played a particularly important part in the expansion of the wheat-growing area, because hitherto a limit had been imposed upon production by the difficulty of caring for the grain after it was grown. In the next decade, the corn-harvester, corn-husker, and fodder-shredder came into use. Increased attention began also to be paid to preserving the soil's fertility through the use of fertilizers and the variation of crops, though, as yet, the Western farmer was less concerned with such matters than his brother in the East or the South.

The various influences that had quickened the westward flow of population after the early sixties led to the organization of the frontier country into self-governing communities. Between 1861 and 1868, territorial governments were erected in Nevada, Colorado, Dakota, Arizona, Idaho, Montana, and Wyoming, leaving only Indian Territory without the usual provision. Nevada was admitted prematurely as a state in 1864 because of Lincoln's need of votes to support his policies in Congress; the state of Nebraska was carved out of the older frontier in 1867; and Colorado followed in 1876. In 1889–1890, six more states were created: North and South Dakota, Montana, Washington, Idaho, and Wyoming.

Utah was denied statehood until 1896 when the Mormon Church satisfied the government at Washington that the national laws against polygamy were being enforced. In 1890 the territory of Oklahoma was formed largely out of lands which the government had purchased from the tribes in Indian Territory, and opened to white settlement (see pages 477–478). New Mexico and Arizona, with populations relatively stationary and with a preponderant Mexican element in their citizenry, continued in their territorial status.

By 1890 the last of the fertile public domain had passed into private hands, and the last Western frontier was at an end. Never before in recorded history had so great a wilderness been peopled in so short a time. The disappearance of the free lands was not due entirely to rapid settlement. The princely grants to railway enterprises had absorbed about 214,000,000 acres, an area about six times the size of Illinois. Some of this land, however, about 51,000,000 acres, was recovered by the government under President Cleveland, because certain railways had not been completed on contract time. Much land had also slipped through the government's fingers as a result of the careless administration of the Homestead Act. Thousands of homesteads were granted to persons who did not intend to occupy the land themselves, but were acting as agents for land engrossers. Though the Cleveland administration likewise labored to correct such abuses, the chief damage was already done.

The steady dwindling of the open frontier from the Civil War to about 1890 meant the disappearance of a social force that had been potent in American history since earliest times. The poor man of pluck and ambition, as well as the social misfit, had always been able to escape oppressive conditions in the older parts of the country by going west and making a "new start." In this way the frontier had served succeeding generations as a source of economic rejuvenation and a cradle of robust Americanism. Furthermore, by draining off the restless and dissatisfied spirits from the congested Eastern centers into a land of abundant opportunity, it had acted as a safety-valve of social discontent.

With the vanishing of the frontier, the people, for the first time, faced the necessity of working out their economic and social destiny where they dwelt, without recourse to the largess of the government. Accordingly, life became a severer struggle for existence, a condition tending to create social unrest and to intensify class feeling. Thus, toward the close of the century, social conditions in America began to resemble those in the Old World.

SELECT BIBLIOGRAPHY

The Economic Revolution. Suggestive discussions of the significance of the Economic Revolution in American history may be found in J. C. Malin,

The United States, 1865–1917: An Interpretation (in *University of Kansas Humanistic Studies*, III, no. 2, Lawrence, 1924); C. E. Merriam, *American Political Ideas, 1865–1917* (New York, 1920), chapter i; and A. M. Schlesinger, *New Viewpoints in American History* (New York, 1922), chapter xi. Students should also be familiar with F. J. Turner's brilliant essay, "Social Forces in American History," in his *The Frontier in American History* (New York, 1920). The Socialist point of view is set forth, with partisan warmth, in A. M. Simons, *Social Forces in American History* (New York, 1911); Austin Lewis, *The Rise of the American Proletarian* (Chicago, 1907); and James Oneal, *The Workers in American History* (New York, 1921). For the facts of the Economic Revolution, see later bibliographical notes of this and the next chapter.

The Opening of the Great West. For the adoption of the Homestead Act, G. M. Stephenson, *The Political History of the Public Lands from 1840 to 1862* (Boston, 1917), and J. T. Du Bois and G. S. Mathews, *Galusha A. Grow, the Father of the Homestead Law* (Boston, 1917), are valuable. The best general presentation of this and related topics is F. L. Paxson, *History of the American Frontier, 1763–1893* (Boston, 1924).

Special works on the transcontinental railways are L. H. Haney, *A Congressional History of Railways in the United States, 1850–1887* (2 v., *University of Wisconsin Economics and Political Science Series*, III, no. 2, VI, no. 1, Madison, 1908–1910); E. V. Smalley, *History of the Northern Pacific Railroad* (New York, 1883); J. P. Davis, *The Union Pacific Railway* (Chicago, 1894); and E. L. Sabin, *Building the Pacific Railway* (Philadelphia, 1919). J. G. Pyle, *The Life of James J. Hill* (Garden City, New York, 1917), is also of importance.

The Pacification of the Indians. The best connected narrative of the border warfare is in F. L. Paxson, *The Last American Frontier* (New York, 1910). For shorter accounts, Emerson Hough, *The Passing of the Frontier* (in *The Chronicles of America*, XXVI, New Haven, 1918), and P. L. Haworth, *The United States in Our Own Times* (New York, 1920), are good.

Westward Migration and the Agricultural Revolution. The white penetration of the Great West is treated in J. B. McMaster, *A History of the People of the United States*, VIII (New York, 1913); E. P. Oberholtzer, *A History of the United States* (2 v., New York, 1917–1922); and the works of Hough and Paxson, previously cited. Salient features of Western life are dealt with, in a popular style, in C. H. Shinn, *The Story of the Mine* (New York, 1896), and Emerson Hough, *The Story of the Cowboy* (New York, 1897), volumes in Ripley Hitchcock, ed., *The Story of the West Series*. The most authentic portrait of the cowboy is given in P. A. Rollins, *The Cowboy* (New York, 1922).

L. B. Schmidt, "Some Significant Aspects of the Agrarian Revolution in the United States" (in the *Iowa Journal of History and Politics*, XVIII [1920], 371–395), is a special study of that subject. Of value in this connection, also, are E. L. Bogart, *An Economic History of the United States* (New York, 1922), and H. W. Quaintance, *The Influence of Farm Machinery on Production and Labor* (Madison, 1904).

CHAPTER XVI

INDUSTRIAL FOUNDATIONS OF THE NEW NATION, 1860–1890

The Revolution in Manufacturing, Transportation, Mining, and Communication

The revolution in agriculture was paralleled by equally profound changes in the domains of manufacturing, transportation, mining, and communication. According to the *Report* of the United States Industrial Commission in 1902, the progress in manufacturing since the Civil War constituted "probably the most rapid change in the methods of industry observable at any time in history." The essence of the revolution in factory production was the substitution of machines for men in the processes of industry. By the use of improved mechanical appliances, more efficient methods were possible, human labor became vastly more productive, and a great cheapening resulted in the cost of manufacturing. At the same time, the efficiency of the machines was multiplied by the widespread use of steam as motive power.

While in some branches of industry American inventors simply improved upon processes borrowed from abroad, most of the inventions were original and new. The records of the Patent Office throw some light on the matter. In the entire period before 1860, something less than 36,000 patents had been granted for all purposes; in the remaining years of the century, the number reached the astonishing total of 640,000.

Statistics showing the expansion of manufacturing are not very instructive, for the figures are so large as to beggar the imagination. Yet it may be worth noting that the output of American factories, valued at $1,885,861,676 in 1860, more than doubled by 1870, trebled by 1880, and quintupled by 1890. The share of labor-saving machinery in this progress appears in the fact that, though the number of factory-hands only trebled from 1860 to 1890, the output increased fivefold. The rate of growth in particular industries was even more astounding. Between 1860 and 1880, cotton manufactures doubled in value, woolen manufactures trebled, and the value of silk textiles increased sevenfold. In the same period, the production of pig iron increased almost five times, and that of steel one hundred and fifty-five times. The phenomenal expansion of the steel industry was caused by the rapid substitution of steel for iron in the manufacture of locomotives, rails, and factory machinery; and the growth was made possible by the opening up of abundant and cheap deposits of iron and coal, and by more scientific methods of converting iron ore into steel.[1]

The chief manufacturing development occurred in eastern Pennsylvania, southern New York, New Jersey, and southern New England, which now became thoroughly industrialized sections. But with the growth of large cities in the old Northwest, factories spread in increasing numbers to that region. Pittsburgh, lying in an area rich in coal, petroleum, and natural gas, and situated on the Ohio River at the forks of the Allegheny and Monongahela, became the principal center of iron and steel manufacturing. It was in these years, too, that cotton mills, iron foundries, and steel plants, stimulated by Northern capital, began their invasion of the South.

As a consequence of this rapid and diversified industrial development, the United States soon outdistanced all her competitors in the volume and value of her manufactures. From fourth place in 1860 she attained first rank in 1894. In the latter year she produced more manufactures than the British Isles and Germany combined.

The revolution in transportation facilities was equally remarkable. To be sure, we lost our important position as carriers of the commerce of the world. The hazards connected with the Civil War enabled the British to take over much of the trade hitherto transported in American vessels, and after the war, American capitalists preferred the certainty of large profits from invest-

[1] Among these processes may be noted the substitution of coke for anthracite coal, and the introduction of the Bessemer process (named after Henry Bessemer, an Englishman) in 1864, and of the Siemens-Martin process in 1868. By the former system a blast of cold air is forced through the molten iron, thereby eliminating the carbon impurities. The latter method is superior in the case of less pure ore, and became most extensively used after 1900.

ments in factories and railways to the doubtful enterprise of rebuilding the merchant marine.

On the other hand, railway construction progressed at an amazing rate. In 1860 there were 30,000 miles of railway in the United States; this number almost doubled by 1870, and more than trebled by 1880. Between the last date and 1890 the mileage nearly doubled again, increasing from 93,267 to 163,597. It reached a total of 193,346 miles by the close of the century, equivalent to an eight-track railway encircling the globe, and exceeding considerably the combined mileage of all the countries of Europe. Not only had the great continental lines been built to the Pacific Coast, but railways had multiplied in the older parts of the North, and pushed southward to assist the industrial development of that section.

The expansion of mileage was attended by important improvements in service. The use of steel rails in place of iron rails began in the late sixties, thereby insuring greater safety and heavier carrying capacity. Pullman "palace cars," described by one enthusiastic traveler as "gorgeous traveling hotels," were introduced by their ingenious inventor in 1864. In 1872 George Westinghouse took out his first patent on the automatic air-brake, and about the same time automatic car coupling began to be used.

Another improvement in service resulted from the linking of independent short lines into "through lines." Before 1870 a traveler from the Atlantic Coast to the Mississippi might be required to make no less than half a dozen bodily transfers from one railroad to another; a road a few hundred miles in length was regarded as the maximum for efficient operation. Thereafter small companies tended to merge into larger units, so that continuous journeys soon became possible between all important points.

Similar dynamic forces were at work in the mining world. Before the close of the Civil War, the enormous mineral resources of the United States were, with the exception of gold in California, either unknown or else only imperfectly utilized. The industrial transformation of the country was both responsible for, and facilitated by, the first energetic exploitation of this mineral wealth. For example, coal had earlier been used in manu-

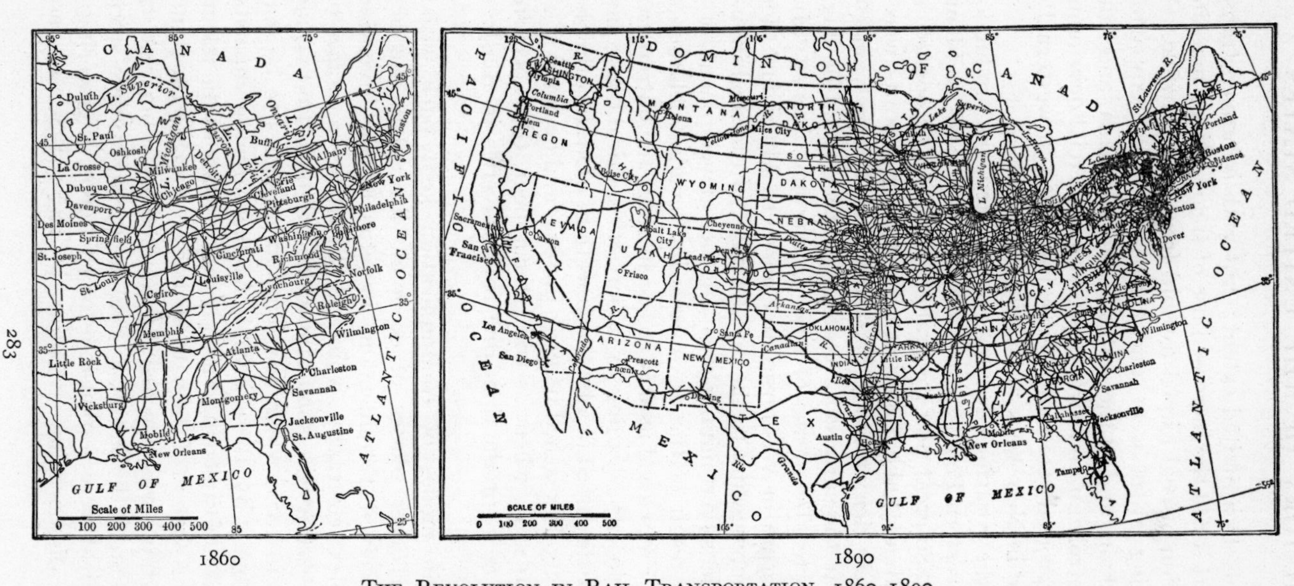

1860

1890

THE REVOLUTION IN RAIL TRANSPORTATION, 1860–1890

Not only were the transcontinental lines built in these years but also the great roads from the Atlantic Seaboard to Chicago as well as countless minor roads. The railway attained an importance in the United States greater than in any other country of the world.

facturing only to a limited extent; but with improved transportation facilities and the increased use of steam-driven machinery, the production of coal leaped fivefold from 1860 to 1880. Vast coal-producing areas were uncovered along the Appalachian Mountain chain, and in the states of Ohio, Indiana, and Illinois. Likewise, petroleum underwent its first commercial development, great underground reservoirs being discovered in western Pennsylvania and in New York and Ohio.

To meet the voracious demands of industry, the production of iron ore in western Pennsylvania advanced by leaps and bounds, and about 1880 great new iron ranges began to be opened up in the region about Lake Superior. These new deposits were not only extremely rich and pure, but unlike the Pennsylvania beds, they lay near the surface. Accordingly, they could be dug out and transported by means of labor-saving machinery. Mining towns sprang up in Wisconsin and northern Michigan, thereby giving new momentum to the development of the steel industry.

Large-scale silver mining was another development of this period, as a result of the discoveries in Nevada, Colorado, and elsewhere. From a value of $150,000 in 1860, the output rose to $36,000,000 in 1873, leading to important political consequences which will be discussed in a later connection. On the other hand, the output of gold reached its peak in 1854, and declined steadily from 1872 to 1893, when, as will later appear, there occurred a rapid increase in production, due to discoveries in Alaska and elsewhere.

Progress in modes of communication kept pace with the advances in other phases of economic life. The use of the telegraph received a tremendous impetus by the invention in 1872 of duplex telegraphy, which permitted two messages to be sent over the same wire simultaneously, and of Edison's quadruplex system in 1874, which enabled four messages to be sent at the same time. By these inventions the carrying capacity of the wires was multiplied, and men began to think of the telegraph as the nervous system of the nation's body. In 1866 the principle of the telegraph was successfully applied to submarine cable communication with Europe. The energy and public spirit of Cyrus W. Field were responsible for this great engineering feat after three discouraging attempts in 1857–1858. Under the assaults of science, of steam and electricity, the vast distances of the world were beginning rapidly to shrink.

At the same time the postoffice facilities of the country were greatly improved and extended. Free city delivery was installed in 1863, and the system of postal money orders a year later. In 1883 postage rates were reduced from three to two cents per half-ounce, and in 1885, to two cents an ounce. Cheap and efficient postal service was an invaluable adjunct to the business growth of the country as well as to its social solidarity.

These tremendous upheavals in industry and commerce were accompanied by a rapid cityward drift of population. Villages grew into towns and towns sprang into cities almost over night. In the transforming industrial order, they were indispensable as labor reservoirs for factories and mines, or as distributing centers of domestic or foreign trade. In 1830 the population living in cities of 8,000 or over was but one fifteenth of the whole; in 1860 it was nearly one sixth, and in 1890 almost one third. From a population of nearly one and one-fifth millions in 1860, New York and Brooklyn advanced to about two millions in 1880, and to more than two and one-half millions a decade later. In the same years, the population of Chicago rose from 100,000 to a half million, and then to a million. Philadelphia and Baltimore doubled in population from 1860 to 1890, Detroit and Milwaukee grew fourfold, San Francisco sixfold, Cleveland ninefold, and Minneapolis sixty-fourfold (from 2,564 to 164,738).

Due to the multitudinous mechanical inventions and better transportation facilities, urban life began to assume a standardized aspect the country over. Cities on the advancing frontier shared with Eastern centers the conveniences of modern civilization, and tended to exhibit the same striking contrasts between affluence and poverty. The advent of great cities meant the appearance of new problems, social and economic, in American life.

The Panic of 1873 and the Granger Movement

The sheer rapidity with which these changes occurred in all the great fields of business enterprise denoted a feverish and unhealthful condition of the body politic. With the opportunities for making money apparently unlimited, business men became unduly optimistic, and particularly in the years immediately after the Civil War, borrowed money at high interest rates for purposes of investment and speculation. In their mad scramble to share in the accelerating prosperity, they forgot the distinction between "possible" and "impossible." Capital poured into flour mills, factories, and iron works, many of which were built far in advance of immediate needs and therefore certain to yield no profit for many years.

More than one billion dollars were invested in railway construction alone during the decade following the incorporation of the Union Pacific. Since this construction outran the development of the country by many years, the railway companies became embarrassed for want of means wherewith to meet the interest on their bonded debt, or for that matter, their current expenses. Even the pioneer farmers shared the craze for speculation, and in their eagerness to improve their little properties, borrowed heavily from Eastern capitalists, mortgaging their lands as security.

Finally the bubble burst. Much of the business development had been financed from abroad; and a panic on the Vienna Bourse in May, 1873, two months after Grant's second inauguration, caused the withdrawal of much of this support. As a result, the financial burden fell chiefly upon the New York bankers, who were unprepared to carry the additional load. The panic was precipitated in September, 1873, by the failure of the great stock brokerage house of Jay Cooke and Company, which had invested too heavily in the projected Northern Pacific Railway.

There was a perfect frenzy of excitement and consternation in the financial world, the Grant administration was helpless before the storm, and the foundations of credit began to crumble. Banks and business houses failed on every hand, and the industrial regions of western New York, Pennsylvania, and the Middle West were afflicted as if by a paralysis. In all, more than 5,000 failures occurred during the panic year with an aggregate loss of about $228,500,000. More than three million wage-earners were thrown out of work, and the Western farmers found their grain a drug on the market and themselves without the means to meet their mortgage payments.

So severe was the shock to the economic structure that the country did not recover until 1878. This prolonged period of hard times, of declining markets, constant bankruptcies, and widespread unemployment, provided fertile soil for the propagation of all sorts of schemes of economic and social redemption. Both conservatives and radicals found in the existing depression evidence to confirm their belief in their pet ideas of reform. A tremendous impetus was, accordingly, given to the growing agitation of such diverse projects as railway regulation, greenback inflation, tariff protection, "free silver," labor organization, and Socialism.

A spectacular consequence of the Panic of 1873 was the rise of the first great farmers' movement in American history. For a number of years, the pioneer farmers in the West, notwithstanding many natural advantages, had found their path to economic well-being beset with serious obstacles. The great increase in the number of farms following the war had caused an overproduction of crops and a consequent dwindling of the prices of agricultural produce. Another difficulty rose from the excessive prices — sometimes netting the dealer forty per cent profit — which were charged for agricultural implements and other supplies. Even more serious was the remoteness of the farmer from the localities in which he expected to sell his crops. This condition fixed his attention upon the problem of transportation facilities, and although the advancing lines of rail were intended to give him relief, he felt that the railways charged extortionate rates, and frequently discriminated between communities, as well as between individual shippers, in the matter of freight charges.

The bad times accompanying the Panic made these conditions seem intolerable, and led to the meteoric rise of a secret ritualistic order, calling itself the "Patrons of Husbandry" but known popularly as the "Grange." This order had been in nominal existence since 1867, chiefly as a vehicle of rural social activity, but during the Panic it satisfied a new need and grew at a phenomenal rate, attaining in 1875 a maximum strength of about 30,000 "granges" and 2,500,000 members of both sexes. The movement was confined almost entirely to the states of the Upper Mississippi Valley, being especially strong in Illinois, Wisconsin, Iowa, and Minnesota.

The Grangers undertook to alleviate price conditions through coöperative activities. In numerous localities, the farmers pooled their funds, and effected great savings by ordering their implements and supplies in wholesale lots direct from the manufacturer. Central agencies were set up by the order to promote the sale of farm products, and coöperative creameries and grain elevators, operated at cost, are said to have saved Grange members thousands of dollars in several states. The State Grange of Iowa even established factories for the manufacture of plows and harvesters, which were sold to members at the cost of production. But by 1875 or 1876 most of these enterprises were abandoned. Many of them had failed for lack of adequate support or proper business direction. Nevertheless, the widespread interest in coöperation had frightened private merchants and manufacturers into establishing fair prices.

Meantime, the farmers waged successful war for cheaper transportation. New political parties sprang up in the states of the Middle West, deriving their inspiration from "Farmers' Declarations of Independence," and pledged to effect "the emancipation of white slaves from the Slave-Power of Monopoly." Through their influence, laws were adopted, for the first time, for regulating railroad rates, either by direct legislative decree or through the action of railway commissions set up for the purpose. Illinois led the way in 1870, and within a few years, her example was followed by Minnesota, Iowa, Wisconsin, Georgia, and California. These laws were based upon the then novel principle that railways should be treated as public-service enterprises, and not as mere private businesses for the enrichment of their stockholders.

The railroads bitterly denounced the "Granger Laws" as unjustifiable, ruinous, and unconstitutional, and it cannot be denied that some of the legislation was ill-wrought, or else colored by a desire for revenge. In the case of Munn *v.* Illinois, however, the United States Supreme Court in 1876 upheld fully the principle of government regulation when the rates established were not confiscatory, and in another decision, even declared that, until Congress acted under its interstate-commerce powers, rates might be fixed on shipments passing outside the state. Soon afterward, the Granger movement, having accomplished its main objective, lost its vitality as a political force.

Public Morals and National Politics, 1869–1872

The public life of Grant's presidency reflected the unstable political and economic conditions of the times. With sectional animosities as yet unabated, American politics began to show the effects of the tugs and pressures exerted by the leaders of the new capitalistic order, seeking to extort special favors from the government and to secure legislative protection for their investments. Unfortunately, these new political forces became active at a time when the country was suffering from a general lowering of its moral tone, as a reaction from the lofty idealism of war days. In the South the Carpetbaggers were beginning their pernicious career of misrule, and conditions equally discreditable existed in the North.

Referring to the new materialistic trend of politics, Senator Henry Wilson of Massachusetts declared in the *Independent* of June 10, 1869: "The power of wealth, individual and associated, concentrated and diffused, constitutes the new danger that is threatening us with its portentous and increasing dimensions. . . . The new danger is seen in the more obvious and obtrusive forms of monopoly, bribery, and the various forms of corruption characteristic of our times. Capitalists and active business men, . . . intensely earnest and anxious to succeed, and without much regard for the Golden Rule, avail themselves of whatever gives promise of success." As if to corroborate this statement, an investigating committee of Congress reported in 1873: "The country is fast becoming filled with gigantic corporations wielding and controlling immense aggregations of money and thereby commanding great influence and power. It is notorious in many state legislatures that these influences are often controlling, so that in effect they become the ruling power of the State."

The fast-growing cities of the East, with their polyglot populations, were rank festering spots of political disease. During these years, the "boss" and the "political machine" rose to a position of dominance in local politics, and James Bryce was obliged to confess, when he visited America some years later, that "the government of cities is the one conspicuous failure of the United States." One of the sensations of Grant's first term was the exposure of the machinations of the "Tweed Ring" in New York

City. In that metropolis "Boss" William M. Tweed and his clique constituted the Democratic machine, known popularly as "Tammany Hall." These men, while in control of the city government for a space of two and one-half years, increased the city debt by $70,000,000, the bulk of which went as loot into the pockets of the Ring. For instance, by ingenious book-keeping, the taxpayers were charged $11,000,000 for an uncompleted court house, whose cost of construction to that time amounted actually to $3,000,000. According to one entry on the books, a plasterer earned $138,187 in two days! Tweed was finally brought to justice in 1871, partly through the efforts of Samuel J. Tilden, who thereby first attracted national attention. But most of his confederates escaped to Europe, where they lived in luxury.

Grant possessed neither the experience nor the skill to stem the rising flood of materialism in American politics. Indeed, as a man who had himself struggled unsuccessfully against poverty, he readily accepted the dollar-mark as a standard of success, and thereby placed himself in harmony with the sordid ideals of the time. Although his own probity was undoubted, he was easily imposed upon by self-seeking and ambitious men, and while in the presidency, set a bad example to the country by accepting expensive gifts from persons whose motives were questionable, if not corrupt.

Grant's cabinet appointments, with one or two exceptions, were determined by personal predilection rather than by public need. His first selection as Secretary of State was Elihu Washburne of Illinois, who had gotten him into the army at the beginning of the war, and when Washburne resigned shortly afterward, his choice fortunately fell upon a statesman of real ability, Hamilton Fish of New York. To Fish belongs large credit for the successful negotiation of the Treaty of Washington (see pages 253–254). As Secretary of the Treasury, he chose A. T. Stewart, known to the country as a wealthy New York drygoods merchant, and when a law was discovered disqualifying the new Secretary because of his business connections, he named as his successor George S. Boutwell of Massachusetts, a routine politician with no special fitness for the place. Of the remaining appointees only ex-Governor J. D. Cox of Ohio, Secretary of the Interior, and

Judge E. R. Hoar of Massachusetts, Attorney-General, possessed the qualifications usually expected of cabinet members.[1]

Grant's entry into office coincided with the rise of a new generation of political leaders. The giants of the Civil-War era were fast passing away: Stevens died in 1868, Stanton in 1869, Vallandigham in 1871, Seward in 1872, Chase in 1873, Sumner (from whom Grant became estranged as early as 1870) in 1874, and Johnson in 1875. Their places were taken by men of lesser stature and of dissimilar ideals and interests. It is not unlikely that the men of vision and organizing genius — the natural leaders of the time — felt the challenge of the transforming economic life of the country, and renounced politics to become architects of the new industrial order. At any rate, the men who rose to national political eminence — Roscoe Conkling of New York, James A. Garfield of Ohio, James G. Blaine of Maine, Samuel J. Randall of Pennsylvania, W. D. ("Pig-Iron") Kelley of Pennsylvania, and their like — were eager to assist by subsidies, charter grants, and tariffs the vigorous exploitation of the nation's resources, and they were sometimes personally interested as stockholders or corporation attorneys in business enterprises which might be affected by their actions as lawmakers.

According to the easy-going standards of the time, such practices, however, were not as reprehensible as the outright bribery and corruption which, during Grant's second term, reached even into the sacred precincts of the President's cabinet. Corruption, declared that staunch Republican, Senator George F. Hoar of Massachusetts, at a later time — corruption "never got so dangerous a hold upon the forces of the Government, or upon a great political party, as in the Administration of General Grant."

Much of the dishonesty and bad government was due to the demoralized state of the civil service. The system of partisan appointments had been in vogue since Jackson's day, and in consequence of the great expansion of the government service during the Civil War, an unusually large number of worthless persons had gotten into official positions. Of Grant's attitude toward the patronage, the New York *Nation* could say in Sep-

[1] In addition to those already mentioned, the original cabinet consisted of J. A. Rawlins of Illinois, Secretary of War; A. E. Borie of Pennsylvania, Secretary of the Navy; and J. A. Cresswell of Maryland, Postmaster-General.

tember, 1869, no doubt with exaggeration, that he had "not only made bad appointments but probably some of the worst ever made by a civilized Christian government." In June, 1870, he dismissed Attorney-General Hoar, one of his ablest advisers, because the latter had become obnoxious to the politicians, and in October of the same year, Cox resigned as Secretary of the Interior because the President would give him no support in introducing the merit system into his department.

Nevertheless, in December, 1870, the President called upon Congress to enact a law for basing appointments upon personal fitness as determined by competitive examinations. Such a plan was already in operation in England, France, and elsewhere; and the reform had been pushed with great urgency by Thomas A. Jenckes of Rhode Island in the House of Representatives since 1865, and by Carl Schurz when he entered the Senate early in 1870. Congress heeded Grant's recommendation, and in March, 1871, authorized him to apply the merit system to federal appointments at his discretion. On January 1, 1872, he declared the new rules to be in force in the federal offices in Washington and New York. His tardy action undoubtedly savored of eleventh-hour virtue for the coming presidential campaign. Indeed, Grant soon chafed under the restrictions, and in 1873 Congress omitted to renew the appropriation for the supervisory commission, upon which the success of the plan depended.

During Grant's presidency the new and growing capitalistic interests, born of the Economic Revolution, completed the process of converting the Republican party from a party of humanitarian idealism to one of bourgeois conservatism. When the problem arose after the war of reorganizing the national finances on a peace basis, steady progress was made under Secretary of the Treasury Hugh McCulloch (1865–1869) and his successor Boutwell in lowering the internal-revenue taxes, in reducing and in 1872 abolishing the income taxes, and in converting the war debt into bonds bearing lower interest rates. But when it was proposed to reduce the tariff duties, an outcry arose from the vested manufacturing interests that had grown up during the war period, and every effort was put forth not only to maintain the wartime protection but to increase it in behalf of special industries.

In 1866 a swarm of lobbyists descended upon Washington, headed by John L. Hayes, representative of the newly formed National Association of Wool Manufacturers. Although no Republican national platform had ever declared for tariff protection save for a passing allusion in the platform of 1860, Congress raised the rates on wool and woolens in 1867, on copper in 1869, and on steel rails, nickel, and marble in 1870. In the words of a contemporary critic of this policy, the country had advanced from the five and ten per cent protection of Alexander Hamilton to the twenty and thirty per cent level of Clay and Webster, and now, with the tariff ranging from 30 to 500 per cent, still higher rates were being demanded.

In 1870 the call for tariff reduction was so strong in the agricultural West that Congress made a pretense of lowering or abolishing customs duties, but upon examination, these reductions proved to be, almost without exception, on such articles as tea, coffee, wines, and spices in which no domestic manufacturing interest was involved. The Act of 1870 left the tariff-reform sentiment unappeased, and the Republican leaders, fearing dissensions within the party on the eve of the presidential campaign, proceeded to enact a new system of duties in May and June, 1872.

By these Acts, sweeping reductions were made on nonprotective duties, and the demand for lower rates on manufactured goods was met by a slight horizontal cut of ten per cent on the products of the great protected industries of the country. The deficit in the national revenues caused by the Panic of 1873 led, however, to a restoration of the protective duties in 1875. At this point they were permitted to remain until the general tariff revision of 1883.

As early as 1870 there were signs of a developing sentiment within the Republican ranks to prevent the reëlection of Grant. In that year a group of Republicans in Missouri, disgusted with the unrelenting policy of the state government toward former Confederate sympathizers, led a bolt from the party. Adopting the name of "Liberal Republicans," they swept the state elections with the aid of the Democrats. Senator Schurz was the real leader of this movement, and under his influence, the new party in Missouri declared not only for a policy of Southern conciliation but also for civil-service reform and tariff revision.

The Missouri incident excited wide national attention among those Republicans who were restive under the Grant sway. Similar bolts from the party ensued in other states, and by 1872 the Liberal Republican movement had gathered such proportions that a national convention met in Cincinnati on May 1 to nominate candidates for the impending election. The convention consisted of diverse elements — tariff reductionists, civil-service reformers, opponents of Grant's policy of federal intervention in Southern politics (see page 251), and disgruntled politicians who had personal grievances.

With antagonism to Grant as the chief bond of union, the proceedings quickly became snarled in a tangle of personalities and politics, which caused the Republicans to call the gathering the "Convention of Cranks." The platform, after a savage arraignment of the administration, declared for civil-service reform and the restoration of home rule in the South, but in consequence of frankly confessed "irreconcilable differences," the platform failed to commit the party on the tariff. In selecting a candidate they made the preposterous mistake of naming Horace Greeley of the *New York Tribune*, a life-long foe of the Democrats and an ardent protectionist. Governor B. Gratz Brown of Missouri was nominated as his running-mate.

The Democrats who had hoped for a less partisan and opinionated nominee felt obliged, nevertheless, to indorse the Liberal Republican ticket. The Republicans, meeting in convention on June 5, unanimously renominated Grant on a platform which justified the administration's Southern policy, declared for tariff protection, and paid sanctimonious respects to civil-service reform. Henry Wilson of Massachusetts was chosen for Vice-President.

The outcome of the contest was at no time in doubt. Even with a stronger candidate than Greeley the Liberal Republican movement could hardly have triumphed, for despite his deficiencies as Chief Executive, Grant was idolized by the masses as the savior of the Union. Many Democrats absented themselves from the polls rather than to vote for Greeley. The victor was chosen by an electoral vote of 286 to 62 and by a popular majority of almost 56 per cent to 44 per cent. Greeley died a broken-hearted man a few weeks later.

In the history of the Republican party, the campaign was notable as marking the formal adoption of tariff protection as an article of party faith. The campaign also signalized the entry of labor into politics in the guise of the short-lived Labor Reform party. No presidential contest since then has been without a minor party devoted to the welfare of the urban or rural workingman.

SELECT BIBLIOGRAPHY

The Revolution in Manufacturing, Transportation, Mining, and Communication. E. L. Bogart, *An Economic History of the United States* (New York, 1922), gives a compact treatment of the subject. Of value, also, are Isaac Lippincott, *Economic Development of the United States* (New York, 1921), H. U. Faulkner, *American Economic History* (New York, 1924), E. R. Johnson and others, *History of Domestic and Foreign Commerce of the United States* (2 v., in Carnegie Institution, *Contributions to American Economic History*, Washington, 1915), I; and C. M. Depew, ed., *One Hundred Years of American Commerce* (2 v., New York, 1895).

The Panic of 1873 and the Granger Movement. Excellent accounts of the Panic may be found in J. F. Rhodes, *History of the United States*, VII (New York, 1906); T. E. Burton, *Financial Crises and Periods of Industrial and Commercial Depression* (New York, 1902); and E. P. Oberholtzer, *Jay Cooke, Financier of the Civil War*, II (Philadelphia, 1907). The standard work on the first farmers' uprising is S. J. Buck, *The Granger Movement* (in *Harvard Historical Studies*, XIX, Cambridge, 1913).

Public Morals and National Politics, 1869–1872. The materialistic political trend is portrayed in J. F. Rhodes, *History of the United States*, VI (New York, 1906); W. A. Dunning, *Reconstruction, Political and Economic* (in *The American Nation*, XXII, New York, 1907); and E. P. Oberholtzer, *A History of the United States*, II (New York, 1922). Of special value for the Tweed Ring exposé are A. B. Paine, *Th. Nast* (New York, 1904); John Bigelow, *The Life of Samuel J. Tilden* (2 v., New York, 1895); and S. P. Orth, *The Boss and the Machine* (in *The Chronicles of America*, XLIII, New Haven, 1919). For civil-service policy, C. R. Fish, *The Civil Service and the Patronage* (in *Harvard Historical Studies*, XI, New York, 1905) is useful. E. D. Ross, *The Liberal Republican Movement* (New York, 1919), is a special study of that incident.

Postwar financial reorganization is treated compactly in D. R. Dewey, *Financial History of the United States* (New York, 1922). A. D. Noyes, *Forty Years of American Finance* (New York, 1909), is also helpful in this connection. Ida M. Tarbell, *The Tariff in Our Times* (New York, 1911), emphasizes the political and social forces in tariff making; Edward Stanwood, *American Tariff Controversies in the Nineteenth Century* (2 v., Boston, 1903), is especially good for the legislative history of tariff measures; and F. W. Taussig, *The Tariff History of the United States* (New York, 1923), gives a scholarly, nonpartisan account from the standpoint of an economist.

CHAPTER XVII

THE POLITICAL TREND, 1872–1885

"The Nadir of National Disgrace"

No sooner was the election of 1872 past than the country was shocked by a political scandal which smirched the fame of some of the highest officials of the government. Investigating committees of the House and Senate discovered that the outgoing Vice-President and a number of members of Congress[1] were on the books of the Credit Mobilier, construction company for the Union Pacific, as holders of stock that had been sold them on credit at a price considerably below the market value. It was ascertained that Oakes Ames, a Congressman who was an official of the company, had distributed 343 shares of Credit Mobilier stock where, as he wrote confidentially, they would "protect us" and "do the most good" in averting a possible inquiry into the company's affairs. The report of the House committee generously absolved most of the members involved of "any corrupt motive or purpose," and the House contented itself with a formal censure of Ames and another member.

Other revelations of wrongdoing followed with almost clocklike regularity throughout Grant's second administration. Only a few of the more conspicuous incidents need to be noticed. For example, in May, 1874, the Secretary of the Treasury, W. A. Richardson, and two of his associates hastily resigned in order to escape a vote of censure by the House. It appeared that Richardson had grossly abused his authority in order to divert some of the funds of the Department, through unearned commissions, into the pockets of J. D. Sanborn, a political henchman of the notorious Benjamin F. Butler.

In the fall elections, the people, though unaware as yet how far the contagion of corruption had spread, cast a mighty vote of

[1] Including James A. Garfield, "Pig Iron" Kelley, John A. Logan, and William B. Allison.

protest against the party in power, giving the Democrats their first victory since before the war. Although the Senate continued Republican, the composition of the House changed from two-thirds Republican to three-fifths Democratic, a fact which was to give administration politicians sleepless nights when the returns of the next presidential election were counted. Twenty-three out of thirty-five states went Democratic, including Ohio, Massachusetts, and Pennsylvania, all Republican strongholds, and in New York Samuel J. Tilden was elected Governor on a platform of political reform.

In the next two years came the floodtide of corruption and dishonor. The fearlessness of B. H. Bristow, Richardson's successor in the Treasury Department, led in 1875 to the unearthing of a "Whisky Ring," composed of revenue officers and leading distillers, which had been engaged since 1870 in defrauding the government out of millions of dollars of taxes. The President's private secretary, O. E. Babcock, was guiltily involved in the conspiracy, but at the trial Grant, through mistaken zeal, managed to save him from conviction. This affair was followed in March, 1876, by the precipitate resignation of the Secretary of War, W. W. Belknap, in order to escape impeachment proceedings on the charge of receiving an annual bribe since 1870 from an office-holder anxious to avoid removal.

A few weeks later another scandal came to light which was forever to tarnish the reputation of James G. Blaine, who had been Speaker of the House from 1869 to 1875. The investigation disclosed that, while holding his powerful office, he had acted as bond salesman for a land-grant railway, and that he had later permitted the Union Pacific and certain other land-grant corporations to relieve him of a large block of the bonds at a sum far in excess of their market value. By a trick, Blaine got possession of the incriminating evidence, the so-called "Mulligan Letters," and though refusing to allow the documents to be examined, he made a brilliant speech in the House, which, if it left the critical public unsatisfied, at least convinced all orthodox Republicans of his innocence. But Blaine's penalty was to be a heavy one, for his connection with this affair was to prevent him in later years from attaining the goal of his ambition, the presidency.

The Greenback Question

The chief redeeming feature of Grant's second administration was the action taken by the government to bring about a renewal, or resumption, of specie payments. Since the early days of the war, the business of the country had been transacted largely in debased greenbacks which the government refused to redeem at face value in gold. The substantial business classes of the East clamored for the withdrawal of all this "cheap money," or at least the establishment of conditions under which all forms of money should have full gold value. Upon authorization by Congress, a start was made in 1866 at taking the greenbacks out of circulation by gradual stages; but this process had to be discontinued two years later, when the amount of greenbacks was reduced to $356,000,000, because of the outcry of Western farmers and Southern planters.

These men saw in contraction one cause of the prevailing low prices of crops. Furthermore, since their farms were heavily mortgaged for sums borrowed from Eastern money centers, they felt they were intolerably handicapped if, before their debts fell due, the volume of greenback currency became smaller. With money less abundant, greenbacks became harder to get, or, to put it differently, their value increased. If paper dollars, borrowed when they were worth sixty-five cents in gold, were repaid in paper dollars worth ninety-five or one hundred cents in gold, the debtor was repaying in principal considerably more than he had borrowed. Many members of the "debtor class" began to demand that the greenbacks should be retained as a permanent part of the monetary system.

During the Panic of 1873, the Secretary of the Treasury, as a temporary measure of relief, reissued some of the greenbacks that had been retired, to the amount of $26,000,000. The demand becoming more insistent, Congress in 1874 passed the "Inflation Bill," designed to increase the total volume of greenbacks to $400,000,000. President Grant courageously vetoed this bill, though it was the act of his own party. When the fall elections of 1874 assured the Democrats control of the next House, the Republicans made use of their remaining months of tenure by enacting a plan for the resumption of specie payments.

The Resumption Act of January 14, 1875, has been called, not inaptly, the "deathbed repentance of the Republican party." Far from radical, its provisions sought to appease both the greenback notions of the West and the gold-standard sentiment of the East. John Sherman was its chief author. The Act provided that on and after January 1, 1879, the government should accept greenback dollars as equivalent to gold dollars, and that meantime, in preparation for the event, the government should retire a part of the greenbacks and, at the same time, accumulate a gold reserve through the sale of bonds. The purpose of this store of gold was to assure the full specie value of the greenbacks remaining in circulation. The gold reserve was subsequently fixed at a minimum of $100,000,000, and Congress decided in 1878 that greenbacks to the amount of $346,681,016 should remain permanently as a part of our money supply. The plan proved entirely practicable in execution. After the date of resumption, the full value of the greenback in terms of gold was never again subject to question. The public credit was vastly strengthened, and the confidence of the investing public in the value of paper currency proved to be an invaluable aid to the industrial development of the nation.

Grant's veto of the Inflation Bill incensed the small group of extreme greenbackers in the country, and the passage of the Resumption Act added to their anger. These persons subscribed to the doctrine of "absolute money"; that is, they contended that money derived its value solely from the stamp (or "fiat") of the government — not from its intrinsic value or the fact that it was exchangeable for gold or some other precious metal. Hopeless of winning the support of either of the old parties, they organized the National Greenback party in May, 1875, which presented candidates in the three following presidential elections. Their platforms demanded the repeal of the Resumption Act, and the establishment of a national legal-tender currency, redeemable only in low-interest United States bonds. Though attaining some popularity in the farming sections of the Middle West and in Eastern labor centers, and commanding 1,000,000 votes in the Congressional elections of 1878, the party never cast an electoral vote. It gradually succumbed to the rising tide of sentiment in favor of an unlimited silver coinage.

The Disputed Election of 1876

Quite content with the Resumption Act, the mass of the voters were thinking of other things as the campaign of 1876 drew near. Although Roscoe Conkling's ambition to secure a third term for Grant was checked in December, 1875, by a protest of the Democratic House of Representatives, in which two thirds of the Republican members joined, the fact helped to fix anew the attention of the public upon the malodorous record of the party in power. What could the Republicans do to avert disaster in the election? Blaine, himself the chief contender for the nomination, pointed the way in January, 1876, when he delivered in the House a violent "bloody-shirt" speech which goaded the Southern members into passionate and ill-considered replies. The Republicans promptly took advantage of the opportunity to frighten the public with the spectacle of an unrepentant South about to ride into power on the back of the Democratic party.

When the Republican convention assembled in Cincinnati on June 14, Blaine was the favorite in the balloting, but he failed of success because of the implacable opposition of the reformers, who wanted to nominate Secretary Bristow of Whisky-Ring fame, and of Conkling, who cherished a vindictive personal dislike for Blaine. The prize went on the seventh ballot to Rutherford B. Hayes, a Civil-War veteran of irreproachable character, then serving his third term as Governor of Ohio. W. A. Wheeler of New York was nominated for Vice-President. The platform bristled with "bloody-shirt" allusions, declared for tariff protection, and repeated its promise of four years before for civil-service reform.

The Democrats, meeting on June 27 in St. Louis, proceeded without hesitation to the choice of Governor Samuel J. Tilden, who, by reason of his success in destroying the corrupt "Canal Ring" in New York politics, had come to symbolize the reform spirit in the eyes of the nation. The vice-presidential nomination went to Thomas A. Hendricks of Indiana. The paramount issue, according to the Democratic platform, was that of reform — financial, tariff, civil-service, and administrative — a duty which could not safely be intrusted to a party "honey-combed with incapacity, waste, and fraud."

In the ensuing campaign, the Democrats sought energetically to focus public attention upon the urgent need for reform, whereas, to quote James Russell Lowell, a Hayes supporter, "The worst element of the Republican party has got hold of the canvass, and everything possible is done to stir up the old passions of the war." Republican orators even asserted that the Democrats, if elected, planned to pay the Confederate war debt and to compensate the former slaveholders. The hard times continuing since 1873 were a strong factor making for Democratic success.

On the morning after the election, Tilden's victory was almost universally conceded by the newspapers, but the Republican national headquarters stoutly claimed the success of Hayes. Within a few days it became clear that, with 185 electoral votes necessary for election, Tilden had the unquestioned right to 184, including the usually decisive states of New York, New Jersey, Connecticut, and Indiana, and that Hayes in like manner was entitled to 165 undisputed votes. Twenty votes, comprising one from Oregon, seven from South Carolina, four from Florida, and eight from Louisiana, were in doubt.

The difficulty in Oregon was of a technical character. One of the duly chosen Republican electors was, after the election, discovered to be ineligible. The state law provided, in such a case, that the remaining electors should appoint a successor, but the Democratic Governor insisted that the highest Democratic candidate for elector should be given the place.

In the three Southern states the question was more complicated. There the native whites, engaged in a final desperate effort to dislodge the Carpetbaggers from power, had, in countless instances, resorted to intimidation and violence to keep the negroes from the polls. But the state election machinery, capped by the famous or infamous "Returning Boards," was under control of the Carpetbaggers, who from their seats of authority could manipulate the election returns as they pleased. The worst situation was presented by Louisiana, where the four members of the Returning Board refused to add a Democratic member as required by statute, offered at one stage to sell out to Tilden for $1,000,000, and ended up by rejecting Democratic votes in wholesale lots in order to create a popular majority for Hayes. To this end, the Democratic popular vote in Louisiana was cut down by 13,213 and the Republican by 2,415, leaving the Hayes electors with a safe margin of 3,437 or more.[1]

From each of the four states double sets of election returns went to Congress. Unfortunately the Constitution makes no adequate provision for such a contingency. Since the two houses of Congress were controlled by opposite parties, compromise was necessary. Accordingly, a law was passed on January 29, 1877, to create a special "Electoral Commission" of five Senators, five Representatives, and five Justices of the Supreme Court, the fifth Justice to be chosen by the four named in the law. The Commission's decisions on disputed returns were to be binding upon Congress unless rejected by the two houses voting separately. When the Electoral Commission was authorized, it was known, of course, that seven of the members would be Republicans and seven Democrats, but it was expected that the unselected Justice would be David Davis, a free lance in politics. Davis's unexpected election by the Democratic legislature of Illinois as United States Senator now caused the appointment of a third Republican Justice, Joseph P. Bradley, the most acceptable to the Democrats of the remaining members of the Court.

The Electoral Commission sat throughout the month of February, 1877. The time was drawing perilously near to inauguration day, suppressed excitement pervaded the country, and President Grant quietly strengthened the military forces in and about Washington. Forty-two ex-Confederate members of the House of Representatives, bent on averting the possibility of another terrible civil war, took a solemn pledge to oppose all attempts to frustrate the counting of electoral votes.

Meantime, the Electoral Commission took cognizance, in turn, of the cases of Florida, Louisiana, Oregon, and South Carolina. On all crucial points the decision was in favor of the Hayes electors by a ballot of eight to seven, and on March 2, Hayes was formally pronounced victorious by an electoral vote of 185 to 184. The disappointment of the Democrats is indescribable,

[1] James Ford Rhodes concludes, "If Hayes had envisaged the facts as I now do he would have refused to accept the presidency from the Louisiana Returning-Board." *History of the United States*, VII, 236. But another historian, while conceding the "grossly partisan and illegal acts" of the Returning Board, expresses the belief that "in an absolutely fair and free election the state would have gone Republican by five to ten thousand." P. L. Haworth, *The Hayes-Tilden Disputed Election of 1876*, 116, 121.

but with many angry mutterings, they yielded grudging acquiescence. It is perhaps not too much to say that, in the peaceful acceptance of Hayes's election, the supremacy of the law won the greatest victory in the history of popular government.

Republicans and Reform, 1877–1881

The portentous revival of Democratic strength, culminating in the election of 1876, badly frightened the professional politicians, and gave a strategic advantage to those Republicans who wished to purify the party. Each age has its own crying abuses which demand correction, and as might be expected, the reformers of the seventies and eighties were interested, above all else, in the honest, efficient, and economical conduct of the government. Alarmed by the ominous creaking of the governmental machinery under the manipulation of unskilled or unscrupulous hands, they were fearful lest the theory of democracy might be discredited by its evil practices.

Their constructive program embraced the adoption of civil-service reform, the abolition of campaign assessments on office-holders, and the prompt punishment of all delinquent public officials. Individuals among them labored also for tariff reduction. Foremost among the reformers were Carl Schurz, George W. Curtis, editor of *Harper's Weekly*, E. L. Godkin, editor of the New York *Nation*, and Dorman B. Eaton, a New York lawyer and publicist. They represented particularly the views of the educated classes of the East.

Since their purposes clashed with those of the organization leaders, the reformers or "Independents" could not always attain their objects within the party. This led them to assume an attitude of independence, whenever occasion demanded, as a rebuke to their party.[1] Their potential freedom of party restraints, their insistence that parties were merely instruments for the public good and not ends in themselves, enraged the professional politicians. But their example helped gradually to establish a tradition of independent voting at a period when the fetish

[1] Some of them had participated in the Liberal Republican movement in 1872, but the disastrous outcome of that adventure apparently convinced them of the futility of third-party undertakings.

of party regularity was stronger than at any other time in our history. The orthodox conception of party duty was, for the Republicans, summed up in the saying, "The men who saved the Union should govern it."

Though acquiring office under dubious circumstances, President Hayes sought earnestly to live up to the maxim, announced in his inaugural address, that "he serves his party best who serves his country best." He was a simple, dignified man, conscientious and hardworking, but devoid of the qualities of leadership. He gathered about him an unusually able group of advisers, including William M. Evarts of New York as Secretary of State and John Sherman of Ohio as head of the Treasury Department. To the horror of the party leaders, the post of Secretary of the Interior was given to Carl Schurz, civil-service reformer and an active campaigner against Grant four years earlier, and David M. Key, a Tennessee Democrat and an ex-Confederate veteran, was appointed Postmaster-General.[1]

These appointments were followed by other acts which showed that the new President expected to tread a path apart from Conkling and the practical politicians who had surrounded Grant. His refusal to accord further military support to the Carpetbag governments in the South, resulting in their overthrow, and his zeal for civil-service reform both offended and outraged these men. They soon began to refer to Hayes as a man who was only a "halfbreed" Republican in contrast with their own "stalwart" Republicanism. The names, "Halfbreed" and "Stalwart," clung to the two wings of the party throughout this administration and the next.

President Hayes made a resolute effort to secure administrative efficiency and to weed out dishonesty. Although his repeated appeals to Congress to renew the civil-service appropriation, which had lapsed under Grant, came to naught, nevertheless he made progress, upon his own authority, in reducing the ravages of the spoils system. Secretary Schurz placed the Department of the Interior on a merit basis, and in the face of bitter opposition from the Stalwarts, Hayes next sought to apply the reform to the

[1] The other members of the cabinet were: George W. McCrary of Iowa, Secretary of War; Richard W. Thompson of Indiana, Secretary of the Navy; and Charles Devens of Massachusetts, Attorney-General.

federal offices in New York City. He reappointed T. L. James, a vigorous exponent of civil-service reform, to the postmastership there in spite of Conkling's protests, and gave him firm support.

He found the New York Custom House, which handled nearly three fourths of the import trade of the country, riddled with incompetency and corruption. Other means of reform failing, he removed Chester A. Arthur, the Collector, and A. B. Cornell, the Naval Officer, the latter being Chairman of the Republican National Committee. The Senate, incensed, declined for two months to confirm their successors. Hayes's devotion to the cause undoubtedly won popular favor for civil-service reform, and helped to hasten its final accomplishment.

Although the President's worst enemies were in the house of his friends, the Democrats in Congress strove ceaselessly to discredit him as "Old Eight-to-Seven" and the "*de facto* President." Their purpose was not to unseat him, but, by stressing Tilden's martyrdom, to sweep the country in 1880 in a dramatic campaign of vindication. They interpreted the President's abandonment of the Carpetbag governments as an admission that his own majorities in those states had been fraudulently secured, and they placed the most injurious construction upon his appointment to federal positions of the members and clerks of the Louisiana Returning Board. In May, 1878, the Democratic House of Representatives directed the so-called Potter Committee to investigate the title of Hayes to the presidency, and after examining over 200 witnesses concerning conditions in Florida and Louisiana in 1876, the Committee decided by a strict party vote that Tilden had been rightfully elected.

The edge of the Democratic disclosures was, however, dulled by the success of a Republican Senate Committee in unearthing a large batch of cipher telegrams which had been sent, or received, by Democratic leaders during the heat of the campaign. These, when decoded, revealed efforts on the part of the Democrats to bribe the Florida and South Carolina Returning Boards. As a result of someone's foresight, Republican telegrams sent at the same time could nowhere be located! Most of the Democrats implicated by the "Cipher Despatches" did not deny the essential charges against them, and in hearings before the Potter Committee, justified their course on the plea that they were merely trying to "ransom stolen property from thieves." Tilden himself was shown to be innocent of any complicity. It was clear that the garments of both parties were soiled, and the "political crime" as a Democratic campaign issue was robbed in advance of much of its vitality.

The Democrats also displayed partisan activity in a stubborn effort to repeal the Force Acts of 1870–1871, passed during the Ku Klux troubles to enable the Washington government to supervise and guard the voting places during federal elections (see page 251). Under this legislation, or at least under such parts of it as had not been annulled by the Supreme Court, the United States had spent from $60,000 to $100,000 on each Congressional election from 1870 to 1878, and had actively interfered in the conduct of elections in certain parts of the North as well as in the South. By refusing to pass the army appropriation bill, the Democratic House finally forced the Senate and the President on June 18, 1878, to accept a bill prohibiting the use of troops at the polls.

The Democrats obtained control of both houses of Congress in the fall elections of 1878, and from this vantage-ground they waged bitter warfare for the abrogation of the remainder of the legislation. Their efforts usually took the embarrassing form of "riders" on appropriation bills, but Hayes, unshaken, vetoed eight different attempts at repeal. Though rendered innocuous by disuse, these last vestiges of the old Reconstruction machinery survived on the statute book until repealed by a Democratic Congress and President in 1894.

The aggressive tactics of the opposition party helped the Republicans, despite their internal differences, to present a united front in preparation for the coming election. Tired of too much virtue, the professional politicians, under Conkling's imperious leadership, resolved to reassert their control of the party, and chose as their candidate for that purpose none other than ex-President Grant, who had just returned from a spectacular tour around the world. The Halfbreeds and Independents were thoroughly alarmed. The anti-Grant forces organized "No-Third-Term" leagues in many parts of the country, and even held a national "Anti-Third-Term" convention.

When the Republicans convened in Chicago on June 2, 1880, 306 of the 757 delegates were pledged to Grant, but though they voted unswervingly for their idol, the "Grant Phalanx" was never able to add appreciably to its strength after the first ballot. Blaine, who enjoyed a reputation as an eleventh-hour Halfbreed, stood second in the contest until the thirty-sixth ballot when the convention in desperation stampeded to a "dark horse," James A. Garfield of Ohio. Garfield was a veteran of the Civil War who had seen continuous service in Congress since 1863; he was regarded as a Halfbreed of a moderate type. The convention made a peace-offering to Conkling and the Grant Phalanx by selecting Arthur of New York, the recently dismissed Collector of Customs, for Vice-President. The platform consisted largely of self-laudation and of disparagement of the Democrats, but included an indorsement of the protective system and, with evident reluctance, of Hayes's civil-service policy.

The Democrats found themselves in a dilemma. Tilden was not available as a candidate because of ill-health and the powerful opposition of "Boss" John Kelly of Tammany Hall. Meeting in Cincinnati on June 22, the convention decided on the third ballot in favor of General Winfield S. Hancock, and selected as his running-mate W. H. English of Indiana. Hancock's nomination was an attempt to refute the customary Republican charge of disloyalty, and at the same time to capitalize the popularity of a faithful war veteran. "The great fraud of 1876–77" was urged by the platform as the issue that "precedes and dwarfs every other," and demands were made for civil-service reform and a tariff for revenue only.

In the campaign, the "great fraud" seemed to have little popular appeal notwithstanding the fact that the Republican candidate had been a member of the Electoral Commission of 1877. Nor did the efforts to discredit Garfield because of his dubious connection with the Credit Mobilier and other scandals yield any greater success.[1] The Republicans made the most of their nominee's rise from humble beginnings as a barefoot canal-boy in Ohio, and scoffingly dismissed Hancock as "a good man weighing two hundred and forty pounds." Hancock's chief campaign utterance was a repudiation of the Democratic tariff

[1] At one stage of the campaign, the figure "329" (the amount of a Credit Mobilier dividend which Garfield had received) was displayed everywhere — on sidewalks, walls, and Democratic newspapers.

plank, on the score that the tariff was necessarily a "local issue." The return of prosperity for the first time since 1872 undoubtedly helped the Republicans. Garfield was victorious by an electoral majority of 214 to 155, though he polled only 48.3 per cent of the popular vote as compared with 48.23 per cent for his opponent.

Sealing the Doom of the Spoils System

The announcement of Garfield's cabinet reopened the Republican breach which had closed during the period of the campaign. The selection of Blaine, the Halfbreed, as Secretary of State was regarded by Conkling as a personal affront, and the other cabinet appointments were scarcely more to his liking.[1] When the President sent the Senate his nominations for federal positions in New York, the Stalwart boss learned that his wishes had been again disregarded. His rage knew no bounds for it had long been customary for Presidents to follow the advice of Senators of their own party in regard to federal appointments within their states.

Conkling determined to make an issue of W. H. Robertson's nomination as New York Customs Collector. Not only was the office the most lucrative in the gift of the government, but Robertson was a Halfbreed and a Blaine man. When in spite of all his efforts he perceived that the nomination would be confirmed, Conkling and his fellow-Senator, T. C. Platt, resigned their seats, and appealed to the New York legislature for reëlection in vindication of their course. But to their mortification and the country's amusement, they were both defeated after fifty-six ballots had been cast. Conkling retired permanently to private life, "Me Too" Platt to a temporary oblivion.

Meanwhile the reforming zeal of James, the new Postmaster-General, uncovered a nest of corruption in the postal service, involving T. W. Brady, who since Grant's time had been Second Assistant Postmaster-General, ex-Senator S. W. Dorsey of Arkansas, and others. Brady attempted to block the investigation by threatening the President with unpleasant consequences.

[1] William Windom of Minnesota, Secretary of the Treasury; Robert T. Lincoln of Illinois, Secretary of War; W. H. Hunt of Louisiana, Secretary of the Navy; Wayne McVeagh of Pennsylvania, Attorney-General; T. L. James of New York, Postmaster-General; and S. J. Kirkwood of Iowa, Secretary of the Interior.

When Garfield remained unmoved, he made public the famous "My dear Hubbell" letter, wherein Garfield as a presidential candidate had expressed approval of the practice of levying campaign assessments on officeholders. The trials of the conspirators in the "Star Route" frauds, as they were called, dragged on until 1883, when, due to technicalities, the chief culprits were acquitted. Some good resulted, however, for the ring was broken up, and public attention was called anew to the need of better federal officials.

Garfield had been in office only four months when the nation was stricken by the news that he had been shot on July 2, 1881, by a disappointed office-seeker, who, in his diseased mind, believed the President's death needful to heal party differences. At the time, Vice-President Arthur was with Conkling and Platt at the New York capital, working for their reëlection; and when Garfield after a brave fight died on September 19, the first feeling of many people was doubtless similar to that of the man who exclaimed, "Chet Arthur President of the United States! Good God!" Yet the new President, despite his long identification with machine politics, was a man of undeveloped possibilities. In office he displayed unexpected firmness and sagacity, and to the surprise of his erstwhile associates, devoted himself earnestly to the task of forwarding the cause of reform.

Arthur presently reconstituted the cabinet, appointing F. T. Frelinghuysen of New Jersey Secretary of State in succession to Blaine before the end of the year. Only Secretary of War Lincoln, a son of the martyred President, was permanently retained.[1] Otherwise, most of Garfield's appointees remained undisturbed, including Robertson whose selection as Customs Collector had been responsible for Conkling's resignation. Nor did Arthur's devotion to the public welfare stop here. In the summer of 1882 the Republican Congress adopted a rivers-and-harbors bill, appropriating almost $19,000,000 for public improvements in nearly five hundred different localities — the first of the modern "pork-barrel" measures. The President rejected the measure

[1] The other new appointments were: C. J. Folger of New York, Secretary of the Treasury; W. E. Chandler of New Hampshire, Secretary of the Navy; B. H. Brewster of Pennsylvania, Attorney-General; T. O. Howe of Wisconsin, Postmaster-General; and H. M. Teller of Colorado, Secretary of the Interior.

as extravagant and unwise, though it was promptly passed over his veto by a bipartisan majority.

His chief interest, however, was civil-service reform. In his messages of 1881 and 1882 he urged upon Congress suitable legislation to that end. Fifteen years of agitation had created an intelligent public opinion on the subject, and the President's efforts were reënforced by the agitation of state and national Civil Service Reform Associations and by countless articles in the *Nation*, *Harper's Weekly*, and other magazines. Revelations of a Senate investigating committee in 1879 to the effect that the Republicans had collected nearly $100,000 from federal employees by virtual compulsion in the Congressional elections of 1878, touched the public on the raw, as did likewise the knowledge, derived from the "My dear Hubbell" letter and other sources, that this practice had been repeated in the campaign of 1880. Garfield's death at the hands of a thwarted spoilsman seemed to give an irrefutable and tragic answer to all objections to the immediate adoption of the reform — yet the politicians in Congress continued to find excuses for delay.

In the fall elections of 1882, the Democrats won control of the new House of Representatives, as well as sweeping victories in thirteen of the sixteen states in which gubernatorial elections were held. While Republican factionalism helped to bring about this result, the failure of the party to reform the public service was an important contributing factor. In the important state of New York, Grover Cleveland, a Democrat and ardent civil-service reformer, was elected Governor by an unprecedented plurality of 192,000. The expiring Republican Congress resolved to enact the desired legislation, both in order to propitiate public sentiment and to protect Republican officeholders from the effects of the severer act which the incoming Democrats were almost certain to propose.

The result was the Pendleton Act of January 16, 1883, drafted by Dorman B. Eaton, and introduced, as it happened, by Senator G. F. Pendleton, an Ohio Democrat. Briefly expressed, the statute provided for a system of competitive examinations as a test of fitness for appointment to federal office, and it further declared that no federal employee should ever lose his position for failure to contribute to political funds. By direction of the law, the new rules were to apply at once to all custom districts and post offices employing fifty or more persons, and the President was empowered to extend this "classified list" (as it was called) from time to time at his discretion. Provision was made for a Civil Service Commission of three members to direct and administer the new system, subject to the President's authority.

The statute left much to be desired, of course. For example, the rules applied only to future appointments and, at first, to only about 14,000 positions, leaving eighty-nine per cent of the offices still subject to partisan politics. Nevertheless, the Pendleton Act has rightly been called "the Magna Charta of civil-service reform," for through its provision for future enlargements of the classified list, subsequent Presidents have progressively extended the merit plan of appointment until, at the present time, approximately sixty per cent of the vast army of federal employees are under its protection. While idealism contributed to this steady diminution of the spoils system, gross partisanship played its part as well, for a party going out of power often increased the classified list in order to protect its followers from being dismissed by its successful rival.[1] Few backward steps have been taken, on the whole. The rapid extension of the reformed system has owed most, perhaps, to the exertions of Presidents Roosevelt, Taft, and Wilson.

Arthur was frankly an aspirant for the Republican nomination in 1884, but his chances were slight, for he had lost his former Stalwart support without entirely convincing the Halfbreeds of the genuineness of his conversion. With Conkling out of politics, the old-line politicians began to rally to the support of Blaine, and even "Me Too" Platt cried, "Blaine's turn has come." To the reform wing of the party, however, Blaine's candidacy promised a negation of all the progress toward good government that had been made since Grant left office. When the national convention assembled in Chicago on June 3, 1884, Blaine's nomination was secured on the fourth ballot, though against the resolute opposition of George W. Curtis and of younger delegates like Theodore Roosevelt and Henry Cabot Lodge. Since his candidacy lacked

[1] This practice has prompted the cynical remark, "To the vanquished belong the spoils!" for, when the civil-service rules are extended to a new class of officers, the incumbents are included within their protection either without an examination, or else with a noncompetitive examination.

the customary Republican qualification of service in the Civil War, amends were made by the nomination of General John A. Logan of Illinois for Vice-President.

Shortly after the convention, a conference of Independent Republicans adopted resolutions condemning the ticket and calling upon the Democrats to offer candidates whom they could support. The Democrats were prepared, and at their Chicago convention, on July 8, chose Grover Cleveland of New York on the second ballot. Thomas A. Hendricks of Indiana, Tilden's running-mate in 1876, was named for Vice-President in a feeble effort to resurrect the old "fraud" issue.

Cleveland's nomination admirably met the requirements of the situation. With none of the qualities of the dashing political cavalier or the wiles of the professional intriguer, he had impressed himself upon the people of his state through his blunt and aggressive honesty and his painstaking devotion to the public weal, and they had raised him from Mayor of Buffalo in 1881 to the chief magistracy of the state in 1882. A second conference of Independents indorsed the Democratic candidate as a man "whose name is the synonym of political courage and honesty and of administrative reform," and stigmatized Blaine as "a representative of men, methods, and conduct which the public conscience condemns."

The platforms of the two parties presented no real points of difference. Both promised a revision of the tariff without injury to domestic industries, both indorsed civil-service reform, and both dangled additional pensions before the old-soldier vote. Accordingly, the contest turned upon the pervasive influence of party loyalty and the personal attributes of the candidates. In bitter contempt the Republican bolters were dubbed "Mugwumps" by the regulars. The electioneering activities of Schurz, Curtis, Henry Ward Beecher, Benjamin H. Bristow, and other Mugwump leaders, covering the states from Rhode Island to Iowa, undoubtedly drew many thousands of voters to Cleveland's support, particularly in the case of the young voters who had grown to manhood since the war. Other Republicans, unwilling to desert to the traditional enemy, compromised by voting for J. P. St. John of Kansas, the Prohibition candidate. The great majority of the Republicans, however, remained loyal — captivated by Blaine's magnetic personality as other hundreds of thousands had once been by Henry Clay's, or else believing with Roosevelt and Hamilton Fish that reform should come from within the party.

The old embers of the "Mulligan Letters" scandal were fanned into flame by new accusations of Blaine's illicit financial dealings with privilege-seeking corporations, and Democratic orators made effective use of Cleveland's precept, "Public office is a public trust." On the other hand, Cleveland, charged with being the father of an illegitimate son, admitted the truth of the accusation. A charge against Blaine as a drunkard was refuted by a certificate of Neal Dow, the Maine prohibitionist. Declared the *Nation*, "The campaign is one worthy of the stairways of a tenement-house."

Blaine tried once more to consolidate Republican strength in the Middle West by "waving the bloody shirt." Both parties put forth special efforts to cultivate the Irish-Catholic vote, and Blaine had the ardent support of the *Irish World*, the American organ of the Irish Land League. But the Democrats had the better of the argument when, in the final week of the campaign, the Rev. S. D. Burchard, chairman of a Protestant ministerial gathering in New York, introduced Blaine as the opponent of the party of "Rum, Romanism, and Rebellion" — a remark promptly attributed by the Democratic press to Blaine himself. Business depression and widespread unemployment were other factors favorable to a change of party.

On the day after the election, the Associated Press announced that Blaine had won, and it was not until three days later that a Democratic victory was conceded. The outcome was exceedingly close, Cleveland receiving 219 electoral votes to 182 for Blaine, and 48.9 per cent of the popular vote to 48.3 for Blaine. Had New York gone Republican, its thirty-six electoral votes would have given the presidency to Blaine; yet Cleveland's lead in that state was barely 1149 popular votes out of a total of more than 1,160,000! Thus the cause of good government was again successful, though this time under the ægis of the Democratic party. It remained to be seen, however, whether Cleveland with all his dogged determination could shape his heterogeneous following into an effective instrument for political reform.

SELECT BIBLIOGRAPHY

"The Nadir of National Disgrace." Detailed accounts may be found in J. F. Rhodes, *History of the United States*, VII (New York, 1906), and W. A. Dunning, *Reconstruction Political and Economic* (in *The American Nation*, XXII, New York, 1907). For a friendly view of Blaine's involvements, see *James Gillespie Blaine* (Boston, 1905) by Edward Stanwood, a relative of Mrs. Blaine.

The Greenback Question. The treatments in D. R. Dewey, *Financial History of the United States* (New York, 1922), A. B. Hepburn, *A History of Currency in the United States* (New York, 1915), A. D. Noyes, *Forty Years of American Finance* (New York, 1909), M. S. Wildman, *Money Inflation in the United States* (New York, 1905), and W. C. Mitchell, *A History of the Greenbacks* (*Chicago University Decennial Publications*, second series, IX, Chicago, 1903), are accurate and helpful. The political aspects of the Greenback movement are sketched in S. J. Buck, *The Agrarian Crusade* (in *The Chronicles of America*, XLV, New Haven, 1920), and F. E. Haynes, *Third Party Movements since the Civil War* (Iowa City, 1916).

The Disputed Election of 1876. The most thorough study is P. L. Haworth, *The Hayes-Tilden Disputed Presidential Election of 1876* (Cleveland, 1906), but excellent accounts appear in the works by Rhodes and Dunning, previously cited. See also John Bigelow, *The Life of Samuel J. Tilden* (2 v., New York, 1895), and C. R. Williams, *The Life of Rutherford Birchard Hayes* (2 v., Boston, 1914).

Republicans and Reform, 1877–1881. Good general treatments may be found in J. F. Rhodes, *History of the United States*, VIII (New York, 1919), E. E. Sparks, *National Development* (in *The American Nation*, XXIII, New York, 1907), and J. W. Burgess, *The Administration of President Hayes* (New York, 1916). A connected account of the Independent movement in politics is given in M. Ostrogorski, *Democracy and the Party System* (New York, 1910). Williams's biography of Hayes, previously cited, is also of much value. F. L. Paxson's single-volume work, *Recent History of the United States* (Boston, 1921), begins with 1877, and continues to its date of publication.

Sealing the Doom of the Spoils System. Rhodes and Sparks continue to be serviceable for the Garfield-Arthur administration. For civil-service reform, C. R. Fish, *The Civil Service and the Patronage* (in *Harvard Historical Studies*, XI, New York, 1905), should be consulted. H. C. Thomas, *The Return of the Democratic Party to Power in 1884* (in *Columbia University Studies*, LXXXIX, no. 2, New York, 1919), is excellent for civil-service reform, as well as the best study of party politics.

CHAPTER XVIII

HUMANITARIAN STRIVING AND SOCIAL PROGRESS, 1872–1890

The Renascence of the Woman's-Rights Movement

Political concerns were not the sole interest of the American people in the generation following the Civil War. Indeed, some of the most significant developments during the years from Grant to the close of Cleveland's presidency were only remotely related to political controversy. The period was, in many respects, one of moral agitation and humanitarian endeavor, yielding results of enduring importance in the annals of American social progress. The interests of the social reformers were broad, and the evils they attacked many; but it is to be noted that, for the most part, they were not concerned with the growing misery of the laboring classes. This subject is therefore reserved for discussion in another place.

The earlier movement for sex equality (see pages 73–75), which had been shoved into the background by the exciting issues of the Civil War, now experienced a revival. At the close of the war the feminist leaders had hoped to obtain for their sex the right to vote at the time that the ballot was extended to colored men by the Fourteenth and Fifteenth amendments. They made desperate but futile efforts to that end, flooding Congress with petitions and making countless personal appeals. Their disappointment was intense, for the franchise seemed a logical reward for the priceless services which the women had rendered during the war.

Realizing that a long and difficult struggle loomed ahead, the suffragists resolved to leave no stone unturned which would advance their cause. In May, 1869, the National Woman Suffrage Association was formed with Mrs. Elizabeth Cady Stanton as President, pledged to strive for the ballot through state action. Later in the year the American Woman Suffrage Association was organized, under the leadership of Henry Ward Beecher, for the purpose of securing equal suffrage through a federal amendment.

Other conditions, different in character and ultimately more potent, were working to change the position of women in American society, and were, in the long run, to bring about the emancipation of the sex. The Economic Revolution ruthlessly violated the traditional seclusion of the home, and forced an ever increasing number of women and girls to seek employment as factory-hands and as bookkeepers, clerks, and helpers in offices and stores. Between 1870 and 1890 the number of women over sixteen years engaged in such occupations grew from 364,819 to 1,199,640, and in 1900 to 1,707,415.

At the same time the portals of higher education began to open to women as never before. In 1865 the first women's college possessing ample funds was opened at Poughkeepsie by Matthew Vassar, consecrated to the ideal of maintaining educational standards equal to those of the best men's colleges. The Western state universities urged forward the movement. Under a law of 1867 Wisconsin admitted girls to the normal department of the university, and three years later the University of Michigan reversed the practice of almost thirty years by offering all the regular courses to women. When the Ohio State University began operations in 1870, women were admitted on equal terms with men. In 1869 private beneficence endowed Boston University on a coeducational basis — the first college of the kind in Massachusetts. Soon coeducation became the rule, rather than the exception, in the liberal arts colleges of the country.

With the ever-broadening facilities for higher education, women began to enter the professions. Before the close of the century they had largely displaced men as schoolteachers. Their progress in medicine, law, and theology was slower because of the reluctance of professional schools to admit them as students. Nevertheless, women were allowed to plead before the federal Supreme Court by 1879, and by the end of the century there were in the United States 1,010 women lawyers, 7,387 physicians and surgeons, 807 dentists, and 3,373 clergywomen. By the force of circumstances, the time-honored argument against woman's rights, summed up in the saying, "Woman's sphere is the home!" was losing its validity.

Another factor working in the interests of feminine emancipation was the rise and development of women's clubs throughout the United States. Beginning in 1868 with the founding of the Sorosis in New York and the New England Woman's Club in Boston, the number of clubs increased as household conveniences multiplied and the housewife gained more time from domestic duties. As the years wore on, such clubs gave less attention to art, literature, and religion and more to civic and social problems, and some of them became centers of agitation for woman's rights and equal suffrage. By 1890 the clubs were so numerous and so widespread that they became linked together in a great national organization called the "General Federation of Women's Clubs."

The expansion of women's activities in so many directions led to reforms in the laws which regulated their position in American life. Such changes were brought about only with the greatest difficulty, for the feminist leaders had to combat not only the inertia, prejudice, and active hostility of the men but also that of many of their own sex. In this long uphill battle the names of Mrs. Elizabeth Cady Stanton, Miss Susan B. Anthony, Mrs. Lucy Stone (Blackwell), Dr. Anna Howard Shaw, and Mrs. Carrie Chapman Catt bear a special luster. The storm center of the struggle was the suffrage question. Opponents of univeral suffrage protested that woman would lose her charm in masculine eyes, that sex equality would lead to the breaking-up of family life, and that the feminine intellect was unfitted to cope with problems of state. The American movement was in harmony with the enlightened conception of women that was making headway in many parts of the world, and the American leaders received encouragement and inspiration from feminist victories in other lands.[1]

The progress toward legal equality was gradual but certain. Although in 1900 the laws of California, the Dakotas, Idaho, New Mexico, Ohio, and Georgia still expressly designated the

[1] In 1862 Sweden gave unmarried women taxpayers a vote for all officials except members of Parliament. Widows and spinsters received local voting rights in Finland in 1865. In 1866 the woman suffrage movement began in Great Britain, and desperate efforts were made to insert equal suffrage in the Reform Bills of 1867 and 1884. In 1869 Parliament granted the municipal franchise to women taxpayers; and later, women received the ballot in school elections and certain other local matters. Iceland gave taxpaying widows and spinsters the municipal ballot in 1882. Parliamentary suffrage was extended to the women of New Zealand in 1893 and of South Australia two years later.

husband as head of the family and the wife subject to him, notable strides toward personal freedom had been made in the great majority of the states. For example, married women could own and control their property, make contracts, engage in business, and retain their own earnings in most states. Accordingly, as the century drew to a close, the *principle* of sex equality in ordinary civil matters had gained general recognition, although many actual inequalities in civil status survived.

Progress was also made toward the enfranchisement of women. While the Economic Revolution was at its height, some Middle Western states ventured to grant suffrage to women in a local and limited sense. Following the example of Kansas in 1861, Michigan and Minnesota bestowed the ballot on women in school elections in 1875, and similar action was taken in the next twenty years by fourteen other states, representing all parts of the country save the old Confederacy. Kansas conferred municipal suffrage in 1887, and Montana (1887) and Iowa (1894) permitted women to vote in elections involving bond issues or taxation questions. Complete equality in voting was not granted in any state until Wyoming, which as a territory had allowed full woman suffrage since 1869, was admitted to the Union in 1890. Colorado followed in 1893, and Utah and Idaho in 1896.

Meantime, determined efforts had been made to secure favorable action from the national government. The great political parties ignored the question, but in 1878 Senator A. A. Sargent of California introduced an equal-suffrage proposal, drafted by Susan B. Anthony, which forty-two years later was to become the Nineteenth Amendment. Between 1878 and 1896 committees of the Senate reported four times in favor of a suffrage amendment, and House committees twice; but action went no further. Then there came such a complete check to further advances that, for a space of fifteen years, universal suffrage appeared to be merely an aberration of the remote and undeveloped West.

The Fight against the Liquor Evil

A reform movement, closely connected with the increasing influence of women in American life, was the fight against the "Rum Evil." In the fifties statewide prohibition had been enacted by a number of legislatures (see page 76), but the Civil War sapped public interest in this cause as in many other reform enterprises. In fact, the drink traffic attained a respectability during the war that it had never hitherto enjoyed, since the United States government, for the first time, used it as a productive source of revenue.

In spite of the burden of taxation, the liquor business throve mightily. The capital invested grew from $29,000,000 in 1860 to $67,000,000 in 1870 and $269,000,000 in 1890. This unprecedented prosperity inevitably caused the liquor manufacturers to become a political factor. With an enormous financial investment to protect against the possibility of more drastic taxation and even of prohibitory legislation, they began to enter politics and to wield power in state and local affairs. In the case of the Whisky-Ring frauds under Grant, they were able to reach degrading hands to the very threshold of the White House.

The earlier hostility to the use of intoxicants had been due to moral and hygienic objections. This opposition was now powerfully reënforced by an argument of a different kind, directed against the organized liquor traffic as a sinister and reactionary influence in American politics. Symptomatic of the new attitude was the formation of the Prohibition party in 1869, on a platform demanding statutory suppression of the liquor traffic and the adoption of woman suffrage as the most effective means to that end. Though never casting an electoral vote, the party has taken part in every presidential contest since 1872, and by reason of its strength in New York state in 1884 was an important factor in bringing about the defeat of Blaine.

In 1874 the women decided to wage warfare against the "Rum Evil" through an organization of their own, the Women's Christian Temperance Union. Under the leadership of Frances E. Willard, branches were established in each state and territory. Campaigns were waged for statewide prohibition, and every state was induced to pass laws to require scientific temperance instruction in the public schools. Many of the religious denominations formed special societies to assist the cause, and in 1893 a new and aggressive organization, the Anti-Saloon League, was established in order to coördinate the efforts of all existing agencies.

The great national parties avoided the prohibition question, for the most part, since they feared either to risk a new and uncertain issue or to lose campaign contributions from the liquor interests. Moreover, a majority of the people were, as yet, opposed to any curbing of their "personal liberty" in the use of intoxicants. This feeling was especially strong among persons

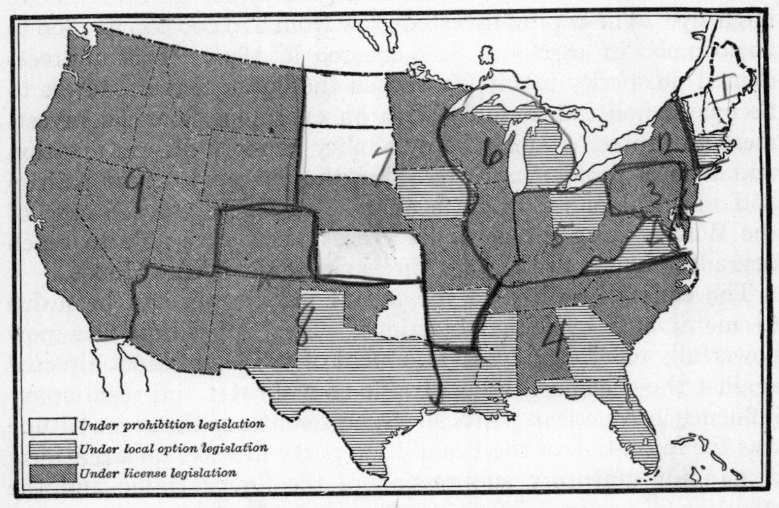

THE PROHIBITION MOVEMENT IN 1893

of German descent. President Hayes, however, gave the cause his moral sanction when he banished alcoholic beverages from all White House functions during his administration, and in 1887 Alaska was placed under prohibition by executive order of President Cleveland.

The reform made steady progress in other respects as well. Between 1880 and 1890, statewide prohibition was established in Kansas, Iowa, and North and South Dakota. In many other states, much of the territory was voted "dry" by means of local option, that is, through self-denying regulations adopted by the popular vote of local communities. Saloons elsewhere were forced to operate under high licenses, costing from $500 to $1000 annually. Yet, notwithstanding the multiplying restraints on the liquor traffic, the *per capita* consumption of alcoholic stimulants for the country in general doubled from 1870 to 1890. The most optimistic prohibitionists hardly dreamed that their cause would be triumphant within the span of another generation.

The Formation of the Red Cross

In harmony with the new humanitarian conceptions was the movement to mitigate the horrors of war. Following a preliminary conference of 1863, a convention representing sixteen nations met at Geneva, Switzerland, in August, 1864, and drew up a treaty for establishing the International Red Cross Society. By its provisions, there should be formed, in every country signing the treaty, organizations to coöperate in times of war with the army medical service. All such societies should wear a red cross (the Swiss national emblem reversed) as a distinguishing mark, and in time of war be free from hostile attack in their care of the sick and wounded. Although the success of the United States Sanitary Commission in the Civil War, then being waged, proved to be a source of great inspiration to the Geneva convention, the American government was not represented by official delegates, and through indifference, it refused to adhere to the treaty.

To Clara Barton, a heroine of mercy in the Civil War, belongs the credit of inducing the government to reverse its attitude. Convinced of the tremendous value of the Red Cross through her relief activities in the Franco-Prussian War (1870–1871), she returned to the United States, and as soon as her health permitted, began a persistent campaign, as she said, "to wipe from the scroll of my country's fame the stain of imputed lack of common humanity." Success finally crowned her efforts. President Garfield promised to recommend ratification of the Geneva Treaty in his first annual message, and under Arthur the Senate took the desired action in March, 1882, thereby lighting "bonfires that night . . . in the streets of Switzerland, France, Germany, and Spain." The United States was the thirty-second nation to sign.

When success was in sight, the American Red Cross Society was established in July, 1881, with Clara Barton as President. As a result of her efforts, the "American Amendment" was added to the Geneva Treaty in 1884, expressly authorizing the Red Cross to engage in peacetime humanitarian work in connection with floods, earthquakes, and other public disasters. Between 1881 and 1890, the American Red Cross carried on relief work during the Michigan forest fires in 1881, the Mississippi River floods in 1882, the cyclone in Louisiana and the Ohio River floods of 1883, the overflow of the Mississippi and Ohio rivers in 1884, the drought in Texas in 1886, the cyclone at Mt. Vernon, Illinois, in 1887, the yellow-fever pestilence in Florida, and the Johnstown (Pennsylvania) flood in 1889. Its hold on the gratitude of the American people was undoubted, and with the passage of years the scope of its activities tended steadily to enlarge.

The Intellectual Revival

The generation following the Civil War witnessed vast improvements in educational opportunities for the masses. In the North the schools were greatly improved, and the curriculum expanded to include forms of manual training like agriculture and home economics. "Kindergartens," first introduced into this country in 1855 by Mrs. Carl Schurz, spread to thirty states by 1880. Free public high schools multiplied, and much more attention than formerly was devoted to teacher-training. At the same time, as has already been seen, the public-school system took firm root in the Southern states; and with the assistance of Northern benefactions like the Peabody Fund (1867) and the Slater Fund (1882), a special effort was made to cope with the problem of negro education. The enrollment of pupils for the entire country assumed an enormous total, increasing from about seven millions in 1870 to nearly thirteen millions in 1890.

In the field of higher education the most striking development was the rise of the great state universities. A strong impetus in this direction had been given by the Morrill Act, passed by Congress in 1862, which offered each state a large grant of land for the purpose of endowing a college devoted chiefly to instruction in agriculture and the mechanic arts. Every state accepted the proffered lands, and applied them either to a preëxisting private college or state university, or to an especially created institution. Between 1865 and 1890, sixteen new state universities were founded, most of them in the Middle and Far West. Everywhere the cause of higher education was quickened.

A remarkable generation of university presidents came on the scene, such men as Andrew D. White at Cornell (1867), James McCosh at Princeton (1868), Charles W. Eliot at Harvard (1869), J. B. Angell at Michigan and Noah Porter at Yale (1871), D. C. Gilman at Johns Hopkins (1876), and Alice Freeman (Palmer) at Wellesley (1882). In 1888 James Bryce declared, "The seats of learning and education are at present among the most potent forces making for progress and the formation of sound opinion in the United States, and they increase daily in the excellence of their teachers no less than in the number of their students."

American journalism also entered a new era. The war had accustomed publishers to lavish outlays of money, and had created many new readers whose subscriptions could not be retained by the old-fashioned editorial discussion and ponderous literary style. Instead, editors began to fill their columns with items, selected not because of their intrinsic importance but because of their human interest or sensational qualities, and written in vigorous and pungent style. Charles A. Dana, who became editor of the *New York Sun* in 1868, set the new pattern, and it reached its full development in this period when Joseph Pulitzer, a brilliant journalist of Hungarian birth, took over the *St. Louis Post-Dispatch* in 1878 and five years later extended his operations to the *New York World*. Pulitzer's purpose was to make the *World* a vehicle of popular opinion for the achievement of social and political reforms. In a few years his journal was the most profitable and the most widely imitated newspaper in the country.

Newspapers of this new type had many of the characteristics of presentday journalism, and were deliberately designed to cater to the increasing numbers of wage-earners — the least literate section of the population. Large headlines, and "feature stories" of scandal and crime, became the rule. Increased attention was given to sports, to amusements, and to the special interests of women and children. The new trend reached its climax in the ubiquitous Sunday supplement, which, to the distress of the pious and the grief of the fastidious, regaled an ever-widening circle of readers with its pictures, sensational fiction, and colored "comics."

Even more significant was the transformation of the larger journals into vast business enterprises. Newspapers ceased to be the external embodiments of great editors as in Greeley's time. As a result of the Economic Revolution and the enormous development of retail stores, the newspapers tended to become, first and foremost, advertising sheets and only secondarily vehicles of news. The great metropolitan dailies passed into the hands of newspaper corporations, for they represented too heavy a financial investment to be borne by a single person or small group of men. Gradually the controlling interest in newspaper policy shifted from the editorial sanctum to the office of the business manager, with a corresponding loss to the freedom of the press.

Better processes and new mechanical devices made it possible for the newspapers to meet the huge leaps in circulation. Notable among these were cheaper methods of making print paper, improved printing presses, and Ottmar Mergenthaler's invention of the linotype machine (1884). At the same time, newspapers, in the interest of economy and efficiency, began to coöperate with each other in news-gathering. Though the original Associated Press was organized prior to 1860, in the years after the war numerous competing news-associations sprang up, and waged hot war with each other. Finally, in 1900, the various interests consolidated, and the presentday Associated Press resulted.

While newspapers in general continued to be strong party organs, the leaven of independent thought and action was at work in the journalistic as well as in the political world. This tendency was greatly strengthened by certain weekly journals that were established, or which became prominent, shortly after the war, such as the *Independent*, the *Christian Union* (now the *Outlook*), *Harper's Weekly*, and the *Nation*. Of the free-lance editors the most significant was E. L. Godkin of the *Nation*, an Irish immigrant, whose good temper and mental acuteness set a new standard for the free and intelligent criticism of public affairs in the period from 1865 to 1899.

These weeklies had a circumscribed reading public, composed chiefly of the educated classes of the East, but indirectly their influence extended far. When Blaine ran for President in 1884, the spirit of independent journalism had made such headway that many of the great Republican dailies supported the Democratic ticket, among them the *Times*, the *Evening Post*, and the *Herald* of New York, the *Boston Transcript*, the *Times* and the *News* of Chicago, and the *Springfield Republican*. In the columns of *Harper's Weekly*, Thomas Nast, whose cartoons had helped to expose the Tweed Ring and other frauds, laid the foundations of modern American political caricature, contributing to our political zoo the familiar figures of the Republican elephant, the Democratic donkey, and the Tammany tiger.

In the loftier realms of literary expression, the years from 1870 to 1890 marked a new creative epoch, comparable to that of the thirties and forties, but surpassing it in originality, variety, and sheer volume of output. The new writers wrote with the rush and thrill of a new nation about them. They saw American life undergoing kaleidoscopic changes, and sought to preserve in their pages impressions of a social organization fast altering beyond recognition. Impatient with the bookishness and fastidious diction of their predecessors, their spirit was social, virile, realistic; they strove to depict men and women in all their crudity and strength as they actually were.[1] Never before had American literature been so distinctively a product of the soil, never so truly a mirror of the life of the people. Every section, almost every region, had its photographer, interpreter, or bard; dialect and local-color writing were the distinguishing marks of the new school.

S. L. Clemens ("Mark Twain") gave a broadly humorous picture of the early days in Middle America, and, with Bret Harte and Joaquin Miller, made memorable the picturesque frontier life of California and the Great West. Edward Eggleston depicted the primitive society of Indiana. With an accomplished pen George W. Cable celebrated the survivals of the old Spanish and French civilizations in Louisiana, Alice French ("Octave Thanet") wrote of the dwellers in the Arkansas cane-brakes, and Mary N. Murfree ("Charles Egbert Craddock") told of the scenery and mountains of Tennessee. The chivalry and folklore of the Old South were made to live again in the pages of

[1] Rooted though this new movement was in the changing foundations of American life, it had its counterpart in Europe where Thomas Hardy in England, Björnson in Norway, and Tolstoi in Russia were finding new and vital literary material in the simple annals of village and peasant life.

Thomas Nelson Page, Joel Chandler Harris, and F. Hopkinson Smith.

More than all others perhaps, Walt Whitman, whose earlier work had failed of an audience, and "Mark Twain," whose first notable work *Innocents Abroad* appeared in 1869, were the incarnate spirit of America, voicing its ideals of democracy, its passion for improvement, its desire for fair play. Of the new age, too, were two authors of a different stamp: William Dean Howells and Henry James, realists like the others in their fidelity to truth but careful and precise students of artistic form. The literary awakening found its unique expression in the short story, "literature in small parcels," a form peculiarly adapted to the needs of the hurrying, breathless people who constituted the new nation. It is not too much to say that through the short story America has made her greatest contribution to world literature.

New Social Conveniences and Pastimes

The new opportunities for educational and literary self-improvement came at a time when the intellectual life of the masses was being quickened by certain epochmaking inventions. Foremost among these was the telephone, invented in 1876 independently by Alexander Graham Bell and Elisha Gray, and made practicable for general use a few years later by the adoption of the central exchange system. Social communication was thereby facilitated, business transactions expedited, and the barriers of isolation among the rural inhabitants began to crumble. In 1924 there were between fourteen and fifteen million telephones in the United States, more than three fifths of the world's supply, and about one for every eight persons in the Union.

Important discoveries were made in lighting, thus tending to erase the difference between day and night for individuals and communities. Improving upon the experiments of others, C. F. Brush of Cleveland devised an arc light in 1878, which attained its effect by passing a flame from one carbon to another, and proved suitable for illuminating streets and public places. In 1879 Thomas A. Edison, the most versatile inventor in history, perfected the first practicable incandescent electric light,[1] and

[1] Between 1870 and 1900 Edison took out 727 United States patents.

when Garfield was inaugurated two years later, the national capital was widely admired for its brilliant illumination.

Of equal significance in a different field was the invention of a mechanical substitute for the old-fashioned penman and copyist. In 1873 Remington and Sons of Ilion, New York, began the manufacture of a typewriter that had been devised five years earlier mainly by C. L. Sholes of Milwaukee. In the ensuing years, the typewriter transformed office work, modified literary style, and was responsible for a new vocation which gave employment and economic independence to thousands of women.

Great progress was also made in photography, most notably perhaps by the invention of the small portable snapshot camera by George Eastman of Rochester, New York, in 1888. Photography was henceforth to play an important part in science, in advertising, and in the general diffusion of intelligence. Another marvel of the period was the talking-machine, invented by Edison in 1877 and exhibited to President and Mrs. Hayes in the White House the following year. At first the phonograph possessed little practical utility, for the records were made of tinfoil and easily perishable. But when C. A. Bell and Sumner Tainter in 1886 substituted wax records for tinfoil, the machine presently entered on a career of wide popularity, and began to furnish amusement and recreation for thousands of homes. These and countless minor inventions of household utility made life easier and more enjoyable for all classes of the population. Even poor people possessed advantages and conveniences which the wealthiest citizen lacked half a century earlier and which Lincoln and his generation knew nothing of.

These years also saw the rise of organized recreations and sports. The piling up of population in great cities, the increased leisure resulting from shorter workdays, the patronage of athletics by the wealthy, and the natural zest of the American people for competitive games were chiefly responsible for this development. Baseball, which in a somewhat primitive form had enjoyed a local vogue since the Civil War, was placed upon a national and professionalized basis with the formation of the National League in 1876. Other leagues followed, and soon baseball won its position as the chief American sport. In 1884 the first "World Series" was played in this country.

Football developed somewhat more slowly, being closely associated with the growth of collegiate athletics. The American game was an adaptation of the English game Rugby, and the first intercollegiate contest occurred between Princeton and Rutgers in 1869. In 1876 the American Intercollegiate Football Association was formed by Columbia, Harvard, Princeton, and Yale; and in the next twenty years the game, under constantly changing rules, spread to nearly all the colleges and most of the high schools of the country. Lawn tennis was imported into America from England about 1875, and soon attracted an increasing number of devotees, leading to the formation of a national association in 1881.

The modern bicycle came into vogue about the same time. An earlier contrivance consisted practically of one large front wheel, over which the rider was precariously mounted, balanced by a smaller wheel in the rear. In 1884, however, the "safety" bicycle was devised with two moderate-sized wheels of equal dimensions, similar to the presentday model. A League of American Wheelmen had been formed in 1880, but the introduction of the "safety," and later of pneumatic tires in place of the solid rubber ones, led to a cycling craze that infected every city and village of the land. Other sports enjoyed a similar development. Professionals and amateurs alike took part in this new play life of the nation, and the well-to-do signified their approval by the establishment of luxurious country clubs, yacht clubs, and athletic clubs.

SELECT BIBLIOGRAPHY

The Renascence of the Woman's-Rights Movement. Belle Squire, *The Woman Movement in America* (Chicago, 1911), and H. A. Bruce, *Woman in the Making of America* (Boston, 1912), present interesting popular accounts of the revival of the feminist movement. On the entry of women into the business world and its social effects, Edith Abbott, *Women in Industry* (New York, 1910), and A. W. Calhoun, *A Social History of the American Family* (3 v., Cleveland, 1917–1919), III, should be consulted. Good discussions of the expansion of feminine education appear in E. G. Dexter, *A History of Education in the United States* (New York, 1904), and C. F. Thwing, *A History of Higher Education in America* (New York, 1906). The spread of woman's clubs is traced in Mrs. J. C. Croly, *The History of the Woman's Club Movement in America* (New York, 1898), and Mary I.

Wood, *The History of the General Federation of Women's Clubs* (New York, 1912). The contest for legal and political equality may be followed in Jennie L. Wilson, *The Legal and Political Status of Women in the United States* (Cedar Rapids, 1912), or, from a different point of view, in Ida H. Harper, *The Life and Work of Susan B. Anthony* (3 v., Indianapolis, 1898–1908).

The Fight against the Liquor Evil. Much of value on the temperance movement may be gleaned from Daniel Dorchester, *The Liquor Problem in All Ages* (New York, 1888), J. G. Woolley and W. E. Johnson, *Temperance Progress of the Century* (Philadelphia, 1903), and E. H. Cherrington, *The Evolution of Prohibition in the United States of America* (Westerville, Ohio, 1920).

The Formation of the Red Cross. Laura M. Doolittle, *The Red Cross* (Washington, 1895), and W. E. Barton, *The Life of Clara Barton, Founder of the American Red Cross* (2 v., Boston, 1922), are important in this connection.

The Intellectual Revival. For educational expansion, C. F. Thwing, *A History of Education in the United States since the Civil War* (Boston, 1910), and E. P. Cubberley, *Public Education in the United States* (Boston, 1919), are useful.

The new journalism is dealt with in J. M. Lee, *History of American Journalism* (Boston, 1923), G. H. Payne, *History of Journalism in the United States* (New York, 1920), and F. W. Scott, "Newspapers since 1860" (in *The Cambridge History of American Literature*, III, 319–336, New York, 1921). For particular newspapers, consult Elmer Davis, *History of the New York Times* (New York, 1921), J. L. Heaton, *The Story of a Page* [*New York World*] (New York, 1913), Allan Nevins, *The Evening Post* (New York, 1922), and F. M. O'Brien, *The Story of the Sun* (New York, 1918). Rollo Ogden, *Life and Letters of Edwin Lawrence Godkin* (2 v., New York, 1907), gives an illuminating account of the New York *Nation* and its editor.

The facts concerning the literary awakening have been brought together in F. L. Pattee, *A History of American Literature since 1870* (New York, 1915), and in *The Cambridge History of American Literature*, III and IV (New York, 1921).

New Social Conveniences and Pastimes. The best compact account of American inventions is E. W. Byrn, *The Progress of Invention in the Nineteenth Century* (New York, 1900). George Iles, *Leading American Inventors* (New York, 1912), and Holland Thompson, *The Age of Invention* (in *The Chronicles of America*, XXXVII, New Haven, 1921), discuss several outstanding inventors and their work. W. Kaempffert, ed., *A Popular History of American Invention* (2 v., New York, 1924), is the latest treatment of the subject. For particular inventions, the following volumes are important: H. N. Casson, *The History of the Telephone* (Chicago, 1910), Charles Bright, *The Story of the Atlantic Cable* (New York, 1903), C. E. Weller, *The Early History of the Typewriter* (La Porte, Indiana, 1918), F. L. Dyer and T. C. Martin, *Edison; His Life and Inventions* (2 v., New York, 1910), and F. E. Leupp, *George Westinghouse, His Life and Achievements* (Boston, 1918).

The great mine of information on the history of organized sports and recreations is the *Encyclopedia of Sport and Games* (4 v., the Earl of Suffolk and Berkshire, ed., London, 1911). The best history of football is Walter Camp and L. F. Deland, *Football* (Boston, 1896); of baseball, A. G. Spalding, *America's National Game* (New York, 1911). F. L. Paxson first called attention to the vital place of athletic recreation in American social history in his article, " The Rise of Sport " (in *Mississippi Valley Historical Review*, IV [1917], 143–168).

CHAPTER XIX

THE ALIEN PEOPLES, 1872–1890

The New Indian Policy

By the decade of the eighties the spirit of national unity had begun to permeate the people of the United States as never before. All the significant currents in American life since the war had tended to make people forgetful of state boundaries and think in terms of the country as a whole. The Economic Revolution, the waning of war issues, the revolt against political corruption, the great inventions, the new trend in education, the broad appeal of the new literature — these were nationalizing influences of far-reaching importance. Nor can the widespread interest in organized sports be ignored as a solvent of local prejudices and sectional animosities. Edward Freeman, the English historian, traveling in the United States in 1883, noticed that "where the word 'federal' used to be used up to the time of the civil war or later, the word 'national' is now used all but invariably. It used to be 'federal capital,' 'federal army,' 'federal revenue,' and so forth. Now the word 'national' is almost always used instead."

True national unity, however, is a product of mutual understanding among all groups and classes of the population, and this, in turn, is closely connected with their freedom to make use of the normal avenues of living a full life and attaining economic independence. Accordingly, one of the vital problems before the United States was occasioned by the existence of undigested alien elements in the population, notably the Indians in the Great West, the negroes in the South, the Chinese on the Pacific Coast, and the increasing horde of European immigrants. The period from Grant to Cleveland marked a turning point in the relationship of the government to these peoples. Although the solutions attempted met with varying degrees of success, they nevertheless formed the foundations of American policy toward these races, which have continued to the present day.

The Indians constituted the most pressing problem. After a quarter-century of desperate combat they were reduced to a subject people by the middle of the eighties. At that time they numbered about 260,000, exclusive of the bands in Alaska. A small portion of them were civilized or taxable Indians who had abandoned their tribal relations and settled in white communities; but the vast majority dwelt on western reservations, where the land was owned collectively by the tribe, and they subsisted partly or almost wholly upon the largess of the United States. According to President Cleveland's annual message of 1885, these Indian lands, aggregating an area almost as large as France, "are included in the boundaries of 171 reservations of different dimensions, scattered in 21 States and Territories, presenting great variations in climate and in the kind and quality of their soils. Among the Indians . . . exist the most marked differences in natural traits and disposition and in their progress toward civilization," some being "vicious and stupid" and others industrious, peace-abiding, and capable of self-government.

Since 1819 the federal government had made modest appropriations to aid missionary schools among the Indians, but about 1873 Congress inaugurated a new policy by appropriating money to be used directly by the government in their education. From $20,000, the annual subsidy increased until it passed the million-dollar mark within fifteen years. Three types of government schools were developed: neighborhood day-schools for elementary instruction, reservation boarding-schools, and non-reservation boarding-schools. The special object of Indian education was to instruct the boys and girls in agriculture, housework, and other practical pursuits necessary to fit them for a part in complex modern life. In 1880 more than 7000 Indian children were in school, and not less than twice that number of adults were engaged in occupations for which they had been trained in the schools.

It was fully realized by Grant and his successors in office that education in itself could not civilize the savages, so long as the old reservation life continued with its tribal ownership of property, dependence on governmental rations, and other enervating influences. But repeated recommendations for reform were, for a number of years, unheeded by Congress. Two sets of influences, however, led eventually to a change of policy. One of these was a strong humanitarian protest on the part of Easterners who where shocked at the wholesale disregard of the red man's rights both by the frontiersmen and the government. This sentiment found its strongest emotional expression in Helen Hunt Jackson's book, *A Century of Dishonor*, published in 1881, and was responsible for the formation of the Indian Rights Association in 1882. Such people desired to free the Indian from the guardianship of the government and set his feet firmly upon the path to civilization. The other influence was the growing conviction that, with the rapid exhaustion of the open frontier country, the uneconomic use of millions of acres given over to Indian occupancy should no longer be tolerated.

Sometime before entering the presidency, Mrs. Jackson's book fell into Cleveland's hands, and he was deeply affected by its pathetic portrayal of Indian mistreatment. Consequently, as President, he actively interested himself in the question, and made the recommendation to Congress, which resulted in the passage of the Dawes Severalty Act on February 8, 1887, the "Emancipation Act of the Indians." According to its provisions, the President might, whenever he deemed proper, terminate the tribal government and communal ownership of land in the case of any tribe, and divide the land among the tribesmen at the rate of a quartersection to each head of family and smaller allotments to others.[1] As a safeguard against improvident management the individual owners were denied the right to mortgage or sell their property for a space of twenty-five years. In all other respects, however, they should be on an equal footing with white citizens, and the adult males were to possess the right to vote. If any tribal land remained after the allotments were made, the government reserved the right to buy the surplus and open it to settlement, the purchase money to be held in trust by the United States with annual interest payments to the Indians.

Steady progress was made under the Dawes Act in bridging the

[1] A supplementary Act of 1891 provided for allotments of 80 acres, share and share alike. The Dawes Act did not apply to the Five Civilized Tribes in Indian Territory, which were dealt with under separate arrangements.

gap between barbarism and civilization. Between 1887 and 1906, 150,123 Indians were given allotments under this law and certain special enactments, aggregating 21,255,391 acres. At the same time, 53,314,220 acres were opened to white settlement or set aside as forest preserves. But experience revealed some serious defects in the statute. Many of the individuals to whom the Act was applied were unprepared for the abrupt assumption of the franchise, and fell an easy prey to unscrupulous white politicians. Moreover, as citizens, they enjoyed the right to buy liquor, and this led to a great increase of drunkenness. When Congress in 1897 forbade the sale of intoxicants to them, the Supreme Court in 1905 held the law unconstitutional.[1]

On the other hand, the twenty-five-year period of apprenticeship necessary for final ownership proved a discouragement to ambitious and capable Indians. In consequence, a supplementary act was passed in 1906, the Burke Law, which empowered the Secretary of Interior thereafter to bestow full property title upon deserving individuals, whenever satisfied of their fitness, without waiting for the expiration of the usual period. It also postponed American citizenship and the ballot until full ownership was granted, and thereby rendered illegal the sale of intoxicants to Indians during the period of probation.

The new policy of assimilation has been amply justified by the results. By 1923, nearly 185,000 of the 345,000 Indians achieved citizenship under the Dawes and Burke Acts. Despite the tendency of the old "blanket" Indians to resist change, marked improvement appeared in health, sanitation, housing conditions, marital relations, and the position of women. Increasing numbers of children received instruction in the special Indian schools, and as the reservations were gradually broken up, they attended the regular public schools side by side with white children. Somewhat more than half of the 65,000 Indian boys and girls in school in 1923 were enrolled in the public schools. In 1924 Congress took the significant step of granting citizenship to every Indian born in the United States.

Equally noteworthy has been the red man's material progress, particularly in farming and stockraising. Unexpected riches came to many Indians with the discovery of oil and gas in Okla-

[1] United States *v.* Heff.

homa early in the twentieth century. The typical Indian today is a settled landholder and homebuilder. The pure strain is rapidly becoming diluted through intermarriage with the whites, and the day will doubtless come when the American aborigine, like many another conquered race, will disappear in the blood of his conqueror.

The Riddle of the Negro

The negroes offered a problem of a somewhat different character, due to their greater number, their racial traits, and their former condition of slavery. In 1880 there were six and one-half million colored people in the United States. The great bulk of them dwelt in the old slave states where they formed more than one third of the population. By the Fourteenth and Fifteenth amendments, their civil and political rights were under the care of the national government, but after the withdrawal of the troops from the South by Hayes in 1877, the authorities at Washington were disinclined to interfere further in their behalf. The North, a little tired of the negro problem, a little doubtful of the wisdom of its Reconstruction policy, and increasingly absorbed in its own affairs, was coming to feel that the race question was one for the Southern whites to solve. Furthermore, the Republican party was at no time in complete control of Congress and the presidency from 1875 to 1889.

Under these favoring circumstances, the native whites in charge of the Southern state governments proceeded systematically to deprive the colored race of the suffrage through discriminatory legislation and ingenious electoral regulations. For example, the illiterate negro was effectively discouraged in South Carolina by the requirement that, with eight or more ballot boxes before the voter, he must select the proper ballot for each one in order to insure its being counted. A common practice in some states was to establish the polling places at points remote from the negro settlements, or else to change the location of the polls on the eve of an election without notice to the blacks. In Mississippi, negro representation in the legislature was kept at a minimum by the creation of the famous "shoestring district," three hundred miles long and about twenty wide, embracing nearly all the densest colored communities of the state. Stuffing of the ballot box by the whites was also resorted to without compunctions of conscience.

Encouraged by their success in reducing the vote by irregular means, the Southern states after 1890 undertook boldly to alter those provisions of their constitutions, which, since Reconstruction times, had guaranteed political equality to the negroes. Mississippi set the pace in that year by a constitutional requirement that a citizen, in order to vote, must have paid his taxes for the preceding two years, and must, in addition, "be able to read any section of the Constitution of this State, or to understand the same when read to him, or give a reasonable interpretation thereof." The flexible intelligence qualification was adopted confessedly in order to enable the election officials to disfranchise illiterate blacks without disfranchising illiterate whites.

The new scheme, with modifications and variations, was presently adopted by South Carolina, Louisiana, Alabama, North Carolina, Virginia, and Georgia. When the Mississippi provision was attacked before the Supreme Court as contrary to the Fifteenth Amendment, the court held that proof must be given that the actual administration of the suffrage clause was evil and not simply that evil was possible.[1] Under the new restrictions the proportion of colored voters continued to decline. Torn from his giddy heights of Reconstruction times, the negro became a negligible factor in Southern politics.

In most respects, the negro was permitted to enjoy the same civil rights as those of the white man, but where the races were apt to come into social contact, barriers were erected. Tennessee passed the first "Jim Crow" law in 1881 by requiring separate compartments or coaches on railways for the two peoples. Presently the negroes in most Southern states found themselves

[1] Williams *v.* Mississippi (1898). Southern ingenuity was not yet exhausted. Beginning in 1898, Louisiana, North Carolina, and Oklahoma (1910) amended their constitutions in order to exempt from the onerous educational and taxpaying tests all male adults whose ancestors had voted prior to the adoption of the Fifteenth Amendment. In the two former cases, the persons so qualifying were given a limited period for registration, whereupon their names were placed upon a permanent voting list. Oklahoma imposed no time limit for registration. The "grandfather clauses" were held unconstitutional by the Supreme Court in 1915 as a clear violation of the Fifteenth Amendment. Guinn *v.* United States; Myers *v.* Anderson. Closely analogous to these clauses was the "old-soldier clause," adopted by Alabama, Virginia, and Georgia from 1901 to 1908, which exempted from the usual qualifications all propertyless soldiers and sailors, who had fought in wars prior to 1902, and their descendants.

compelled, by law or custom, to accept separate accommodations in public conveyances, restaurants, and theaters. Laws were also enacted against intermarriage.

The color line was likewise applied to the public schools, where special and usually inferior training and facilities were provided for black children. Nevertheless, negro illiteracy declined from seventy per cent in 1880 to fifty-seven per cent in 1890 and forty-four in 1900. Active race friction leading to lynchings and burnings usually developed in localities where the two peoples were about evenly divided or where the worst elements of the two races came into collision. Such disgraceful affrays, however, have been the exception rather than the rule.

Fortunately, the right to acquire property and establish a home, perhaps the greatest privilege of all, was in no way abridged by the dominant race. In the cultivation of the habits of thrift and industry, the negroes owed much to the teachings of Booker T. Washington, a great colored leader, who in 1881 founded a Normal and Industrial Institute at Tuskegee, Alabama, for his people. Deploring the tendency of negro demagogues to agitate incessantly for equality, he constantly urged the race to "make itself so valuable to the community in which it lives that it will not merely be tolerated, like a poor relative, but rather welcomed and sought after." "The opportunity to earn a dollar in a factory," he declared, "is just now worth infinitely more than the opportunity to spend a dollar in an opera house."

The majority of the negroes continued to live on the land, as in slavery times, and acquired full ownership as rapidly as circumstances permitted. As early as 1874 colored farmers owned 338,769 acres, and in the next decade this acreage doubled. By 1890, nearly one fifth of all the homes occupied by colored heads of families were owned by their tenants. The value of the agricultural land owned by negroes aggregated more than $100,000,000 in 1900. In that year they farmed more than one sixth of the improved acreage of the South, and raised more than one sixth of the gross products. This progress was a substantial testimonial to a people who were practically landless in 1860.

Domestic and personal service proved to be the next most popular occupation. The number engaged in manufacturing and mechanical pursuits and in professional callings was small in comparison. The colored population increased after 1880 at the rate of one million a decade, a smaller ratio than the dominant race, and there was a steadily growing appreciation on the part of the whites of the important place that the negro wage-earner occupied in Southern economic life.

The New Immigrant Invasion

A third race problem, unlike that of either the Indians or the negroes, was presented by the increasing numbers of Chinese on the Pacific Coast. When Chinese laborers first went to California in the fifties and sixties, they were welcomed as a source of cheap labor; Leland Stanford and other captains of industry gladly imported whole shiploads of them. By 1870 there were 56,000 Chinese in the United States. While this feeling of cordiality was still uppermost, the Burlingame Treaty was made with China in 1868, which explicitly recognized the "inalienable right of man to change his home and allegiance, and also the mutual advantage of the free migration and emigration" of persons between the two countries.

Almost at once public sentiment on the Coast underwent a change. The number of unskilled white laborers grew rapidly in California with the completion of the transcontinental railways. In the competition for work, the whites found themselves pitted against a people who lived on a lower plane of subsistence, and who eagerly accepted working conditions that were repugnant to Caucasians. Racial differences, of course, served to sharpen the feeling of antagonism. In 1871 a race riot in Los Angeles ended in the killing of twenty-one Orientals, and for the next ten years, the Chinese question was one of commanding importance in California politics. A special political party was formed with the slogan, "The Chinese must go"; mob attacks were made upon the Chinese quarter of San Francisco; and discriminatory laws were passed by the legislature, though most of these were subsequently annulled by the courts.

The violence of the agitation in time excited the attention of Congress. In 1879 the Democratic House and Republican Senate, vying with each other for the electoral vote of California, passed an act restricting Chinese immigration and abrogating the Burlingame Treaty. Though sympathetic with the purpose of the measure, President Hayes deprecated the peremptory mode of procedure. Therefore, while attaching his veto to the bill, he dispatched a special commission to China, which presently effected a new understanding with that country. By the Treaty of 1880, the United States was permitted to "regulate, limit, or suspend," though not absolutely to prohibit, the future admission of Chinese laborers.

Two years later Congress adopted the first Chinese Exclusion Act, suspending the immigration of Chinese workingmen for a space of ten years. Subsequent laws renewed the period of suspension from time to time, and in 1902 Congress made the prohibition of indefinite duration. Though China in 1904 refused to give further treaty sanction to the practice, the American government has felt justified in continuing Chinese exclusion on its own authority as a measure of domestic welfare.

European immigration had been permitted without let or hindrance since colonial times, but early in the eighties occurred a change in the character of the alien arrivals which led to the adoption of a new national policy toward them. Before that time the bulk of the newcomers consisted of peasants from Germany, the British Isles, and, more latterly, the Scandinavian countries. Of the total foreignborn population numbering 6,680,000 in 1880, 1,967,000 were Germans, 1,855,000 Irish, 717,000 Canadians, 664,000 English, and 440,000 Scandinavians. These people, the Irish excepted, generally became farmers, and in 1880 more of them were to be found in the states of the Upper Mississippi Valley than in any other part of the country. These alien stocks, however, were easily assimilated, for they represented the same racial strains as those from which the Anglo-Saxon people had originally sprung, and with plenty of land open for settlement, their coming caused little shock to the economic structure.

The year 1882 stands as a landmark in the history of European immigration. In that year the number of arrivals reached the unprecedented figure of nearly 790,000, a total not again equaled until 1903; the influx from western and central Europe reached its climax; and immigrants first began to appear in noticeable numbers from eastern and southern Europe. After 1882 the arrivals from Italy, Austria-Hungary, southern Russia, and other Mediterranean countries increased steadily until, by 1896, they exceeded in volume the immigrants of the older type.

Many influences were responsible for the changed makeup of

EUROPEAN SOURCES OF AMERICAN IMMIGRATION IN THE LATE NINETEENTH AND EARLY TWENTIETH CENTURIES

immigration, none more important perhaps than the overcrowded conditions in southern and eastern Europe, the anti-Semitic persecution in Russia beginning about 1881, the opening of direct steamship connections between the Mediterranean ports and the United States, the unexampled opportunities for manual labor in the new American mines and factories, and the decline of the older immigration because of unwillingness to compete with laborers maintaining a lower plane of existence. Steamship companies stimulated the new immigration to the extent of their advertising ability, and labor agents representing American corporations often prepaid the passage of the newcomers.

The new immigration marked a sharp divergence from the earlier type in economic standards, racial traits, education, and familiarity with democratic institutions and ideals. The most wretched working conditions represented an improvement over those to which these men were accustomed in their homelands, with the consequence that native American wage-earners found it difficult to compete with them. Crowding into the great cities and the industrial centers, they usually formed special communities of their own, with their peculiar institutions and foreign-language newspapers, and vastly complicated the problems of policing, sanitation, and housing for the municipal authorities.

Moreover, approximately one third of them returned to their places of origin after they had accumulated a little money. They, accordingly, lacked the incentive to learn American ways, or to work for the improvement of American laboring conditions. More than thirty-five per cent of them were illiterate, as compared with three per cent in the case of the old immigrant class. Individuals among them were, of course, equal to the best that the older immigration produced; and it is only fair to say of the mass of the newer arrivals that, according to an extensive governmental inquiry, they were "not recruited in the main from the lowest economic and social strata" of the European population.

Indeed, just as the older immigrants had accelerated the agricultural expansion of the nation, the Slavs, Magyars, Poles, Greeks, Russian Jews, and Italians hastened its industrial and commercial development, being available at a time when thousands of Americans were taking up Western lands. Furthermore, the children of the immigrants, born in the United States, generally showed marked progress over their parents, an improvement due largely to the Americanizing influence exerted by compulsory attendance in the public schools.

The swelling tide of immigration from southern and eastern Europe coincided with the adoption of a new national policy toward incoming aliens. There was, as yet, no desire on the part of the United States to relinquish its historic rôle as a refuge for the oppressed of all lands, but the conviction was growing that, with the filling up of the country and the dwindling of the open frontier, some form of selective immigration was desirable. The first important restrictive law, that of 1882, excluded from entry into the United States lunatics, idiots, persons likely to become public charges, and criminals. Three years later the Alien Contract Labor Law, enacted at the behest of organized labor, forbade American employers to import foreign workingmen under a previous contract of labor.

Every few years saw the adoption of additional restraints until in the early years of the twentieth century the excluded classes embraced physical, mental, and moral defectives of all kinds, professional beggars, polygamists, and anarchists. A strong sentiment developed for the application of a literacy test to the newcomers, but this was as vigorously opposed by persons who insisted that the ability to read would be a test of youthful opportunity rather than of mental endowment. A bill for this purpose, adopted by Congress in 1897, was rejected by President Cleveland, and failed of passage over his veto only by a few votes in the Senate.

The sheer magnitude of the immigration after 1865 is a source of amazement. Between that year and 1900 no less than 13,260,000 foreigners of all kinds entered the United States, enough to populate Illinois or Holland twice over today, and the volume became larger in the opening years of the new century. What effect these alien infusions, particularly those from Mediterranean Europe, may have upon American character and ideals, it is too early to say. A hot controversy has raged over the question whether the net result will be to debase or to enrich the earlier native stock.

Modern immigration has caused the racial complexion of certain sections to change in startling ways. For example, as early as 1888, James Bryce noticed in the case of New England that the "old race of New England yeomen" were moving out and giving way to Irish immigrants and French Canadians, and "thus that which was the most purely English part of America is now becoming one of the most Celtic." Students of the subject are agreed that the great influx of foreigners has not enlarged our total population, for by increasing the competition for employment, it has tended to encourage late or childless marriages among native families and thereby to retard the growth of the old American stock.

SELECT BIBLIOGRAPHY

The New Indian Policy. The most nearly satisfactory exposition is *The Indian and His Problem* (New York, 1910) by F. E. Leupp, former Commissioner of Indian Affairs. G. E. E. Lindquist, comp., *The Red Man in the United States* (New York, 1923) presents the results of an inquiry, made under the auspices of the Interchurch World Movement, into the present situation of the Indians, and is especially good as a picture of their economic and social conditions.

The Riddle of the Negro. The process of negro disfranchisement is sketched in W. A. Dunning, *Essays on the Civil War and Reconstruction* (New York, 1904), and Holland Thompson, *The New South* (in *The Chronicles of America*, XLII, New Haven, 1919).

The question of race adjustments and relations is discussed, from the negro point of view, in Benjamin Brawley, *A Social History of the American Negro* (New York, 1921), C. G. Woodson, *The Negro in Our History* (Washington, 1922), Kelly Miller, *Race Adjustment* (New York, 1908), and W. E. B. Du Bois, *The Negro* (in *Home University Library*, New York, 1915). The white man's viewpoint is set forth in an extensive literature, of which the following books may be mentioned: M. S. Evans, *Black and White in the Southern States* (New York, 1915), Holland Thompson, *The New South* (previously cited), R. S. Baker, *Following the Color Line* (New York, 1908), and A. H. Stone, *Studies in the American Race Problem* (New York, 1908). The story of Tuskegee may be found in convenient form in M. B. Thrasher, *Tuskegee* (Boston, 1900).

The New Immigrant Invasion. An excellent sketch of the problems raised by Chinese immigration is included in E. E. Sparks, *National Development* (in *The American Nation*, XXIII, New York, 1907). Mary R. Coolidge, *Chinese Immigration* (New York, 1909), is detailed and authoritative. Valuable discussions of the new influx from Mediterranean Europe may be found in J. R. Commons, *Races and Immigrants in America* (New York, 1920), P. F. Hall, *Immigration, and its Effects upon the United States* (New York, 1906), H. P. Fairchild, *Immigration, a World Movement and its American Significance* (New York, 1913), J. W. Jenks and W. J. Lauck, *The Immigration Problem* (New York, 1922), S. P. Orth, *Our Foreigners* (in *The Chronicles of America*, XXXV, New Haven, 1920), Peter Roberts, *The New Immigration* (New York, 1912), E. A. Ross, *The Old World in the New* (New York, 1914), and F. J. Warne, *The Tide of Immigration* (New York, 1916). Some of the newer immigrant elements have received special study, as in Emily G. Balch, *Our Slavic Fellow Citizens* (New York, 1910), C. S. Bernheimer, ed., *The Russian Jew in the United States* (Philadelphia, 1905), Thomas Burgess, *Greeks in America* (Boston, 1913), and Eliot Lord, J. J. D. Trenor and S. J. Barrows, *The Italian in America* (New York, 1905).

CHAPTER XX

PARTY CONFLICT AND THE TARIFF QUESTION, 1883-1897

Cleveland as Party Leader

In some of the humanitarian movements that have been described, President Cleveland played a part, at times a conspicuous one, as in the case of the Dawes Severalty Act. But the activities of his administration which aroused party rancor and caused him to leave an indelible impress upon American political history were of a different character. Cleveland rode into office upon a wave of protest against reactionary Republicanism rather than because of a popular preference for the Democrats. Countless voters who had personal confidence in the new Chief Executive cherished a deep distrust of his party. Indeed, many unreconciled Republicans in the North looked upon the victory of the Democrats as tantamount to a rebel triumph, and gloomily predicted the payment of the Confederate debt and the reëstablishment of slavery.

While such notions were manifestly absurd, it is true that the Democrats had been out of power for so long a time that their ranks contained many discordant elements. The party had been guided by opportunism rather than by principle in the elections of the past twenty years. To Cleveland fell the choice — as many years before it had fallen to Jackson — of allowing his followers to continue to be infirm of purpose and torn with internal strife, or of reorganizing them upon an uncompromising program of principles. Cleveland was happily situated to pursue the sterner course. A newcomer in national politics, he was unhampered by political entanglements; and by temperament, he was equally impervious to flattery and to threats. Possessing few preconceptions as to public questions when he entered office, he arrived at his convictions as the result of unremitting study, and his conclusions, once reached, became his inflexible guide of conduct.

The touchstone of all his political thinking was unmistakably indicated in his inaugural address when he declared, "The people demand reform in the administration of the government and the application of business principles to public affairs." Like the reform leaders in the Republican party, he was interested principally in questions of administrative efficiency, and was largely indifferent to those profound influences which were already making for labor unrest and class friction. The opportunity of the Democrats, however, either for good or ill was seriously limited, for the Senate remained Republican throughout Cleveland's term. The new policies, therefore, did not take the form of statutes, but were embodied in presidential recommendations, executive orders, and veto messages.

Cleveland's cabinet, while containing men unknown to the nation, compared favorably with any selected by his Republican predecessors in ability and integrity, being headed by Thomas F. Bayard of Delaware as Secretary of State. The "Solid South" was expressly recognized by the appointment of two Southern Senators, A. H. Garland of Arkansas and L. Q. C. Lamar of Mississippi, to the offices of Attorney-General and Secretary of the Interior.[1]

The President's sincerity as a civil-service reformer was subjected to a severe test by the Democratic hunger for "spoils." Old-time party spokesmen, like A. P. Gorman in the Senate and Samuel J. Randall in the House, openly flouted the "Goody Two-Shoes" reform, and even introduced bills for the repeal or modification of the Pendleton Act. Being almost alone in his party as a champion of the cause, Cleveland had to make progress slowly if he were to avoid party dissensions which would be fatal to the success of other things he hoped to accomplish. Judged by the results, his policy was to appease the politicians with appointments and removals in the unclassified service, and to do this most freely in those parts of the country where there was little local support for the merit system. He even defended

[1] The other members were: Daniel Manning of New York, Secretary of the Treasury; W. C. Whitney of New York, Secretary of the Navy; W. C. Endicott of Massachusetts, Secretary of War; and W. F. Vilas of Wisconsin, Postmaster-General.

this policy on the plea that, with the offices monopolized by Republicans, an "equalization" of appointments was in the interests of a nonpartisan service.

Upon occasion he won the unstinted praise of civil-service reformers by resisting party pressure, and then again he sorely disappointed them by his apparent surrender to the spoilsmen. In a letter to Dorman B. Eaton in 1885, he spoke feelingly of "the conditions which bound and qualify every struggle for a radical improvement in the affairs of government." Despite his frequent concessions to the politicians, he preserved the classified service almost intact, and strengthened the reformed system materially in 1887 by extending the competitive principle to include promotions within the public service. By the close of his term he had succeeded in doubling the number of positions under the merit rules.

Cleveland's desire to apply efficient business standards to governmental operation led to a determined effort to do away with laxness and fraud in the granting of pensions. One of the worst abuses was the practice of Congress of passing special pension acts to satisfy claimants whose applications had been, or were likely to be, rejected by the Pension Bureau. The President vetoed 233 bills of this character after painstaking examination.[1] More than one hundred others became law without his signature because there was not time for proper investigation.

When Congress in 1887 passed a general pension bill applying to all dependent veterans who had served three months or more, Cleveland vetoed it on the ground that its loose phraseology would make the pension list a refuge for the dishonest instead of a roll of honor. Coming in close conjunction with an executive order (later revoked) for returning the captured Confederate battle-flags, the veto was regarded by the old-soldier element as proof of the unpatriotic character of the party in power.[2] Nevertheless,

[1] In his veto messages Cleveland set forth the fraudulent or worthless character of these claims. For example, one applicant who alleged "long and faithful service" was shown to have spent most of his period of service in prison on the charge of desertion. In another case a pension was sought by the widow of a veteran whose death had been the result of accidental shooting by a neighbor who was trying to kill an owl. Another soldier applied for a pension, alleging permanent injuries sustained from falling into a cellar while on a furlough.

[2] In a public address in 1887, Senator John Sherman termed the Democratic party "the left wing of the new Confederate army." It is worth noting that, when Congress ordered the return of the battleflags in 1905, the act was looked upon as "graceful" instead of "disgraceful."

Cleveland signed many more private pension bills than he vetoed, and in his four years the aggregate annual appropriation for pensions grew from $56,000,000 to $81,000,000.

Cleveland's desire to keep expenditures within reasonable bounds was further evinced by his refusal to sign an extravagant river-and-harbors bill of 1887, and by his rejection of a measure passed in December, 1888, for returning to the states the direct tax of 1861, amounting to $15,000,000. In all his vetoes, he was rebuking a House of Representatives controlled by his own party, as well as a Senate controlled by the opposition.

The Surplus Revenue and the Tariff Question

The President's interest in "the application of business principles to public affairs" caused him to devote increasing attention to the tariff, a subject concerning which he knew little when he entered office. Commencing in 1881, a surplus had begun to pile up in the treasury at the rate of more than $100,000,000 annually, representing the excess of government income over current expenditures. The existence of a surplus revenue indicated, of course, that the people were paying heavier taxes than was necessary, and that money needed for business development was being kept out of circulation. Moreover, the overflowing treasury tempted Congress to intemperate and ill-considered expenditures — "surplus financiering," as it was called. Some of the money was devoted to reducing the national debt, but more characteristic of the period were the "pork-barrel" measures, such as Arthur and Cleveland vetoed, and the lavish outlays for pensions.

The Republicans, by extravagant appropriations, hoped to divert attention from the Tariff of 1875, which was chiefly responsible for the excessive revenue. In the face of a growing popular demand, however, President Arthur urged upon Congress the need of relieving "industry and enterprise from the pressure of unnecessary taxation." In May, 1882, Congress, somewhat reluctantly, provided for a special commission to study American industries and propose a revision of the tariff "that would be just to all interests." All the members appointed were protectionists by conviction. Indeed, four of the nine were directly connected with important protected industries, including the Chairman, John L. Hayes, Secretary of the National Association of Wool Manufacturers. After investigating conditions in many parts of the country, the Tariff Commission, to the surprise of many, recommended reductions averaging from twenty to twenty-five per cent.

Since Congress had the final word in the matter, a great throng of lobbyists now descended upon Washington, including Hayes himself, who, in his capacity as spokesman for the wool manufacturers, endeavored now to defeat the recommendations which he, as Chairman of the Tariff Commission, had favored. Senator Morrill, Senator Nelson W. Aldrich, Representatives "Pig Iron" Kelley, William McKinley of Ohio, and others, rallied to the protectionist cause; and as finally enacted, the Tariff of 1883 left the protective system virtually unchanged. Substantial cuts were made in internal-revenue duties, but the reductions in import duties averaged less than five per cent, and these were made on manufactures which were least affected by foreign competition.

The attitude of the Democrats on the tariff question had been wavering and ill-defined since the Civil War. Indeed, prominent leaders of the party, like Randall of Pennsylvania, who voted for the Tariff of 1883, were ardent protectionists. Although the Democrats had controlled the House of Representatives from 1875 to 1881, no bills had been passed for tariff reduction. Nevertheless, there was a growing sentiment in the party, particularly in the farming regions, for tariff reform.

This feeling was well represented in the new Democratic House, which met in December, 1883, by John G. Carlisle of Kentucky, who defeated Randall for Speaker, and by W. R. Morrison of Illinois, Chairman of the Ways and Means Committee. A bill was introduced by Morrison early in 1884 for a horizontal reduction of twenty per cent upon most import duties, but notwithstanding a Democratic plurality of seventy-eight in the House, it failed because of a combination of the Republican minority with forty-one Randall Democrats. In the Democratic convention of 1884 the protectionists were ascendant, and as has been seen, Cleveland was elected on a platform which pledged tariff revision that would not "injure any domestic industries."

Cleveland was a man little given to abstract theories, and at no time did he have any sympathy with that extreme form of tariff doctrine known as "free trade." But his sense of propriety was outraged by the annual appearance of a large excess of revenue, and after assiduous study of the problem, he determined to attack the evil at its source. His resolution was stiffened by the continued success of the Randall Democrats in the House in defeating efforts to lower the tariff. From a rather vague and casual indorsement of tariff reduction in his message of 1885, he became more definite in 1886, and finally in December, 1887, he defied all precedent and startled the country by devoting his entire annual message to the imperative need of immediate action.

Stigmatizing the Tariff of 1883 as "the vicious, inequitable and illogical source of unnecessary taxation," he declared that the surplus revenue would inevitably produce business stagnation. He charged that the high tariff had already raised the cost of living for the masses in order to give "immense profits" to an exclusive class of manufacturers. As a remedy, he proposed "a readjustment" which would eliminate the "hardships and dangers" of the present tariff without, however, "imperiling the existence of our manufacturing interests." He excluded theoretical considerations as irrelevant, for, he added, in a phrase quick to catch the public ear, "It is a *condition* which confronts us, not a theory." A careful reading of the message makes clear that the President contended for a tariff for revenue primarily, the protective features to be confined within the narrowest possible limits.

Cleveland's thunderclap cleared the air for his party. The Mills bill of 1888, framed in accord with his recommendations, enlarged the free list, and provided for a general reduction of protective duties. Support of the measure was made a quasi-test of party loyalty. It passed the House in July with only four Democrats dissenting. Since the Senate was Republican, further action on the tariff awaited the outcome of the presidential election.

Cleveland was renominated by acclamation at the Democratic national convention, meeting in St. Louis on June 5, 1888. The platform was largely devoted to commendation of his stand on the tariff, and Allen G. Thurman of Ohio was named for

Vice-President. The Republicans were without an outstanding candidate, for Blaine refused to allow his name to be considered. When their convention met in Chicago on June 19, the nomination finally went on the eighth ballot to ex-Senator Benjamin Harrison of Indiana, a Civil-War veteran and strong protectionist. Levi P. Morton of New York was chosen for second place. The platform contained a resounding indorsement of the "American system of protection," promised additional pensions "in the presence of an overflowing treasury," and declared that reduction in the revenue should be accomplished, if need be, by abolishing all internal-revenue taxes.

The campaign was the first one in American history to turn mainly on the tariff issue. Eager to discredit the position of their opponents, Republican orators dubbed the Democrats "free traders," although the Democratic platform expressly declared that the tariff rates should make "due allowance for the difference between the wages of American and foreign labor." Strong appeals were made to the protected manufacturers for funds for the Republican cause. A circular letter, issued by the Philadelphia merchant, John Wanamaker, as spokesman for the Republican national committee, asked: "If you were confronted with from one to three years of general depression by a change in our revenue and protective methods, what would you pay to be insured for a better year?" The manufacturers responded with the utmost liberality. In Indiana and other close states, it appears that large sums of money were spent by the Republicans with an unsparing and not too scrupulous hand.[1]

Neither party forgot the influence of the Irish vote in the election of 1884, and both platforms feelingly, though prematurely, congratulated the Irish-Americans upon the approach of "home rule" in Ireland. This time the advantage lay with the Republicans, for Democratic tariff reform was susceptible of being represented as a surrender to British manufacturing interests. A popular campaign document presented the names of the Democratic candidates under the British flag and the Republican ticket under the Stars and Stripes, and printed a statement,

[1] One good result of the corruption of the campaign was the impetus given to the adoption of the Australian ballot system, providing for secret, uniform, and officially printed ballots. Massachusetts acted in May, 1888, and by 1896 the reform had spread to thirty-eight states, and in a partial form, to four others.

falsely ascribed to the *London Times*, "The only time England can use an Irishman is when he emigrates to America and votes for free trade."[1]

Next to the tariff, Cleveland's pension vetoes came in for bitter Republican condemnation. The President received only half-hearted backing from the professional politicians within his own party, and in New York there is good reason to believe that Tammany Hall threw its support to his opponent. In the election, Harrison carried the large states by small pluralities and thereby secured an electoral majority of 233 to 168, though in the popular vote Cleveland was the favorite, polling nearly 48.7 per cent to 47.8 per cent for Harrison.

Extreme Republicanism and Tariff Protection

Harrison's chief claim to distinction prior to his elevation consisted in his long and faithful service to his party. As President he shrank from leadership, and although gentle by nature, the coldness of his demeanor tended to antagonize even his political friends, and gave coinage to the saying, "Harrison sweats ice-water." From the outset he leaned heavily upon the men identified with the Republican organization: Blaine, who had been influential in bringing about his nomination; Speaker Thomas B. Reed of Maine, whose iron rule of the new House of Representatives won for him the sobriquet of "Czar"; and to a lesser extent, on large-state "bosses" like Senator Matthew S. Quay of Pennsylvania, and Senator Platt of "Me Too" fame. Harrison made Blaine head of his cabinet, and rewarded Wanamaker for his doughty campaign services with the office of Postmaster-General.[2]

In his dispensing of patronage, he permitted the spoilsmen to have almost unobstructed sway in the unclassified service. J. S.

[1] In pursuance of the same purpose, Lord Sackville-West, the British Minister at Washington, was tricked into writing a letter to a supposed former fellow-countryman, in which he declared that Cleveland, if elected, would be friendly to England. This correspondence was given wide publicity by the Republicans.

[2] The other members were: William Windom of Minnesota, Secretary of the Treasury; Redfield Proctor of Vermont, Secretary of War; W. H. H. Miller of Indiana, Attorney-General; B. F. Tracy of New York, Secretary of the Navy; J. W. Noble of Missouri, Secretary of the Interior; and J. M. Rusk of Wisconsin, Secretary of Agriculture (a cabinet portfolio created in 1889).

Clarkson of Iowa, First Assistant Postmaster-General, fairly won the title of "headsman" by changing thirty thousand officials in a single year before he himself was beheaded. In emulation of Grant, Harrison himself conferred a long list of appointments upon his relatives by blood and marriage. On the other hand, after waiting two years, he extended the merit system to certain new classes of offices. His greatest service to the cause, however, was the appointment, as Chairman of the Civil Service Commission, of Theodore Roosevelt, whose aggressive championship of the reform made his name a source of real terror to the politicians of both parties during his six years' tenure.

Congress, now Republican in both branches, quickly set about to deal with the problem of the surplus revenue. The platform allusion to "the overflowing treasury" was not forgotten, and James ("Corporal") Tanner of New York, when he took up his duties as Commissioner of Pensions, is reputed to have cried, "God help the surplus revenue!" At any rate, in the six months during which he was permitted to remain, he encouraged new claimants, reopened cases that had formerly been rejected, and increased the amounts of allowances already granted.

In June, 1890, the general pension bill, which had been vetoed by Cleveland, was repassed by Congress. This act embodied a new principle, that of granting pensions to veterans and their families where the disability was not due to military service. During Harrison's administration the annual outlay for pensions rose from $81,000,000 to $135,000,000. In 1891 Congress also repassed the bill to refund the direct tax to the states, which Cleveland had vetoed, and thereby made away with $15,000,000 more of the surplus. Increased appropriations for naval purposes account for other expenditures of this "billion-dollar" Congress.

The Republican leaders well understood that such methods dealt with symptoms rather than with causes; but, committed as they were to the high-tariff system, they were unwilling to tamper with the source of the exuberant revenue at the cost of impairing protection. Accordingly, their problem was to find some way of reducing the surplus without reducing protection. The solution was worked out by William McKinley, former disciple of "Pig Iron" Kelley and now Chairman of the Ways and Means Committee. As a son and grandson of iron manufacturers, McKinley had for many years made high protection the central article of his political faith. His philosophy may thus be summed up in his own words: "We lead all nations in Agriculture, we lead all nations in Mining, and we lead all nations in Manufacturing. These are the trophies which we bring after twenty-nine years of a Protective Tariff. Can any other system furnish such evidences of prosperity?" Elsewhere he gave frequent utterance to his conviction that protection also assured steady employment and high wages to the laboring class.

The McKinley Tariff of 1890 lifted the general level of duties from 38 to 49.5 per cent. Yet, in consequence of ingenious arrangements, the result was a less abundant revenue than before. For example, the sum of $50,000,000 was eliminated by removing the duty on raw sugar, though American growers continued to be protected by the new device of a bounty of two cents on each pound of sugar raised. This subsidy represented another slice of $10,000,000 from the surplus revenue. In other cases, such as cotton and woolen textiles and metal products, the tariff rates were raised to the point of practically excluding foreign importations. A further cut in the revenues resulted from the removal of the internal-revenue taxes on tobacco and alcohol.

In other respects, as well, the law was unique. At President Harrison's suggestion, an effort was made to extend the benefits of protection to the farmer as well as to the manufacturer. Accordingly, the duties on farm products were substantially increased. A second novel feature, that of reciprocity, was introduced at the urgency of Blaine, who charged that the original bill disregarded the interests of our growing export trade, and particularly the possibilities of commerce with Latin America. By this arrangement, certain articles commonly imported from Latin-American countries, such as molasses, tea, coffee, and hides, were placed on the free list, with the proviso that the President might impose duties on them in the case of any nation which levied "unjust or unreasonable" duties on American products.

The high rates prescribed by the new Tariff Act were quickly reflected in retail prices, and caused widespread dissatisfaction. The fall elections of 1890, coming about a month after the

McKinley Tariff went into effect, resulted in a stinging defeat for the Republicans. They lost nearly one half of their strength in the House, and the Democrats lacked but a few votes of a three-fourths majority. McKinley himself was among the defeated candidates. While this popular verdict came as a surprise, the law met the expectations of its framers in drying up the source of superabundant revenue. The provisions for revenue reduction, together with Congress's lavish expenditures, rapidly wiped out the surplus, and in Harrison's last months in office a deficit appeared.

The Democrats, balked of effective legislative action by a hostile Senate and President, used the House of Representatives as a citadel from which to assail the works of Republicanism in preparation for the approaching presidential campaign. Commencing in April, 1892, they passed a series of separate tariff bills for the purpose of exposing the weakest spots in the McKinley Act, and although these "popgun" bills all failed in the Senate, they kept public attention focused upon the tariff question.

Under the circumstances, Cleveland, who had been quietly practicing law in New York City since his retirement, was again the logical candidate of his party. Persistent efforts were, however, put forth by the professional Democratic politicians, and particularly by the Tammany cohorts of his own state, to prevent this. But when the national convention met in Chicago on June 21, 1892, he was nominated on the first vote. A. E. Stevenson of Illinois was named for the second place. As framed by the committee on resolutions, the platform reiterated the declaration of 1888 for tariff reduction without injury to "any domestic industries," but the radical tariff-reformers induced the convention to substitute a plank which declared that any tariff, except for purposes of revenue only, was unconstitutional.

Harrison's candidacy was regarded without enthusiasm by his party. Platt and Quay had become estranged from him, and even Secretary of State Blaine, who had hitherto disclaimed presidential aspirations, made himself available for nomination by resigning from the cabinet three days before the convention gathered. Nor was there any outside demand for Harrison.

Nevertheless, the Republican leaders were fearful of the political consequences of repudiating a President of their own party, and the national convention, meeting at Minneapolis on June 7, renominated him on the first ballot. Whitelaw Reid, editor of the *New York Tribune*, was chosen for the vice-presidency. On the leading question of the day, the platform contained a ringing reaffirmation of the "American doctrine of protection."

The contest was unusually devoid of incident. The storm center of campaign oratory was, as four years before, the tariff. In his speech of acceptance, Cleveland declared, with oblique reference to the doctrinaire tariff utterance of the Democratic platform, "We need not base our attack upon questions of constitutional permission." A violent labor disturbance at the Carnegie steel works in Homestead, Pennsylvania, reacted strongly for Democratic success, for, since the trouble was an outgrowth of wage decreases, it appeared that the much-vaunted connection between tariff protection and high wages was disproved in the case of one of the best protected industries.

The election resulted in a sweeping victory for Cleveland, who polled 277 votes in the electoral college as compared with 145 for Harrison, and 46 per cent of the popular vote as compared with less than 43 per cent for his rival. The remaining 22 electoral votes were cast for a third-party candidate — James B. Weaver of Iowa, presidential nominee of the People's party. The sudden rise of this party was ominous for the future, for it denoted the emergence of new forces and issues with which the major parties had failed to cope. The story of the "Populists" and of the silver movement with which they were inseparably identified may, however, be better considered in a later connection (see pages 393–394).

The Triumph of Protectionism

Cleveland took up the presidential reins once more in 1893, heartened by the popular indorsement of tariff reform and by the confidence of the people in his own unflinching honesty and courage. Moreover, the way seemed clear for the Democrats to adopt a program of constructive legislation, since, for the first time since Buchanan's day, they commanded a majority in both houses. But appearances were deceptive. Cleveland's second presidency was a time of crosscurrents and countercurrents in American political and social life, of severe business depression, mighty labor conflicts, and spirited currency agitation (see pages 395–399). These events roused all of the President's fighting qualities; but what had formerly been termed his strength of character now sometimes appeared to be mere stubbornness, and to his opponents his independence of public opinion seemed quite like indifference to public welfare. Time, however, has softened the judgment of Cleveland's contemporaries, and has revealed him, in spite of his limitations, as an honest, fearless, and patriotic executive.

In selecting his cabinet, Cleveland named John G. Carlisle Secretary of the Treasury, and W. Q. Gresham of Illinois Secretary of State, in express recognition of the low-tariff elements in Democratic and Republican parties.[1] The President's civil-service policy resembled that of his first administration in his willingness to use as "spoils" the offices not yet under the merit system, and in his subsequent enlargements of the classified list. The number of positions under the merit system was more than doubled from 1893 to 1897, reaching a total of nearly 82,000 out of somewhat more than 200,000 offices.

The preparation of a new tariff bill was begun at a special session of Congress in August, 1893, under the direction of William L. Wilson of West Virginia, Chairman of the Ways and Means Committee. In contrast with the purpose of the framers of the McKinley Act, the object of Wilson's committee was to increase the revenue and diminish protection. The bill, as adopted by the House in December, embraced certain principles that, in a general way, have guided all subsequent Democratic efforts at tariff legislation. Basic raw materials essential to manufacturing and construction, such as lumber, wool, sugar, and iron ore, were placed on the free list. Since this enabled manufacturers to lower their costs of production, the existing protective duties on manufactures were generally reduced. In order to make up for losses in revenue, new internal duties were

[1] The other members were: D. S. Lamont of New York, Secretary of War; Richard Olney of Massachusetts, Attorney-General; W. S. Bissell of New York, Postmaster-General; H. A. Herbert of Alabama, Secretary of the Navy; Hoke Smith of Georgia, Secretary of the Interior; and J. S. Morton of Nebraska, Secretary of Agriculture. On Gresham's death in June, 1895, Olney became Secretary of State.

placed on liquors, tobacco, and other luxuries, and for the first time since Civil-War days, a tax was levied on incomes. This last provision, which imposed a two-per-cent tax on all incomes above $4,000, was the price paid by the Democrats for Populist support of the bill, and was championed as a means of shifting the tax burden to those best able to pay.

Industries affected adversely by the House bill hastened to exert every possible pressure upon the Senate to emasculate the bill. Ugly rumors were soon afloat of the corruption of Senators by the Sugar Trust, and Senator Quay, among others, admitted to an investigating committee that he had speculated in sugar stock for a rise when the sugar duty was under consideration. Indeed, he added, "I do not feel that there is anything in my connection with the Senate to interfere with my buying or selling the stock when I please; and I propose to do so."

Under Senator Gorman's leadership, 634 amendments were attached to the House bill, and the measure was altered not only in detail but also in principle. The most important articles, including sugar, were removed from the free list, and the protective duties were generally advanced. Only the income tax and the internal-revenue duties remained without material change. After stubborn opposition by the House, the Gorman version was finally accepted; and in August, 1894, the President, who bitterly assailed the Senate's action as "party perfidy and party dishonor," permitted the measure to become a law without his signature. By the Wilson-Gorman Act the general scale of duties was lowered to about forty per cent.

The Democrats suffered another blow from a Supreme Court decision in 1895, which held that the income-tax provision was unconstitutional. The validity of the tax had been assumed by the Democrats, and had been explicitly declared by the Court itself in 1880 in a case involving the Civil-War income tax. Now the judges decided, by a vote of five to four, that a tax on incomes was a "direct" tax and, under the Constitution, must be apportioned among the states according to the number of their inhabitants.[1] This requirement, of course, defeated the very purpose for which the tax had been devised, since wealth is concentrated

[1] Pollock *v.* Farmers' Loan and Trust Company. All subsequent income taxation by Congress awaited the adoption of the Sixteenth Amendment in 1913.

in certain districts and bears little relation to the distribution of population.

The inconsistencies of the new tariff, the widespread depression continuing from the Panic of 1893, and the upsetting of the income tax, all helped to discredit the Wilson-Gorman Act in the eyes of the public. Although the tariff question was only a minor issue in the campaign of 1896, President McKinley, when he entered office in March, 1897, summoned a special session of Congress to revise the tariff according to the Republican pattern. The outcome was the adoption of the Dingley Tariff in July, 1897 — a thoroughgoing protective measure, which raised the tariff wall to the highest point it had yet reached, an average of 57 per cent. The principle of reciprocity, abandoned by the Democrats, was again recognized but in so complicated a form as to be virtually unworkable.

After a decade of almost ceaseless controversy over the tariff, the victory thus rested with the ultraprotectionists. The remarkable prosperity, which burst upon the country shortly after 1897, was declared by the Republicans to vindicate their most extravagant claims for the protective system. For ten years the tariff disappeared as a public question. In the thronging of new interests, the great parties turned their attention to problems such as the Spanish War of 1898 and trust regulation.

SELECT BIBLIOGRAPHY

Party Conflict and the Tariff Question, 1883–1897. The events of this period have been studied in a number of general works, among them, D. R. Dewey, *National Problems* (in *The American Nation*, XXIV, New York, 1907), H. T. Peck, *Twenty Years of the Republic, 1885–1905* (New York, 1906), H. J. Ford, *The Cleveland Era* (in *The Chronicles of America*, XLIV, New Haven, 1919), and J. F. Rhodes, *History of the United States*, VIII (New York, 1919).

Cleveland as Party Leader. H. C. Thomas, *The Return of the Democratic Party to Power in 1884* (in *Columbia University Studies*, LXXXIX, no. 2, New York, 1919), throws light on Cleveland's political course. On pensions, W. H. Glasson, *Federal Military Pensions in the United States* (New York, 1918), is valuable. Two important biographies are Robert McElroy, *Grover Cleveland* (2 v., New York, 1923), and Henry James, *Richard Olney and His Public Service* (Boston, 1923).

The Surplus Revenue and the Tariff Question. The financial questions of the time are ably discussed in D. R. Dewey, *Financial History of the*

United States (New York, 1922), A. D. Noyes, *Forty Years of American Finance* (New York, 1909), and W. R. Lawson, *American Finance* (Edinburgh, 1908). For the evolution of tariff legislation and the triumph of protection, see the works by Taussig, Stanwood, and Tarbell referred to in the Select Bibliography of Chapter XVII. On Reed's ascendancy in the House, consult Mary P. Follett, *The Speaker of the House of Representatives* (New York, 1896), and S. W. McCall, *The Life of Thomas Brackett Reed* (Boston, 1914). Presidential elections are compactly treated in Edward Stanwood, *A History of the Presidency*, I (Boston, 1898).

CHAPTER XXI

THE EVOLUTION OF "BIG BUSINESS"

The Trend toward Large-scale Industry

The latter part of Cleveland's first administration and the early years of Harrison's presidency saw the adoption of a new national policy toward railway corporations and industrial combinations. Unlike the tariff settlement, this event was not the product of party controversy. It can be understood only in the light of the trend toward large-scale operation which had been going on in the basic industries of the country since the early days of the Economic Revolution.

Prior to 1865, the railroads and manufacturing establishments had come into being in a more or less haphazard way, usually in response to real or fancied local needs. A length of a few hundred miles was regarded as best adapted for efficient railway management, and only one road exceeded one thousand miles. Eight different widths of track were in use, with the result that it was often impossible for the cars of one line to use another, even when the owners were otherwise agreeable. A similar diffusion of economic effort and lack of efficiency resulted from the numerous, scattered factories, most of which operated in a small way on limited capital.

After 1865, the trend in the economic world was strongly toward the consolidation of smaller units into larger ones, the elimination of competition, and the concentration of control in relatively few hands. Many influences contributed to this end. The high protective tariff helped to divert capital into such channels, especially in mining and manufacturing. The rapidly expanding web of railways enlarged the market for the sale of goods by energetic business men. Furthermore, the advantages of large-scale operation made it possible for the railways and manufacturers to satisfy the clamor of investors for greater dividends, and in the long run, to meet the public demand for cheaper and better service. Viewed from another standpoint, the movement may be regarded as one phase of the new nationalism that was beginning to flood American life.

Large-scale management made possible vast improvements and savings in the operation of both railways and factories. For instance, it became possible to install improved and costly machinery, employ highly trained managers and superintendents, purchase supplies on advantageous terms, and reduce the cost of competitive advertising and salesmanship. A large manufacturing plant had the additional advantage of being in a position to make use of refuse and byproducts, usually neglected by smaller concerns.

So long as business was conducted on a small scale, the *partnership* was the favorite form of organization, but under the new conditions, the *corporation* rose to its dominant place in modern life. The corporate form was better adapted to the limitless opportunities of the new world of business. Unlike a partnership, the continuance of a corporation does not depend upon the life of its original members. Accordingly, it is possible to carry out a program of development extending beyond the lifetime of any group of men. Moreover, through the sale of shares of stock, a corporation ordinarily has greater financial resources, and the pecuniary burden of vast undertakings may be distributed among many stockholders. In case of business failure — an important consideration in speculative enterprises — the stockholders are usually liable merely to the amount of their stockholdings, whereas a member of a partnership is generally responsible for the entire indebtedness of the firm.

On the other hand, if a corporation is making excessive profits and wishes to conceal the fact from the public, it ordinarily has the power to "water its stock," or, in other words, to distribute additional shares to its stockholders and thus reduce the nominal rate of dividend. For example, a corporation with a capital stock of $1,000,000, earning a twelve-per-cent dividend, may, by doubling the amount of stock held by each stockholder, lower the rate of dividend to six per cent, and yet give each stockholder his full profits. As a result of such action the business would show only a moderate return, and the board of directors could, with a show of sincerity, combat the demands both of the public for lower prices and of the wage-earners for better pay. As might be expected, "watering" is also resorted to by financiers who wish to foist inflated capitalization on the gullible public. A railroad expert estimated that, out of an indebtedness of seven and one half billions which the roads of the country were carrying in 1883, two billions represented "water."

The actual process of consolidation and absorption was directed by commercial geniuses who, by reason of their broad vision, creative energy, and relentless driving power, were termed by common consent "steel kings," "coal barons," "railway magnates," and "Napoleons of finance." Of this group perhaps the foremost names were Cornelius and William H. Vanderbilt, J. Edgar Thomson, Jay Gould, and James J. Hill in railway reorganization; John D. Rockefeller, Henry H. Rogers, and H. M. Flagler in oil development; Andrew Carnegie, H. C. Frick, and Charles M. Schwab in the steel industry; and Jay Cooke, J. P. Morgan, and E. H. Harriman in banking and finance.

They and their associates were men who saw things in the large, and whose imagination was equaled only by their boldness in execution. The story of their activities is a singular mixture of the heroic and splendid with the sordid and grotesque. For the most part, they were free to carry out their plans without let or hindrance from the government, for the American people at this time were steeped in the doctrine of individualism or *laissez faire*, that is, the right of individual enterprise to function without governmental interference.[1] This belief was an inheritance from pioneer days, when the doors of opportunity were wide open for everybody, and only gradually did the public come to realize that, under the new conditions, unbridled individualism threatened economic servitude for the masses.

The philosophy of the new order was a hard one, and may be summed up in the phrase, "everyone for himself." "Law!" roared Cornelius Vanderbilt, the unlettered founder of the Vanderbilt millions, "What do I care about law? Hain't I got the power?" Or in the briefer expression attributed to W. H.

[1] It is to be noted, however, that, as applied by "Big Business," *laissez faire* was a one-sided doctrine. At the same time that the industrial leaders rejected political interference which might work to their detriment, they eagerly sought favors from the government in the form of tariff protection, subsidies, and land grants.

Vanderbilt, who succeeded to his father's shoes, "The public be damned!" Yet, with all their cynicism, the best of these men were spurred on by the conviction that they were laying the foundations of a new America, and that the accumulation of colossal wealth in a few hands would indirectly benefit the less fortunate classes of society.

The Growth of Railway Consolidation

Although local mergers of railways had taken place in earlier years, a period of rapid and extensive amalgamation began about 1865. Cornelius Vanderbilt was one of the first to realize the importance of railway consolidation. Already past middle age, and the possessor of a fortune amassed in water traffic, he sold out his steamboats in 1865 for what they would bring, and gave his whole attention to the development of a direct steam route from the Atlantic Seaboard at New York to the heart of the Middle West at Chicago. Starting with a short line connecting New York and Albany, he acquired the New York Central in 1867, making possible continuous traffic from New York to Buffalo. In 1873 he extended the road to Chicago by leasing the Lake Shore and Michigan Southern. At the time he embarked on his railway career, Vanderbilt's fortune amounted to about $10,000,000; when he died twelve years later at the age of eighty-three, he left $104,000,000, the first of the great modern American fortunes. Much of this wealth came from the unscrupulous manipulation of railway stocks and from methods of competition not far removed from the ethics of the jungle.

Meantime, the Pennsylvania Company, which in 1865 merely possessed a main line from Philadelphia to Pittsburgh with a few branches, underwent a rapid expansion. Under J. Edgar Thomson's leadership, it reached out tentacles toward Chicago and St. Louis, and gained entry to these cities in 1869. It also established connections with New York City. Thomson's business methods, however, were in welcome contrast with those of Vanderbilt. By 1875 three other trunk lines had been completed between Atlantic ports and Lake Michigan: the Erie, the Baltimore and Ohio, and the Grand Trunk. Similar mergers took place in the Mississippi Valley. There were three through lines between Chicago and St. Louis in 1870, and others were later completed.

The formation of great rail arteries, while reducing the number of competing roads, intensified competition. It is doubtful whether enough business existed, as yet, to support all these railways. At any rate, the rival companies engaged in furious warfare for the control of traffic between important shipping centers. In the scramble for business, certain practices grew up that were detrimental both to the companies and to the public. For example, in 1869 and again in 1874, 1875, and 1876, relentless rate wars were waged by the trunk lines between Chicago and the Seaboard. A standard freight charge of $1.88 per hundred pounds in 1868 was forced down to twenty-five cents in 1869; rates were sometimes fixed at a point below the cost of operating the trains. Such transportation wars were in the nature of endurance contests, and as a consequence of the losses sustained, were never of long duration.

Another scheme was to discriminate between cities in traffic charges. Freight rates were based not on the cost of service but on "what the traffic would bear." If two important commercial centers were connected by more than one line, competition drove the transportation charges down to the lowest possible figure. On the other hand, undue rates were likely to be charged between cities which were joined by a single road. For example, it was cheaper for Pittsburgh merchants to ship their merchandise by boat to Cincinnati and thence by rail to Philadelphia than to send it directly over the Pennsylvania Railroad from Pittsburgh to Philadelphia. The "long-and-short-haul" device roused public indignation, but the extortionate charges for traffic between local points enabled the roads to make up for their losses elsewhere.

Discriminations between places were, on the whole, less objectionable than the surreptitious and unfair discriminations between persons. Large shippers were favored with secret rebates from the published freight charges when such action was necessary to keep traffic from going to a rival railway. Moreover, railway corporations were themselves often interested in other businesses, such as coal mining, and when this was so, forced possible competitors to pay higher rates.

Such conditions were unsatisfactory to the railways themselves, and led to various coöperative attempts to lessen competition and keep up prices. "Rate agreements" were formed, whereby rival companies covenanted to maintain uniform charges, but these invariably broke down for want of mutual confidence. A somewhat similar device, known as "pooling," was more successful. By this scheme the freight business, hitherto competed for, was amicably divided among the companies on some prearranged basis; or according to another variation, the total earnings from this traffic went into a common fund for similar distribution.

The first pool of any consequence was established in 1870 by the railroads connecting Chicago and Omaha — the Northwestern, the Rock Island, and the Burlington lines. Under an agreement, which eventually lasted fourteen years, each road was to retain about one half of its earnings on the through traffic, and the balance was to be shared equally by the three companies. During the lifetime of this agreement, pooling arrangements were extensively entered into by railways in all parts of the country, their duration depending very largely upon the willingness of erstwhile competitors to trust each other.

The practices of the railways were viewed with growing disfavor by the public at large. In the early seventies the demand of the Western farmers for cheaper transportation had led to the adoption of the so-called "Granger Laws" for the regulation of railway charges within state borders (see pages 287-288). A similar movement, spreading in a modified form through the East, had caused the establishment of state railway commissions with investigative and advisory powers. The transportation question, however, was by its very nature a national rather than a state problem, and it soon became the subject of Congressional discussion and investigation.

A Senate committee, headed by William Windom of Minnesota, proposed in 1874 that the government should build and operate a freight line from the Mississippi to the Seaboard as a means of keeping down the charges of private companies. In 1874, 1878, and 1885, the House passed bills for the national regulation of railways, and in the last year the Senate acted likewise, though the two chambers were unable to agree on the same bill. Final action was hastened by a decision of the Supreme Court in 1886, which, reversing its earlier view, forbade individual states to fix transportation charges on shipments passing outside their own borders. In other words, the decision held that the ever increasing volume of interstate traffic could be regulated only by Congress.[1]

Under this spur, Congress passed the Interstate Commerce Act, which received Cleveland's signature on February 4, 1887. This measure prohibited excessive charges, rebates, the long-and-short-haul discrimination, and pools. It required the advance publication of transportation rates, and provided for an Interstate Commerce Commission of five members to guard against violations of the law. The powers of this body were, however, largely investigative. The Commission was not given the authority to fix railway rates, nor did it possess the power to enforce its own decisions. If a railway company declined to execute its orders, the Commission must bring action in the federal courts to compel obedience. The law, being based upon the interstate-commerce clause of the Constitution, had, of course, nothing to do with traffic carried on entirely within the limits of a single state.

This first experiment in the national supervision of railways proved a disappointment in many respects. In cases of appeal, the Supreme Court was apt to uphold the companies rather than the orders of the Interstate Commerce Commission. By still other decisions, the powers of the Commission were restricted within the narrowest bounds. The railways, for the most part, continued their evil ways though with greater regard for external appearances than before. For example, since pooling was forbidden, the companies abandoned the practice, and formed "traffic associations" which regulated rates and punished disobedient members.

When the Supreme Court decided (1897) that these rate agreements violated the Sherman Anti-Trust Act of 1890 (see page 370), a strong impetus was given to a new movement for combination, which resulted in the consolidation of many hitherto competing lines. By 1900 the great railway systems had come

[1] Wabash, St. Louis, and Pacific Railway Company *v.* Illinois. At this time practically three fourths of the rail traffic of the country was interstate in character. For the earlier decision, see page 288.

into being, having as their aim the entire control of all the roads in a particular section of the country. More than half of the mileage of the United States was controlled by six dominant financial groups, the Vanderbilt, Morgan, Harriman, and Pennsylvania interests each owning a mileage of approximately 20,000, the Gould group 16,000, and the Hill group 5,000.

Yet the Act of 1887 was not without benefit. It paved the way for a better understanding of the railway problem; the right of national regulation, at first disputed, was thoroughly established in principle; and a better adjustment of transportation charges was brought about. Moreover, the statute created official machinery for railway control, which Congress could strengthen and enlarge whenever public opinion should demand stronger action from the government.

The Movement for Concentration in Manufacturing

The movement for the consolidation of manufacturing ran parallel to that of railway combination. Manufacturing enterprises were at first organized in small separate concerns without governmental regulation. Under aggressive leadership and favorable economic conditions, they developed into larger establishments in the period after 1865, and engaged in cutthroat rivalry for the control of business. Then followed an era when the stronger competitors in a given industry sought to effect secret arrangements with each other for the establishment of uniform prices and the restriction of output, the results appearing in price agreements, pools, and a device, unknown to railway reorganization, called the "trust." Finally, with public opinion at full tilt against "Big Business," both the individual states and the nation intervened with restraining laws. But the great combinations managed to survive, and at the turn of the century, entered on an epoch of superconsolidation. The unifying trend was stronger in some branches of manufacturing than in others, though it left untouched few industries that were of basic importance to the nation.

As one of the earliest and most powerful of industrial combinations, the career of the Standard Oil Company may serve as an illustration of the process of concentration in other fields. In

1865 John D. Rockefeller, then a young man of twenty-six years, was the leading spirit in the Standard Oil Company of Cleveland, Ohio, a concern capitalized at $100,000. Joining hands with powerful capitalists in Cleveland and New York, he augmented his operations, attained ownership of rival establishments, and in 1870 organized the Standard Oil Company of Ohio with a capitalization of one million dollars. At this time his company produced four per cent of all the oil refined in the United States.

Now began a career of conquest that was Napoleonic in its daring, magnitude, and execution. By 1872 the Standard absorbed all but five of the twenty-five independent plants in Cleveland. Two years later Rockefeller and his associates acquired mastery of the greatest refineries in New York and Philadelphia; the largest companies in Baltimore surrendered in 1875. Within the next few years the Standard obtained control of the refining business of western Pennsylvania. Thus, in the course of a decade ninety per cent of all the refineries in the United States had passed into the hands of the Rockefeller group.

Many elements, good and evil, had made possible this brilliant campaign. Not the least of these was the remarkable group of men who gathered about Rockefeller — business geniuses like Flagler, Rogers, and J. D. Archbold, who spent their waking moments planning, plotting, fighting for the Standard, and exacted from their subordinates the last ounce of energy and devotion. Another factor was the sheer industrial efficiency attained through the conduct of business on a great scale. The Company established factories to make its own barrels and manufacture its own acids; it acquired tank cars and great underground mains, or pipe lines, for the transportation of crude oil; it created its own selling agencies and, instead of paying large storage charges, erected its own storage tanks at strategic points. In addition to its main product, kerosene or coal oil, it utilized and popularized many byproducts that ordinarily would have been discarded, such as lubricating oils, gasoline, paraffin, and vaseline products.

Its success was further assured by unfair practices and unethical methods of competition. In the former category were the special transportation rates exacted from the railways. In 1872 the

Standard and certain other refining companies joined together in an agreement with the railways whereby they were to receive secret rebates not merely on their own oil but also on all shipments by their competitors. The conspiracy was discovered before the arrangement became operative, and in the face of a mighty public wrath, all parties to the agreement disowned it. Subsequently the Standard on its own account obtained discriminating rates from the railways, a practice that continued for thirty years or more.

Before public exposure upset the agreement of 1872, agents of the Standard used its existence as a club to force the sale of rival refineries. This illustrates the ruthless methods which the Company employed in dealing with competitors. Another practice consisted in price-cutting campaigns. In order to crush a competitor, the Company would temporarily reduce the price of oil, even perhaps below the cost of production, and then, when its object was accomplished, raise the price again.

The entire country was divided into districts, over each of which presided a Standard agent, who in turn subdivided his territory into smaller divisions with special men in charge. Each agent was commanded to acquire the entire oil-selling business of his district. His methods in doing so were left to his own discretion, but his success was rewarded with salary increases, his failure by curt dismissal.

By 1882 the Standard interests owned fourteen separate companies outright, and held a majority of the stock in twenty-six other concerns. In the effort to harmonize the operation of these plants, price agreements and pooling arrangements had been tried from time to time; but since a more unified control was desired, a new form of industrial organization was devised in 1879, called a "trust." The scheme, as revised in 1882, provided for a federation of the Standard and the related companies, whereby all the stock of these concerns was confided to a board of nine trustees, who, in this way, attained to a position of supreme control. In return for their stock, the original holders received "trust certificates," which entitled them to their proportionate share of the earnings of the combined Standard Oil Trust. The device proved so successful in securing unity of management that it led to the formation of the "Whisky

Trust" and the "Sugar Trust" and to similar organizations in other industries.

Since the prevalent belief in the doctrine of *laissez faire* had hitherto prevented the government from doing anything to curb or restrain corporations, during the eighties the public outcry against "Big Business" reached a climax. The idea of monopolies had always been abhorrent to the American mind; and now it appeared that not only the comforts of existence but the very necessities of life — "from meat to tombstones," declared Henry Demarest Lloyd — were drifting into the control of "soulless corporations."

The benefits which accrued to the public from the improved quality and generally lower prices of commodities were obscured by the evil practices of "Big Business" in strangling competition, tampering with legislatures, exacting excessive profits, watering stock, and opposing labor welfare. In 1884 an Anti-Monopoly party appeared in the national campaign, though with little success. Four years later the platforms of the major parties, recognizing for the first time the presence of the new industrial problem, condemned capitalistic combinations.

As it happened, the first steps toward corporation control were taken by the states. In 1889 and 1890, fifteen states adopted legislation to prevent conspiracies or agreements in restraint of free competition. Before the movement spent its force, all but New Jersey, Delaware, and West Virginia had followed their example. Unfortunately, the remissness of these three proved fatal, since an industrial corporation chartered in one of them might trade unmolested across state lines. In order to shut off all means of escape, Congress on July 2, 1890, passed a national prohibitory law, known as the "Sherman Anti-Trust Act." It declared illegal "Every contract, combination in the form of trust or otherwise, or conspiracy, in restraint of trade or commerce among the several States, or with foreign nations."

Adopted in response to an imperious popular demand, the statute was drafted in such haste that the meaning of its apparently simple and direct language was, for many years, the subject of impassioned controversy. Should the words be taken literally, it followed that virtually every large commercial enterprise in the country was illegal, since, by its superior efficiency, such a business tended to be in restraint of competitive trade. If this were the true meaning, then the law aimed to prevent the benefits of large-scale operation as well as its evils, and all industrial combinations were equally under the ban.

But it was contended by others that, inasmuch as the terms used in the statute had been employed since ancient times in the common law, they had acquired a technical meaning different from their everyday usage. If this were so, then acts in restraint of trade, when reasonable and fair, were not intended to be outlawed by the language of the statute.[1] Other obscurities lurked in the law as well. For example, were railway combinations forbidden along with the other kinds? were labor organizations prohibited as well as capitalistic combinations? These and similar questions had to be decided eventually by the Supreme Court.

The Anti-Trust Law, in its commonly accepted meaning, was too dangerous a weapon for the innocent to be used freely against the guilty. Largely for this reason, little effort was made by the government to enforce it in the first ten years or so after its enactment. Furthermore, the Supreme Court, as in the case of the Interstate Commerce Law, took a very conservative position, and in most instances, construed the act as narrowly as possible.

In reality, the decade beginning with the year 1890 saw the formation of more industrial combinations than in the entire preceding period. Between 1860 and 1890, twenty-four combinations had been organized with a total nominal capital of $436,000,000, but in the next ten years 157 new combinations were formed with a total nominal capital of $3,150,000,000. The years 1898–1901 were particularly prolific, and ushered in an era of superconsolidation, signalized by the formation of the United States Steel Corporation (1901), a combination of combinations, capitalized at more than one billion dollars.

The special type of organization known as the "trust" was, however, a thing of the past, in consequence of hostile decisions of a New York court against the Sugar Trust in 1890 and of the Ohio Supreme Court against the Standard Oil Trust two years

[1] This view was eventually adopted by the Supreme Court in 1911 in the case of the Standard Oil Company *v.* United States. See page 462. The contrary view was upheld by Mr. Justice Harlan's separate opinion in the same case.

later.[1] But the word itself continued, in popular parlance, to denote any form of "Big Business" which in size threatened to become a monopoly. In deference to the law, the great capitalistic organizations now adopted a different legal framework. Many of them, like the Sugar Trust and the Whisky Trust, reorganized as single huge corporations in states where the laws were negligent.[2]

For a time, the Standard Oil Trust accomplished the same purpose in a different way. When the trust was dissolved in 1892, the various holders of trust certificates, including the nine trustees who in their own right owned a majority interest in the trust, were given a proportionate share of control in each one of the twenty corporations into which the business was divided. As a result, without any formal organization among themselves, the ex-trustees were enabled to continue the former unity of management. In 1899, however, the Standard interests became a single great corporation under the laws of New Jersey.

The numerous alterations in structure apparently had no hurtful effect on the Standard Oil business. The earnings of the Standard Oil Trust from 1882 to 1891 never fell below $8,000,000 annually. The combined profits of the severed units of the trust in the years from 1892 to 1896 ranged from $19,000,000 to $34,000,000 a year. When organized as a single corporation, the Standard earned an annual profit of from $34,000,000 to $57,000,000 in the period from 1899 to 1905.

The trend toward consolidation in transportation and manufacturing was symptomatic of a similar irresistible movement in almost every sphere of commercial activity. By 1900 the telephone, telegraph, and express businesses had gravitated into the hands of a very few corporations. At the same time, in the mining industry, the Amalgamated Copper Company acquired control of sixty per cent of the copper produced in the United States. A few years later the United States Steel Corporation controlled about seventy per cent of the iron and steel production.

[1] The New York decision held that the combination of sugar refiners partook of the nature of a partnership of corporations and hence violated the common law. In the Ohio case, the decision rested explicitly on the contention that the object of the oil combination was to form a monopoly.

[2] Another form of organization was the "holding company," that is, a corporation organized primarily for the purpose of buying stock in other corporations. This was usually a transitional form, since holding companies tended to become absorbing corporations.

The same tendency was at work in the sphere of banking. By 1900 the Rockefeller interests and the Morgan group dominated banking to such an extent that it was doubtful whether any large business enterprise could be started without the aid of one or the other of them. The country was confronted with the spectacle of combinations and monopolies on nearly every hand, and thoughtful people were beginning to wonder how long democratic institutions could withstand the strain.

SELECT BIBLIOGRAPHY

The Growth of Railway Consolidation. E. R. Johnson and T. W. Van Metre, *Principles of Railroad Transportation* (New York, 1921), Eliot Jones, *Principles of Railway Transportation* (New York, 1924), W. Z. Ripley, *Railroads: Rates and Regulation* (New York, 1912), and Stuart Daggett, *Railroad Reorganization* (in *Harvard Economic Studies*, IV, Boston, 1908), though primarily technical treatises, touch upon historical phases. John Moody, *The Railroad Builders* (in *The Chronicles of America*, XXXVIII, New Haven, 1919), gives the best outline history of leading railways. Informing chapters may be found in E. E. Sparks, *National Development*, and D. R. Dewey, *National Problems* (in *The American Nation*, XXIII and XXIV, New York, 1907), and in C. R. Lingley, *Since the Civil War* (in *The United States*, III, New York, 1920).

The Movement for Concentration in Manufacturing. A general picture of the trend is given in two articles by W. F. Willoughby: "The Concentration of Industry in the United States" (in *Yale Review*, VII [1898], 72–94), and "The Integration of Industry in the United States" (in *Quarterly Journal of Economics*, XVI [1902], 94–115). John Moody, *The Truth about the Trusts* (New York, 1904), is a statistical survey of capitalized industry and finance as it existed at the apex of the consolidation movement. Less technical, and therefore more valuable for the general reader, are B. J. Hendrick, *The Age of Big Business*, and John Moody, *The Masters of Capital* (in *The Chronicles of America*, XXXIX and XLI, New Haven, 1919). Excellent summaries appear in Dewey and Lingley, cited above.

Among the histories of individual corporations are Ida M. Tarbell, *The History of the Standard Oil Company* (2 v., New York, 1904) — detailed and painstaking; G. H. Montague, *The Rise and Progress of the Standard Oil Company* (New York, 1903) — scholarly and brief; Abraham Berglund, *The United States Steel Corporation* (in *Columbia University Studies*, XXVII, no. 2, New York, 1907) — primarily an economic study; H. N. Casson, *The Romance of Steel* (New York, 1907) — popular; and Eliot Jones, *The Anthracite Coal Combination in the United States* (in *Harvard Economic Studies*, XI, Cambridge, 1914) — scholarly and accurate. An outline of the story of the Morgan banking house may be reconstructed from Carl Hovey's eulogistic *The Life Story of J. P. Morgan* (New York, 1911).

CHAPTER XXII

THE RISE OF ORGANIZED LABOR

THE GROWTH OF LABOR SOLIDARITY

The rise of combinations in the domains of transportation and industry was matched by a parallel trend in the field of labor. By the time of Cleveland and Harrison, organized labor stood prepared to measure its strength with organized capital, and indeed, with the government itself. To this height the working class had climbed from lowly levels. In the thirties the first labor movement in American history had been wrecked by the Panic of 1837, and sporadic efforts made in subsequent years to consolidate wage-earners in various occupations and crafts had been without enduring results. It is no exaggeration to say that, when the Civil War broke out, there was no effective labor organization in the country, though four national unions had a nominal existence.

The next twenty years, however, wrought a tremendous change, due chiefly to the greatly increased numbers of workingmen employed in factories, mines, and rail transportation. In 1860 there were about one and one-third million wage-earners in the United States; in 1870, well over two millions; in 1880, nearly two and three-quarter millions; and in 1890, over four and one-quarter millions. These persons had hitherto labored at local occupations where they were their own masters, or else had been employed in small factories, where the monotony of the toil was alleviated by personal association with the owners, who often worked along with them.

But with the rapid spread of the factory system and large-scale methods of production, wage-earners discovered a radical alteration in their status. No longer employed as self-respecting craftsmen, they became mere adjuncts to great machines. Their working conditions were dictated by managers representing impersonal and absentee corporations. When stockholders clamored for larger dividends or employers engaged in price-cutting competition, the toilers' earnings were the first to suffer. The workday, which had in many branches been reduced to ten hours thirty years earlier, tended to grow longer instead of shorter. Moreover, the employees performed their work in great gloomy factories amid unsanitary conditions and dangerous unguarded machinery. The rapacious demand for cheap labor drew increasing numbers of women and children into the factories, and the plight of the native workingmen was further aggravated by the hordes of immigrant laborers who contended with them for jobs.

In the United States, an aggrieved class has, under ordinary circumstances, been able to win redress through legislative action. But to the working class, the prospect for such relief seemed hopeless, since the government was dominated by the *laissez faire* doctrine, and in any case, the legislatures were likely to have a corporation bias. Some optimistic souls did, indeed, endeavor to launch labor parties from time to time; but the shrewder labor leaders, mindful of the successes attained by capital through organized economic effort, devoted their energies to the promotion of similar combinations among the workingmen.

The new movement for labor organization began in the later years of the Civil War. Local unions were formed in many branches of industry, and in a growing number of cases, the scattered unions of a particular trade or occupation joined hands in a national union. For example, in 1864 and 1865 ten national unions came into being, including the plasterers, cigar-makers, bricklayers, and carpenters. In cities where unions were numerous, the local bodies often formed central trade assemblies to look after their common interests in the community. By 1870 at least thirty-two national trade unions were in existence, commanding a total membership of perhaps 300,000. Many of these did not survive the Panic of 1873, but others arose to take their place.

The national organization of wage-earners by special trades and occupations was preliminary to ambitious attempts to unify all the labor forces of the country in a single body. W. H. Sylvis of the Iron Molders' Union was the prime mover in the first of such enterprises. As a result of his efforts, a loose federation of local unions, city trade assemblies, and national unions was effected in 1866 under the name of the "National Labor Union."

Several annual congresses were held, at which resolutions were adopted in favor of the eight-hour day, the substitution of arbitration for strikes, and the establishment of coöperative shops in which the workingmen would supply the capital and share the profits. Sylvis's own union opened ten or more stove foundries on a coöperative plan, and most of the leading trades made similar attempts, all of which failed for lack of proper business direction. By 1872 the movement died, because of internal dissensions between those who preferred industrial action pure and simple and those who desired to form a political party.

Meantime, a second and more successful attempt to consolidate the labor movement saw light under the name of the "Noble Order of the Knights of Labor." Organized in Philadelphia in 1869 by Uriah S. Stephens and six other garment-cutters, the new undertaking, unlike the National Labor Union, was based upon the principle that all toilers, skilled and unskilled, organized and unorganized, should band together in one mighty partnership without distinctions of trade or vocation. The local units of the order were known as "assemblies," and they usually included a mixture of all kinds of workingmen. In the early years secrecy was adopted to protect the members from persecution by employers. Even the name of the order was withheld from the public. The avowed purpose of the Knights of Labor was to foster class solidarity among wage-earners, to free poor people from capitalistic greed by means of coöperative industries, and to agitate for the eight-hour day, arbitration, the abolition of child labor, and other industrial reforms.

Meeting with small success at the start, the order benefited in membership and strength from the hard times of 1873–1878, and after the abandonment of its secret features in 1881, began a career that was truly meteoric. Its membership reached a highwater mark of perhaps seven hundred thousand in 1886. A fund to assist coöperative enterprises was established in 1882, and under encouragement of the Knights, no less than 135 coöperative stores and factories were founded, most of them in the mining, cooperage, and shoe industries, where wages were exceptionally low. These undertakings, however, were invariably short-lived, because of inexperienced management and the unscrupulous opposition resorted to by private business concerns.

In spite of their avowed attachment to arbitration as a cure for labor ills, the Knights became embroiled in an increasing number of strikes and boycotts, many of which ended disastrously. Moreover, the rapid expansion of membership after 1881 brought into the order many Socialists, radicals, and other jangling elements, and created ceaseless internal discord. The failure of some important railway strikes in 1886 cast further discredit on the order, and caused it to enter a period of decline, from which it has never recovered.

Another factor in the collapse of the Knights was the rise, at this time, of a rival labor body based upon a different principle of organization. Established originally in 1881 under a somewhat different name, this body reorganized on a broader basis in 1886, adopted a new constitution, and assumed the name of the "American Federation of Labor." The organization was modeled upon the British Trades Union Congress, which had been in successful operation since 1868.

As its name implies, the American Federation of Labor was, and is, a national confederation of self-governing trade bodies, supervised by a central board of officials. The fundamental basis of membership is the national union, though city trade assemblies, state federations, and local unions lacking national affiliations are admitted to membership. Since the workers in the constituent labor organizations enjoy home rule, the chief duties of the officers of the American Federation of Labor are to strengthen existing labor bodies and organize new ones, to act in an advisory capacity during industrial conflicts, and to agitate constantly for new and better labor laws. The purposes of the Federation are similar, in many respects, to those avowed by the Knights of Labor, and include the eight-hour day, the legislative prohibition of child labor, and the establishment of more humane working conditions in factories and mines.

From the outset, the constructive statesman of the American Federation of Labor was Samuel Gompers, an English immigrant of Dutch-Jewish lineage, who, entering the tobacco trade in New York in the early sixties, had helped to make the Cigar Makers' Union a model of its kind. The history of the Federation has been inextricably bound up with Gompers' own career. As President from 1882 almost uninterruptedly until his death in 1924, he built up a powerful organization. From a membership of 150,000 in 1886, it grew to 200,000 in 1890 and 550,000 in 1900. A man of forceful personality, his character mingled fearlessness and executive skill with conservative idealism. Largely through his influence, the Federation has resisted all efforts to commit it, on the one hand, to Socialism, or on the other, to the formation of an American labor party. At the present time, the Federation has more than 3,000,000 members, and is probably the strongest labor combination in the world.

As a result of its peculiar structure, the American Federation of Labor automatically excluded from membership the great mass of unorganized and unskilled workers, perhaps ninety per cent of the entire laboring class. Moreover, certain trade unions, notably the four Railway Brotherhoods (engineers, conductors, firemen, and brakemen), preferred to remain unaffiliated. These so-called Brotherhoods originated as mutual insurance associations, in consequence of the refusal of commercial companies to insure the lives of trainmen, but subsequently they took on ordinary trade-union activities. Their independent course toward the American Federation of Labor was a natural consequence of the strategic position they as railway workers held in American economic life — they had everything to lose and nothing to gain by casting in their fortunes with those of other labor groups.

Industrial Conflicts, 1873–1900

The chief bone of contention between capital and labor concerned wages, the workday, and the right of employees to organize. Labor's demands betokened not merely a desire of the common man to augment his creature comforts, but also an aspiration to live a better, fuller, and freer life — to share more richly in the graces and opportunities afforded by modern civilization. To labor's champions, it appeared that the proletariat were not getting their due share of the immense wealth which their dexterity and brawn had helped to create.

Employers, on the other hand, looked upon wages as one among a number of necessary items in their operating expenses, to be regulated according to market conditions rather than by humanitarian considerations. To them, labor's contribution in industry was of small importance as compared with the indispensable part played by financial resources, inventive genius, machinery, managerial ability, and business enterprise.

With two antagonistic philosophies struggling for dominance, a long series of costly and bloody conflicts was inevitable before either side could perceive that the other performed an essential rôle in production. Moreover, both parties, blinded by self-interest, regarded industrial disturbances as a private matter, concerning themselves alone. Not for many years did the American people come to realize that, whoever may be the victor in a strike, the general public is the loser, because of the unsettlement of business conditions, the added cost of police protection, and the temporarily increased prices.

While instances of labor disorders may be found throughout the period of national independence, the modern period of frequent and gigantic strikes began with the depression attending the Panic of 1873. Neither side was wholly blameless in these encounters, for irresponsibility, greed, and criminality entered, in varying degrees, into the actions of both. According to statistics compiled by the United States Bureau of Labor, approximately 24,000 strikes and lockouts of all kinds took place in the twenty years from 1881 to 1900, involving nearly 128,000 establishments and more than 6,600,000 wage-earners, at a total cost to employers and employees of $450,000,000. Strikes were likely to be successful in times of material prosperity when the employers were least willing to suspend business operations, and to fail when the opposite conditions prevailed.

As labor organizations grew in strength and improved in leadership, they were slower to resort to methods of coercion and violence, and the employers, on the other hand, betrayed a greater readiness to meet their demands. As the years wore on, there appeared a tendency, slight at first but of growing proportions, to settle industrial differences through joint conferences concluding in "trade agreements," which fixed wage-scales and other conditions of employment, or if such adjustment was impossible, through peaceful arbitration by disinterested parties.

Certain labor conflicts were of such magnitude and importance as to be termed "historic strikes." The first of these industrial outbreaks was the outgrowth of a general wage reduction of ten per cent on the Pennsylvania, New York Central, and Baltimore and Ohio railways in June and July, 1877. This cut came on top of an earlier ten-per-cent reduction after the Panic. Between July 16 and 31, 1877, there was rioting, destruction of property, and loss of life at Martinsburg in West Virginia, Baltimore, Pittsburgh, Chicago, St. Louis, and elsewhere. At the request of the respective Governors, President Hayes sent troops into West Virginia, Maryland, Pennsylvania, and Illinois to assist in quelling the disturbances.

At Pittsburgh the contest resembled a pitched battle. The state guardsmen living in the vicinity were called to arms, but fraternized with the strikers. When a division of Philadelphia militia arrived on the scene and killed about twenty rioters, the soldiers were besieged for twelve hours in a roundhouse by an infuriated mob. About 1600 cars, 126 locomotives, and nearly all the railway shops and supplies were destroyed during the strike. Order was finally restored by patrols of citizens, though not until damages had been inflicted estimated at $5,000,000. Here and elsewhere the strikers failed to accomplish their purpose.

The lawlessness that characterized the strikes of 1877 was greater than in most subsequent labor convulsions. This was due partly to the immaturity of trade-unionism at the time, and even more, to a new type of man which four years of unemployment had bred in the United States — the tramp or hobo. Alarmed by the reign of anarchy, the general public feared for a time that the country was on the verge of a social eruption similar to the Paris Commune of 1871.

Less than ten years later occurred the "Great Upheaval" of 1885–1886, when twice as many industrial conflicts took place as in any previous two-year period. Three of them involved the Gould railway system in the Southwest. The strike of March, 1885, was precipitated by a ten-per-cent wage reduction, and ended successfully for the workers. Another disturbance, six months later, was occasioned by the unfriendly attitude of the railway authorities toward employees who belonged to the Knights of Labor, and terminated in another victory for the strikers. The third and greatest of the disorders grew out of the discharge, for alleged incompetency, of a shop foreman prominent in the Knights of Labor. In the first days of March, 1886, the strike broke out simultaneously over the entire Gould system, throwing out of work nearly 9,000 shopmen, yardmen, and section hands in Nebraska, Kansas, Missouri, Arkansas, and Indian Territory. The strike was managed by the Knights, and after two months of sporadic violence and of much local suffering for want of food and fuel, it ended in utter failure for the employees.

The year 1886 was also signalized by a nationwide movement for an eight-hour day, sponsored by the American Federation of Labor. May 1 was set as the time for a general strike, although the constituent trade unions were permitted to determine their own attitude toward it. The main argument for shorter hours was the need to provide work for the unemployed. No fewer than 340,000 men took part in the movement. One hundred and fifty thousand of them secured a shorter day (eight or nine hours) without a demonstration; the remainder actually struck, though of these only 42,000 gained their point. In many cases, the concessions were subsequently lost through the aggressive activities of "employers' associations," which began to be formed about this time, in combating the claims of labor. Notwithstanding these setbacks, the conception of an eight-hour day aroused wide popular interest, and soon came to be regarded by the public as a just demand.

The next memorable outbreak was the Homestead strike of July, 1892, involving the employees of the Carnegie Steel Company at Homestead, Pennsylvania. The source of difficulty was the familiar one of the wage-scale and recognition of the union. Three hundred armed Pinkerton detectives were employed by the corporation to guard the plant during the troubles, and their coming on July 5 precipitated a fierce battle, which resulted in the death of ten men and the wounding of over sixty others. A few days later, 8,000 state militia arrived upon the scene. Under their protection, the Carnegie Company gradually resumed operations with non-union men, and the strike was finally declared off in November. Thereby the trade-union cause suffered a defeat in the steel industry from which it has not recovered to the present time.

On the day that the militia arrived at Homestead (July 11).

another bloody affray occurred between the organized miners of the Cœur d'Alene silver-mining district in Idaho and the strike-breakers whom the employers had imported to take their place. Successive wage reductions, growing out of the continuous drop in the market price of silver, were responsible for the troubles. The miners succeeded in seizing control of the property, and drove the strike-breakers out of the district. At the Governor's request, President Harrison dispatched troops to the seat of the disorders; martial law was declared; and the strike came to an end. This affair, however, proved to be the forerunner of a series of grave disturbances which ravaged the Cœur d'Alene district for many years.

The year 1894 was another eventful year in labor annals. The widespread unemployment resulting from the Panic of 1893 gave to industrial disorders the explosive qualities of a genuine class conflict. The numerous disturbances, deranging many trades and industries, involved nearly 750,000 workingmen, an even larger number than in 1886. The most serious of these affrays was the great Chicago strike.

This affair began in a small way in May, in consequence of the unwillingness of certain employees of the Pullman Palace Car Company to accept a general wage cut of from twenty to twenty-five per cent. The strikers were members of the American Railway Union, a new organization formed by Eugene V. Debs for the purpose of amalgamating all railway workers into one union. Accordingly, this body in June espoused the cause of the strikers, and ordered its 150,000 members to stop handling Pullman cars on the railways of the country unless the Pullman Company should consent to arbitration. This threat proving to be without avail, the strike spread after June 26 to the twenty-three lines radiating from Chicago, and soon affected traffic operations in twenty-seven states and territories.

The vortex of the storm, however, was Chicago. There, until the United States government took a hand in the affair, the principal antagonists were the General Managers' Association, representing the railway owners, and the American Railway Union. The damages, direct and indirect, inflicted by the strike on the property and business of the country were later estimated at $80,000,000. The lawless elements in Chicago took advantage of the disturbed conditions to rob, burn, pillage, and kill. Openly sympathetic with the strikers, Governor J. P. Altgeld refused to exercise his constitutional privilege of appealing for federal troops, and since the state legislature was not in session to make application, it appeared that the reign of violence would continue unchecked.

Such a conclusion, however, did not make sufficient allowance for the stubborn-willed Chief Magistrate of the nation. On July 2, the federal government secured a "blanket" injunction from the United States Circuit Court, which forbade Debs and the other strike-leaders and "all other persons whomsoever" to interfere in any manner, direct or indirect, with the operation of the railways. This was followed on the next day by the ordering of 2,000 United States troops to Chicago. The constitutional basis for President Cleveland's unexpected action was his obligation to prevent obstruction in the transmission of the mails, to protect interstate commerce, and to safeguard the processes of the federal courts.

On July 10 Debs was arrested on the charge of conspiracy in restraint of trade under the Sherman Anti-Trust Act; and being released on bail, he was rearrested a week later on a new charge — contempt of court, that is, violation of the judicial injunction of July 2. The government's bold intervention broke the morale of the strikers; and this circumstance, along with the refusal of the great unions in the American Federation of Labor to join the strike, caused its complete collapse before the end of the month.

Other than as a great labor insurrection, the strike of 1894 is historic because of the new legal conceptions and practices which issued from it. The employment of United States troops without the consent of the state authorities marked a new and impressive development of national authority. The application of the Sherman Anti-Trust Act to labor combinations — later upheld by the courts — threw unexpected light on that law.

Perhaps most significant of all was the part played by the judiciary in using the injunction as a weapon in industrial warfare. By organized labor, this was denounced as "judicial tyranny" — unjust because it seemed to range the might of the government on the side of the employers, and illegal because men arrested for violating the court order were sentenced without trial by jury and subjected to penalties not prescribed by statute. Opposition to "government by injunction" became a leading issue of the American Federation of Labor, and an attempt to restrict the operation of the injunction was eventually made during the first Wilson administration (see page 472).

Political Aspects of the Labor Movement

The cause of labor made great strides as a result of trade-union activities, and the victories won by industrial warfare were supplemented by legislative safeguards extended by the state and national governments. Eight-hour laws were passed in Connecticut, New York, Illinois, Wisconsin, Missouri, and California in 1867 and 1868. It must be confessed, however, that the advantage to the workingman was more illusory than real, since longer days were permitted by these statutes whenever the contract of labor so provided. In the latter year, an eight-hour law was adopted by Congress, applicable to all federal employees.

Steady progress was made in the subsequent years in the enactment of factory legislation. The advances seem meager, however, as compared with thoroughgoing statutes that were being enacted in Great Britain and Germany during these years for the welfare of the working class. Wage-earning children and women were the first beneficiaries of the new American laws, since public sympathy responded most readily to their needs. Massachusetts set a shining example for that time with a statute of 1874, which established a ten-hour day in factories for children under eighteen and women above that age. During the eighties similar legislation was passed in most of the manufacturing states. The number of child-workers in factories fell off one third during that decade, but grew again after 1890 with the increase of cotton mills in the South.

In the late eighties and early nineties, acts began to be passed for the safeguarding of dangerous machinery, for better sanitary arrangements in factories, and for government inspection of conditions. But when statutes were adopted in certain states for the absolute restriction of the length of the workday of men in private industries, such acts were invariably held to be unconstitutional, except in especially hazardous employments, on the ground that they interfered with the individual's freedom of contract.

The formidable proportions of the "Great Upheaval" of 1885–1886 elicited the first special message dealing with labor ever sent by a President to Congress. In 1886 Cleveland proposed the creation of a national commission to assist in the settlement of all controversies between capital and labor. Finally in October, 1888, Congress enacted a law for the arbitration of disputes between railway corporations and their employees with the consent of both parties and without obligation upon either party to abide by the decision reached. The law proved to be of little utility, and was superseded in 1898 by the Erdman Act, which provided, among other things, that after a difference was once submitted to arbitration, the decision of the arbitrators should be binding. Fifteen of the states also passed laws in this period, providing for voluntary arbitration and nonenforceable decisions in the case of industrial disturbances occurring wholly within their jurisdiction.

The ceaseless agitation of labor organizations played an important part in the enactment of factory laws. The American Federation of Labor was especially successful in lobbying for better legislation. Though independent labor parties offered candidates in almost every presidential campaign, beginning with 1872, it is doubtful whether their activities counted for much. Those parties which, in imitation of the Knights of Labor and American Federation of Labor, proposed mere piecemeal reform were short-lived, and polled only a handful of votes.[1]

In 1892 a labor party of a different type, the Socialist Labor party, took part in the presidential election. Socialism in its modern form was introduced into this country by the German immigrants of mid-century; and after 1867, Socialist parties began to operate locally in New York, Illinois, and elsewhere under leaders who could scarcely speak the English language. In 1877 the various Socialist groups united in forming the Socialist

[1] The following parties were of this type: the Labor Reform party (1872), an outgrowth of the National Labor Union; the Greenback-Labor party (1880 and 1884), which sought to combine the interests of rural and urban labor; the Anti-Monopoly party (1884); and in 1888, the Union Labor party and the United Labor party.

Labor party, but being small in numbers and needing time for propaganda, they refrained from nominating candidates until 1892.

The Socialists flouted all efforts to patch up or reform the existing economic order as puerile, and proposed nothing less than a fundamental reconstruction of society and industry. According to their creed, the opportunity of private individuals and corporations to amass colossal fortunes and acquire vast economic power is the root of all evil in modern capitalistic civilization. They therefore advocate the socialization of all the great industries, transportation systems, and important natural resources, or in other words, that the people collectively shall own these enterprises and, in conjunction with the workers employed in them, operate them for the good of the public and of the employees.

The Socialist Labor candidates secured only 22,000 votes in their first campaign, and but 36,000 in 1896. The slow growth of the party was due partly to the fact that its policies were dictated by men unfamiliar with American life and institutions. In an effort to broaden the appeal of the cause, a rival party, the "Socialist" party, was founded a few years later by Eugene V. Debs, recently of the American Railway Union. Debs himself was the first candidate for President, polling nearly 88,000 votes in 1900. In every campaign since then, both parties have been active.

SELECT BIBLIOGRAPHY

The Growth of Labor Solidarity. The most detailed historical treatment is J. R. Commons and others, *History of Labour in the United States*, II (New York, 1918). Selig Perlman, *A History of Trade Unionism in the United States* (New York, 1922), S. P. Orth, *The Armies of Labor* (in *The Chronicles of America*, XL, New Haven, 1919), and Mary R. Beard, *A Short History of the American Labor Movement* (New York, 1924), are well-connected accounts and briefer in compass.

Important monographic studies are M. A. Aldrich, " The American Federation of Labor " (in American Economic Association, *Economic Studies*, III, no. 4, New York, 1898); D. D. Lescohier, *The Knights of St. Crispin* (in *University of Wisconsin Economic and Political Science Series*, VII, no. 1, Madison, 1910); B. M. Rastall, *The Labor History of the Cripple Creek District* (in *University of Wisconsin Economic and Political Science Series*, III, no. 1, Madison, 1908); and E. C. Robbins, *Railway Conductors; a Study in Organized Labor* (in *Columbia University Studies*, LXI, no. 1, New York, 1914).

Industrial Conflicts, 1873–1900. The conditions which have produced friction between capital and labor are described and analyzed in T. S. Adams and Helen L. Sumner, *Labor Problems* (New York, 1905), and F. T. Carlton, *The History and Problems of Organized Labor* (Boston, 1920). A systematic and interesting narrative of the historic strikes may be found in C. D. Wright, *The Industrial Evolution of the United States* (New York, 1895). J. F. Rhodes, *History of the United States*, VIII (New York, 1919), is particularly good on the railway strikes of 1877 and the Molly Maguires' affair.

Political Aspects of the Labor Movement. Nearly all the general works on the labor movement pay attention to the evolution of factory legislation. F. E. Haynes, *Social Politics in the United States* (Boston, 1924), gives a succinct account of the American Socialist movement; a fuller treatment is Morris Hillquit, *History of Socialism in the United States* (New York, 1910).

CHAPTER XXIII

THE SILVER CRUSADE, 1873–1900

THE RISE OF THE SILVER MOVEMENT

The new social forces and class antagonisms, engendered by the Economic Revolution, found unfettered expression, for the first time, in Cleveland's second administration. The turbulence attending the Chicago strike of 1894 had awakened, in the minds of many people, fears of the durability of democratic institutions, but no sooner did the nation weather this storm than it was projected into the midst of a bitter conflict between the debtor and creditor classes over the question of "free silver."

This controversy had its rise in a statute of 1873, which, among other things, omitted the silver dollar from the list of authorized coins for domestic use. At the time, the Act attracted little attention since silver dollars had not been in circulation for forty years. Greenbacks and national-bank notes were the only forms of money in actual use by the people, for the scarcity of silver metal caused the bullion value of a dollar to exceed its face-value, and hence none of it was presented at the mints for coinage.

It was not long, however, before the law was brought to an angry public notice. The Act was denounced as the "Crime of 1873," and in the political discussions of the next twenty years or so, the charge was freely made and widely believed that the silver dollar had been demonetized through the sinister and corrupt influence of "Wall Street" and "Big Business." Several influences conspired to bring about this state of affairs. Quickly following the passage of the law there occurred an enormous and unexpected increase in the world supply of silver bullion. New mines were opened up in Nevada, Utah, Colorado, and Montana, and at about the same time, several European countries, deciding to adopt the single gold standard, melted all their important silver coins and offered the metal for sale.[1] Coincident with these developments, the United States entered a five-year period of uninterrupted hard times, unemployment, and falling farm prices.

As a result, there were two classes of people who became vitally interested in the restoration of the historic silver dollar. One of these was the small but energetic group of silver-mine owners in the Far West, who saw the market price of the bullion content of the old dollar drop from $1.02 in 1872 to 96 cents in 1875, and subsequently to 82 cents in 1885, with the downward trend still unchecked. If the government could again be induced to purchase all the bullion brought to the mint for coinage into dollars, they reasoned that the market price of the metal and the profits of silver production would rise in response to the unlimited demand.

The chief outcry, however, came from the poor people of the country — the hardworking farmers of the West and the South and the wage-earning population of the Eastern cities, many of whom were mired in debt because of the financial depression. In reality, the lean years of 1873–1878 were a revulsion from an era of feverish industrial expansion, aggravated by a falling-off of the European demand for grain. But these people, unaccustomed to thinking in the broader terms of the economist, attributed their ills to a shortage of circulating medium. They cited not only the "Crime of 1873" but also the fact that the annual world production of gold was virtually stationary. By enlarging the volume of money in circulation, they believed that the government would indirectly help them to get higher prices for farm crops and better wages in industry, and make it easier for them to pay their debts.

Although for a few years the greenback demand occupied the center of the stage, the chances of new paper issues rapidly waned after the passage of the Resumption Act of 1875. Silver, moreover, had the advantage of being a metal, a legal coin of the United States for many years, and still a standard coin in certain foreign lands. Accordingly, "free silver" — the coinage of

[1] Germany demonetized silver in 1871, Denmark, Sweden, and Norway in 1873. In the latter year the Latin Union, composed of France, Italy, Belgium, Switzerland, and Greece, limited the coinage of silver.

standard silver dollars under the same unlimited arrangement as gold — became the paramount demand of the money inflationists, though the greenback alternative was never entirely lost sight of. The chief opposition came from the men of capital and large business interests, who had no desire to try an experiment which would, in their opinion, diminish the purchasing power of their incomes, and enable their debtors to discharge their obligations in "cheap money."

The silver question was not a party issue for many years, indeed not until the eve of the campaign of 1896 in the case of the major parties. Each party was divided internally on the issue, roughly between East and West, between creditor and debtor. Consequently, the platform declarations on the money question were conveniently vague. But notwithstanding the nonpartisan character of the agitation, few questions of the time were more violently contested in the halls of Congress.

One of the earliest champions of free silver was Richard P. Bland, a Missouri Democrat whose convictions represented the fruit of his experiences in Western mining regions as well as his familiarity with the hardships of his farmer constituents. Under his leadership, a bill passed the House of Representatives in November, 1877, providing for the restoration of the silver dollar and its coinage in unlimited quantities as before 1873. The Senate demurred; and an amendment, offered by W. B. Allison of Iowa, directed the Treasury Department to purchase only from two to four million dollars' worth of silver bullion each month and coin it into dollars. Even in this modified form the measure was unacceptable to President Hayes, who held that, in the case of debts contracted since 1873, it substituted a less valuable form of payment and, therefore, involved a violation of contract. But the bill was easily passed over his veto in February, 1878.

As a compromise settlement, the Bland-Allison Act had the effect of allaying further agitation of the money question for several years, though both Arthur and Cleveland recommended the repeal of the law. The least amount of bullion permitted by the statute was purchased and coined each month, adding about $31,000,000 annually to the circulating medium. As the people disliked to handle the heavy coins, Congress in 1886 authorized the issuance of silver certificates in small denominations, and by means of these paper representatives, most of the money passed into circulation.

Toward the end of the decade, however, the silver movement sprang to life again. The reasons were various. For one thing, the United States government, under spur of the surplus revenue, was actively engaged in retiring its war bonds; and the dwindling of the bonded indebtedness, on which the national-bank notes were based, caused a shrinkage of these notes from $359,-000,000 in 1882 to $186,000,000 in 1890. At the same time, the political effectiveness of the silver elements in Congress was greatly strengthened by the granting of statehood to the Dakotas, Montana, Washington, Idaho, and Wyoming in 1889 and 1890. Most significant of all, however, was the momentum given to the cause by a reappearance of farmers' organizations.

Like the Granger uprising of the seventies, the strength of this new agrarian movement sprang from the economic difficulties which beset the rural population. The price of agricultural products, which had been falling almost continuously since the war, now reached new depths. Corn which sold for 63 cents per bushel in 1881 was selling for 28 cents nine years later. The average price of a bushel of wheat from 1883 to 1889 inclusive was 73 cents, of oats 28 cents. The farmer was further harried by a long series of droughts, which, beginning in 1887, parched his fields and withered his annual plantings for a space of ten years in South Dakota, Nebraska, and the western half of Kansas. The annual corn production of Kansas and Nebraska fell from 287,816,000 bushels in 1885 to 110,579,000 bushels in 1889.

Unable to make ends meet, the farmers borrowed heavily from Eastern capitalists and bankers at ruinous rates of interest. The mortgage indebtedness of the agricultural lands of the nation increased from $343,000,000 in 1880 to $586,000,000 in 1890. In the latter year, the farms of Kansas, Nebraska, and the Dakotas were mortgaged to one fourth of their value. In Kansas and South Dakota, counties were to be found in which ninety per cent or more of the agricultural land was under mortgage.

Under these circumstances, the farmers turned their thoughts to organized action as a means of bettering their situation. Early in the eighties local farmers' associations began to spring up in various parts of the West and South. After a time these merged into state bodies, and presently, into interstate federations. Two great organizations grew up in this manner in the cotton belt: the National Farmers' Alliance, founded in 1880, and the Agricultural Wheel, established in 1882. They combined forces in 1888 to form a body known popularly as the "Southern Farmers' Alliance." Meantime, a Northern Farmers' Alliance, founded in 1880, rose to a dominant position among the agricultural bodies of the Middle West.

In the first years, the organized farmers were nonpolitical in their outlook, and gave their attention to projects for self-help, such as joint-stock stores and coöperative cotton yards, grain elevators, and creameries. But when, through inexperienced direction, these enterprises collapsed, as most of them did, the farmers began to seek legislative remedies for their ills. They demanded of the government such measures as lower interest rates, free silver and greenback inflation, an income tax on the rich, and public ownership of railways. Their ceaseless propaganda proved a potent force in inducing Congress to pass a new coinage act in July, 1890.

The Senate was willing to go the whole length and establish free silver, but the House preferred to let matters rest as they were under the Bland-Allison Act. The Republican leaders, however, were chiefly concerned with the adoption of a new tariff, and by delaying the passage of the McKinley bill, the silverites in the House forced the Eastern manufacturers to yield ground on the money question. McKinley himself, who had supported the original Bland bill in November, 1877, now advocated the passage of the new silver measure as the next best thing to free coinage. In its final form, the Sherman Silver Purchase Act, as it was termed, required the Treasury Department to buy 4,500,000 ounces of silver bullion each month (nearly twice as much as had been coined before), and to issue in payment therefor treasury notes of full legal-tender character, redeemable in either gold or silver at the option of the government.

Populism and the Panic of 1893

Unlike the Bland-Allison Act, no respite of silver agitation followed the Act of 1890. The bullion value of the dollar declined from 81 cents in 1890 to 60 cents in 1893, notwithstanding the greater absorption of silver by the government. Moreover, after 1890, there began another downward trend in the price of grain and live stock. An investigation, made by the Department of Agriculture in 1893, showed that under the existing conditions the cost of raising wheat and corn exceeded the prices received. More than 11,000 farm mortgages were foreclosed in Kansas between 1889 and 1893, and two years later, from 75 to 90 per cent of the land was owned by loan companies in fifteen counties of the state. The South shared in the current distress. Cotton, which had averaged nearly 11 cents a pound for the decade ending in 1890, dropped to less than 9 cents in 1891, and below 8 cents in 1892.

A wave of despair swept over the West and the South, on the crest of which the aggrieved classes turned instinctively to direct political action for relief. Hamlin Garland, who studied the phenomenon at first hand, wrote many years later, "As ten-cent corn and ten per cent interest were troubling Kansas, so six-cent cotton was inflaming Georgia — and both were frankly sympathetic with Montana and Colorado whose miners were suffering from a drop in the price of silver."

The new spirit was exemplified in the person of Mrs. Mary E. Lease of Kansas, a stirring speaker who went up and down the state, exhorting the farmers to "raise less corn and more hell"; and the effect of the agrarian uprising on conservative Easterners was reflected in the caustic comment of the *New York Evening Post*, "We don't want any more states until we can civilize Kansas." Leaders new to politics began to make their appearance, like "Sockless" Jerry Simpson of Kansas, whose nickname rose from a personal habit that was ascribed to him, and B. R. Tillman of South Carolina, a "poor white" leader of the backcountry, whose violent speech won him the sobriquet of "Pitchfork Ben."[1]

[1] As was true of most Southerners who espoused the farmers' cause, Tillman carried on his fight within the ranks of the Democratic party.

Less than four months after the passage of the new silver law, the Farmers' Alliances took part in the fall elections of 1890, carrying a number of Western and Southern states, and electing three United States Senators and fifty Representatives. Fired by these initial successes, plans were at once begun to bring the urban wage-earners into the movement, and thereby enable the manual workers of the nation to present a united front to the old parties at the approaching presidential election.

Under the name of the "People's party," the new party was formally launched at Omaha on July 2, 1892, at a mammoth convention, made up of representatives of the moribund Knights of Labor and a number of civic reform associations as well as of the organized farmers. The delegates were animated by an unquenchable zeal, and the adoption of the platform was greeted, according to one observer, by "cheers and yells which rose like a tornado . . . and raged without cessation for thirty-four minutes, during which women shrieked and wept, men embraced and kissed . . ., marched back and forth, and leaped upon tables and chairs in the ecstasy of their delirium."

The major parties were denounced by the platform as pawns of the capitalistic interests, and on behalf of the "plain people," demands were made for free silver, greenbacks, a graduated income tax, government ownership of the railways and telegraphs, a shorter workday for urban laborers, direct election of United States Senators, and the initiative and referendum. The veteran campaigner, James B. Weaver of Iowa, who had been the Greenback nominee in 1880, was chosen as the Populist candidate for President, and in the ensuing election the new party amazed the old-party leaders by polling twenty-two electoral votes and more than one million popular votes. For the first time since the birth of the Republican party, a third party won representation in the electoral college.

Nevertheless, Cleveland had been elected by an enormous majority on the tariff issue, and with an improvement of economic conditions, it seemed probable that the political stream would subside quietly into its customary banks once more. But such was not to be the case. No sooner did the new President enter office than a panic crashed upon the country, which, in its destructive effects, rivaled that of 1873.

The disaster of 1893 was the product of a complication of causes. Overinvestment in railways and industrial combinations, including too many of a highly speculative character, was a leading factor. Widespread depression in Europe since 1889, involving Great Britain, Germany, and France among other countries, had its influence, for it led to a withdrawal of a part of the gold which foreign capitalists had invested in American enterprises. But most serious of all was the growing fear of the business classes that the rising tide of silver inflation, under the Sherman Act, would sweep the government off of a gold basis and cause a suspension of gold payments.

The Sherman Law did, indeed, direct the redemption of the new treasury notes in either gold or silver, but while the monthly purchases caused the piling up of a vast hoard of silver bullion in the treasury, no provision had been made for additions to the gold supply. It will be recalled that this gold reserve of $100,000,000 had originally been accumulated as a sustaining fund for the $346,681,016 worth of greenbacks when specie payment was resumed; now it must serve, in addition, as a redemption fund for the treasury notes that were being issued at an annual rate of more than $50,000,000 under the Sherman Act.[1]

Indeed, since the law had not expressly separated it from the other funds in the treasury, there was always a possibility that the gold reserve might be drawn upon for the routine expenses of the government. While the Act of 1890 authorized the government to redeem the treasury notes in silver if it chose, the provision was highly impracticable, for the refusal to pay gold would have impaired the confidence of the people in the government's financial integrity and toppled down the whole edifice of public credit.

In the last months of Harrison's administration, the amount of gold in the treasury fell rapidly, largely because of lavish appropriations of Congress and the diminished revenues caused by the McKinley Tariff Act. Six weeks after Cleveland entered office, the gold reserve itself was dipped into to meet the current expenses of the government. The decline of the gold reserve below $100,000,000 created intense alarm among the business

[1] The 378,166,000 silver dollars issued under the Bland-Allison Act were not redeemable in gold, according to law.

classes, and incited people everywhere to present treasury notes for redemption in gold. It created further demands upon the treasury from foreign capitalists and merchants, who called for prompt settlement of their American accounts in gold, the only metal used in international trade.

Even a sounder commercial structure could not have withstood this shock to public confidence. As it was, a paralysis of fear seized upon the business world. More than 8,000 commercial concerns failed between April 1 and October 1, 1893, with liabilities of nearly $285,000,000. Many banks went under, particularly in the West and the South; and one hundred and fifty-six railways fell into the hands of receivers, including the Erie, the Union Pacific, and the Northern Pacific. In the population centers the problem of unemployment became acute. The farmers were likewise involved in the universal ruin, wheat touching bottom in 1894 with an average price of 49 cents a bushel.

Cleveland's policy of dealing with the crisis was twofold: first, to stop the increasing strain upon the already overburdened gold reserve by a cessation of silver purchases, and secondly, to continue gold payments at all hazards. In pursuance of the first purpose, he summoned a special session of Congress for August 7, 1893, and at his insistence, the House rushed through a bill for repealing the Sherman Silver Purchase Act. But the silver forces in the Senate were not to be taken by storm, and utilizing their advantage of unlimited debate, they sought to prevent action through "filibustering." On one occasion the Populist Senator, W. V. Allen of Nebraska, held the floor for fourteen hours. Another persistent opponent was a Republican, Senator H. M. Teller of Colorado. The majority eventually prevailed, however, and the repeal bill was signed by Cleveland on November 1, 1893.

In order to protect the gold reserve without suspending gold payments, the government proposed to borrow the yellow metal faster than it was drained from the treasury for redemption purposes. Unfortunately, paper money presented for redemption had to be paid out by the government for running expenses, and it was then promptly turned in again for gold by its recipients. "We have an endless chain in operation constantly depleting the Treasury's gold," Cleveland bitterly told Congress. After this fashion, the gold fund dwindled from $95,000,000 at the close of June, 1893, with fluctuations to $65,000,000 a year later.

Congress, inspired in part by silver arguments, refused to authorize bond issues to maintain the reserve, whereupon Cleveland, acting under authority of an almost forgotten statute, sold $50,000,000 worth of bonds to the public for gold in January, 1894, and a similar amount again in November. Only temporary relief resulted, however, for the bonds were purchased, in large part, with gold that had been drawn out of the treasury itself by the presentation of paper currency for redemption.

In the quest for more substantial relief, the government in February, 1895, arranged with J. P. Morgan and a financial syndicate for the purchase of $65,000,000 worth of gold with bonds bearing a high interest rate. The unusual conditions were affixed that at least one half of the metal must be procured abroad, and that the bankers should exert their influence to protect the gold reserve against further depletion. As a result, the financial strain on the government relaxed for the next four or five months, though the Populists and radical Democrats, embittered against capitalistic greed, charged Cleveland with betraying the masses by allowing the bankers an excess profit of $16,000,000 in the transaction. The peak of the financial crisis was passed; but normal conditions did not return until the next year, when they were assisted by a fourth bond sale — this time directly to the public — of $100,000,000 in January, 1896, and by a widespread improvement of business.

The Battle of 1896

When the bill repealing the Sherman Law passed the House of Representatives, Bland proclaimed that the struggle had but begun, and would conclude only with the establishment of free coinage. The events of the next few years made this prediction seem anything but an idle boast. The wage reductions and bread-lines of 1893 produced a harvest of labor outbreaks in the spring of 1894, of which the great Chicago strike was only the most portentous instance (see pages 382–384). Among the unemployed, the social contagion spread rapidly, and organized gangs of tramps and men out of work began a march on Washington to make a personal presentation of their grievances.

One "petition in boots" under "General" L. C. Frye started from Los Angeles, and at one time numbered about eight hundred men. Another, under "General" C. T. Kelly, gathered nineteen hundred followers on its picturesque journey eastward from San Francisco. The third and best known "army," commanding a maximum strength of six hundred, was led by "General" J. S. Coxey of Massillon, Ohio. Other bands, of fluctuating strength, were recruited in Seattle, St. Louis, and Chicago. In all, perhaps twelve hundred men straggled into Washington during May, June, and July, 1894. Coxey himself was arrested on the technical charge of trespassing on the Capitol lawn, and the motley bands, lacking provisions and constantly worried by the authorities, soon melted away.

Popular suspicion of the overweening power of "Big Business" was intensified by the Senate's betrayal of Cleveland's tariff policy in the framing of the Wilson-Gorman Act in 1894, and when the Supreme Court declared the income-tax provision unconstitutional in 1895, the resentment of the discontented exceeded all bounds (see pages 357–358). As Mr. Justice Harlan recalled many years later in the course of a Supreme Court decision, the people in these years were stirred by "a deep feeling of unrest. The Nation had been rid of human slavery . . . but the conviction was universal that the country was in real danger from another kind of slavery, . . . namely, the slavery that would result from aggregations of capital in the hands of a few . . . controlling, for their own . . . advantage exclusively, the entire business of the country. . . ."

Under these circumstances, the controversy over the money standard ceased to be a technical financial question, and became a symbol of the underlying, irrepressible conflict between the "masses" and the "classes." The friends of the masses instinctively rallied to the silver cause, whereas those in the opposition were classed as the tools of "Wall Street" and the "plutocracy." The growing enthusiasm for free coinage rapidly developed into something resembling a mighty religious revival, and in 1894 the Bible of the new faith appeared in the form of a yellow-backed, paper-bound book, entitled *Coin's Financial School,* written by W. H. Harvey.

This little volume, enlivened with pertinent caricatures and addressed to the simplest understanding, set forth cogently the main silver arguments, and skillfully played upon the prejudices of the poor against the rich. Early in 1895, it attained a sale of more than 100,000 copies a month, and undoubtedly won thousands of converts to the silver cause. With the ardor of crusaders, the people assembled in ten thousand schoolhouses throughout the West and the South to debate the absorbing question — not only the politician and the farmer, but the small merchant and the workingman, the preacher and the schoolteacher. Organized labor took a hand in the matter, and conventions of the American Federation of Labor in 1893, 1894, and 1895 warmly indorsed free silver.

The old parties were badly frightened, but knew not what to do. Their bewilderment was revealed in their state conventions of 1894 prior to the fall elections. Official utterances, both of the Republicans and Democrats, varied from ambiguous generalities to whole-hearted advocacy of free coinage. A significant demonstration of silver sentiment among Western Democrats took place in June at Omaha, where, under the leadership of William Jennings Bryan of Nebraska, a monster convention declared for the immediate adoption of free coinage. In the elections, the Democrats, burdened with Cleveland's unpopularity, suffered severe losses. The Republicans were the chief gainers, but the Populists elected six United States Senators, and increased their popular vote over that of 1892 by 42 per cent.

On the heels of the election, the silver Democrats began to make plans to cast off Eastern control in the forthcoming presidential campaign, and commit the party unequivocally to free coinage. During 1895 numerous conferences of silverites were held, organizations formed, speeches made, pamphlets circulated. When the national convention assembled at Chicago on July 7, 1896, the triumph of the silver Democrats was assured. A platform was adopted which contained a ringing indorsement of free coinage — the question "paramount to all others at this time," assailed the income-tax decision, and denounced federal interference in labor disturbances. All favorable mention of Cleveland, the party's own President, was omitted.

While the platform was before the convention, there occurred one of the most exciting debates ever held on such an occasion. Amidst hissing and jeering, "Pitchfork Ben" Tillman of South Carolina, now a United States Senator, shouted that the silver question was as truly sectional as the slavery question, and that the South now joined hands with the West to restore the government to the people. Senator David B. Hill of New York ably championed the cause of gold and the East, and ended his address with an appeal not "to drive old Democrats out of the party who have grown gray in the service, to make room for a lot of Republicans and Populists, and political nondescripts."

Other speakers participated, and then the debate reached a dramatic climax in the concluding speech of the youthful Bryan of Nebraska. Speaking with a full-toned, richly modulated eloquence unmatched in his generation, he presented the free-coinage question as "a cause as holy as the cause of humanity," called for another Jackson to lead the Democratic hosts "against the encroachments of organized wealth," and brought his hearers in a frenzy to their feet with his closing defiance to the gold adherents, "You shall not press down upon the brow of labor this crown of thorns; you shall not crucify mankind upon a cross of gold." Bland had been considered the logical candidate for President before the convention gathered, but now his fame was eclipsed by that of the young Nebraskan. In the balloting Bryan was chosen on the fifth trial, most of the Eastern delegates abstaining from voting. Arthur Sewall, a Maine banker and shipbuilder of free-coinage convictions, was nominated for Vice-President.

When the Republicans convened at St. Louis on June 16, their ranks were divided among advocates of the gold standard, those who preferred the customary policy of noncommittalism, and a resolute minority from the Far West bent upon a free-silver declaration. The leading aspirant for the nomination was ex-Governor McKinley of Ohio, a Civil-War veteran, known to the public chiefly as an ardent protectionist. For his prominence before the convention he was largely indebted to the tireless efforts of his friend Marcus A. Hanna. The latter was an Ohio capitalist, who in his early years had found political manipulation an indispensable tool for amassing a fortune in mines, banking, and street railways, but who later became addicted to the political game for its own sake.

Hanna's efforts and money had facilitated McKinley's election as Governor in 1891, and when two years later McKinley became involved in financial obligations to the extent of $100,000, Hanna, Carnegie, Frick, and others supplied the funds that saved him from bankruptcy. In preparing the way for McKinley's nomination by the Republican convention, Hanna spent not less than $100,000 in a campaign of publicity and personal canvass among the delegates.

The monetary issue presented serious difficulties for McKinley, for he had been a supporter of free silver until 1891, when, in his gubernatorial campaign, he upheld limited coinage, as provided by the Sherman Act, in preference to unlimited coinage. By temperament as well as by previous conviction, McKinley wished the party to straddle the money question, as in earlier campaigns, and to focus all attention on the tariff. He believed, furthermore, that this policy of conciliation was necessary to cement the majority necessary for his nomination by the convention. Hanna, sinking the business man in the politician, assented to the plan, but not so the powerful Eastern leaders who demanded a gold declaration as the price of their support.

The outcome of many secret conferences between the factions was a skillfully constructed plank, which read in part: "We are . . . opposed to the free coinage of silver except by international agreement . . . , which we pledge ourselves to promote, and until such agreement can be obtained the existing gold standard must be preserved." Taken literally, the platform declared for international free silver, but since international conferences in 1878, 1881, and 1892 had amply demonstrated the unwillingness of European countries to depart from the single gold standard, the plank was rightly construed by the silverites as a repudiation of free coinage. Thirty-four delegates with Senator Teller of Colorado at their head withdrew from the convention in protest. In the completed platform, the money plank occupied an inconspicuous position in the middle, the first nine paragraphs being devoted to disparagement of the Democrats and praise of the protective system. McKinley was easily nominated on the first ballot, and with his name was coupled that of G. A. Hobart of New Jersey.

The decision of the major parties led to a disruption of party loyalties comparable only to the effect of the slavery issue on the voters of 1860. Certain old-school Democrats, acting with Cleveland's approval, held a convention, indorsed the gold standard, and nominated their own candidates. Had the Republican platform been less emphatic on the tariff question, the McKinley ticket might have received their support. The Republican irreconcilables, calling themselves the "National Silver party," gave their formal indorsement to Bryan and Sewall. As was to be expected, the People's party also indorsed Bryan, though for Vice-President they nominated one of their own followers in preference to the Maine banker. Even the Prohibitionists were affected by the all-absorbing issue, and broke into two parties, with separate platforms and candidates.

The contest was unique and sensational to the end. Fearful of further defections from their ranks, Republican campaigners at first avoided the monetary question, and placed all stress upon "Bill McKinley and the McKinley Bill." But the lead was taken out of their hands when Bryan undertook a remarkable stumping tour of eighteen thousand miles, addressing nearly five million people in twenty-nine states in fourteen weeks, and everywhere preaching free silver and the doctrine of discontent. Gompers and other leaders of organized labor exerted themselves on his behalf. The Democratic cause was also aided by the "yellow press," which, under Hearst's leadership, was beginning its rise about this time. Of very great influence were Homer Davenport's cartoons, which pictured "Mark" Hanna as an obese man of brutalized aspect, clad in a suit checkered with dollar-signs, and leading the child McKinley by a string. For campaign funds the Democrats leaned heavily upon the silver-mine owners, and something over a half-million dollars was subscribed in all.

To checkmate the efforts of the opposition, Hanna as Chairman of the Republican National Committee collected from the great banking and business interests an election fund of unknown amount, probably between three and four million dollars, and launched a mammoth campaign of popular education. A small army was organized to address rallies, disseminate literature, and distribute campaign buttons. More than 250,000,000 copies of documents were distributed among the voters, printed in German, French, Spanish, Italian, Swedish, Norwegian, Finnish, Dutch, and Yiddish as well as in English.

A circular letter was even sent to the various religious denominations, pointing out the harm which, according to the gold-standard doctrine, free coinage would inflict upon those engaged in church work. Over five hundred different posters were prepared, one of the most popular being a lithograph of McKinley, bearing the inscription, "The Advance Agent of Prosperity." The candidate himself remained at home, delivering from his front porch in Canton, Ohio, impressive set addresses to visiting delegations.

Most of the leading students of finance and political economy were against Bryan on the money question, and the veteran independent, Carl Schurz, threw all his enormous influence to the Republican ticket. But as a writer in the *Arena* magazine remarked with much truth, "The real meaning of this campaign lies far deeper than any question of one metal or two for a monetary base. It is a question of entrusting Federal power to men in hearty sympathy with the great common people or to men in sympathy with Wall Street."

As the campaign drew to a close, the excitement of the country became intense. The moneyed interests exerted economic pressure on behalf of the Republican ticket. Manufacturers made contracts contingent upon McKinley's election, and wage-earners were notified that the factories would close in the event of Democratic success. By such newspapers as the *New York Tribune*, Bryan was reviled as a "demagogue," an "anarchist," and a "madman." Even so sober an organ as the *New York Evening Post* characterized the contest as one between "the great civilizing forces of the republic" and "the still surviving barbarism bred by slavery in the South and the reckless spirit of adventure in the mining camps of the West." A rise in the price of wheat, due to crop failures in Russia, South America, and elsewhere, occurred a few weeks before election day, and by mitigating the farmers' dissatisfaction, served to aid the Republican cause.

The outcome of the election was decisive. McKinley received 51 per cent of the popular vote as compared with less than 47 per cent for his opponent, the largest majority since Grant's victory over Greeley. His preponderance in the electoral college was considerably greater than in the popular vote: 271 to 176. In general, the industrial and older grain-growing states supported McKinley as against the cotton states, prairie states, and silver-mining states. The immediate issue, that of silver coinage, was conclusively settled, but the future was to disclose that the campaign marked the entry of new and dynamic social forces into American politics.

The new President went into office with Republican majorities in both branches of Congress. In marked contrast with his Democratic predecessor, McKinley's distinguishing traits were affability, tact, patience, and a desire to keep in step with his party. He wished to make Hanna Postmaster-General, but the latter's ambitions looked toward the Senate. McKinley therefore promoted Senator John Sherman to the office of Secretary of State, so that Hanna might succeed to the vacant senatorship. Because of advanced years and mental impairment, Sherman was presently replaced by William R. Day of Ohio, and the latter in turn retired late in August, 1898, to make way for John Hay, one of the ablest men who ever occupied the office.[1]

In spite of an apparently clear popular verdict against silver, President McKinley chose to interpret his victory as primarily a mandate for tariff protection. The fact was that Republican ranks remained divided notwithstanding the united front displayed at the election, and it seemed to McKinley and his advisers the part of wisdom to let well enough alone, so far as monetary reform was concerned. However, an official commission was dispatched to France and Great Britain in 1897 to confer in regard to the establishment of free silver by inter-

[1] Other than Sherman, the members of the original cabinet were: L. J. Gage of Illinois, Secretary of the Treasury; R. A. Alger of Michigan, Secretary of War; Joseph McKenna of California, Attorney-General; J. A. Gary of Maryland, Postmaster-General; J. D. Long of Massachusetts, Secretary of the Navy; C. N. Bliss of New York, Secretary of the Interior; and James Wilson of Iowa, Secretary of Agriculture.

national action, as promised by the Republican platform. The absolute refusal of Great Britain, followed presently by the distracting effects of the Spanish-American War, eased the path for the gold advocates.

Indeed, nature itself was working in their behalf. After 1896 a period of bewildering prosperity burst on the country. Harvests were generous and prices ample, thereby making agriculture profitable again, and gladdening the heart of the farmer. Most important of all was the discovery of new sources of gold supply in Alaska, Australia, and elsewhere. The world's annual production of gold, which had averaged between five and six million ounces since 1860, began to show an increase after 1890, reaching nearly eleven and one half millions in 1897. It continued to mount steadily until 1910, when it reached twenty-two millions, a level at which it has since remained nearly stationary. With prosperity widely diffused and all reasonable fear of the scarcity of gold removed, the argument for silver inflation collapsed.

On March 14, 1900, the Gold Standard Act was adopted. This statute definitely established the gold standard by declaring other forms of money redeemable in gold on demand. It also enlarged the gold redemption fund to $150,000,000. In order to avoid the difficulties which had vexed the Cleveland administration, the law made the gold reserve a separate and distinct fund, not to be drawn upon by the government to meet deficiencies in the revenue, and it provided further that, when paper notes were offered for redemption, they should not be paid out again except for gold. Thus the war of the standards closed, leaving for the next generation the solution of certain knotty problems arising from imperfections of the circulating medium, notably its inelastic character.

SELECT BIBLIOGRAPHY

The Silver Crusade, 1873–1900. Illuminating descriptions of the silver movement and the election of 1896 may be found in S. J. Buck, *The Agrarian Crusade* (in *The Chronicles of America*, XLV, New Haven, 1920), C. A. Beard, *Contemporary American History* (New York, 1914), H. T. Peck, *Twenty Years of the Republic* (New York, 1906), and D. R. Dewey, *National Problems* (in *The American Nation*, XXIV, New York, 1907). The money question is discussed in its technical aspects in J. L. Laughlin, *The History* *of Bimetallism in the United States* (New York, 1900), A. B. Hepburn, *A History of Currency in the United States* (New York, 1915), A. D. Noyes, *Forty Years of American Finance* (New York, 1909), D. R. Dewey, *Financial History of the United States* (New York, 1922), and Horace White, *Money and Banking* (Boston, 1914).

The rise of Populism is traced in Buck's work (previously cited), F. E. Haynes, *Third Party Movements since the Civil War* (Iowa City, 1916), and, in the case of a particular state, A. M. Arnett, *The Populist Movement in Georgia* (in *Columbia University Studies*, CIV, no. 1, New York, 1922).

A special study of the Panic of 1893 is W. J. Lauck, *The Causes of the Panic of 1893* (Boston, 1907). For an enlightening account of the Coxey movement, consult D. L. McMurry, *The Industrial Armies and the Commonweal* (in the *Mississippi Valley Historical Review*, X [1923], 215–252). Herbert Croly, *Marcus Alonzo Hanna* (New York, 1912), is important for an understanding of the Republican management of the campaign of 1896.

CHAPTER XXIV

THE RISE OF THE UNITED STATES AS A WORLD POWER

The New Stakes of Diplomacy

Foreign affairs claimed the chief attention of the McKinley administration. Since the Civil War, the diplomatic interests of the United States had been undergoing a gradual and almost unconscious change. The new trend was, in large part, a result of the transformation which the Economic Revolution had wrought in American life. So long as the nation was engaged in building commonwealths in its own lands to the west, the government was largely engrossed with domestic problems, private capitalists found ample opportunity for profitable investment in the undeveloped country, and Eastern manufacturers, operating as yet on a moderate scale, could sell their surplus wares to advantage.

But these conditions altered in the generation following the Civil War. With the rapid filling up of the frontier country, the government at Washington was freer to give heed to external problems. Opportunities to invest money for unusual returns at home became rarer, and with more excess capital in private hands than ever before in American history energetic capitalists began to look beyond the national borders for chances of investment.

At the same time occurred the enormous material development of the country, yielding a volume of production far beyond domestic needs. American manufacturers began to seek new markets for their surplus output, and to reach out for their share of the world's trade. The tin cans used by the Standard Oil Company became familiar utensils in Arabia, China, and the heart of Africa. Perhaps half the women of the civilized world fell under the spell of the American sewing machine.

Between 1860 and 1900 the rank of the United States as an exporting nation rose from fourth place to second in all the world, and manufactures, which formed but one eighth of our exports in 1860, constituted one third of the total in 1900.

But materialistic motives were not the only reasons for this widening horizon. In past times, zeal for expansion, due partly to economic self-interest but partly also to a popular zest for adventure, had directed the march of the people from the original settlements on the Atlantic shore across the continent to the edge of the Pacific Ocean. With the subjugation of the frontier country, this national passion for excitement and achievement had to seek new avenues of expression, and readily responded to the challenge of a "Manifest Destiny" in far climes. Furthermore, for many years the activities of American missionaries, particularly in the Pacific islands and the Orient, had acquainted unnumbered Americans with the conditions of these backward peoples, and thereby tended to glorify overseas expansion as a sort of governmental missionary enterprise — a means of bringing Christian civilization to less favored races.

Sensitive to these broadening diplomatic interests, the Secretaries of the Navy throughout the eighties undertook an aggressive campaign for the enlargement and modernization of the American navy.[1] Other powers had profited from the lesson of the *Monitor-Merrimac* encounter in 1862, but the American navy had remained upon a wooden basis. While Arthur was President, Congress in 1883 provided for the construction of four steel cruisers. The new naval program was energetically carried forward under Cleveland, embracing the construction of additional steel vessels, improvements in armament, the establishment of a naval ordnance plant, and the strengthening of seacoast defenses. Under Harrison, the first first-class battleships were built, and the total number of modern steel vessels in commission increased to twenty-two. By 1893 the United States had advanced from twelfth to fifth place as a naval power.

As compared with the great European powers, the United States was late in showing an interest in overseas dominion.

[1] W. H. Hunt under Garfield, W. E. Chandler under Arthur, W. C. Whitney under Cleveland, and B. F. Tracy under Harrison.

Beginning about 1880, a wave of imperialism swept over Europe, caused by the desire of the powers to open up new markets, secure investment opportunities, colonize their surplus population under their own flags, and enhance their national glory. Most of Africa was partitioned among Great Britain, France, and Germany before 1890, with smaller portions for Italy and Belgium. In the late eighties, the energies of the imperialists turned to the stagnant countries of Asia, particularly China. The astounding weakness of China, revealed by her war with Japan in 1894–1895, seemed to be an open invitation to Europe to join in the spoils. Between 1870 and 1900 the British Empire grew by about five million square miles exclusive of spheres of influence, and France and Germany added three and one-half million and one million square miles respectively to their possessions.

The history of American diplomacy in the years from the Civil War to the close of the century reveals a growing absorption in the problems of extending commerce and acquiring dependencies in two widely separated parts of the world — in Latin America, on the one hand, and in the Pacific and the Far East, on the other. Protected by the Monroe Doctrine, Latin America had escaped the fate of Africa at the hands of the Great Powers; and traditional reasons, as well as geographic proximity and economic interest, impelled the United States to strengthen her position in this part of the world. The other great field for exploitation, the Pacific islands and the Orient, was just becoming the prey of European imperial designs in the early nineties, and, in any case, was opulent enough in territorial and trading opportunities to satisfy the cravings of a number of powers. Here, too, the United States enjoyed a natural advantage by reason of being the only important Occidental country with a front on the Pacific.

Since an aggressive policy of overseas expansion and conquest ran counter to the temper of the American people, the new program was undertaken at first hesitantly and in piecemeal fashion. But it gained momentum from its own success, and as will presently appear, the United States rose to the position of a world power before the close of McKinley's first term, with insular possessions in two hemispheres and a potential voice in the affairs of Asia, Africa, and Europe.

The United States and the Latin-American Republics

Since the issuance of the Monroe Doctrine in 1823, the interest of the United States in Latin America had been largely a negative one — to prevent the military or political interference of Europe with the free nations of the New World. Boundary disputes formed a prolific source of friction in the relations of the American republics both with each other and with European nations, and in the seventies and eighties, the United States government sought to minimize the danger of armed clashes by offering to serve as mediator in controversies among them. For example, in 1876 a territorial dispute between Argentina and Paraguay was referred to the United States for arbitration. In 1880 Colombia and Chile agreed to make the President of the United States a permanent arbitrator between them when disagreements could not be settled by direct negotiations. In 1881, the American government aided in the settlement of boundary differences between Chile and Argentina, and between Mexico and Guatemala. The Garfield administration, however, was unsuccessful in its attempt to stop a war, already of two years' duration, in which Chile was fighting Peru and Bolivia for the possession of an important nitrate tract (Tacna and Arica), situated near the junction of their national boundaries.[1]

As thus conceived, the Monroe Doctrine was mainly a political policy. The question of commercial relations between the United States and the southern republics had been permitted to go by default. Meantime, Great Britain captured the lion's share of their import trade, with France, Spain, and, somewhat later, Germany as her chief competitors. Between 1860 and 1880, the United States actually lost ground in her export trade with Latin America, though the period was one of intense economic development at home.

No American statesman of the time understood better than Blaine the threatening aspects of this European trade activity to the future industrial growth of the United States. He believed

[1] By the treaty of peace of 1883, Chile was granted occupation of Tacna and Arica for ten years when a plebiscite should determine the eventual ownership of the region. The plebiscite was not held, however. Finally, in 1922, Chile and Peru referred their differences to the United States for arbitration. President Coolidge's decision, rendered in 1925, provided for a plebiscite under American supervision.

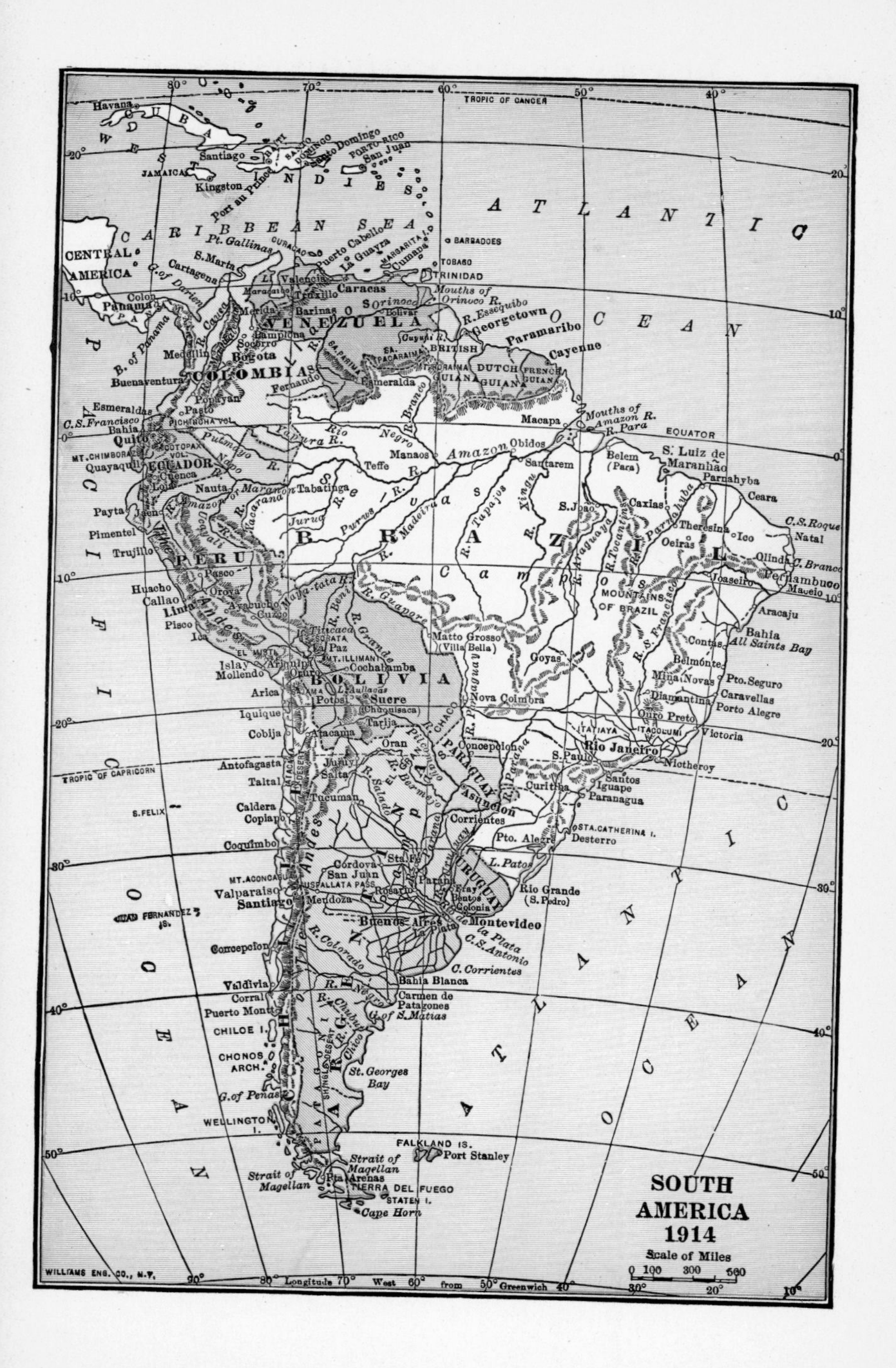
SOUTH AMERICA 1914
Scale of Miles
0 100 300 500
TROPIC OF CANCER
TROPIC OF CAPRICORN
EQUATOR
Longitude 70° West 60° from 50° Greenwich 40°
WILLIAMS ENG. CO., N.Y.
ATLANTIC OCEAN
ATLANTIC OCEAN
PACIFIC OCEAN
CARIBBEAN SEA
WEST INDIES
CUBA
Havana
Santiago
JAMAICA
Kingston
Port au Prince
HAITI
SANTO DOMINGO
Santo Domingo
PORTO RICO
San Juan
BARBADOES
TOBAGO
TRINIDAD
MARGARITA I.
CURACAO
CENTRAL AMERICA
Colon
Panama
B. of Panama
G. of Darien
Pt. Gallinas
S. Marta
Cartagena
Maracaibo
Valencia
Puerto Cabello
La Guayra
Caracas
Cumana
Bolivar
Merida
Barinas
Truxillo
VENEZUELA
Mouths of Orinoco R.
R. Orinoco
R. Essequibo
Georgetown
Paramaribo
Cayenne
BRITISH GUIANA
DUTCH GUIANA
FRENCH GUIANA
Esmeralda
Fernando
Pamplona
Socorro
Bogota
Medellin
Buenaventura
COLOMBIA
Popayan
Pasto
Esmeraldas
C.S. Francisco
Bahia
Quito
PICHINCHA VOL.
COTOPAXI VOL.
MT. CHIMBORAZO
Quayaquil
ECUADOR
Cuenca
Loja
Nauta
Payta
Pimentel
Trujillo
PERU
Pasco
Huacho
Callao
Lima
Pisco
Ica
Oroya
Ayacucho
Cuzco
Andes
R. Maranon
R. Ucayali
R. Napo
R. Putumayo
R. Yapura
Tabatinga
Teffe
Manaos
Rio Negro
R. Branco
Amazon
Obidos
Santarem
Macapa
Mouths of Amazon R.
R. Para
Belem (Para)
S. Luiz de Maranhão
Parnahyba
Ceara
C.S. Roque
Natal
Olinda
C. Branco
Pernambuco
Maceio
Aracaju
Bahia
All Saints Bay
Caxias
Theresina
Oeiras
Ico
Joaseiro
S. Joao
R. Tapajos
R. Xingu
R. Madeira
R. Purus
R. Jurua
BRAZIL
Campos
MOUNTAINS OF BRAZIL
R. Araguaya
R. Tocantins
R. Parnahyba
R. S. Francisco
Contas
Belmonte
Minas Novas
Pto. Seguro
Caravellas
Porto Alegre
Diamantina
Ouro Preto
Victoria
Matto Grosso (Villa Bella)
Goyas
Nova Coimbra
R. Guapore
R. Beni
R. Grande
Titicaca
SORATA
La Paz
MT. ILLIMANI
Cochabamba
BOLIVIA
Oruro
Arequipa
Islay
Mollendo
Arica
Iquique
Cobija
Potosi
Sucre (Chuquisaca)
Tarija
Atacama
CHACO
R. Paraguay
R. Pilcomayo
Oran
PARAGUAY
Concepcion
Asuncion
ITATIAYA
ITACOLUMI
Rio Janeiro
Nictheroy
S. Paulo
Santos
Iguape
Curityba
Paranagua
R. Parana
Antofagasta
Taltal
Caldera
Copiapo
S. FELIX
Coquimbo
Jujuy
Salta
Tucuman
R. Bermejo
R. Salado
Corrientes
Pto. Alegre
STA. CATHERINA I.
Desterro
L. Patos
Rio Grande (S. Pedro)
URUGUAY
Cordova
San Juan
Sta. Fe
Parana
Rosario
USPALLATA PASS
MT. ACONCAGUA
Valparaiso
Santiago
Mendoza
Fray Bentos
Colonia
Buenos Aires
Montevideo
La Plata
Rio de la Plata
C.S. Antonio
C. Corrientes
JUAN FERNANDEZ IS.
Concepcion
R. Colorado
Bahia Blanca
Valdivia
Corral
Puerto Montt
R. Negro
Carmen de Patagones
G. of S. Matias
R. Chubut
R. Chico
CHILOE I.
CHONOS ARCH.
G. of Penas
WELLINGTON I.
St. Georges Bay
PATAGONIA
ARGENTINA
CHILE
SHINGLE DESERT
FALKLAND IS.
Port Stanley
Strait of Magellan
Strait of Magellan
Pta. Arenas
TIERRA DEL FUEGO
STATEN I.
Cape Horn

that, without sacrificing the political side of the Monroe Doctrine, that policy might be fashioned into an effective instrument for welding closer commercial bonds between the United States and the other American republics, thereby assuring an outlet for the growing surplus of our factories and farms. As Secretary of State during Garfield's short term (1881) and later under Harrison (1889–1892), Blaine bent his efforts to this end. To him, also, is due great credit for the modern trend of the Monroe Doctrine in the direction of New-World solidarity, or "Pan-Americanism," under the leadership of the United States.

In answer to his tireless endeavors, the first Pan-American Congress assembled in Washington in 1889 with Blaine as its presiding officer.[1] Among the subjects discussed were the adoption of a customs union or American *Zollverein*, the standardization of trademarks and patents, improved railway and steamship communication among the American republics, the creation of a Pan-American monetary union, and finally, a definite scheme for the arbitration of international disputes. The sole tangible results of the conference were the naming of a committee to report on an intercontinental railway, and the establishment in Washington, at the joint expense of the several countries, of the Bureau of American Republics (subsequently called the "Pan-American Union") as a clearing-house of commercial information. Nevertheless, the discussion of common problems did much to dispel mutual jealousies and suspicions, and caused the Congress of 1889 to be the forerunner of a series of later conferences among the New-World republics.[2]

Unhappily, Blaine's nature contained much of the mountebank as well as of the statesman. In consequence, his handling of certain difficulties arising out of the Chilean civil war of 1890–1891 had the effect of undoing temporarily much of the good will which he had been laboring to foster. The American minister in Chile, Patrick Egan, swayed by strong anti-English feeling, assumed an unfriendly attitude toward the triumphant

[1] This gathering had an interesting precursor in the ill-fated Panama Congress of 1826, in which Clay and Adams were interested. The purpose of the earlier conference, however, was political rather than economic.

[2] At Mexico City in 1901–1902, at Rio de Janeiro in 1906, at Buenos Aires in 1910, and at Santiago, Chile, in 1923. Apart from these gatherings of a general character, a number of Pan-American scientific congresses and financial conferences have been held.

insurgents, apparently because their victory gratified the English residents in Chile. Blaine, perhaps with an eye on the Irish-American vote in the next presidential election, upheld him in this. Other incidents followed.

Finally, on October 16, 1891, a number of sailors from the United States ship *Baltimore* fell to quarreling with some Chilean sailors in a saloon in Valparaiso. In the ensuing riot, the Americans were outnumbered, and one was killed and several wounded. Blaine adopted a high-handed policy, declining to regard the affair as a mere sailors' brawl. Equally defiant, the provisional government of Chile refused to accord any sort of satisfaction. For a time the countries were on the brink of war, but the election of a new government in Chile led to a change of attitude. Ample apologies and reparation followed.

The Venezuela Boundary Dispute

The next significant development of the Monroe Doctrine was the byproduct of a long-standing disagreement between Venezuela and British Guiana over their common frontier. The merits of the controversy were far from clear, for, like many other South American boundaries, this one had never been clearly established. Indeed, the question had been in dispute long before the present owners had come into possession.

For more than fifty years, both Great Britain and Venezuela asserted extravagant claims to land held by the other. After a time, Venezuela, as the weaker power, began to insist that the matter be settled by arbitration, a request which Great Britain invariably refused. About 1876 the United States became interested in the matter, but her proposals for arbitration, reënforcing those of Venezuela, left Britain unmoved. The conviction not unnaturally gained ground in governmental circles at Washington that Great Britain, by bullying tactics, was seeking to defraud a defenseless country of its rights.

When gold was discovered in the disputed area in 1888, a settlement of the question became imperative. Several hostile encounters took place in the frontier region, and the appeals of Venezuela during the next few years to the United States for protection grew increasingly insistent. American consular representatives in Venezuela also urged active intervention by the United States for the sake of securing trade advantages. President Cleveland, whose acquaintance with the trouble dated back to his first administration, decided in 1895 that the situation admitted of no further paltering.

In a famous dispatch of July 20, composed by Secretary of State Olney, Great Britain was warned that her failure to submit the dispute to arbitration would lead to grave consequences. He declared that the conduct of the British government bore the guilty appearance of an attempt to encroach upon the territory of a free American nation, and accordingly came within the purview of the Monroe Doctrine. If, encouraged by our silence, other powers should follow Britain's example, "it is not inconceivable that the struggle now going on for the acquisition of Africa might be transferred to South America." Britain was further told that "today the United States is practically sovereign on this continent," and in consequence of its "infinite resources combined with its isolated position," it is "practically invulnerable against any or all other powers."

This dispatch, blunt, aggressive, and provocative, elicited a reply from Lord Salisbury, the British Foreign Minister, on November 26 to the effect that the Monroe Doctrine was not applicable to the controversy, and that the United States was wholly unwarranted in interfering. Cleveland now took the question out of the diplomatic channel. Appealing directly to Congress, he declared in a message of December 17, 1895, that the Monroe Doctrine was in jeopardy, and asked authority for the appointment of a boundary commission whose findings the United States should, if need be, enforce against any counterclaims of Great Britain. "In making these recommendations," he added, "I am fully alive to the responsibility incurred and keenly realize all the consequences that may follow." Congress promptly acceded to the President's wishes, and unanimously voted funds for the expenses of the proposed commission.

To the general public in both nations, ignorant of the diplomatic crisis, Cleveland's peremptory message came like a bolt from the blue. Evidences began to appear on every hand that the two English-speaking peoples were resolved to avert the war which the rashness of their rulers had made imminent. Leading

American newspapers criticized the President's extreme position as unjustified by the circumstances. Thirteen hundred British authors sent an appeal to their brethren in America to exert every effort to prevent fratricidal conflict. Prominent public men in both countries, including the Prince of Wales and the Bishop of London, threw their influence on the side of conciliation.

Joseph Chamberlain, an influential member of the cabinet, expressed official British opinion when he declared in a speech at Birmingham in January, 1896, "We do not covet one single inch of American territory. War between the two nations would be an absurdity as well as a crime. . . . The two nations are allied and more closely allied in sentiment and in interest than any other nations on the face of the earth." Indeed, with continental Europe already separating into antagonistic military alliances,[1] British statesmen realized the folly of unnecessarily making an enemy of the most powerful non-European nation in the world. There was prophetic insight in Chamberlain's concluding sentiment: "I should look forward with pleasure to the possibility of the Stars and Stripes and the Union Jack floating together in defence of a common cause sanctioned by humanity and justice."

Accordingly, it happened that, though the American boundary commission had already begun its work, Great Britain signified to the United States her willingness to submit the boundary dispute to international arbitration. A treaty for this purpose was drawn up in February, 1897. The American commission thereupon ceased its labors; and much to British satisfaction, the new tribunal, rendering its decision in 1899, awarded to British Guiana the larger share of the disputed area.

Great Britain's yielding did much to vindicate Olney's boastful claim of the supremacy of the United States in the Western Hemisphere.[2] In the eyes of the world the Monroe Doctrine gained new prestige. The incident is equally significant in

[1] The Triple Alliance, composed of Germany, Austria, and Italy, was formed in 1882, and renewed from time to time. Russia and France entered into the so-called Dual Alliance in 1891. Great Britian, possessing interests apart from either coalition, held aloof until 1904 when she formed an *Entente Cordiale* with France, and three years later, with Russia.

[2] It is noteworthy that a dispute between British Guiana and Brazil over their common frontier was referred to arbitration by Great Britain in 1901 without controversy.

marking the adoption of a systematic policy on the part of Great Britain to cultivate closer relations between the two English-speaking powers. The fruits of this policy became amply evident in the international policies of the ensuing years.

American Policy toward Cuba

Following closely upon the Venezuela episode, the United States became gravely involved with another European power owning American colonies — Spain. After the wars for independence in the early nineteenth century, two Caribbean islands, Cuba and Porto Rico, formed the sole remnants of Spain's once splendid western empire. But Spain learned nothing from the revolt of her other colonies, and continued her autocratic rule in these islands, exploiting the natives both politically and economically.

The larger dependency, Cuba, was governed by a Captain-General, invested with virtually unlimited power, who was assisted by numerous, high-salaried officials, all appointed by the Spanish Crown. Of self-government, there was none. Taxes were both capricious and exorbitant, very little of the revenues being spent for education or local improvements. The despotic character of the administration was equaled only by its corruption. Moreover, though about one third of the inhabitants were negro slaves, Spain refused to follow the example of other civilized nations by setting them free. In addition, governmental restrictions hampered the development of Cuba's chief source of wealth, sugar cane. The best market for this basic crop was the United States, but the mother country, by placing discriminating duties on American exports into the island,[1] provoked the United States to retaliate by imposing high duties on Cuban sugar.

The discontent of the native population waxed with the years, tending to crystallize in a sentiment for Cuban independence. From time to time there were sporadic outbreaks, but it was not until 1868 that the first great revolutionary uprising

[1] For example, the import duty on foreign flour at Cuban ports was $10.00 a barrel, though its market price in the United States was only $4.50. As a result, American flour was sent by way of Spain, and entered Cuba as "Spanish" flour in Spanish ships.

took place. The precipitating cause was the disappointment of patriot leaders when a short-lived revolutionary republic, set up in Spain in 1868, failed to carry out reforms in the island. The "Ten Years' War," as it was called, was marked by cruelty, treachery, and irregular methods of warfare on both sides. Though the Spanish authorities succeeded in confining the fighting to the eastern end of the island, they were unable to end the revolt with a crushing blow.

The contest was followed with eager interest in the United States. The nearness of Cuba to the United States, our traditional interest in Spanish-American struggles for independence, and the important trading interests at stake combined to excite wide popular sympathy for the Cubans. In spite of the protests of the Spanish Minister at Washington, numerous filibustering expeditions were clandestinely fitted out in American ports. The tension between the United States and Spain almost reached a breaking point in consequence of the *Virginius* affair in 1873. This vessel, while sailing under American colors and carrying men and supplies to the insurgents, was captured outside of Cuban waters by a Spanish gunboat. The crew and passengers were haled before a court at Santiago, and fifty-three of the prisoners, including eight American citizens, were summarily executed.

An outcry for war went up in the United States. The government demanded of Spain an apology and suitable indemnity and reparation. While the United States acknowledged the unlawful nature of the expedition, she maintained that, so long as the *Virginius* remained on the high seas, only the American government might restrain the lawbreakers. The discovery, presently made, that the *Virginius* was improperly carrying the American flag did not change the essential character of the American demands. Early in 1875 Spain accepted these terms, but the good impression thereby created was largely effaced by the ill grace with which the conditions were actually executed.

Three years later the Spanish General, Martinez Campos, induced the insurgents to lay down their arms. The terms of the peace included forgetfulness of the past, the abolition of slavery, Cuban participation in the government of cities, and the admission of insular delegates to the Spanish *Cortes*. Had these provisions been carried out in a truly liberal spirit, Spanish control of the island might have lasted indefinitely. In reality, the government continued to be a thinly veiled military despotism. The right to vote was restricted to men paying an annual tax of $25, whereby the elections were thrown into the hands of the Spanish residents in Cuba and the masses were little better off than before. Of the deputies sent by the island to the *Cortes*, only about one fifth were Cuban born. Meantime, the financial burden borne by the natives grew heavier, for the whole expense of the Ten Years' War was placed on their shoulders. In the words of Estrada Palma, a patriot leader, "the native Cubans have been left with no public duties whatsoever to perform except the payment of taxes to the government and blackmail to the officials."

The kindling wrath of the insular population burst forth into a new war for independence in February, 1895. The event was hastened by a severe depression of the sugar industry, caused by the repeal in 1894 of the McKinley Tariff, which for four years had permitted the free entry of Cuban sugar into the United States (see page 353). In an effort to forestall the insurrection, Spain at the eleventh hour authorized the establishment of a "Council of Administration" for the island. But since this body was given advisory powers only, and was to consist one half of Crown appointees and the remainder of persons chosen under the existing franchise, the only effect was to fortify the revolutionists in their resolution to cast off the Spanish yoke.

Unlike the Ten Years' War, the new uprising quickly spread to all parts of the island. Great barbarism marked the progress of hostilities. The plan of the insurgents was to avoid open battle, but to fight constant skirmishes and devastate the country, with the purpose either of exhausting Spain or of bringing about the favorable intervention of the United States. Unable to distinguish friend from foe among the Cuban people, the Spaniards adopted the scheme of herding the rural inhabitants into the great *reconcentración* camps, which quickly became pestholes filled with starving and diseased unfortunates.

The course of the struggle was watched in the United States with growing concern. Besides historic and geographic reasons, the United States was deeply involved from an economic point of view. American citizens owned plantations, mines, and railways in Cuba valued at perhaps $50,000,000, and at the beginning of the revolt, American commerce with Cuba amounted to $100,000,000 annually. These pecuniary interests were placed in serious jeopardy by the civil strife. Moreover, American humanitarianism was outraged by the cruel methods of warfare, particularly the suffering inflicted on the *reconcentrados*.

Nevertheless, so long as Cleveland remained President, every effort was put forth to keep the United States a disinterested spectator. Official vigilance succeeded in stopping most of the expeditions which Cubans or Cuban agents fitted out in the United States, though some, of course, eluded the authorities. In his last annual message to Congress (December, 1896), however, President Cleveland broadly intimated that, unless Spain soon satisfied the rebels with a grant of genuine home rule, America might feel compelled to intervene because of her "higher obligations" in the affair.

The McKinley administration began to pursue the more aggressive policy hinted at by Cleveland. Partly in response to American protests, Spain modified somewhat the policy of *reconcentración* in October, 1897, and offered the natives a larger share of self-government, with their own constitution and legislature, to become effective upon ratification by the *Cortes*. Granted three years earlier, the concession might have assured a peaceful solution of Cuban difficulties; but coming after more than two years of relentless warfare, the revolutionists, suspicious of Spanish good faith, were unwilling to accept anything short of complete independence.

Moreover, two incidents now occurred which raised popular sentiment in the United States to a war pitch, and made it increasingly difficult for President McKinley to preserve the attitude of impartial friend. Through the columns of a sensational New York newspaper, the American public on February 9, 1898, was acquainted with the contents of a confidential letter written by the Spanish Minister in Washington, Dupuy de Lome, to a friend in Spain. In this missive, de Lome set McKinley down as a tricky politician, and admitted his own duplicity in certain commercial negotiations, then under way with the United States.

Spain refused to make a formal disavowal of the utterances, and instead of dismissing de Lome, permitted him to resign.

Of graver import was the destruction of the United States warship *Maine* on February 15, while lying peacefully at anchor in Havana Harbor. The vessel was sunk and 260 men killed. A naval court of inquiry, appointed by the President, ascribed the disaster to an external explosion, but was unable to fix responsibility upon any person or persons. A similar board, appointed by Spain, found the cause of the catastrophe in the explosion of one of the ship's forward magazines. The conclusions of the American board were subsequently confirmed in 1911 when the hulk was uncovered, though it will probably never be known whether the destruction was perpetrated by some overzealous Spanish subordinate or by a Cuban patriot intent on precipitating war, or whether it was merely the result of accident.

The outburst of popular feeling was unlike anything since 1861. "Remember the Maine!" began to appear in huge headlines in the sensational dailies, and soon the slogan was echoed in public gatherings throughout the land. Even Congress was aflame with war spirit. But McKinley, oppressed, as he said, with "the thought of human suffering that must come into thousands of homes," seemed resolved at this stage to avert hostilities, if possible.

On March 29, 1898, he demanded of Spain the complete abandonment of *reconcentración*, and the establishment of an armistice in Cuba, preparatory to peace negotiations to be conducted through himself. By this latter measure he hoped to secure Cuban independence. The first demand was promptly granted, but national pride and a deep-rooted habit of procrastination caused Spain to meet the second issue evasively. Nevertheless, the American Minister in Madrid cabled the President his conviction that the Spanish government and people sincerely desired peace, and that with a few months' delay, "I will get peace in Cuba, with justice to Cuba and protection to our great American interests." On April 6, the Washington representatives of Great Britain, Germany, France, Austria-Hungary, Russia, and Italy made a joint appeal to the President for a continuance of peaceful negotiations. Four days later, Spain informed our government that, at the solicitation of the Pope, the Queen had acceded to the American demand for an armistice.

By this time, however, McKinley had experienced a change of heart. Perhaps he doubted the good faith of Spain's compliance, and felt that war was the only real solution. Perhaps, as has been charged, he was frightened by the clamor of the war faction in Congress, and feared a serious rupture in his own party. At any rate, on April 11, he sent a message to Congress, recommending intervention in Cuba for the sake of humanity, for the protection of American lives and property, and for the purpose of ending a needless and costly war.[1]

Congress responded on the nineteenth with three resolutions authorizing the employment of force on behalf of Cuban independence. A fourth resolution, adopted at the same time on the motion of Senator Teller, assured an incredulous world that "the United States hereby disclaims any disposition or intention to exercise sovereignty, jurisdiction or control over said Island except for the pacification thereof, and asserts its determination, when that is accomplished, to leave the government and control of the Island to its people."

European powers observed these developments with mixed feelings. In Germany and France, public opinion was distinctly hostile to the United States, and talk was rife of a joint European intervention on behalf of Spain. British sentiment was mirrored in a widely quoted sentiment of the *London Spectator* of April 9, 1898: "If America were really attacked by a great Continental coalition, England would be at her side in twenty-four hours." President McKinley took occasion early in the war to thank the *London Times* for its hearty advocacy of the American cause. In reality, all the powers observed an official neutrality toward the two belligerents, although at one juncture, presently to be described, it seemed possible that the war might develop into a general European conflict.

[1] "We may rest assured that if Mark Hanna had been President there would have been no war with Spain," says Rhodes in his *McKinley and Roosevelt Administrations*, p. 64. "To his dying day Mr. Cleveland never believed that the war with Spain was necessary," states his personal friend, George F. Parker, writing in the *Saturday Evening Post*, November 10, 1923. On the other hand, Theodore Roosevelt, impatient with the President's slowness to resort to war, exclaimed at the time, "McKinley has no more backbone than a chocolate éclair."

SELECT BIBLIOGRAPHY

The Rise of the United States as a World Power. The subject is discussed in its general aspects in C. R. Fish, *American Diplomacy* (New York, 1924), and his *The Path of Empire* (in *The Chronicles of America*, XLVI, New Haven, 1919); R. G. Adams, *A History of the Foreign Policy of the United States* (New York, 1924); J. B. Moore, *The Principles of American Diplomacy* (New York, 1918); J. H. Latané, *America as a World Power* (in *The American Nation*, XXV, New York, 1907); W. F. Johnson, *America's Foreign Relations* (2 v., New York, 1916); and A. E. McKinley, *Island Possessions of the United States* (in *The History of North America*, XX, Philadelphia, 1907). For a luminous exposition of the fundamental forces behind these new developments in American policy, consult A. C. Coolidge, *The United States as a World Power* (New York, 1908). Very suggestive, also, is Achille Viallate, *Economic Imperialism and International Relations during the Last Fifty Years* (New York, 1923), part i.

The United States and the Latin-American Republics. Of the many works on the Monroe Doctrine, D. Y. Thomas, *One Hundred Years of the Monroe Doctrine* (New York, 1923), and A. B. Hart, *The Monroe Doctrine: an Interpretation* (New York, 1916), are among the most recent and best. Somewhat more inclusive in scope are J. H. Latané, *The United States and Latin America* (Garden City, 1920), and W. S. Robertson, *Hispanic-American Relations with the United States* (*Carnegie Endowment Publications*, New York, 1923).

The Venezuela Boundary Dispute. Besides the books already noted, J. B. Henderson, *American Diplomatic Questions* (New York, 1901), Robert McElroy, *Grover Cleveland* (2 v., New York, 1923), and Henry James, *Richard Olney and His Public Service* (Boston, 1923), are important in this connection.

American Policy toward Cuba. See the works cited in the Select Bibliography of the next chapter.

CHAPTER XXV

THE RISE OF THE UNITED STATES AS A WORLD POWER (*Concluded*)

The Spanish-American War and Its Fruits

Unlike most previous conflicts of the United States, the naval arm of the nation was of paramount importance in the war with Spain, and the military operations were subsidiary thereto. Those publicists who had persuaded Congress in the eighties to modernize the navy now won complete vindication. For the immediate state of preparedness, however, much credit was due to the energetic foresight of Theodore Roosevelt, McKinley's Assistant Secretary of the Navy.

In sad contrast was the condition of the army. Politics entered into the appointment of officers; and mismanagement, lack of plans, and general confusion interfered seriously with the mobilization, provisioning, and transport of troops. Moreover, no adequate cognizance was taken of the fact, in the arrangements for either food or clothing, that the operations would be conducted in a tropical climate. The regular army was enlarged to 62,000 men; and in April and May, the President called for 200,000 volunteers, most of whom it was eventually unnecessary to send out of the country. A picturesque feature of the volunteer cavalry was a regiment known as the "Rough Riders," recruited from among cowboys, ranchers, Indians, and college athletes by Roosevelt, who presently became their Colonel.

The actual hostilities were swift and decisive, lasting four months in all. The chief sphere of operations was the West Indies. Cuba was promptly placed under blockade in order to prevent the arrival of men and supplies for the enemy forces. Nevertheless, on May 19, a fleet from Spain under Admiral Pasqual Cervera succeeded in reaching Santiago, which had rail connections with Havana. Santiago was at once placed under a close blockade by Rear-Admiral W. T. Sampson, and in the ensuing weeks, troops under General W. R. Shafter were assembled for a land attack on the city. On July 1, El Caney and San Juan Hill, the outer defenses of Santiago, were successfully assaulted by the American land forces.

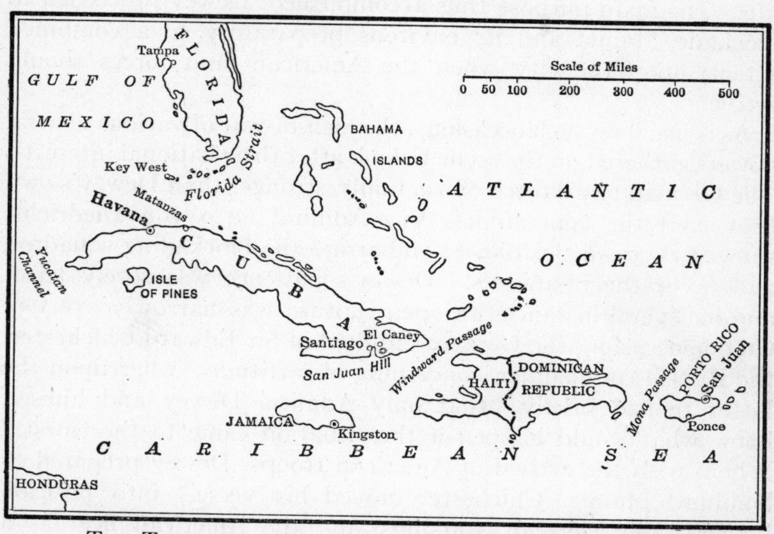

THE THEATER OF WARFARE IN THE WEST INDIES, 1898

The city was now doomed. In order to avoid capture, Cervera's fleet sought to escape on July 3, but as the warships steamed out of the harbor, they were engaged, one by one, by the blockading vessels, and either captured or destroyed. Sampson's absence on an official errand left Commodore W. S. Schley in actual command during the engagement. The fall of Santiago quickly followed. Shortly afterwards, an army commanded by General Miles began the occupation of the nearby island of Porto Rico.

Meantime, the Americans had successfully carried the fighting against the Spaniards in a different quarter of the globe. Immediately upon the outbreak of war, Commodore George Dewey, then at Hong Kong, was ordered to take his squadron of six vessels to the Philippine Islands, and by capture or destruction, incapacitate the Spanish fleet there for operations in American waters. Although his nearest base was 7,000 miles away, Dewey, trained in the school of Farragut, executed his orders with boldness and efficiency. Before daybreak on May 1, he ran the batteries of Manila Bay, and by high noon, he had destroyed the entire Spanish fleet without the loss of an American life. His main purpose thus accomplished, Dewey proceeded to blockade Manila and its environs preparatory to a combined attack upon the city when the American land forces should arrive.

As is usual on such occasions, the men-of-war of various neutral powers gathered on the scene to look after their national interests. The German naval force was actually stronger than Dewey's own fleet, and the commander, Vice-Admiral Otto von Diedrichs, showed every disposition to embarrass the blockading squadron and favor the Spaniards. Dewey's patience was sorely tried, and in several instances an open rupture was narrowly averted. On one occasion, the German inquired of Sir Edward Chichester, the British commander, concerning his attitude; whereupon the latter replied briefly "that only Admiral Dewey and himself knew what would happen if the situation came to the worst." When, with the arrival of American troops, Dewey prepared to bombard Manila, Chichester moved his vessels into position between the German warships and the American fleet as a precaution against possible interference. The whole conduct of the Germans suggests not merely partiality for Spain but also a design to secure a foothold in the Philippines at the conclusion of the war. It is evident that the British government was resolved to prevent any such outcome.

During July and early August the reënforcements from the United States arrived. The city was invested with the aid of the Filipinos, who, under the leadership of Emilio Aguinaldo, were fighting for independence. On August 13, Manila surrendered after a joint naval and land attack. Meanwhile, in June, the United States had come into possession of the Ladrone Islands, 1,500 miles east of the Philippines, when the cruiser *Charleston* on its way to Manila secured the surrender of the Spanish authorities on Guam, the main island.

The war was a popular one among the American people at home. War funds were derived principally from a bond issue of $200,000,000 offered in denominations as low as twenty dollars, and from the imposition of a wide variety of internal-revenue duties. For example, special taxes were levied upon banks, amusement places, tobacco, wines, medicinal preparations, documents used in businesss transactions, and the like. The American Red Cross under Miss Barton had its first opportunity to demonstrate its wartime efficiency, and nobly met the requirements of the situation, beginning its ministrations in Havana as early as six days before the *Maine* disaster.

Much popular dissatisfaction, however, was excited because of the inadequate arrangements made by the government for the provisioning and the sanitary protection of the troops. Malaria and typhoid fever made their inroads on the unseasoned troops about Santiago in the early weeks, and on August 3 Shafter reported that seventy-five per cent of his command were sick. At the same time his general officers signed a "Round Robin" protest, insisting on the removal of the army to the United States before it was exterminated by that dreadful tropical scourge, yellow fever, then just beginning the toll of its victims. The government acquiesced. Notwithstanding the widespread criticism, it is only fair to note that the percentage of deaths from disease was about three fifths as great as during the first year of the Civil War. Moreover, due to the progress of medical science since the earlier conflict, comparatively few amputations proved necessary.

An epochal consequence of this first contact of American science with the tropics was the discovery, made in 1900 by an official medical board of which Major Walter Reed was head, that yellow fever was transmitted by the female *Stegomyia* mosquito.[1] Acting on this knowledge, the disease was soon banished from the island by the efforts of Major Reed and Major W. C. Gorgas; and, potentially at least, tropical life the world over was relieved of one of its terrors.

After the war had been under way about three months, Spain asked France to ascertain peace terms from the United States.

[1] In his official report as Secretary of War, Elihu Root declared in 1902, "The name of Dr. Jesse W. Lazear, contract surgeon, who voluntarily permitted himself to be inoculated with the yellow fever germ in order to furnish a necessary experimental test . . . and who died of the disease, should be written in the list of the martyrs who have died in the cause of humanity."

An armistice, signed on August 12 by the belligerent powers, foreshadowed the settlements of the peace treaty, save in regard to the disposition of the Philippines, which was left undetermined. The final negotiations took place in Paris, William R. Day acting as head of the American peace delegation. Since we stood in a position to demand what we wanted, the negotiations were the simplest in which our government had ever engaged. The outcome was the treaty of December 10, 1898. Spain transferred Cuba to the United States for temporary occupation, preliminary to Cuban independence. Porto Rico and Guam were ceded to the United States in lieu of war indemnity, and the Philippines on payment of $20,000,000. The civil and political rights of the native inhabitants of the ceded islands were left to the determination of Congress.

American ownership of Porto Rico was a logical consequence of the war; and the annexation of Guam, for use as a coaling and cable station, was not surprising. But the acquisition of the entire Philippine Archipelago marked a new and not wholly popular innovation in American policy. These islands formed a part of the coastline of Asia, and being inhabited by a people alien in race, language, and institutions, were not likely ever to achieve statehood. Moreover, they could not be expected to furnish room for the expansion of the American people, though it was hoped that they might supply profitable openings for American capital and commerce. Prior to the Paris conference, McKinley had been undecided concerning the wisdom of taking the islands, but strong pressure was brought to bear upon him by commercial organizations and missionary bodies. There was, moreover, a fear that, if we did not annex the Philippines, they would fall to Germany, one of our chief trade rivals in the Orient.

Strenuous objections, however, were urged by certain Senators against this feature of the peace settlement. For example, G. C. Vest of Missouri denied the constitutional authority of the United States "to acquire territory to be held and governed permanently as colonies." Hoar made much of the fact that the Filipinos had declared their independence, and that annexation would occur without "the consent of the governed." The vote ratifying the treaty was accompanied by the passage of the McEnery resolution, which declared, in effect, that the treaty provision should not be deemed a final determination of our attitude toward the Philippines. Since, however, the resolution received a mere majority vote, it had no validity as an act of the treaty-making power.

In the light of earlier history, the great significance of the Spanish-American War was the final expulsion of Spain from the Western Hemisphere. From a prospective point of view, however, the war marked a turning-point in American policy. The next few years were to disclose whether, as the opponents of the treaty charged, the United States was committed to a policy of overseas dominion and imperialism.

American Expansion in the Pacific

The annexation of the Philippines was accompanied by other acquisitions in the Pacific. These came as the natural fruit of our growing commercial and diplomatic interests in that region. Since the last decade of the eighteenth century, American merchantmen and whalers had been plying a brisk trade with the Pacific islands and the Orient. It was concern for this commerce that impelled President Tyler in 1842 to affirm our opposition to the seizure of the Hawaiian Islands by any foreign power, and that provoked Commodore M. C. Perry's naval demonstration in 1854, whereby the ancient seclusion of Japan was broken down and the island brought into intercourse with the world. American missionaries, both Protestant and Catholic, penetrated these non-Christian lands at an early time, and their activities constituted another lodestone of interest in this quarter of the globe.

American trade in the Pacific suffered a setback during the Civil War, only to be followed by a commercial revival in the years thereafter. As a halfway stop across the Pacific, the Hawaiian Islands had long been of peculiar interest to the United States. Moreover, American missionaries had reduced the native language to writing and helped to modernize the government — many of their children became landowners and sugar planters. In 1875 a reciprocity treaty was concluded, whereby sugar and other Hawaiian products gained free access to the American market, and the insular King covenanted not to lease or dispose of any of his territory to another country. This was followed in 1884 by the lease of Pearl Harbor, near Honolulu, as an American naval station.

The harmonious relations of the two countries were interrupted in January, 1893, when the recently installed Queen abolished the liberal constitution, which had been set up under American influences, and proclaimed a new one, based on absolutism and native home rule. At once a revolt occurred, which received moral backing, at least, from the presence of United States marines landed for that purpose from a cruiser in the harbor. The revolutionary government, headed by an American, proceeded without delay to negotiate a treaty of annexation with the United States, but Harrison's term expired before it could be acted upon by the Senate. An anti-imperialist by nature, Cleveland promptly withdrew the treaty from the Senate, and when an official investigation disclosed the guilty connection of the American minister at Honolulu (J. L. Stevens) with the revolt, he denounced the whole proceeding, and even sought to bring about a restoration of the Queen.

Events now awaited the return of the Republicans to power. Meantime, the growing strength of the Japanese elements in Hawaii, coupled with a readiness of the Tokio government to uphold their demands, roused American fears of the designs of that power. The outbreak of the Spanish-American War gave sharp emphasis to the arguments that had been urged concerning the naval advantages of owning Hawaii, and accordingly, the islands were annexed by joint resolution on July 7, 1898.[1] "Annexation," declared McKinley, "is not a change; it is a consummation."

Shortly afterwards, the United States acquired a new insular dependency in the Pacific, south of the equator. The Samoan Islands lie on the direct trade route between San Francisco and Sidney, Australia, about 5,000 miles from the former port. In 1872 an American naval officer secured from a native chief permission for the United States to establish a coaling station at Pago-Pago, in Tutuila, the finest harbor in the South Pacific Ocean. Germany and Great Britain were also keenly alive to the

[1] While the negotiations were in progress, Japan protested vigorously on the ground that American annexation would "disturb the *status quo* in the Pacific."

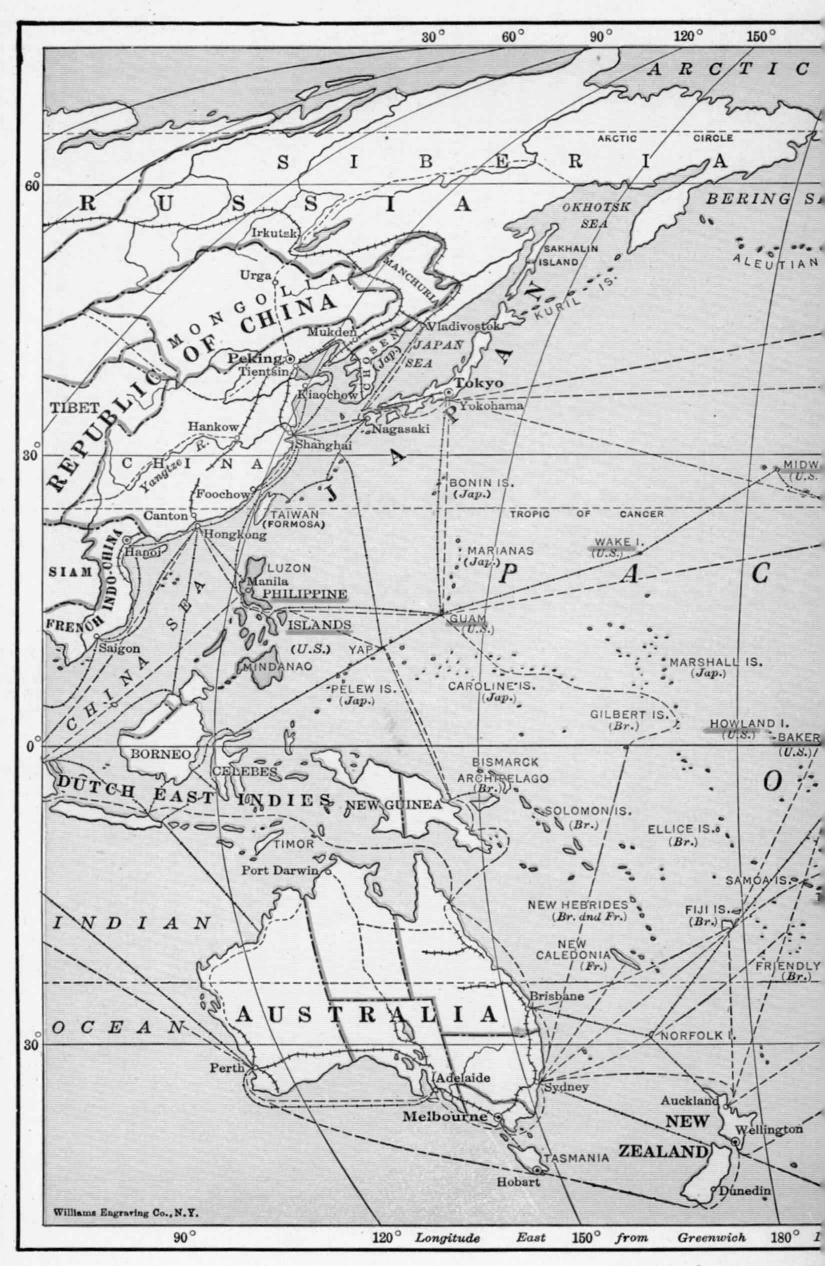
ARCTIC
ARCTIC CIRCLE
SIBERIA
RUSSIA
BERING SEA
OKHOTSK SEA
SAKHALIN ISLAND
ALEUTIAN
Irkutsk
Urga
MONGOLIA
MANCHURIA
REPUBLIC OF CHINA
KURIL IS.
Vladivostok
Mukden
CHOSEN (Jap.)
JAPAN SEA
Peking
Tientsin
Tokyo
Yokohama
TIBET
Kiaochow
Hankow
Nagasaki
Shanghai
JAPAN
CHINA
Yangtze R.
MIDWAY (U.S.)
BONIN IS. (Jap.)
Foochow
TAIWAN (FORMOSA)
TROPIC OF CANCER
Canton
Hongkong
Hanoi
MARIANAS (Jap.)
WAKE I. (U.S.)
PACIFIC
SIAM
FRENCH INDO-CHINA
LUZON
Manila
PHILIPPINE ISLANDS (U.S.)
GUAM (U.S.)
CHINA SEA
Saigon
YAP
MARSHALL IS. (Jap.)
MINDANAO
PELEW IS. (Jap.)
CAROLINE IS. (Jap.)
GILBERT IS. (Br.)
HOWLAND I. (U.S.)
BAKER (U.S.)
BORNEO
BISMARCK ARCHIPELAGO (Br.)
CELEBES
DUTCH EAST INDIES
NEW GUINEA
SOLOMON IS. (Br.)
OCEAN
ELLICE IS. (Br.)
TIMOR
Port Darwin
SAMOA IS.
NEW HEBRIDES (Br. and Fr.)
FIJI IS. (Br.)
INDIAN OCEAN
NEW CALEDONIA (Fr.)
FRIENDLY (Br.)
Brisbane
AUSTRALIA
NORFOLK I.
Perth
Adelaide
Sydney
Auckland
Melbourne
NEW ZEALAND
Wellington
TASMANIA
Hobart
Dunedin
Williams Engraving Co., N.Y.
30° 60° 90° 120° 150°
60° 30° 0° 30°
90° 120° Longitude East 150° from Greenwich 180°

AMERICAN I

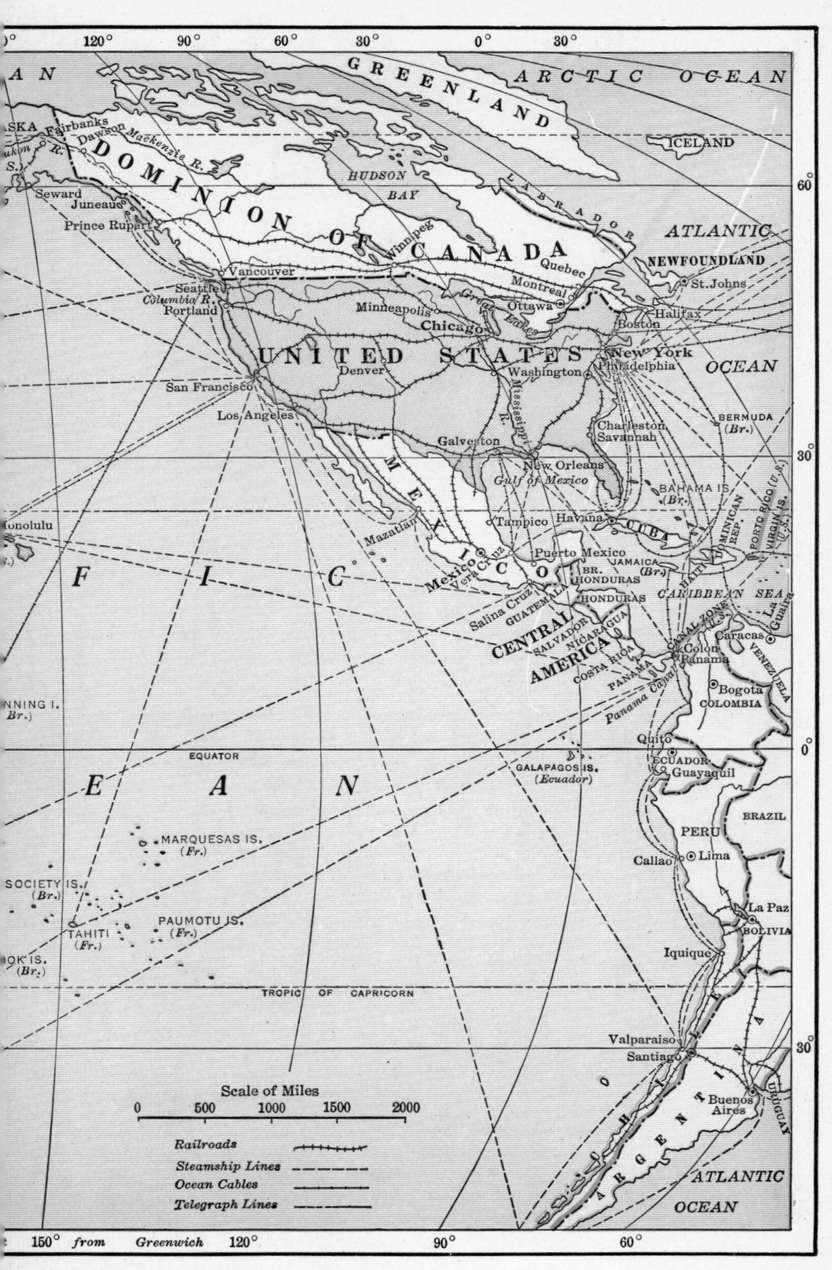

120°
90°
60°
30°
0°
30°
GREENLAND
ARCTIC OCEAN
ICELAND
Fairbanks
Dawson
Mackenzie R.
DOMINION OF CANADA
HUDSON BAY
LABRADOR
Seward
Juneau
Prince Rupert
Winnipeg
Quebec
ATLANTIC
NEWFOUNDLAND
St. Johns
Vancouver
Seattle
Columbia R.
Portland
Montreal
Ottawa
Great Lakes
Minneapolis
Chicago
Halifax
Boston
UNITED STATES
New York
Philadelphia
Denver
Washington
OCEAN
San Francisco
Mississippi R.
Los Angeles
BERMUDA (Br.)
Charleston
Savannah
Galveston
MEXICO
New Orleans
Gulf of Mexico
BAHAMA IS. (Br.)
Tampico
Havana
CUBA
PORTO RICO (U.S.)
VIRGIN IS. (U.S.)
DOMINICAN REP.
HAITI
Mazatlan
Puerto Mexico
JAMAICA (Br.)
Mexico
Vera Cruz
BR. HONDURAS
HONDURAS
F
I
C
CARIBBEAN SEA
La Guaira
Salina Cruz
GUATEMALA
CENTRAL AMERICA
SALVADOR
NICARAGUA
COSTA RICA
PANAMA
CANAL ZONE (U.S.)
Colon
Panama
Caracas
VENEZUELA
Panama Canal
Bogota
COLOMBIA
(Br.)
Quito
EQUATOR
ECUADOR
GALAPAGOS IS. (Ecuador)
Guayaquil
E
A
N
BRAZIL
PERU
MARQUESAS IS. (Fr.)
Callao
Lima
SOCIETY IS. (Br.)
La Paz
BOLIVIA
TAHITI (Fr.)
PAUMOTU IS. (Fr.)
Iquique
TROPIC OF CAPRICORN
Valparaiso
Santiago
CHILE
ARGENTINA
Buenos Aires
URUGUAY
Scale of Miles
0 500 1000 1500 2000
Railroads
Steamship Lines
Ocean Cables
Telegraph Lines
ATLANTIC OCEAN
60°
30°
0°
30°
150° from Greenwich 120°
90°
60°

THE PACIFIC

opportunities offered by the islands, and jangling national interests led to constant intrigues with the native rulers. In 1886 the American consul, to block German designs, proclaimed a protectorate, but the act was at once disavowed by President Cleveland.

Germany continued aggressive; and in anticipation of trouble, all three powers hurried warships to the scene in March, 1889. A tropical hurricane, inflicting widespread destruction and suffering, swept away the hostile feelings for the time, and led to an agreement of the powers in April, whereby the independence and neutrality of Samoa were guaranteed under a tripartite protectorate. This arrangement proving impracticable, the powers in 1899 decided on a partition of the islands. The United States received Tutuila, the most important island, Germany the remaining islands, and Great Britain was given compensation elsewhere in the Pacific.

Besides these more notable acquisitions, the United States in the eighties and nineties asserted jurisdiction over many scattered small islands in the Pacific. Some of these were hardly more than rocks or coral reefs, but were valuable for guano, for use as relay cable stations, or for other purposes. The largest of them are Wake, Christmas, Gallego, Starbuck, Penrhyn, Phœnix, Midway, Palmyra, Howland, Baker, Johnston, Gardner, Morell, and Marcus.

The United States and China

European powers also engaged in the game of acquiring Pacific possessions. Germany, for instance, purchased Spain's remaining Pacific dependencies after the Peace of 1898, and extended her dominion in other ways as well. But the real rivalry among these powers occurred for territorial and economic advantages in China.

In retaliation for the murder of two missionaries, Germany in 1898 extorted from China a long-time lease of Kiaochow, the chief port of the Shantung Peninsula in northern China, including the right to work mines and build railways in the region. In the same year, Russia coerced China into the lease of the important harbor of Port Arthur, which dominated the sea approaches to Peking.[1] Great Britain, learning of these transactions, exacted the lease of Wei-Hai-Wei, which lay between the acquisitions of Germany and Russia, and in 1899 made an agreement with the latter country for a division of railway concessions in China. Not to be outdone, France obtained control of Kwang-Chow-Wang Bay in southeastern China, and secured special mineral rights in the adjoining provinces.

Such was the situation when the United States, having annexed the Philippines, looked expectantly to a vigorous development of business and financial relations with China. In almost every desirable part of China, the mining and railway rights were preëmpted long years in advance by foreign interests, and it seemed likely that, before long, American commerce would likewise be hampered in the leased ports by discriminatory regulations. Self-interest, as well as a sense of justice, required the United States to demand of the interloping powers equality of trading opportunity, an "open door" for all, in the areas they controlled. In this position she could count on the support of Great Britain, for, in spite of British aggression in China, that country's commercial interests demanded a policy which would freely admit her manufactures to all ports.[2]

In the fall of 1899, Secretary of State John Hay asked the powers to pledge themselves to the maintenance of the open-door principle in China in matters of trade and navigation.[3] Great Britain, Germany, France, Italy, and Japan acceded — Russia also, though in somewhat evasive language. The sincerity of the pledges, however, remained yet to be tested.

A violent outbreak against foreigners and foreign innovations in China the next year furnished opportunity for a further development of Hay's diplomacy. In June the insurgents, known as "Boxers," seized Peking and laid close siege to the foreign legations there. The United States coöperated with the other powers in organizing a punitive expedition against the Boxers, sending about 6,000 troops for this purpose. Fearing,

[1] As a result of the Russo-Japanese War in 1904, Port Arthur was transferred to Japan.

[2] Indeed, in 1898, the British government made overtures to the United States for an alliance for the guarantee of the "open door" in China; but our then ambassador, John Hay, discouraged the project because of the certain opposition of "that unspeakable Senate of ours."

[3] That is, that no regulations on commerce and shipping should be imposed except by the Chinese government.

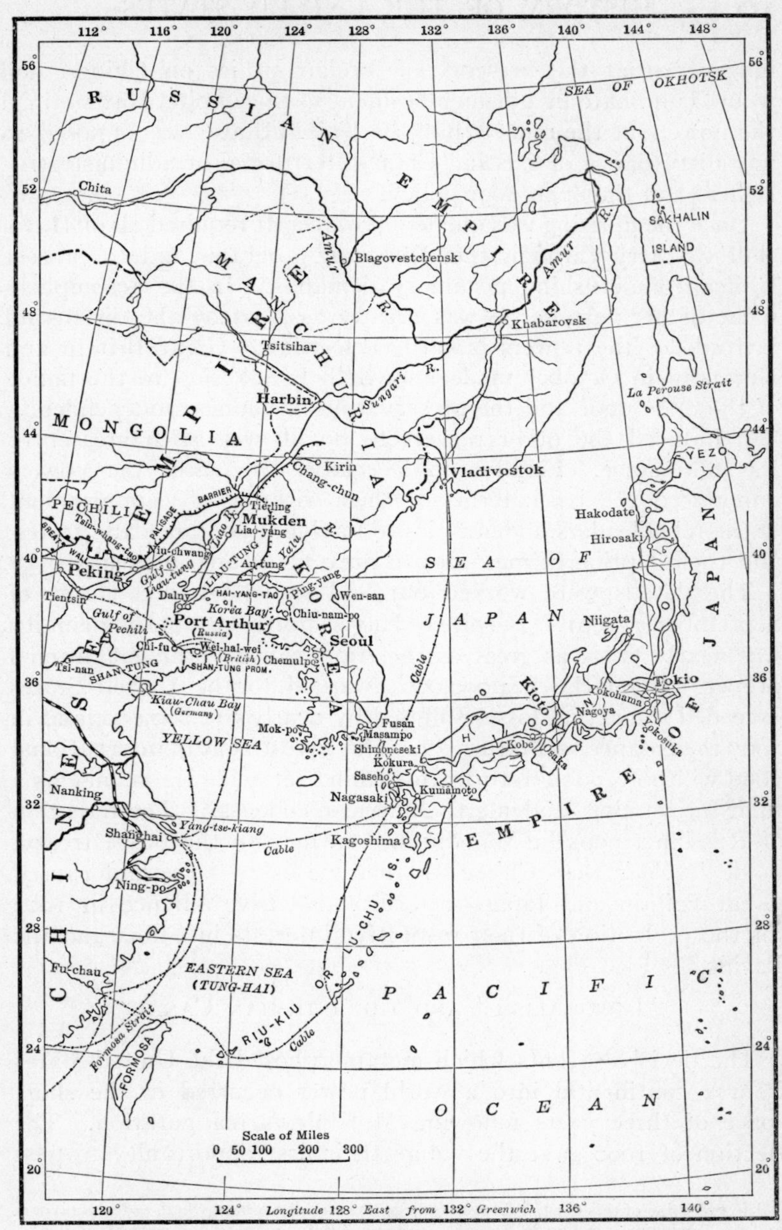

EASTERN ASIA AT THE OPENING OF THE TWENTIETH CENTURY

however, that the presence of foreign armies on Chinese soil would culminate in a dismemberment of the empire, Hay notified the powers at the outset that the United States was opposed to any disturbance of existing Chinese territorial or administrative rights or of the open-door policy.

Once the uprising was quelled, however, it required all of Hay's skill to carry through the American program, and to protect China from crushing pecuniary demands. In the accomplishment of his purpose he was greatly assisted by the distrustful attitude of the powers toward each other. Great Britain and Germany in October made known their adhesion to the policy of the open door and the preservation of Chinese independence, and induced the other powers to do likewise with greater or less reluctance. Finally, on December 22, 1900, the powers announced the basic terms of their withdrawal — punishment of the rebel leaders, indemnities to foreign individuals and states, and the adoption of measures to prevent future outbreaks.

The details were worked out and embodied in a treaty of September 7, 1901. In spite of Hay's efforts, the total indemnity was nearly twice as great as the American government deemed proper. Even the $24,000,000 awarded to the United States exceeded the actual losses suffered by nearly $11,000,000, and in 1907 the balance was returned. This investment in international good will bore noble returns, for China set aside the money as a fund for sending students to American colleges.[1] The retention of Russian troops in Manchuria, contrary to the peace treaty, made it clear that China still had perils to face, and caused Great Britain and Japan to form a defensive alliance in 1902 for the protection of their respective interests in China and the Pacific.

"Imperialism" and the Isthmian Canal

The decisive events which metamorphosed the United States from a continental into a world power occurred in the short space of three years following McKinley's inauguration. The election of 1900 gave the voters their first opportunity to pass

[1] In execution of this trust, Tsin Hua College was established in Pekin in order to prepare students for junior standing in American colleges. Between sixty and seventy graduates are sent annually to the United States.

judgment upon the new departure. Meeting at Philadelphia on June 19, the Republicans expressed jubilation over the war with Spain "for liberty and human rights," the acquisition of insular dependencies, and the effort to "obtain new markets" through "the policy of the open door." As a matter of course, President McKinley was renominated; the second place on the ticket went to Governor Theodore Roosevelt of New York, a war hero. The chief reason for Roosevelt's nomination was the desire of Platt and the Republican machine in New York to rid the state of an energetic and self-willed Chief Executive. Roosevelt's own reluctance was overcome only by the genuine enthusiasm which his name excited among the Western delegates.

The opponents of overseas expansion rallied to the Democratic standard. The fact that the Filipinos since February, 1899, had been waging a war for independence against American authority affected public opinion at home, and placed the United States in the position of imposing its dominion upon an unwilling people. When the Democratic convention assembled at Kansas City on July 4, the platform declared that "the paramount issue of the campaign" was "imperialism," that is, "the seizing or purchasing of distant islands to be governed outside the Constitution and whose people can never become citizens." After affirming that "no nation can long endure half republic and half empire," the Democrats further condemned the entry of the United States into "so-called world politics, including the diplomacy of Europe and the intrigue and land grabbing in Asia." Bryan was unanimously renominated for President, and at his behest, the platform contained a perfunctory reassertion of Democratic advocacy of free silver. A. E. Stevenson, Cleveland's former Vice-President, was chosen as his running-mate.

More than the usual number of minor parties appeared in the campaign. As in 1896, Bryan's candidacy was indorsed by the Populists and the Silver Republicans, and reverberations of the silver question served somewhat to confuse the main issue before the voters. Hanna, once more in charge of McKinley's campaign, ascribed the return of prosperity to Republican supremacy, and everywhere might be found campaign emblems and posters of the "Full Dinner-Pail." In spite of Bryan's eloquent condemnations of "imperialism," the policy of overseas dominion struck a responsive chord among the voters. Fewer popular votes were cast than in the preceding election, but McKinley received a larger proportion of them — 51.6 per cent to 45.5 for Bryan. The electoral vote stood 292 to 155.

McKinley was not destined long to enjoy his victory. On September 6, 1901, while attending the Pan-American Exposition at Buffalo, he was shot by an anarchist, and eight days later he died. His death placed in the presidential chair Theodore Roosevelt, the most aggressive and picturesque character to reach that position since Andrew Jackson.[1] Although the new President's energies were largely engaged in domestic problems, it fell to him to bring to fruition an enterprise which the new international position of the United States rendered imperative — the construction of an interoceanic canal.

His path of accomplishment was strewn with diplomatic obstacles, hitherto insurmountable, dating back to the middle of the century. For many years the United States had been dreaming of, and planning for, a Central-American canal, either through the Isthmus of Panama or across Nicaragua. By a treaty of 1846 with Colombia, the United States had received a free and equal right of passage across the Isthmus of Panama, in return for which the American government guaranteed the "perfect neutrality" of the right of way and Colombia's "rights of sovereignty and property" in the Isthmus.

A few years later the United States became apprehensive at the encroachments of the British authorities in Belize (British Honduras) on nearby Central-American territory. This alarm assumed definite form in 1848 with the British seizure of Greytown at the mouth of the San Juan River in Nicaragua. Not only were such activities a violation of the Monroe Doctrine, but the San Juan River formed an essential part of a possible Nicaragua canal. Protests of the United States resulted in the negotiation of the Clayton-Bulwer Treaty of 1850, whereby Great Britain yielded her recent territorial claims, and the United States agreed,

[1] Roosevelt retained McKinley's cabinet, composed at this time of John Hay, Secretary of State; L. J. Gage of Illinois, Secretary of the Treasury; Elihu Root of New York, Secretary of War; Philander C. Knox of Pennsylvania, Attorney-General; C. E. Smith of Pennsylvania, Postmaster-General; J. D. Long of Massachusetts, Secretary of the Navy; E. A. Hitchcock of Missouri, Secretary of the Interior; and James Wilson of Iowa, Secretary of Agriculture. In 1904 William H. Taft of Ohio was appointed Secretary of War, and upon Hay's death in 1905, Root succeeded to his place. Numerous other changes were made.

in return, that she should share in pledging the neutrality of any future interoceanic route and enjoy equal rights in its use with American citizens. Other nations were invited to join in the guarantee.

As this treaty indicates, the United States at this time conceived of the canal as an international highway, whose neutrality should be under international protection and whose benefits should be open equally to all nations. Interest in the project declined during the Civil War, and for a time thereafter, because of the construction of the transcontinental railways, which seemed to meet the essential needs. In the eighties, however, the discontent over railway rates drew attention anew to the advantage of establishing an artificial waterway between the two coasts.

That the United States bitterly rued her bargain of 1850 with Great Britain now became amply evident. In a message of March 8, 1880, President Hayes declared, "The policy of this country is a canal under American control. The United States cannot consent to the surrender of this control to any European power or to any combination of European powers." His Secretary of State, as well as those of Garfield and Arthur, labored with Great Britain to recast the Clayton-Bulwer Treaty, but without success.

Other events fortified the resolution of the United States to secure a canal under exclusive American control. In 1879 a private company was chartered by the French government to construct a canal under the leadership of Ferdinand de Lesseps, builder of the Suez Canal. For this purpose it obtained from Colombia the exclusive privilege of building a canal across Panama without, however, impairing the rights of the United States under the Treaty of 1846. The French company spent $260,000,000 on the enterprise between 1881 and 1889; but gross financial irregularities and unexpected engineering difficulties impeded operations, and forced the company into bankruptcy. Several interested Frenchmen then reorganized the company in order to keep alive its franchises and to salvage the canal equipment.

Although the French government had no official part in the de Lesseps undertaking, the project occasioned misgivings in the United States, and proved a potent incentive to the formation of a rival American syndicate to build a Nicaragua canal. The Maritime Canal Company, incorporated by Congress in 1889, began excavation at Greytown the following year, but its work was brought to an abrupt close by the Panic of 1893. The leaders of the syndicate sought to obtain financial backing from Congress; but though official commissions reported favorably on the practicability of the Nicaragua route in 1895 and 1899, the government was unwilling to proceed further under the chafing restrictions of the Clayton-Bulwer Treaty.

Nevertheless, the acquisition of American dependencies in two hemispheres in 1898 and 1899 necessitated prompt action as a measure of naval defense. Both political parties advocated immediate steps to that end in their platforms of 1900, and fortunately the British government, true to her recent policy of cultivating American good will, was now favorably disposed. The outcome was the Hay-Pauncefote Treaty of November 18, 1901. By its provisions, the Clayton-Bulwer Treaty was explicitly abrogated, and the United States was granted "exclusive" control over any canal that might be built. Although the "general principle of neutralization" received nominal recognition, the United States was authorized to maintain "military police" along the canal adequate for its protection.

Further developments now awaited the selection of a canal site. President Roosevelt was a warm partisan of the Panama route as being shorter and cheaper to build than a canal through Nicaragua. On the other hand, advocates of the rival route pointed to the superior advantages to be derived from the use of Lake Nicaragua and the San Juan River as links of a canal. After considerable debate, Congress instructed the President in the Spooner Act of June, 1902, to proceed with the Panama route if "within a reasonable time and upon reasonable terms" he could reach an agreement with the French canal company and also with the government of Colombia; otherwise, he should undertake a canal through Nicaragua.

The moribund French company, whose remaining interest in the canal was to sell out its rights before their expiration in 1904, promptly reduced its former exorbitant figure of $109,000,000 to $40,000,000. Arrangements with Colombia, however, proved a more difficult matter. By the Hay-Herran Treaty of January 22, 1903, the United States was granted an indefinite lease of a belt of land, six miles wide, across the Isthmus in return for an initial payment of $10,000,000 and an annual rental of $250,000. But in August the Colombian Senate, acting within its undoubted constitutional rights, unanimously rejected the treaty. The feeling of that body was strong that Colombia was surrendering too much authority in the canal strip, and that, in any case, the compensation was too small as compared with the amount offered the French company.

The decision of Colombia enraged Roosevelt. As he said at a later time, "I did not intend that any set of bandits should hold up Uncle Sam." The people of Panama seethed with discontent at the prospect of becoming a languishing province out of the course of world trade. To the leaders of the French company the outlook was equally desperate since the failure of the negotiations threatened them with a loss of $40,000,000. Here were the combustibles for a conflagration, and the rapid succession of events in November, 1903, bears eloquent testimony to the unity of purpose which actuated the several interested parties.

On November 2, the United States cruiser *Nashville* arrived in the harbor of Colon. On the next evening occurred a bloodless revolution in the City of Panama, at the opposite side of the Isthmus. On the fourth, United States marines from the *Nashville* prevented the rail transportation of five hundred Colombian troops from Colon to the seat of the trouble. Two days later, the American government recognized the new Republic of Panama, and on November 18, a canal treaty was arranged. The United States was granted perpetual use and control of a zone ten miles wide across the Isthmus in return for the money payments which Colombia had spurned and an American guarantee of independence. Philippe Bunau-Varilla, former chief engineer of the French company, represented the Isthmian government in these negotiations.

In a message to Congress President Roosevelt subsequently made a brilliant defense of the part played by the United States. Denying that the American government had fomented the revolution, he claimed justification for the actions of November on three grounds: "First, our treaty rights; second, our national interests and safety; and, third, the interests of collective civilization." By preventing the use of the Panama railway by Colombian troops, he asserted that the United States was merely executing its treaty pledge of 1846 to protect the "perfect neutrality" of the right of passage. The President disposed of the correlative treaty obligation — to protect Colombia's ownership of the Isthmus — by insisting that this guarantee held only against external aggression. His further contentions — that transcendent interests of national and world import were involved in an interoceanic canal — no one could deny, but his critics maintained that these grand purposes would have been served equally well by a canal through Nicaragua pursuant to the Spooner Act.

Discarding the earlier plan of employing a private corporation to build the canal, the government decided to assume the burden directly, and chose the War Department as its agency for the purpose. Excavation started in 1906, and the work was completed eight years later at a cost of $375,000,000. As an engineering feat, it was comparable in this new age with the transcontinental railway of forty years before. James Bryce declared, "It is the greatest liberty man has ever taken with nature." Yet the problem of obtaining labor, questions of sanitation, and the task of stamping out yellow fever and malaria were difficulties almost commensurate with the engineering problems.

Colombia's resentment over the high-handed procedure of the United States continued unabated for a number of years. When the Democrats returned to power under Wilson, a treaty of 1914 was negotiated, wherein the United States expressed "sincere regret that anything should have occurred" to cause ill will, and agreed to pay Colombia the sum of $25,000,000. In return the Colombian government agreed to recognize the independence of the Republic of Panama with specified boundaries. Roosevelt, then in private life, denounced the treaty as "blackmail," and a militant Republican minority in the Senate prevented ratification. When the Harding administration came into office, steps were taken to eliminate the expression of apology from the document, though the money payment was retained. In this modified form, the treaty was ratified in 1921 with the support of both Democrats and Republicans.

SELECT BIBLIOGRAPHY

The Spanish-American War and Its Fruits. Accurate and detailed accounts of the war and its antecedents may be found in F. E. Chadwick, *The Relations of the United States and Spain* (3 v., New York, 1909–1911). Of great importance, also, are H. E. Flack, *Spanish-American Diplomatic Relations preceding the War of 1898* (in *Johns Hopkins University Studies*, XXIV, nos. 1–2, Baltimore, 1906), E. J. Benton, *International Law and Diplomacy of the Spanish-American War* (Baltimore, 1908), and J. M. Callahan, *Cuba and International Relations* (in *Johns Hopkins University Studies*, extra vol. XXI, Baltimore, 1899). Good summaries appear in J. F. Rhodes, *The McKinley and Roosevelt Administrations* (New York, 1922), C. S. Olcott, *The Life of William McKinley* (2 v., Boston, 1916), C. E. Hill, *Leading American Treaties* (New York, 1922), and in the general works on diplomatic history cited in the Select Bibliography of the preceding chapter. The European background of the war is made clear in Bertha A. Reuter, *Anglo-American Relations during the Spanish-American War* (New York, 1924), and Jeannette Keim, *Forty Years of German-American Political Relations* (Philadelphia, 1919), chap. vi.

American Expansion in the Pacific. In addition to the accounts in the general diplomatic histories, some special studies are available. Early contacts with Japan are treated in P. J. Treat, *Japan and the United States, 1853–1921* (Boston, 1921). W. F. Blackman, *The Making of Hawaii* (New York, 1899), is useful. A detailed treatment of the partition of Samoa may be found in J. B. Henderson, *American Diplomatic Questions* (New York, 1901).

The United States and China. Tyler Dennett, *Americans in Eastern Asia* (New York, 1922), is a detailed and authoritative work, covering the period to 1901. Earlier studies are J. M. Callahan, *American Relations in the Pacific and the Far East* (in *Johns Hopkins University Studies*, XIX, nos. 1–3, Baltimore, 1901), J. W. Foster, *American Diplomacy in the Orient* (Boston, 1903), and P. S. Reinsch, *World Politics at the End of the Nineteenth Century as Influenced by the Oriental Situation* (New York, 1900).

"Imperialism" and the Isthmian Canal. Good descriptions of the election of 1900 may be found in Rhodes, *The McKinley and Roosevelt Administrations* (previously cited), and Edward Stanwood, *A History of the Presidency*, II (Boston, 1916). Besides the discussions in the general diplomatic histories, the following books on isthmian-canal diplomacy are valuable: Harmodio Arias, *The Panama Canal, a Study in International Law and Diplomacy* (London, 1911), Mary W. Williams, *Anglo-American Isthmian Diplomacy* (Washington, 1916), L. Oppenheim, *The Panama Canal Conflict between Great Britain and the United States of America* (Cambridge, England, 1913), I. E. Bennett, *History of the Panama Canal* (Washington, 1915), and Norman Thomson, *Colombia and the United States* (London, 1914). See also J. B. Bishop, *Theodore Roosevelt and His Time* (2 v., New York, 1920), I.

CHAPTER XXVI

THE BEGINNINGS OF THE PROGRESSIVE MOVEMENT, 1901–1908

THE COMING OF THE MUCKRAKERS

Roosevelt's accession to the presidency coincided with the dawn of a new epoch in American political life. As a distinguished conservative (William Howard Taft) remarked in 1915 concerning this time, "For thirty years we had [had] an enormous material expansion in this country, in which we all forgot ourselves in the enthusiasm of expanding our material resources and in making ourselves the richest nation on earth. We did this through the use of the principle of organization and combination, and through the development of our national resources. In the encouragement of the investment of capital we nearly transferred complete political power to those who controlled corporate wealth and we were in danger of a plutocracy."

Indeed, to many thoughtful people in the opening years of the century it seemed that the United States, in ironical perversion of Lincoln's words at Gettysburg, had come to be a government of the corporations, for the corporations, and by the corporations. Organized wealth was active in the state and national governments, the laws to restrain railways and trusts were openly flouted, and a spirit of unbridled materialism infected every branch of business and society.[1] The tocsin of revolt, sounded in 1896 against "Wall Street" and "Big Business," had been hushed by the thronging of new and bewildering national interests as a result of the Spanish-American War, and in 1900 the "Vested Interests" appeared more firmly intrenched than ever before.

[1] As late as 1906, Roosevelt credited Harriman with saying that "he could buy a sufficient number of Senators and Congressmen or State Legislators to protect his interests, and when necessary he could buy the Judiciary."

By the people as a whole the situation, though galling, was deemed inevitable; they were oppressed with the hopelessness of battling against the evil. Aggressive and sensational measures were required to awaken the nation from its lethargy and to rejuvenate the old spirit of American democracy. To this mission a new generation of Americans dedicated themselves. The protest first found expression through the newspapers and popular magazines; it was assisted by budding novelists, and was given a practical turn by aspiring political reformers, including the new incumbent of the presidency.

The campaign of agitation and education inevitably bred individuals who purveyed sensation for sensation's sake, and this fact led Roosevelt to liken such persons to the Man with the Muckrake in *Pilgrim's Progress*, whose absorption in the filth on the floor caused him to refuse a celestial crown. Though the term was unfair to a majority of the writers, it was seized upon by them as a badge of distinction, and they are known in history as the "Muckrakers."

The period of muckraking, properly so-called, extended from 1902 to 1908. Of the countless articles and serials, only a few of the epochmaking contributions can be mentioned. Beginning late in 1902, *McClure's* published Ida M. Tarbell's "History of the Standard Oil Company," based on three years' study of Congressional reports, court records, and the like, and exposing relentlessly the Standard's methods toward competitors, consumers, and the government. In 1904 and 1905 appeared Thomas W. Lawson's trenchant serial, "Frenzied Finance," in *Everybody's*. The author, a well known stockmarket operator, purported to reveal, in realistic detail, the inner workings of the gigantic financial "System" which held the nation's economic and political life by the throat.

In 1905 Upton Sinclair, using fiction as his medium, published a novel entitled *The Jungle*, which presented ugly pictures of unsanitary conditions in the great Chicago packinghouses, and told of the grip of the Beef Trust on the nation's meat supply. The railways came in for their share of the onslaught because of their unfair manipulation of traffic rates, one of the notable series being Ray Stannard Baker's "The Railroads on Trial" in *McClure's* during 1905 and 1906. The fulminations against trust-controlled government reached their climax in David Graham Phillips' articles on "The Treason of the Senate" in the *Cosmopolitan* during 1906–1907. The leaders of that body were considered one after the other, and the sensational conclusion reached that seventy-five of the ninety members were in the control of the railways, the beef and sugar trusts, and the Standard Oil and steel interests.

The activities of the Muckrakers extended to other phases of American life as well. Two series by Lincoln Steffens appeared in *McClure's* under the titles, "The Shame of the Cities" and "Enemies of the Republic," which laid bare disgraceful conditions in municipal and state government. *Collier's* gave aggressive attention to the fraudulent claims and injurious ingredients of patent medicines. In like fashion, many articles were published to expose the unscrupulous practices of banking and insurance companies, the immoral traffic in women, food adulteration, the evil results of child labor, and the appalling number of unnecessary industrial accidents.

It was a characteristic of the Muckrakers to make their accusations of wrongdoing specific and to name names. Some light is therefore thrown upon the substantial correctness of their charges by the fact that few of the writers were ever found guilty of libel. On the other hand, their exposures of corruption and knavery led to court proceedings to rectify some of the worst abuses.[1] The most beneficial effect, however, of the literature of protest was the moral awakening of the masses. In growing numbers they gave their support to a new group of political leaders who fought to restore government to the people.

An Era of Social Politics

The first battles for reform were waged in the arena of state politics. Thus the states again proved their utility as laboratories of governmental and social experimentation. Under the

[1] For example, Joseph W. Folk, incited by Steffens' articles, conducted municipal graft prosecutions in St. Louis in 1903, which raised him to the governorship of the state the following year. The mismanagement of the great New York insurance companies, charged by leading Muckrakers, led to a legislative investigation in 1905, which first brought Charles E. Hughes, one of the attorneys for the state, to favorable national attention. During 1906 the Standard Oil Company was indicted by federal grand juries in two different states for receiving rebates, and the New York Central Railroad was convicted of illegal rebating.

lead of such men as Robert M. La Follette of Wisconsin, A. B. Cummins of Iowa, J. W. Folk of Missouri, Charles E. Hughes of New York, and Hiram Johnson of California, steady progress was made in the betterment of conditions, though, of course, with varying degrees of success. The new leadership was met at every turn with uncompromising opposition from the professional politicians and from persons of a conservative cast of mind — "standpatters" they were called from a phrase first used by Senator Hanna. As might be expected, the new spirit spread most rapidly in the trans-Mississippi West. It infected both parties, and led to growing internal differences which were in time to divide each party into progressive and conservative wings. Much of the confusion today in regard to the meaning of party labels arises from this fact, since the corresponding factions of the two parties often have more in common than the opposing wings of the same party.

One principal point of attack of the reformers was the party nominating convention, another the legislature, for in these bodies the "bosses" and the special interests they represented had their strongholds. In place of the convention method of making nominations, the progressives sought to substitute "direct nominations" through popular vote of the party membership in advance of the general election. Wisconsin adopted the first statewide primary law in 1903; seven other commonwealths followed in 1907. From these beginnings the system spread to the great majority of the states.

As checks on the legislature, the reformers advocated the initiative and referendum, a dual arrangement long in use in democratic Switzerland. The latter is a device whereby the electorate may approve or reject by popular vote laws enacted by the legislature; the former, a method by which the voters themselves may propose laws, either for action of the legislature or for submission to popular vote. Although Oregon adopted the initiative and referendum in 1902, the movement did not get well under way until four or five years later. Today the system of "direct legislation," in some form or other, prevails in nearly half the states.

As a further step in the democratization of government, the progressives demanded for the voters the right to "recall" officials who were out of harmony with the popular will. The scheme, however, was not widely adopted by the states, perhaps because under the American system of frequent elections the people felt they already had ample opportunity to change officials. The legislatures also took action to curb the lavish and corrupt expenditures of money in state elections. By 1911, thirty-five commonwealths had enacted some sort of legislation for this purpose.

The widespread distrust of the United States Senate led to proposals that its members be elected by popular vote, instead of by the state legislatures, as hitherto. On several occasions the Senate blocked efforts of the House to secure a constitutional amendment for that purpose. But the rising democratic tide was not so easily stayed. Beginning with Nevada in 1899, various states adopted legislation, which pledged the members of the state legislature to elect, as United States Senator, the candidate who received indorsement in a statewide primary election. By 1910 three fourths of the states were operating under this system, in one form or another, and it was only a question of time until the Senate should consent to a formal amendment of the Constitution.

At the inception of the progressive movement, the leaders strove principally for the democratization of the machinery of government. But under the hammering impact of the Muckrakers, they came to concern themselves increasingly with legislation to ameliorate the conditions under which the mass of the people lived and worked. As a result, more social legislation was passed in the first fifteen years of the century than in all previous American history.

The existing state laws in regard to child labor were strengthened, and new ones adopted, raising the age limits, shortening the hours, restricting night work, closing dangerous trades to minors, and requiring better opportunities for school attendance. By 1912 child-labor laws were to be found in thirty-eight states, the South being the most backward section in this respect. In the same period, twenty-eight states enacted legislation limiting the number of hours per day or per week which a woman wage-earner might work.

Some progress was also made in shortening the workday for

men. Large numbers of cities and more than one half the states provided an eight-hour day for labor on public works by 1912. In certain especially hazardous employments, such as mining and railway transportation, the workday was likewise made subject to legislative regulation. For example, in the single year 1907 no less than twenty-three states passed laws of this character.

Beginning with Maryland in 1902, employers' liability (or workingmen's compensation) laws were adopted, whereby, contrary to the old common-law doctrine, employers were made responsible for injuries sustained by employees while at work. By 1917, all but ten states had set up state insurance systems for this purpose, either optional or compulsory in character. In addition, the scope of the existing laws for factory inspection and regulation was broadened, provision was made in a number of states for pensions for destitute mothers, and further safeguards were established for women in industry.

Renewed efforts were made by the states to control the corporations and railways operating within their boundaries. A great wave of passenger rate regulation began in Ohio in 1906, spread over the South and the Middle West, and reached its height in 1907. Some of these acts were admirable, but most of them erred in being too severe. In many states, passenger rates were fixed so low as to hamper the roads in making needed repairs and extensions. New revenue laws were also enacted, which, by taxing inheritances, incomes, and the property or earnings of corporations, sought to place the burden of government on those best able to pay.

The new body of social and economic legislation ran counter to the old *laissez faire* conception of government, which had usually guided legislatures and courts in the past. Accordingly, the courts at first invalidated many of the laws as contrary to the Fourteenth Amendment, alleging either that the employers were being deprived of "property without due process of law" or that the wage-earners were being denied the "liberty" to work under any conditions they chose. Much popular dissatisfaction resulted, criticism of the judiciary became rife, and public denunciations of the courts often equaled in vehemence the Northern outcry against the judiciary at the time of the Dred Scott decision.

In time, however, a more liberal view prevailed among the

judges. The courts began to sustain the new acts on the ground that a state possesses, under that vague authority known as the "police power," ample power to promote the health, morality, and welfare of the people as opposed to special privilege. The yielding of the *laissez faire* attitude to the new doctrine of social responsibility was perhaps the most valuable advance made by the new generation.

Notwithstanding the great avalanche of social legislation, certain types of laws common in the countries of Western Europe made little headway in the United States. Such, for example, were the minimum-wage acts, provisions for health and unemployment insurance, and old-age pensions. Moreover, during the first decade of the century, the reformers, in spite of constant agitation by the women, were, on the whole, indifferent to the demand for equal suffrage. On the other hand, a great revival of temperance enthusiasm swept over the West and South, with occasional victories elsewhere. Through the operation of local or statewide prohibition enactments, two thirds of the territory and almost one half of the people of the United States were "dry" by 1909.

Roosevelt and Reform

Although many, if not most, of the reforms sought by the new leadership lay within the realm of state authority, certain of them required action by the nation. For example, the regulation of railways and industrial corporations, in so far as they were interstate in their operation, fell to Congress. The same held true of the transportation of adulterated foods and the regulation of expenditures in federal elections.

In Roosevelt the new democratic aspirations found a knight errant. Unlike many of the progressive leaders, Roosevelt had had long experience in public life. His entire earlier career, moreover, had evinced a natural bent toward reform. He had opposed Blaine's nomination in 1884, though not to the extent of becoming a Mugwump. When civil-service reform was the dominant ideal, he had, as a member of the Civil Service Commission, labored zestfully to further that cause. Although a determined opponent of free silver, he had been sensitive to the fundamental social conflict underlying the McKinley-Bryan campaign.

He confessed subsequently in his *Autobiography* that in 1896 he "was already growing to understand that mere improvement in political conditions by itself was not enough," and that a few years later, when he became President, he "had grown to feel with deep intensity of conviction that governmental agencies must find their justification largely in the way in which they are used for the practical betterment of living and working conditions among the mass of the people."

Indeed, "deep intensity of conviction" was Roosevelt's outstanding trait, second only to his breadth of interest, and to a versatile scholarship hitherto unknown in American Presidents.[1] As President, he did not at once embrace all the articles of the progressive creed, for he was schooled in the old order of politics. Moreover, unlike the ultraprogressives, he was always willing to work with the professional politicians whenever it served his purpose to do so. But when once he espoused one of the new reforms, he did so with all the evangelistic fervor and bulldog tenacity of his dynamic nature. Well-meaning people sometimes accused him of insincerity and inconsistency; but the masses rallied increasingly to his support, for his virile personality and pungent utterances helped to dramatize, in the common mind, the struggle between the forces of democracy and of special privilege.

In his first message to Congress (December, 1901), the President devoted much space to the "serious social problems" resulting from the "tremendous and highly complex industrial development which went on with ever accelerated rapidity during the latter half of the nineteenth century." Acclaiming industrial concentration as a natural and desirable evolution, he opposed the policy of trust prohibition, and demanded legislation to eliminate the evils, while retaining the advantages, of large-scale business enterprises. He recommended broader powers for the Interstate Commerce Commission in regulating railways, and directed attention to the need of conserving the nation's natural resources. Law-abiding labor unions received his

[1] On entering office, Roosevelt already possessed a reputation for notable attainments in the fields of natural history, literature, and historical writing.

approval, and he declared for protective legislation for women and children in federal employment.

The program was too radical for immediate accomplishment. While it elicited widespread popular approval, it roused no answering chord in Congress, where stolid conservatism held sway under Speaker Cannon's leadership in the House and that of Aldrich and Hanna in the Senate. During the summer of 1902 the President carried his message directly to the people, making speeches in New England and the Middle West. Everywhere he urged his policy of government regulation, and demanded a "square deal" for all — for labor, for capital, and for the public.

The great Pennsylvania anthracite coal strike, which began in May, 1902, called attention to corporate selfishness in an impressive manner, and lent strength to the President's cause. The miners demanded a reduction of the workday from ten to nine hours, a twenty-per-cent increase in wages, and recognition of the union. Although the United Mine Workers was one of the best managed unions in the country, the mine owners refused to negotiate. The resulting strike involved nearly 150,000 men, and a total loss to miners and operators of almost $100,000,000. As winter approached, the East faced a terrible coal famine, and Roosevelt decided to intervene in the affair on behalf of the public, whose interests transcended those of either of the contending parties.

Though confessing privately at the time that "there is literally nothing . . . which the National Government has any power to do in the matter," early in October he urged the owners and the miners to submit their differences to arbitration. The former flatly refused, and denied the President's right to interfere. Thereupon he let it be known that, if necessary, he would operate the mines with federal troops, and meantime appoint an arbitration board whose findings he expected Congress to support with appropriate legislation.

J. P. Morgan and other New York financiers at once exerted strong pressure on the operators, and the strike ended on October 23, with an agreement that the controversy should be arbitrated by a board appointed by the President. The subsequent arbitral award was a substantial victory for the strikers, who received a ten-per-cent increase in wages and the shorter workday. In the settlement, provision was also made for the adjustment of future difficulties in the anthracite industry by a board of conciliation, representing equally the operators and the organized workers, with final appeal to the federal judge of the circuit.

Under the spur of an aroused public sentiment, Congress in February, 1903, made important concessions to Roosevelt's demands for the curbing of "Big Business." A law was adopted, providing for a Secretary of Commerce and Labor with membership in the cabinet. Included in the new department was a Commissioner of Corporations, who was authorized to investigate the organization and methods of corporate enterprises. His function was not to prosecute offenders but to provide data for the use of the Attorney-General and of Congress.

A few days later, the Elkins Act was passed as an attempt to cure the evil of railway rebates, which the Interstate Commerce Act of 1887 had sought in vain to stop. The new statute forbade variations from published rates, and in cases of violation, inflicted pecuniary penalties not only on the railway and its officers but also on shippers who accepted special favors. The general power of rate-fixing, however, was left exclusively in the hands of the railways, as hitherto, notwithstanding a strong popular feeling that transportation charges were unreasonably high.

Congress in this session also made a special appropriation of $500,000 for the stricter enforcement of the Sherman Anti-Trust and the Interstate Commerce Acts. Earlier decisions of the Supreme Court had tended to narrow the scope of these laws, and rendered difficult the successful prosecution of offenders. In the case of the Northern Securities Company in 1904, which involved an attempt of the Morgan and Hill interests to unite the management of two transcontinental railways through the device of a holding company, the court reversed a previous decision in regard to holding companies, and by a vote of five to four, dissolved the merger as a combination in restraint of trade. Encouraged by this new attitude of the judiciary, other prosecutions were pushed by the government. For instance, in January, 1905, the Court required the break-up of the "Beef Trust," and presently the General Paper Company was ordered to dissolve.

The year 1904 found "Teddy," as he was fondly termed,

firmly intrenched in the affections of the rank and file of the Republican party. The financial interests and the organization politicians, deprived of Hanna's leadership by the latter's death in February, 1904, dared not oppose Roosevelt's nomination. At the national party convention, which met in Chicago on June 21, he was named by acclamation, and C. W. Fairbanks of Indiana was chosen for Vice-President. The influence of the stand-patters, however, appeared in the platform, which was devoted largely to a eulogy of the past achievements of the party. On the trust question, the platform declared simply that combinations of capital and labor "are alike entitled to the protection of the laws, . . . and neither can be permitted to break them."

For the first time since 1892, Democrats of the Cleveland stamp were in control of the national convention of that party at its St. Louis meeting on July 6. Against the fierce opposition of Bryan, the nomination went to Judge Alton B. Parker of New York, an utterly respectable gentleman of conservative convictions, hitherto unknown to national politics. H. G. Davis of West Virginia was named for second place. The platform called for the prohibition of capitalistic monopolies and for augmented powers for the Interstate Commerce Commission. Roosevelt was berated for his "executive usurpation of legislative and judicial functions," and his whole course as President written down as "erratic, sensational, spectacular, and arbitrary."

"Rooseveltism," rather than any specific public question, proved to be the decisive factor in the voters' minds. Like Andrew Jackson, "Teddy" possessed the quality of exciting passionate devotion or fanatical antagonism, and the masses voted according as they loved or feared him. Parker represented, on the whole, the conservative elements, but the certainty of Roosevelt's success caused the great corporations to contribute to the Republican campaign chest as before. The progressive Democrats were drawn more to Roosevelt than to their own party candidate, although Bryan himself gave Parker a lukewarm support. The abounding prosperity of the country was another influence making for Republican victory.

The outcome was an extraordinary testimonial of public confidence in the President. He received 56.4 per cent of the popular vote to 37.6 for Parker, and 336 electoral votes as compared with 140 for his opponent. Incidentally the result was a vindication for the new-school Democrats, for in both 1896 and 1900 Bryan polled over a million more votes than the conservative Parker in 1904. When Roosevelt was notified of his sweeping victory, he declared in a statement to the press, "The wise custom which limits the President to two terms regards the substance and not the form, and under no circumstances will I be a candidate for or accept another nomination."

The Fight for Reform Renewed

Roosevelt entered his second administration with redoubled energy for the work of reform. In his first annual message he called for more drastic regulation of the railways in particular. His proposal met with dogged opposition from the railway interests, who pointed out that transportation charges in the United States were the cheapest in the world, but won enthusiastic support from the small shippers and the traveling public. The House responded promptly with a bill giving to the Interstate Commerce Commission the absolute right to fix interstate railway rates, but the Senate was unwilling to go to that length.

In the end, the Hepburn Act was passed on June 29, 1906. This measure gave the Commission the power to substitute fair rates for unreasonable rates in interstate commerce, and declared that the orders of the Commission should have binding effect unless set aside by a federal court. Notwithstanding the disappointment of the supporters of the House bill, the new law was an advance over the Act of 1887, for the burden of initiating litigation to test the validity of the Commission's orders now rested upon the railways, in place of the Commission as hitherto.

The Hepburn Act also enlarged the authority of the Commission to include the control of express and sleeping-car companies and pipe lines. Free passes, which had hitherto been an insidious source of political corruption, were forbidden except under strict limitations. In addition, the Commission was empowered to prescribe the methods of bookkeeping and accounting which the roads must follow. The last provision was due, in part, to the practice of certain companies in concealing corrupt expenditures through a manipulation of book entries.

Other measures of Congress carried the principle of government regulation to new limits. In response to the Muckrakers' crusade against patent medicines and adulterated foods, the Pure Food Law of 1906 was enacted for prohibiting the use of any "deleterious drug, chemical or preservative" in prepared medicines or preserved foods that were sold in interstate commerce. This measure was presently reënforced by an act requiring the federal inspection of all meats shipped from one state into another.

An employers' liability act for interstate transportation companies was also passed in 1906. When declared unconstitutional by the Supreme Court, a law which met the Court's objections was adopted in April, 1908. In 1907 the question of the relationship of "Big Business" to national politics was taken up, and a law enacted forbidding corporations to make campaign contributions in federal elections. A sister bill, providing for publicity of campaign funds and expenditures, was, however, defeated.

Meantime, active steps were taken by the Attorney-General to assure the enforcement of the regulatory laws. In 1907 it was discovered that the American Sugar Refining Company had defrauded the government out of a large amount of import duties. The resulting legal actions led to the recovery of over $4,000,000 from the Company and the conviction of several of its officials. In the same year the Standard Oil Company of Indiana, a subsidiary of the Standard Oil Company of New Jersey, was indicted for receiving rebates on petroleum shipped over the Chicago and Alton Railroad. The changed spirit of the times was reflected in the fine imposed by Judge K. M. Landis of the federal District Court, amounting to $29,240,000 on 1,462 separate counts. To thoughtful people it seemed that Judge Landis's decision was actuated by a desire for retaliation rather than a spirit of justice, and the case was subsequently dismissed by a higher court.

Next to his program of corporation control, President Roosevelt gave chief attention to the conservation of the nation's natural resources. Although the last of the desirable farming lands had passed into the hands of settlers in the late eighties, powerful private interests had been acquiring, often through fraud, great tracts valuable for mineral deposits or timber or as irrigation sites. The result was the selfish exploitation or waste of raw materials and natural advantages which should have been utilized over a long period of years for the greatest good of the greatest number. At the turning of the century it was estimated that, at the current rate of consumption, the forests would last about thirty years longer, anthracite coal about fifty years, and bituminous perhaps a century. The supplies of petroleum, iron, and natural gas were already showing signs of depletion. Furthermore, great tracts of land regarded as worthless needed only proper attention from the government in order to become tillable.

In the nineties Congress took some tentative steps to conserve our natural resources. By a statute of 1891, the President was authorized to set aside from time to time, as public reservations, any government lands bearing forests. The Carey Act of 1894 offered government aid, in the form of arid lands, to any state that would agree to irrigate them and open them to settlers at reasonable prices. On these beginnings President Roosevelt enlarged. Commencing with his annual message of 1901, he preached the gospel of conservation in public and in private until the masses came to understand the relationship between public-land policy and national welfare.

His actions suited his words. Where his predecessors had set aside 45,000,000 acres of forest land under the law of 1891, Roosevelt increased the timber area by 148,000,000 acres, and through Gifford Pinchot, Chief of the Division of Forestry, began systematic efforts to prevent forest fires and to retimber denuded tracts. By the close of his presidency, the larger part of the great forests remaining on the public lands in the Pacific and Rocky Mountain states had been set apart to be used perpetually in the interest of the whole nation.

Important progress was made in the reclamation of unproductive agricultural lands. The Carey Act had been meager of result; and in consequence, the Newlands Reclamation Act of 1902 was enacted, which reserved the proceeds of public-land sales in sixteen semiarid Western states and territories as a fund to assist the construction of irrigation works. Soon one important project after another was undertaken, great dams and reservoirs

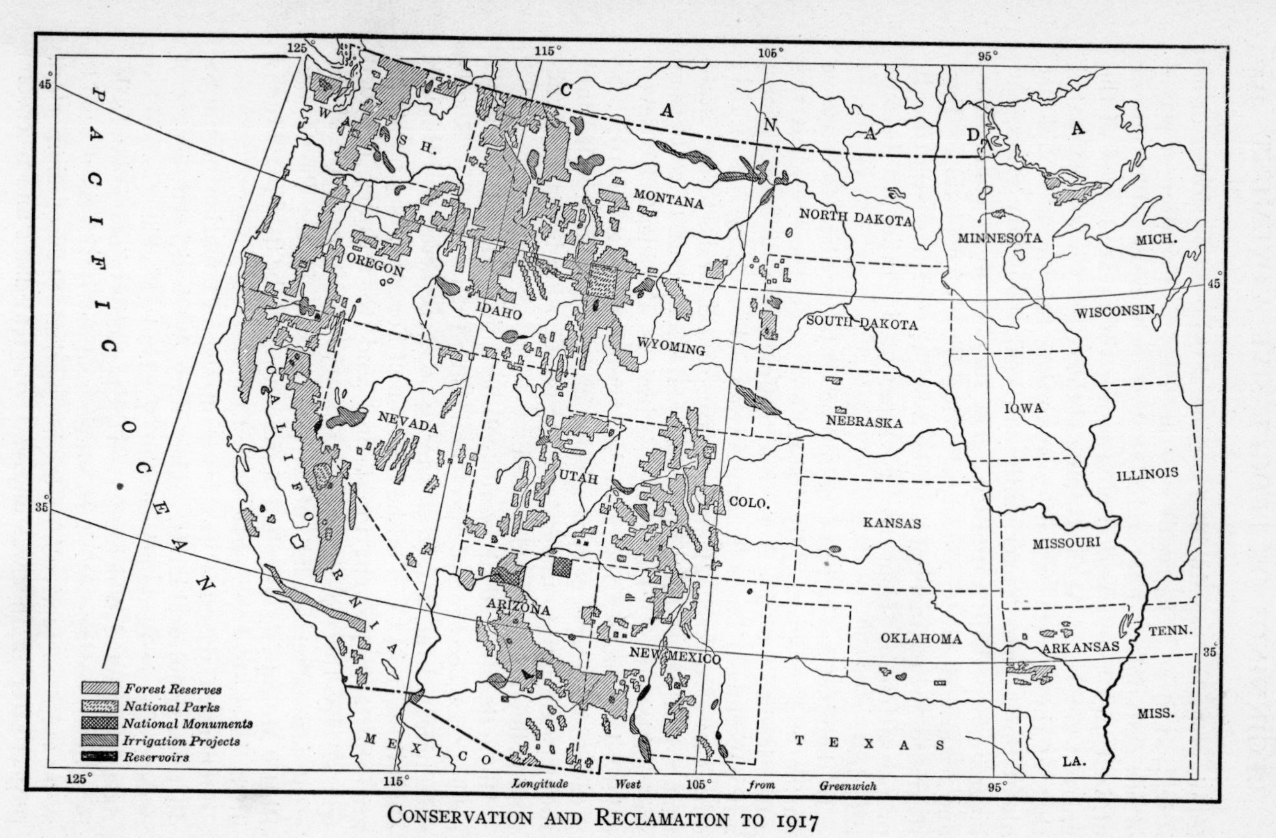

CONSERVATION AND RECLAMATION TO 1917

were constructed, and great thirsty tracts were supplied with water by irrigation. Steps were also taken to reclaim swamp or overflowed lands when they were of an interstate character. In order to protect mineral resources, Roosevelt withheld from sale and settlement a total of 64,000,000 acres that contained oil, coal, and other subsurface wealth.

Another phase of conservation concerned the waterways. It was becoming increasingly apparent that, in order to relieve the congestion of the railways, the public must make greater use of water transportation. Furthermore, the destructive effects of the periodical floods on the Mississippi and elsewhere called for preventive measures on the part of the government. In 1907 Roosevelt appointed an Inland Waterways Commission to study the problem from all angles, and on the basis of their report, appropriations began to be made for a systematic development of the nation's rivers, lakes, and canals.

The success of conservation required whole-hearted coöperation by the states. In full realization of this fact, the President inaugurated a new precedent by summoning the Governors of the states to a conference on conservation in 1908. Within eighteen months after its adjournment, forty-one state conservation commissions were appointed and in active operation. Though sometimes disappointing in immediate accomplishment, President Roosevelt's efforts undoubtedly had the effect of establishing conservation as a permanent American policy. Every succeeding Chief Executive has sought to build upon the foundations which he laid.

As the campaign of 1908 approached, Roosevelt was at the full tide of his popularity. His great service to his country had consisted, not in the specific additions made to the statute book, but in giving the nation new faith in itself. Furthermore, at a time when labor and capital were ready to leap at each other's throats, his voice declared with growing emphasis, "The corporation has come to stay just as the trade union has come to stay," but he unfailingly added, both must bow to the will of the public. Conservatives who thought him too radical and radicals who thought him too conservative failed to perceive that he sought to hold the balance evenly between the contending elements in modern society. Always deeply indebted to the pioneer work of the Muckrakers, he gave the prestige of his great office to the view that between the two extremes of unbridled individualism and paternalistic Socialism lay the middle path of intelligent social control.

SELECT BIBLIOGRAPHY

An Era of Social Politics. The most valuable single study of the new tendencies is B. P. De Witt, *The Progressive Movement* (New York, 1915). Well-balanced accounts may be found in F. A. Ogg, *National Progress* (in *The American Nation*, XXVII, New York, 1918), and F. E. Haynes, *Third Party Movements since the Civil War* (Iowa City, 1916), and his *Social Politics in the United States* (Boston, 1924). The philosophical basis of the reform movement is made clear in C. E. Merriam, *American Political Ideas, . . . 1865–1917* (New York, 1920), and W. E. Weyl, *The New Democracy* (New York, 1912).

For changes in the structure and methods of government, D. F. Wilcox, *Government by All the People* (New York, 1912), is important. The inevitability of reform in the mode of electing Senators is made evident in G. H. Haynes, *The Election of Senators* (New York, 1906). General descriptions of recent labor legislation appear in T. S. Adams and Helen L. Sumner, *Labor Problems* (New York, 1905), F. T. Carlton, *The History and Problems of Organized Labor* (Boston, 1920), and J. R. Commons and J. B. Andrews, *Principles of Labor Legislation* (New York, 1920). Significant studies of a more restricted scope are G. G. Groat, *Attitude of American Courts in Labor Cases* (in *Columbia University Studies*, XLII, New York, 1911), G. E. Barnett and D. A. McCabe, *Mediation, Investigation, and Arbitration in Industrial Disputes* (New York, 1916), and C. H. Mote, *Industrial Arbitration* (Indianapolis, 1916).

Roosevelt and Reform. The main events of Roosevelt's two administrations are outlined in Harold Howland, *Theodore Roosevelt and His Times* (in *The Chronicles of America*, XLVII, New Haven, 1921), and J. F. Rhodes, *The McKinley and Roosevelt Administrations* (New York, 1922). A biographical approach is afforded by J. B. Bishop, *Theodore Roosevelt and His Time* (2 v., New York, 1920). A brief character sketch, written with admirable detachment, is included in S. P. Sherman, *Americans* (New York, 1922). The Roosevelt as envisaged by the public is shown in Albert Shaw, *A Cartoon History of Roosevelt's Career* (New York, 1910). W. R. Thayer, *The Life and Letters of John Hay* (2 v., Boston, 1915), and Herbert Croly, *Marcus Alonzo Hanna* (New York, 1912) are also of value here.

The best general exposition of conservation problems is C. R. Van Hise, *The Conservation of Natural Resources in the United States* (New York, 1910), which should be supplemented by R. P. Teele, *Irrigation in the United States* (New York, 1915), and G. F. Swain, *Conservation of Water by Storage* (New Haven, 1915).

CHAPTER XXVII

PROGRESSIVISM AT FLOOD TIDE, 1908–1917

Taft as Party Leader

As the presidential election of 1908 approached, Roosevelt sternly repelled all suggestions of a "second elective term," and threw his support to William Howard Taft of Ohio, who had been Secretary of War since 1904. Taft had consistently supported the President's policies in public and private, and he knew the insular dependencies as no other American. Nevertheless, Roosevelt's preference occasioned considerable public surprise, and among the progressive Republicans, distrust, for Taft in his earlier career as federal judge had shown pronounced conservative tendencies.

They bowed to the judgment of their chief, however; and the latter, by adept management of the federal patronage and manipulation of the Southern delegates, succeeded in working his will on the first roll-call of the party convention at Chicago in the middle of June. J. S. Sherman of New York was nominated for Vice-President. The platform praised Roosevelt's record in combating "the abuse of wealth and the tyranny of power," called for ampler national regulation of trusts, and favored restrictions on the granting of injunctions in labor disputes. Recognition was accorded the growing demand for tariff reform by a pledge for "a revision of the tariff," to be based on the difference between "the cost of production at home and abroad, with a reasonable profit to American industries."

The disastrous defeat suffered by the candidate of the conservative Democrats in 1904 brought the progressive wing strongly to the fore again. There followed naturally the triumphant nomination of the veteran progressive, Bryan, on the first ballot of the party convention, meeting in Denver on July 7. J. W. Kern of Indiana was named for the second place. "Shall the people rule?" was, according to the platform, "the overwhelming issue," forced on the nation by Roosevelt's dictation of his successor, the "absolute domination of the Speaker" over the House, and the grip of the predatory interests on the party in power. Stigmatizing the Republican tariff plank as belated and insincere, the Democrats pledged themselves definitely to tariff "reduction." The platform took a stronger position than had the Republicans against injunctions in labor disputes, and further demanded the destruction of capitalistic monopolies.

In the ensuing campaign, both Taft and Bryan made long stumping tours. Chief stress was laid on the tariff question, and Taft was forced by Bryan to declare that the Republican plank meant revision downwards. For the first time in history, organized labor sought officially to influence the outcome of a presidential election when the officers of the American Federation of Labor invited support of the Democrats because of their anti-injunction plank. In harmony with the new political morality, the Democrats before the election made public all individual contributions received in excess of $100, and both parties issued postelection statements.

Taft proved the victor, receiving 321 electoral votes to 162 for Bryan, and 51.6 per cent of the popular vote as compared with 43 per cent for his opponent. Afterwards, in explaining his defeat, Bryan declared ruefully that the Republican cause had enjoyed the unfair advantage of two presidential candidates — Taft the progressive who swept the West, and Taft the conservative who carried the East. The Republicans also won majorities in both branches of Congress.

Events quickly revealed that Roosevelt was mistaken in his judgment of Taft. Left to his own devices by Roosevelt's departure on an African hunting-trip, the new President quickly reverted to his naturally conservative outlook on public questions. It is likely that he believed, without conscious disloyalty to his former chief's policies, that the country needed time for recuperation and reflection after seven years of incessant agitation. At any rate, his kindly nature and imperturbable good humor inclined him to conciliate the powerful party leaders whom his predecessor had antagonized, and soon convinced the progressive Republicans that he was deliberately engaged in betraying the cause so close to their hearts.

The most urgent problem that faced the new administration was tariff revision, a question in which Roosevelt had shown little or no interest.[1] The rising cost of living since 1900 had created deepening dissatisfaction with the Dingley Tariff of 1897, which was blamed with allowing the Eastern manufacturers to exact extortionate profits from the purse of the public. The stronghold of this sentiment was the great grain-growing region of the Middle West, which formed the main support of the progressive movement.

The President summoned a special session of Congress to deal with the question, and in accordance with his recommendations, the House passed the Payne bill providing for tariff revision in a downward direction. But under Aldrich's leadership, the Senate promptly pounced upon the bill, and made 847 amendments, most of them for increased duties. The outcome of the differences was the Payne-Aldrich Act, signed by the President on August 5, 1909, which raised the average rate on all dutiable goods approximately one per cent over the Dingley law. Besides the normal rates, the President was empowered to impose a maximum scale of duties on imports from countries which discriminated against American trade. The law also levied a two-per-cent tax on the net earnings of corporations, and provided for a bipartisan tariff board.

The bill had been stubbornly fought by the progressive leaders of the party, including Senators Cummins and J. P. Dolliver of Iowa, La Follette of Wisconsin, B. H. Bristow of Kansas, and A. J. Beveridge of Indiana. The fact that the duties on wool and woolens were left virtually unchanged created special resentment at a time when woolen manufacturing companies were declaring dividends up to fifty per cent. Even President Taft did not defend "Schedule K," as it was called, though in a public address at Winona, Minnesota, he pronounced the new tariff as a whole "the best the country ever had."

The breach between the progressives and the administration

[1] Taft's cabinet consisted of P. C. Knox of Pennsylvania, Secretary of State; F. MacVeagh of Illinois, Secretary of the Treasury; J. M. Dickinson of Tennessee, Secretary of War; G. W. Wickersham of New York, Attorney-General; F. H. Hitchcock of Massachusetts, Postmaster-General; G. von L. Meyer of Massachusetts, Secretary of the Navy; R. A. Ballinger of Washington, Secretary of the Interior; James Wilson of Iowa, Secretary of Agriculture; and C. Nagel of Missouri, Secretary of Commerce and Labor. Meyer and Wilson were holdovers from Roosevelt's cabinet.

was presently widened by two other events. One of these appeared to involve Taft's good faith toward the conservation of natural resources. In the summer of 1909, Gifford Pinchot, the Chief Forester, openly accused Secretary of the Interior Ballinger of lack of zeal in the protection of water-power sites and coal lands. The President stood by Ballinger, and dismissed Pinchot for insubordination. In consequence, the situation of the administration became so intolerable that presently Ballinger was "permitted" to resign. The incident as a whole deepened a widespread impression that Taft was a dupe of the "Special Interests."

Reform sentiment was further outraged by the failure of the President to aid the Western Republicans in their fight to reduce the powers of Speaker Joseph G. Cannon. In the course of many years, the presiding officer of the House had come not only to appoint all the committees of the House, but also, through his domination of the Rules Committee, to fix the limits of debate and to control the entire course of law-making. A man of confirmed standpat views, Speaker Cannon used his autocratic authority to the prejudice of the progressives. Consequently, on March 19, 1910, the dissatisfied Republican group joined forces with the Democratic minority in a successful effort to curb the Speaker's powers. Though Cannon was permitted to retain the speakership, his right to appoint the Rules Committee and to act as one of its members was taken from him. When the Democrats came into control the next year, they went a step further, and made all committees elective by the House.

The revolution in the House foreshadowed a greater one in the fall elections. On the issues of tariff reform and "Cannonism," the Democrats won decisive victories in all sections of the country, and gained control of the new House by a majority of 227 to 173 Republicans and one Socialist. Roosevelt, once more in the United States, made a long speaking tour, and though not openly hostile to the administration, his efforts were mainly directed in favor of progressive Republican candidates. Even New Jersey, a boss-ridden Republican state which had hitherto been the despair of the reformers, placed in the Governor's chair a progressive Democrat, Woodrow Wilson, recently President of Princeton University.

The lesson of the election was not lost upon Taft. In an effort to appease low-tariff sentiment, the President in January, 1911, proposed to Congress a reciprocity pact with Canada, whereby the United States should remove or reduce the duties on many Canadian food products and raw materials in return for similar concessions on American farm implements and certain other commodities. The measure was supported by the Eastern Republicans, since it left the duties on manufactures untouched, but it roused a whirlwind of protest from the farming and lumbering interests of the Middle and Far West, who feared the consequences of Canadian competition in these products.

Under the astute leadership of Oscar W. Underwood of Alabama, Chairman of the Ways and Means Committee of the House, the Democrats proceeded to take advantage of this new breach in their opponents' ranks. Seeing in Canadian reciprocity an entering wedge for general tariff reduction, they helped the President carry his scheme through Congress in July, 1911. Taft's victory, as it turned out, was short-lived because Canada subsequently rejected the terms.

To offset the displeasure of the progressive Republicans, the Democrats next combined with them to pass a number of bills for lowering the tariff on Eastern manufactured articles. In succession, a "farmers' free-list bill" was passed, the notorious "Schedule K" was revised, and bills were carried to scale down the duties on cotton goods, chemicals, and iron and steel. All these ran afoul the President's veto, and served further to increase his unpopularity both within and without the party.

Legislative Progress under Taft

Despite its shortcomings, the Taft administration had, in reality, done much in a quiet way to further the cause of reform. The dust raised by the Ballinger-Pinchot affair obscured the fact that Congress in 1911 appropriated a large sum of money for the purchase of forest lands lying in the vicinity of the headwaters of navigable streams in the White Mountains and the Southern Appalachian System. Likewise, in 1910 and 1911, Congress passed legislation for limiting the total amount of money which a candidate might spend in running for the House or the Senate, and requiring the publication of all receipts and expenditures before and after both primaries and elections.[1]

In a similar spirit, the Mann-Elkins Act, passed in 1910, brought telegraph and telephone companies under the jurisdiction of the Interstate Commerce Commission, and amended the Hepburn Act so as to make the Commission's orders for lower railway rates immediately effective, even when an investigation of their reasonableness was being conducted by the courts. In addition, the public-land laws were improved (1910), acts requiring the use of safety appliances on railways were strengthened (1910), a Bureau of Mines was established to study the welfare of the miners (1910), a parcels-post law was enacted (1912), and a Department of Labor was created with membership in the cabinet (1913).

Prosecutions were also actively conducted against combinations under the Sherman Act. In May, 1911, the Supreme Court ordered the dissolution of the Standard Oil Company, and also of the American Tobacco Company, into separate competing units. The immediate rise in the value of Standard Oil stock indicated that the decision was of slight practical consequence. Indeed, the Court in these two decisions betrayed a conviction of the undesirability of reckless attempts to break up large-scale enterprises. This appeared in the new construction which it placed upon the Sherman Act. Where that statute had outlawed "every" contract or combination "in restraint of trade" (see page 370), the Supreme Court now interpreted the words to mean the prohibition merely of *undue* or *unreasonable* restraints of trade.

Perhaps most important of all was the initiation of two new amendments to the Constitution. The controversy, begun in 1895 by a Supreme Court decision against the federal income tax (see page 357), was solved, once for all, by the Sixteenth Amendment, submitted by Congress to the states in 1909. By its provisions, Congress was empowered to levy an income tax without the necessity of apportioning it among the states according to population. The Seventeenth Amendment, proposed by

[1] The Supreme Court in 1921 held the Act of 1910 unconstitutional in so far as it sought to regulate the expenditures of Senatorial candidates in primary elections. Newberry *v.* the United States.

Congress in 1912, represented the climax of the popular demand for a reconstitution of the Senate. By its terms, United States Senators were made elective by popular vote of the state instead of by the state legislature.

The income-tax amendment was ratified by the state legislatures shortly before Taft left office, and the other amendment shortly thereafter. The adoption of these changes gave new hope to the reformers, who had long been contending that the federal Constitution was, for all practical purposes, unamendable. It was significant of the changed outlook of America that the Taft administration should clothe with constitutional sanction two reforms which had first been brought to prominent national attention by the Populists in 1892.

The Presidential Election of 1912

Had the President possessed qualities of leadership, he might have capitalized these constructive achievements to his political advantage. As it was, plans began to be made by progressive Republican leaders as early as January, 1911, to prevent his renomination. A formal organization was effected, and with some misgivings, Senator La Follette was presently indorsed as the logical Republican candidate. Although "Fighting Bob's" life-long battle for popular rights had placed him at the van of the progressive Republicans, he had never made the same appeal to the popular imagination as Roosevelt, and the feeling grew among the progressives that he lacked the vote-getting qualities necessary to unseat Taft in the national party convention.

Increasing pressure was therefore exerted upon the ex-President to identify himself unreservedly with the movement against Taft. Finally, in February, 1912, Roosevelt in a speech before the Ohio constitutional convention made clear his support of those items of the progressive creed, which he had hitherto ignored or opposed. A few days later, following a temporary breakdown in La Follette's health, he announced his readiness to contest Taft's nomination at the hands of the convention.

Both the President and the ex-President went on the stump to present their claims to the party membership, and soon these former devoted friends became involved in an unedifying personal controversy. The President denounced Roosevelt's "explosive inconsistencies," and warned the people against "political emotionalists" intent on plunging the country "into a condition that would find no parallel except in the French Revolution." In scathing rejoinder, Roosevelt declared, "It is a bad trait to bite the hand that feeds you," and charged Taft with being the beneficiary of "pure political brigandage."

The contest was not an uneven one. Although Roosevelt had a wider personal following, the President's supporters controlled the party machinery for selecting delegates in most of the states, and absolutely controlled the South where the delegates were usually federal officeholders. In the twelve states, however, where preferential primaries were established by law, Roosevelt won 278 delegates, Taft 46, and La Follette 36. Elsewhere Taft was generally the favorite, though there was an unusually large number of contested seats.

When the national convention assembled in Chicago on June 18, 1912, the Republican National Committee, employing what the progressives called "steamroller tactics," awarded most of the contested seats to Taft delegates, and constructed a majority which renominated Taft and Sherman on the first ballot. Three hundred and forty-four Roosevelt delegates, representing one third of the membership, refused to vote, though critics unkindly pointed out that Roosevelt himself had secured Taft's nomination four years before by similar methods. The platform, while declaring for a "self-controlled representative democracy," carefully skirted questions provocative of factional bitterness. The chief planks called for a federal commission to regulate trusts, a "readjustment" of the tariff with the aid of a commission of experts, and a reformation of the monetary system. The Roosevelt supporters, unappeased, prepared to carry their case directly to the public.

The Republican schism lent unusual interest to the proceedings of the Democratic convention, which assembled in Baltimore on June 25. For the first time in sixteen years the Democrats felt confident of victory, and emboldened by this circumstance, the conservative forces and professional politicians made a desperate effort to regain mastery of the party. Either Governor Judson Harmon of Ohio or Congressman Underwood was acceptable to them as a candidate, and they resolved at all costs to defeat the nomination of Woodrow Wilson, who, as Governor of New Jersey, had shown himself to be a militant progressive. A fourth candidate, Speaker Champ Clark, flirted with both factions, and on the tenth ballot actually polled a majority of the votes.

That Clark failed of the requisite two-thirds vote was due to the energy and skill of William Jennings Bryan, who sat as a member of the Nebraska delegation. He fought the "predatory interests" at every turn, and kept the outside public constantly informed of his plans, with the result that thousands of approving telegrams poured in to the delegates. The long balloting concluded with Wilson's nomination on the forty-sixth trial. Governor T. R. Marshall of Indiana was named for the vice-presidency. The platform attributed the high cost of living to the Republican tariff, pledged "immediate downward revision," repeated the labor-injunction plank of 1908, asked that the Sherman Act be restored to its original vigor, and demanded revision of the banking and currency laws.

At the close of the Republican national convention, the Roosevelt delegates held a mass meeting with other dissatisfied Republicans, and decided upon the formation of a new party. The new organization was formally launched under the name of the "Progressive party" at a national convention held in Chicago on August 5. Amid scenes of high emotional excitement, Roosevelt and Governor Hiram Johnson of California were named to head the party ticket, and a platform was adopted which was perhaps the most unusual ever framed by any party having a chance for success. Its keynote was the pledge "to sweep away old abuses" and "build a new and nobler commonwealth." To this end the platform advocated (1) such political reforms as direct primaries, the "short ballot," initiative, referendum and the recall, equal suffrage, and a referendum on court decisions nullifying state legislation; (2) such economic reforms as a federal commission to regulate industrial combinations, tariff revision by an expert commission without sacrifice of the protective principle, and an overhauling of the banking and currency laws; and (3) a wide variety of laws to secure "social and industrial justice." Among the last-named proposals were the eight-hour day, a "living wage," the prohibition of child labor, and measures for the prevention of industrial accidents and occupational diseases.

The campaign was surprisingly quiet in view of its dramatic prelude. Roosevelt was inevitably the central figure. His followers were nicknamed "Bull Moosers" from a chance expression dropped by their leader, and he himself was censured for his unbounded ambition and egotism in seeking a third term. The most startling incident was the attempt of an insane man in Milwaukee to assassinate him. Although the Progressive program was widely condemned as radical and socialistic, the ticket received warm support from certain well-known capitalists, who saw in the elaborate provisions for government control of industrial conditions the best hope for an efficient and contented labor-force. It is significant that Gompers, as in 1908, called on organized labor to support the Democrats; indeed, the Progressive platform nowhere definitely affirmed the right of the wage-earners to organize and strike. Wilson's dignified and well-phrased utterances won growing favor with thoughtful people, who came to regard him as standing midway between candidates of extremist tendencies — "a progressive with the brakes on."

In any case the divided opposition made Democratic success inevitable. Many Republicans refrained from voting on election day, but a greater number of them rallied to their old idol, "Teddy." Wilson received 435 electoral votes, Roosevelt 88, and Taft 8. But the distribution of the popular votes mirrored the situation more accurately, Wilson winning 41.8 per cent, Roosevelt 27.4, and Taft 23.2. In fact, the victor received one and one-third million votes less than the total polled by his two rivals, and fewer votes than Bryan had commanded in any of his three candidacies. The remarkable showing made by the new party promised to give it a permanent place in American politics, if, indeed, the Progressive strength represented anything more than personal attachment to a brilliant chief.

The Reform Program of the Democrats, 1913–1914

The new President embodied the best traditions of the party that elected him. A Virginian by birth, he had spent his mature years in the North, serving as professor, and then President, of

Princeton University since 1890. Like Jefferson, he was a philosopher and student of political institutions; his works on political science laid the foundations of the modern study of that subject in America. In common with Jackson, he was a militant believer in democracy, and possessed an intuitive understanding of the spiritual yearnings of the common people. His unvarying self-command and stubborn courage recalled Cleveland, whose neighbor he had been at Princeton.

Unlike all these, however, he surveyed the world with the serene detachment of a man ever alert to discover the basic principles which govern the thoughts and activities of mankind. His espousal of popular rights, it is not too much to say, sprang from his head rather than his heart. Moreover, he possessed a literary style, which made of his messages and speeches fine tapestries woven of noble and luminous phrases. His hold on the American people rested, in large part, on their growing confidence in his high-mindedness and penetrating intelligence rather than on a devotion to his personal qualities, though he was deeply loved by his intimates. His intellectual aloofness proved a constant irritation to his political opponents, and often to his own party leaders, and in the end, contributed powerfully to his defeat in the greatest battle of his career, that for the ratification of the League of Nations.

The election of 1912 was a victory for progressivism if not for the Progressives. Wilson showed no disposition to evade or straddle any of the urgent questions of the time. He felt a solemn mission to commit the Democrats unalterably to the progressive position, and by the appointment of Bryan as Secretary of State, he served notice, at the outset, of his open alliance with the reform wing of his party.[1] In any case, this course was the part of political wisdom, for thereby the President might hope to undermine the strength of the Progressive party, and win

[1] The other members of the cabinet were: W. G. McAdoo of New York, Secretary of the Treasury; L. M. Garrison of New Jersey, Secretary of War; J. C. McReynolds of Tennessee, Attorney-General; A. S. Burleson of Texas, Postmaster-General; Josephus Daniels of North Carolina, Secretary of the Navy; F. K. Lane of California, Secretary of the Interior; D. F. Houston of Missouri, Secretary of Agriculture; W. C. Redfield of New York, Secretary of Commerce; and W. B. Wilson of Pennsylvania, Secretary of Labor. Wilson was a former secretary of the United Mine Workers. The indebtedness of the Democratic party to the "Solid South" was evidenced by the fact that five of the appointees, including McAdoo, were natives of ex-slave states.

for his administration that majority support among the people, which had been lacking in the presidential election.

For the accomplishment of his task he possessed Democratic majorities in both branches of Congress. But the party as a whole was lacking in cohesion and in responsible leaders. Moreover, for many years, Wilson as a student of government had maintained that the Chief Executive should not be a mere presiding officer of the government but an active and aggressive director of public policy, bearing a relationship to the party and the people comparable to that of the Prime Minister in Great Britain.

Accordingly, he frankly assumed the reins of leadership, revived the custom, abandoned by Jefferson, of reading his messages to Congress, and in other ways enhanced the prestige of his position, even in a greater degree than had Roosevelt. In accounting for his legislative achievements, however, it must always be remembered that his administration was the beneficiary of all the agitation for democratic reform that had occurred since the opening of the century.

Summoned in special session on April 7, 1913, the new Congress proceeded to carry through a legislative program which was one of the most notable in American history in scope and importance. Its first task was tariff revision. To safeguard their interests, agents of the protected manufacturers — the so-called "third house of Congress" — gathered from far and near to press their special claims, as on previous occasions. Their efforts, however, came to nought and they themselves decamped in haste when the President, in a trenchant public statement, exposed the "extraordinary exertions" of the "insidious and numerous lobby."

The Underwood Tariff Act, as signed by the President on October 3, provided substantial reductions in the duties on important raw materials and foodstuffs, cotton and woolen goods, iron and steel, and other commodities, and abolished the tariff on more than one hundred items. Though primarily a tariff for revenue, many protective features were retained. In order to make up for the certain loss of revenue, advantage was taken of the recent Sixteenth Amendment, and a graduated tax was levied on all net incomes in excess of $3,000, with an additional exemption of $1,000 in the case of married persons.

The new tariff was well received by the public. Its actual fiscal effects were never fairly tested, for the outbreak of the World War in 1914 caused a sharp decline of imports and of customs revenue. The Underwood Act did not provide for a revival of the tariff board, established in 1909; but agitation in favor of such a body became subsequently so strong that in September, 1916, Congress created a bipartisan commission of six members to assist in tariff legislation.

The second item on the Democratic program was a reorganization of the banking and currency system. The Act of 1900 had firmly established the gold standard, but had left unaltered another serious defect of the monetary system — its lack of elasticity. Under the then existing system, the amount of greenbacks, treasury notes, and silver certificates was virtually stationary, and the quantity of national-bank notes, being based upon the ownership of government bonds by the banks, showed little fluctuation. Although the volume of gold varied from time to time, its movements were governed by the demands of international trade and had no relation to domestic needs. Consequently, the currency of the country did not expand and contract as busy times demanded more, or dull times required less, of the circulating medium.

In November, 1907, the country was overtaken by a severe financial panic. Speculation had been rife for several years, particularly in trust development, and many industrial securities were selling far above their real value. Yet the blow fell with little warning. Most banks were in excellent condition, industries flourishing, and labor fully employed. Suddenly, however, confidence became impaired, "runs" on banks started, factories shut down, and business generally became paralyzed. Thirteen banks failed in New York City alone. To afford relief, payroll checks and other substitutes for money were put into circulation, gold was imported from Europe, and the national treasury poured its surplus into banks of deposit in all parts of the country. By the middle of January, 1908, confidence was again restored.

Other than overspeculation, the fundamental cause of the financial collapse seemed to be the inability of the national banks to enlarge the volume of their currency in a period of money stringency. Many business concerns which possessed ample resources failed through their impotence to convert their assets into ready money and thus meet their obligations. An important contributory cause was the fact that each bank had to meet the crisis substantially alone. Although throughout the Panic there were ample funds in the vaults of the stronger banks, they were inclined to hoard their cash for fear of being themselves left in the lurch.

Students of finance also pointed to the unscrupulous activities of certain great financiers at the nation's money center, New York. If these men did not actually form a "money trust," they were nevertheless in a position to manipulate the available money supply in such a way as to serve their own ends and embarrass the public. The crisis left a trail of indictments and suicides in high financial circles.

Spurred to action by the financial breakdown, Congress in the Aldrich-Vreeland Act of May, 1908, authorized the creation of a National Monetary Commission to investigate the currency systems of the world as the basis for a reformation of the American system. For the next six years, the law empowered the national banks to increase their circulation in times of stringency by the issue of emergency bank notes, properly secured. These emergency issues should be guaranteed by the government, and be taxed on a graduated scale to insure their retirement as soon as the urgent need should cease. In 1912 the Monetary Commission made an elaborate report, but its scheme of reorganization received a cool reception, since private banking interests, instead of the government, were given control of the proposed system. Nevertheless, its investigations proved of great aid to the Democrats when, on President Wilson's recommendation, they turned their attention to currency reform.

On December 23, 1913, the Federal Reserve Act was adopted, representing the joint labors of Secretary McAdoo, Senator R. L. Owen, and Representative Carter Glass. The law was designed to cure the chief faults which experience had revealed in the old monetary system: (1) lack of coöperation among banks during crises; (2) inelasticity of the currency supply; and (3) the concentration of power in the hands of a few financial magnates.

By the provisions of the new act, the country was divided into twelve districts, within each of which a "Federal Reserve Bank" was established at some principal city.[1] These regional banks serve as central reservoirs for the cash reserves of the national banks in their respective districts and of such state banks as choose to join the system.[2] Their primary function is to act as a bank for banks. Under strict regulations, it is possible to use the funds of the Federal Reserve Banks to assist individual local banks in periods of temporary embarrassment.

Greater elasticity is given to the currency supply through the issuance of "Federal Reserve notes" in times of money shortage. For this purpose, local banks may deposit with the Federal Reserve Bank, approved commercial paper (for example, promissory notes of reliable business concerns), and receive in exchange a supply of Federal Reserve notes. When the emergency is over, the process is, or may be, reversed. The Federal Reserve notes are expected eventually to replace the old national bank notes. To prevent manipulation by private bankers, the delicate and complicated machinery of the new banking plan was placed under the general supervision of a Federal Reserve Board, made up of the Secretary of the Treasury, the Comptroller of the Currency, and five presidential appointees,[3] and under the immediate oversight of the special governing boards of the Reserve Banks of the several districts.

The system quickly demonstrated its utility, and even won favor among those who, like the private banking interests, had originally fought its adoption. The regional banks operated harmoniously with each other; currency demands were promptly met; crop-moving difficulties, notably in the South, were overcome; and progress was made toward unifying the basic banking resources of the nation. Though the new plan was not fully in operation till November, 1914, it helped greatly toward relieving the commercial strain caused in America by the outbreak of the World War.

The next important task of the Democrats was trust regulation. Experience commended a system of control similar to that of the Interstate Commerce Commission over the railways, but it

[1] Boston, New York, Philadelphia, Richmond, Atlanta, Cleveland, Chicago, Minneapolis, St. Louis, Kansas City, Dallas, and San Francisco.

[2] The United States government also deposits its funds in the Federal Reserve Banks, thus abandoning the subtreasury system which had been in use since the forties.

[3] A sixth appointed member was added in 1923.

required vigorous leadership by the President to secure legislation along the lines that he desired. The results were embodied in two laws. An act passed on September 26, 1914, abolished the office of Commissioner of Corporations, created in 1903, and transferred its powers of investigating corporate abuses to a new body, the Federal Trade Commission, consisting of five appointed members. In addition, the Federal Trade Commission was given authority to issue orders prohibiting the use of "unfair methods of competition" by business concerns in interstate trade. In cases of disobedience, the Commission was empowered to seek aid from the federal courts in the enforcement of its orders.

A second law, the Clayton Anti-Trust Act of October 15, forbade many corporate practices which had thus far escaped specific condemnation by federal statute, such as interlocking directorates, discriminations in prices among purchasers, and the ownership by one corporation of stock in other similar enterprises. Other provisions dealt with labor grievances dating back at least as far as the Pullman strike of 1894. The Clayton Act exempted from antitrust prosecution all labor and agricultural organizations "lawfully carrying out the legitimate objects thereto." It proclaimed that strikes, peaceful picketing, and boycotting were not violations of any federal law. It also prohibited injunctions in labor disputes growing out of the terms and conditions of employment, unless necessary to prevent irreparable injury, and required jury trial for contempt of court, except when the offense was committed in the presence of the judge.

The public at large greeted the new trust legislation with high satisfaction. In labor circles the elation was unexampled. Subsequent decisions of the Supreme Court, however, tended to restrict narrowly the application of the labor clauses, and to rob the unions of many of the immunities which they had believed to be theirs. For instance, in one notable decision, that of the Duplex Printing case in 1921, the Court upheld an injunction, issued by a lower court, to prevent the membership of a national union from boycotting an employer. The decision was based upon the view that the benefits of the Clayton Act extend only to the employees immediately and directly involved in an industrial controversy, and not to the members of their union throughout the country, who, by order of the national officers, join them in the boycott. Again in the Coronado decision in 1922, the Supreme Court held that unions, although unincorporated, are in every respect like corporations, and are liable for damages in their corporate capacity, including triple damages under the Sherman Anti-Trust Law.

The Congressional elections of 1914 gave the people a chance to pass judgment on the President's masterful course. The voters were also given an opportunity to declare whether, upon sober second thought, they wished to abandon the Republican party for the Progressive party. On both points the outcome was clear. The Progressives revealed startling weaknesses all along the line, polling less than one half their number of votes in 1912. As a result of Republican gains, the Democratic majority in the House fell from 147 to 29; but the Democrats had cause for rejoicing, for they had maintained their control of Congress in what was essentially a two-party contest. It was evident that large numbers of Progressives had already made their transition into the President's following.

Further Social and Economic Legislation, 1915–1917

Although foreign affairs, especially the great conflict in Europe, occupied increasing attention during the second half of the administration, the Democrats, nevertheless, proceeded energetically to the task of rounding out their program of economic and social legislation. In 1915 the Seamen's Act, sponsored by La Follette, was adopted for the improvement of the living and working conditions of employees on ocean-going vessels and on lake and river craft.

In the same year a bill passed Congress, denying the right of immigration to adult aliens who were unable to read English or some other language. This device of a "literacy test" was espoused by those who viewed with alarm the newer immigration from Mediterranean Europe, for a very high percentage of these arrivals consisted of illiterates. By organized labor it was welcomed as an effective means of reducing the competition for work. Similar bills had been vetoed by Cleveland in 1897, and by Taft in 1913, and now Wilson added his name to theirs, affirming that, where youthful educational opportunities were lacking, illiteracy did not argue an absence of natural capacity. Two years later, however, the advocates of the literacy test had their way. A bill for this purpose became a law over Wilson's veto in February, 1917.

In 1916 the Rural Credits Law was enacted. Its purpose was to give farmers credit facilities equal to those extended by the Federal Reserve System to manufacturers and merchants. Under the general administration of a Federal Farm Loan Board, named by the President, farmers were enabled to borrow money from Federal Land Banks on farm-mortgage security over long periods of time, at a lower rate of interest than an ordinary commercial bank would charge. Another measure of 1916, the Federal Workingmen's Compensation Act, authorized a federal allowance to civil-service employees during periods of disability.

Congress also tackled the problem of child employment. Although most of the states had laws to restrict child labor, others were notoriously laggard in this regard. Notwithstanding the fact that the Constitution was silent on the subject, the need to improve the situation through national action was urgent. Accordingly, in a law of 1916 Congress, stretching to the utmost its power to regulate interstate commerce, excluded from interstate transportation the products of factories employing children under fourteen years. Only about 150,000 working children fell directly within the scope of the law, but it was hoped that the example would indirectly benefit the 1,850,000 child laborers beyond the reach of the national authority.

The Supreme Court, however, by a vote of five to four declared the law unconstitutional. Thereupon Congress, not to be balked, tried another scheme, and in 1918 imposed a tax of ten per cent on the net profits of factories employing children under the age of fourteen. This law was likewise held unconstitutional in 1922.[1] At once a demand developed for a child-labor amendment to the Constitution, and in June, 1924, Congress took the desired action, submitting to the states a proposal to give Congress the "power to limit, regulate, and prohibit the labor of

[1] The two cases were Hammer *v.* Dagenhart and Bailey *v.* Drexel Furniture Company.

persons under eighteen years of age." The proposed Twentieth Amendment is now before the states for action.

The administration's friendly attitude toward labor was further demonstrated in a threatened railway strike of 1916. Since the passage of the Erdman Act in 1898 (see page 385), many labor troubles on the railways had been adjusted by the means of conciliation provided in that law. The Act contained imperfections, however, and in July, 1913, the Newlands Act set up a permanent Board of Mediation and Conciliation with broader powers to assist in the settlement of railway labor controversies. Although the Board lacked compulsory powers, a total of sixty-one disputes were adjusted under its direction by October, 1916.

Nevertheless, when the four great Railway Brotherhoods, representing 325,000 engineers, firemen, conductors, and trainmen, made a concerted demand for a standard eight-hour workday in March, 1916, they refused to submit the matter to the Board of Mediation and Conciliation. In the old days, when organized labor was weak, capital had refused arbitration; now, with labor holding the whip-hand, the railway executives championed the cause of arbitration. The demand of the Brotherhoods embraced not merely a shorter day, but also the same pay as for the existing ten-hour day, with a time-and-a-half rate for overtime. By the employers, who denied that the business could be reorganized on an eight-hour basis, this was denounced as a covert demand for higher wages by a group of the best-paid skilled workers in America.

Other means of adjustment failing, President Wilson in August intervened in the controversy on his own initiative. Acting with the approval of the Brotherhoods, he appealed to the railway executives to accept the basic eight-hour day, leaving to arbitration merely the question of overtime pay. The refusal of the latter brought matters to a deadlock. With a nationwide railway tie-up imminent on September 4, involving grave consequences for the public, the President went before Congress on August 29, and asked for the immediate enactment of a law granting ten-hours' pay for the first eight hours of work each day, with proportionate additional compensation for overtime. Wilson, in defending his action, declared that "the eight-hour day now undoubtedly has the sanction of the judgment of society in its favor."

Within exactly one hundred hours after the President's appearance at the Capitol, the Adamson Law was passed, embodying his proposals. He had also urged an amendment to the Newlands Act, declaring illegal henceforth any strike or lockout while a government investigation of a labor controversy was pending. This recommendation, however, was ignored. The crisis was averted, but critics of the administration pronounced the "surrender" of the government to organized labor a precedent fraught with serious consequences for the future.

SELECT BIBLIOGRAPHY

Taft as Party Leader. The legislative achievements and political controversies of the Taft administration are sketched in some detail in F. A. Ogg, *National Progress* (in *The American Nation*, XXVII, New York, 1918), and C. A. Beard, *Contemporary American History* (New York, 1914). The legislative history of the trust question is presented in O. W. Knauth, *The Policy of the United States toward Industrial Monopoly* (in *Columbia University Studies*, LVI, no. 2, New York, 1914). E. R. Johnson and T. W. Van Metre, *Principles of Railroad Transportation* (New York, 1921), and Eliot Jones, *Principles of Railway Transportation* (New York, 1924), are excellent for an understanding of the problems of government regulation of railways.

The Reform Program of the Democrats. A sympathetic study of Wilson's career by a trained historian is W. E. Dodd, *Woodrow Wilson and His Work* (Garden City, 1920). The principal social and economic legislation is treated in F. A. Ogg, *National Progress* (previously cited). The working of the new fiscal system is summed up in E. W. Kemmerer, *The A. B. C. of the Federal Reserve System* (Princeton, 1920). A special work on the new trust policy is G. C. Henderson, *The Federal Trade Commission* (New Haven, 1924).

CHAPTER XXVIII

THE DEVELOPMENT OF A COLONIAL EMPIRE

Completing the Forty-Eight States

In the opening years of the twentieth century the last of the continental domain of the United States was laid out into states. Oklahoma was the first of the three remaining territories to gain this coveted distinction. Early in 1889, the Creeks and Seminoles sold to the United States an unoccupied district near the center of Indian Territory known as "Oklahoma," and on April 22, 1889, this tract, consisting of more than one million acres, was thrown open to white settlement. At noon of that day, thousands of would-be homesteaders — on foot, on horseback, in every conceivable vehicle — rushed frantically over the border to claim fertile quartersections or choice town-lots. By nightfall Guthrie had sprung into being with a tented population of 10,000, and Oklahoma City and other places had made robust beginnings. Additional tracts were subsequently opened to settlement, and similar scenes enacted.

In 1890 the territory of Oklahoma was formally erected, embracing an irregular area in the western part of old Indian Territory, together with a narrow rectangular strip ("No Man's Land"), bordering upon the most northern section of Texas. Agitation for statehood commenced almost at once, but eventual admission was delayed by the question whether two states should be organized, one Indian and one white, or a single unified commonwealth. In 1907 the entire area, including all of Indian Territory, was finally admitted into the Union as a single state.

In that year, Indians and negroes formed one eighth of the population as compared with one third in 1890. During the territorial period the white population had increased from 172,554 to 1,054,376, more than six-fold. The constitution of the new state excited wide interest. Enjoying free scope in the modeling of their government, the members of the constitutional convention put into the instrument practically all the radical democratic innovations of the day.

The forty-seventh and forty-eighth states followed in 1912. The original territory of New Mexico had been created in the stormy days of the Compromise of 1850, and had been subdivided into the territories of Arizona and New Mexico in 1863 at the time of the discovery of precious minerals. The population of the two regions grew but slowly, though a new era opened with the progress of irrigation and the spread of large-scale mining toward the close of the century.

As in the case of Oklahoma, the constitutions proposed for the two new states reflected the democratic idealism of the times, and the Arizona constitution even included a provision for the recall of judges by popular vote. Congress, upon President Taft's recommendation, refused to complete the act of admission for Arizona until this objectionable feature should be removed. Arizona acceded, but only to restore the offending provision by a constitutional amendment as soon as full statehood was achieved.

The Evolution of a Colonial Policy

The admission of New Mexico and Arizona completed, for the time at least, the process of state-building and federal integration which had its origins in the early colonial settlements. In the period since the Civil War, the United States had gathered colonial possessions — "in a fit of absent-mindedness," as Seeley once remarked of Great Britain — in widely separate parts of the world. But these lands contained peoples of diverse races and religions, in all stages of cultural and political progress; their historical traditions and political institutions and ideals were totally unlike those of the American stock. The United States, in consequence, was confronted with the problem whether these new accessions should, in harmony with long-established practice, be granted large powers of home rule as a training school for eventual statehood, or whether they should be held permanently as provinces.

The problem became urgent with the numerous acquisitions

made after 1898. Publicists and statesmen gave earnest consideration to the question. Its solution was inextricably entangled with considerations of political expediency and with questions of historic American ideals, and in last analysis, it devolved upon the Supreme Court to decide whether any departure from customary American practice was warranted by the Constitution.

In 1900 and 1901, a series of cases came before the Supreme Court involving the position of the insular annexations in our political system.[1] In answer to the basic question, "Does the Constitution follow the flag?" the Court decided "yes" but with important and sweeping qualifications. The Constitution was held to consist of two kinds of provisions, "fundamental" and "formal," only the former of which applied to the dependencies. The Court intimated that it would declare from time to time, as specific cases arose, which provisions possessed this "fundamental" quality.

In deciding the concrete issues then before it, the trend of the Court's thinking became apparent. According to the "Insular Cases," the inhabitants of these scattered possessions are not citizens of the United States unless and until Congress expressly confers citizenship on them. The constitutional guarantees enjoyed by citizens, such as indictment by grand jury and trial by jury, do not belong to them unless and until Congress so provides. As respects tariff laws, duties may be imposed on commerce between the United States and its overseas dependencies.

In other words, Congress was, for all practical purposes, left free to administer the new acquisitions as it saw fit. Accordingly, Congress was able, without hampering restrictions, to work out a colonial policy which, in many striking respects, resembled that of the modern British Empire. Diversity, rather than uniformity, became the guiding principle. In each case, an effort was made to legislate in accord with the special needs of the dependency, and to suit the regulations to the political and economic progress of the people.

[1] Downes *v.* Bidwell (1900), De Lima *v.* Bidwell (1900), Dooley *v.* the United States (1901), Pepke *v.* the United States (1901), Hawaii *v.* Mankichi (1901), Dorr *v.* the United States (1904).

Hawaii and Alaska

Where the circumstances seemed to justify, full territorial status was granted after a suitable period of probation. Hawaii was the first of the outlying possessions to receive this boon. By the Organic Act of April 30, 1900, American citizenship was conferred on the inhabitants,[1] an elective legislature was authorized, and the franchise was bestowed on all male adults who could read, write, and speak the Hawaiian or the English language. The Governor and Secretary of Hawaii are appointed by the President and the Senate.

Under the American régime the territory made steady progress. An excellent school system was developed, capped by the state-supported University of Hawaii. English is the language generally used in the schools. The principal industry of the islands is the culture of sugar cane and the production of raw sugar, the yield per acre being larger than that of any other country. Next in importance is the growing and canning of pineapples. The product of this industry increased 1,094 per cent from 1909 to 1919.

Standing at the crossroads of the Pacific, the islands have received infusions from many nationalities. Of the total population of 255,912 in 1920, there were 109,274 Japanese, 27,002 Portuguese, 23,723 Hawaiians, 18,027 part-Hawaiians, 23,507 Chinese, 21,031 Filipinos, and 19,708 Americans. The native stock has steadily dwindled since early times, chiefly through intermarriage with other strains. As a result of the literacy qualification on the suffrage, the political power is largely in the hands of the English-speaking inhabitants.

The next noncontiguous possession to become an organized territory was Alaska, whose annexation, it will be remembered, dated back to the Treaty of 1867.[2] "Seward's Ice-Box" showed little sign of development for many years. The bulk of the inhabitants was Indian and Eskimo, and the chief sources of wealth were the fur-seal industry and the fisheries. Not until 1884 was Alaska given a resident civil government and then

[1] That is, all persons who were "citizens of the Republic of Hawaii on August 12, 1898."

[2] By this treaty, the rights and immunities of American citizenship were conferred upon the inhabitants, excepting the uncivilized native tribes.

without powers of self-rule. In the years thereafter, penetration of the Alaskan interior by whites gradually unlocked its geographical secrets. The finding of gold on Klondike Creek in 1896, on the Canadian side of the border, precipitated a gold-rush from all parts of the world, which soon led to the discovery of valuable deposits in American territory — along the Yukon, around the head of Cook Inlet, and about Nome, near Bering Strait. This new treasure-trove yielded $320,000,000 in gold, from American sources alone, up to 1921. Few of the gold-seekers, however, became permanent settlers.

In 1903 the Homestead Act was extended to the dependency, though for many years there was little demand for land for settlement. Increasing knowledge of Alaskan natural resources caused this subject to loom large in the national conservation program. The best timber lands were set aside as national reserves, and efforts were made to protect coal and other mineral lands from unlawful seizure. With the gradual growth of a settled white population, Congress, by the Organic Act of August 24, 1912, granted Alaska territorial status. The first legislature of the new territory extended the suffrage to women.

Inadequate transportation facilities continued to hamper Alaska's development; and in default of other means, Congress provided in 1914 for the government construction and operation of a railroad, not to exceed one thousand miles in length. This is the first time the United States ever essayed the rôle of railway owner and operator in times of peace.[1] The population continued small, numbering 54,899 in 1920, of whom a slight majority were whites. With many difficulties yet to be overcome, there can be little doubt that Alaska is a great natural storehouse, which, with prudent management, will serve the people of the nation for ages to come.

The Philippines under American Rule

The Philippines were the third outlying possession to achieve a large measure of autonomy. The archipelago embraces no less than 7,083 islands, of which the most important are Luzon,

[1] In 1924, the line was in operation from Seward to Fairbanks, 467 miles, with spurs to coal mines that brought the total to 541 miles.

Mindanao, Samar, Negros, Palawan, and Panay. Its total land area is slightly larger than that of England, Scotland, and Ireland. Racially of Malayan stock, the native population of 11,000,000 persons contains representatives of about thirty different tribes, speaking a wide variety of dialects. When annexation took place, the civilized inhabitants were nearly all of the Catholic faith, and ranged in culture from educated and wealthy Spaniards to illiterate and degraded natives. The "wild tribes" made up perhaps one tenth of the entire population.

At the time the Senate ratified the Spanish-American Peace Treaty (February, 1899), the Filipinos were engaged in a war for independence against the United States under the leadership of Aguinaldo. Lacking sufficient arms, ammunition, and military experience, the odds were heavily against the insurrectionists. The native forces were always badly defeated in pitched battles, and they therefore resorted to guerilla warfare, laying waste the fields, and surprising and massacring American outposts and detachments. The American troops, angered by the barbarisms inflicted upon captive comrades, were often guilty of cruelties in return.

In March, 1901, Brigadier-General Frederick Funston with a small party captured Aguinaldo by a daring exploit, and the latter presently issued a proclamation to his followers to give up the struggle. But it was not until July 4, 1902, that President Roosevelt officially declared the islands pacified. Even afterward, sporadic outbreaks occurred, notably among the Moros and other wild tribes. The cost of pacifying the Philippines amounted to $170,000,000, more than eight times the purchase price.

At the outset, the islands were placed under a strict military government. In March, 1900, however, President McKinley appointed a Commission of five civilians, headed by Taft, then a federal Judge, to assist the Military Governor in the capacity of a legislative body. On July 4, 1901, the military régime was abandoned, and all powers of government were transferred to the Philippine Commission under Taft as Civil Governor. The Commission was enlarged a few months later to include three native members, appointed by the President. Under the Commission's authority, energetic steps were taken to reorganize the provincial and municipal governments in the more civilized sections. The suffrage was granted in local elections to males, twenty-three years of age, who were taxpayers or property-owners, or who could speak, read, and write English or Spanish, or who had once held municipal office.

The aim of the American government was to accord rights of self-rule as rapidly as the conditions seemed to warrant. In harmony with this policy, the Organic Act of July 1, 1902, declared the inhabitants to be "citizens of the Philippine Islands, and as such entitled to the protection of the United States." Most of the constitutional guarantees for the protection of life, liberty, and property were extended to them, except trial by jury, which could not easily be grafted on to the old Spanish legal system. The authority of the Civil Governor and the Commission was continued, but the Act provided for the eventual creation of a bicameral legislature. In 1907 this pledge was fulfilled. The Commission became the upper house, and the lower house was elected by the voters.

Under American rule the islands made rapid progress. One longstanding native grievance had been the vast economic and political power wielded by three Roman Catholic orders, which owned great tracts of fertile land and controlled much of the local government. The Filipinos hated the friars so bitterly that, during the revolt, they had expelled them from the islands with great cruelty. With the establishment of American authority, the friars reasserted their legal rights, though the natives generally ignored their claims. As a way out, Governor Taft took up the matter with the papal authorities in Rome in person, and in 1903 the United States purchased the 410,000 acres for $7,239,000.

One of the most important reforms was the development of a public school system, culminating in the state-supported University of the Philippines. Hundreds of young American men and women went to the islands and taught Filipino children, while the normal school at Manila was greatly enlarged, and many native teachers trained there. With 200,000 children in the schools in 1902, the number more than doubled by 1907, and reached the surprising total of nearly one million in 1920. This phenomenal expansion often made it difficult to secure properly qualified teachers. Through the channel of schoolroom instruction, English is, with the full consent of the Filipinos, on the way to becoming the universal language of the islands. With the population divided by speech barriers, the natives see in a common language a necessary basis of Philippine national solidarity.

The social and economic advance has likewise been great. A currency system was established, and a comprehensive program of public works carried on, including the construction of highways, bridges, port improvements, lighthouses, irrigation works, and government buildings. With the aid of American capital, agriculture made rapid strides, notably in the cultivation of rice, cocoanuts, sugar, and hemp. The rich mineral resources of the islands, however, have scarcely been touched. Public order was assured by the establishment of an able native constabulary, and prison administration was reorganized. There remained, however, insufficient provision for public health, sanitation, and hospitals.

In all these reforms the Filipinos warmly coöperated. Keenly aware of their own political inexperience, they sought to derive a maximum of benefit from this intimate contact with a progressive Western people. In return, the American officials placed natives in positions of trust and responsibility as rapidly as circumstances seemed to justify. Never once, however, did the Filipinos yield their aspirations for national freedom. The chief issue between the two main political parties, the Nacionalista and the Nacional Progresista, has been merely the question of how soon independence should come. The Nacionalistas, advocating immediate independence, have controlled the House of Representatives since its creation in 1907.

In the United States the cause of Philippine freedom has been most actively supported by the Democratic party. In 1913 President Wilson appointed Filipinos for the first time to a majority of the nine seats in the upper chamber, or Commission, thereby insuring full native control of the insular legislature. This was followed on August 29, 1916, by a new organic law, the Jones Act, which gave the islands what was, in many respects, a territorial status. Both houses of the Philippine legislature were made elective, and the number of voters was trebled by including all male adults who could read and write a native dialect. The chief executive functions remained in the Governor-General, appointed by the United States. American citizenship was withheld, however, since the Philippines were not regarded as a permanent possession.

The preamble of the Jones Act further stated the purpose of the United States to recognize the independence of the islands "as soon as a stable government can be established therein." While the bill was before Congress, a Senate amendment proposed the granting of national freedom within from two to four years, but the House insisted upon the conditional pledge. Under the new Organic Act, the Filipinos were confronted almost at once with a severe test of their capacity for self-rule, due to the financial and economic disturbances attendant upon the World War. Hostile critics saw evidences of governmental incompetence on every hand. Nevertheless, President Wilson in his message of December 2, 1920, declared that the Philippine people, having "succeeded in maintaining a stable government," were ready for independence.

With the accession of the Republicans to power a few months later, a different influence became ascendant. President Harding sent Major-General Leonard Wood and former Governor-General W. C. Forbes to make a thorough survey of Philippine conditions. In their report, these men, while recognizing the many solid achievements of the Filipinos, recommended "that the present general status . . . continue until the people have had time to absorb and thoroughly master the powers already in their hands," and "that under no circumstances should the American government permit to be established in the Philippine Islands a situation which would leave the United States in a position of responsibility without authority." Under the Republican sway, therefore, the policy of the United States is to postpone further the granting of Philippine freedom, and that event will doubtless have to await the return of the Democrats to a complete control of the government at Washington. Meantime the agitation for a separate national existence continues at full blast in the Philippines. The suggestion that eventual independence should be under American protection has wide support among the Filipinos themselves.

Porto Rico and Other Overseas Dependencies

Six months after the granting of autonomy to the Philippines, Porto Rico was given full territorial status. This island has an area nearly three times as great as that of Rhode Island. Unlike most Caribbean countries, the population was largely white in 1899, and the insular resources enabled the people to maintain a standard of living unusually high for the tropics. The new domain remained under American military authority until a civil government was set up by the Foraker Act of April 12, 1900. Under the new system, the Governor and the upper house of the legislature were appointed by the President, and the lower house elected by the qualified voters. The people were declared to be "citizens of Porto Rico."

As elsewhere, American control brought vast improvements in government, education, and social and economic conditions. In 1899 there were but 430 miles of completed highways; in 1919, 1914 miles. In 1899 there were practically no public-school buildings; twenty years later there were 529, erected at a cost of more than $2,500,000. In the same period, illiteracy declined from 79.6 per cent to 55 per cent. Public-health agencies, including sewage systems, quarantine regulations, hospitals, and other sanitary measures, were introduced, and such scourges as yellow fever and smallpox were almost completely stamped from the island. Before the American occupation, coffee was the chief crop, but now sugar cane holds first rank, with coffee and tobacco as the next most valuable industries. The total population in 1920 was 1,299,809, of whom 948,709 were whites and the rest mulattoes and negroes.

The Porto Ricans assisted wholeheartedly in these advances. Nevertheless, they were discontented because they had not been granted American citizenship or a sufficiently large measure of home rule. In 1914 President Wilson reconstructed the upper house so as to give the natives a majority of the appointments, and on March 2, 1917, their demands were more fully met by the passage of a new Organic Act. This law continued the authority of the American Governor, but made the upper legislative chamber elective as well as the lower. Full American citizenship was conferred on the people with manhood suffrage. No other nation ever set up, in a tropical colony, an electoral system of such liberality. Nevertheless, or perhaps because of this fact, restiveness continued among the population, an active minority favoring independence and the larger number membership in the Union. The situation will be greatly clarified when Congress makes a definite declaration of its future intentions toward Porto Rico.

In addition to these noncontiguous organized territories, a host of smaller overseas possessions have continued to be governed directly by the United States without local legislatures. In American Samoa, all governmental authority resides in the Commandant of the United States Naval Station at Pago-Pago, who in turn appoints native Governors in the three political subdivisions. The natives, numbering 8,068 in 1920, are of the highest type of the Polynesian race, and can all read and write.

The same system of administration by naval commandant prevails in the island of Guam. The present generation of natives, numbering 13,698 in 1920, are a mixed race with the Malayan strain uppermost. Instruction in the English language is compulsory. In the case of the Panama Canal Zone, the administration is in charge of a Governor appointed by the Secretary of War. Wake, Midway, Howland, Baker, and the numerous guano islands, containing few or no inhabitants, have not been placed under any organized form of government.

In 1917 the insular area of the United States was increased by the addition of the Danish West Indies or Virgin Islands. This group, situated sixty miles east of Porto Rico, consists of St. Thomas, St. Croix, and St. John, and of about fifty smaller islands, mostly uninhabited. Attracted by the splendid harbor of St. Thomas, Secretary of State Seward had attempted to purchase the islands in 1867, but the treaty failed in the United States Senate.

The desirability of American ownership became increasingly apparent to the government at Washington with the progress of our isthmian-canal plans. A treaty of annexation was approved by the American Senate in 1902, but was rejected by the upper chamber of the Danish *Rigsdag*. A third attempt, however, in 1916, resulted in the formal transfer of the islands to the United

States the next year for $25,000,000. By the Organic Act of March 3, 1917, the islands were placed under the authority of an American naval or military officer as Governor. The people were permitted to enjoy home rule in purely local matters as heretofore. In 1917 the population was 26,051. Education is compulsory, and the language of the people is English.

The Caribbean Protectorates

In the early years of the twentieth century the American political system, as a result of the new colonial policy, came to assume the distinguishing characteristics of a colonial empire. Attached to the federal union of self-governing states were the outlying organized territories, inhabited by alien populations enjoying a large share of home rule. Whether these territories might expect eventual statehood was an unsettled question. On a plane below these were the numerous insular possessions, comparable to the "Crown Colonies" of Great Britain, which were under direct rule of the Washington government with little or no rights of self-government. A few of the subject peoples, one notably, were held against their desires, and longed for independence; but everywhere the extension of American rule had been attended by marked improvements in the condition of the mass of the people. Nor did the resemblance end here. The imperial structure was rounded out by the development of a sphere of influence in the Caribbean Sea, involving the creation of political and financial protectorates.

The first impulse toward the development of American protectorates came as a result of the responsibilities which the United States assumed toward Cuba under the Spanish-American Peace Treaty. When the American military administration took charge on January 1, 1899, the island was disorganized politically and economically. Furthermore, two thirds of the population could neither read nor write. The task fell to Major-General J. R. Brooke and his successor, Major-General Leonard Wood, to introduce order into the chaos. Under their direction, emergency relief was afforded the destitute, far-reaching sanitary reforms introduced, order established, the legal system reorganized, and highway construction begun on an extensive scale. Likewise, church and state were separated, and the educational system was renovated and extended.

In July, 1900, Wood set in motion the machinery for the establishment of the Cuban Republic. The constitutional convention assembled at Havana on November 5, and framed a national constitution modeled on that of the United States. Despite Wood's urgent representations, nothing in the proposed instrument defined the future relations of Cuba with the United States. The American Congress, however, held the whiphand. By the Platt Amendment to the Army Appropriation Act of March 2, 1901, the President was instructed to continue the military occupation until certain specified provisions were inserted in the Cuban Constitution.

These included a pledge that Cuba should never allow any foreign power to impair her independence or territorial integrity in any manner, nor contract any debt for which her ordinary revenues were inadequate, and also an express recognition of the right of the United States to intervene at any time to preserve the island's independence or orderly government. In addition, Cuba was required to accord the United States the privilege of acquiring naval bases on the island.[1] With great reluctance, the convention made the required concessions, and two years later, the stipulations were embodied in a treaty.

The government of the Republic of Cuba was formally installed on May 20, 1902. Handicapped by a bad heritage, the people were slow to accept the ballot as superior to the bullet in the settlement of public issues. Civil disorders growing out of the presidential election of 1906 led to a second military occupation of the island, under the Platt Amendment, which lasted from September 26 of that year to January 28, 1909. In his message to Congress on December 3, 1906, Roosevelt made it clear that, while the United States had no desire to annex Cuba, it was "absolutely out of the question" for the island to continue independent should the "insurrectionary habit" become "confirmed." One of the important reforms accomplished by the second military occupation was the promulgation of a new and improved election law.

[1] Such stations were presently leased at Bahia Honda and Guantanamo, but the former was abandoned in 1912.

Again during the presidential contest of 1912 serious riots caused the United States to concentrate a fleet at Key West, though more decisive measures proved unnecessary. A revolt of 1917, provoked by a disputed election of 1916, caused American marines to be landed at Santiago, Camaguey, and elsewhere for the preservation of order. The detachment at Camaguey remained until January, 1922. To prevent a recurrence of such tumults, a new electoral law, drafted with the assistance of Major-General E. H. Crowder of the United States Army, was adopted by the Cuban Congress in August, 1919. The conduct of the election of 1920 showed little improvement, however, and Crowder had to return to Cuba in order to effect the peaceable seating of the successful candidate. At his instance, also, the insular Congress in 1922 undertook an extensive program of governmental reform, designed to do away with financial irregularities and extravagance, and to improve the administration of justice.

The steadying hand of the Washington government undoubtedly saved Cuba from a career of turbulence and chronic revolution. Nevertheless, the Platt Amendment has continued to cause resentment among important elements of the Cuban people, who believe that they should be allowed to work out their national destiny without foreign interference. Cuba has, on the whole, prospered mightily as an American protectorate. Commercially and economically, she is bound up very closely with the United States since seventy-five per cent of her business is now done with us.

Shortly after the establishment of republican Cuba, a second event in the Caribbean demonstrated the importance of firm American control in that region. In December, 1902, Germany, Great Britain, and Italy undertook a blockade of Venezuela in order to compel the payment of longstanding obligations to their subjects. Venezuela promptly agreed to submit the claims to arbitration, but Germany, seeing a chance to secure lodgment on Latin-American soil, refused to withdraw her warships. When ordinary diplomatic means failed, President Roosevelt, after notifying the American fleet in the West Indies to be prepared for instant action, gave Germany forty-eight hours to accept arbitration. The German government promptly yielded.

The moral of the episode was evident if Latin-American territory was to be protected from the danger of foreign aggrandisement. As Roosevelt informed Congress in December, 1904, "Chronic wrongdoing . . . may in America, as elsewhere, ultimately require intervention by some civilized nation, and in the Western Hemisphere, the adherence of the United States to the Monroe Doctrine may force the United States, however reluctantly, . . . to the exercise of an international police power."

A third reason for the extension of American authority in the Caribbean arose from the acquisition of the Panama Canal Zone in November, 1903. The canal was the jugular vein of American sea power, and every means had to be taken to insure its invulnerability. As a measure to insure stability in the adjoining territory, the United States guaranteed the independence of the new Republic of Panama, in return for the constitutional privilege of intervening with armed force whenever necessary "for the reëstablishment of constitutional peace and order." This constituted the second application of the Platt-Amendment principle to a Caribbean republic.

Accordingly, by early 1904, the Caribbean sphere of influence was already taking shape. As the foregoing incidents have shown, the new policy was based on the necessity, felt by the United States, (1) of maintaining stable governments in these volatile, tropical countries, (2) of removing the pretext for unfriendly European intervention in the "American Mediterranean," and (3) of strengthening the military position of the United States in respect to the isthmian canal. The penetration of American capital into the region served to wed economic to political interest. American investors were taking an active part in the exploitation of sugar, fruit, coffee, asphalt, and petroleum. In addition, trade with the United States was growing by leaps and bounds, increasing from $195,000,000 in 1900 to more than one billion in 1919.

Under Roosevelt and his successors the policy of protectorates was applied to new areas. The Dominican Republic on the Island of Santo Domingo was heavily indebted to European bondholders; and in order to avert the possibility of foreign intervention, Roosevelt, at the request of the Dominican government, placed an American financial expert in charge of the insular revenues in 1905, with authority to arrange for the progressive payment of the debt. In 1907, the stipulations were embodied in a treaty, the United States receiving authority to accord "such protection" to the American General-Receiver and his staff as might "be requisite for the performance of their duties."

Under this vague grant, American representatives supervised the Dominican elections of 1913, and three years later United States marines landed for the purpose of subduing a revolt against the existing government. The intervention quickly grew into a complete military occupation. The American administration restored peace to the country, enforced sanitary measures, reorganized and extended the school system, and undertook an elaborate program of good roads and public works.

Resentful of outside interference in their domestic affairs, the natives insisted again and again upon the termination of the occupation. In June, 1921, President Harding announced that withdrawal would occur only when the Dominican government agreed to a treaty ratifying all the acts of the military régime and enlarging the powers of the General-Receiver of the Customs. These terms became the subject of indignant comment in Santo Domingo, but were eventually accepted. American evacuation occurred in July and August, 1924.

In 1915 the adjoining negro Republic of Haiti was converted into a protectorate. Following a revolutionary outbreak early in that year, United States marines took possession of the chief towns. As a consequence, a treaty was arranged in September, which established American supervision of Haitian finances, provided for a native constabulary under command of American officers, and empowered the United States to intervene with military force when necessary for the preservation of Haitian independence or an orderly government. The American administration, with characteristic efficiency, carried through extensive sanitary, monetary, and governmental reforms, and stabilized political and economic conditions.

Bitter resentment, however, was caused among the natives by the revival in 1917–1918 of the *corvée* system of forced labor on the roads, and by alleged abuses of authority on the part of members

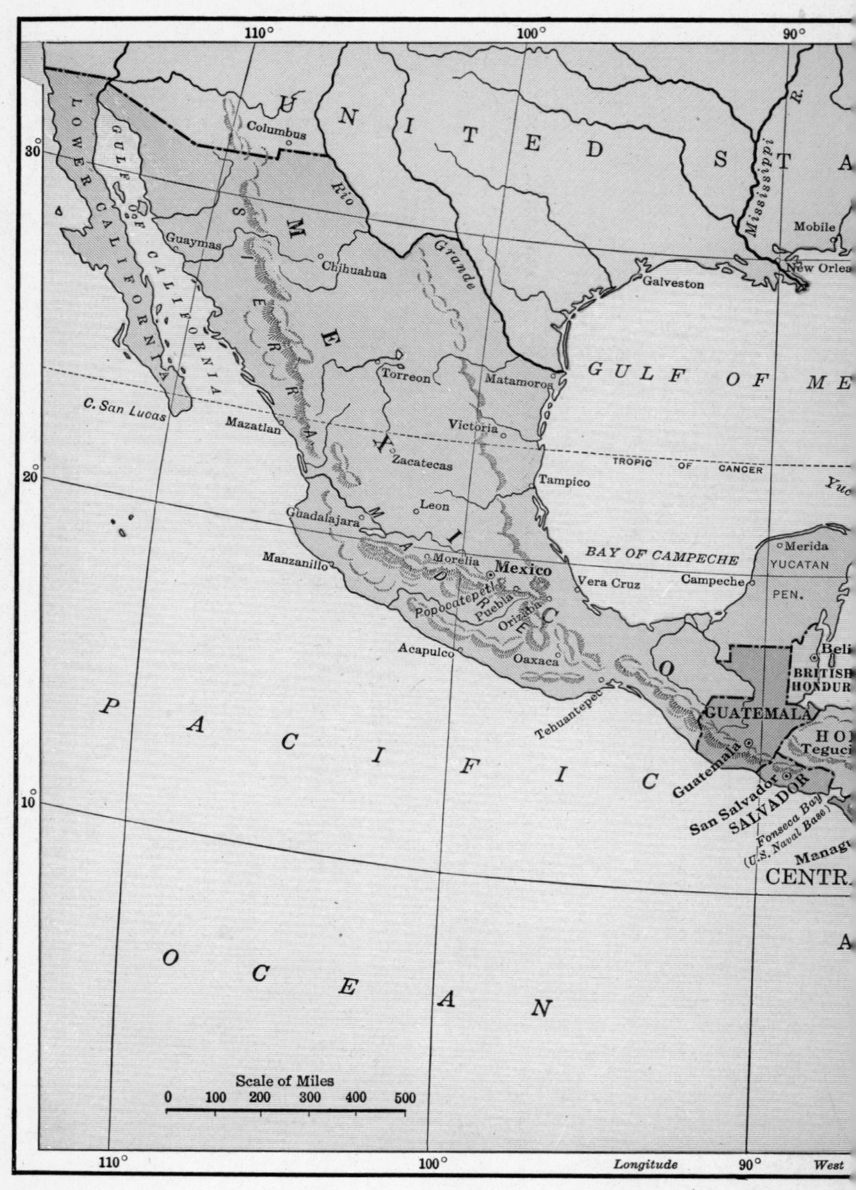

Mexico, the Cari

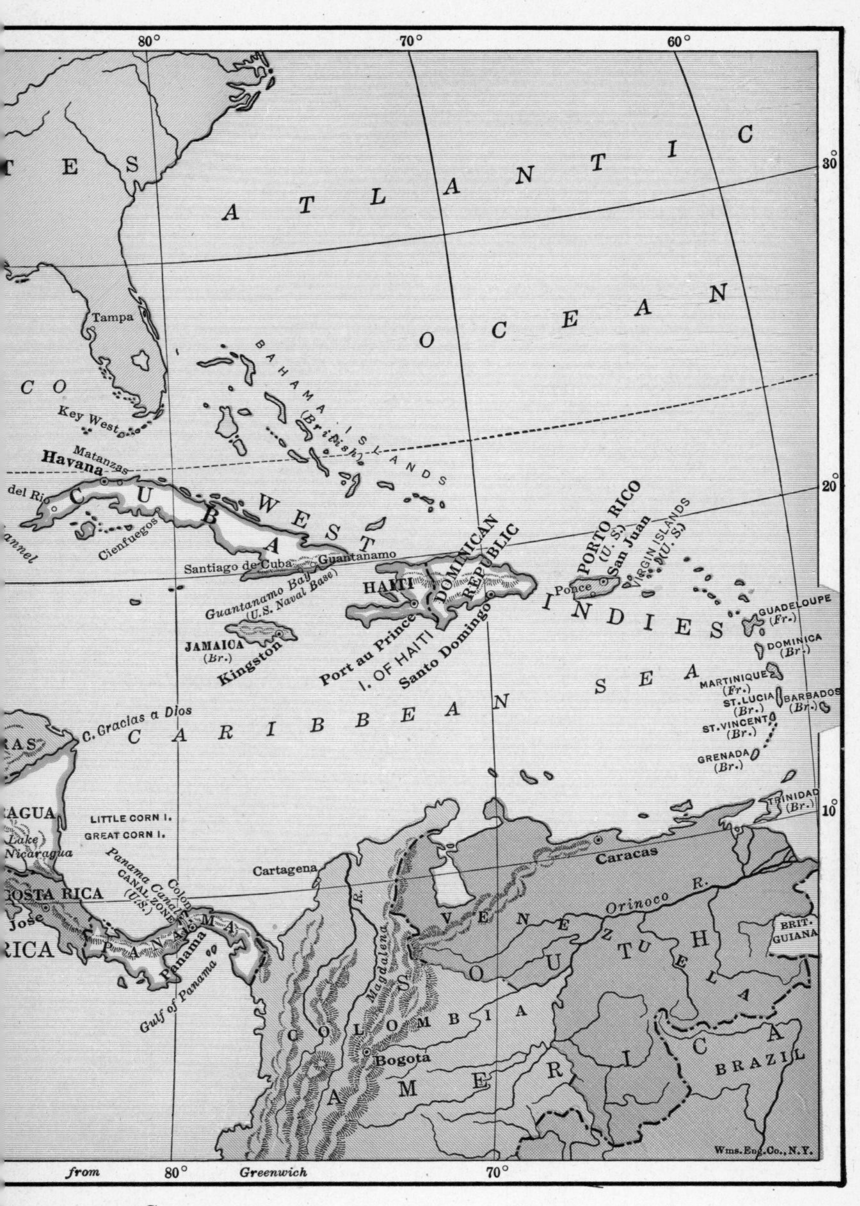

N, AND THE CANAL

of the marine corps. Indeed, to Haitian patriots the mere presence of the American uniform was a denial of their cherished right of national freedom. A special committee of the United States Senate, after investigating Haitian conditions at first hand, recommended unanimously in June, 1922, that the military occupation continue for an indefinite period.

Treaties designed to place the Central American republic of Nicaragua under American tutelage failed of ratification by the United States Senate in 1911 and 1914. Nevertheless, Nicaragua in 1911 put her customs in charge of an American financial expert as the price of securing a loan from certain powerful New York banking houses. In August, 1912, American marines were landed to quell civil disorders, and subsequently remained until 1925 as a legation guard at the capital. Order was preserved at the elections during this period with the aid of American bayonets. A treaty of 1916, negotiated two years before, granted to the United States the exclusive and perpetual right to build a canal through Nicaragua, empowered the United States to acquire naval bases, and stipulated a payment of $3,000,000 for these privileges. Although express treaty provisions are lacking, Nicaragua is, to all intents and purposes, an American protectorate.

That the protectorate movement has yet reached a pause is quite unlikely. The whole policy has been variously regarded in the United States as an altruistic assumption of the "White Man's Burden," as an ungrateful task imposed by considerations of national safety, and as an ugly manifestation of economic and financial imperialism. Doubtless all of these elements entered into the working out of the program. In any case, the systematic development of the policy was a product of the efforts of Presidents of both parties.

The United States and Mexico

When President Roosevelt first proposed to the Senate the establishment of a fiscal protectorate over the Dominican Republic, he justified the plan as a "practical test of the efficiency of the United States in maintaining the Monroe Doctrine." Indeed, the protectorate policy is to be regarded as a significant twentieth-century addition to the original doctrine. It marks a new stage in its evolution, whereby a policy of noninterference by Europe in the affairs of the Western Hemisphere has become a policy of unmistakable interference by the United States.

Although the new policy affects only the north tropical zone of Latin America, its application, along with the "seizure" of the canal zone in 1903, has produced the greatest uneasiness throughout the Latin-American world. Resentment against "Monroeism" has been especially warm among the peoples of Argentine, Brazil, and Chile, the so-called "A. B. C." powers, who feel that their political stability and cultural progress entitle them to freedom from North-American tutelage. Accordingly, a powerful sentiment has developed for a "Pan-American Doctrine," which would replace the United States as sole interpreter and guarantor of the Monroe Doctrine with a league of American republics. Naturally, a "Pan-American Doctrine" would act as a curb on the "Colossus of the North" as well as on European powers.

In order to allay Latin-American apprehensions, President Roosevelt solemnly avowed in his message of December 5, 1905, that "under no circumstances will the United States use the Monroe Doctrine as a cloak for territorial aggression." The pledge was renewed, from time to time, by subsequent administrations. But the acid test of American good faith came with the outbreak of a prolonged reign of anarchy in Mexico, beginning in 1911.

The circumstances were peculiarly provocative since Mexico borders directly upon the United States. Moreover, many American citizens were extensively engaged in business there, and American investments in Mexican mines, railways, and ranches amounted to billions of dollars. Nevertheless, the conduct of the Wilson administration showed unexampled forbearance, and during the course of the troubles, the President established a new precedent by calling on Latin-American powers, at critical junctures, to coöperate with the United States in the settlement of Mexican difficulties. Only the future can disclose whether these were the first steps toward the development of a "Pan-American Doctrine."

Since 1877 Mexico had been almost continuously under the iron rule of Porfirio Diaz. Popular government existed in name only; but peace and order prevailed, foreign capital was welcomed, and the country experienced a wonderful material transformation. Nevertheless, while Mexico became rich, the mass of Mexicans remained poor and ignorant. Native dissatisfaction increased to a dangerous pitch, and the eighth "election" of Diaz in 1910 was the signal for a popular uprising led by Francisco Madero, a Mexican patriot. In 1911 Diaz fled to Europe, and Madero became his successor. The tide of lawlessness, however, still ran strong. In February, 1913, General Victoriano Huerta, supported by the old Diaz faction, overturned the new government, and, there is good reason to believe, instigated the assassination of Madero. Once more Mexico was plunged into anarchy with Venustiano Carranza leading the insurgent bands as Madero's political heir.

The Huerta régime was promptly recognized by leading European powers, but Wilson declined, justifying his course on the ground that the new government was rooted in force and murder. Persuaded that Huerta's authority would soon collapse without American recognition and financial aid, the President notified Congress that his policy would be one of "watchful waiting." Meantime, the destruction of life and property continued, and Wilson was savagely denounced as an impractical idealist by American interests striving for armed intervention or annexation.

As it happened, the arrest of a party of United States marines at Tampico, coupled with Huerta's refusal to tender a suitable apology, led to the American seizure of Vera Cruz on April 21, 1914. President Wilson readily accepted an offer of the A. B. C. governments in May to mediate the difficulties. This action, however, proved of little practical consequence, for Huerta, overwhelmed by his enemies, fled Mexico almost at once. Carranza, the chief insurgent leader, succeeded to his place, and in November Vera Cruz was evacuated by the American troops.

With the popular party once more in control, the situation assumed a new aspect, for the victors fell to quarreling among themselves. Francisco Villa, a former bandit chieftain, was the chief disturbing element, and so fierce was the ensuing struggle that Mexico City changed hands thrice in a single month. Even Wilson's patience was sorely tried. Once more he turned to Latin America for counsel. An inter-American conference, composed of representatives of Bolivia, Uruguay, Guatemala, the A. B. C. powers, and the United States, decided in October, 1915, on the recognition of Carranza as head of the true Mexican government.

Carranza's government was immeasurably strengthened thereby, but Villa succeeded in continuing his turbulent career for more than a year longer. In a spirit of retaliation, he crossed into New Mexico in March, 1916, and raided the town of Columbus, killing seventeen persons. A punitive expedition under command of General J. J. Pershing was sent in pursuit; and although Villa succeeded in eluding capture, many lawless bands were dispersed, and Villa himself was forced to cease his activities. While the regulars were still in Mexico, guerilla raids into Texas caused President Wilson to call out 150,000 state militiamen to guard the international border. In January, 1917, the forces were withdrawn.

Carranza, well-meaning and patriotic, served Mexico to the limit of his abilities. His greatest achievement was the adoption of a new Constitution in January, 1917, which was designed to accomplish a radical economic and social reconstruction of the country. Elaborate provision was made for the welfare of the working classes; and the much-discussed Article XXVII provided for the breaking-up of the great landed estates, and asserted national ownership of all oil and other mineral resources. But Carranza's efforts to dictate the election of his successor provoked a new uprising in May, 1920, which culminated in his own assassination.

In spite of his statesmanlike qualities, the United States refused to recognize the new President, Alvaro Obregon, for several years. The chief difficulty centered in Article XXVII, which vitally affected American property rights in Mexico. This obstacle, however, was removed by a treaty of August, 1923, wherein the Mexican government gave assurance that Article XXVII of the Constitution would not work the confiscation of American mineral rights acquired under the previous Constitution, and agreed further to compensate American citizens whose estates had been seized and partitioned. Two other conventions, negotiated a month later, provided for the settlement of American claims for damages during the revolutionary disturbances and for the adjustment of Mexican pecuniary claims growing out of the Vera Cruz and Pershing expeditions. Each of the claims commissions consisted of three members, one appointed by each government and one by joint agreement.

In the single term allowed him by the Constitution, Obregon gave Mexico the best, most democratic government the people had ever enjoyed, and the country attained something approaching political and economic stability. That many difficulties still lie ahead of Mexico is easy to believe, and it may be that the revolutionary fever is checked rather than cured. The chief impediment to real progress is the apathy and ignorance of the illiterate Indians and halfbreeds, who make up nearly eighty per cent of the population.

The New Peace Movement

The rising tide of democracy throughout the world, the new value placed by governments upon the welfare of the common man, the incessant internationalist agitation of the Socialists, the tightening network of financial and commerical ties among the nations, the staggering cost of national armaments — influences such as these smoothed the way for the growth of a powerful world peace movement in the first decade of the twentieth century. In this enterprise the United States took an energetic part. Indeed, no other country had done more in the past to encourage the pacific settlement of international difficulties.

At the suggestion of the Czar of Russia, twenty-six leading powers conferred at The Hague in 1899 on the possibility of limiting armaments and promoting universal peace. This body adopted certain principles to govern the conduct of war on land and sea, and established a Permanent Court of Arbitration to sit at The Hague. In 1907 a second Hague conference of forty-four states, held at the instance of President Roosevelt, adopted additional rules to abate the horrors of war, reorganized the Court, and indorsed the principle that the contract debts of one country to another should not be collected by force.

In the ordinary sense, the Permanent Court of Arbitration was not a court but a list of judges, selected by the several countries, from which special courts might be composed with the consent of the governments directly concerned, whenever specific cases arose. Although the submission of cases was optional with the countries and the machinery of adjustment somewhat cumbersome, the establishment of the Hague Court was an important move in the right direction, and colored the world's thinking favorably to international conciliation. Twelve cases were decided by the tribunal between the years 1902 and 1912, and to three of these the United States was a party. The most notable case involved the long-standing question of the rights of Americans on the fishing grounds off Newfoundland and Labrador; and the decision, rendered in 1910, was favorable to the claims of the United States.

Private efforts were being made along the same line. In the United States, Andrew Carnegie, Edwin Ginn, and other wealthy persons furnished large sums for "foundations" to investigate and promote the cause of peace. American peace societies multiplied, peace literature received wide circulation, and international exchange lectureships were created by the great universities.

Supported by a robust public opinion, President Roosevelt submitted to the Senate in 1904 a group of treaties, which went beyond the original arrangement, and *obligated* the United States and the contracting powers to submit all their disputes to the Hague Court, save those involving vital interests, independence, or national honor. An unfortunate quarrel between the President and the Senate prevented the ratification of the treaties in a form acceptable to him, and the matter hung fire until 1908–1909, when the United States became a party to twenty-two agreements of this kind.

The eager interest of the American people in universal peace caused Roosevelt in 1905–1906 to depart from that strict aloofness which had usually characterized the attitude of the United States toward Old-World embroilments. In the former year he was instrumental in bringing to a close the Russo-Japanese War. The peace conference was held at Portsmouth, New Hampshire, and the President took an active part in facilitating the arrangement of terms. During the same year a controversy broke out between Germany and France over the latter's claims to Morocco. The situation was a critical one for the peace of Europe, and in January, 1906, the United States joined with ten European nations in a conference at Algeciras in Morocco to compose the differences. In ratifying the act of settlement, the American Senate cautiously disclaimed any "purpose to depart from the traditional American foreign policy which forbids participation . . . in the settlement of political questions which are entirely European in their scope."

The chief menace to American peace in these years, the Mexican imbroglio excepted, was the growing tension of our relations with Japan. That power was inclined to resent the enlarging influence of America in the Pacific and Far East. On the other hand, the United States suspected Japan, victorious in her recent war with Russia, of desiring to dominate China economically and politically and thus close the "open door." Relations were further strained by a delicate situation which developed in California as a result of the increasing immigration of Japanese laborers in the first years of the century.

These immigrants were mostly farmers, and being thrifty and accustomed to a lower standard of living, soon began to displace white farmers and laborers. As in the days of the Chinese invasion, talk became rife of the "yellow peril," organized labor demanded Japanese exclusion, and the people of the state gave hearty support. California fears looked to the future rather than the present, for the Japanese numbered only two per cent of the population in 1910. It was also true that, by federal law, Japanese and other Orientals had for many years been excluded from the privilege of naturalization, though, of course, their children born in America acquired citizenship under the Fourteenth Amendment.

In 1906 the antagonism flared forth in the form of an order of the San Francisco Board of Education to segregate the Asiatics in a special building apart from the white children. At this time there were 93 Japanese in the schools out of a total enrollment of 25,000. The action was protested by Japan as a violation of her treaty with the United States, and although the question of state rights was involved, President Roosevelt exerted himself to secure justice for the Japanese residents on the Coast.

Two agreements resulted, which sought to compose the chief differences between the two countries. By the "Gentlemen's Agreement" of 1907, Japanese children below sixteen years were admitted to the regular public schools, and the Japanese government on its part contracted to prevent the emigration of laborers to the United States. In the following year, the Root-Takahira Agreement pledged the two powers, "uninfluenced by any aggressive tendencies," to respect each other's territorial possessions in the Pacific Ocean, and to support "by all pacific means" Chinese independence and the maintenance of the open-door policy. Both arrangements partook of the nature of gentlemen's agreements, since the stipulations were not embodied in the form of a treaty and no action was required of the Senate.

Anti-Japanese feeling persisted in California, however, and in 1913 led the legislature, over President Wilson's protest, to pass the Webb Act. This law forbade aliens ineligible to citizenship to own agricultural land in the state. In operation, its purpose was quickly defeated by the formation of land corporations in which Japanese were the chief stockholders, and also by the practice of aliens acting as guardians for their American-born children in the ownership of land. The upshot was the enactment of the Asiatic Land Law of 1920, which expressly forbade such attempts at evasion.

Japan entered vigorous protests against these discriminatory measures, but the American government insisted that no actual treaty rights were denied, and proposed to leave the question to the Supreme Court. In 1923 the Supreme Court affirmed the constitutionality of the Webb Act and of a similar statute of the state of Washington.[1] Japan at once made energetic efforts to secure the negotiation of a new treaty.

The cause of world peace was given new hope by Wilson's appointment of William Jennings Bryan as Secretary of State in 1913. For many years he had been preaching the irrationality of war as a method of settling international differences. He believed that most wars might be prevented if the nations concerned could be induced to postpone hostilities until their passions had a chance to subside. At his prompting, President Wilson

[1] The Act of 1920 remained to be passed upon. It is perhaps significant that the guardianship clause was declared unconstitutional by the California Supreme Court in 1922.

in April, 1913, asked the governments of the world to form treaties with the United States, providing in each instance that, when diplomacy failed, the two nations should refrain from war until the dispute "of whatever character" had been investigated by an international commission and the facts determined; thereafter the countries should be free to act as they wished. The plan was so well received that by the close of the year thirty-one governments signified their willingness to enter "cooling-off" treaties.[1] The dawn of a new era of world brotherhood seemed to be at hand when suddenly, almost without warning, the glittering dream was shattered by the outbreak of the great European war of 1914.

SELECT BIBLIOGRAPHY

Completing the Forty-Eight States. Roy Gittinger, *The Formation of the State of Oklahoma* (in *University of California Publications in History*, VI, Berkeley, 1917), is a standard work.

The Evolution of a Colonial Policy. The legal and constitutional considerations involved are analyzed in W. F. Willoughby, *Territories and Dependencies of the United States* (New York, 1905), and C. F. Randolph, *The Law and Policy of Annexation* (New York, 1901), and, more briefly, in such manuals as C. A. Beard, *American Government and Politics* (New York, 1924), W. W. Willoughby, *The Constitutional Law of the United States* (2 v., New York, 1910), and F. A. Ogg and P. O. Ray, *Introduction to American Government* (New York, 1922).

Hawaii and Alaska. A general discussion of the administration of dependencies down to 1907 is A. E. McKinley, *Island Possessions of the United States* (in *The History of North America*, XX, Philadelphia, 1907). Much information on Hawaii may be gotten from W. R. Castle, *Hawaii, Past and Present* (New York, 1917). On Alaska, the best work is Jeannette P. Nichols, *Alaska* (Cleveland, 1924).

The Philippines under American Rule. Three important works on American administration in the Philippines are D. C. Worcester, *The Philippines, Past and Present* (2 v., New York, 1914), J. A. LeRoy, *The Americans in the Philippines* (2 v., Boston, 1914), and C. B. Elliott, *The Philippines to the End of the Commission Government* (Indianapolis, 1917). More restricted in scope is J. S. Reyes, *Legislative History of America's Economic Policy toward the Philippines* (in *Columbia University Studies*, CVI, no. 2, New York, 1923). The Filipino nationalist viewpoint is strongly presented in M. M. Kalaw's books: *The Case for the Filipinos* (New York, 1916), *Self-Govern-*

[1] Such treaties were signed with the United States by thirty countries up to the end of 1916.

ment in the Philippines (New York, 1919), and *The Present Government of the Philippines* (Manila, 1921). See also C. E. Russell, *The Outlook for the Philippines* (New York, 1922).

Porto Rico and Other Overseas Dependencies. An early work, L. S. Rowe, *The United States and Porto Rico* (New York, 1904), should be supplemented by Meyer Bloomfield, *A Study of Certain Social, Educational and Industrial Problems in Porto Rico* (n. p., 1912), and G. H. Stuart, *Latin America and the United States* (New York, 1922). For the Virgin Islands, consult W. C. Westergaard, *The Danish West Indies* (New York, 1917), or for a briefer account, S. J. M. P. Fogdall, *Danish-American Diplomacy, 1776–1920* (in *University of Iowa Studies*, VIII, no. 2, Iowa City, 1922).

The Caribbean Protectorates. The structure of the American colonial empire is described in W. B. Munro, *The Government of the United States* (New York, 1919), C. A. Beard, *American Government and Politics* (New York, 1924), and other similar manuals. A useful popular book is W. D. Boyce, *United States Colonies and Dependencies* (Chicago, 1914). The Socialist point of view is presented in Scott Nearing, *The American Empire* (New York, 1921).

The evolution of the protectorate system is traced in J. H. Latané, *America as a World Power*, and F. A. Ogg, *National Progress* (in *The American Nation*, XXV and XXVII, New York, 1907–1918); also in the general diplomatic histories cited in the Select Bibliography of Chapter XXIV. C. L. Jones, *Caribbean Interests of the United States* (New York, 1916), is a detailed treatment, which, in view of later developments, needs to be supplemented by such works as G. H. Stuart, *Latin America and the United States* (previously cited), J. H. Latané, *The United States and Latin America* (Garden City, 1920), W. S. Robertson, *Hispanic-American Relations with the United States* (*Carnegie Endowment Publications*, New York, 1923), H. G. James and P. A. Martin, *The Republics of Latin America* (New York, 1923), and D. Y. Thomas, *One Hundred Years of the Monroe Doctrine* (New York, 1923). A Central-American view is given in J. M. Moncada, *Social and Political Influence of the United States in Central America* (A. C. Gahan, trans., New York, 1911).

The United States and Mexico. The present-day Monroe Doctrine with its tendencies toward a Pan-American Doctrine is considered in all the foregoing books on our Latin-American relations. Hiram Bingham, *The Monroe Doctrine, an Obsolete Shibboleth* (New Haven, 1913), is a strong presentation of the Latin-American point of view. Of importance, also, is J. B. Lockey, *Pan-Americanism: Its Beginnings* (New York, 1920).

Excellent chapters on the relations of the United States with Mexico since 1910 appear in F. A. Ogg, *National Progress*, and G. H. Stuart, *Latin America and the United States*, previously cited. Some special works are S. G. Inman, *Intervention in Mexico* (New York, 1919), C. L. Jones, *Mexico and Its Reconstruction* (New York, 1921), and E. J. Dillon, *President Obregón — a World Reformer* (Boston, 1923).

The Peace Movement. The work of the two great peace conferences is discussed in the first volume of J. B. Scott, *The Hague Peace Conferences of*

1899 and 1907 (2 v., Baltimore, 1909), and more briefly, in J. H. Choate, *The Two Hague Conferences* (Princeton, 1913). The activities of American peace societies are treated in a sketchy manner in Julius Moritzen, *The Peace Movement of America* (New York, 1912). Roosevelt's efforts for international peace may be followed in J. B. Bishop, *Theodore Roosevelt and His Time* (2 v., New York, 1920).

The Far Eastern relations of the United States and Japan are discussed from varying angles in T. F. Millard, *Our Eastern Question* (New York, 1916), J. A. B. Scherer, *The Japanese Crisis* (New York, 1916), J. F. Abbott, *Japanese Expansion and American Policies* (New York, 1916), P. J. Treat, *Japan and the United States, 1853–1921* (Boston, 1921), and K. K. Kawakami, *Japan in World Politics* (New York, 1917). The controversial character of the question of Japanese immigration is reflected in H. A. Millis, *The Japanese Problem in the United States* (New York, 1915), J. F. Steiner, *The Japanese Invasion* (Chicago, 1917), and S. L. Gulick, *The American Japanese Problem* (New York, 1914).

CHAPTER XXIX

AMERICA AND THE WORLD WAR

The Outbreak of the War

The seeds of the European war were sown at least as early as 1870 when the Germans imposed a drastic peace on their vanquished foe at the close of the Franco-Prussian War. The ground was fertilized by the intense nationalism which, in the same decade, started the Great Powers on strenuous imperialistic careers, involving a worldwide scramble for territory, spheres of influence, raw materials, markets, and trade routes. As a part of the drift of events occurred an ominous drawing apart of Europe into two armed camps, each with its own ambitions and fears, secret treaties and unrecorded commitments — Russia, France, and Great Britain heading one coalition, and Germany and Austria-Hungary the other. An exhausting competition in expenditures for armaments began, leading to the creation of greater and ever greater armies and navies, undertaken perhaps quite as much from the rival powers' dread of each other as from motives of aggression.

By 1914 Europe had become a powder magazine which needed only a careless match to set it off. This spark was provided when on June 28 the heir-apparent to the Austro-Hungarian throne was assassinated, while on his own soil, by a youth belonging to one of the many subject peoples composing the Austro-Hungarian Empire. Without proof for the accusation, the imperial government charged Serbia with being a party to the crime, and having made certain of the German Kaiser's support, declared war on Serbia a month later. Such was the tenseness of feeling and the obligations of alliances that all the Great Powers quickly plunged into the war, with the Central Empires — Germany and Austria-

Hungary — leading one set of belligerents, and the Entente Allies — Russia, France, and Great Britain — the other.[1]

The people of America were stunned. Notwithstanding the rapid advance of the United States as a world power since 1898, the progressive movement in American politics had fastened the attention of the nation on questions of domestic reform, and the people had remained blandly ignorant of the forces that were driving Europe to disaster. On August 4, when five nations had taken up arms, President Wilson issued a Proclamation of Neutrality, which was repeated as successive countries entered the conflict. Two weeks later he made a special appeal to his countrymen to be "impartial in thought as well as action." The former measure was in accord with a century and a quarter of consistent practice, and was justified by the existing circumstances. The latter, however desirable, was impossible of fulfilment.

The United States was, in large part, a nation of immigrants. Of the hundred million people in the country when the war began, one third were foreignborn or American-born of alien parentage. The Central Powers contributed one third of the total number of immigrant residents, and Great Britain and Canada one sixth. Next in order stood the Russians, the Irish (who sided generally with Germany because of their hatred of England), and the Italians, each of whom numbered well above a million. In these peoples, dwelling peaceably with one another in the land of their common adoption, the war roused ardent emotions born of racial attachments, family relationships, and rekindled patriotisms.

The older American stock had its prejudices as well. The traditional dislike of Britain, nourished by school histories, was by no means offset by America's experience with the Kaiser's sabre-rattling conduct at Manila Bay, and later in the Venezuelan incident of 1902, of which the public knew little. On the other hand, the business interests naturally leaned toward Great Britain both because of financial ties and their disapproval and fear of German commercial methods. In general, however, the

[1] Between July 28 and November 5, Austria-Hungary, Germany, and Turkey entered the war on the one side, and Serbia, Russia, Great Britain, Belgium, Montenegro, and Japan on the other. Italy joined the Allies in May, 1915. Smaller states followed.

people were at first ready and eager to maintain a neutral position, viewing the European conflict as something horrible and unclean. The stronghold of pacifist feeling was the Middle West, which had been the breeding ground of progressivism.

The European struggle placed America in somewhat the same position she had occupied during the Napoleonic wars. With German shipping swept from the seas and a large part of Britain's merchant tonnage devoted to military uses, the United States became the chief carrier of the world's commerce. At the same time American export trade increased prodigiously as a result of the derangement of European industry and the unprecedented demand for foodstuffs, munitions, metal products, and raw materials. The country's shipping was unequal to the demands. Therefore Congress on August 18, 1914, adopted a law to encourage the purchase of merchant vessels built in neutral nations by admitting such ships to immediate registry without the former five-year restriction. A statute of September 2 authorized the government to set up a Bureau of War Risk Insurance in order to keep marine insurance charges within reasonable limits.

These measures, while helpful, failed to meet the real need of the situation: the construction of additional ships. Accordingly, the administration next proposed that the government itself should engage in the business, but Congress was slow to act through fear of foreign complications and dislike of government ownership. Finally, by the Shipping Act of September 7, 1916, official machinery was provided for the lease, purchase, construction, and operation of merchant vessels, directly or indirectly by the government. The new system was headed by a Shipping Board of five members; and while government ownership was limited to five years after the war, the Board was granted permanent powers to regulate private vessels engaged in interstate or foreign commerce. It was thus given a footing similar to the Interstate Commerce Commission and the Federal Trade Commission. Unfortunately the Act came too late to be of much use before America's entry into the war, but thereafter the Board was virtually given control of the entire shipbuilding resources of the nation and, in that capacity, performed indispensable service.

The Defense of Neutral Rights

As in Napoleon's time, along with the flood of business prosperity came grave perils to the maintenance of American national security. Neither Great Britain nor Germany was disposed to allow the rights of countries at peace to endanger its chances of victory. Accordingly, as the leading power not engaged in war, the United States was forced once more to assume her historic rôle as the champion of neutral rights.

Britain's invasion of American rights consisted chiefly in arbitrary interruptions of commerce between the United States and neutral countries bordering on the Teutonic states. Perceiving that war materials were thereby finding their way into enemy territory, she freely seized cargoes of contraband. The United States, however, upheld the right of neutrals to absolute freedom of the seas in trading with other neutrals, and denounced the interferences as illegal. Seizures, nevertheless, continued. For example, before the close of 1914, thirty-one cargoes of copper valued at $5,500,000 had been taken over by the British. Partly to obviate American objections, Britain in March, 1915, adopted a policy which amounted to a blockade of the German coast and nearby neutral ports. This move was likewise protested by the President as "illegal and indefensible," since under international law countries at peace were not subject to blockade. Again Britain, pleading the law of national self-preservation, declined to abandon her course.

Great Britain also extended the list of contraband articles greatly beyond those tentatively agreed to by a conference of ten maritime powers at London in 1909. In March, 1915, she even forbade the shipment of foodstuffs to the civil population of Germany, alleging that a recent German regulation for nationalizing the food supply made it impossible to distinguish between provisions intended for noncombatants and those destined for the army.

However vexatious and unlawful, such practices inflicted merely property losses, whereas the troubles which developed with the Central Empires involved, in addition, conspiracies against our domestic tranquillity and the destruction of American lives on the high seas. Since German military success required that the Allied shortage in munitions should not be replenished from other sources, German agents in the United States undertook a vigorous propaganda to induce Congress to place an embargo on munitions. The government, however, was not to be persuaded, since the munitions trade was fully sanctioned by international law, and it was Germany's fault, not America's, that she was not in a position to buy in the American market.

Thwarted at this point, the Central Empires undertook to accomplish their purpose through a campaign of terrorism and violence. "It is my impression," wrote the Austrian Ambassador, Dr. Constantin Dumba, boastfully to his government in August, 1915, "that we can disorganize and hold up for months, if not entirely prevent, the manufacture of munitions in Bethlehem and the Middle West." Under the direction of German and Austrian agents, explosions and incendiary fires damaged or destroyed munition plants, bombs were concealed aboard vessels carrying cargoes to the Allies, and strikes were instigated among seamen and munition workers. Much property was destroyed, and many lives taken. The federal authorities apprehended most of the individual culprits, and soon managed to trace their devious trails back to the Teutonic embassies in Washington. In September, 1915, the President demanded and secured the recall of Dumba, and three months later, of the German naval and military attachés at Washington, Karl Boy-Ed and Franz von Papen, because of their nefarious activities.

Along the sea lanes the Central Empires were engaged in an even more desperate attempt to prevent shipments to the Allies. Outmatched by the British navy on the ocean's surface, Germany had developed undersea craft, as an instrument of destruction, to a point of perfection undreamed of in earlier wars. The use of submarines, though sanctioned by the international law of 1914, was subject to severe restrictions. A merchant or passenger vessel must not be attacked unless it refused, after warning, to submit to visit and search, and under no circumstances should it be destroyed without safeguarding the lives of passengers and crew.

Germany's unwillingness to abide by these regulations was the source of all the difficulties that arose with the United States over submarine warfare. In justification, the former pleaded the inability of undersea craft to accommodate additional passengers, and contended that, by rising to the surface to give warning, the vessel would place itself in unreasonable jeopardy from the possibility of hostile gunfire. The United States, however, maintained that, if the new weapon could not be used according to the well-established rules, that was an argument for abandoning the weapon rather than for scrapping the rules.

Germany began her submarine operations with a proclamation that, after February 18, 1915, she would destroy every enemy merchant vessel found in the waters about the British Isles without regard to the safety of passengers or crew, and that even neutral vessels plying these waters might, through accident, meet with like treatment.[1] At once Wilson replied that, if such conduct resulted in the destruction of American vessels or lives, Germany would be held to a "strict accountability." Nevertheless, an American was drowned in March by the submarining of the British steamer *Falaba*, and on May 1 the *Gulflight*, an American steamer, was sunk in the same manner. Six days later occurred the most shocking incident of all when the great British trans-Atlantic liner *Lusitania*, carrying military supplies and nearly 2,000 people, was sent to the bottom without warning, with a loss of more than 1,100 of her passengers and crew, including 114 American men, women, and children.

America blazed with resentment, and a war of revenge might at once have followed had not the President taken the situation firmly in hand. In a series of diplomatic dispatches, he demanded that the German government disavow her lawless practices, make all possible reparation, and take prompt steps to prevent their recurrence. The only immediate result was the resignation of Bryan as Secretary of State (June), who felt, with a large section of American opinion, that citizens should not travel on vessels carrying munitions and that the difficulties with Germany should be settled according to the principle of the "cooling-off" treaties (see page 501).

Meantime the submarine depredations continued, culminating on August 18, 1915, in the sinking of the British liner *Arabic*, involving the loss of two American lives. Fearful of the con-

[1] The pretext for this proclamation was the British blockade upon foodstuffs, then recently issued.

sequences, Germany on August 27 gave the definite pledge that "Liners will not be sunk by our submarines without warning and without safety of the lives of noncombatants," and in October offered apologies and indemnity for the *Arabic* disaster. Wilson had won a diplomatic victory, but its edge was somewhat dulled by a lack of confidence in Germany's good faith. Thus, in February, 1916, Germany offered indemnity for the lives lost in the *Lusitania*, but refused to admit the illegality of the act.

On March 24 a new crisis was precipitated by the destruction of the *Sussex*, a French passenger ship, with a loss of American lives. An outright violation of the *Arabic* pledge, the President refused to accept the German excuse that the submarine commander had merely made an unfortunate mistake. In a note of April 18, 1916, he delivered an ultimatum to the effect that, unless unrestricted submarine attacks ceased, diplomatic relations would be severed. Germany, convinced at last of the aroused state of American public opinion, grudgingly made the concession demanded. The crisis was over, at least for the time being. For the next nine months relations between the two nations showed less tension than at any time since the war began.

From Spectator to Participant

When the war opened in 1914, it had seemed remote from the ordinary concerns of American life. But successive incidents, such as British interferences with American trade, German plots against American industry and domestic security, and the ruthless submarine depredations, had gradually caused the people to think of the conflict as a concrete reality affecting intimately their own comfort and happiness. Moving westward from the Atlantic Seaboard, a strong pro-Ally sentiment began to envelop the people. Its spread was assisted not only by the greater enormity of Teutonic infractions of American neutrality, but also by disapproval of the brutal invasion of Belgium at the beginning of the war and the reports, often grossly exaggerated, of German atrocities committed on captive or helpless civilians.[1]

[1] American interest in the plight of Belgium was greatly stimulated by the important part played by Herbert Hoover, an American, in organizing food relief for the people. As the head of the Commission for the Relief of Belgium, he secured widespread financial support in the United States, obtained the much-needed food, and provided for its effective distribution in spite of many hindrances.

A growing number of people came to fear a triumphant Germany as a certain menace to the United States itself.

As the German cause lost favor in America, its supporters, led by the widespread German-language press, grew more strident in their claims and assertions. The nation became, as it were, a vast and vociferous debating society, with the President a somewhat lonely figure, intent on avoiding war except as a last resort. He became increasingly a target for acrid criticism from "hyphenated Americans," both pro-Germans who accused him of dealing too gently with Great Britain, and pro-Allies who charged him with weakness toward Germany.

Inspired by Roosevelt, Leonard Wood, and the recently organized National Security League, an active agitation was begun early in the war for a stronger army and navy to protect American rights. The President was at first averse, for, like many of his countrymen, he believed that the demand was a product of hysteria. Convinced finally by the multiplying dangers which beset the nation, he advocated "preparedness" in his annual address of December, 1915, and even made a speaking tour in the Middle West to educate public sentiment on the question.

Already in August Congress had adopted a three-year naval program, embracing the construction of ten dreadnaughts, six battle cruisers, one hundred submarines, and other war craft, and making provision for a government-owned armorplate plant. Now, under spur of the President's insistence, Congress on June 3, 1916, adopted the Hay Act to strengthen the military department. Provision was made for enlarging the regular army by five annual accessions, and for increasing and placing under federal control the state militia. Though assuring substantial improvement in many respects, the measure was condemned as too mild by Secretary of War Garrison, an ardent preparedness advocate, who resigned in protest while the bill was still before Congress. On August 29, Congress authorized the creation of a "Council of National Defense," consisting of six cabinet members, as a board of strategy for the industrial mobilization of the country in case of war.

With Wilson military preparedness represented a sober second thought. He had, from the beginning of hostilities, devoted his chief efforts to a different mode of meeting the international crisis. The healing methods of diplomacy, he believed, could be made to cure the troubles that imperiled the United States and plagued the world. Thus, while, on the one hand, he sought time and again to vindicate American neutrality by peaceful means, on the other, he endeavored to attack the evil at its source by repeatedly offering the good offices of the United States to end the war. His confidential agent in these transactions was usually Colonel E. M. House of Texas, a man of wide acquaintance abroad and of unusual ability as a diplomat. In 1915 the President's program advanced another step as a result of the activities of an organization called the "League to Enforce Peace," formed at Philadelphia in June of that year. Its main proposal, that of a world confederation to prevent war, found a ready convert in Wilson, as it also did in ex-President Taft and many other Americans irrespective of party.

Seeing how the European struggle might be turned into a war to end war, he sent a formal note to the belligerents on December 18, 1916, asking for "their respective views as to the terms upon which the war might be concluded, and the arrangements which would be deemed satisfactory as a guarantee against its renewal." On January 22, 1917, he reported the results to the Senate in an address intended for the whole world to hear. The Central Powers, he said, had refused to define peace terms; the Allies had stated what they regarded as "indispensable conditions." Since "the war puts in constant jeopardy" the rights of neutral countries, he asserted the vital interest of the United States in a righteous and enduring peace — not "a victor's terms imposed upon the vanquished," provocative of future wars, but "a peace without victory." The peace settlement must embrace such principles as the right of self-determination, freedom of the seas, the limitation of armaments, and a league of nations to safeguard peace.

Through the President's efforts, the United States was rapidly attaining to the moral leadership of the world. At home, however, the address exposed him to fresh volleys of scorn and execration because of the expression, "peace without victory," which was interpreted by "hyphenates" as a confession of weakness and indecision. In reality, the conception underlying the phrase remained the essence of America's purpose even as a belligerent, though in view of the altered circumstances and his certainty of direct participation in the peace negotiations, Wilson changed the expression to a "peace of justice."

Before the President sent his formal request to the warring powers, the presidential election of 1916 had taken place. At the outset of the campaign the Republicans and the Progressives held their national conventions in Chicago on the same day (June 7), in the hope that the two parties might unite upon a single ticket. However, the passions of four years before had not yet sufficiently cooled. The older organization proposed Charles E. Hughes who, as a member of the Supreme Court since 1910, had escaped the embroilments of party factionalism; but the Progressives, despite Hughes' earlier reform record as Governor of New York, demanded Roosevelt's nomination. In the end, each side named its own favorite, the Republican ticket being completed by the addition of C. W. Fairbanks of Indiana. The Republican platform stigmatized the President's foreign policy as one of "phrase-making" and "shifty expedients," promised thoroughgoing preparedness, and pledged a "strict and honest neutrality between the belligerents."

Roosevelt, who had no liking for lost causes, declined to run after the Progressive convention had adjourned, and urged his followers to support Hughes. His running mate, J. M. Parker of Louisiana, however, declared for Wilson. The Democrats, convening at St. Louis on June 14, renominated their ticket of 1912 by acclamation. For the first time in many years, the party could point to a record of actual achievement. After recalling the epochmaking economic and humanitarian measures of the Wilson administration, the platform condemned "hyphenism," pledged adequate preparedness, and vaunted the President's diplomatic victories in dealing with the European belligerents.

The ensuing campaign proved close and exciting. As the "Outs," the Republicans brought all their batteries to bear upon the shortcomings of the "Ins." The pro-Germans, urged on by an organization called the "German-American Alliance," bitterly denounced Wilson; and until the last week of the campaign, Hughes avoided saying anything that might alienate their support. In the words, "He kept us out of war," Democratic orators found an effective vote-getting slogan, especially in the case of the women who now possessed the franchise in twelve states. Wilson's own speeches, however, contained nothing to justify an expectation that peace would necessarily continue. The American Federation of Labor advocated his reëlection, and as the campaign wore on, the independent voters of the country began to turn to him, largely because of Hughes' lukewarmness toward social and economic reforms.

The outcome of the contest was in doubt for several days after the election. The President received 277 electoral votes to 254 for his opponent, and 49.2 per cent of the popular vote as compared with 46 per cent. The Democratic ticket swept the South and the Far West, including nearly all the woman-suffrage states. For the first time in almost fifty years, if the Hayes-Tilden contest be excepted, a candidate was successful without the electoral vote of New York.

The significance of the election was misunderstood in the Central Empires. "The Germans," declared the American Ambassador, J. W. Gerard, at a subsequent time, "believed that President Wilson had been elected with a mandate to keep out of war at any cost, and that America could be insulted, flouted, and humiliated with impunity." Consequently, they redoubled the secret exertions already begun for the most extensive and destructive submarine campaign within their resources. On January 31, 1917, Germany abruptly informed the United States that thereafter, in utter disregard of the *Sussex* pledge, she would sink on sight all vessels, neutral as well as belligerent, found in the waters about the British Isles or in the Mediterranean Sea.

At once, in accordance with his ultimatum on the former occasion, Wilson severed diplomatic relations, and followed this action on February 26 by asking Congress to authorize a policy of armed neutrality. The House promptly responded, but in the Senate a group of eleven men, led by La Follette, succeeded through filibustering in preventing action before the end of the session a few days later. Nevertheless, the President, by authority of an almost forgotten statute, directed the mounting of guns on merchant ships, and provided them with expert marksmen from the navy. Meantime, Teutonic ruthlessness was taking its toll of victims. From February 3 to April 1, eight American vessels were submarined with a loss of forty-eight American lives. Armed neutrality was fast proving its futility, and Wilson called a special session of Congress for April 2.

Before that date, two new events helped further to clarify the mind of the country in regard to the issues at stake. One of these was the so-called "Zimmermann note," whose contents were made public on February 28 through the enterprise of the British intelligence service. In this document the German foreign minister, under date of January 19, instructed the German minister in Mexico City to urge that government to attack the United States in case the latter declared war on Germany, and to offer as inducements, "general financial support" and the opportunity to recover "the lost territory of New Mexico, Texas, and Arizona." The American people were deeply shocked by the proposal, and alarmed anew by the danger which German militarism held for their own safety and peace. The other event was the news, which came in the middle of March, of the Russian Revolution and the setting up of a republican government. By the overthrow of the Czar the chief Entente Allies all became exponents of popular government, leaving to the Teutonic states and Turkey the dubious distinction of being the last strongholds of military autocracy.

When the special session assembled, President Wilson addressed Congress, and in words that deeply stirred the nation, asked that the recent conduct of Germany be declared to constitute war against the United States. He recited the submarine depredations and the conspiracies against American national unity culminating in the Zimmermann note, and pictured these as the inevitable accompaniments of "autocratic governments backed by organized force which is controlled wholly by their will, not by the will of their people." The United States, he said, would battle for the rights of mankind, "for the ultimate peace of the world and for the liberation of its peoples, the German peoples included." And he added, in a phrase that rang throughout the world, "The world must be made safe for democracy."

Thus the period of indecision came to an end. After three years of unexampled forbearance, Wilson led the nation into the conflict when the people were deeply convinced that no other course remained. Moreover, he made the fateful choice turn not on motives of revenge or the possibilities of national aggrandisement, but the opportunity to extend traditional American ideals to oppressed peoples. By overwhelming majorities, Congress on April 6 voted to back up the President, La Follette being one of the six Senators in the opposition. A declaration of war against Austria-Hungary was delayed until December 7, in the vain hope that meantime she might be weaned away from her alliance with Germany.

America's entry into the conflict was a signal for similar action by many other neutral countries. The response of the republics of the New World was particularly significant for the light it threw upon Pan-American solidarity. In the ensuing months, Brazil, Cuba, Panama, Guatemala, Costa Rica, Honduras, Haiti, and Nicaragua declared war on Germany, and most of the other countries, not wishing to go so far, severed diplomatic relations.

A Nation in Arms

The World War of 1914 was the eighth world struggle in which the American people had participated, and the fourth since the declaring of national independence.[1] Indeed, no great international conflict involving operations in the Atlantic had taken place, to which America was not forced, sooner or later, to become a party. When the United States entered the lists against Germany, the war had been raging two years and eight months. At the outset the Germans had sought to win a speedy decision, but after getting within sight of Paris, they had been turned back at the Battle of the Marne. Since then, in spite of titanic exertions on the part of the Allies, they had remained in possession of most of Belgium and an important section of northern France. In addition to the fighting on the western front, operations were also being conducted on the Russo-Austrian frontier, and after the spring of 1915, on the Austro-Italian frontier as well. The advantage on land lay everywhere with the Central Powers. Their commerce had been swept from the seas, however, and nearly all of the German colonies had been captured.

[1] This statement has reference, of course, to the fact that the following wars were merely American phases of greater international struggles: the four intercolonial wars with the French; the Revolutionary War following the French Alliance of 1778; the naval defense of neutral rights against France from 1798 to 1800; and the War of 1812–1815.

The war had developed along lines quite different from any preceding conflict. Involving unprecedented millions of soldiers, open-field fighting was out of the question, and trench warfare on a vast scale took its place. Moreover, mechanisms and discoveries that had been developed within the period of a generation to promote human happiness were now converted to the hideous purposes of human destruction. Chief among these was the automobile, which, rendered practicable through the perfection of the internal-combustion engine, had spread throughout the civilized world after 1900. The motor car in its various forms proved an essential means for the rapid transportation of troops and supplies, and in the form of armored "tanks," was even effective as an engine of warfare.

Of great importance also was the heavier-than-air flying machine, invented in 1903 by Orville and Wilbur Wright of Dayton, Ohio. Though the contrivance was hardly regarded as more than a toy before the war, the combatants quickly developed it to a new point of efficiency. Airplanes were found indispensable for reconnoitering and bombing, and even successful for combat purposes. Among other recent inventions, wireless telegraphy (devised in 1895 by Guglielmo Marconi, an Italian) was valuable for keeping the many units of the gigantic armies in constant communication, and the beneficent peacetime discoveries of the world's chemists were utilized in the manufacture of explosive bombs and clouds of poisonous gases.

The new machinery of warfare gave an unexpected importance to petroleum, which furnished life-giving fluid to all conveyances on land, in the air, and under the water. Because of its greater economy and effectiveness, oil was even beginning to displace the use of coal on naval vessels. It "is as necessary as blood in the battles of tomorrow," wrote Georges Clemenceau, the French Premier, to President Wilson shortly after the United States entered the struggle.

The entry of the United States placed at the disposal of the Allies not only a vast unplumbed reservoir of man-power but also unlimited quantities of foodstuffs, minerals, manufactures, money-wealth, shipyards, and material resources of all kinds. But perhaps most significant of all was the fresh enthusiasm and ardent idealism which America brought to the struggle. Nevertheless, the government refrained from entering a formal alliance with the Entente Allies, preferring to regard them officially as merely "Associates" in a common war.

However remiss the government may have been in forearming against war, it sought now to make up for lost time by organizing the nation on a war basis with a thoroughness and on a scale unprecedented in American annals. Under Wilson's compelling leadership and against the fierce opposition of leaders of his own party, Congress on May 18, 1917, adopted the Selective Service Act. It empowered the President to raise by selective conscription, in two installments, one million troops from men between the ages of 21 and 30 inclusive.[1] Exemptions or deferred classification were authorized for public officials, clergymen, members of religious sects opposed to war, persons engaged in employments essential to military success, men upon whom others were dependent, and physical and mental defectives. Though running counter to usual American practice in such matters, the Act was based upon the essentially democratic principle — to use the President's words — "that there is a universal obligation to serve and that a public authority should choose those upon whom the obligation of military service shall rest, and also in a sense choose those who shall do the rest of the nation's work."

Without loss of time the men of draft age were registered throughout the country, and this, with the subsequent enrollment of youths coming of age later, made available more than ten millions under the original service law. From this body the names of those who were first called to the colors were drawn on July 20. The operation of the draft occasioned local protests, but unlike Civil-War times, no serious disturbances.[2] By the close of the year about a half-million draftees, known as the "National Army," were mustered in. The Act of May 18 also authorized an increase of the regular army to 287,000, and the mustering of the entire national guard into the federal service. With these additions the total number of troops at the end of 1917 reached one and a quarter millions, and of officers more than 100,000.

[1] The draft age was lowered to 18 and raised to 45 years inclusive on August 31 of the following year.

[2] The record of desertions from the army shows that the total was smaller than in previous wars, and a smaller proportion occurred among drafted men than among those who volunteered.

The problem of assembling the elements of an army was less difficult than that of fitting them for the ugly business ahead of them. Sixteen great tent-camps were established in the South as training quarters for the augmented National Guard, and a similar number of cantonments in various parts of the country for the

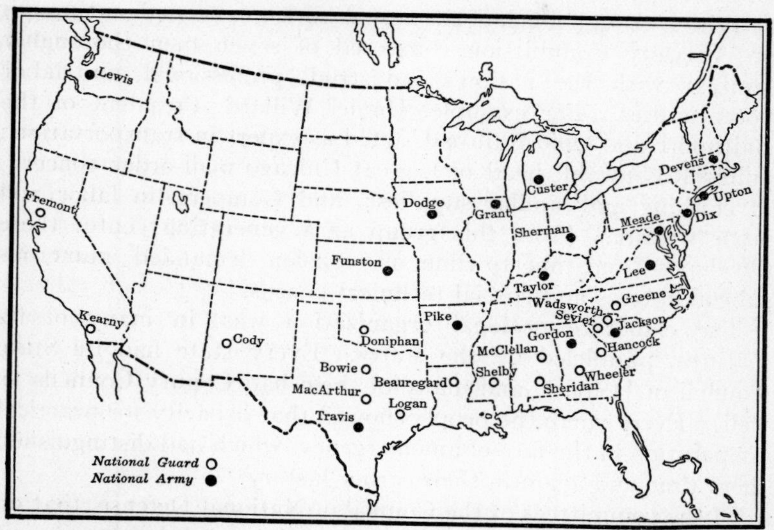

Location of Camps and Cantonments, 1917–1918

National Army. Springing up like mushrooms, these cantonments consisted of a thousand or more frame structures capable of housing an average of 48,000 men, and were amply equipped with sewers, water supplies, camp newspapers, libraries, theaters, laundries, and hospitals. Here, as a result of able direction and conscientious devotion to duty, the men were prepared for active service in an average period of six months.

Officers were supplied through special training camps, of which the best known was that at Plattsburg, New York. The curse of political appointments, which had marred the conduct of earlier wars, was avoided by the adoption of a scientific rating system, designed to recognize ability and experience. Even the colleges of the country were formed into training schools, and ultimately about 170,000 young men below the draft age, in five hundred institutions of higher learning, joined the Students' Army Training Corps.

Simultaneously with the creation of an army, thoroughgoing measures were taken to mobilize the material resources of the country. The Council of National Defense, authorized in August, 1916 (see page 511), assumed general charge of such activities, though much of the actual work was carried on through an Advisory Commission composed of seven men thoroughly familiar with the nation's industrial, professional, and labor potentialities. For example, Daniel Willard, President of the Baltimore and Ohio Railroad, acted as expert in transportation; Julius Rosenwald, head of a great Chicago mail-order concern, in clothing and similar supplies; and Gompers, in labor and labor welfare. From this group as a generating center there developed from time to time, as occasion demanded, numerous subcommittees and special technical boards.

The elaborate national organization was, in many of its features, paralleled by the states. Every state had its State Council of Defense, and many of them had County Councils as well. Everywhere the people showed that capacity for practical coöperation in the face of an emergency, which had distinguished them time and again in their earlier history.

Of the committees of the Council of National Defense, that on munitions developed such importance that on July 28, 1917, it was reorganized as the "War Industries Board." It possessed far-reaching powers over the processes of manufacture, and bent every effort toward speeding up the production of military supplies. At the close of the war it was estimated that the industrial capacity of the country had been increased twenty per cent through its efforts. For heavy artillery, machine guns, and airplanes, however, the United States was forced to depend largely upon the French and British.

America had hoped to make her distinctive contribution in aerial hostilities, for in the large-scale manufacture of aircraft, the mechanical and organizing genius of the nation would have full play. Moreover, the prospect of fighting above the clouds appealed to the imagination of a people accustomed to frontier warfare and displays of personal daring. In July, 1917, the government formulated a plan for building 11,500 combat planes before the following summer, besides a large number of training craft. Unfortunately no American factories were equipped to turn out combat planes, and this fact, along with other delays and difficulties, some of them avoidable, prevented the execution of the program, greatly to the public's exasperation. Not until well into the second year did the government's plans begin to yield substantial results, though when the armistice was signed only about 12,000 planes had been completed, of which a third were service planes.

Another committee of the Council of National Defense, that on food supply, derived its importance from a dangerous shortage of food in the Allied countries and the need to collect huge supplies to feed the American forces. This committee, headed by Herbert Hoover of Belgian-relief fame, at first lacked adequate authority, but on August 10, 1917, the Food and Fuel Control Act was passed, which gave Hoover as Food Administrator practically unlimited power in the stimulation of agriculture and the conservation of food. To assist him, subordinate Food Administrators were appointed in the states and local subdivisions.

The problem centered mainly in wheat, meat, sugar, and fats. In order to increase production, every effort was exerted to expand the existing cultivated acreage. Farmers were encouraged to make extensive plantings by the government's agreement to buy all the wheat raised in 1918 at two dollars a bushel. Even the dwellers in cities converted their yards and nearby vacant lots into "war gardens," and by consuming their own produce, lessened their daily demands on the grocer.

In the campaign to secure economy in the domestic consumption of food, the Food Administration resorted both to official regulations of wholesalers and retailers and to the encouragement of voluntary coöperation by consumers. The slogan, "Food Will Win the War," was spread over the billboards of the country, and a new verb, "to hooverize," entered the vocabulary. Housewives hung cards in their windows to proclaim their fidelity to the war regulations, and showed patriotic zeal in the use of substitutes and the observance of "meatless meals" and "wheatless days." It was a movement of general renunciation such as no country had ever undertaken except at the urge of biting necessity.

The results amply justified the self-denial. In the four summer months of 1918, the American people saved out of their regular consumption and sent abroad half a million tons of sugar. The autumn of 1918 saw an increase of nearly one million tons of pork products over what was available the preceding year. In general, during the crop year of 1918, America doubled the average amount of food exported to Europe immediately before the war. By such means the United States was able not only to feed the Allied armies but also to save their peoples (and later much of central and southeastern Europe) from almost certain starvation.

The Food Administration was hardly set up before it was paralleled by the establishment of a Fuel Administration, authorized by the same law. As in the case of food, the coal problem involved both increased production and economical use. Miners and operators zealously coöperated, and private households observed unwonted domestic economy. The difficulties of distribution were greatly complicated by the congested condition of the railways and the cruelly cold winter of 1917–1918 which delayed transportation and imprisoned coal barges in icebound harbors. At one juncture H. A. Garfield, the Fuel Administrator, ordered a temporary shutdown of industry in the trans-Mississippi region in order that the coal might be diverted to more essential purposes. Attention was also given to oil production, which in 1918 increased fourteen per cent over the yield of 1914. The motoring public reduced pleasure riding to a minimum, and willingly heeded the request for "gasless Sundays."

As the fuel situation made evident, success in industrial mobilization was closely connected with the efficient utilization of rail facilities. The problem of troop movements was similarly involved. The railways, called upon to carry an unprecedented volume of traffic and hampered by long-established habits of rivalry and other conditions, proved, under private management, unequal to the emergency. Accordingly, on December 26, 1917, the President put the railways in charge of Secretary of the Treasury McAdoo.

As Director-General of Railroads, the latter called to his aid experienced railway executives, and proceeded to merge the chief lines into one great system. Arbitrary control of the routing and distribution of traffic relieved the congestion on certain roads, and obtained ampler service from others. Terminals, equipment, repair shops, and other physical facilities were used wherever needed irrespective of ownership. Many other improvements were introduced. Government operation attained the results desired, though the Director-General found it necessary to raise wages by an aggregate sum of more than $600,000,000, and to effect substantial advances in freight and passenger rates. Despite the higher transportation charges, the greatly increased costs caused the railways to be operated at a deficit throughout the period of federal control.[1]

Armed Operations Overseas

In the actual warfare the naval forces were the first to undertake operations. Within eighteen days of the declaration of war, six destroyers were sent to European waters, where, under command of Admiral W. S. Sims, they immediately set about to aid the British navy in chasing and sinking submarines. Battleships and cruisers followed until, at the close of the war, 5,000 naval officers and 70,000 enlisted men were serving abroad. The three-year construction plan, adopted in 1916 as a part of the preparedness program, was accelerated and expanded, private vessels were commandeered, and German ships interned in American ports were taken over. In the first nine months of 1918, no less than eighty-three new destroyers were launched, as compared with sixty-two for the preceding nine years. During the war period the total number of vessels in commission increased from 197 to 2,003.

Among other exploits, the navy, with some British assistance, laid a great mine barrage, 245 miles long and twenty wide, from the Norwegian coast to the Orkney Islands, thereby making it increasingly hazardous for German submarines to reach the high seas. Likewise with British coöperation, it performed an indispensable service in protecting American troop-ships crossing the Atlantic from the raids of German submarines. The results

[1] In July, 1918, the Postmaster-General, by direction of the President, took over the operation of all telephone and telegraph lines, and later extended his authority to marine cables. In a similar fashion the express business was placed under government management in November.

were a tribute to Anglo-American naval efficiency. In all, only six transports were torpedoed, and two of these managed to make port.

Shortly after the declaration of war, General John J. Pershing, who had recently conducted warlike operations across the Mexican border, was sent to France to act as Chief of the American Expeditionary Force (the "A. E. F."). At the urgent representation of the French government, a division of regulars followed in June and July as a visible symbol of the hosts which were to come later. These hosts, however, were still in course of training, and by the end of the year 1917, only 195,000 troops had reached France. Thereafter their numbers rapidly increased. More than one million soldiers made the overseas trip during the four months from May to August, 1918.

To look after the multifarious needs of these arrivals, colossal preparations were made by an organization known as the "Services of Supply," formed by Pershing in February, 1918, with headquarters at Tours. The "S. O. S." was responsible for securing, organizing, and distributing all the food, equipment, building materials, and other necessities required for the A. E. F. It built gigantic docks at the ports of arrival, constructed 1,000 miles of railroad and more than 100,000 miles of telegraph and telephone communication, and erected great hospitals and warehouses. As an indication of the magnitude of its work, one supply station consisted of 300 buildings, covering six square miles, operated by 20,000 men, and housing supplies worth $100,000,000.

The fighting forces, as they arrived in France, were usually given a month or more of training before going to the front, and then, brigaded with French or British troops, were kept for another month in a quiet section of the line. But in January, 1918, Pershing collected the scattered fragments of his command, which thereafter operated as a unit, though, of course, in harmony with the Allied forces.

Between America's entry into the war and the beginning of the spring campaign of 1918, the Allies had suffered severe reverses. Fearful of the strength of the Western giant when fully roused, Germany had endeavored to end the war with a series of crushing blows before that event occurred. Italy had been demoralized by a terrific defeat at the hands of the Austrians at Caporetto in October, 1917. War-weary Russia, now dominated by Socialist extremists or Bolshevists, concluded an inglorious peace with the Central Empires at Brest-Litovsk in March, 1918. Rumania, left in the lurch by Russia's defection, had little choice but to follow her example, which she did the same month.

Free to concentrate their armies in the western theater of warfare, the Central Empires made gigantic preparations for a smashing drive against the Allied forces in France. Since the preceding autumn, President Wilson had been urging upon the Allies the necessity of entrusting all the forces in France to the supreme command of one man; and in March, 1918, as the new German offensive was getting under way, the powers sank their national jealousies and adopted the plan. This responsible post was given to Marshal Ferdinand Foch, an experienced French commander and perhaps the foremost military genius of the time.

Prior to the beginning of the German offensive, the United States troops had engaged in nocturnal raids on the enemy trenches and occasional concerted attacks. But now, inured to the new conditions of warfare and eager to get into the fray on their own account, they played their full part, along with the veteran forces of the Allies, in resisting the terrific German onslaughts. It is possible here to make only brief allusions to the American phases of the contest.

On May 28 the American First Division took Cantigny. Three days later, on June 1, the Third Division assisted the French in checking the Teutonic advance at Château-Thierry, located on the Marne River only forty miles from Paris. Nearby, enemy forces occupied a densely forested tract known as Belleau Wood, and six days of furious hostilities, involving hand-to-hand fighting, were required before the marines of the Second Division could eject them on June 11. A new assault by the Germans on July 14 brought the Third Division into action again, and on the following day a Franco-American charge drove the enemy back one mile and led to the capture of the villages of Chezy and Montlevon.

The Teutonic offensive, as the sequel was to show, was a gambler's last throw. In their powerful effort, the enemy forces

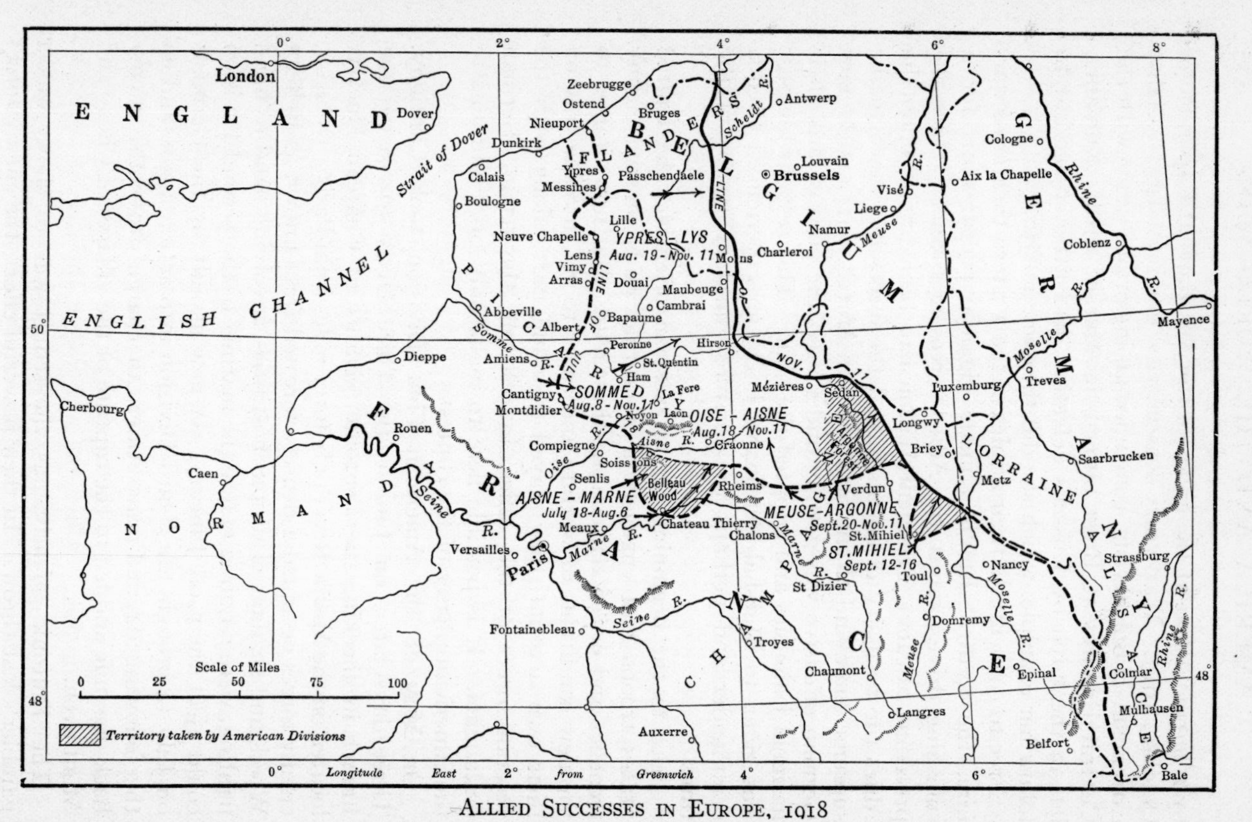

ALLIED SUCCESSES IN EUROPE, 1918

not only failed to win a decisive victory, but suffered irreplaceable losses in men, equipment, and *morale*. As their exertions came to a lull, Foch in mid-July unexpectedly launched a mighty counter-offensive. Once more the American troops contributed their utmost toward victory. On the eighteenth, in coöperation with picked French troops, they made a successful drive on Soissons. In the following weeks they were almost continually in action until, on August 30, they were given entire responsibility for a section of the front, about 85 miles in length. From this position of vantage they succeeded on September 12–15, against feeble resistance, in capturing the St. Mihiel salient, a triangle of enemy ground jutting into Allied territory. About 550,000 American soldiers were engaged in this battle — a number five and one half times as large as the Union army at Gettysburg.

The most important action, however, in which the United States participated was the Meuse-Argonne offensive. The goal of the attack was a four-track railroad, which ran parallel to the front and formed a main supply line of the enemy. From the standpoint of magnitude, this battle was the greatest ever fought by American troops. Beginning on September 26, it proceeded with little abatement and increasing success for forty-seven days. A total of 1,200,000 Americans, as well as 840 airplanes and 324 tanks, were engaged. In the first week of November, a portion of the coveted railway passed into the possession of the French and the Americans. In Pershing's words, "We had cut the enemy's main line of communications, and nothing but surrender or an armistice could save his army from complete disaster."

By the close of the fighting on November 11, 1918, the American army at home and abroad totaled more than 3,500,000. Of this number, 1,390,000 troops had seen active service, or two out of every three soldiers who reached France. During the whole course of the war, the Americans had captured about 44,000 prisoners and 1,400 guns of all kinds. American aviators had brought down 755 enemy planes, and themselves lost nearly half that number. When the war closed, the United States was responsible for 22 per cent, or about 100 miles, of the western front. While American participation was chiefly confined to operations in France, United States soldiers were to be found on other fronts as well. A regiment was dispatched to the Austro-Italian front in July, 1918, at the urgent request of Italy. In October, two divisions were sent to reënforce the French fighters in Belgium.

The United States also became involved in hostilities with the Bolshevists although technically the country was at peace with Russia. The Allies refused to acknowledge the separate peace concluded by the Soviet government with Germany at Brest-Litovsk (see page 525), and were outraged by Russia's cancellation of her foreign indebtedness. Accordingly, they resorted to armed intervention in order to assist anti-Bolshevist insurrectionary movements and to protect from confiscation large stores of military supplies in northern Russia. About 5,000 Americans became members of an Allied expedition, which fought a series of minor engagements in the vicinity of Archangel and Murmansk from September, 1918, until May, 1919, when their withdrawal began. Another force of about 10,000 men was sent, as part of an Allied expeditionary force, to Vladivostok and eastern Siberia. They were withdrawn in January, 1920.

Of every 100 American soldiers who served in the war, two were killed or died of disease during the period of hostilities.[1] In the Union army during the Civil War, the number was about ten, and among the other great powers in the World War between twenty and twenty-five. The American deaths from all causes totaled 125,000, of which about 10,000 were in the navy. That the losses in battle were not greater was due largely to the fact that the heavy fighting lasted only for two hundred days. For every man killed in battle, six were wounded, and of these five were cured and returned to duty.

This was the first war of the United States that showed a lower death-rate from disease than from battle. In the case of the A. E. F. more than twice as many died from battle as from disease; but for the army as a whole, almost half the total losses were from disease. The health record would have been even more creditable but for a dreadful epidemic of influenza-pneumonia, which swept through the country during the fall and

[1] The total battle deaths for all countries in the World War were greater than all the deaths in all wars for more than a century previous.

winter of 1918 and took its heaviest toll in the crowded camps and cantonments.

The remarkable record in combating disease was due largely to the great advances which had been made in medical science in recent years, to a highly trained medical *personnel,* and to the completeness of hospital facilities.[1] With 2,089 commissioned medical officers at the beginning of the war, 31,251 physicians from civil life were inducted into the Medical Corps during the course of the struggle. Among them were the foremost leaders of the profession, who not only facilitated the adoption of the most recent methods for the prevention and cure of disease, but themselves made new discoveries of vast human benefit. The main preventive measures involved thorough camp sanitation and control of drinking water, and compulsory vaccination against typhoid fever. Intestinal disorders, such as dysentery, typhus, cholera, and the typhoids, which had ravaged armies in the past, were practically eliminated as causes of death.

While war still raged unabated on the several battle fronts, President Wilson renewed his efforts, begun as a neutral, to make of the most terrible war in history an instrument for an enduring world peace. To him military victory was not an opportunity for vengeance but rather to secure a peace settlement which would prevent future wars from growing out of the bitterness engendered by the present one. He became by common consent the spokesman of the powers fighting Germany. If they did not subscribe to all his lofty idealism, they at least believed that his utterances might have the useful effect of weakening the hold of the military class on the war-weary Teutonic peoples and thereby shorten the struggle.

In an address to Congress on January 8, 1918, he set forth, under fourteen headings, the most complete statement he had yet made of an acceptable peace settlement. The first five of the Fourteen Points were designed to curb or obviate three of the deeper causes of the existing conflict: secret diplomacy, militarism, and imperialism. He demanded the abandonment of secret international understandings, freedom of the seas, the removal of economic barriers between nations, the reduction of

[1] The death-rate from disease in the Mexican War was 110 per year in each 1,000 men; in the Civil War, 65; in the Spanish-American War, 26; in the A. E. F., 19.

national armaments, and an adjustment of all colonial claims with due regard to the interests of the populations concerned. Next followed eight points, more specific in character but all concerned with assuring to European nationalities rights of self-rule and unhampered development. The conquered areas of Belgium, France, Russia, Rumania, Serbia, and Montenegro should be evacuated and restored; the oppressed nationalities of Austria-Hungary and Turkey, accorded home rule;[1] an independent Poland, created out of German, Austrian, and Russian territory; and the Franco-German and Austro-Italian frontiers, readjusted along lines of nationality.

For his fourteenth point Wilson reserved the keystone of his arch of peace — the formation of an association of nations to afford "mutual guarantees of political independence and territorial integrity to great and small states alike." He intimated in the final portion of his address that the Allies would be unwilling to conclude a peace with a government which spoke for the military party rather than for the people of Germany.

However, it required the great Allied offensive of the summer of 1918 to convince Germany that she faced certain disaster. Elsewhere her allies, hemmed in on every side, their *morale* shattered, were preparing to give up the fight with or without her consent. In her own country the people were seething with revolution, and the Kaiser was about to abdicate and flee. On October 4 Germany asked Wilson to take steps toward peace on the basis of the Fourteen Points. After the President had assured himself that the request came from representatives of the people rather than of the military clique, he conferred with the Allies, who acceded to the German proposal, subject to reservations as to the freedom of the seas and to an explicit admission of German obligation for all damages to civilian life and property. On this basis an armistice was concluded on November 11.

SELECT BIBLIOGRAPHY

America and the World War. J. S. Bassett, *Our War with Germany* (New York, 1919), J. B. McMaster, *The United States in the World War* (2 v., New York, 1918–1920), and Charles Seymour, *Woodrow Wilson and*

[1] Wilson subsequently changed this demand to political independence in the case of the subject peoples of Austria-Hungary.

the World War (in *The Chronicles of America*, XLVIII, New Haven, 1921), are reliable general accounts by trained historians, and deal also with the problems of neutrality.

The Defense of Neutral Rights. In addition to the books already cited, a well-connected discussion may be found in F. A. Ogg, *National Progress* (in *The American Nation*, XXVII, New York, 1918). A special study is J. B. Scott, *A Survey of International Relations between the United States and Germany, August 1, 1914–April 6, 1917* (New York, 1917). The main facts in regard to the German plots appear in J. P. Jones and P. M. Hollister, *The German Secret Service in America* (Boston, 1918).

A Nation in Arms. Benedict Crowell and R. F. Wilson, *How America Went to War* (6 v., New Haven, 1921), is a comprehensive account, devoted chiefly to economic mobilization. W. F. Willoughby, *Government Organization in War Time and After* (New York, 1919), C. R. Van Hise, *Conservation and Regulation in the United States during the World War* (Washington, 1917), P. R. Kolbe, *The Colleges in War Time and After* (New York, 1919), E. A. Powell, *The Army behind the Army* (New York, 1919), and G. B. Clarkson, *Industrial America in the World War* (Boston, 1923), are valuable for their respective subjects. I. L. Pollock, *The Food Administration in Iowa* (2 v., Iowa City, 1923), is a detailed study for a single state.

Armed Operations Overseas. Besides the general discussions by Bassett, McMaster, and Seymour (already cited), the following should be consulted: R. J. Beamish and F. A. March, *America's Part in the World War* (Philadelphia, 1919) — popular and interesting; L. P. Ayres, *The War with Germany* (Washington, 1919) — valuable as a statistical summary; Colonel de Chambrun and Captain de Marenches, *The American Army in the European Conflict* (New York, 1919) — a French view; Shipley Thomas, *The History of the A. E. F.* (New York, 1920); I. F. Marcosson, *S. O. S.* (New York, 1919) — a journalist's account; and W. S. Sims and B. J. Hendrick, *The Victory at Sea* (Garden City, New York, 1920).

CHAPTER XXX

PEACE AND ITS PROBLEMS

The War and the American Public

In no previous conflict had the American people given such wholehearted support to the prosecution of the war. Preëxisting differences of opinion as to the relative deserts of the European belligerents were drowned in a swelling tide of loyalty to the national cause. Customary party lines were wiped away, though the Republicans reserved the right to insist on a more vigorous conduct of the war and grew increasingly restive under what they termed Wilson's "dictatorial" political methods. Organized labor rallied strongly to the support of the government. Even the citizens of German and Austro-Hungarian origin, almost without exception, made America's cause their own. In Congress the President found them among his most zealous supporters. Hundreds of thousands of them fought valiantly on the field of battle.

As a force for unifying and invigorating public opinion, the Committee on Public Information played an important part. Created by executive order on April 14, 1917, with George Creel as Chairman, it gave out news concerning the war activities of the government, withholding such as might aid the enemy. It also carried on a mammoth campaign of popular education regarding the dangers of German imperialism and America's objects in the war. For these purposes, it published a daily newspaper, issued pamphlets by the million, produced patriotic films, directed countless speakers, and established press agencies in Allied and neutral countries.

Notwithstanding the unexampled unity of opinion, unanimity, of course, was not to be found. The farmers of the Upper Mississippi Valley retained some of their earlier pacifism; but the chief dissent came from the Socialists, who met in party convention at St. Louis on April 7, 1917, to deliberate on the international crisis. After branding America's entry as a crime of the capitalist class against the people, the convention pledged a "continuous, active and public opposition to the war through demonstrations . . . and all other means within our power." Though their position was anticapitalistic and antimilitaristic rather than pro-German, the public generally refused to recognize a distinction. Even many prominent Socialists, including Allan Benson, the party candidate in 1916, bolted the party in protest.

In order to cope with this and similar situations, Congress on June 15, 1917, adopted the Espionage Act. This statute, among other things, provided severe penalties for wilful attempts to obstruct recruiting or to "cause insubordination, disloyalty . . . or refusal of duty" among the armed forces. It further gave the Postmaster-General authority to exclude from the mails all matter deemed seditious or treasonable. A year later, on May 16, the law was strengthened by the Sedition Act, which amplified the list of crimes, including among them abusive utterances, written or oral, about the government, the Constitution, or the flag.[1] This was followed on October 16 by a third statute, which empowered the Secretary of Labor to deport, without jury trial, aliens who "believe in or advocate" the forcible overthrow of government, or who advocate the unlawful destruction of property, or who belong to organizations holding such views.

All three measures were assailed, while in course of passage, as infringements of the constitutional rights of free speech and free press, and it was freely charged that they outdid the Alien and Sedition Acts of 1798 in severity. As in the case of the Civil War, however, the real or fancied rights of the individual were not suffered to hamper the will of the majority. The federal authorities undertook a systematic campaign to suppress objectionable Socialist activities, censoring and suppressing their newspapers, prosecuting their speakers, and raiding and preventing their meetings. Debs, four times Socialist candidate for President, was among those sentenced to prison. In all, over 1,900 judicial proceedings were brought against Socialists

[1] Many states enacted similar and even more drastic laws of their own.

and other offenders up to July 1, 1919. About half of the cases resulted in convictions.

There can be little doubt that the zeal of the federal authorities sometimes outran their judgment. For example, Mrs. Rose Pastor Stokes, a Socialist speaker, received a ten years' sentence for saying, "I am for the people, and the government is for the profiteers." Men were imprisoned for arguments or profanity used in the heat of private altercation, on a railway train, or at a boarding-house table. In a number of such cases, and that of Mrs. Stokes, the judgments were subsequently set aside in the upper courts.

The close of hostilities seemed to increase rather than to abate the fires of intolerance. The popular mind continued to be keenly sensitive to criticism of the government from whatever source. Furthermore, many persons feared the effects of Russian Bolshevist propaganda on the radical elements in the United States, and seemed to see their fears confirmed in the adoption of communistic views by the "Left Wing" of the Socialist party in 1919. Consequently, Attorney-General A. M. Palmer and his assistants devoted their attention frankly to the suppression of unorthodox political and social opinions, whether concerned with the war or not. In many of the states the authorities were equally active. Serious doubts of the wisdom of such practices were, however, roused in the minds of persons, rooted in the older American tradition of free speech.

On April 1, 1920, five duly elected members of the lower house of the New York legislature were expelled because of their membership in the Socialist party, a body recognized under the state laws. The incident challenged the attention of the country. In a ringing protest, Charles E. Hughes, former Justice of the Supreme Court, asserted, "This is not, in my judgment, American government. . . . I count it a most serious mistake to proceed, not against individuals charged with violation of law, but against masses of our citizens combined for political action, by denying them the only resource of peaceful government; that is, action by the ballot box and through duly elected representatives in legislative bodies." His protest had the desired effect. Though the expelled legislators were not restored to their seats, the country was shocked into a realization of the serious consequences of the drift of events, and the tide turned toward customary American tolerance of minority rights.

Without an ardent public support of the war it would have been difficult to raise the immense sums necessary for its prosecution. From the first of April, 1917, through April, 1919, the war cost the United States considerably more than $1,000,000 an hour, or a total of $21,850,000,000. In addition, loans were advanced to the Allies at the rate of nearly half a million dollars an hour, amounting in all to $8,850,000,000. The expenditures arising from these two sources were almost three times as great as the total outlay of the government for all purposes during the first century of its existence. Of the total war revenue, the government raised about one third by taxation, and the remainder by borrowing.

The proportion secured from taxation exceeded that in any previous war, and indeed, that of any other power in the World War. Income taxes were greatly increased, with the heaviest burdens falling upon the largest incomes (amounting to 67 per cent in the case of incomes of $2,000,000 and over). In like fashion corporation profits in excess of normal prewar earnings were taxed on a progressive scale. Besides these, the chief resources of taxation, taxes were laid upon inheritances, postage rates were raised, and internal-revenue duties were expanded until they touched practically all the luxuries and many of the necessaries of life. Tariff revenue, which had so long been the mainspring of the government's receipts, contributed less than five per cent.

Five great bond issues were made, in denominations as low as $50. The first four were called "Liberty Loans," and the fifth, floated after the armistice, the "Victory Loan." Campaigns of publicity, such as had never been seen in America, were undertaken to popularize the bond issues and secure subscriptions. In the fourth loan, 21,000,000 subscribers responded, nearly one for every family in the population. While the design of the government was to tap every available source of revenue, almost equally important was the desire to give a maximum number of people a financial stake in the outcome of the war. These purposes were further served by the sale of "War Savings Certificates" in denominations of $5, and "Thrift Stamps" as low as twenty-five cents. In the end, there was hardly a man, woman, or child in the entire population who had not contributed a "silver bullet" toward military victory.

The government set a new standard in humane legislation for the soldiers and their dependents. By an act of October, 1917, the sum of $15, or one half the pay of a private, was to be sent home each month as an "allotment," and the government thereupon increased the sum by an "allowance," which normally amounted to $15 or more according to nearness of kin and the number of the dependents. The maimed soldier was promised vocational training at national expense in case he was unable to resume his former private employment. In addition, the War Risk Insurance plan provided means whereby the soldiers could, at low cost, take out government insurance against death or disability. It was hoped that these provisions would prevent a repetition of the pension abuses that had followed the Civil War.

Voluntary organizations appeared on every hand to befriend the soldiers and sustain the national *morale*. Chief among these was the American Red Cross. To its activities only a brief allusion can be made. It safeguarded the interests of the soldiers' families at home; it took charge of the sanitary conditions in the civil districts adjoining the camps; it distributed comfort articles among the soldiers; it aided refugees outside of the war zone; it recruited ambulance companies, trained and directed vast numbers of nurses, and organized great base hospitals. On March 1, 1919, Henry P. Davison, Chairman of the Red Cross War Council, reported that the American people had, in the preceding twenty-one months, given $400,000,000 toward the cause in cash and supplies — "by far the largest voluntary gifts of money, of hand and heart, ever contributed purely for the relief of human suffering."

Scarcely less important was the work of other civilian agencies, notably the Young Men's Christian Association, Young Women's Christian Association, National Catholic War Council of the Knights of Columbus, Jewish Welfare Board, Salvation Army, American Library Association, and War Camp Community Service. These organizations carried on their service of humanity in no spirit of narrow sectarianism, and their efforts were sustained by an unexampled financial support from the public at large.

The heightened sense of social responsibility, evoked by the war, was significantly evinced by the addition of two new amendments to the Constitution. The first of these had to do with the much agitated question of prohibition. Since the close of the preceding century, the efforts of temperance advocates had received strong reënforcement from the action of certain great corporations which, desiring to reduce the number of industrial accidents for which they were held accountable under the new Workingman Compensation laws (see page 445), adopted the practice of refusing employment to persons addicted to drink. By 1915 there were only three states that had neither state-wide prohibition nor some form of local option. Approximately seventy-five per cent of the area of the United States was "dry."

The war situation created a new interest in the reform. As a measure of grain and coal conservation, Congress on November 1, 1917, forbade the manufacture of all liquors except beer and wine, and in the following year, the President cut off the output of beer. The fact that the breweries and distilleries were largely owned by persons of German origin helped to sharpen public resentment against the drink traffic and to prepare the way for the adoption of the Eighteenth Amendment by Congress on December 18, 1917. This amendment, providing for the prohibition of the manufacture, transportation, and sale of intoxicating beverages one year after its ratification, became a part of the Constitution on January 16, 1919. Before the wave of public interest subsided, all but two of the legislatures passed resolutions of ratification.

The adoption of national prohibition was a bold social experiment, the merits of which caused unceasing controversy. By the Volstead Act of 1920 Congress declared all beverages containing one half of one per cent of alcohol to be intoxicating and hence forbidden. Enforcement involved serious difficulties, especially in the great population centers where local sentiment was strongly hostile. The immediate effect was a great increase in illicit distilling and a brisk smuggling traffic along the coasts and across the international borders. As time wore on, however, the regulations were amended, the machinery of enforcement was improved, and "bootlegging" became an increasingly hazardous occupation.

The Nineteenth Amendment granted the long-sought boon of nationwide equal suffrage. Its adoption was prompted largely by a heartfelt appreciation of the indispensable war services rendered by the women. They had played their full part, not only in food production and conservation and in Red Cross workrooms, but also as patriotic speakers and as workers in munition plants and other essential industries. Moreover, thousands of them had accompanied the Expeditionary Force, serving in a great variety of capacities from ambulance-drivers and Red Cross nurses to office clerks and Y. M. C. A. entertainers.

Earlier content with the extension of the suffrage through state action, Wilson became an outspoken champion of a federal amendment after the outbreak of the war. He contended that it was not merely an act of justice, but also a measure required to convince the world of the thoroughgoing character of American democracy.[1] After considerable delay, Congress submitted the Nineteenth Amendment to the states on June 5, 1919, and it was proclaimed a part of the Constitution on August 18, 1920, in time for the women to take part in the presidential election. Thus the movement for feminine enfranchisement, after many long years, attained victory. Women became a part of American society literally and directly, not merely as represented by men to whom they "belonged" in some relation.

Wilson and the Peace Settlement

Although the American President in the days preceding the armistice was spokesman for the world, he was already beginning to lose his right to speak for his own countrymen. The accumulating discontent of Wilson's political opponents with his imperious wartime leadership found an opportunity for unrestricted expression for the first time in the election of a new Congress in November, 1918. Notwithstanding his personal appeal to the voters

[1] Though a pioneer in the movement, the United States had been outdistanced during the war period by many foreign countries. In 1917, woman suffrage was granted in Russia and Mexico; in 1918, in Austria, Germany, Hungary, Poland, Czecho-Slovakia, England, Scotland, Wales, Ireland, and Canada; and in 1919, in Belgium, Luxemburg, Sweden, Iceland, British East Africa, and Rhodesia.

to elect a Democratic majority as a vindication of his leadership, the Republicans were successful in winning majorities in both houses of Congress.

Undeterred by this event, the President turned his attention to the approaching peace negotiations at Paris. As author of the Fourteen Points, he decided, in defiance of unbroken precedent, to attend the Peace Conference in person, and associated with himself, as fellow commissioners, Robert Lansing, who had succeeded Bryan as Secretary of State, Henry White, a retired diplomat, Colonel House, and General T. H. Bliss. The group as a whole was not a strong one. White, the only Republican, was not prominent in the party counsels, and many felt that the Senate should have had representation. To this delegation was added a host of technical, economic, historical, geographic, and military experts, who had been engaged for many months in compiling an enormous mass of pertinent information under the direction of Colonel House.

From the moment of his landing in France in mid-December till the opening of the Peace Conference on January 18, 1919, the President enjoyed a triumphal progress through Western Europe such as no man in history had ever known. Everywhere he was acclaimed by the populace as the savior of humanity, and showered with gifts and honors. When the Conference began its labors, the victors proceeded frankly on the assumption that the vanquished should have no part. Indeed, representatives of the latter were not allowed to come to Paris until the peace terms were ready.

Although thirty-two nations participated in the proceedings, the real work was done chiefly by Great Britain, France, the United States, and Italy, and to a lesser extent, by Japan. From the outset the American President strove tirelessly to secure an idealistic basis for the settlement — that "peace of justice" so dear to his heart and which he believed to be essential for future world stability. But his purpose, however exalted, quickly partook of the nature of the quixotic. The very air of Paris was surcharged with hatred and fear of Germany. Moreover, the broad principles enunciated in the Fourteen Points were often susceptible of differing, or even conflicting, interpretations when applied to concrete situations, a fact of which the President's antagonists were not slow to take advantage.[1] Finally, in spite of Wilson's example and their own lofty professions, the victors were resolved, true to time-honored diplomatic practice, on a division of the enemy spoils. Some, indeed, had received advance assurance of their share by means of secret treaties, and each nation had its own special necessities, jealousies, and aspirations to gratify.

While the discussions proceeded behind closed doors, starvation was spreading over half the continent, Bolshevism was gaining new adherents throughout Central Europe, and nearly a score of little fires of war, left over from the great one, still burned fiercely. As David Lloyd George, the British prime minister, declared later in the House of Commons in a vivid figurative passage, "We had to . . . work crowded hours, long and late, because, while we were trying to build, we saw in many lands the foundations of society crumbling into dust, and we had to make haste. . . . I am doubtful whether any body of men with a difficult task have worked under greater difficulties, with stones crackling on the roof and crashing through the windows, and sometimes wild men screaming through the keyholes."

Wilson's chief antagonist in the negotiations was the French premier, Clemenceau, grim, grizzled, and determined — an uncompromising representative of the old diplomacy. Lloyd George, who reminded Americans in many ways of their own Roosevelt, usually supported the President's position but was not to be relied upon. On behalf of Italy, Vittorio Orlando played a less important rôle, though at one juncture the Italian claim to the Adriatic port of Fiume, at the expense of Jugo-Slavia, led to an open clash with Wilson. The Italian delegation actually withdrew from the Conference temporarily, and subsequently negotiated a compromise. The Japanese, watchful and assertive where their own interests were involved, took little part in the strictly European settlements. As for the smaller nations, each lifted a piping voice, and accepted such crumbs of satisfaction as fell to its lot.

As the weeks went by, the President felt obliged to make

[1] For example, the Poles resolutely demanded the application of Point 13 which promised them "a free and secure access to the sea," but in order to accord this to them, it was necessary to include a million or more Germans within Polish borders, an arrangement which violated the spirit of the principle of self-determination which animated Points 6–13.

repeated concessions to his associates, and under their ceaseless hammering, many of the Fourteen Points began to crumble.[1] Yet, in spite of the inconsistencies and injustices that found lodgment in the treaty, its character would have been considerably more punitive and imperialistic but for Wilson's presence at the peace table. On one critical occasion, when the tide of reaction ran unusually strong, he summoned his vessel, the *George Washington*, to take home the American delegation. This threat of withdrawal had the desired effect, for there resulted an immediate toning down of demands.

The President stood firm as a rock against all attempts to tamper with Point 14, which promised an "association of nations." In this international mechanism he saw an opportunity to repair the mistakes and inequities of the Peace Treaty as well as to insure future world tranquillity. On February 14, 1919, the Conference formally adopted a constitution, or "Covenant," for the proposed League of Nations, which had been evolved chiefly by Lord Robert Cecil of England and General Jan Smuts of the South African Union. The President sailed on the next day for America in order to consult leading Senators, and distinguished publicists like Hughes, ex-President Taft, and Elihu Root, in regard to the Covenant. Armed with their comments, he returned to Paris and succeeded in incorporating in the document an explicit recognition of the Monroe Doctrine and certain other changes that they had suggested. By these alterations he believed that he had assured American adhesion.

As thus revised, the Covenant declared that the main object of the new organization was to "achieve international peace and security by the acceptance of obligations not to resort to war." The machinery of the League was to consist of an Assembly, in which each country in the League should have an equal voice; a Council, composed of representatives of the five great Allied and Associated Powers together with four other members elected by the Assembly; and a permanent Secretariat or business office at Geneva, Switzerland. The League was granted general supervision of the administration of the former enemy colonies, though

[1] For example, Point 4 (pledging an effective reduction of national armaments) was abandoned. Likewise, the fate of enemy territory and colonies was determined with little or no regard to the principle of self-determination or the interests of the native inhabitants.

these were placed directly in charge of various powers in the capacity of trustees or "mandatories." It was also authorized to seek improvement in labor conditions throughout the world and to assist in certain other humanitarian reforms of international concern.

Most significant of all, however, were the powers conferred for the purpose of minimizing the possibility of international conflicts. Two prolific causes of war were aimed at in the provision outlawing secret treaties and in the authority given the Council to recommend plans for the reduction of national armaments. Provision was also made for the creation of a Permanent Court of International Justice. It was further declared to be the "friendly right" of any country in the League to call attention to "any circumstance whatever" inimical to international peace. If, in spite of these precautions, war should threaten anywhere in the world, the League was empowered to "take any action that may be deemed wise and effectual to safeguard the peace of nations."

More specifically, the countries in the League agreed, in harmony with the Bryan "cooling-off" plan, that when diplomatic means failed they would submit their differences to arbitration, and in no case, declare war until three months after the award was made. Violation of this provision subjected the offending nation to a drastic international boycott. If armed coercion proved necessary, the Council would "recommend" the amount of armed force each country should furnish the League.

Article X, designed by its author, President Wilson, as an additional guarantee of peace, pledged the countries in the League "to respect and preserve as against external aggression the territorial integrity and existing political independence of all members of the League. In case of any . . . danger of such aggression, the Council shall advise upon the means by which this obligation shall be fulfilled." Another section asserted that "regional understandings like the Monroe Doctrine" were in no wise affected by the Covenant. No important decisions could be made without the unanimous vote of the members of the Assembly and Council, and no amendment to the Covenant without the consent of all the nations represented in the Council.

On June 28, 1919, representatives of the new German Republic in great bitterness signed the treaty which they denounced as intolerably severe and contrary to the Fourteen Points. President Wilson on July 10 submitted it to the American Senate for ratification.[1] At once a tempest of protest and denunciation, which had been gathering strength for several months, broke loose in the Senate, and only to a less degree, in the country at large.

The opposition had a variety of sources, personal, partisan, and racial. Part of it was due to Wilson's characteristic aloofness and self-assurance, which had become intensified under the stress of wartime exigencies. Furthermore, Republican leaders perceived a strong party advantage in advertising the defects of the treaty and their own efforts to "Americanize" it by means of amendments. The Irish-American section of the population was antagonistic for fear that Article X would preclude the possibility of Irish independence, and their hostility was reënforced by the indignation of German-Americans because of the harshness of the treaty and the exclusion of the German Republic from the League. Beneath these sources of opposition, however, lay a deepseated and sincere hesitation of many Americans to depart from what they believed to be the traditional national policy of abstention from European entanglements.

Out of the storm and fury of controversy there gradually emerged certain definite groupings among the Senators: those who, like Wilson himself, demanded ratification of the treaty without material change; those who were willing to accept mild reservations; those who insisted on amendments or strong reservations; and lastly, the "irreconcilables" who opposed ratification in any form. The first two groups were predominantly Democratic in complexion; the latter two, Republican. The two central groups were led respectively by G. M. Hitchcock, a Democrat of Nebraska, and Henry Cabot Lodge, the Republican Chairman of the Foreign Relations Committee. Though few in number, the irreconcilables were singularly fortunate in

[1] This treaty, known as the "Treaty of Versailles," contained 80,000 words, and was the pattern for similar pacts with the other enemy powers. As a result of the several treaties, the conglomerate empire of Austria-Hungary was broken up, and three independent governments were created: Austria, Hungary, and Czecho-Slovakia. The remainder of the territory was distributed among various adjoining countries. Poland was also erected as an independent nation. Representatives of the United States signed the peace treaties with Austria and Hungary on September 10, 1919, and June 4, 1920.

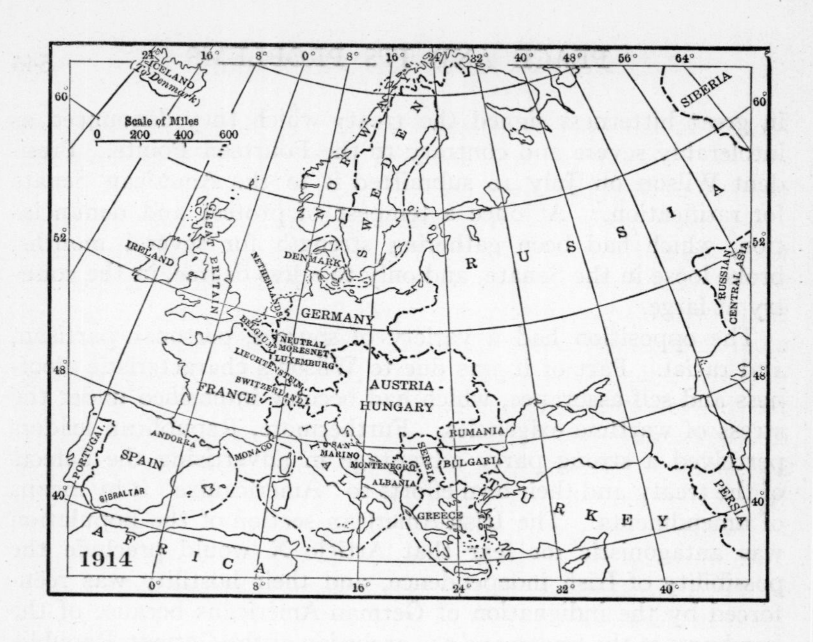

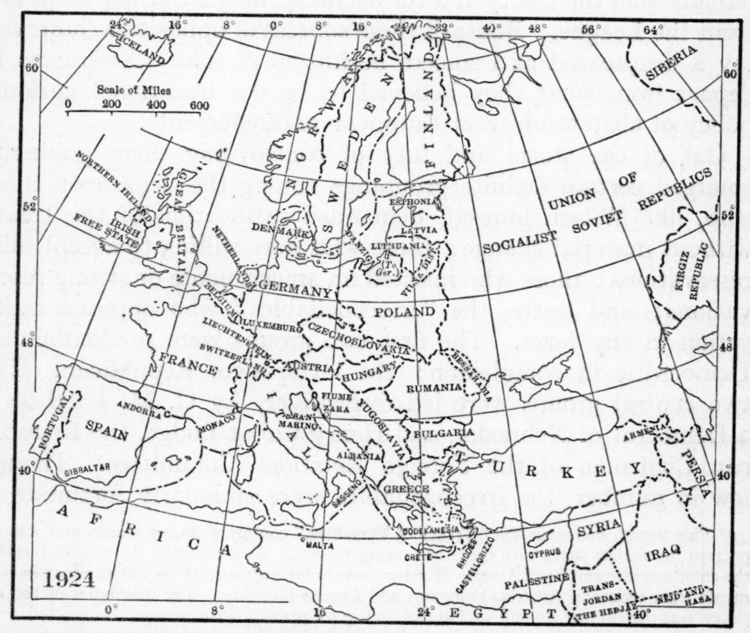

Europe and Asia Minor before and after the World War

having as their spokesmen such Senators as Johnson of California and W. E. Borah of Idaho, long known to the public as persistent champions of popular rights.

On September 10, 1919, Senator Lodge, acting on behalf of the Foreign Relations Committee, recommended the ratification of the treaty with thirty-eight amendments and four reservations, which were subsequently reduced to fourteen. The principal changes concerned certain features of the League Covenant, notably Article X which, in its existing form, was held to guarantee the *status quo* and to obligate the United States, at the behest of the League, to send troops to defend even unjust territorial settlements (see page 542). This obligation was expressly repudiated except in cases where Congress should specifically authorize to the contrary.

In anticipation of the Lodge report, the President left Washington a week before on a stumping tour to arouse public sentiment in behalf of unqualified ratification. The effort, however, proved too great for a physique worn by many months of fearful strain and terrible responsibility. While in Colorado he suffered a paralytic stroke on September 25, which caused the immediate close of his tour and confined him to the sickroom for most of the remainder of his presidency. Thereby the pro-League forces lost their commanding general, and the way was cleared for the ultimate triumph of the opposition.

The Senate discussions continued throughout the succeeding weeks with increasing rancor. When the treaty came up for vote on November 19, it proved impossible to secure the necessary two-thirds majority for it either with or without reservations. Had the spirit of acrimony been less intense or President Wilson more amenable, it is possible that the requisite majority for ratification might even then have been secured by a process of compromise. Senator Hitchcock, on behalf of the Democrats, did indeed offer a series of reservations which differed from the Lodge set chiefly in details of phraseology; but on the eve of a presidential election, neither party was willing to yield to the other the credit of saving the peace. On March 19, 1920, the treaty came up for vote a second time, modified by fifteen Lodge reservations. Once more ratification failed though the vote stood 49 to 35 in favor. The minority consisted of a combination of the irreconcilables with those Democrats who stood squarely by the President.

Pleading the impossibility of ratifying the Wilson treaty by a two-thirds Senate vote, the Republicans set about to make a separate peace with the enemy powers by means of a majority vote of the two houses. Accordingly, the Knox Resolution, repealing the declarations of war, was passed on May 27; but it was promptly vetoed by the President. The question of peace was at a deadlock so far as the American government was concerned, and further action awaited an expression of the popular will in the approaching election, which, Wilson asked, should take "the form of a great and solemn referendum."

Postwar Readjustments, Economic and Political

Other factors, besides the League question, were, however, to play a part in the campaign of 1920. America's participation in the war had been attended at home by a widespread and dazzling prosperity, in fitting climax to the great industrial revival of the period of neutrality. To the insistent call of the European belligerents for foodstuffs, manufactures, and munitions was added the imperative need of the American government for these supplies. Heroic efforts were made to meet the demands. In order to stimulate production, the banks freely loaned money to borrowers, and the government added the inducement of exceptionally high prices. Meantime, as a result of the abnormal trade relations with Europe, our sales abroad vastly exceeded our purchases, the position of the United States changed from a debtor to a creditor nation, and each year saw an increasing flow of gold into America available for investment.

In consequence, every nerve of industry was quickened, speculation became rife, and prices began to soar. The cost of living by the middle of 1919 had advanced 77 per cent beyond that of 1913. With the rise in prices, wage-earners demanded higher pay, and employers, suffering from a shortage of labor and hampered by the falling off of European immigration, felt obliged to meet their demands. Indeed, the government at Washington, unlike previous administrations, exerted constant pressure on employers during the war to secure larger rights and better wages for the unions. To this end the American Federation of Labor was given representation on the Council of National Defense, the War Industries Board, and other important boards and commissions. Never before had organized labor attained such great power and so large a membership.

One result of the abnormal demand for labor was the migration of thousands of negro workers from Southern plantations to better paid jobs in Northern mills, with a consequent improvement in the economic status of those left behind. In great manufacturing cities like Cleveland, Detroit, and Akron, the colored population increased anywhere from 300 to nearly 800 per cent in the decade from 1910 to 1920. The farmer shared in the general well-being, receiving prices for his crops beyond his wildest dreams of a few years before. The chief benefits of the highly stimulated prosperity, however, fell to business men whose rapidly mounting profits permitted them to keep safely ahead of the advancing costs of operation. It is significant that the ranks of American millionaires increased twenty-five per cent from 1917 to 1920, growing from 16,000 to 20,000.

The cessation of hostilities had no immediate effect on the situation. With her industries still badly deranged, Europe continued to stand in need of American exports, and in the United States the people, made gay by unwontedly fat purses and the sudden relaxing of the war strain, engaged in an orgy of extravagant buying and fast living. Overexpansion, speculation, and inflated prices were carried to new extremes both in industry and agriculture.

From the standpoint of labor troubles, the year 1919 proved to be one of the most eventful in recent times. Most of the strikes were actuated by a desire to keep wages abreast the ascending cost of living, but it was widely remarked that the labor program was fast becoming tinged with Socialism and that the older leadership, personified by President Gompers, was beginning to give way to a new and more radical leadership. More than four million wage-earners took part in strikes and lockouts, with an aggregate cost to employees of over $800,000,000, and to employers of $1,300,000,000 or more.[1] Among the gravest

[1] The total duration of these strikes was 57,885 days as compared with 28,779 days in 1918 and 25,077 days in 1917.

disturbances were the walkout of 125,000 wage-earners in the building trades in New York City in February, the railway shopworkers' strike in August, involving 250,000 men, the strike of 367,000 iron and steel employees in September, and the walkout of 435,000 bituminous coal miners in November. An ominous feature of the situation was the great number of "outlaw" strikes — strikes undertaken against the wishes of the national unions — which in 1919 involved one fourth of the total number of strikers.

The whole structure of prosperity rested on an insecure basis, and in the spring of 1920, the edifice began to topple. The immediate cause was the diminished ability of Europe to buy American products. At the same time domestic purchases rapidly fell away, for the public was beginning to recover its mental equilibrium and think again in terms of prudent living. The products of factory, mine, and farm became a glut on the market, and the inflated prices began to collapse. As a result, factories and mines curtailed their operations, farmers found themselves with produce they could not sell, and millions of laborers suffered wage reductions or were thrown out of work.

The Crisis of 1920 differed, however, from those that had occurred before in that there was no sudden panic followed by widespread bankruptcies and business failures. For this outcome the Federal Reserve System, with its extensive control over bank credit, was largely responsible. The general business depression continued until 1922 and later, and like other periods of hard times, was productive of widespread social unrest and radical plans for social amelioration. The process of readjustment was slowest among the Western farmers, who, as on earlier occasions, attributed their troubles to the machinations of "Big Business" and prepared once more to enter the political arena as an organized group.

As steps toward the restoration of normal conditions, Congress passed two important laws in 1920. The Transportation Act (Esch-Cummins Law) of February 28 fixed the terms upon which the railways should be handed back to private ownership and management. Enacted after much controversy, it embodied certain new principles which had been discovered as a result of the period of government operation. The idea that competition must be enforced among railways was abandoned. Pooling, hitherto forbidden, was legalized under supervision of the Interstate Commerce Commission, and plans were authorized for the ultimate consolidation of the railways into a limited number of systems. To the Commission was granted the power of fixing minimum as well as maximum rates, so that the railways would be assured a fair profit at the same time that they would be prevented from obtaining an excessive one. Other provisions of the Act created special tribunals to deal with railway labor difficulties.

In the Merchant Marine Act of June 5, Congress declared its policy in regard to the fleet of 1500 merchant vessels which the Shipping Board (see page 506) had acquired during the war. The law put an end to further shipbuilding by the Board, but continued temporarily the experiment of government ownership and operation. The Board was empowered, at its discretion, to dispose of the vessels from time to time to private American purchasers, and to accumulate out of its profits a fund from which loans might be made to private shipbuilders. By such means it was hoped that America might recover some part of her earlier importance in the carrying trade.

As the presidential campaign of 1920 approached, the temper of the people was strongly favorable to a change of party. All over the world the war governments had been swept out of power on a tide of accumulating resentment because of the hardships which the conflict produced. In America the cause of the Democrats was further prejudiced by the unpopularity of Wilson's stubborn stand on the ratification of the Peace Treaty and by the blight which had fallen on the economic life of the nation.

A widespread but unorganized public sentiment favored the Republican nomination of Herbert Hoover, the only American connected with the war who had captured the popular imagination. But when the party convention met in Chicago on June 8, its proceedings were dominated by the Senatorial clique which had conducted the fight against the Treaty. The Hoover sentiment had little following among the delegates; and of the leading contestants before the convention, General Leonard Wood and Governor F. O. Lowden of Illinois, neither could obtain a majority vote. As a result, on the tenth ballot, the prize went to Senator Warren G. Harding of Ohio, a Lodge-reservationist and reliable organization man. The second place on the ticket fell to Governor Calvin Coolidge of Massachusetts whose part in suppressing a policemen's strike in Boston had attracted national notice. The platform assailed "executive autocracy," promised governmental economy, measures for farm relief and the return of prosperity, and in language designed to satisfy all shades of opinion on the League question, declared "for agreement among the nations to preserve the peace of the world." [1]

In their San Francisco convention on June 28, the Democrats nominated Governor James M. Cox of Ohio on the forty-fourth ballot after a hot three-cornered contest in which Attorney-General Palmer and the President's son-in-law, W. G. McAdoo, were his leading rivals. Franklin D. Roosevelt of New York, a distant relative of the former President, was named for Vice-President. The platform eloquently defended Wilson's domestic and foreign policies, promised farm betterment, and declared for immediate ratification of the Peace Treaty without material reservations. As usual, other parties participated in the election. The Socialists, for the fifth time, nominated Eugene V. Debs although he was still behind the bars in the Atlanta Penitentiary. A newly organized group, the Farmer-Labor party, offered candidates in the hope of crystallizing the growing discontent of the rural and industrial classes.

The result of the campaign was clear from the start. The action of the American Federation of Labor in indorsing the Democratic ticket did little to help it. The public was in a captious mood and eager to lay all its troubles at the door of the party in power. In regard to the League question the Republicans succeeded in befuddling the issue. Leading irreconcilables like Hiram Johnson maintained that Harding's election would mean the repudiation of the Peace Treaty. On the other hand, thirty-one distinguished Republicans, including Hughes, Root, and Hoover, assured the public in a joint statement on October

[1] This section of the platform was very long and involved a constant restatement of the Republican position on the League, the last one being: "We pledge . . . such agreements with the other nations . . . as shall meet the full duty of America to civilization and humanity . . . without surrendering the right of the American people to exercise its judgment and its power in favor of justice and peace."

14 that "the true course to bring America into an effective league" was through a Republican victory. Harding's own speeches, though somewhat ambiguous, indicated his own preference for "an association of nations," based possibly on a modification of the Covenant.

The election was a Republican landslide. The Republican plurality of nearly 7,000,000 was due in part to the women voters who had just received the ballot by federal amendment. In the electoral college the vote stood 404 to 127, and Harding received 60.3 per cent of the popular vote as compared with 34.2 per cent for Cox. Even the Solid South was badly shaken, Tennessee deserting to the enemy for the first time since Carpetbag days.

The Republicans and the Peace Problem, 1921–1924

The new President had had a long career in Ohio politics, where he had identified himself with conservative views and purposes, but he was virtually unknown to the country at large. Of modest and conciliatory temperament and ordinary ability, his elevation was hailed with satisfaction by countless persons who sought relief from an aggressive personality at the helm of state. As if to make up for his own shortcomings, he placed in his cabinet three men of distinguished ability: Hughes as Secretary of State, A. W. Mellon, a Pittsburgh millionaire, as Secretary of the Treasury, and Hoover as Secretary of Commerce. Some of his other choices, however, were less happy, being dictated by considerations of personal friendship. Thus ex-Senator A. B. Fall of New Mexico, a pronounced anticonservationist, was made Secretary of the Interior, and H. M. Daugherty, an Ohio machine politician, Attorney-General.[1] Harding established a precedent by inviting Vice-President Coolidge to attend the cabinet meetings, and in June paid a graceful compliment to the only living Republican ex-President, Taft, by appointing him Chief Justice of the Supreme Court.

Though the Republicans commanded substantial majorities in both houses of Congress, strong factional differences existed

[1] The remaining members of the cabinet were: J. W. Weeks of Massachusetts, Secretary of War; W. H. Hays of Indiana, Postmaster-General; Edwin Denby of Michigan, Secretary of the Navy; H. C. Wallace of Iowa, Secretary of Agriculture; and J. J. Davis of Pennsylvania, Secretary of Labor.

within the party, and President Harding's task would have been a difficult one even if he had been more amply endowed with the attributes of leadership. Seeking to placate the two principal opposition groups, he yielded to the irreconcilables in the matter of foreign relations, and endeavored to secure the domestic legislation desired by the conservative Eastern wing.

On the President's recommendation, the new Congress, which met in special session on April 11, 1921, revived the Knox Resolution, which Wilson had vetoed, and repassed it in somewhat modified form on July 2. The war was thereby declared to be at an end, the United States reserved all the rights and advantages which would have come to it as a signatory of the Treaty of Versailles, and all enemy property seized by the government in the war period was to be retained until the enemy powers provided by treaty for the satisfaction of America's war claims.[1] Treaties with Germany and Austria expressed assent to these terms in August. One year later Germany and the United States arranged for a joint commission to determine the amount of American losses from submarine depredations and other causes.

With the formal ending of the war, the President, under spur of a resolution introduced into Congress by Senator Borah, called a Conference on the Limitation of Armament to meet at Washington on November 11, 1921. Besides the five Great Powers, China, Belgium, Holland, and Portugal were represented. The deliberations were dominated by the conviction that the greatest threat to world peace lay in the disturbed conditions and international rivalries of the Pacific and Far East. The outcome was embodied in a great variety of treaties and other agreements.

The open-door policy, which had been seriously weakened during the war by aggressive demands which Japan had imposed on China, was given a more secure status than ever before by a pledge of the powers to respect Chinese independence and to maintain "the principle of equal opportunity for the commerce and industry of all nations" there.[2] In a Four-Power Treaty,

[1] Exclusive of forty German vessels, the property sequestrated during the war was valued at $400,000,000.

[2] Another source of irritation was removed by the agreement of Japan to restore to China the former German-leased territory of Kiaochow in Shantung, together with the special economic privileges enjoyed there. This area had been transferred to Japan by the Treaty of Versailles.

Great Britain, Japan, France, and the United States agreed to respect each other's possessions in the Pacific Ocean, and if danger threatened from some outside power, to confer "as to the most efficient measures to be taken, jointly or separately." Though reassuring to all the signatories, from the standpoint of the United States the Four-Power Treaty disposed of the popular fear that Japan cherished aggressive designs toward the Philippines.

The United States, Great Britain, Japan, France, and Italy also signed a treaty, restricting the number of their battleships and fixing a relative strength in accordance with the ratio of 5 : 5 : 3 : 1.75 : 1.75 respectively until the end of 1936. By this agreement a new balance of sea power was established, and the two English-speaking powers were assured a combined strength greater than that of the other three. In a separate declaration the five powers condemned unrestricted submarine warfare and the use of poisonous gas. The dominant figure in the Conference was Secretary of State Hughes, who served as one of the four American delegates. The results of the Conference, though rightly hailed as a signal victory for international peace, fell short of the hopes of the American government in that nothing was done to limit the size of armies or the number of submarines.

In spite of America's failure to ratify the Peace Treaty, the League of Nations had been duly organized in January, 1920, and soon commanded a membership of fifty-four nations, including seventeen republics of the New World. The United States was confronted with the question of what its official attitude should be toward the multifarious international activities and decisions that were sponsored by the League and which often affected vital national interests.

For the first six months Secretary Hughes did not so much as answer communications from the League, but thereafter the administration hesitantly adopted the practice of appointing "observers" to attend conferences where matters of concern to the United States were under consideration. They were authorized to present the American viewpoint but had no vote in the final decisions reached. In this manner, for example, the United States attached observers to the committees of the League on Health, the Opium Trade, Anthrax, the Traffic in Arms, Customs

Formalities, Communications and Transit, and the Traffic in Women and Children. The policy was stigmatized by pro-Leaguers as "furtive," and as placing the administration in the undignified position of making use of League facilities without contributing a penny to their upkeep.

Unofficial American coöperation was even greater, for American experts in law, medicine, and finance, acting in their private capacities, freely accepted important League appointments. Thus Henry Morgenthau headed the committee to provide an international loan to Greece, Norman Davis of New York presided over the commission which settled certain boundary differences between Poland and Lithuania, and Professor John Bassett Moore of Columbia University was appointed a judge of the Permanent Court of International Justice.

The creation of the last-named body, popularly termed the "World Court," caused the government at Washington to depart even further from its original policy of aloofness. Authorized by Article XIV of the Covenant, this tribunal had been organized at The Hague in January, 1922, in accordance with a plan drafted by Elihu Root and other eminent jurists of the world and adopted by the League Council and Assembly. Unlike the earlier Hague tribunal (see page 498), it was an actual court with a fixed *personnel* and always open to litigants. It had jurisdiction over "any dispute of an international character which the parties thereto submit to it," and the judges were selected by the Council and the Assembly from nominations made by the old Hague Court. In a message to the Senate, President Harding on February 24, 1923, recommended American participation in the World Court on condition that the United States be given an equal voice with other countries in the selection of judges. The proposal roused the ire of the irreconcilables, but was warmly supported by pro-League members of both parties. Ratification, coupled with a number of reservations, finally occurred in January, 1926.

The growing interest in European affairs was further evinced by Secretary Hughes' suggestion to France and Great Britain, made in December, 1922, that an international commission of experts be appointed to determine Germany's capacity to pay reparations. The sum had not been fixed in the Treaty of Versailles, but had been referred to a special Reparation Commission for determination. Germany's slowness in making payments led France in January, 1923, on her own initiative to take forcible possession of the Ruhr Valley in order to work the German factories and mines located there. Late in 1923 France finally accepted the Hughes proposal, and the United States agreed to designate American experts for the commission.

The so-called "Dawes Report" resulted, named after one of the two American representatives, Charles G. Dawes, a Chicago banker. By this plan, a method, too detailed for consideration here, was outlined whereby Germany might recover her former industrial and fiscal vitality and at the same time be compelled to pay a maximum indemnity over a long period of years. The plan also provided for the immediate economic, and the eventual military, evacuation of the Ruhr. Acceptance of the scheme was accorded by the several interested powers at a conference in London in the summer of 1924, in which Secretary Hughes and Secretary of the Treasury Mellon took an active but unofficial part.

Domestic Problems of the Republicans, 1921–1924

In domestic affairs President Harding, in his first message to Congress, strongly urged the adoption of a budget system. According to time-honored practice, revenue bills originated in many different committees of Congress; there was no competent scrutiny of the departmental requests for funds, and no coördination between income and outgo. President Taft had made efforts to secure a budget system, and in 1920 a bill for this purpose had been vetoed by Wilson. The confused condition of the national finances resulting from the war made further delay of this reform unwise. The Budget and Accounting Act of June 10, 1921, created a Budget Bureau in the Treasury Department, headed by a Director armed with authority, under the President's direction, to prepare estimates of income and to recommend expenditures. It was further provided that all requests for appropriations must go to the Bureau rather than directly to Congress. Dawes was appointed first Director, and the new plan quickly demonstrated its utility in curbing governmental extravagance.

The most difficult problem with which the administration had to deal grew out of the bad situation of the rural population after the war. From the dizzy heights of wartime prosperity the Crisis of 1920 had plunged them into a slough of starvation prices, heavy debts, and bankruptcy. At the heart of their difficulties lay the fact that, with the falling off of the European market after the war, agricultural production vastly exceeded domestic needs; and prompt readjustment to the new conditions was difficult, if not impossible. Their plight was aggravated by their greatly increased taxes, the high freight rates lasting over from the war, and the difficulty of borrowing money to tide over the bad times. Moreover, when conditions in the urban business world began gradually to return to normal, the situation of the farmer remained as before, except that he was forced to pay higher prices for the goods he purchased. Data collected by the Department of Agriculture in 1922 showed that the cost of producing a bushel of wheat or oats was greater than the average sale price.

The war period had witnessed a revival of farmers' organizations — such as the Farmers' National Council, the American Cotton Association, the United Farmers of America, the Wheat Growers' Association, and, most important of all, the American Farm Bureau Federation — and these now took an active part in agitating plans for agricultural relief. Even before the depression they had done much to promote coöperative enterprises among the rural population. In 1919, more than a half-million farmers marketed coöperatively products valued at $722,000,000, and over 300,000 farmers made purchases amounting to $84,000,000 through common buying associations. Moreover, the coöperative societies were organized with such care and were conducted so efficiently that, unlike earlier experiments of a like kind, they promised to become a permanent part of the economic structure of the nation.[1]

Since the Harding administration displayed little interest in the hardships of the farmer, the American Farm Bureau Federation, with a membership of over a million, took the initiative in the matter. Largely through its influence, a small bipartisan group of Senators and Representatives, mostly from the West, organized

[1] Coöperative marketing was applied most extensively to grain, milk, cream, butter, fruit, and truck crops.

a "farm bloc" in the spring of 1921 for the purpose of securing effective laws for agricultural betterment. Notwithstanding the obstructive tactics of administration leaders, the Bloc wielded great influence from the start, for, led by such Senators as W. S. Kenyon of Iowa, Arthur Capper of Kansas, and La Follette of Wisconsin, it held the balance of power between the two old parties.

The outstanding objects of the Farm Bloc were to improve agricultural credit facilities, reduce the power of the middlemen, and protect the American farmer from Canadian competition. The program met with substantial success. In furtherance of the first purpose, Congress in 1921 revived the War Finance Corporation and authorized it to assist in financing the exportation of farm products. In the twelve months following December 1, 1921, the sum of $433,447,000 was advanced in this manner in thirty-seven states. Congress also increased the capacity of the Federal Land Banks (see page 474) to lend on farm mortgages, and in the Agricultural Credits Act of March 3, 1923, provided means whereby farmers might borrow on live-stock and farm products on their way to the market.

Three important measures were directed against the middleman and designed to reduce the great discrepancy between the small price paid the farmer and the high price charged the public. By the Packers and Stockyards Act of August 15, 1921, the Secretary of Agriculture was given supervision of the packing houses, stockyards, and commission merchants, with power to correct price manipulation or other unfair practices. The Grain Futures Act, signed several days later, gave the same official authority to prevent improper speculation upon the grain exchanges in regard to grain sold for future delivery.[1] In the Capper-Volstead Act of February 18, 1922, Congress expressly legalized the formation of coöperative associations in interstate commerce, and empowered the Secretary of Agriculture to see that they were not used as monopolies to enhance prices unfairly.

In the effort to obviate the competition of low-priced Canadian grain, Congress on May 27, 1921, enacted an Emergency Tariff

[1] Though declared unconstitutional by the Supreme Court, it was replaced on September 21, 1922, by a new Grain Futures Act, which was based on the interstate commerce clause instead of the taxation clause as in the former case.

Act, which imposed high import duties on wheat and corn along with meat, wool, sugar, and certain other farm products. This was followed presently by a general tariff revision in which the manufacturing interests shared. The Fordney-McCumber Act of September 21, 1922, was the highest protective measure ever passed. The effect of the excessive rates was, however, somewhat tempered by the provision that, upon recommendation of the Tariff Commission, the President might raise or lower duties as much as fifty per cent in order to equalize the costs of production in the United States and competing foreign countries.

Though the urban wage-earners fared better than the farmers, the process of readjustment nevertheless caused prolonged unemployment and numerous strikes, and created acute discontent. Two industrial disturbances in 1922 were of peculiar interest, partly because of their magnitude, and partly because of the light they threw upon the administration's labor policy. In April a great coal strike commenced, the first in history to embrace both anthracite and bituminous miners. The chief grievance centered in the question of wages, and 640,000 workers were involved. In July President Harding proposed a plan of settlement which the operators rejected. Matters were then allowed to drift on until fall when the two sides adjusted their difficulties by mutual concessions.

On July 1 began a nationwide strike of 400,000 railway shopmen as a result of wage reductions ordered by the Railway Labor Board. The strike proceeded with intermittent disorders though none of threatening proportions. President Harding made several fruitless attempts to end the trouble through mediation, and on September 1, Attorney-General Daugherty, alleging the need of protecting the mails and interstate commerce, obtained from the federal court in Chicago a "blanket" injunction against the strikers. It was the most sweeping decree of the kind ever issued. Under its terms the strikers could not even use peaceful argument or moral suasion to induce employees to cease work. It was bitterly denounced by labor leaders and others as an infringement of labor's rights and of the Clayton Anti-Trust Act. Though not the decisive factor, the Attorney-General's move hastened the conclusive defeat of the strikers.

While the attention of the nation was engaged with such problems, the people were deeply shocked by the unexpected news of Harding's death. Overtaxed by the burdens of office, the President succumbed to a stroke of apoplexy on August 2, 1923, in San Francisco while returning from a trip to Alaska. His successor in office was a matter-of-fact, hard-working man with an unusual aptitude for reticent speech. Though little known to the public in general, Coolidge had shown himself to be a shrewd and competent executive while Governor of Massachusetts. He was the first native New Englander to reach the presidency since Arthur's succession under similar circumstances.

Unfortunately, the new President inherited from his predecessor a legacy of official corruption and betrayal of public trust. The main facts, as revealed by special Senate committees after Harding's demise, disclosed a record of wrongdoing in high places unequaled since Grant's day. The first notable scandal grew out of C. R. Forbes' activities as Director of the Veterans' Bureau, an agency which had succeeded to the functions of the Bureau of War Risk Insurance and certain other government bureaus charged with the welfare of disabled ex-service men. In the two years he was permitted to remain in office, his record (according to the Senate committee) was one of "almost unparalleled waste, recklessness and misconduct," involving questionable methods in the purchase of hospital sites, the payment of excessive fees to architects and contractors, and fraud in the buying of supplies and equipment.[1] The losses sustained by the government were estimated at more than $200,000,000. In February, 1924, Forbes was indicted by a federal grand jury for conspiracy and fraud, and subsequently convicted of the charge.

Close on the heels of this exposure came startling revelations involving members of the cabinet. The evidence showed that in May, 1921, Secretary Denby of the Navy Department had, with Harding's approval, transferred to Secretary of the Interior Fall the administration of certain petroleum reserves which had been set apart during the Taft and Wilson administrations for the exclusive use of the navy. In 1922 Fall, without seeking

[1] For example, according to the testimony submitted, he bought $70,000 worth of floor cleaner — enough to last nearly one hundred years — paying for it ninety-eight cents a gallon when it could be manufactured for less than four cents a gallon. Likewise, it appears, he sold 84,000 new bed sheets, which had cost $1.37 apiece, at about twenty-seven cents each, and at the same time, bought 25,000 more new sheets at $1.03 each.

competitive bids, secretly leased Reserve No. 3 (Teapot Dome), near Casper, Wyoming, to the H. F. Sinclair interests, and another and larger reserve at Elk Hills, California, to the E. L. Doheny interests. Though the government in each case reserved a moderate royalty on the oil extracted, the fluid itself was by these leases diverted from its intended purposes, to the enormous prospective profit of private commercial interests.

However unwise, the transactions bore no sinister aspect until the Senate committee, headed by T. J. Walsh of Montana, discovered that late in 1921 Doheny had loaned Fall $100,000 on an unsecured note bearing no interest, and that after Fall's retirement from the cabinet in March, 1923, Sinclair had similarly loaned him $25,000. Though President Coolidge was inclined to move slowly, an outraged public demanded strong action from the administration. Early in 1924, the government instituted suits for the cancellation of the oil leases, and in June, secured grand jury indictments against Fall, Sinclair, and Doheny for bribery and conspiracy. Meantime, Denby, whose chief fault had been inattention to the public interest, resigned from the cabinet in February amid a storm of popular criticism.

While the public was still stirred by these disclosures, another committee, headed by Senator B. K. Wheeler of Montana, was engaged in bringing to light unsavory facts concerning Daugherty's record as Attorney-General. The testimony, which was of a highly sensational character, tended to support the charges that the Attorney-General had surrounded himself with bribe-takers and other disreputable characters, and that the Department's activities had been subject to corrupt influences. When Daugherty refused the committee access to certain official files, Coolidge dismissed him on March 28, 1924.

The President's unruffled calm in the face of these shocking disclosures excited unfriendly criticism at the time, but in the long run, his steadiness won him a growing measure of public confidence. He devoted his chief efforts to completing the program of fiscal retrenchment and reorganization which his predecessor had begun. On the plea of economy, Harding had vetoed a soldiers' bonus bill in 1922 designed to benefit World-War veterans, and also a measure, passed the following year, for increasing the pensions of survivors of earlier wars. When

Congress in May, 1924, once more adopted the same bills in somewhat modified form, Coolidge imitated Harding's example.

Under spur, however, of the American Legion, composed of ex-service men, Congress passed the bonus bill over his veto. This measure created a system of prepaid insurance policies, to be issued by the government to World-War veterans, with the stipulation that at the end of twenty years the principal should be given to the holders. The President was more successful in his efforts for tax reduction, although the measure adopted by Congress in May, 1924, retained a higher rate on large incomes than either he or Secretary Mellon had favored. The immediate relief in the nation's tax burden amounted to nearly $360,000,000 a year.

Another subject for Congressional action was immigration. The intense nationalism engendered by the war, the fear of a deluge of undesirable immigrants from war-stricken Europe, the opposition of the unions to cheap foreign labor — all combined to create a strong demand for tightening the clamps on immigration. As a fantastic offshoot of this sentiment, a new nativist movement appeared in the South, and spread over the country like wild fire. Though assuming the name and employing the mystifying ceremonials of the Ku Klux Klan, the organization, in reality, more nearly resembled the Know-Nothing movement of the fifties, for it exalted the virtues of white Protestant native Americanism against the supposed machinations of Catholics, Jews, immigrants, and negroes. It displayed considerable political strength in certain states, notably in the South and Middle West, and occasioned real concern in the minds of politicians.

Under pressure of public opinion, Harding attached his signature to a bill on May 19, 1921, which limited the annual immigration from any European (or African) country to three per cent of the number of its nationals in the United States in 1910. The measure accomplished a dual purpose. It not only insured a reduction of the total number of arrivals from the Old World, but also made possible a correspondingly larger proportion from Western and Northern Europe than from the southern and eastern parts.

The restrictive features, however, were not drastic enough to satisfy public sentiment, and on May 26, 1924, a new law (the

Johnson Act) placed the annual quota of each nation at two per cent of the number of its immigrants in the United States in 1890.[1] By naming an earlier census year the discrimination in favor of the older immigration became even greater. It was further provided that after July 1, 1927, no more than 150,000 immigrants should

IMMIGRATION RESTRICTION UNDER THE QUOTA LAWS

	2% Quota Act of 1924	3% Quota Act of 1921	Immigrants Admitted 1913
Italy	3,845	42,057	265,542
Russia	2,248	34,284	291,040
Austria	785	7,451	254,825 (Austria and Hungary)
Hungary	473	5,638	
Poland	5,982	25,827	
Germany	51,227	68,059	34,329
United Kingdom	62,574	77,342	88,204
Sweden	9,561	20,042	12,688
All countries	164,667	356,995	1,092,442

Because of the changed map of Europe, it should be noted that the figures in the third column are not exactly comparable with those in the others.

be admitted annually, and that this number should be apportioned among the several nations according to the relative strength of the various foreign stocks represented in the American population in 1920.

Although the Johnson Act applied primarily to Europe, one section barred from the United States immigrants ineligible to citizenship. The President had tried in vain to keep this provision out of the bill, for it involved an abrogation of the Gentleman's Agreement of 1907 with Japan, which the latter country had observed in good faith. Its inclusion in the law drew a sharp protest from that power.

Convinced that the Harding-Coolidge lease of power had been a failure, the Democrats made their preparations for the election of 1924 in high enthusiasm — too high, in fact, for they exhausted much of it in their national convention in New York in June when W. G. McAdoo, Wilson's Secretary of the Treasury, and

[1] But each nation is allowed an irreducible annual minimum of one hundred immigrants, and under certain circumstances, near relatives of recent immigrants are permitted entry to the United States in excess of the quota.

Governor Alfred E. Smith of New York, the two leading aspirants for the nomination, deadlocked the gathering for ten days in a contest productive of great bitterness. Finally, in desperation, the delegates stampeded on the one hundred and third ballot to John W. Davis, a distinguished New York corporation lawyer and former ambassador. To offset his conservatism, Governor C. W. Bryan of Nebraska, a brother of William Jennings Bryan, was named for Vice-President. The platform denounced Republican corruption and incapacity, promised legislation to restore rural prosperity, and favored adhesion to the League of Nations after a popular referendum.

Coolidge was nominated without opposition by the Republican convention, meeting at Cleveland on June 10. For the second place Dawes of Illinois, former Director of the Budget, was chosen. The platform pointed with pride to Republican retrenchment and tax reduction, the nation's recovery from the Crisis of 1920, and the administration's success in promoting international peace without the entanglements of the League of Nations.

Under the leadership of Senator La Follette and some of the more radical trade unions and farmers' organizations, an ambitious effort was made to fuse the various reform groups of the country into a new "Progressive" party. At a convention in Cleveland on July 4, La Follette himself was nominated for President on a platform assailing private monopoly and pledging radical measures for agricultural relief, public ownership of railways, and a constitutional amendment to give Congress the power to reverse Supreme-Court decisions. In order to widen the appeal of the new party, B. K. Wheeler, the Democratic Senator from Montana, was named for Vice-President. The Progressive ticket was promptly indorsed by the Socialist party, the Farmer-Labor party, the American Federation of Labor, many national unions and state federations, and by the Steuben Society (successor to the German-American Alliance).

The campaign that followed proved singularly apathetic. For the first time the candidates made systematic use of the radio in reaching the public; indeed, by this means, countless thousands of people attended the several party conventions. Republican orators made the most of the slogan, "Keep Cool with Coolidge," and by focusing their efforts on the La Follette campaign, maintained (in the President's language) that the vital issue was "whether America will allow itself to be degraded into a Communistic and Socialistic state, or whether it will remain American."

The Progressive cause was further harmed in the rural sections by a fortuitous rise in the prices of wheat, corn, and live stock, which somewhat alleviated the farmers' discontent. Democratic efforts were seriously hampered by lack of unity within party ranks as a result of the New York convention. In the closing weeks it became plain that the voters were not disposed to blame Coolidge for the political sins of his predecessor. The outcome was a signal victory for conservatism. Of the electoral votes, Coolidge received 379, Davis, 139, and La Follette 13 — his own state of Wisconsin. The victor had behind him 54 per cent of the popular votes as compared with 28.7 and 16.5 per cent respectively for his rivals.

SELECT BIBLIOGRAPHY

The War and the American Public. The work of the Committee on Public Information is portrayed in George Creel, *How We Advertised America* (New York, 1920). Zechariah Chafee, Jr., *Freedom of Speech* (New York, 1920), deals critically with the policy of the government toward political offenders. War finances receive detailed treatment in E. L. Bogart, *War Costs and Their Financing* (New York, 1921). The services of the American Red Cross and the Y.M.C.A. are described respectively in H. P. Davison, *The American Red Cross in the Great War* (New York, 1919), and Katherine Mayo, "*That Damn Y*" (Boston, 1920). For the exertions of an embattled people in a typical Middle-Western state, consult E. S. Fullbrook, *The Red Cross in Iowa* (2 v., Iowa City, 1922), N. R. Whitney, *The Sale of War Bonds in Iowa* (Iowa City, 1923), M. L. Hansen, *Welfare Campaigns in Iowa* (Iowa City, 1920), and the same author's *Welfare Work in Iowa* (Iowa City, 1921).

Wilson and the Peace Settlement. American participation in the Peace Conference is authoritatively treated in R. S. Baker, *Woodrow Wilson and World Settlement* (3 v., Garden City, 1922), C. H. Haskins and R. H. Lord, *Some Problems of the Peace Conference* (Cambridge, 1920), E. M. House and Charles Seymour, eds., *What Really Happened at Paris* (New York, 1921), and B. M. Baruch, *The Making of the Reparation and Economic Sections of the Treaty* (New York, 1920). A good summary of the Senate's course on the treaty may be found in G. A. Finch, *The Treaty of Peace with Germany in the United States Senate* (in *International Conciliation*, no. 153, Greenwich,

1920), or in W. A. Phillips, "The Senate and the Covenant" (in *Edinburgh Review*, vol. 232 [1920], 1–29).

Postwar Readjustments, Economic and Political. Wartime and postwar economic conditions are set forth in E. S. Cowdrick, *Industrial History of the United States* (New York, 1923), and H. U. Faulkner, *American Economic History* (New York 1924). The status of labor receives special consideration in Selig Perlman, *A History of Trade Unionism in the United States* (New York, 1922). E. R. Johnson and T. W. Van Metre, *Principles of Railroad Transportation* (New York, 1921), is valuable for the Esch-Cummins Act; E. W. Zimmermann, *Zimmermann on Ocean Shipping* (New York, 1921), for the Merchant Marine Act.

The Republicans and the Peace Problem. The most notable event of this epoch of foreign relations, the Washington Conference, led to the writing of several extensive accounts, the best of which is perhaps Mark Sullivan, *The Great Adventure at Washington* (Garden City, 1922).

Domestic Problems of the Republicans. On the agrarian revolt there is already a considerable literature, including H. A. Gaston, *The Nonpartisan League* (New York, 1920) — favorable; A. A. Bruce, *Nonpartisan League* (New York, 1921) — unfavorable; O. M. Kile, *The Farm Bureau Movement* (New York, 1921); Arthur Capper, *The Agricultural Bloc* (New York, 1922); and C. B. Fisher, *The Farmers' Union* (in University of Kentucky, *Studies in Economics and Sociology*, I, no. 2, 1920). A convenient summary of the situation may be found in F. E. Haynes, *Social Politics in the United States* (Boston, 1924). Edward Wiest, *Agricultural Organization in the United States* (in University of Kentucky, *Studies in Economics and Sociology*, II, 1923) should also be consulted. On the tariff measures of 1921–1922, see F. W. Taussig, *The Tariff History of the United States* (New York, 1923). M. E. Ravage, *Teapot Dome* (New York, 1924), gives a detailed account of one of the worst scandals.

Aids in Linking Current Events with Recent History. For this purpose the following annual compilations will be found particularly useful: *The New International Year Book* (1898–); *The Americana Annual* (1923–); the special supplement, entitled "Record of Political Events," published each September by the *Political Science Quarterly; The American Labor Year Book* (1916–); and *The World Almanac* (1891–). Of the quarterly periodicals, *Foreign Affairs*, the *Political Science Quarterly*, the *American Political Science Review*, the *American Journal of International Law*, the *American Journal of Sociology*, the *American Economic Review*, and the *Quarterly Journal of Economics* are very valuable in their respective fields, as is also the bimonthly *Journal of Social Forces*. Among the monthly magazines, the *Congressional Digest*, *Current History Magazine*, and the *Monthly Labor Review* are particularly helpful, though much of value is also to be found in *Current Opinion* and the *American Review of Reviews*. *Time* and the *Literary Digest* are two of the best weeklies that chronicle history in the making; the *Independent*, the *Nation*, the *New Republic*, and the *Survey* offer critical and interpretative comments.

INDEX

circa 2000

gay fiction at the millennium

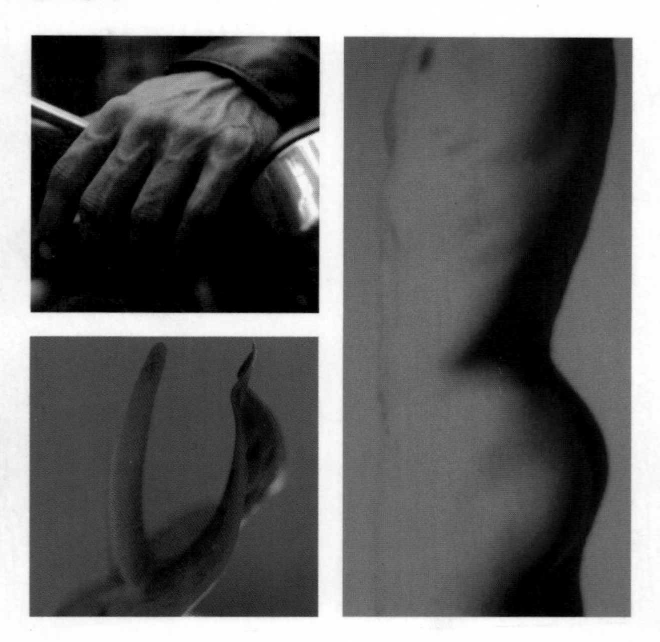

edited by

robert drake & terry wolverton